Lecture Notes in Computer Science 13983

Founding Editors

Gerhard Goos
Juris Hartmanis

The series Lecture Notes in Computer Science (LNCS), including its subseries Lecture Notes in Artificial Intelligence (LNAI) and Lecture Notes in Bioinformatics (LNBI), has established itself as a medium for the publication of new developments in computer science and information technology research, teaching, and education.

LNCS enjoys close cooperation with the computer science R & D community, the series counts many renowned academics among its volume editors and paper authors, and collaborates with prestigious societies. Its mission is to serve this international community by providing an invaluable service, mainly focused on the publication of conference and workshop proceedings and postproceedings. LNCS commenced publication in 1973.

Shujun Li · Mark Manulis · Atsuko Miyaji
Editors

Network and System Security

17th International Conference, NSS 2023
Canterbury, UK, August 14–16, 2023
Proceedings

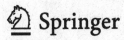

Editors
Shujun Li 🄳
University of Kent
Canterbury, UK

Mark Manulis 🄳
Universität der Bundeswehr München
München, Germany

Atsuko Miyaji
Osaka University
Suita, Osaka, Japan

ISSN 0302-9743   ISSN 1611-3349 (electronic)
Lecture Notes in Computer Science
ISBN 978-3-031-39827-8   ISBN 978-3-031-39828-5 (eBook)
https://doi.org/10.1007/978-3-031-39828-5

This Springer imprint is published by the registered company Springer Nature Switzerland AG
The registered company address is: Gewerbestrasse 11, 6330 Cham, Switzerland

Preface

NSS (International Conference on Network and System Security) is an annual conference focusing on all theoretical and practical aspects related to network and system security. Its 17th edition, NSS 2023, took place from 14th to 16th August, 2023, in Canterbury, Kent, United Kingdom. It was organized by the Institute of Cyber Security for Society (iCCS) at the University of Kent, and co-located with the 9th International Symposium on Security and Privacy in Social Networks and Big Data (SocialSec 2023).

NSS 2023 received 64 submissions. Each Technical Program Committee (TPC) member was assigned an average of two submissions for review. Each paper was assigned to at least three reviewers. The TPC was helped by the reports and opinions of four external reviewers. The submission process was anonymous and author names were not visible to the reviewers. Received reviews were also anonymised to other TPC members, as well as to the paper's authors. The review process was organized and managed through EasyChair. The reviewers were asked to declare any conflicts of interest for all submissions at the beginning of the process, and the EasyChair system was configured to ensure that TPC members (including TPC chairs) could see neither reviewer assignments nor reviews of papers for which they had a confict of interest. For several papers, one TPC Co-Chair had a conflict of interest, and the discussion on each of the papers was held, and the decision was made, between the other two TPC Co-Chairs without a conflict of interest. The selection process was competitive and after highly interactive discussions and a careful deliberation, 12 full papers (18.8%) were selected by the TPC for presentation at the conference. In addition, 9 papers were selected for presentation as short papers, resulting in the overall acceptance rate of 32.8%.

NSS 2023 and the co-located SocialSec 2023 shared three invited talks for both conferences' participants, given by Julia Hesse from IBM Research Zurich, Nishanth Sastry from University of Surrey and Lorenzo Cavallaro from University College London.

The NSS 2023 TPC selected one paper to receive the Best Paper Award and another one to receive the Best Student Paper Award. The Best Paper was awarded to Aurélien Greuet, Simon Montoya and Clémence Vermeersch for their paper "Modular Polynomial Multiplication Using RSA/ECC coprocessor". The Best Student Paper went to Mahshid Mehr Nezhad, Elliot Laidlaw and Feng Hao for their paper "Security Analysis of Mobile Point-of-Sale Terminals". Both awards include a certificate and a cash prize. The cash prizes were kindly sponsored by the Institute of Cyber Security for Society (iCCS), University of Kent.

The NSS 2023 TPC was co-chaired by Shujun Li, Mark Manulis and Atsuko Miyaji who selected the TPC members and led their efforts in selecting the papers that appear in this volume. The organization of NSS 2023 and the co-located SocialSec 2023 was led by Budi Arief, Robert Deng and Elena Ferrari as both conferences' joint General Co-Chairs. The conferences were also made possible due to the professional work of Yuntao Wang, Yulei Wu and Zhe Xia as the Publicity Co-Chairs, Shujun Li as the Publication

Chair, and Haiyue Yuan as the Web Chair. The NSS 2023 TPC was also advised by a Steering Committee chaired by Yang Xiang.

We would like to thank everyone who contributed to the success of NSS 2023. We are grateful to all TPC members and external reviewers for their commitment, hard work and enthusiasm, which ensured that each submitted paper went through a thorough and fair review process. We thank all members of the Organizing Committee of both NSS 2023 and the co-located SocialSec 2023 for their professional work that supported us, the TPC and all participants of both conferences. Last but not the least, we also wish to thank all authors who submitted to NSS 2023 and all conference participants for making NSS 2023 an enjoyable experience.

June 2023

Shujun Li
Mark Manulis
Atsuko Miyaji

Organization

General Chairs

Budi Arief   University of Kent, UK
Robert Deng   Singapore Management University, Singapore
Elena Ferrari   University of Insubria, Italy

Program Committee Chairs

Shujun Li   University of Kent, UK
Mark Manulis   Universität der Bundeswehr München, Germany
Atsuko Miyaji   Osaka University and Japan Advanced Institute of
     Science and Technology, Japan

Steering Committee

Yang Xiang (Chair)   Swinburne University of Technology, Australia
Elisa Bertino   Purdue University, USA
Robert Deng   Singapore Management University, Singapore
Dieter Gollmann   Hamburg University of Technology, Germany
Xinyi Huang   Hong Kong University of Science and
     Technology, China
Kui Ren   Zhejiang University, China
Ravi Sandhu   University of Texas at San Antonio, USA
Wanlei Zhou   City University of Macau, China

Publicity Co-chairs

Yuntao Wang   Osaka University, Japan
Yulei Wu   University of Exeter, UK
Zhe Xia   Wuhan University of Technology, China

Publication Chair

Shujun Li   University of Kent, UK

Web Chair

Haiyue Yuan   University of Kent, UK

Program Committee

Sridhar Adepu   Singapore University of Technology and Design,
                                       Singapore
Chuadhry Mujeeb Ahmed   Singapore University of Technology and Design,
                                       Singapore
Nadeem Ahmed   Cyber Security Cooperative Research Centre,
                                       Australia
Magnus Almgren   Chalmers University of Technology, Sweden
David Arroyo   Spanish National Research Council (CSIC), Spain
Joonsang Baek   University of Wollongong, Australia
Diogo Barradas   University of Waterloo, Canada
Osman Biçer   Koç University, Turkey
Silvia Bonomi   Sapienza University of Rome, Italy
Alessandro Brighente   University of Padova, Italy
Emiliano Casalicchio   Blekinge Institute of Technology, Sweden and
                                       Sapienza University of Rome, Italy
Luca Caviglione   CNR - IMATI, Italy
Koji Chida   Gunma University, Japan
Sherman S. M. Chow   Chinese University of Hong Kong, China
Nora Cuppens-Boulahia   Polytechnique Montréal, Canada
Bernardo David   IT University of Copenhagen, Denmark
Keita Emura   National Institute of Information and
                                       Communications Technology, Japan
Wenjun Fan   Xi'an Jiaotong-Liverpool University, China
Davide Ferraris   University of Malaga, Spain
Afonso Ferreira   CNRS - Institut de Recherches en Informatique
                                       de Toulouse, France
Amrita Ghosal   University of Limerick, Ireland
Stefanos Gritzalis   University of Piraeus, Greece
Jinguang Han   Southeast University, China
Guillaume Hiet   CentraleSupélec, France

Shoichi Hirose — University of Fukui, Japan
Darren Hurley-Smith — Royal Holloway, University of London, UK
Sokratis Katsikas — Norwegian University of Science and Technology, Norway
Stefan Katzenbeisser — University of Passau, Germany
Hiroaki Kikuchi — Meiji University, Japan
Shinsaku Kiyomoto — KDDI Research Inc, Japan
Veronika Kuchta — Florida Atlantic University, USA
Shane Li — Cardiff University, UK
Wanpeng Li — University of Aberdeen, UK
Yingjiu Li — University of Oregon, USA
Xiapu Luo — Hong Kong Polytechnic University, China
Taous Leila Madi — King Abdullah University of Science and Technology, Saudi Arabia
Mohammad Mamun — National Research Council Canada, Canada
Kalikinkar Mandal — University of New Brunswick, Canada
Daisuke Mashima — Advanced Digital Sciences Center, Singapore
Wojciech Mazurczyk — Warsaw University of Technology, Poland
Florian Mendel — Infineon Technologies, Germany
Kazuhiko Minematsu — NEC Corporation, Japan
Antonio Muñoz — University of Malaga, Spain
Rolf Oppliger — eSECURITY Technologies, Switzerland
Daniela Pöhn — Universität der Bundeswehr München, Germany
Chen Qian — Shandong University, China
Fatemeh Rezaeibagha — Murdoch University, Australia
Ruben Rios — University of Malaga, Spain
Sankardas Roy — Bowling Green State University, USA
Corinna Schmitt — Universität der Bundeswehr München, Germany
Siamak Shahandashti — University of York, UK
Paria Shirani — University of Ottawa, Canada
Mohammad Shojafar — University of Surrey, UK
Luisa Siniscalchi — Danmarks Tekniske Universitet, Denmark
Simone Soderi — IMT Scuola Alti Studi Lucca, Italy
Juraj Somorovsky — Paderborn University, Germany
Chunhua Su — University of Aizu, Japan
Erik Tews — University of Twente, The Netherlands
Yangguang Tian — University of Surrey, UK
Zhihong Tian — Guangzhou University, China
Ehsan Toreini — University of Surrey, UK
Jacques Traore — Orange Labs, France
Luca Viganò — King's College London, UK
Yongge Wang — University of North Carolina at Charlotte, USA

Steffen Wendzel	Worms University of Applied Sciences, Germany
Yongdong Wu	Jinan University, China
Zhe Xia	Wuhan University of Technology, China
Jinbo Xiong	Fujian Normal University, China
Toshihiro Yamauchi	Okayama University, Japan
Kuo-Hui Yeh	National Dong Hwa University, Taiwan
Kazuki Yoneyama	Ibaraki University, Japan
Tsz Hon Yuen	University of Hong Kong, China
Melek Önen	EURECOM, France

Additional Reviewers

Asmaa Hailane
Weihan Li
Thomas Poeppelmann
Harry W. H. Wong

Contents

Attacks and Malware

Evaluating Rule-Based Global XAI Malware Detection Methods 3
   Rui Li and Olga Gadyatskaya

Whitelisting for Characterizing and Monitoring Process Control
Communication 23
   Andreas Paul, Franka Schuster, and Hartmut König

Detection of Malware Using Self-Attention Mechanism and Strings 46
   Satoki Kanno and Mamoru Mimura

KDRM: Kernel Data Relocation Mechanism to Mitigate Privilege
Escalation Attack 61
   Hiroki Kuzuno and Toshihiro Yamauchi

The Effectiveness of Transformer-Based Models for BEC Attack Detection 77
   Amirah Almutairi, BooJoong Kang, and Nawfal Fadhel

Blockchain

Resilience of Blockchain Overlay Networks 93
   Aristodemos Paphitis, Nicolas Kourtellis, and Michael Sirivianos

Provably Secure Blockchain Protocols from Distributed
Proof-of-Deep-Learning 114
   Xiangyu Su, Mario Larangeira, and Keisuke Tanaka

Security Model for Privacy-Preserving Blockchain-Based Cryptocurrency
Systems 137
   Mayank Raikwar, Shuang Wu, and Kristian Gjøsteen

Cryptography and Privacy

Group Oriented Attribute-Based Encryption Scheme from Lattices
with the Employment of Shamir's Secret Sharing Scheme 155
   Maharage Nisansala Sevwandi Perera, Toru Nakamura,
   Takashi Matsunaka, Hiroyuki Yokoyama, and Kouichi Sakurai

New LDP Approach Using VAE 177
Andres Hernandez-Matamoros and Hiroaki Kikuchi

Machine Learning

Privacy-Preserving Federated Learning with Hierarchical Clustering
to Improve Training on Non-IID Data 195
Songwei Luo, Shaojing Fu, Yuchuan Luo, Lin Liu, Yanxiang Deng,
and Shixiong Wang

RRML: Privacy Preserving Machine Learning Based on Random
Response Technology 217
Jia Wang, Shiqing He, and Qiuzhen Lin

SPoiL: Sybil-Based Untargeted Data Poisoning Attacks in Federated
Learning 235
Zhuotao Lian, Chen Zhang, Kaixi Nan, and Chunhua Su

Agnostic Label-Only Membership Inference Attack 249
Anna Monreale, Francesca Naretto, and Simone Rizzo

ppAURORA: Privacy Preserving Area Under Receiver Operating
Characteristic and Precision-Recall Curves 265
Ali Burak Ünal, Nico Pfeifer, and Mete Akgün

Security Through Hardware

Modular Polynomial Multiplication Using RSA/ECC Coprocessor 283
Aurélien Greuet, Simon Montoya, and Clémence Vermeersch

T3E: A Practical Solution to Trusted Time in Secure Enclaves 305
Gilang Mentari Hamidy, Pieter Philippaerts, and Wouter Joosen

Decentralized SGX-Based Cloud Key Management 327
Yunusa Simpa Abdulsalam, Jaouhara Bouamama, Yahya Benkaouz,
and Mustapha Hedabou

Security in the Wild

Spying on the Spy: Security Analysis of Hidden Cameras 345
Samuel Herodotou and Feng Hao

Security Analysis of Mobile Point-of-Sale Terminals 363
Mahshid Mehr Nezhad, Elliot Laidlaw, and Feng Hao

On the Design of a Misinformation Widget (MsW) Against Cloaked Science ... 385
  David Arroyo, Sara Degli-Esposti, Alberto Gómez-Espés,
  Santiago Palmero-Muñoz, and Luis Pérez-Miguel

Author Index 397

Attacks and Malware

Evaluating Rule-Based Global XAI Malware Detection Methods

Rui Li and Olga Gadyatskaya(✉)

LIACS, Leiden University, Leiden, The Netherlands
{r.li,o.gadyatskaya}@liacs.leidenuniv.nl

Abstract. In recent years explainable artificial intelligence (XAI) methods have been applied for interpreting machine learning-based Android malware detection approaches. XAI methods are capable of providing Android malware analysts with some explanations of why a certain sample has been classified as malicious or benign. However, human analysts also have domain-specific requirements, i.e., expectations of how XAI methods should behave. For example, analysts expect that similar malware samples will be explained in a similar way. Recent works by Warnecke *et al.* [41] and Fan *et al.* [13] have proposed domain-specific properties for *local* XAI methods that provide explanations for a single sample.

In this work, we formulate three domain-specific properties for *global* XAI rule-based malware detection methods: *stability*, *robustness* and *effectiveness*. We evaluate performance of five explanation approaches (SIRUS, deepRED, REM-D, ECLAIRE and inTrees) using these metrics. Our experimental results show that the SIRUS method outperforms the other five state-of-the-art methods, with stability, robustness, and effectiveness values of 96.15%, 95.56%, and 91.65% respectively. Our study provides valuable insights for Android malware analysts seeking reliable explanation approaches.

Keywords: Explainability · Android malware · Rule extraction · Evaluation metrics

1 Introduction

In recent years, smartphones have become one of the most indispensable products. According to the report by StatCounter, the Android operating system dominates the smartphone operating system market with a market share of 67.56%, as of June 2023[1]. The flexibility and openness of the Android system have brought great convenience to developers and users. For example, developers can freely develop and upload applications (apps for short) to an application market, and users can download apps from many markets at will.

---

[1] StatCounter, Mobile Operating System Market Share Worldwide, https://gs.statcounter.com/os-market-share/mobile/worldwide, accessed on 19/06/2023.

Supported by Chinese Scholarship Council.

However, Android provides no assurance of the trustworthiness of apps installed from sources other than Google Play, the official market owned by Google. This makes users vulnerable to malicious software. As reported in the *Mobile malware evolution 2021* report, in that year Kaspersky detected more than 3 million malicious mobile installation packages. Moreover, attacks on mobile users are becoming more sophisticated in terms of both malware functionality and attack vectors[2]. Driven by the need to protect security of the Android operating system and privacy of Android device users, Android malware detection has become a booming research field in recent years [32]. Several effective techniques have been proposed to counter the sheer volume and sophistication of Android malware, frequently based on machine learning (ML) [9,12,22,33].

Nevertheless, most of the machine learning methods applied to malware detection are *black-box*, which means that these methods do not explain how and why certain classification decisions are made. Due to the size of training data and the complexity of the learned model, malware analysts can find it hard to interpret the detection model and explain the decision reasons [15,43]. Moreover, adversarial analyses have shown that only a few changes to the content of a malicious Android app may suffice for evading detection by a ML-based detector [6,10]. Therefore, the analysts can start distrusting the detection results, and doubt whether the detection model can be deployed in practice [7,30,37,44,46].

To make analysts and users trust the ML-based methods, a variety of interpretable models has been proposed to explain predictions. An interpretable model should be *human-simulatable*, which means that a user can "take in input data together with the parameters of the model and in reasonable time step through every calculation required to produce a prediction" [21]. In the mobile security domain, many XAI methods interpret the detection model by identifying important features or extracting important rules [1–3,14,16,18,24,28,31,34,35,40,42,47].

XAI methods can be generally categorized into *local* and *global* methods depending on *what* they strive to explain [5,8,46]. The *local* explanation approaches provide short, human-accessible explanations why a certain *sample* was classified as malicious or benign, while *global* explanations compute a short representation of important indicators across a set of samples, for example, a malware family or a category.

Moreover, there are some domain-specific requirements for XAI methods applied to cyber security in general and to interpretable malware detection in particular [7,30]. Security analysts, for example, can reasonably expect that the provided explanations will be similar for similar apps, and that they will stay similar across different runs of the model. Thus, there is a need to ensure that the explainable ML techniques proposed for malware detection satisfy these requirements.

Addressing this problem, Warnecke *et al.* [41] and Fan *et al.* [13] have proposed formalizations of several domain-specific requirements for Android mal-

---

[2] Kaspersky https://securelist.com/mobile-malware-evolution-2021/105876/, accessed on 19/06/2023.

ware detection. They have independently proposed several metrics that can be used to assess the quality of local explainable ML techniques when applied to Android malware, i.e., the explanation approaches applied to the classification of individual samples. For example, Fan et al. [13] have shown that explanation results provided by five local explanation approaches for the same Android malware sample cannot achieve a consensus in general. However, to the best of our knowledge, there has so far been no investigation of properties for global explainability Android malware detection methods, i.e., methods that provide a single explanation for a set of samples, and there has been no evaluation of existing global XAI techniques with respect to the domain-specific requirements of Android security analysts.

In this paper, we aim to close this gap. Specifically, we make the following contributions:

1. We formulate three metrics – *stability*, *robustness*, and *effectiveness*– to assess the fundamental properties that rule-based global explainable Android malware detection methods should satisfy. These metrics are crucial for evaluating the performance of such methods.
2. We evaluate performance of five state-of-the-art explanation methods, namely, SIRUS [4], DeepRED [48], REM-D [36], ECLAIRE [45], and inTrees [11], for Android malware detection using the CICMalDroid dataset [25, 26]. Our experimental results show that SIRUS outperforms the other four state-of-the-art global XAI methods in terms of detection performance, stability, robustness, and effectiveness.

2 Related Work

As mentioned, the explainable Android malware detection methods can be divided into *local* explanation methods and *global* explainable methods [5]. Another dimensions to categorize XAI methods refer to the connection of the interpreter to the ML model: some XAI approaches are *intrinsic*, as it is the ML model itself that is interpretable [7, 8, 46]. All linear classifiers are intrinsically interpretable. In the Android malware research such approaches are, for example, Drebin [2], Traffic AV [40], LUNA [3], and CASANDRA [31], where linear Support Vector Machine, Decision Tree, Bayesian Classifier, and Online CW Classifier are used, respectively. Other XAI approaches are *post-hoc/extrinsic*, as they can be applied to any ML model after training.

The local explanation methods explain why a single Android application was labeled as malware or benign via a detection model. Several research teams have investigated application of local XAI methods for Android malware detection. For example, Fan et al. [13] have applied five widely-used *post-hoc* explanation approaches – LIME [34], Anchor [35], LORE [14], SHAP [24] and LEMNA [16] – to Android malware detection. Alani and Awad [1] present the PAIRED lightweight Android malware detection system that integrates SHAP as an interpreter. Morcos et al. [29] propose a surrogate-based technique to interpret Random Forest models that integrates SHAP for interpreting the data exfiltrating behavior in Android malware samples.

Martin *et al.* [18] propose a method to explain convolutional neural networks (CNNs) by calculating network activations to identify locations deemed important in an Android app's opcode sequence. Zhu *et al.* [47] develop a backtracking method to infer important suspicious features of apps for explaining classification results.

Melis *et al.* [28] identify the most influential malicious local features by leveraging a gradient-based approach, which enables using nonlinear models to increase accuracy without sacrificing the interpretability of decisions. Lu and Thing [23] develop the PhilaeX method to identify a subset of features for explaining decisions of different AI models, including Support Vector Machines implemented by Drebin [2] and BERT (a transformer-based deep neural network classifier).

The global explanation methods let analysts understand how the whole model makes decisions. Some approaches do this based on a holistic view of model's features and the learned components, such as weights, parameters, and structures. For example, Bozhi *et al.* [42] propose a global XAI approach called Xmal that not only pinpoints the key features most related to the classification result by hingeing the multi-layer perceptron and attention mechanisms, but also automatically produces natural language descriptions to help analysts to interpret malicious behaviours within apps.

Other global XAI methods extract a rule-based representation of the targeted set from the model. For example, AdDroid [27] is based on various combinations of artefacts called rules to analyze and detect malicious behaviour in Android applications. Jerby *et al.* [17] develop the BMD method for malware detection rules generation using a Bi-Level optimization problem. Both AdDroid and BMD are *intrinsic* XAI methods.

Still, explanation methods in security need not only to be accurate but also to satisfy domain-specific requirements, such as complete and robust explanations [41]. This is arguably especially important when *post-hoc* XAI methods are being applied to malware detection, as they are by design not aware of the underlying classification problem. To evaluate how well this problem is addressed by the existing XAI methods in the field, Warnecke *et al.* propose general evaluation criteria, which include descriptive accuracy and sparsity, and security (domain-specific) evaluation criteria, which include stability, robustness, and efficiency. Independently, Fan *et al.* [13] propose stability, robustness, and effectiveness to evaluate the Android malware detection explanation results. We discuss these metrics in more detail in Sect. 5.3. However, they have been developed only for local explanation methods. Our work aims to close this gap and to formulate domain-specific quality metrics to be used in conjunction with rule-based global XAI methods.

3 Candidate XAI Methods and Evaluation Metrics

3.1 Evaluated XAI Methods

In this work we focus on evaluating the *post-hoc* XAI methods, as we were not able to find implementation of the intrinsic XAI approaches AdDroid [27] and BMD [17]. The following global rule-based XAI methods have been selected for experiments:

- The **SIRUS** algorithm [4] is a stable and interpretable rule-based classifier that consists of two main processes: training a black-box model, such as Random Forest (RF), and constructing an *agent* model that extracts rules and generates a rule-based malware detector. The goal of SIRUS is to identify a concise set of non-overlapping detection rules that capture robust and strong patterns in the data [4].
- The **inTrees** method [11] extracts, measures, prunes, selects, and summarizes rules from a tree ensemble (such as RF and Boosted Trees), the rules can be ranked by length, support, error, or a combination of multiple metrics.
- The **deepRED** method [48] extracts rules from deep neural networks by mimicking the internal logic of neural networks at each layer and neurone. This makes hidden logic and features accessible, and also exploits deep structures to improve the efficacy of rule extraction and induction process.
- The **REM-D** (Rule Extraction Methodology-Deep Neural Network) method [36] approximates a deep neural network (DNN) with an interpretable ruleset model and uses that ruleset to explain the results of the DNN. For approximation, REM-D first decomposes the trained DNN into adjacent layers and then uses the C5.0 classification algorithm to extract rules from pairs of layers in the network.
- The **ECLAIRE** (Efficient CLAuse-wIse Rule Extraction) method [45] is a polynomial-time decompositional method applicable to arbitrary DNNs; it exploits intermediate representations in parallel to build an ensemble of classifiers that can then be efficiently combined into a single rule set.

Interpreted Classifiers. Note that the selected interpreters work with two types of classifiers: either the RF or DNNs. These classifiers are quite different from one another, and rules generated with them will be quite distinct. One of the goals of our work is to understand whether the established domain-specific requirements previously considered for local methods can be expected at all from deep neural network interpreters.

The RF algorithm builds multiple independent decision trees following the bagging strategy, using both sample and attribute selection to prevent overfitting. This decision-making tree generation process helps to avoid the problem of under-fitting caused by single tree judgments and significantly improves discrimination. Finally, the model combines the predictions of multiple trees to make category determinations through a voting method, resulting in higher accuracy.

A DNN consists of a sequence of multiple layers of interconnected neurones. Each neurone in a layer receives input from the previous layer's neurones and performs a computation that typically involves a weighted sum of the inputs followed by a nonlinear activation function. The network's neurones collectively implement a complex nonlinear mapping from the input to the output, which is learned from data by adjusting the weights of each neurone using error back-propagation. This technique involves propagating the prediction error back through the layers of the network to adjust the weights of the connections between neurones. By adjusting the weights in this way, the DNN is able to learn complex patterns and relationships within the data, leading to improved accuracy and robustness in many machine learning tasks.

To explain a *black-box* detection model (an RF or a DNN-based classifier), we apply one of the above explanation methods to extract rules, select rules and generate a new *rule-based detector*, which is now an intrinsically interpretable (*white-box*) classification model. These detectors are then evaluated based on their detection performance and also the proposed domain-specific properties, as we discuss further.

Rules. Rules produced by the considered XAI methods are in the format "if $f_1 \& f_2 \& ......f_n$ then p_1 else p_2", where the conjunction of conditions $f_1 \& f_2 \& ......f_n$ is the detection rule body, p_1 is the model's confidence that the sample is malware under the given condition in the rule body, and p_2 is the confidence that the sample is malware when the condition is not satisfied.

3.2 Evaluation

The literature [13,41] proposes domain-specific metrics for local XAI methods applied to malware detection. However, these metrics are based on feature sets, rather than rules, and are only suitable for local explanation methods. In our study we consider global, rule-based explanation methods. Thus we propose new definitions of the *stability*, *robustness*, and *effectiveness* metrics previously defined in [13,41] to suit rule-based global explanation methods. Table 1 lists the used notations.

Intuition 1. *Stability requires that the generated explanations result do not vary between multiple runs* [41].

Since the explanation results remain similar on the same pre-trained models, good stability requires that an explanation approach can really capture the actual reason for an individual classification decision. Otherwise, the analyst would be confused and would not trust the explanation results [13]. The stability of an explanation method m, denoted as $stb(m, T)$, is measured on a target testing dataset T as follows.

$$stb(m, T) = \frac{1}{C_n^2} * \sum_{i,j \in n,} sim(e_{n_i}(g), e_{n_j}(g)) \tag{1}$$

Table 1. Notations and definitions

Notation	Definition
C_n^k	the number of combinations for selecting k elements out of n
f	a classifier model constructed on a training dataset
m	an explanation approach
$g = m(f)$	a specific interpreter constructed based on an explanation method m and a trained classifier f
$e(g)$	the explanation results of the samples with interpreter g
$stb(m, T)$	stability of explanation approach m on testing dataset T
$rob(m, T)$	robustness of explanation approach m on testing dataset T
$eff(m, T)$	effectiveness of explanation approach m on testing dataset T

$$g = m(f) \tag{2}$$

$$sim(e_{n_i}(g), e_{n_j}(g)) = 2 * \frac{e_{n_i}(g) \cap e_{n_j}(g))}{|e_{n_i}(g)| + |e_{n_j}(g)|)} \tag{3}$$

where n is the number of times that the experiment is repeated; C_n^2 denotes the number of pre-trained models and is bigger than two. g is a specific interpreter constructed based on an explanation method m and a trained classifier f, and $e_{n_i}(g)$ is the n_i-th explanation results of the samples with the interpreter g. $sim(e_{n_i}(g), e_{n_j}(g))$ is the similarity between $e_{n_i}(g)$ and $e_{n_j}(g)$ based on the Dice coefficient.

The main difference between our stability metric and the one in [13] is that we measure the malware explanation results for all the samples jointly rather than each sample individually. Moreover, we compare all rules in different runs rather than the top-k features.

Intuition 2. *Robustness is an ability of the explanation method to remain unaffected when slight variations are applied* [13].

Robustness is used to measure how similar the explanation results are for similar instances. Intuitively, the explanation results of similar malware instances should be highly similar. The robustness formula proposed in [13] requires that every sample has an individual explanation, which is not suitable for our work. So according to the intuition of robustness, we propose a new robustness evaluation metric that is based on variations in the whole dataset.

The dataset $T_t(x)$ ranges from $sampleX_{0+(t-1)*u}$ to $sampleX_{r+(t-1)*u}$, $t \in (0, \beta)$, β is equal to total number of samples minus r, and then divided by u. The robustness of an explanation approach p on the dataset T is calculated as below. For example, if $i = 0$, that means we should calculate the similarity of $[X_0, X_1, X_2 ......X_r]$ and $[X_1, X_2, X_3 ......X_{r+1}]$.

$$rob(p, T) = \frac{1}{t} * \sum_{i \in t} sim(T_i(g), T_{i+1}(g)), t \in (0, \beta)] \tag{4}$$

Intuition 3. *Effectiveness measures whether the explanation results are important to the decision-making* [13]. *If the explanation results are really the decision basis for an individual prediction, the classification result would change after mutating rules* [13].

To compute effectiveness, we mutate the produced rules. First, the confidence score of rules above 0.5 will be set 1 (indicates malware), otherwise set to 0 (indicates benign). For instance, a rule "if `android.permission.DISABLE_KEYGUARD` < 1 & `android.permission.SEND_SMS` < 1 then *0.0031* else *0.95*" will change to "if `android.permission.DISABLE_KEYGUARD` < 1 & `android.permission.SE-ND_SMS` < 1 then *0* else *1*".

The effectiveness $eff(m, T)$ of an explanation approach m on testing dataset T is then calculated as below.

$$eff(m,T) = \frac{1}{|T|} * \sum_{x_i \in T} eff(m, x_i) \tag{5}$$

$$eff(m, x_i) = \begin{cases} 1, \hat{y_i^*} \neq \hat{y_i}, \hat{y_i^*} \in \hat{Y^*} \\ 0, \hat{y_i^*} = \hat{y_i}, \hat{y_i^*} \in \hat{Y^*} \end{cases} \tag{6}$$

$$\hat{Y^*} = f(X^*) \tag{7}$$

$$X^* = mutate(x, e_{(g)}) \tag{8}$$

where $eff(m, x_i)$ denotes the effectiveness of explanation results for the sample x_i with m. The hat sign $\hat{}$ denotes the classification result. X^* is a new ruleset for the samples by mutating the original ruleset X, $\hat{Y^*}$ are classification results of X^*; it is a vector with values 0 or 1. If the *mutate* classification result $\hat{y_i^*}$ is not equal to the original classification result $\hat{y_i}$, $eff(m, x_i)$ is assigned to 1, indicating that rules are important to the current decision-making. Otherwise, $eff(m, x_i)$ is set to 0, indicating that rules are useless to predict malware.

The *mutate* operator in [13] changes the value of a feature that appears in the explanation results. However, in our method, *mutate* applies the logical negation to the rule body by, for instance, changing the rules from the AND condition to the OR condition. Moreover, the conflicting rules are deleted.

As en example, the above rule "if `android.permission.DISABLE_KEYGUARD` < 1 & `android.permission.SEND_SMS` < 1 then *0* else *1*" will be mutated into a set with two rules: 1) "if `android.permission.DISABLE_KEYGUARD` >= 1 then *0* else *1*"; and 2) "if `android.permission.SEND_SMS` >= 1 then *0* else *1*".

4   Methodology

In this section, we introduce our set-up for evaluating the global rule-based XAI Android malware detection methods according to the proposed definitions

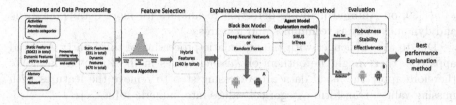

Fig. 1. Our set-up for evaluating global rule-based XAI Android malware detection methods

of stability, robustness and effectiveness, and their performance as white-box classifiers.

Our process is divided into 4 steps: data and feature preprocessing, feature selection, explainable Android malware detection process, and evaluation, as shown in Fig. 1. These steps are further detailed in the remainder of this section. In a nutshell, we first preprocess the data by treating the missing and outlier values. Next, we select the important features using the Boruta algorithm [20]. Then, a black-box malware detection model based on the Random Forest algorithm or Deep Neural Network is trained (the detection task A), and we use the five selected agent models (explanation methods) – SIRUS [4], DeepRED [48], REM-D [36], ECLAIRE [45], and inTrees [11] – to produce rule-based detectors which can detect Android malware (the detection target B). Finally, we evaluate the rules extracted by the considered XAI methods based on their robustness, stability, effectiveness, and also the performance of rule detectors.

4.1 Features and Data Preprocessing

Android apps are software applications running on the Android platform. A typical Android app contains different components: activities, fragments, services, content providers, and broadcast receivers. Most of these app components should be declared in the special Manifest file. This file is used to decide how to integrate the app into the device's overall user experience by the Android OS. The apks (Android application packages) are used to install Android apps onto device. Different properties of apks are used to detect malicious apps as features. These features are usually extracted using some program analysis techniques [39].

For static analysis of Android apps, apks should be unzipped and decompiled. The Manifest file (`AndroidManifest.xml`) and the code file (`classes.dex`) are usually used in static analysis. *Static features* like sensitive permissions, names of activities, and intents are extracted from the Manifest file, while sensitive API calls are extracted from the code file [2].

For dynamic analysis of the Android apps, apps should be executed in a dedicated analysis environment, like, e.g., CopperDroid [38], to automatically reconstruct low-level OS-specific and high-level Android-specific behaviours of Android apps [26]. *Dynamic features* like system calls and Binder calls could be extracted in dynamic analysis. We refer the interested reader to a survey by Tam *et al.* [39] on Android malware detection techniques for more details on static and dynamic analysis techniques and features.

Due to the challenges with the automatic processing of third-party Android apps [19], there might be outliers or missing values in the collected data. We therefore apply the usual data preprocessing step to remove the features with missing values, transform categorical values into numeric values, etc.

4.2   Feature Selection

After completing the data collection and preprocessing steps, we apply the Boruta algorithm [20] to eliminate redundant and irrelevant features from our dataset. The Boruta algorithm is effective in minimizing the impact of random fluctuations and correlations during feature selection [20]. The approach involves augmenting the original features with a set of shadow features, which are randomized copies of the original features. To identify the most important features in the dataset, the Boruta algorithm trains a classifier using the extended feature set. It then compares the importance of each original feature with that of its corresponding shadow feature. If a feature has higher importance than its corresponding shadow feature, it is considered important. This process is repeated until all features are either confirmed as important, rejected as unimportant, or remain uncertain.

5   Experimental Evaluation

5.1   Dataset

A generic Android malware detection pipeline requires automated app analysis tooling to extract static and dynamic features. In our work we use the CICMalDroid [25,26] dataset, which already contains static and dynamic features extracted from 1795 benign and 9803 malware samples. The samples were collected from December 2017 to December 2018. The dataset includes five distinct categories: Adware, Banking, SMS malware, Riskware and Benign, as shown in Table 2.

The dataset includes 470 dynamic features, such as frequencies of system calls, Binder calls, and composite behaviours; and 50,621 static features, such as intent actions, permissions, sensitive APIs, services, etc. To balance the dataset for experiments, we randomly subselected 1795 benign and 1795 malware samples.

5.2   The Experiment Procedure

To ensure the integrity of the dataset and minimize the impact of outliers and missing values, we undertook the preprocessing steps before analysis. The dataset initially included 50,621 static features and 470 dynamic features. We removed features with missing values exceeding 90%, and converted object-type features

Table 2. The details of CICMalDroid dataset categories

Category	Description	# of samples
Adware	Adware can infect and root-infect a device, forcing it to download specific Adware types and allowing attackers to steal personal information	1253
Banking	Mobile Banking malware is a specialized malware designed to gain access to the user's online banking accounts by mimicking the original banking applications or banking web interface	2100
SMS malware	SMS malware exploits the SMS service as its medium of operation to intercept SMS payload for conducting attacks. They control attack instructions by sending malicious SMS, intercepting SMS, and stealing data	3940
Riskware	Riskware refers to legitimate programs that can cause damage if malicious users exploit them. Consequently, it can turn into any other form of malware such as Adware or Ransomware, which extends functionalities by installing newly infected applications	2546

such as `incognito.is valid` APK (with values of `True` or `False`) to integer-type values. After these preprocessing steps, we reduced the number of static features to 231, while retaining all 470 dynamic features.

With the resulting 701 features, we have applied the Boruta algorithm for feature selection that has identified 240 important features[3].

Then, the 10-fold cross-validation method is used to do the experiment. We use the training set to train a Random Forest detection model and a Keras DNN model[4].

Next, we extract rules from the trained black-box detection models using the studied SIRUS, deepRED, REM-D, ECLAIRE and inTrees methods. The maximum rule number of the SIRUS algorithm was set to 200; the hyperparameter $p_0 = \langle p_0.pred, p_0.stab \rangle$ is used to select rules, where $p_0.pred$ minimizes the error and $p_0.stab$ finds a tradeoff between error and stability. In the SIRUS algorithm, the error means 1-AUC for classification and the unexplained variance for regression, and stability refers to the average proportion of rules shared by two SIRUS

---

[3] The settings of the Boruta algorithm were: the Random Forest classifier, auto estimators, `verbose` is set to 2, `random state` is set to 1, number of trees is set to 200.

[4] The parameters of Keras included: last-layer activation – softmax, loss function – softmax_xentr, and learning rate – 0.001.

models fit on two distinct folds in the cross-validation. We choose $p_0.pred$ as an optimal hyperparameter.

In the REM-D method, *trials* (the number of sampling trials to use when using bagging for C5.0 rule extraction) is set to 1, *min_cases* ((the minimum number of samples we must have to perform a split in a decision tree)) is set to 30. In the ECLAIRE method, *min_cases* is set to 30, *block_size* (the hidden layer sampling frequency) is set 1, *ccp_prune* (whether or not we perform the post-hoc cost complexity pruning in the trees we extract with CART before rule induction) is set to `True`. In the deepRED method, *min_cases* is set to 20, *ccp_prune* is set to `True`, *trials* is set to 1.

5.3 Evaluation Metrics

We will evaluate the performance of black-box models, white-box models and rules using detection performance metrics and domain-specific metrics. Specifically, we will use detection performance metrics, such as accuracy, precision, recall, and F-measure, to evaluate the performance of both black-box models (i.e., RF, DNNs) and white-box models (i.e., rule detectors). To do so, we will use the standard confusion matrix, which summarizes the number of true positives, false positives, true negatives, and false negatives (see Table 3). Using this matrix, Table 4 provides the definitions of accuracy, precision, recall, and F-measure, which are commonly used to evaluate the performance of classification models and rule detectors. In addition to these metrics, we will use domain-specific metrics that we proposed (see Sect. 5.3) to evaluate the stability, robustness, and effectiveness of rules extracted from the black-box models using five explanation methods.

5.4 Experimental Results

The performance of black-box models (RF and DNNs) in the 10-fold validation scheme on the pre-processed CICMalDroid dataset is presented in Table 5. The performance of agent models (the considered explanation methods) on the same dataset are shown in Table 6, where stability, robustness, effectiveness are evaluated on the produced rulesets, while accuracy, precision, recall, and F-measure are evaluated on the generated rule detectors.

Table 3. Confusion matrix

Truth	Prediction	
	Malware	Benign
Malware	True Positive (TP)	False Negative (FN)
Benign	False Positive (FP)	True Negative (TN)

Table 4. Definitions of detection performance evaluation metrics

Term	Description
Precision	$\frac{TP}{TP+FP}$
Recall (Detection Rate)	$\frac{TP}{TP+FN}$
Accuracy	$\frac{TP+FN}{TP+TN+FP+FN}$
F-measure	$\frac{2*Recall*Precision}{Recall+Precision}$

Table 5. Performance of black-box models

Metric	RF	DNN
Accuracy	98.97%	95.54%
Precision	99.22%	96.73%
Recall	98.72%	93.94%
F-measure	98.74%	95.32%

Table 6. Performance of the chosen explanation methods

Metric	SIRUS (RF)	inTrees (RF)	deepRED (DNN)	REM-D (DNN)	ECLAIRE (DNN)
# of rules	55	12	3	2	2
Stability	96.15%	0%	0%	0%	0%
Robustness	95.56%	0%	0%	0%	0%
Effectiveness	91.65%	86.64%	–	–	–
Accuracy	92.47%	88.19%	88.99%	86.35%	92.34%
Precision	87.20%	91.70%	88.29%	87.85%	86.87%
Recall	99.82%	87.11%	89.05%	76.08%	93.95%
F-measure	93.09%	87.75%	88.67%	81.54%	91.16%

To compute the robustness score according to the Eq. 4 in our experiments, the variation parameter u was set 10, the r was set to 2000, the total number of samples is 3580 (1790 malware and 1790 benign samples).

The deepRED, REM-D, and ECLAIRE methods output less than 5 rules; the inTrees method produces 12 rules; and SIRUS produces 55 rules. Although the ECLAIRE method only has 2 rules, they contain above 100 features per rule. In contrast, SIRUS contains less than 3 features per rule.

The stability and robustness of SIRUS are above 95%. The other considered XAI methods all have very low stability and robustness (0%). These results suggest that SIRUS has higher potential as explainable Android malware detection method, as it shows high stability and robustness. It is known that the stable and robust XAI methods will improve the human trust and will not confuse the analyst [13]. At the same time, the state-of-the-art methods inTrees, deepRED, REM-D and ECLAIRE seem to have much higher variability of the rule conditions. It will be interesting to investigate how to improve stability and robustness of such methods. Otherwise, explanation results provided by these methods can be regarded by human analysts as meaningless as they would not understand how the detection model works [13].

The effectiveness of SIRUS is 91.65%, which is higher than the inTrees method. We note that we could not compute effectiveness of deepRED, REM-D and ECLAIRE as they use transformed features to generate rules, which do not correspond to the app features from the original dataset. Thus, we could not define a meaningful mutation procedure for them. As an example, the explanation results produced by these DNN-based methods can look like the following: " if $(0.4975 \mid 1.0000)[(h\_0\_0 \leq 9805)$ AND $(h\_0\_263 \leq 25)]$ ... OR $(0.9746 \mid 1.0000)[(h\_0\_143 > 40002)]$ then 1". Therefore, we can conclude our formulation of the effectiveness metric needs to be improved in the future to cover this case.

We examined the accuracy, precision, recall and precision of black-box models (RF and DNN) and the produced rule-based classifiers (agent models). Compared to black-box models, detection performance of agent models has decreased. This is understandable, as the agent models are based on rules extracted from black-box models. For the rules to be readable and less complex, the neural network or trees should be pruned, which leads to loss of detection performance compared to the black-box models.

We note that accuracy of SIRUS is 92.47%, which is higher than the other considered methods. The precision of inTrees is 91.70%, which is the highest in all methods. The value of recall and F-measure of SIRUS is 99.82% and 93.09%; higher than the other comparison methods. Overall, these results suggest that SIRUS has acceptable stability, robustness, effectiveness, and detection performance (as measured by accuracy, recall, and F-measure). The inTrees method has better precision in malware detection.

6   SIRUS Rules

We have demonstrated in our experiments that the SIRUS method could be considered a viable XAI solution for Android malware detection. We now give examples of some detection rules produced by SIRUS.

The detection rule body produced by SIRUS is a conjunction of logic conditions f_i in the path from the root node to the current node in the tree. We note that SIRUS takes care of removing overlapping rules. Therefore the generated 55 rules are not redundant. Five examples of the extracted rules are shown in Table 7. To help understand how to read the rules, they are explained below.

Rule 1: If TelephonyManager.getLine1Number < 2 & TelephonyManager. getSubscriberId < 1 then *0.04* else *0.87*.

Explanation: TelephonyManager.getLine1Number is an API that obtains a phone number, TelephonyManager.getSubscriberId is an sensitive API that gets device information. The value of these features represents the count of API calls in the code. These are all sensitive behaviors, that might lead to private user data leakage. So this rule means: if an application tries to access the phone

Table 7. Example rules extracted by the SIRUS method

ID	Rules
1	if `TelephonyManager.getLine1Number` < 2 & `TelephonyManager.getSubscriberId` < 1 then *0.04* else *0.87*
2	if `Android.permission.SEND_SMS` < 1 & `removeAccessibilityInteractionCon nection` < 3 then *0.012* else *0.97*
3	If `TelephonyManager.getCellLocation` < 3 & `TelephonyManager.getSubscriberId` < 1 then *0.05* else *0.88*
4	if `Android.intent.action.PACKAGE_ADDED` < 1 & `getInstallerPackageName` ≥ 1 then *0.0089* else *0.76*
5	if `Android.permission.READ_PHONE_STATE` < 1 & `target_sdk` < 19 then *0.24* else *0.52*

number at least 2 times or calls for device information, then there is a 87% possibility that it belongs to malware.

Rule 2: If `Android.permission.SEND_SMS` < 1 & `removeAccessibilityInteractionConnection` < 3 then *0.012* else *0.97*.

Explanation: `Android.permission.SEND_SMS` is a permission that is required to send SMS messages, the value of this feature is 0 means the app without requesting this permission, otherwise means the app has been granted the corresponding permissions. `RemoveAccessibilityInteractionConnection` is a dynamic behavior to consume lots of system memory, which can reduce the app's speed or lead to crashes. So this rule means: if the application request the SEND_SMS permission or makes the system unstable by removing the accessibility interaction connection more than 3 times, there is a 97% possibility that it belongs to malware. It indicates that this is a strong rule to identify malware.

Rule 3: If `TelephonyManager.getCellLocation` < 3 & `TelephonyManager.getSubscriberId` < 1 then *0.05* else *0.88*.

Explanation: `TelephonyManager.getCellLocation` is an API that obtains the location information; `TelephonyManager.getSubscriberId` is an API that obtains device information. The value of these features represents the count of API calls in the code. This rule means that if an application calls for the user's location more than 3 times or tries to access the phone number, then there is a 88% possibility that it is malware.

Rule 4: If `Android.intent.action.PACKAGE_ADDED` < 1 & `getInstallerPackageName` ≥ 1 then *0.0089* else *0.76*.

Explanation: `Android.intent.action.PACKAGE_ADDED` is an action that notifies of an apk package added to the system; `GetInstallerPackageName` is an API that obtains the source of the package, it could be from Google Play or other third-party markets. The large number of these features might be indicate there are abnormal frequent application installation behaviors or a large number of installations of untrusted application packages.

This rule means that if an application is notified about added more than one packages or the app does not show the source of the apk package, then there is a 76% possibility that it is malware.

Rule 5: If `Android.permission.READ_PHONE_STATE` < 1 & `target_sdk` < 19 then *0.24* else *0.52*.

Explanation: `Android.permission.READ_PHONE_STATE` is a permission that allows read-only access to phone states, such as phone numbers, network information, and device identifiers. The value of 0 for this feature indicates that the app has not requested the `READ_PHONE_STATE` permission, while a non-zero value indicates that the app has been granted this permission. `Target_sdk` is the app Android SDK target version. This rule means that if an application tries to access the phone state or has the target SDK version above 19, there it is a 52% possibility that it is malware. So it is not a very strong rule for the analysts to distinguish the malware.

7   Conclusion

In this study, we aimed to evaluate the quality of rule-based global XAI methods in the context of Android malware detection and to provide useful insights for malware analysts regarding the existing post-hoc XAI approaches. To achieve this goal, we formulated three domain-specific properties to measure the quality of the detection methods: *stability*, *robustness*, and *effectiveness*. Using these metrics, we evaluated five state-of-the-art explanation approaches using the CICMalDroid dataset. Our work investigating domain-specific evaluation metrics for global rule-based explanation methods extends the elegant works by Fan *et al.* [13] and Warnecke *et al.* [41]. They proposed domain-specific properties for *local* XAI methods that provide explanations for a single sample. However, we now focus on rule-based *global* XAI methods.

Our experimental results demonstrate that these evaluation metrics can assess the rule-based global XAI approaches, providing valuable insights for researchers and practitioners. Specifically, we found that the SIRUS method can generate stable, robust, and effective rules with high detection performance, outperforming other state-of-the-art methods that were evaluated in our study. Indeed, in our experiments, the deepRED, REM-D, and ECLAIRE methods show zero stability and robustness: this means that with every run the produced rules are different and any small change will change the explanation results. These methods can still provide valuable malware-related information to human analysts, but the analysts might become confused receiving constantly changing explanations.

Our findings highlight the importance of evaluation metrics in assessing the quality of rule-based global XAI Android malware detection methods. The proposed metrics can provide useful guidance for researchers and practitioners working in this field, helping them to select the most effective and reliable detection methods.

In the future work, we intend to focus on improving the proposed metrics in discussion with practitioners, to be able to propose new domain-specific metrics definitions that will capture important properties while being computable for the vast majority of available XAI methods. In addition, we are interested in exploring the impact of the number of rules on the performance of explanation methods. This is an important consideration, as it can help us to better understand the trade-offs involved in using larger rulesets versus smaller ones, and to identify the optimal ruleset size. Finally, we are interested in extending our metrics definition to cover global XAI methods relying on interpretations in terms of significant features rather than rules.

Acknowledgements. This research was partially supported by the Chinese Scholarship Council (CSC).

References

1. Alani, M., Awad, A.: PAIRED: an explainable lightweight Android malware detection system. IEEE Access **10**, 73214–73228 (2022)
2. Arp, D., Spreitzenbarth, M., Hübner, M., Gascon, H., Rieck, K.: DREBIN: effective and explainable detection of android malware in your pocket. In: Symposium on Network and Distributed System Security (NDSS) (2014)
3. Backes, M., Nauman, M.: LUNA: quantifying and leveraging uncertainty in Android malware analysis through Bayesian machine learning. In: 2017 IEEE European Symposium on Security and Privacy, Los Alamitos, CA, USA, pp. 204–217. IEEE (2017)
4. Bénard, C., Biau, G., Da Veiga, S., Scornet, E.: SIRUS: stable and interpretable rule set for classification. Electron. J. Stat. **15**(1), 427–505 (2021)
5. Burkart, N., Huber, M.F.: A survey on the explainability of supervised machine learning. J. Artif. Intell. Res. **70**, 245–317 (2021)
6. Calleja, A., Martín, A., Menéndez, H.D., Tapiador, J., Clark, D.: Picking on the family: disrupting Android malware triage by forcing misclassification. Expert Syst. Appl. **95**, 113–126 (2018)
7. Capuano, N., Fenza, G., Loia, V., Stanzione, C.: Explainable artificial intelligence in cybersecurity: a survey. IEEE Access **10**, 93575–93600 (2022)
8. Charmet, F., et al.: Explainable artificial intelligence for cybersecurity: a literature survey. Ann. Telecommun. **77**, 1–24 (2022)
9. Dashevskyi, S., Zhauniarovich, Y., Gadyatskaya, O., Pilgun, A., Ouhssain, H.: Dissecting Android cryptocurrency miners. In: Proceedings of the Tenth ACM Conference on Data and Application Security and Privacy, pp. 191–202 (2020)
10. Demontis, A., et al.: Yes, machine learning can be more secure! a case study on android malware detection. IEEE Trans. Dependable Secure Comput. **16**(4), 711–724 (2017)

11. Deng, H.: Interpreting tree ensembles with intrees. Int. J. Data Sci. Anal. **7**(4), 277–287 (2019)
12. Dhalaria, M., Gandotra, E.: Android malware detection techniques: a literature review. Recent Patents Eng. **15**(2), 225–245 (2021)
13. Fan, M., Wei, W., Xie, X., Liu, Y., Guan, X., Liu, T.: Can we trust your explanations? Sanity checks for interpreters in Android malware analysis. IEEE Trans. Inf. Forensics Secur. **16**, 838–853 (2020)
14. Guidotti, R., Monreale, A., Ruggieri, S., Pedreschi, D., Turini, F., Giannotti, F.: Local rule-based explanations of black box decision systems. arXiv preprint arXiv:1805.10820 (2018)
15. Guidotti, R., Monreale, A., Ruggieri, S., Turini, F., Giannotti, F., Pedreschi, D.: A survey of methods for explaining black box models. ACM Comput. Surv. (CSUR) **51**(5), 1–42 (2018)
16. Guo, W., Mu, D., Xu, J., Su, P., Wang, G., Xing, X.: LEMNA: explaining deep learning based security applications. In: proceedings of the 2018 ACM SIGSAC Conference on Computer and Communications Security (CCS), pp. 364–379 (2018)
17. Jerbi, M., Chelly Dagdia, Z., Bechikh, S., Ben Said, L.: Android malware detection as a bi-level problem. Comput. Secur. **121**, 102825 (2022)
18. Kinkead, M., Millar, S., McLaughlin, N., O'Kane, P.: Towards explainable CNNs for Android malware detection. Procedia Comput. Sci. **184**, 959–965 (2021)
19. Kong, P., Li, L., Gao, J., Liu, K., Bissyandé, T.F., Klein, J.: Automated testing of Android apps: a systematic literature review. IEEE Trans. Reliab. **68**(1), 45–66 (2018)
20. Kursa, M.B., Jankowski, A., Rudnicki, W.R.: Boruta - a system for feature selection. Fund. Inform. **101**, 271–285 (2010)
21. Lipton, Z.C.: The mythos of model interpretability: in machine learning, the concept of interpretability is both important and slippery. Queue **16**(3), 31–57 (2018)
22. Liu, K., Xu, S., Xu, G., Zhang, M., Sun, D., Liu, H.: A review of Android malware detection approaches based on machine learning. IEEE Access **8**, 124579–124607 (2020)
23. Lu, Z., Thing, V.L.: PhilaeX: explaining the failure and success of AI models in malware detection. arXiv preprint arXiv:2207.00740 (2022)
24. Lundberg, S.M., Lee, S.I.: A unified approach to interpreting model predictions. In: Advances in Neural Information Processing Systems, vol. 30 (2017)
25. Mahdavifar, S., Alhadidi, D., Ghorbani, A.A.: Effective and efficient hybrid Android malware classification using pseudo-label stacked auto-encoder. J. Netw. Syst. Manage. **30**, 1–34 (2022)
26. Mahdavifar, S., Kadir, A.F.A., Fatemi, R., Alhadidi, D., Ghorbani, A.A.: Dynamic Android malware category classification using semi-supervised deep learning. In: 2020 IEEE International Conference on Dependable, Autonomic and Secure Computing(DASC/PiCom/CBDCom/CyberSciTech), pp. 515–522. IEEE (2020)
27. Mehtab, A., et al.: AdDroid: rule-based machine learning framework for Android malware analysis. Mob. Netw. Appl. **25**(1), 180–192 (2020)
28. Melis, M., Maiorca, D., Biggio, B., Giacinto, G., Roli, F.: Explaining black-box Android malware detection. In: 2018 26th European Signal Processing Conference (EUSIPCO), pp. 524–528 (2018). https://doi.org/10.23919/EUSIPCO.2018.8553598
29. Morcos, M., Al Hamadi, H., Damiani, E., Nandyala, S., McGillion, B.: A surrogate-based technique for Android malware detectors' explainability. In: 2022 18th International Conference on Wireless and Mobile Computing, Networking and Communications (WiMob), pp. 112–117. IEEE (2022)

30. Nadeem, A., et al.: SoK: explainable machine learning for computer security applications. arXiv preprint arXiv:2208.10605 (2022)
31. Narayanan, A., Chandramohan, M., Chen, L., Liu, Y.: Context-aware, adaptive, and scalable Android malware detection through online learning. IEEE Trans. Emerg. Top. Comput. Intell. 1(3), 157–175 (2017)
32. Odusami, M., Abayomi-Alli, O., Misra, S., Shobayo, O., Damasevicius, R., Maskeliunas, R.: Android malware detection: a survey. In: Florez, H., Diaz, C., Chavarriaga, J. (eds.) ICAI 2018. CCIS, vol. 942, pp. 255–266. Springer, Cham (2018). https://doi.org/10.1007/978-3-030-01535-0_19
33. Qiu, J., Zhang, J., Luo, W., Pan, L., Nepal, S., Xiang, Y.: A survey of Android malware detection with deep neural models. ACM Comput. Surv. (CSUR) 53(6), 1–36 (2020)
34. Ribeiro, M.T., Singh, S., Guestrin, C.: "Why should I trust you?" Explaining the predictions of any classifier. In: Proceedings of the 22nd ACM SIGKDD International Conference on Knowledge Discovery and Data Mining, pp. 1135–1144 (2016)
35. Ribeiro, M.T., Singh, S., Guestrin, C.: Anchors: high-precision model-agnostic explanations. In: Proceedings of the AAAI Conference on Artificial Intelligence (2018)
36. Shams, Z., et al.: REM: an integrative rule extraction methodology for explainable data analysis in healthcare. medRxiv (2021)
37. Srivastava, G., et al.: XAI for cybersecurity: state of the art, challenges, open issues and future directions. arXiv preprint arXiv:2206.03585 (2022)
38. Tam, K., Fattori, A., Khan, S., Cavallaro, L.: CopperDroid: automatic reconstruction of android malware behaviors. In: NDSS Symposium 2015, pp. 1–15 (2015)
39. Tam, K., Feizollah, A., Anuar, N.B., Salleh, R., Cavallaro, L.: The evolution of Android malware and Android analysis techniques. ACM Comput. Surv. (CSUR) 49(4), 1–41 (2017)
40. Wang, S., et al.: TrafficAV: an effective and explainable detection of mobile malware behavior using network traffic. In: Proceedings of 24th International Symposium on Quality of Service (IWQoS) (2016)
41. Warnecke, A., Arp, D., Wressnegger, C., Rieck, K.: Evaluating explanation methods for deep learning in security. In: Proceedings of European Symposium on Security and Privacy (EuroS&P), pp. 158–174. IEEE (2020)
42. Wu, B., Chen, S., Gao, C., Fan, L., Liu, Y., Wen, W., Lyu, M.R.: Why an Android app is classified as malware: toward malware classification interpretation. ACM Trans. Softw. Eng. Methodol. (TOSEM) 30(2), 1–29 (2021)
43. Xu, F., Uszkoreit, H., Du, Y., Fan, W., Zhao, D., Zhu, J.: Explainable AI: a brief survey on history, research areas, approaches and challenges. In: Tang, J., Kan, M.-Y., Zhao, D., Li, S., Zan, H. (eds.) NLPCC 2019. LNCS (LNAI), vol. 11839, pp. 563–574. Springer, Cham (2019). https://doi.org/10.1007/978-3-030-32236-6_51
44. Yan, F., Wen, S., Nepal, S., Paris, C., Xiang, Y.: Explainable machine learning in cybersecurity: a survey. Int. J. Intell. Syst. 37(12), 12305–12334 (2022)
45. Zarlenga, M.E., Shams, Z., Jamnik, M.: Efficient decompositional rule extraction for deep neural networks. arXiv preprint arXiv:2111.12628 (2021)

46. Zhang, Z., Hamadi, H.A., Damiani, E., Yeun, C.Y., Taher, F.: Explainable artificial intelligence applications in cyber security: state-of-the-art in research. arXiv preprint arXiv:2208.14937 (2022)

47. Zhu, D., Xi, T., Jing, P., Wu, D., Xia, Q., Zhang, Y.: A transparent and multimodal malware detection method for Android apps. In: Proceedings of the 22nd International ACM Conference on Modeling, Analysis and Simulation of Wireless and Mobile Systems (MSWIM), New York, NY, USA, pp. 51–60. ACM (2019). https://doi.org/10.1145/3345768.3355915

48. Zilke, J.R., Loza Mencía, E., Janssen, F.: DeepRED – rule extraction from deep neural networks. In: Calders, T., Ceci, M., Malerba, D. (eds.) DS 2016. LNCS (LNAI), vol. 9956, pp. 457–473. Springer, Cham (2016). https://doi.org/10.1007/978-3-319-46307-0_29

Whitelisting for Characterizing and Monitoring Process Control Communication

Andreas Paul[1]([⊠]), Franka Schuster[2], and Hartmut König[2]

[1] Codewerk GmbH, Karlsruhe, Germany
andreas.paul@codewerk.de
[2] Brandenburg University of Technology Cottbus-Senftenberg, Cottbus, Germany
{franka.schuster,hartmut.koenig}@b-tu.de

Abstract. In recent years, industrial control systems (ICS) used in critical infrastructures have come under the spotlight as a powerful target to potentially harm broader segments of society. Although there is a growing body of anomaly detection approaches in this field, the homogeneous network traffic narrative that is supposed to justify their potential success is poorly proven. At the same time, more and more machine learning (ML) schemes have been developed for this purpose neglecting though that ML is not the ideal approach for various profound detection aspects in operational technology (OT) networks. In this paper, we present and evaluate a communication whitelisting approach for anomaly detection in OT networks and point out advantages of this allegedly ancient monitoring method compared to machine learning. For this, we introduce measures to express the variability of network traffic and use them to quantify the communication dynamics of traffic for different OT infrastructures and network layers. We show that due to the static network communication in the OT domain the detection capability is sufficiently high without whitelist explosion or runtime concerns.

Keywords: Intrusion Detection · Industrial Networks · Whitelisting · Traffic Ananlysis

1   Introduction

In recent years, information technology (IT) and operational technology (OT) have converged very closely. This trend has serious implications for the protection of critical infrastructures from external and internal threats. In contrast to office networks, the traffic in OT environments is commonly expected to be static and homogeneous regarding the involved devices and their communication characteristics. Hence, many approaches assume regular network communication for the training phase to apply *anomaly detection* for the analysis. This reflects today's attack trends, which are increasingly characterised by polymorphic aspects, but at the same time must address the need to identify unknown (zero-day) attacks, which is not possible with the complement misuse detection approach.

S. Li et al. (Eds.): NSS 2023, LNCS 13983, pp. 23–45, 2023.
https://doi.org/10.1007/978-3-031-39828-5_2

For this, machine learning (ML) has meanwhile become the dominant app-roach because it is considered to be more efficient for the definition of normality than rule-based approaches. From the domain perspective, however, network-based attack detection relies in no small part on communication aspects that ML cannot model effectively. This comprises the precise characterization of *commu-nication relations* which includes both the devices involved and the protocols and message types used for data transmission. Here, the strength of ML to generalise is simultaneously its weakness. Since this capability arises from abstractions of the training data, it means that some important aspects are not reflected accu-rately enough in the model. This leads to incorrect classifications for aspects that can be expressed with rules. Especially in OT networks, which are less dynamic than IT networks, it is an essential requirement to be able to precisely and com-pletely recognise the devices seen in the training phase and their communication relations[1] and without any generalization[2] for the detection. Consequently, the question is not whether to apply machine learning *or* rules for attack detection. It is actually, which method is the right one for which aspects. While rules allow a precise monitoring of well-defined communication behavior, machine learning is supposed to be applied to traffic parts for which it is not reasonable or feasi-ble to express them by rules, e. g., the application payload of packets spanning a comparably much broader space of information which is in general challeng-ing to model. Apart from precise detection, communication rules can effectively support a key problem in OT network security research: they enable the analysis of characteristics and dynamics of OT network traffic to prove or disprove com-mon assumptions of OT network communication compared to IT traffic. The following essential contributions of this paper are derived from this:

- We present an approach for the automated generation of communication rules from raw network traffic usable as whitelists in anomaly detection for a wide range of OT protocols independent of their underlying protocol stack.
- We apply the rule generation on six datasets taken from *real* OT networks and compare them to traffic from an OT [8] and an IT [22] testbed that are prominent in research. By quantifying the emergence of the rules over time, we measure the dynamics in network communication and express the static nature of OT network traffic that are commonly expected in the literature, but to the best of our knowledge have not been demonstrated so clearly, yet.
- We show that different OT network layers can be identified by a statistical clustering applied on the metrics derived from the rule generation process that allows us in turn to identify network layers from an unknown domain.
- We evaluate the efficiency of the rules regarding detection capability and runtime. The former is done through attacks in a public OT dataset prominent in research [8], the latter by converting the rules into a rule set for a widely

---

[1] A communication observation $dev_A \rightarrow dev_B$ and $dev_B \rightarrow dev_C$ may not be part of the abstraction without proper reflection in the model when using ML.

[2] The same two observations could lead to a model reflecting also $dev_A \rightarrow dev_C$ when applying ML.

used Intrusion Detection System (IDS) [21] and their application on real networks.

- In the course of the discussion regarding the attack detection capability of our rules we precisely explain the impact of the attacks contained in the used public OT data set on the network traffic. We conclude that in turn our whitelisting can be used both for packet-based labeling of anomalous data and as a baseline for more advanced detection mechanisms.

The remainder of this paper is organised as follows. In Sect. 2, we give background information of OT infrastructures and preliminary considerations for communication whitelisting. The method for whitelist generation is explained in Sect. 3. After introducing the datasets used for our evaluation in Sect. 4, the approach and the results for measuring communication dynamics are presented in Sect. 5. Practical results of the whitelist application are presented in Sect. 6. We discuss related work in Sect. 7 before concluding this paper with some final remarks in Sect. 8.

2   Preliminaries

Before presenting our approach we dive into necessary background and terminology for assessing the concepts of the paper. There are two types of industrial control systems (ICSs): distributed control systems (DCSs) and supervisory control and data acquisition (SCADA) networks [23]. In the energy sector, for example, local energy production processes in power plants employ DCSs, while SCADA networks are deployed for the power distribution to consumers spanning up to thousands of dispersed assets. For the explanations of process control networks, we use the generic term operational technology (OT), which describes hardware and software for controlling physical processes.

2.1   OT Network Hierarchy

The field of process control involves particular constraints and trends leading to major security issues that have already been identified for a decade from now [12], but which still unaltered exist due to the long-term design and operation of most networks. Regardless of the specific type, OT networks are typically divided into multiple sub-networks, resulting in an organisation in different layers. A simplified architecture of OT networks is presented in Fig. 1. On the lowest layer, i. e. the *fieldbus*, sensors and actuators measure and adjust physical parameters, e. g., pressure, temperature, or speed values, that are used by programmable logic controllers (PLCs) to fulfill a control-loop-based task. Data from several PLCs are collected in the *control network* for evaluation by servers that aggregate all activities of sub-processes and prepare these data for visualization. By connecting the (dual homed) servers with a second *supervisory network*, the data are made available there. Operators can interact with the processes via human-machine interfaces (HMI) by monitoring the data and manually adjusting sub-processes.

Nowadays, OT networks are connected to public networks, such as the Internet, to provide remote access to certain services provided by dedicated servers, e.g., data historians or maintenance servers, which are placed in a demilitarised zone *(DMZ network)*. Firewalls are used as major prevalent security measure to restrict access to these servers or to the OT network. To extend this basic protection, we propose monitoring *within* the subnets, which takes effect, for instance, when the firewall has been penetrated or an attack is launched within the network. The monitoring is based on a simple whitelisting of network communication. A set of rules defines the allowed communication behaviour, more precisely, which components are allowed to communicate with each other and how (with which protocols and message types).

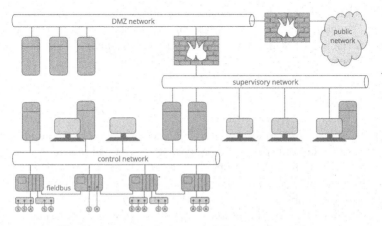

Fig. 1. Example of a typical OT network topology

2.2   Aspects of the Whitelist Use

Whitelisting has several advantages and disadvantages compared to alternative anomaly detection methods, which are discussed below regarding four aspects.

Completeness. Even in the case of a comprehensive learning, it cannot be guaranteed that a *complete* whitelist representing all legal network communication can be generated. An incomplete whitelist leads to the generation of false positives (FPs) that quickly cause an unacceptable administrative effort due to the necessary assessment of the alarms' relevance and the consideration of whitelist extensions. We conduct a detailed investigation of this in Sect. 5.

Monitoring Coverage. Whereas the completeness is associated with FPs, the monitoring coverage is linked to the false negatives (FNs) problem. Thus, attacks can occur in traffic parts not captured by the monitoring. Machine learning approaches in particular are usually limited to monitoring a specific traffic type, e.g., by targeted analysing process data or flow meta-information. In contrast, we follow a complete monitoring of the network traffic, independent of the protocol stack, up to the application-oriented protocol level.

Interpretability. Since the generation of FPs cannot be precluded, the application of systems that automatically initiate countermeasures, such as intrusion prevention systems, is usually not considered acceptable in OT networks. It is therefore more important that generated alerts are in a format that can easily be interpreted by a human being, so that a direct identification of the attack causes is possible. Compared to ML, whitelists offer great advantages here because the rule-based expression of detection references is inherently comprehensible.

Efficiency. Attack steps have to be logged at the shortest possible time interval after execution, so that countermeasures can immediately be initiated. It is likely that both the memory and the computing capacity required for the analysis are influenced by the size of the whitelist. Since the number of rules required for the desired monitoring cannot be estimated in advance, it is questionable whether a real-time monitoring can be achieved. We examine both the attack detection capability and the practical application of whitelisting in detail in Sect. 6.

3   Methodology

The proposed approach for whitelist generation from raw network traffic and the use for analysing the communication dynamics is shown in Fig. 2. Network traffic is first preprocessed to collect all information for specifying regular communications in the form of so-called *communication graphs* [19] (Sect. 3.1). A communication graph is first mapped to a *general whitelist* (Sect. 3.2) from which a *specific whitelist* (Sect. 3.3) is generated subsequently. The latter is adapted to a specific tool, here the IDS Snort [21], which can immediately be used for the monitoring. The whitelist application to analyse the communication dynamics and the experiments to investigate practical aspects are described in Sect. 5 and Sect. 6.

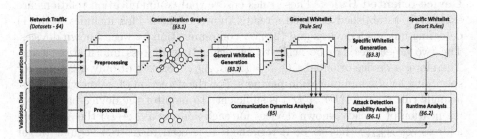

Fig. 2. Methodology overview

3.1   Communication Graphs

A communication graph is a directed graph used to represent network devices and their *logical* connections, also referred to as *communication relations*. Formally, a directed graph $D = (V, E)$ consists of a set of nodes (vertices)

$V = \{v_1, ..., v_n\}$ representing the network devices and a set of edges $E = \{e_1, ..., e_m\}$ for the communication relations. The addresses determined for a node v are represented by $A(v) = \{a \mid a \in \mathtt{A_{IP}} \cup \mathtt{A_{MAC}}\}$ with $\mathtt{A_{IP}}$ and $\mathtt{A_{MAC}}$ representing the domain of IP and MAC addresses. The set of all addresses of a communication graph D is referred to as $A(D)$:

$$A(D) = \bigcup_{i=1}^{n} A(v_i), v_i \in V(D)$$

An edge $e = (v_{src}, v_{dst}, M)$ contains the source and target vertices v_{src} and v_{dst} as well as a set of messages $M = \{m_1, ..., m_o\}$. A message $m = (a_{src}, a_{dst}, t, p, u)$ is characterised by the transmission protocol t, the payload protocol p, and the message type u. Since multiple addresses can be assigned to a vertex, the source and destination addresses used for message transmission are available in a_{src} and a_{dst}. We refer to all messages of a graph D as set $M(D)$:

$$M(D) = \bigcup_{i=1}^{m} M(e_i), e_i \in E(D)$$

A communication graph can directly be used as a reference to detect undesired communication. Next, we explain this procedure.

3.2   Generation of the General Whitelist

The message set $M(D)$ contains all information for describing legitimate network communications. Hence, it forms the initial rule set: $R = M(D)$. From this, more meaningful rules can be derived that focus on single aspects of communication. So, it is possible to distinguish between different types of whitelist violations.

Device-oriented Rules. These rules ensure that communication relations are exclusively established between already known devices. This includes both (1) detecting unknown devices and (2) new communication between known devices. The two objectives can be achieved by evaluating address information alone. Therefore, a device-oriented rule $r = (A_{src}, A_{dst})$ consists of only a 2-tuple for specifying legal communication partners. For the detection of unknown devices, a single rule $r_U = (A(D), A(D))$ is sufficient. To monitor the device-based communication of already known devices for each address $a \in A(D)$ the associated address set $A_{dst}(a)$ has to be determined. It is used to restrict regular target components that can be addressed by means of a:

$$A_{dst}(a) = \bigcup_{m \in M(D) \mid a_{src}(m) = a} a_{dst}(m)$$

In addition for each address $a \in A(D)$, a rule $r = (\{a\}, A_{dst}(a))$ is generated, resulting in the rule set R_K. We denote the rules for detecting new senders out of the set of already known devices as $R_{K_{src}} = \{r \mid r \in R_K \wedge A_{dst}(a) = \emptyset\}$. The set $R_{K_{dst}} = R_K \setminus R_{K_{src}}$ is used to identify devices that have already acted as senders but addressed different devices during monitoring. We refer to the complete set of device-oriented rules as $R_D = r_U \cup R_K$.

Communication-oriented Rules. After ensuring the legitimacy of device-to-device communication using the R_D rule set, specific communication type are verified. To generate these rules the tuple set $A_C(D)$ is first determined which contains all source and destination address combinations specified by graph D:

$$A_C(D) = \{a_C = (a_{src}, a_{dst})| \bigcup_{m \in M(D)} (a_{src}(m), a_{dst}(m))\}$$

Each address tuple is used to determine the associated message set

$$M(a_C) = \{m \in M(D)|a_{src}(m) = a_{src}(a_C) \wedge$$
$$a_{dst}(m) = a_{dst}(a_C)\}$$

whose elements are subsequently combined in three different ways. First, communication protocols used for data transmission are determined, whereby transport-oriented protocols $T(a_C)$ and application-oriented protocols are distinguished, referred to as $P(a_C)$. In addition, the set of used message types $U(a_C)$ is determined for each application-oriented protocol. These three combination sets are formally described as follows:

$$T(a_C) = \bigcup_{m \in M(a_C)} t(m)$$

$$P(a_C) = \bigcup_{m \in M(a_C)} (t(m), p(m))$$

$$U(a_C) = \{((t, p), U)|(t, p) \in P(a_C),$$
$$U = \bigcup_{m \in M(a_C): t(m) = t \wedge p(m) = p} u(m)\}$$

A separate rule per address tuple is generated from each set:

$$R_T(a_C) = \{(a_{src}(a_C), a_{dst}(a_C), T(a_C))\}$$
$$R_P(a_C) = \{(a_{src}(a_C), a_{dst}(a_C), P(a_C))\}$$
$$R_U(a_C) = \{(a_{src}(a_C), a_{dst}(a_C), U(a_C))\}$$

We name the sets of all rules of these three rule types as R_T, R_P, and R_U, whose union gives the set of communication-oriented rules $R_C = R_T \cup R_P \cup R_U$.

3.3 Generation of Specific Whitelists

The rules describe aspects that are also analysed by existing security methods, such as firewalls or IDSs. Thus, it is straightforward to generate rules from the general whitelist for such tools. We realized that for Snort, a widely used IDS, by mapping the address information of the general rules to device-oriented rules and general communication-oriented rules to Snort header elements and options. We give a detailed demonstration of the generation principle of specific whitelists for Snort in respect of the syntax of Snort's description language in Appendix A.

4 Datasets

For the evaluation of our approach, we use eight datasets from different types of infrastructures that operate both OT networks and standard IT technology. Table 1 summarises the characteristics of the datasets. All are captured via dedicated access points (typically switches). The properties specified in Table 1 refer to the monitoring domain of the sensor used for capturing. As our evaluation is carried out from several aspects, the last column of the table contains information on whether a dataset is used for communication characterization *(com)*, attack detection capability evaluation *(det)*, or runtime analysis *(rta)*.

Table 1. Dataset characteristics

Dataset	Infrastructure type	Network level	Duration (hh:mm:ss)	# Packets (millions)	Packet rate (k/second)	# Devices	Analysis aspect		
							com	det	rta
power1.1	power plant	supervisory	02:39:34	90.53	9.46	114	●	○	●
power2.1		supervisory	02:15:36	66.08	8.12	71	●	○	○
power2.2		control	01:25:40	6.10	1.19	66	●	○	○
power2.3		DMZ	17:36:10	83.89	1.32	682	●	○	○
train1.1	train	control	01:35:44	17.00	2.96	76	●	○	○
train1.2		control	02:41:10	9.96	1.03	155	●	○	○
cicids.17	office	–	08:05:36	11.68	0.40	9,727	●	○	○
swat.a3	water treatment	control	24:12:58	1,248.96	14.00	61	●	○	○
swat.a6		control	03:40:00	321.03	24.00	98	○	●	●

Power Plants. We use several traffic traces that were captured at two coal-fired power plants. They involve two different control systems from leading vendors used worldwide. In our experience, networks of plants using the same control technology have strong similarities in architecture, protocols, and hardware. The dataset labeled as *power1.1* was captured within the supervisory level of a plant consisting of in total four generation units with a combined capacity of 2200 MW. The other datasets *power2.1* to *power2.3* originate from different network layers of a second plant with two generation units of the 800 MW class each.

Local Passenger Train. Two datasets originate from a control network of a train used for urban passenger transport. The train communication network is used for a train series rolled out in Germany at the end of 2018. The concrete train is composed of six coaches including two railcars. The operation is implemented by a network (conform to [5]) spanning all coaches. It is divided into two local networks. The first subnet contains devices of subsystems that are essential to ensure regular train operation. These include, for example, traction/brake and door control, power converters, and safety systems. The second subnet includes devices of various systems whose fault-free operation does not have a decisive influence on the safe operation of the train. They serve organisational and coordination purposes or contribute to passenger comfort. These include the camera surveillance system, passenger counting, intercoms and passenger information devices. Both subnets reflect the control network layer.

Water Treatment. This dataset [8][3] represents a small-scale version of a modern water treatment plant. The network traffic considered in this study was provided in two different datasets. The first one originates from 2016 and covers 136 h of network traffic from continuously running SWaT without performing any attacks. We use the first about 24 h of this data and refer to them as *swat.a3*. The dataset *swat.a6* was provided in 2019 and contains a series of malware infection attacks on the engineering workstation. Due to the network architecture of the testbed, the two datasets are assigned to the control level.

Standard IT Network. In addition to the OT traffic, we use a portion of the popular public dataset CICIDS2017 [22] as an exemplary representative of standard IT traffic for a direct comparison of communication characteristics. The dataset labeled *cicids.17* corresponds to the first day (Monday) of the capture when no attack activity has been observed.

Notes on Private Datasets. The first two datasets contain sensitive information that we are only allowed to describe in abstract form due to non-disclosure agreements. The datasets were captured using the tool `tcpdump`, running on a separate sensor device attached to switches with activated port mirroring.

5   Communication Dynamics Analysis

Besides the whitelist generation, the process depicted in Fig. 2 aims to analyse the communication dynamics of OT networks. Here, we focus on investigating the variability or homogeneity of the traffic and on determining whether (and to what extent) a complete whitelist can be generated from it.

5.1   Multi-step Whitelist Generation

For the communication dynamics analysis, each dataset is first divided into two parts, the *generation data* and the *validation data*. The whitelist is generated in an n-step procedure in which the generation data is further split into n disjoint and consecutive sub-captures. In each step i ($1 \leq i \leq n$), an increasing amount (i sub-captures) of the generation data is used for the whitelist generation. After each step, the validation data is analysed with the derived whitelist and the number of packets that do not match the whitelist is determined. This proportion of packets from the total amount of validation data is called *mismatching packet rate (MPR)*. The MPR in the i-th step is denoted as m_i.

5.2   Measures for MPR Evolution Analysis

The MPR determined in the last sub-step m_n is an indicator of the completeness of the whitelist generated from the generation data used to monitor the validation data. To characterize the communication dynamics within the generation data,

---

[3] https://itrust.sutd.edu.sg/itrust-labs_datasets/dataset_info/.

multiple measures are determined. The basis is the MPR reduction achieved between two sub-steps. Due to the monotonicity of the MPR evolution function, the MPR decrease after the i-th step is determined as difference of the current MPR and the MPR of the next step: $d_i = m_i - m_{i+1}$, with $1 \leq i < n$.

Mean MPR Decrease. As base for the following measures this is defined by:

$$\bar{d} = \frac{1}{n-1} \sum_{i=1}^{n-1} d_i$$

Dispersion Measures. In addition to the mean MPR decrease, the communication dynamics can also be characterized by the distribution around the mean value. A higher distribution indicates significant whitelist extensions within relatively few generation steps. Thus, communication can be considered more static in the case of a comparatively high dispersion than in the case of a relatively low one. The analysis of the dispersion of individual MPR reduction rates around the mean is based on relative measures. First, the relative standard deviation is determined, which is also referred to as the variation coefficient:

$$v = \frac{\sqrt{\frac{1}{n-1} \sum_{i=1}^{n-1} (d_i - \bar{d})^2}}{\bar{d}}$$

As a second measure of dispersion, the normalized Gini coefficient is determined. For this purpose, the MPR decrease values are first sorted in increasing order; we denote the values thus obtained as $\hat{d}_1, ..., \hat{d}_{n-1}$, with $\hat{d}_i \leq \hat{d}_{i+1}$. The normalized Gini coefficient is determined from these as follows:

$$g = \left(\frac{2 \cdot \sum_{i=1}^{n-1} i \cdot \hat{d}_i}{n-1 \cdot \sum_{i=1}^{n-1} \hat{d}_i} - \frac{n}{n-1} \right) \cdot \frac{n-1}{n-2}$$

For the normalized Gini coefficient, it holds $0 \leq g \leq 1$, with the value rising as the inequality dispersion increases. Finally, we introduce a measure to analyse how often the whitelist changes *significantly* during generation. Hence, we define the jump rate j as the fraction of decreasing MPR values that exceed a certain threshold. We use the product of the mean MPR decrease and the variation coefficient as the relative threshold, so that the jump rate is defined by:

$$j = \frac{|\{d | d \in \{d_1, ..., d_{n-1}\} \wedge d > (\bar{d} \cdot v)\}|}{n-1}$$

5.3   Experimental Setup and Results

The whitelist generation process (Sect. 5.1) is applied as follows. The split of a dataset into generation and validation data was performed in a 1:1 ratio and ten sub-steps ($n = 10$) were used to create the whitelist from the generation data. All splits are time-based, so each resulting sub-capture has the same duration.

Table 2. Whitelist information, mismatching packets, and clustered MPR evolution measures for the investigated datasets

Dataset	Network level	# Triggered rules / # Total rules device-oriented			comm.-oriented			# Mism. packets	MPR evolution m_{10}	$\bar{d}$	v	g	j
		r_U	$R_{K_{src}}$	$R_{K_{dst}}$	R_T	R_P	R_U						
power1.1 superv.		$\frac{1}{1}$	$\frac{0}{10}$	$\frac{9}{54}$	$\frac{0}{151}$	$\frac{3}{151}$	-	336	0.000721	0.000532	1.697286	0.827277	0.2
							2/151	47,604	0.102202	0.000534	1.686094	0.819754	0.2
power2.1 superv.		$\frac{1}{1}$	$\frac{0}{9}$	$\frac{13}{83}$	$\frac{2}{226}$	$\frac{8}{226}$	-	366,176	1.166194	0.000731	1.388637	0.772760	0.3
							1/226	367,188	1.169417	0.000731	1.388637	0.772760	0.3
power2.2 control		$\frac{0}{1}$	$\frac{0}{5}$	$\frac{1}{68}$	$\frac{0}{222}$	$\frac{0}{222}$	-	27	0.000917	0.005911	2.747624	0.991066	0.1
							2/222	31	0.001052	0.005911	2.747624	0.991066	0.1
power2.3 DMZ		$\frac{1}{1}$	$\frac{19}{109}$	$\frac{96}{514}$	$\frac{18}{3028}$	$\frac{31}{3028}$	-	9,146,857	19.463888	0.569613	2.312673	0.946033	0.1
							15/3028	9,187,419	19.550202	0.570594	2.309209	0.945694	0.1
train1.1 control		$\frac{0}{1}$	$\frac{0}{34}$	$\frac{0}{67}$	$\frac{0}{207}$	$\frac{0}{207}$	-	0	0.0	0.000631	2.649324	0.985537	0.1
							0/207	0	0.0	0.000631	2.649324	0.985537	0.1
train1.2 control		$\frac{1}{1}$	$\frac{1}{50}$	$\frac{12}{123}$	$\frac{1}{270}$	$\frac{1}{270}$	-	6,252	0.126118	0.397197	2.821426	0.998874	0.1
							0/270	6,252	0.126118	0.397197	2.821426	0.998874	0.1
swat.a3 control		$\frac{1}{1}$	$\frac{0}{21}$	$\frac{8}{53}$	$\frac{1}{272}$	$\frac{0}{272}$	-	57	0.000009	0.000177	2.797246	0.996615	0.1
							6/272	64	0.000011	0.008177	2.827717	0.999923	0.1
cicids.17 -		$\frac{1}{1}$	$\frac{1}{40}$	$\frac{2,796}{7,065}$	$\frac{88}{27,145}$	$\frac{1,326}{27,145}$	-	1,592,881	54.123183	2.941505	0.847902	0.477112	0.4
							16/27,145	1,593,120	54.131304	2.940656	0.848042	0.477112	0.4

The measures introduced in Sect. 5.2 for the individual datasets are presented in Table 2[4] Since the traffic of different networks exhibits a different protocol mix and not every protocol is decoded to distinguish message types, two values per measure were determined for each dataset. The lower line shows the measures that takes the rules for the identification of different message types into account. In comparison, the upper row states the measures from the exclusive application of the remaining rule types. For allowing a quick visual comparison among the datasets, the results are clustered (column-wise) into four coloured groups (corresponding to the number of different network layers) using k-means. Table 2 also states for each rule type (cf. Sect. 3.2) the ratio of rules triggered by mismatching packets to the total number of generated rules. Thus, the sum of the numerators corresponds to the number of rules that would have to be extended to complete the whitelist with respect to a mismatching packet free analysis of the validation data. The evolution of the MPR over the whitelist generation steps and the influence of the different rule classes on the MPR is shown in the bar charts in Fig. 3.

5.4   Characterization Takeaways

Finding 1: Communication Whitelisting is not Suitable for Monitoring Standard IT Networks. With an MPR of over 54%, by far the most incomplete whitelist was generated for the *cicdis.17* dataset. Due to about 4,000 different rules to be extended, it must be concluded that a whitelist cannot be developed with proper effort to a complete one. The values determined for the dispersion measures indicate a uniform development of the MPR reduction and thus a

---

[4] A repository for interactive analysis of the public datasets is provided here: https://gitlab.com/paulandre/ot-whitelisting.

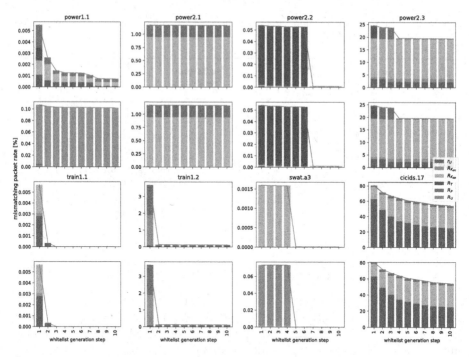

Fig. 3. Evolution of MPRs taking (rows two and four) and not taking (rows one and three) message-type-specific rules into account

high communication dynamics in the generation data. Consequently, we consider communication whitelisting to be unsuitable for standard IT traffic represented by the *cicdis.17* dataset and do not discuss further details for this dataset.

Finding 2: Different OT Network Layers Exhibit Different (measurable) Communication Dynamics. A clustering of dispersion measures shows that communication dynamics differ significantly among OT network layers. Already on the basis of the jump rate measure, the supervisory networks ($j = 0.\overline{2}$, resp. $j = 0.\overline{3}$) can be distinguished from other layers ($j = 0.\overline{1}$). However, as the range of the jump rate is too small, this measure is not suitable for an accurate classification of network domains. In contrast, both the coefficient of variation and the Gini coefficient can be used to clearly refer traffic to OT network layers. Furthermore, the communication dynamics measures indicate that the lower the network layer, the smaller the differences in communication dynamics among different networks of the same layer. While the large difference between the two datasets representing the supervisory layer can even be discerned in the jump rate, the control-layer networks show a comparatively small range in terms of the coefficient of variation (2.65 to 2.83) and the Gini coefficient (0.986 to 0.999).

Finding 3: Strong Correlation between Communication Dynamics and Whitelist Completion Effort. Looking at the communication dynamics in isolation using the measures to describe MPR evolution does not yet allow any conclusions to be drawn about the effort required to extend the whitelist towards a complete one, since in the extreme cases to detect n mismatching packets exactly one, but also n rules may be responsible. By including information on triggering rules, a relatively strong negative correlation can be determined between the proportion of triggering rules from the total amount of rules (r_t for short) and the MPR dispersion measures. Depending on the consideration or exclusion of the message-type-specific rules, a correlation coefficient of -0.79 and -0.83 was determined between r_t and v, respectively. The correlation coefficient between r_t and g is -0.81 (taking message-type-specific rules into account) and -0.84 (when excluding these rules), respectively.

Finding 4: Detection of Whitelist Violations is Dominated by Device-oriented Rules. New device-level communication relations are the most common cause of logging whitelist mismatching packets. Only for dataset *power1.1*, communication-specific rules are dominant, in case message-type-specific rules are considered. For the remaining five datasets, the percentage of messages logged by device-oriented rules ranges from 61% *(train1.2)* to 98% *(power2.3)*. The most common cause of new device-level communication relations involves, between known components, a component already acting as a sender addressing one or more additional devices.

6   Whitelist Application

We discuss the application by detection capability and evaluation performance.

6.1   Attack Detection Capability

The attack detection capability of the whitelists is exemplarily evaluated using the *swat.a6* dataset containing four malicious events. Information on the allocation of these events to the corresponding sub-captures are taken from the documentation of the dataset. A whitelist was generated from the first sub-capture (referred to as *c0*), which does not contain any malicious traffic. Figure 4(a) shows the MPRs derived from the remaining sub-captures *c1-c14*.

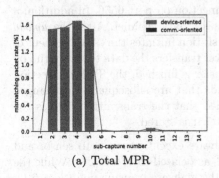

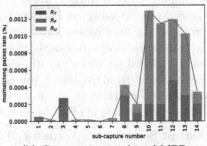

(a) Total MPR   (b) Communication-based MPR

Fig. 4. Mismatching packet rates of the SWaT A6 sub-captures

Infiltrate SCADA WS via USB Thumb Drive with First Malware.
A first malware infection is assigned to $c1$. As the pure infection does not immediately result in changed communication relations, a relatively low MPR (0.000139%) was determined for this capture.

Exfiltrate Historian Data. In a total of four cycles, which are assigned to $c2$ to $c5$, a data exfiltration attack was performed. These result in high MPRs (>1.5%), whereby logged packets mainly belong to the communication of three devices. Figure 5(a) shows a message sequence chart (MSC) representing their communication. The malware apparently enables a remote control of the infected host. The SCADA workstation first establishes a TCP connection on port 6556 (messages *3* to *5*, $m3$ to $m5$ for short) to the device designated as command-and-control (C2) server. After exchanging initial alive messages, the C2 server transmits a command (e5, see $m8$) to the workstation, whereupon the workstation requests current process data from the historian. For this purpose, a TCP connection on port 8080 is established, transferring HTTP packets to request files from the historian *($m14$)*. Subsequently, the historian responds *($m15$)*, transferring the file content in JSON format. This polls the current measurement and status values of all devices involved in the six sub-processes step by step. Afterwards, the data is forwarded with a single TCP packet *($m19$)*. The data polling from the historian and the transmission of the collected values to the C2 server is repeated at regular intervals of about one second. The logging of the associated packets was caused entirely by device-oriented rules. More precisely, the communication between the victim and the C2 server (a so far unknown device) was detected by r_U. In contrast, the communication between the victim and the historian was identified by two rules from set $R_{K_{dst}}$.

Infiltrate SCADA WS with Second Malware, via Downloading from C2 Server. After a rest period of 60 min, represented by $c6$ to $c9$, a secondary infection of the workstation occurs by reloading software from the C2 server. This event is assigned to $c10$, where a slightly increased MPR ($\sim$0.044%) can be observed, that is mainly caused by the communication between the workstation and the C2 server. Packets violating the whitelist are summarised by the MSC shown in Fig. 5(b). This reveals that the malware operates through two different channels. According to the execution of the data exfiltration attack, the control commands are transmitted over a TCP connection on port 6556. In addition, a connection established on port 6001 serves as a data channel. After the *upload* command has been received *($m1$)*, the workstation initiates the establishment of the data connection. Afterwards, the C2 server transfers the data to the victim by sending several packets. Once the data transfer is finished, the TCP connection is closed *($m8$ to $m10$)*. From the commands that are subsequently exchanged over the second channel, it can be concluded that the transmitted data is the malware executable file that is executed after it is stored.

Disrupt Sensor and Actuator. The malware execution tends to sensor and actuator disruption, performed in five cycles associated to $c10$ to $c13$. While the visibly increased MPR to $c10$ is caused by the malware transmission (Sect. 6.1),

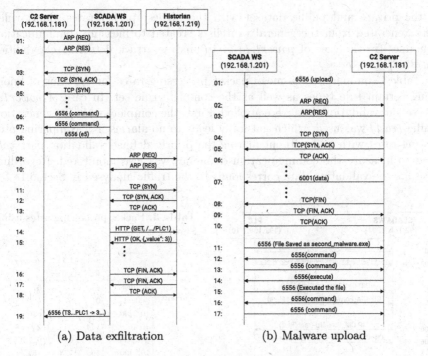

(a) Data exfiltration   (b) Malware upload

Fig. 5. Sequence charts representing analysed attacks

further events cannot be identified from the overall MPR. However, when looking exclusively at the results of the communication-oriented rules (see Fig. 4(b)),
a significantly increased MPR for the sub-captures is evident. Here, the MPR is
dominated by rules of the set R_U used to detect new message types. For $c10$, a total
of 236 associated packets can primarily be assigned to a communication between
the workstation and the primary PLC used to control the first sub-process (P1)
of the SWaT's six-stage process. The logged communication between these components consists of 220 messages transmitted via EtherNet/IP combined with the
Common Industrial Protocol (CIP). There are a combined total of ten different
message types that violate the whitelist. Figure 6 shows the communication. First,
a session is established by means of EtherNet/IP *(m1, m2)*. The application-based
communication between the victim and PLC is realised using CIP, also operating
in a connection-oriented manner. A two-way handshake is used to establish and
terminate the connection ($m5+m6$ and $m9+m10$, respectively). To ensure that no
path to the objects to be accessed exists yet, prior to this *(m3, m4)* an attempt is
made to terminate the connection. Object access by the workstation is executed
by $m7$ and confirmed by the PLC through $m8$.

6.2 Application of a Specific Whitelist

Experimental Setup. We perform a communication monitoring with a runtime
analysis using Snort as an example. Here, we focus on *power1.1* and *swat.a6*

as the private and public dataset with the highest packet rates. Snort rules were generated from the general whitelists created to measure communication dynamics (in the case of *power1.1*) or to analyse attack detection capabilities *(swat.a6)*.

Table 3 summarises the mean packet processing rates for ten runs of Snort using certain rule types as well as the complete rule set. In case of *power1.1* two sets of validation data were applied. First, the complete whitelist generation traffic *(val1)* was used, which naturally leads to no alarms. For comparing processing rates with and without alarms the priorly defined validation part *val2* used to measure the communication dynamics was also monitored. Regarding *swat.a6*, the validation data corresponds to the traffic analysed in Sect. 6.1.

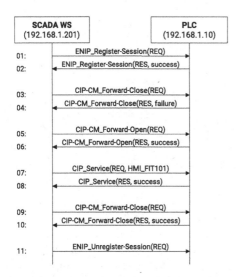

Fig. 6. Sequence chart of process disruption

Table 3. Packet processing rates using Snort

		power1.1		*swat.a6*
		val1	val2	
device-orient.	#rules	43		57
	#alerts	0	87	1,391,094
	10^3 pkts/s	762	773	615
R_T	#rules	144		219
	#alerts	0	0	0
	10^3 pkts/s	563	574	432
R_P	#rules	161		140
	#alerts	0	0	192
	10^3 pkts/s	364	375	294
R_U	#rules	976		22
	#alerts	0	46,126	0
	10^3 pkts/s	2,429	2,416	3,644
all	#rules	1,208		435
	#alerts	0	46,213	1,391,286
	10^3 pkts/s	225	225	113

Performance Results. All rule types allow processing rates in the three-digit thousands range. The rate decreases with an increasing amount of packet header information that has to be analysed. A significantly high processing rate was achieved when only message-type-specific rules were used. This can be explained by the fact that only for a subset of the communication protocols a distinction between different message types is made. Depending on the protocol mix of the analysed data, there is only a very small proportion of end-to-end communication relations (specified by the header of the Snort rules) whose packets need to be analysed at all, so that the analysis of the majority of packets can be terminated at a very early stage. The rule set R_U is significantly smaller in the case of the *swat.a6* dataset, which recognisably results in a higher processing rate. Since there are no relevant differences in the analysis performance of the two *power1.1* validation datasets, we conclude that only the number of rules used is decisive and that the logging effort is of no importance. As all packet processing rates exceed the communication packet rates determined for the datasets (cf. Table 1) by a factor of 4.5 to 23.5, we conclude that our whitelists can be used for a real-time monitoring of OT traffic.

7   Related Work

We aim to contribute to OT security by both characterizing OT traffic and providing a monitoring technique according to these characteristics. Hence, we discuss the state of the art in both areas.

7.1   Characterization of Process Control Traffic

We distinguish two groups for characterizing process control traffic and refer to the terms SCADA and DCS as differentiated in [23].

Aggregated Traffic Characterization. This kind focuses on the quantification of traffic meta information, which is motivated by the need for realistic traffic simulation in research. For SCADA networks, the approaches outline differences to standard IT networks by measuring the periodicity in terms of the frame rate and the number of active connections [2] and investigate the application of standard IT traffic models, which are figured out as not transferable to SCADA traffic [3]. Other research measured the TCP-based DNP3 communication in terms of polling intervals, inter-arrival times, idle and round-trip times per device, (temporal and byte) duration of TCP flows, retransmission rates and timeouts [7]. Other works studied the traffic of the SCADA protocol IEC 60870-5-104 by categorizing the traffic into strongly cyclic, weakly cyclic, stable, bursty, and phase transitional by quantifying distribution changes of event inter-arrival times over time [15,16]. The authors of [13] recently proposed a five-step method for profiling traffic by quantifying communication intensity, recognizing work-cycles by repeated communication patterns, and identifying the work-cycles' states with their subsequent profiling. Regarding DCS, the presence of a rich protocol mix has recently been identified in [18], in contrast to what is stated for SCADA networks. The authors show the feasibility to distinguish proprietary protocols by clustering traffic based on the inter-arrival times and header data of frames.

Structural Traffic Profiling. Related approaches try to model periodic communication patterns. While this was initially examined for supporting single protocols [9,10], other works proposed a protocol-independent modelling of concrete periodic traffic patterns [4,11] exploring message repetition and timing information. They evaluated their approaches for a DCS (Siemens S7 and MMS, respectively) as well as for a SCADA protocol (both Modbus). An analysis of the IEC 60870-5-104 communication of the power distribution backbone network is available in [17]. In addition to the analysis of physical network changes and the communication flow lengths of the SCADA infrastructure, particularly structural traffic analyses are presented in the form of clustering session variants and measurements of the amount and the semantics of message types. A recent publication [6] suggest a deep-packet inspection on OT protocols to generate models of communications between network device pairs, what they demonstrate for three protocols (Modbus/TCP, DNP3, and EtherNet/IP) for SCADA and DCS networks. They, however, admit that the used Discrete Time Markov Chains suffer from state and transition explosion.

Research Gap. The former type of characterizations abstract network activities to aggregated traffic observations. These allows only a topview on OT traffic quantities. The latter type of works analyzes communication frames, but it dives to deep into the perspective of the process (modelling of process variables) and thus loses track of network transactions and runs into state explosion. We target at the gap between the two trends providing (1) a bottom view on the traffic by analyzing frames instead of aggregated traffic properties, (2) by keeping the network perspective as prerequisite for a network operator's understanding and re-use of findings, and (3) by providing a profiling approach capable to incorporate a mix of protocols in the network, as it was figured out to be the case especially for DCS [18] and so-called brownfield systems [13].

7.2   Attack Detection for OT

For the sake of brevity we refer to the recent structured overview given in [25]. Our work falls into the smaller group of communication-based approaches, which has decisive advantages over process state-aware approaches. These include the applicability on networks independent from the existence of (potential vendor-specific) systems for the necessary preprocessing to provide well-structured sensor data. Many detection approaches have been identified as unnecessarily complex [24] which relates to serious problems of interpretability and reliability in real-world scenarios. In contrast, the presented approach provides both, transparency into the modeled detection knowledge in the form of precise rules as well as the possibility to influence the detection by the adaptions of the rules.

8   Conclusion

In this paper, we presented a whitelisting approach for characterizing and monitoring communication in OT networks. We used it for measuring eight datasets to express the homogeneity of OT traffic and differences among OT network layers. We examined that the whitelists meet essential criteria regarding completeness (measured by a *mismatching packet rate*), interpretability (inherent to rule-based approaches), detection capability (identified for a prominent OT dataset), and efficiency (measuring the packet processing rates when using the whitelists with a well-known IDS). Although the generation cannot guarantee complete whitelists even in the OT domain, which can lead to false alarms, the evaluation still proves the whitelists are very effective for process control traffic. Hence, they can serve as an interpretable baseline in the OT domain in order to justify the composition of more complex methods, which is often neglected when proposing new detection schemes [1]. Consequently, up next we will use the whitelist approach to define baselines for the OT domain using public data (e. g., [14,20]) and to transpose current rough time-based packet labelings of public datasets into a precise pattern-based one.

A   Specific Whitelist's Generation for Snort

As a prerequisite to follow the description, an exemplary Snort rule is shown in Fig. 7.

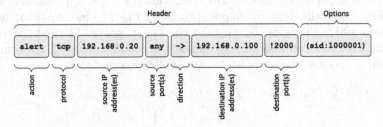

Fig. 7. Example of a Snort rule

Device-orientated Rules. Device-oriented Snort rules are created from the address information of the general rules of this class. Since only IP-based network traffic can be specified by Snort rules, all MAC addresses have to be removed from the applied address sets. A set of addresses A filtered by IP addresses is called $A' = \{a | a \in A \cap A_{\text{IP}}\}$. The mapping of the general rule r_U is done using the set $A(D)' = \{a_1, ..., a_i\}$ as follows:

$$\texttt{alert ip !}[a_1, ..., a_i] \texttt{ any -> any any}$$

As Snort operates in blacklist mode, the exclamation mark as negation operator is used which causes the rule to trigger an alert whenever a device with an unknown IP address acts as a sender. The keyword **any** specifies the complete value range of the respective header element (destination IP addresses, and source/destination ports). Accordingly, the mapping of a rule $r \in R_K$ with a source address $a \in A(D)'$ and the corresponding address set $A_{dst}(a)'$ is done accordingly to (1) in case $A_{dst}(a)' \neq \emptyset$, otherwise to (2):

$$(1) \texttt{ alert ip } a \texttt{ any -> !}[a_1, ..., a_j] \texttt{ any}$$
$$(2) \texttt{ alert ip } a \texttt{ any -> any any}$$

Communication-orientated Rules. To map general communication-oriented rules, Snort header elements and Snort options are used. Since only rules for the specification of IP-based communication can be mapped here as well, further notations of the sets used for the mapping are given first. We denote the set of address tuples $A_C(D)$ filtered by IP addresses as $A_C(D)'$, the set of messages determined for an address tuple a_C' as $M(a_C')$, and the aggregated sets from these as $T(a_C')$, $P(a_C')$, and $U(a_C')$, respectively. For a definition of allowed transport-oriented protocols, the protocol field of the Snort header is used. Since the application of the negation operator is not provided for this element and also no list can be used, the mapping is done by several Snort rules if necessary. To this end, the set of transport protocols to be mapped $T_M = \{t | t \in T_S \backslash T(a_C')\}$ is determined, where $T_S = \{ip, icmp, tcp, udp\}$ corresponds to the set of protocols that can be used in the header. A Snort rule is created for each $t \in T_M$:

$$\text{alert } t \ a_{src} \text{ any } \rightarrow a_{dst} \text{ any}$$

The generation of Snort rules for the specification of legal application-oriented protocols is basically done by mapping the set $P(a_C')$ to the protocol header element as well as the fields source_ports and dest_ports. The first step here is to create a set that contains all port numbers in combination with the transport protocol. It specifies the set of legitimate application protocols:

$$P_S(P(a_C')) = \{(t, P) | t \in t(p_C \in P(a_C')) \cap \{tcp, udp\},$$

$$P = \bigcup_{p_C \in P(a_C'): t(p_C) = t} p(p_C)\}$$

However, a Snort rule can only be created from this set if there is a distinct client-server relationship between the communication partners regarding the packets to be specified by the rule. If the corresponding services are hosted by the destination component the mapping is as follows:

$$\text{alert } t \ a_{src} \text{ any } \rightarrow a_{dst}![p_1, ..., p_n]$$

If the services are provided by the source device the values of the source_ports and dest_ports header fields are swapped. To determine the server component of a specific service the following strategies with descending priority are used:

1. Message types: For typical client-server-oriented services, the observed message types provides immediate information about the device role. For example, in the case of DNS, when a request message is detected, the sender is considered as a client and the target device as a server.
2. Connection establishment: In case of TCP-oriented services, an observed connection establishment can be used for the assignment, whereby for the first (or third) packet of the three-way handshake the sender is considered as the client and the destination as the server.
3. Heuristic: The heuristic role determination is based on the subgraph resulting from the communication graph filtered by the protocol used to transmit the messages used for service provision. If a service is used by multiple clients the server can be identified by the associated node in the graph with the highest node degree (indegree and outdegree).

Since the differntiation of message types relies on the protocol-specific decoding of packet payload data, there is no generalized way to map message types specified by general rules to a set of Snort rules. We present two exemplary ways.

Preprocessor Usage: Some existing preprocessors already allow explicit logging of packets with specific message types being transmitted. For Modbus packets, for example, the option `modbus_func` (Modbus function code) is available for this purpose. Since negation and the specification of multiple values are also not provided when using this option, a rule must be created for each non-permitted Modbus message type. For example, packets sent from a_{src} to a_{dst} to request coils status are logged by the following rule:

```
alert tcp a_src any -> a_dst 502 (modbus_func:read_coils)
```

Use of Payload Detection Options: Snort can be extended by further preprocessors for the detection of message types of arbitrary protocols. However, since the proposed method is primarily intended to support existing unmodified tools, the development of any extensions is omitted. Because the message type is often encoded in the first bytes of the payload, another way to detect different message types is to use options for payload investigation, such as `content` and `byte_test`, which selectively examine byte values for one given pattern. Another possibility is provided by the `pcre` option which can be used to specify a set of patterns of illegitimate message types by means of a regular expression, thus requiring only one rule to be created per PDU-specific communication relation. If, for example, all read requests from a_{src} to a_{dst} should be logged, the following rule can be used as an alternative to four different rules using the `modbus_func` option:

```
alert tcp a_src any -> a_dst 502
(pcre:"/^.{7}(\x01|\x02|\x03|\x04)/s")
```

References

1. Arp, D., et al.: Dos and don'ts of machine learning in computer security. In: USENIX Security Symposium. USENIX Association (2022)
2. Barbosa, R.R.R., Sadre, R., Pras, A.: A first look into SCADA network traffic. In: Network Operations and Management Symposium (NOMS). IEEE (2012)
3. Barbosa, R.R.R., Sadre, R., Pras, A.: Difficulties in modeling SCADA traffic: a comparative analysis. In: Taft, N., Ricciato, F. (eds.) PAM 2012. LNCS, vol. 7192, pp. 126–135. Springer, Heidelberg (2012). https://doi.org/10.1007/978-3-642-28537-0_13
4. Barbosa, R.R.R., Sadre, R., Pras, A.: Exploiting traffic periodicity in industrial control networks. Int. J. Crit. Infrastruct. Prot. **13** (2016)
5. Commission, I.E.: IEC 61375–1:2012 Electronic railway equipment - Train communication network (TCN) - Part 1: General architecture (2012)
6. Faisal, M.A., Cardenas, A.A., Wool, A.: Profiling communications in industrial IP networks: model complexity and anomaly detection. In: Alcaraz, C. (ed.) Security and Privacy Trends in the Industrial Internet of Things. ASTSA, pp. 139–160. Springer, Cham (2019). https://doi.org/10.1007/978-3-030-12330-7_7

7. Formby, D., Walid, A.I., Beyah, R.A.: A case study in power substation network dynamics. In: International Conference on Measurement and Modeling of Computer Systems (SIGMETRICS). ACM (2017)

8. Goh, J., Adepu, S., Junejo, K.N., Mathur, A.: A dataset to support research in the design of secure water treatment systems. In: Havarneanu, G., Setola, R., Nassopoulos, H., Wolthusen, S. (eds.) CRITIS 2016. LNCS, vol. 10242, pp. 88–99. Springer, Cham (2017). https://doi.org/10.1007/978-3-319-71368-7_8

9. Goldenberg, N., Wool, A.: Accurate modeling of Modbus/TCP for intrusion detection in SCADA systems. Int. J. Crit. Infrastruct. Prot. **6**(2), 63–75 (2013)

10. Kleinmann, A., Wool, A.: Accurate modeling of the siemens S7 SCADA protocol for intrusion detection and digital forensic. J. Digit. Forensics Secur. Law **9**(2), 37–50 (2014)

11. Kleinmann, A., Wool, A.: Automatic construction of statechart-based anomaly detection models for multi-threaded SCADA via spectral analysis. In: Workshop on Cyber-Physical Systems Security and Privacy (CPS-SPC). ACM (2016)

12. Krotofil, M., Gollmann, D.: Industrial control systems security: what is happening? In: International Conference on Industrial Informatics (INDIN). IEEE (2013)

13. Lavassani, M., Åkerberg, J., Björkman, M.: Modeling and profiling of aggregated industrial network traffic. Appl. Sci. **12**(2) (2022)

14. Lemay, A., Fernandez, J.M.: Providing SCADA network data sets for intrusion detection research. In: Workshop on Cyber Security Experimentation and Test (CSET). USENIX Association (2016)

15. Lin, C., Nadjm-Tehrani, S.: Understanding IEC-60870-5-104 traffic patterns in SCADA networks. In: Workshop on Cyber-Physical System Security (CPSS). ACM (2018)

16. Lin, C., Nadjm-Tehrani, S.: Timing patterns and correlations in spontaneous SCADA traffic for anomaly detection. In: International Symposium on Research in Attacks, Intrusions and Defenses (RAID). USENIX Association (2019)

17. Mai, K., Qin, X., Silva, N.O., Molina, J., Cárdenas, A.A.: Uncharted Networks: a first measurement study of the bulk power system. In: Internet Measurement Conference (IMC). ACM (2020)

18. Mehner, S., Schuster, F., Hohlfeld, O.: Lights on power plant control networks. In: Hohlfeld, O., Moura, G., Pelsser, C. (eds.) PAM 2022. LNCS, vol. 13210, pp. 470–484. Springer, Cham (2022). https://doi.org/10.1007/978-3-030-98785-5_21

19. Paul, A., Schuster, F., König, H.: Network topology exploration for industrial networks. In: Maglaras, L.A., Janicke, H., Jones, K. (eds.) INISCOM 2016. LNICST, vol. 188, pp. 62–76. Springer, Cham (2017). https://doi.org/10.1007/978-3-319-52569-3_6

20. Rodofile, N.R., Schmidt, T., Sherry, S.T., Djamaludin, C., Radke, K., Foo, E.: Process control cyber-attacks and labelled datasets on s7comm critical infrastructure. In: Pieprzyk, J., Suriadi, S. (eds.) ACISP 2017. LNCS, vol. 10343, pp. 452–459. Springer, Cham (2017). https://doi.org/10.1007/978-3-319-59870-3_30

21. Roesch, M.: Snort: lightweight intrusion detection for networks. In: Conference on Systems Administration (LISA). USENIX (1999)

22. Sharafaldin, I., Lashkari, A.H., Ghorbani, A.A.: Toward generating a new intrusion detection dataset and intrusion traffic characterization. In: International Conference on Information Systems Security & Privacy (ICISSP). SciTePress (2018)

23. Stouffer, K., Pillitteri, V., Lightman, S., Abrams, M., Hahn, A.: Guide to industrial control systems (ICS) security. NIST Spec. Publ. 800–82 (2015). Rev. 2

24. Wolsing, K., Thiemt, L., Sloun, C.v., Wagner, E., Wehrle, K., Henze, M.: Can industrial intrusion detection be SIMPLE?. In: Atluri, V., Di Pietro, R., Jensen, C.D., Meng, W. (eds.) Computer Security – ESORICS 2022. ESORICS 2022. LNCS, vol. 13556. Springer, Cham (2022). https://doi.org/10.1007/978-3-031-17143-7_28
25. Wolsing, K., Wagner, E., Saillard, A., Henze, M.: IPAL: breaking up silos of protocol-dependent and domain-specific industrial intrusion detection systems. In: International Symposium on Research in Attacks, Intrusions and Defenses (RAID). ACM (2022)

Detection of Malware Using Self-Attention Mechanism and Strings

Satoki Kanno$^{(\boxtimes)}$ and Mamoru Mimura

National Defense Academy, Yokosuka, Japan
{em61025,mim}@nda.ac.jp

Abstract. Readable strings that can be extracted from executable files are used to aid in malware analysis. Recent advances in natural language processing technology have made it possible to consider the word order of sentences and use it for machine learning. Previous research has proposed a method for detecting unknown malware by applying natural language processing techniques to readable strings. This method detects unknown malware by applying natural language processing technology to readable strings. This method detects malware by excluding words that occur infrequently and creating a corpus. However, it does not consider word order, and the words that contribute to the recognition are not known. In this study, we propose a method to detect malware using a self-attention mechanism while preserving the order of readable strings. In a experiment, the recall and f-measure of the proposed method that considers word order and the model that considers only the number of occurrences of words were compared using the FFRI Dataset. The maximum F-measure for the proposed method considering word order was 0.904. We also analyzed the weights of the self-attention mechanism to identify the features that contribute to the detection of attacks.

Keywords: Self-Attention · Malware · Natural language processing · Machine learning · Bag-of-Words

1 Introduction

Targeted attacks are one of the ways that organizations and individuals can be targeted to steal critical information. They often attach malware in the form of executable files [13,34]. The computer is infected with malware by executing an executable file sent by the attacker. Thus, the attacker can steal information held by the victim. A countermeasure against targeted attacks is the detection of malware by antivirus software. However, antivirus software sometimes fails to detect malware used in targeted attacks. One reason is that attackers may have confirmed in advance that they will not be detected by antivirus software.

Techniques that combine static or dynamic analysis with machine learning have been proposed to detect unknown malware [2,21,22,27–30]. Although, these have several problems.

S. Li et al. (Eds.): NSS 2023, LNCS 13983, pp. 46–60, 2023.
https://doi.org/10.1007/978-3-031-39828-5_3

Dynamic analysis of untrusted software requires kernel-level privileges [3], virtual machines, and resources. Furthermore, malware typically executes after examining the environment in which it will be run to avoid detection [10,23]. Therefore, when dynamic analysis is performed on a virtual machine, it may not reproduce the environment targeted by the malware [25]. Moreover, performing dynamic analysis on all untrusted software is time-consuming. Static analysis can be performed to avoid these problems.

Some static analysis methods have been proposed to extract features from the results of static analysis of executable files and classify them using machine learning models [8,14,36]. In these studies, features were extracted from metadata extracted from executable files, readable strings, etc., and the similarity between the extracted features was calculated. Thus, it is not possible to identify the features that contributed to the detection. The attention mechanism is an effective way to reveal the features that contributed to the detection. It will assign weights to features that are important to the input features. One method of visualizing malware features using attention mechanisms is to convert binary data into images and visualize the parts of high importance in the images [35]. However, many combined static analysis and machine learning models have been found to be unable to deal with obfuscated or packed software [15,20]. Packing is increasingly used against benign software, increasing the likelihood of misclassifying benign software as malware and reducing detection accuracy [24].

The effectiveness of using NLP for malware detection has been demonstrated by some methods [14,16,17,32]. One of these methods, the study of Mimura et al., demonstrates the effectiveness of using NLP and readable strings to detect obfuscated and packed malware [14]. Mimura et al. believe that the Application programming interface (API) and argument names used for obfuscation are effective for detection. In addition, typical instructions that need to be left for de-obfuscation can be extracted as readable strings.

Therefore, we propose a malware detection method using readable strings and a self-attention mechanism. The use of readable strings allows detection of obfuscated malware, and the use of a self-attention mechanism reveals the readable strings that contribute to detection. In this study, we compare the accuracy of models that consider the word order of readable strings and models that consider only the number of occurrences of words. In addition, we analyze the weights of the self-attention mechanism to identify words that contribute to malware detection.

The contributions of this study are as follows.

1. A new model with a self-attention mechanism was used to detect malware using readable strings. The maximum F-measure was 0.904.
2. We confirmed that removing non-contiguous ASCII from the corpus has a certain effect.
3. The influence of the self-attention mechanism on readable strings was clarified, and it was confirmed that there are words of high importance that contribute to detection.

2 Related Techniques

2.1 Bag-of-Words

Bag-of-Words (BoW) is a model that counts the number of times a word occurs in a sentence and represents it as a vector [26]. In this model, the order of words is not taken into account; if w is a word and n is the number of occurrences corresponding to w, document d can be expressed as in Eq. (1). Based on Eq. (1), if we fix the position of n and omit the word w, we can express d numerically. This allows us to express the document-word relationship in terms of a vector in Eq. (2), which represents the number of times a word appears in each document $\hat{d}_i$. In this study, it is used to compare the word order of sentences. BoW can convert any document into a vector of fixed dimensions with a unique number of words.

$$d = [(w_1, n_{w_1}), (w_2, n_{w_2}), (w_3, n_{w_3}), ..., (w_j, n_{w_j})] \tag{1}$$

$$\hat{d}_i = (n_{w_1}, n_{w_2}, n_{w_3}, ..., n_{w_j}) \tag{2}$$

2.2 Long Short Term Memory

Long short term memory (LSTM) is a model for learning long term dependencies that cannot be considered in Recurrent neural network (RNN) [5]. The LSTM consists of a memory cell, a forget gate, an input gate, and an output gate. As shown in Fig. 1, the output is also used for the next input, and each gate can learn long-term dependencies by selecting past information.

In this study, LSTM is used in validation experiments to compare it with other classifiers.

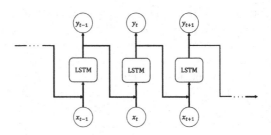

Fig. 1. Conceptual chart of LSTM structure

2.3 Self-attention Mechanism

Self-attention mechanism is a method of expressing input data by focusing on the relationships between its elements [33]. Figure 2 shows an overview of the

Self-attention mechanism, which has three elements, Query, Key, and Value, and is represented by Eq. (3). For each element, Query represents the information to be retrieved in the input data, Key is used to calculate the relevance of Query to the target to be retrieved, and Value is used to output an appropriate value based on Key.

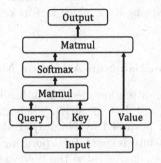

Fig. 2. Conceptual chart of the structure of the self-attention mechanism

$$Attention(Q, K, V) = softmax(\frac{QK^T}{\sqrt{d_k}})V \qquad (3)$$

3   Related Works

Many methods have been proposed to detect executable malware, and many virus vendors use a variety of methods to detect unknown malware. Malware detection methods are categorized into dynamic and static analysis. Our research is categorized as surface analysis. In this section, we describe the studies that are related to this study and discuss the differences between them and this study.

3.1   Malware Detection Using Readable Strings Contained in Executable Files

A variety of methods have been proposed to detect malware using readable strings contained in executable files [9,12,14,36]. Lee et al. [9] proposed a method to detect malware by extracting readable strings from executable files and calculating the similarity of the strings. Their method showed that readable strings are effective for malware detection. Mimura et al. [14] proposed a method for detecting malware by applying NLP to readable strings. Mimura et al. showed that their method was effective against packed malware and anti-debugging techniques. However, these methods were not able to identify the words that contributed to the malware detection.

3.2 Deep Learning Detection

Numerous methods have been proposed for malware detection using deep learning [1,6,8,19]. For example, Pascanu et al. [19] used RNN with API call history to detect malware. Kolosnjaji et al. [8] used a convolutional neural network (CNN) to detect malware using a combination of executable metadata, dynamic linking library (DLL), and operation code. Although, it is difficult for humans to determine from deep learning data which factors contribute to detection and by how much.

3.3 Malware Detection Using an Attention Mechanism

Malware detection using an attention mechanism has been proposed by Yakura et al. [35], Ma et al. [11] and Jian et al [7]. Their method adds an attention mechanism to the method proposed by Nataraj et al. [18] to classify malware by converting binary data into images. Incorporating an attention mechanism into malware detection has demonstrated the potential to reduce the workload of human analysts by using an attention mechanism to visualize regions of high importance in the image. However, these methods can only identify malware based on image characteristics, so when malware is obfuscated, the binary data changes and the image-based characteristics change completely. In this study, obfuscation is handled by using readable strings.

4 Proposed Method

4.1 Outline

Details of the unknown malware detection methods in this study are described. An overview of the proposed method is shown in Fig. 3. The known and unknown executable files contain benign and malicious files, respectively. The model used in this study that combines the self-attention mechanism and LSTM is called LSTM with self-attention mechanism.

For comparison with LSTM with self-attention mechanism considering word order, we also perform the case when BoW is used for feature vector creation and when the classifier is implemented with SVM. Figure 4 shows how the feature vectors used in this experiment are generated and the classifier is applied.

The following is an overview of the proposed method. The numbers correspond to those in Fig. 3.

1. Extract readable strings from known executable files.
2. Split the readable string into words, adjust the number of words in the readable string per file and make the number of words uniform.
3. Create a corpus by extracting words with a high number of occurrences and words that are at least $n(n \geq 1)$ consecutive ASCII strings.
4. Convert the readable strings into feature vectors using the corpus.
5. Train each classifier on feature vectors created from readable strings.

6. Extract readable strings from unknown executable files.
7. Split the readable string into words, adjust the number of words in the readable string per file, and make the number of words uniform.
8. Convert the readable strings into feature vectors using the corpus.
9. Detect unknown executable files, which are converted into feature vectors using the model trained in 5.
10. Extract words weighted by the self-attention mechanism in the executable files classified in 9.

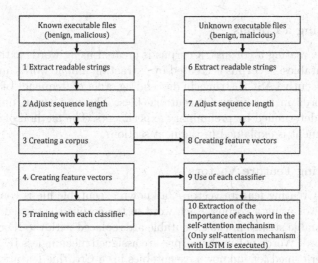

Fig. 3. Chart outlining the proposed method

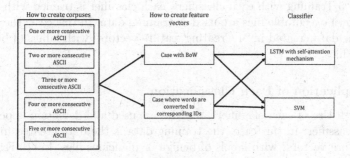

Fig. 4. How to create the corpuses and feature vectors and how to apply the classifiers used

4.2   Extract Readable Strings and Adjust Word Count

In Fig. 3, "1 Extract readable string" and "2 Adjust sequence length" are used to extract readable strings contained in executable files. Readable strings consist of alphabetic characters and symbols, and a sequence of readable strings in a file is considered to be a single sentence. In this case, the readable strings are separated by whitespace and written separately, and then the number of words per file is adjusted by padding or reducing the number of words to a uniform number. The same process is applied to unknown executables for "6 Extract readable strings" and "7 Adjust sequence length" in Fig. 3.

4.3   Creating a Corpus

In Fig. 3, "3 Creating a corpus", a corpus is created using words extracted from known executables. A corpus is created by extracting unique words and $n(n \geq 1)$ or more consecutive ASCII strings in descending order of frequency of occurrence from the words in the known executable files. The number of unique words extracted is determined by preliminary experiments. The method of the preliminary experiment is explained in the next section.

4.4   Creating Feature Vectors

In Fig. 3, "4 Creating feature vectors", a known executable file is converted into a feature vector using a corpus. Each word in the corpus is assigned an ID, and words in readable strings in the executable are replaced with the ID corresponding to the word. Words not in the corpus are assigned meaningless IDs. The same process is performed for unknown executables in "8 Creating feature vectors" in Fig. 3.

4.5   Training with Each Classifier

In Fig. 3, "5 Training with each classifier", each classifier is trained with training data. Known executable files are used as training data. In this case, the training data is the data created in "4 Creating feature vectors" with labels of benign or malicious files.

4.6   Application of Each Classification

In Fig. 3, "9 Use of each classifier", test data is used and detection is performed by each classifier. In this case, the training data is the data created in "8 Creating feature vectors" with labels of benign or malicious files. In "10 Extraction of the importance of each word in the self-attention mechanism", words that have weight in the self-attention mechanism are extracted from the detected executable files. In this case, the words are ranked by the Python rank function in order of increasing weight in each file, and the words with ranks 1 to 10 are extracted. Then the words are extracted in the order of the number of occurrences of the words with ranks 1 to 10 in all files.

5   Experiment

5.1   Dataset

In this study, we used strings extracted from the FFRI Dataset 2020 to FFRI Dataset 2022 [4,31] provided by FFRI Inc. as a dataset. Strings were extracted from both benign and malicious executables, and the data was prepared for detection. The total number of datasets used is shown in Table 1. We used 75,000 benign and 75,000 malicious files each from the FFRI Dataset 2020 as training data for detection. As test data, we used 75,000 benign and 75,000 malicious files each from FFRI Dataset 2021 and FFRI Dataset 2022.

Table 1. Datasets used for experiments

Dataset	Number of files	Number of unique words
FFRI Dataset2020 (cleanware)	75,000	967,075,087
FFRI Dataset2020 (malware)	75,000	162,245,592
FFRI Dataset2021 (cleanware)	75,000	1,001,705,100
FFRI Dataset2021 (malware)	75,000	15,504,0251
FFRI Dataset2022 (cleanware)	75,000	712,981,765
FFRI Dataset2022 (malware)	75,000	298,828,720

5.2   Experimental Environment

The environment used in the experiments is shown in Table 2, and the library is shown in Table 3.

Table 2. Experimental environment

CPU	Core i9-10900X 3.70GHz
Memory	128GB
GPU	GeForce RTX 3090
OS	Windows10 Home
Language	Python3.8.9

Table 3. Python main libraries used for implementation

Library name	Version
TensorFlow	2.4.3
Gensim	4.1.2
scikit-learn	1.0.2

5.3   Evaluation Index

This section describes the evaluation indices used in this study. The values needed to calculate the evaluation index are shown in Table 4. For judgments, a true/false judgment is made based on the true result, and True is used if the result is true and False if the result is false. For example, True Negative (TN) is a judgment of a benign file as a benign file, and False Positive (FP) is a judgment of a benign file as a malicious file. Four types of evaluation indices were used: Accuracy, Precision, Recall and F-measure.

Table 4. Relationship between predicted and true results

		True results	
		Benign	Malicious
Prediction Results	Benign	True Negative(TN)	False Positive(FP)
	Malicious	False Negative(FN)	True Positive(TP)

5.4   Preliminary Experiments

Preliminary experiments are conducted to determine the optimal number of words and the optimal sequence length to be used in the corpus. The corpus is created by extracting words with a high number of occurrences from benign and malicious files. Using the FFRI Dataset 2020 for training and test data, 10-Fold Cross Validation is performed using LSTM with a self-attention mechanism and optimal values are measured using F-measure values. In the preliminary experiment, we used a corpus created by extracting words that were at least 1 consecutive ASCII strings.

Case with BoW. Figure 5 shows the results of changing the number of unique words used in the corpus. Figure 5 shows that the F-measure reached its maximum value of 0.686 when the number of words was set to 500, which is the optimal value for the number of words of the corpus in the case of BoW in this experiment.

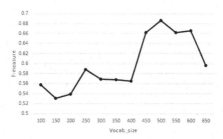

Fig. 5. Number of unique words and length of sequences used in the corpus in the case of BoW

Case Where Words Are Converted to Corresponding IDs. The results of changing the number of unique words used in the corpus are shown in Fig. 6. Figure 6 shows that the F-measure reached its maximum value of 0.826 when the number of words in the corpus was set to 100,000, which is the optimal value for the number of words in the corpus when assigning IDs corresponding to words in this experiment. Figure 8 shows the results of changing the sequence length. Figure 7 shows that the F-measure reached its maximum value of 0.844 when the number of words in a file was set to 120, which is the optimal value for the sequence length when assigning IDs corresponding to words in this experiment.

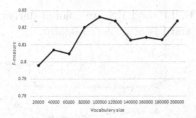

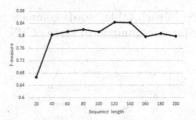

Fig. 6. Number of unique words used in the corpus when IDs are assigned corresponding to words

Fig. 7. Length of the sequence when IDs are assigned to words

5.5   Experiment Contents

In the validation experiment, we use 5 corpus types to create feature vectors for the case with BoW and the case where words are replaced by their corresponding IDs. We compare the results using a classifier based on each feature vector created. We performed five experiments for each classifier and used the average as the result. Moreover, using the corpus with the highest recall value in the experiment, we tabulate the words with high importance in LSTM with self-attention mechanism when replacing the IDs corresponding to the words in the corpus.

5.6   Result

The results for the BoW case are shown in Figs. 8 and 9, and for the case of replacing IDs corresponding to words in the corpus are shown in Figs. 10 and 11. For the horizontal axis in Figs. 8 through 11, it is the minimum word length of ASCII when the corpus is created by extracting ASCII. From Figs. 8 and 10, the highest recall value was obtained when LSTM with a self-attention mechanism was used with FFRI Dataset 2022 and a corpus of at least 2 consecutive ASCII strings in the test data in the case of replacing IDs corresponding to words in the corpus, and the recall value was 0.893. Figure 9 shows that in the case of BoW, the highest F-measure value was obtained when SVM was used with the FFRI Dataset 2021 as test data and a corpus of at least 5 consecutive ASCII strings, resulting in an F-measure value of 0.890. Figure 11 shows that the highest F-measure value when replacing IDs with IDs corresponding to words in the corpus was obtained when LSTM with a self-attention mechanism was used with FFRI Dataset 2022 in the test data and with a corpus of at least 1 consecutive ASCII string, resulting in an F-measure value of 0.904.

Tables 5 and 6 show the results of tabulating the words of high importance in LSTM with self-attention mechanism when substitutions are made to IDs corresponding to words in the corpus. The top 20 words in the order of the number of occurrences of words with ranks 1 to 10 are extracted using the rank function for the weights of the words when they are divided into TN, FP, TP, and

FN. In each table, words common to TN, FP, TP, and FN are colored darker, and words common to three of TN, FP, TP, and FN are colored lighter.

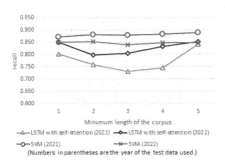

Fig. 8. Result of recall in case of BoW

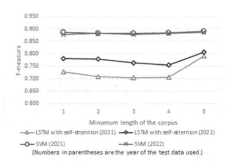

Fig. 9. Result of F-measure in case of BoW

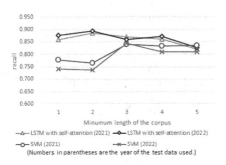

Fig. 10. Result of recall in case where words are converted to corresponding IDs

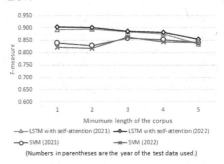

Fig. 11. Result of F-measure in case where words are converted to corresponding IDs

6   Discussion

6.1   Need to Consider Contiguous ASCII Strings in Corpus Creation

Figures. 8 and 9 show that in the case of BoW, the recall and F-measure values initially decreased with increasing the value of n when LSTM with self-attention mechanism was used, but the recall and F-measure values improved in the middle of the process. The SVM did not show a significant change in the reproducibility and F-measure values compared to the LSTM with the self-gazing mechanism, however, they were almost similar. Figures 10 and 11 show that for both LSTM and SVM with self-attention mechanism, when IDs are assigned to words, the recall and F-measure values initially increase and later decrease with increasing value of n for consecutive ASCII strings from the corpus. These results suggest that removing non-consecutive strings from the dictionary has a certain effect.

Table 5. Aggregate results based on word weights (FFRI Dataset2021)

Rank	TN	FP	TP	FN
1	run	run	in	in
2	program	program	run	run
3	be	be	data	up
4	in	in	rd	rs
5	dos	dos	text	data
6	text	must	rs	text
7	rd	under	rich	rd
8	reloc	win32	id	id
9	data	text	reloc	rich
10	rs	rd	this	dll
11	must	data	tls	this
12	bs	up	win32	win32
13	under	rs	under	under
14	win32	rich	boolean	tls
15	id	dll	FALSE	sv
16	tls	as	it	bs
17	xd	wi	TRUE	ad
18	strings	54	integer	as
19	rich	yr	sv	reloc
20	it	reloc	up	4o

Table 6. Aggregate results based on word weights (FFRI Dataset2022)

Rank	TN	FP	TP	FN
1	in	in	cannot	cannot
2	dos	dos	run	run
3	cannot	cannot	rich	rich
4	rd	js	rd	up
5	data	text	data	main
6	bs	data	rs	emu
7	reloc	exe	text	g7
8	rs	rd	be	bs
9	text	z9	under	fv
10	tls	rs	up	dl
11	id	dll	sn	petite
12	be	go	id	ein
13	run	ai	gg	sv
14	win32	kt	reloc	rs
15	core	mp	ad	dll
16	pd	zo	as	5t
17	303	cm	ed	text
18	hh	ds	tls	hd
19	uu	qb	bs	uw
20	sv	ni	le	code

6.2 Effect of Self-Attention Mechanism on Readable Strings

Tables 5 and 6 show that the number of words common to 3 or more of TN, FP, TP, and FN is about 60% when using FFRI Dataset 2021, while it is about 30% when using FFRI Dataset 2022. In addition, when looking at the top words for each of TN, FP, TP, and FN, approximately 50% of the words are common to both FFRI Dataset 2021 and FFRI Dataset 2022 in the test data. This indicates that words of high importance overlap in the data sets used in this study, even when the year of collection is changed. Creating a corpus with only words of high importance may improve recognition accuracy.

6.3 Research Ethics

In this study, the FFRI Dataset provided by FFRI Security, Inc. was used for both benign and malicious files. The experimental environment used, including programming languages, natural language processing techniques, and machine learning libraries such as scikit-learn, are publicly available and easy to implement. This study did not use any data or libraries that are not publicly available and difficult to obtain, and we believe that the reproducibility of the results is high.

6.4 Limitations

In this study, experiments were conducted using the FFRI Dataset, but this does not necessarily mean that the validation reflects the trends of all executables in reality. Although it is impossible to create a dataset from all executables, there is room to consider the validity of the sampling method of the dataset.

7   Conclusion

In this study, we confirmed that the F-measure was at most 0.904 when malware detection was performed using the LSTM model with a self-attention mechanism and readable strings. In addition, we confirmed that removing non-contiguous ASCII strings from the corpus has a certain effect, and identified the words that contributed to the malware detection. There are two issues to be addressed in the future. The first is to improve the detection accuracy by adjusting the value of each parameter. In the validation experiments, default values were set for each parameter except the number of words in the corpus and the sequence length, which could be adjusted to improve detection accuracy. The second is to modify the corpus used for LSTM with the self-attention mechanism. We believe that the detection accuracy can be improved by creating a corpus that extracts only words of high importance using the self-attention mechanism.

References

1. David, O.E., Netanyahu, N.S.: Deepsign: deep learning for automatic malware signature generation and classification. In: 2015 International Joint Conference on Neural Networks (IJCNN), pp. 1–8 (2015). https://doi.org/10.1109/IJCNN.2015.7280815
2. Dube, T., et al.: Malware target recognition via static heuristics. Comput. Secur. **31**(1), 137–147 (2012). https://doi.org/10.1016/j.cose.2011.09.002
3. Egele, M., et al.: A survey on automated dynamic malware-analysis techniques and tools. ACM Comput. Surv. **44**(2), 1–42 (2008). https://doi.org/10.1145/2089125.2089126
4. Group, C.S.: Anti malware engineering workshop. https://www.iwsec.org/mws/datasets.html. Accessed 03 Jan 2023
5. Hochreiter, S., Schmidhuber, J.: Long short-term memory. Neural Comput. **9**(8), 1735–1780 (1997). https://doi.org/10.1162/neco.1997.9.8.1735
6. Huang, W., Stokes, J.W.: Mtnet: a multi-task neural network for dynamic malware classification. In: Caballero, J., et al. (eds.) Detection of Intrusions and Malware, and Vulnerability Assessment, pp. 399–418. Springer International Publishing, Cham (2016). https://doi.org/10.1007/978-3-319-40667-1_20
7. Jian, Y., et al.: A novel framework for image-based malware detection with a deep neural network. Comput. Secur. **109**, 102400 (2021). https://doi.org/10.1016/j.cose.2021.102400
8. Kolosnjaji, B., et al.: Empowering convolutional networks for malware classification and analysis. In: 2017 International Joint Conference on Neural Networks, IJCNN 2017, Anchorage, AK, USA, 14–19 May 2017, pp. 3838–3845 (2017). https://doi.org/10.1109/IJCNN.2017.7966340
9. Lee, J., et al.: A study of malware detection and classification by comparing extracted strings. In: Proceedings of the 5th International Conference on Ubiquitous Information Management and Communication. ICUIMC 2011, Association for Computing Machinery, New York, NY, USA (2011). https://doi.org/10.1145/1968613.1968704

10. Lindorfer, M., Kolbitsch, C., Milani Comparetti, P.: Detecting environment-sensitive malware. In: Sommer, R., Balzarotti, D., Maier, G. (eds.) RAID 2011. LNCS, vol. 6961, pp. 338–357. Springer, Heidelberg (2011). https://doi.org/10.1007/978-3-642-23644-0_18

11. Ma, X., et al.: How to make attention mechanisms more practical in malware classification. IEEE Access 7, 155270–155280 (2019). https://doi.org/10.1109/ACCESS.2019.2948358

12. Mastjik, F., et al.: Comparison of pattern matching techniques on identification of same family malware. Int. J. Inf. Secur. Sci. 4(3), 104–111 (2015)

13. Mimura, M.: Evaluation of printable character-based malicious PE file-detection method. Internet Things 19, 100521 (2022). https://doi.org/10.1016/j.iot.2022.100521

14. Mimura, M., Ito, R.: Applying NLP techniques to malware detection in a practical environment. Int. J. Inf. Sec. 21(2), 279–291 (2022). https://doi.org/10.1007/s10207-021-00553-8

15. Moser, A., et al.: Limits of static analysis for malware detection. In: Twenty-Third Annual Computer Security Applications Conference (ACSAC 2007), pp. 421–430 (2007). https://doi.org/10.1109/ACSAC.2007.21

16. Moskovitch, R., et al.: Unknown malcode detection via text categorization and the imbalance problem. In: 2008 IEEE International Conference on Intelligence and Security Informatics, pp. 156–161 (2008). https://doi.org/10.1109/ISI.2008.4565046

17. Nagano, Y., Uda, R.: Static analysis with paragraph vector for malware detection. In: Proceedings of the 11th International Conference on Ubiquitous Information Management and Communication. IMCOM 2017, Association for Computing Machinery, New York, NY, USA (2017). https://doi.org/10.1145/3022227.3022306

18. Nataraj, L., et al.: Malware images: Visualization and automatic classification. In: Proceedings of the 8th International Symposium on Visualization for Cyber Security, VizSec 2011, Association for Computing Machinery, New York, NY, USA (2011). https://doi.org/10.1145/2016904.2016908

19. Pascanu, R., et al.: Malware classification with recurrent networks. In: 2015 IEEE International Conference on Acoustics, Speech and Signal Processing (ICASSP), pp. 1916–1920 (2015). https://doi.org/10.1109/ICASSP.2015.7178304

20. Perdisci, R., et al.: Mcboost: boosting scalability in malware collection and analysis using statistical classification of executables. In: 2008 Annual Computer Security Applications Conference (ACSAC), pp. 301–310 (2008). https://doi.org/10.1109/ACSAC.2008.22

21. Raff, E., et al.: Learning the PE header, malware detection with minimal domain knowledge. In: Proceedings of the 10th ACM Workshop on Artificial Intelligence and Security, AISec 2017, pp. 121–132. Association for Computing Machinery, New York, NY, USA (2017). https://doi.org/10.1145/3128572.3140442

22. Raff, E., et al.: Malware detection by eating a whole exe (2017). https://doi.org/10.48550/ARXIV.1710.09435

23. Raffetseder, T., Kruegel, C., Kirda, E.: Detecting system emulators. In: Garay, J.A., Lenstra, A.K., Mambo, M., Peralta, R. (eds.) ISC 2007. LNCS, vol. 4779, pp. 1–18. Springer, Heidelberg (2007). https://doi.org/10.1007/978-3-540-75496-1_1

24. Rahbarinia, B., et al.: Exploring the long tail of (malicious) software downloads. In: 2017 47th Annual IEEE/IFIP International Conference on Dependable Systems and Networks (DSN), pp. 391–402 (2017). https://doi.org/10.1109/DSN.2017.19

25. Rossow, C., et al.: Prudent practices for designing malware experiments: status quo and outlook. In: 2012 IEEE Symposium on Security and Privacy, pp. 65–79 (2012). https://doi.org/10.1109/SP.2012.14

26. Salton, G., et al.: A vector space model for automatic indexing. Commun. ACM 18(11), 613–620 (1975). https://doi.org/10.1145/361219.361220

27. Santos, I., et al.: OPEM: a static-dynamic approach for machine-learning-based malware detection. In: Herrero, A., et al. (eds.) International Joint Conference CISIS'12-ICEUTE'12-SOCO'12 Special Sessions. Advances in Intelligent Systems and Computing, vol. 189, pp. 271–280. Springer, Berlin (2013)

28. Saxe, J., Berlin, K.: Deep neural network based malware detection using two dimensional binary program features. In: 2015 10th International Conference on Malicious and Unwanted Software (MALWARE), pp. 11–20 (2015). https://doi.org/10.1109/MALWARE.2015.7413680

29. Schultz, M., et al.: Data mining methods for detection of new malicious executables. In: Proceedings 2001 IEEE Symposium on Security and Privacy, S&P 2001, pp. 38–49 (2001). https://doi.org/10.1109/SECPRI.2001.924286

30. Shafiq, M.Z., et al.: Pe-miner: mining structural information to detect malicious executables in realtime. In: Kirda, E., et al. (eds.) Recent Advances in Intrusion Detection. Lecture Notes in Computer Science, vol. 5758, pp. 121–141. Springer, Berlin Heidelberg, Berlin, Heidelberg (2009). https://doi.org/10.1007/978-3-642-04342-0_7

31. Terada, M., et al.: MWS datasets for anti-malware research contribution to the community and its challenges. Technical report 8, Tokyo Denki University/Hitachi Ltd., NTT Secure Platform laboratories, N.F. Laboratories Inc., Nippon Telegraph and Telephone Corporation, Japan Advanced Institute of Science and Technology (2020)

32. Tran, T.K., Sato, H.: NLP-based approaches for malware classification from API sequences. In: 2017 21st Asia Pacific Symposium on Intelligent and Evolutionary Systems (IES), pp. 101–105 (2017). https://doi.org/10.1109/IESYS.2017.8233569

33. Vaswani, A., et al.: Attention is all you need. In: Guyon, I., et al. (eds.) Advances in Neural Information Processing Systems, vol. 30. Curran Associates, Inc. (2017). https://proceedings.neurips.cc/paper/2017/file/3f5ee243547dee91fbd053c1c4a845aa-Paper.pdf

34. VMware Inc: Global incident response threat report 2022. https://www.vmware.com/content/dam/learn/en/amer/fy23/pdf/1553238_Global_Incident_Response_Threat_Report_Weathering_The_Storm.pdf. Accessed 03 Feb 2023

35. Yakura, H., et al.: Neural malware analysis with attention mechanism. Comput. Secur. 87(C), 101592 (2019). https://doi.org/10.1016/j.cose.2019.101592

36. Ye, Y., et al.: SBMDS: an interpretable string based malware detection system using SVM ensemble with bagging. J. Comput. Virol. 5(4), 283–293 (2009). https://doi.org/10.1007/s11416-008-0108-y

KDRM: Kernel Data Relocation Mechanism to Mitigate Privilege Escalation Attack

Hiroki Kuzuno[1]([⊠]) [iD] and Toshihiro Yamauchi[2] [iD]

[1] Graduate School of Engineering, Kobe University, Kobe, Japan
kuzuno@port.kobe-u.ac.jp
[2] Faculty of Environmental, Life, Natural Science and Technology,
Okayama University, Okayama, Japan
yamauchi@okayama-u.ac.jp

Abstract. A privilege escalation attack by memory corruption based on kernel vulnerability has been reported as a security threat to operating systems. Kernel address layout randomization (KASLR) randomizes kernel code and data placement on the kernel memory section for attack mitigation. However, a privilege escalation attack will succeed because the kernel data of privilege information is identified during a user process execution in a running kernel. In this paper, we propose a kernel data relocation mechanism (KDRM) that dynamically relocates privilege information in the running kernel to mitigate privilege escalation attacks using memory corruption. The KDRM provides multiple relocation-only pages in the kernel. The KDRM selects one of the relocation-only pages and moves the privilege information to the relocation-only pages when the system call is invoked. This allows the virtual address of the privilege information to change by dynamically relocating for a user process. The evaluation results confirmed that privilege escalation attacks by user processes on Linux could be prevented with KDRM. As a performance evaluation, we showed that the overhead of issuing a system call was up to 149.67%, and the impact on the kernel performance score was 2.50%, indicating that the impact on the running kernel can be negligible.

1 Introduction

Memory corruption countermeasures in the operating system (OS) kernel are paramount. In particular, privilege escalation attack and security-feature disabling attacks use memory corruption of kernel data [3,7].

In this regard, kernel address space layout randomization (KASLR) randomly places kernel code and data on the kernel memory at kernel startup as a countermeasure against memory corruption attacks. KASLR makes it challenging to identify the virtual address of the kernel data to be attacked and reduces the possibility of kernel data tampering due to memory corruption. However, the virtual address of kernel data (e.g., privilege information) on the kernel memory is fixed in the running kernel, which poses the following problem.

© The Author(s), under exclusive license to Springer Nature Switzerland AG 2023
S. Li et al. (Eds.): NSS 2023, LNCS 13983, pp. 61–76, 2023.
https://doi.org/10.1007/978-3-031-39828-5_4

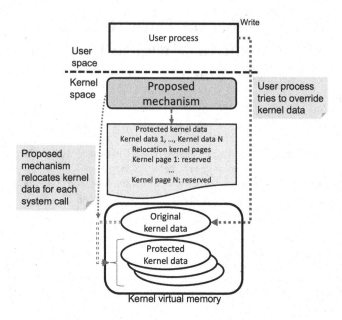

Fig. 1. Overview of the KDRM

Privilege information illegal modification

Assume that an attacking user process has identified the virtual address of the privilege information to be attacked in a running kernel [8].

The privilege information can be tampered with by an attack exploiting the kernel vulnerability. Therefore, an attacker can conduct a privilege escalation attack.

This paper proposes a kernel data relocation mechanism (KDRM) that allows dynamic relocation of privilege information in the kernel memory to provide the kernel with resistance to attacks against privilege escalation attack. The KDRM can be applied to a running kernel with KASLR to improve the attack resistance of the kernel.

Figure 1 provides an overview of the proposed KDRM. The KDRM forces the user process to relocate privilege information when a system call is issued. The relocation of kernel data contains privilege information that makes it challenging to identify the virtual address of privilege information.

The KDRM allocates multiple relocation-only pages (4 KB) for each user process in the kernel memory and uses them to store privilege information to be protected. When a system call is issued, the privilege information to be protected is replicated to a randomly selected relocation page, and the reference to privilege information to be protected is changed to the replicated page. Then, the original page is temporary unmapped by KDRM for the .tampering protection in the kernel memory. The virtual address of privilege information in the running kernel is dynamically changed by changing the page and protected by unmapping the page where the privilege information is stored each time a system call is issued.

Table 1. Types and effects of kernel vulnerability [1]

	Item	Description
Type	Missing pointer check	Lack of pointer variable verification
	Missing permission check	Lack of permission verification
	Buffer overflow	Overwriting of the stack or heap space
	Uninitialized data	Lack of initialization at variable creation
	Null deference	Access to Null variable
	Divide by zero	Zero dividing calculation
	Infinite loop	Occurrence of the infinite loop process
	Data race / deadlock	Occurrence of race condition or deadlock
	Memory mismanagement	Inconsistent allocation of memory allocation and free
	Miscellaneous	Other wrong implementations
Effect	Memory corruption	Modification of kernel data
	Policy violation	Miss implementation of access control decision
	Denial of Service	Forcing kernel to stop running
	OS information leakage	Information leakage from uninitialized data variables

In the proposed approach, the difficulty in identifying the virtual address of privilege information depends on its size to be relocated and the number of relocation-only pages. When the relocation target is 256 bytes (8 bits) and one relocation-only page (4 KB, 12 bits) is set as one page, the privilege information can be protected from brute force attacks in the range of 4 bits (see Sect. 6.7 for details).

Suppose that a user process performing a privilege escalation attack executes vulnerable kernel code that can be used in an arbitrary memory corruption attack. In that case, an attempt to tamper with privilege information can occur. However, the KDRM makes it challenging to locate the exact virtual address of privilege information. Therefore, tampering with privilege information occurs the page fault. In particular, tampering fails, and privilege escalation attacks are prevented.

The research contributions in this paper are as follows:

1. To mitigate memory corruption attacks, we designed and implemented a security mechanism that enables the dynamic relocation of privilege information when a system call is issued. We implemented the KDRM on Linux, which is resistant to privilege escalation attacks.
2. We confirmed that the KDRM could prevent privilege escalation against user processes that attempt privilege escalation attacks. In this regard, the impact of the KDRM on user process and kernel operation was evaluated. The results showed that the overhead to the kernel when issuing system calls ranged from 102.88% to 149.67%, and the impact on the kernel performance score was 2.50%.

2   Memory Corruption Vulnerability

Kernel vulnerabilities are mis-implementations that can be used to attack the kernel. Table 1 lists a classification of 10 types of kernel vulnerabilities and summarizes the effect of four types of attacks using kernel vulnerabilities [1].

```
1    // From Linux kernel v5.18.2
2    // include/linux/sched.h
3    struct task_struct {
4        ...
5        const struct cred __rcu    *cred;
6        ...
7    }
8    // include/linux/cred.h
9    struct cred {
10       ...
11       /* real UID of the task */
12       kuid_t    uid;
13       /* real GID of the task */
14       kgid_t    gid;
15       ...
16   }
17   // include/linux/uidgid.h
18   typedef struct {
19       // typedef __kernel_uid32_t  uid_t;
20       // typedef unsigned int   __kernel_uid32_t;
21       uid_t val;
22   } kuid_t;
23   typedef struct {
24       // typedef __kernel_gid32_t  gid_t;
25       // typedef unsigned int   __kernel_gid32_t;
26       gid_t val;
27   } kgid_t;
```

Fig. 2. Structures related to user ID in Linux [4]

The KDRM is a countermeasure against memory corruption attacks that exploit kernel vulnerabilities related to pointers and variables. A memory corruption attack is an attack that attempts to write an arbitrary virtual address in the kernel memory. If the memory area to be attacked is rewritable, the attack target is overwritten by memory corruption.

Privilege Escalation Attack: For privilege escalation attacks, a kernel vulnerability that takes privilege management omissions to forcibly call kernel code that performs privilege modification operations [14–16] and memory corruption attacks has been reported [17].

The attacker attempts a privilege escalation attack that targets kernel data concerning user process privilege information, which is placed in the kernel memory. As a precondition for a successful privilege escalation attack, the virtual address of the kernel data that stores privilege information must be correctly specified as the attack target. After that, an attacker attempts to tamper with the kernel data that stores privilege information. Furthermore, the attacker can change the user ID of a user process to an administrator user in the case of a memory corruption attack.

Privilege Information: The attack target was kernel data related to privilege information. Figure 2 illustrates the structure definition of user ID in Linux. The `task_struct` structure in Linux manages user processes and stores privilege information. Line 5 shows that the privilege information is stored in the `cred` structure that manages the user process. The user ID is stored in the variable `uid` of the `kuid_t` structure on line 12, which is included in the `cred` structure on lines 9 through 16. The `kuid_t` structure has variable `val` of `uid_t` on lines 18 through 22. In a privilege escalation attack, the variable `val` of the `uid` of the `kuid_t` structure is rewritten to the user ID (0) of the `root`.

3 Threat Model

Attack Target Environment: The threat model in this study considered an attacker attempting a memory corruption via a kernel vulnerability. The attack target environment, assumed as the threat model, is summarized as follows:

- Attacker: Runs a user process with general user privileges. In the user process, the attacker executes the attack code, calls vulnerable kernel code and attempts a memory corruption attack.
- Kernel: Contains kernel vulnerabilities that can be used for memory corruption attacks, allowing user processes to call vulnerable kernel code. No security mechanisms other than access control functions are applied to user processes.
- Kernel Vulnerability: Specify an arbitrary virtual address of kernel data and achieve a memory corruption attack. Receive the virtual address and overwritten data of the attack target from the user process and tamper the kernel data of the attack target.
- Attack target: The attack target is kernel data placed on the kernel memory. The attack target stores user process privilege information.

Attack Scenario: In the assumed attack scenario, the attacker attempts a memory corruption attack against the kernel. In particular, the attacker executes an arbitrary user process as a normal user. The user process invokes vulnerable kernel code to perform memory corruption attacks that can overwrite the kernel data using arbitrary data.

For example, in a privilege escalation attack, an attacker identifies the position of the kernel data containing the privilege information of a user process. Subsequently, the attacker overwrites the privilege information of the user ID to administrative privilege.

4 The Design of the Approach

4.1 Requirement

The KDRM dynamically relocates protected kernel data during kernel operation. The design aims to satisfy the following requirements:

RQ1: The assumed attack is privilege information modification by a memory corruption attack through a kernel vulnerability during the execution of a system call.

RQ2: Relocation control of protected kernel data on the kernel is transparent to user processes.

RQ3: To make it difficult to identify the relocation position of privilege information.

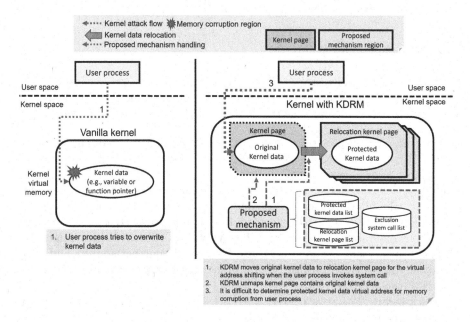

Fig. 3. Design overview of the KDRM

4.2 Concept

The design concepts of the KDRM are defined as follows:

- Concept 1: The protected kernel data relocation handling its performed in the kernel to mitigate attacks from user processes and make it challenging to detect countermeasures.
- Concept 2: The KDRM is designed to mitigate attacks on the protected kernel data relocation handling so that user processes and kernel operations are unaffected.

4.3 Protected Kernel Data Relocation Challenge

The design outline of the KDRM is shown in Fig. 3. Based on the design concepts of the KDRM and to satisfy the requirements, multiple relocation-only pages are provided as relocation destinations of kernel data to be protected in the kernel on the kernel memory. In addition, a list of kernel data to be protected, a list of relocation-only pages, and a list of system calls that are excluded from relocation handling by the KDRM.

Protection Kernel Data: In the KDRM, the protected kernel data to be relocated on the kernel memory. The protected kernel data is privilege information that is created at the time of user process creation.

Relocation-Only Page: In the KDRM, the relocation-only page is kernel page to which the protected kernel data is relocated. The KDRM provides multiple relocation-only pages on the kernel memory.

Table 2. Protected kernel data and Exclusion system call list

(a) Kernel data to be protected in the KDRM implementation		(b) A system call that performs authorization operation that exempts the realization method	
Item	Description	Item	Description
Protected kernel data	User ID (e.g., uid, euid, fsuid, and suid) Group ID (e.g., gid, egid, fsid, and sgid)	Exclusion systemcall list	execve, setuid, setgid, setreuid, setregid, setresuid, setresgid, setfsuid, setfsgid

Relocation Handling: The relocation handling of the protected kernel data in the KDRM is performed before and after the execution of the system call.

- Before system call execution: Protected kernel data is relocated to a relocation-only page and temporary unmapped the original kernel data from kernel memory.
- After executing the system call: The protected kernel data on the relocation-only page is moved to the original kernel data location.

In the KDRM, the relocation destination of protected kernel data is selected randomly from a list of relocation-only pages before executing the system call. The virtual address of the protected kernel data after relocation changes within a specific range, making it difficult to specify the virtual address.

5   Implementation

5.1   Implementation Overview

Linux on the x86_64 CPU architecture was assumed to be the environment for implementing the scheme. An overview of the implementation, the KDRM creates a new page and placed for each user process to make the privilege information of the kernel data to be protected. While processing of the implementation method, the page storing the privilege information is replicated to a randomly selected relocation-only page before the execution of the system call, and the virtual address of the privilege information is changed.

5.2   Protected Kernel Data

In the implementation method, a kernel page (4 KB) is created to store the protected kernel data as the privilege information of the user process.

Table 2a lists the privilege information of the protection target. During the operation period of the user process, each kernel page (4 KB) is subject to relocation handling.

5.3   Relocation Kernel Page

In the implementation, a certain number of relocation-only pages are allocated at kernel startup to reduce the load during user process creation. The `alloc_pages` function is used for allocating relocation-only pages. Multiple relocation-only pages (4 KB) (e.g., 10) are allocated when a user process was created. In addition, the `remove_pagetable` function is used for the unmapping original kernel page from the kernel page table that is the variable `pgd` of `current`.

A specific range of virtual addresses in the kernel memory can be used as relocation destinations for privilege information by allocating multiple relocation-only pages to each user process. In addition, the relocation-only page can be randomly selected, making it difficult to identify the virtual address of the relocation destination.

5.4   Relocation Handling

Relocation control of kernel data that stores privilege information is performed by using a list of relocation-only pages and a list of exempted system calls as follows:

1. Hooks system calls invocations by user processes.
2. Determine if the system call number is included in the list of exempted system calls.
   (a) For exempt system calls: privilege information is not relocated.
   (b) For other than exempt system calls: privilege information is relocated.
       i   Randomly selects a relocation-only page from the list of relocation-only pages as the relocation destination for privilege information.
       ii Duplicate the kernel data storing the privilege information to the relocation-only page by page.
       iii Change the reference from the privilege information in the kernel to the replication destination.
       iv Unmap the privilege information of the original kernel page from the kernel page table.
3. Continue execution of the system call.
4. Terminate system call.

KDRM restores the privilege information of the original kernel page to the kernel page table after the termination of other than exempt system calls.

Page Fault Handling: An attempt to illegally overwrite kernel data that contain privilege. The page fault handler's `handle_page_fault` function catches a privilege escalation attack. The Linux kernel can know the referenced virtual address at the page fault. The implementation method compares the virtual address of the privilege information before relocation handling. As the page fault occurs, a SIGKILL is sent to the target user process with the function `force_sig_info` when considered an illegal write.

Protected Kernel Data Relocation Exemptions: Depending on the type of kernel data to be protected, reference or write failures to kernel data due to relocation in the kernel might affect the kernel and user process operations.

In particular, the KDRM allows the user to specify in advance which system calls are exempted from relocation for each protected kernel data to avoid affecting the kernel and user processes. Moreover, KDRM uses these system calls to determine whether the relocation handling is applicable. The kernel data to be protected is not relocated when the specified exempted system call is executed.

In the implementation, the writing to privilege information may cause page faults; Thus, system calls that explicitly write to privilege information are managed as a list of exemptions in Table 2b, which summarizes the system calls that operate the privilege information.

6 Evaluation

6.1 Evaluation Purpose

We evaluated the kernel with KDRM to investigate the security capability, the overhead to kernel processing, and the attack difficulty by relocating kernel data. The evaluation contents are listed as follows:

1. Privilege escalation attacks security assessment
   We evaluated whether the kernel with KDRM can prevent privilege escalation attacks by introducing kernel vulnerabilities that can be used for memory corruption.
2. Performance evaluation in kernel operation
   We used benchmarking software to calculate the kernel performance score with KDRM.
3. Performance evaluation in issuing system calls
   Using benchmark software, we measured the overhead of relocating kernel data before and after issuing system calls on a kernel with KDRM.
4. Attack difficulty assessment with kernel data relocation
   The granularity of randomization of virtual addresses by the relocation of kernel data using KDRM was compared with KASLR to evaluate the attack difficulty.

6.2   Evaluation Environment

The evaluation device was used for security evaluation and performance evaluations. The evaluation device was an Intel(R) Xeon(R) W-2295 (3.00 GHz, 18 cores, 32 GB memory) running Debian 11.3, Linux kernel 5.18.2. We implemented the KDRM in Linux kernel 5.18.2 with 248 lines of code for nine files. Furthermore, we added 32 lines of kernel vulnerabilities that can be used for memory corruption for security evaluation to three files and implemented the PoC code in 134 lines.

6.3   Kernel Vulnerability

The following system calls were introduced to evaluate the security capability of KDRM:

```
// PoC code running, process id is 1676          13. // relocation kernel pages' region
1.   user $ ./a.out                               14. // ffff888005d82000, ..., ffff8880063e5000
2.   uid=1000(user) gid=1000(user) groups=1000(user)  15. // relocate kernel page of privilege
3.   [*] sys_kvuln01 system call invocation       16. [ 363.704204] uid virtual address: ffff8880063e2000
4.   uid virtual address: ffff888007af9784        17. // Kernel memory corruption
5.   [*] sys_kvuln02 system call invocation       18. [ 363.704204] attack target virtual address: ffff888007af9784
6.   Killed user process                          19. [ 364.216821] #PF: error code (0x0002), virtual address: ffff888007af9784
                                                  20. Page fault error code 2 (0b010)
// Kernel log information                         21. Page fault error code bits: from Linux v5.18.2 : arch/x86/include/asm/trap_pf.h
7.   // set kernel page of privilege at the user process creation  a.   bit 0 == 0: no page found
8.   [ 363.704204] uid virtual address: ffff888007af9784  b.   bit 1 == 1: write access, X86_PF_WRITE
9.   // start system call invocation              c.   bit 0 == 0: kernel-mode access
10.  [ 363.702116] sys_kvuln02 system call invocation  22. // finish system call invocation
11.  [ 363.702179] sysnum: 0x6a (352)             23. // finish user process
12.  [ 363.702204] PID: user process 1676

Red text is the points of kernel memory corruption information
```

Fig. 4. Results of Preventing Privilege Elevation Attacks Using the KDRM.

– Original system call 1: Original system call 1 identifies the virtual address of the kernel data (e.g., the privilege information of the user process), then returns it to the user process.
– Original system call 2: Original system call 2 takes two arguments. The first argument is the virtual address, and the second is the overwritten data. Execution of the original system call 2 attempts to overwrite kernel data of the specified virtual address. A privilege escalation attack is possible if the first argument is the virtual address of the privilege information of the user process and the second argument is root ID (e.g., 0).

6.4   Privilege Escalation Attacks Security Assessment

As a security assessment, the attacking user process uses the original system call 1 to identify the virtual address of the privilege information and then attempts a privilege escalation attack using the original system call 2.

Figure 4 shows the attack prevention results of KDRM when a user process executes a privilege escalation attack.

In the attacking user process, line 2 displays the privilege information of the user process. The value of uid is 1,000, which confirms that the user is a normal user. In line 4, it calls the original system call 1 to specify the virtual address of the kernel data storing the privilege information.

In line 5, the user executes the original system call 2, a privilege escalation attack. In the kernel, line 8 shows the virtual address of the kernel data containing the privilege information. Lines 13 and 14 indicate the range of virtual addresses of the relocation-only page. In lines 15 and 16, KDRM moves the kernel data that stores the privilege information to the relocation-only page. The virtual address is changed before executing the original system call 2.

In line 18, an attempt is made to overwrite the virtual address specified by the original system call 2. A page fault with error number 2 is caught in line 19. This indicates a violation of writing to the page for the virtual address. The writing target is the previous virtual address of privilege information.

Table 3. UnixBench compile performance of implementation

	Vanilla kernel	Implementation
Dhrystone 2	4450.50	4440.50 (0.22%)
Double-Precision Whetstone	1557.54	1552.92 (0.30%)
Excel Throughput	1193.23	1187.14 (0.52%)
File Copy 1024 bufsize	4122.08	3997.08 (3.03%)
File Copy 256 bufsize	2790.40	2698.60 (3.29%)
File Copy 4096 bufsize	7401.80	7192.62 (2.82%)
Pipe Throughput	2109.68	2041.04 (3.25%)
Pipe-based Context Switching	806.02	785.34 (2.57%)
Process Creation	1019.10	1017.92 (0.12%)
Shell Scripts (1 concurrent)	2485.20	2456.13 (1.17%)
Shell Scripts (8 concurrent)	2298.00	2294.36 (0.16%)
System Call Overhead	1771.08	1620.68 (8.49%)
System Benchmarks Index Score	2195.16	2140.24 (2.50%)

6.5   Overhead of Kernel Performance

To evaluate the performance of the kernel, UnixBench version 5.1.3 was run five times on the Linux kernel before and after KDRM was applied, and the performance score was calculated from the average values.

Table 3 lists the UnixBench performance score of each running kernel for numerical computation, file copy, process processing, and system calls. Higher score values indicate high performance. From Table 3, the KDRM had most negligible impact on the score of 0.12% for Process Creation and the most significant impact on the score of 8.49% for System Call Overhead. The overall impact on the performance score was 2.50%.

6.6 Overhead of Kernel Processing

In KDRM, the privilege information is to be protected when a system call is performed. In the evaluation, we ran the benchmark software LMbench version 3.0-a9 10 times on a Linux kernel before and after applying KDRM. We calculated the overhead from the average value of the system call.

Table 4a lists the results of the performance evaluation. In LMbench, the number of system call invocations differs for each evaluation item: fork+/bin/sh is 54 times, fork+execve is 4 times, fork+exit is 2 times, open/close is 2 times, and the others are once.

6.7 Attack Difficulty Assessment by Kernel Data Relocation

A comparison of KDRM and the attack difficulty of Linux KASLR [5,13] is summarized in Table 4b. The randomization granularity of the virtual address was expressed in terms of entropy [19]. Moreover, 32 bits of Linux KASLR are randomized in 2 MB (21 bits) units, 512 MB (29 bits) has 8 bits of entropy, and 1 GB (30 bits) has 9 bits of entropy. In Table 4b, the relocation target is 256 bytes, 8 bits, and the relocation-only pages (4 KB, 12 bits) are 1, 64, and 4096 pages with 4, 10, and 16 bits of entropy.

Table 4. Overhead and randomization entropy comparison

(a) Overhead of KDRM on the Linux kernel (μs)

System call	Vanilla kernel	Implementation	Overhead
fork+/bin/sh	434.2899	446.8079	12.5180 (102.88%)
fork+execve	101.2726	129.0260	27.7534 (127.40%)
fork+exit	89.9990	94.8672	4.8682 (105.41%)
open/close	1.1642	1.4920	0.3278 (128.16%)
read	0.1177	0.1599	0.0422 (135.85%)
write	0.0908	0.1359	0.0451 (149.67%)
fstat	0.1484	0.1953	0.0468 (131.60%)
stat	0.5265	0.6979	0.1714 (132.55%)

(b) The comparison of randomization entropy

Type	Entropy	Range	Align Size
Linux KASLR 32 bits	8 bits	512 MB (29 bits)	2 MB (21 bits)
Linux KASLR 64 bits	9 bits	1 GB (30 bits)	2 MB (21 bits)
KDRM	4 bits	4 KB (12 bits)	256 byte (8 bits)
KDRM	10 bits	256 KB (18 bits)	256 byte (8 bits)
KDRM	16 bits	16 MB (24 bits)	256 byte (8 bits)

The number of attack attempts required for successful memory corruption by a brute-force attack is $\frac{1}{2^{n-1}}$ times for n bits entropy if the virtual address is not changed during the attack attempts. If the virtual address can be randomized for each attack attempt, it is 2^n times [19]. Because Linux KASLR randomizes virtual addresses only at startup, the number of attack attempts, the result is $\frac{1}{2^n}$ times. Moreover, KDRM can randomize the virtual address of the kernel data at each system call of the user process; thus, number of attack attempts is 2^n times for n bits entropy.

7 Discussion

7.1 Evaluation Consideration

Evaluating the resistance to memory corruption attacks confirmed that the kernel with KDRM can mitigate privilege escalation attacks. When implementing

KDRM, kernel data of privilege information is designated as a protection target, relocated, unmapped, and restored in the running kernel. Thus, making virtual address identification of the privilege information difficult.

The performance evaluation results show that the KDRM slightly affects the numerical calculations and process operations. However, the KDRM has a high overhead for processes requiring system calls, such as file copying. As a factor of overhead, we considered the processing time required to duplicate, unmap, and restore the protected kernel data after issuing the system call. The results confirmed that the stability of the kernel operation was not affected through performance evaluation.

7.2   Approach Consideration

Design and Implementation: The design of KDRM allows the relocation of protected kernel data at each system call issued to be transparent to user processes. We specified the user process privilege information stored in the kernel data at the time of user process creation because the privilege information is a target of privilege escalation attacks by memory corruption. To protect kernel data other than privilege information, investigate the writing location for each kernel data and consider the related system calls.

System calls involving changes in privilege information are excluded from the application of KDRM to minimize the impact of KDRM on the kernel operation. In addition, if the kernel data to be protected exceeds the page size (4KB), or if many references in the kernel exist, the applicability of KDRM must be considered for performance impact.

Attack Difficulty: In the KDRM, the number of attack attempts against the protected kernel data is 2^n for n bits entropy. The attack cost is increased to make the memory corruption attack more challenging.

However, the n bit entropy increases or decreases depending on the size of the kernel data to be protected and the number of relocated pages. Thus, it is necessary to consider the difficulty of identifying virtual addresses and calculating the attack cost of memory corruption attacks depending on the type of kernel data.

7.3   Limitation of KDRM

The KDRM does not prevent vulnerable kernel code calls or illegal memory writes. CFI verifies the order of code calls and prevents unauthorized code calls. The Memory Protection Key (MPK) enables the CPU to limit writes on a page-by-page basis [10]. Therefore, we believe that combining CFI and MPK with KDRM can improve the attack resistance of the kernel.

7.4   Portability

The KDRM relies on managing the kernel memory per page to protect kernel data and the privilege information per user process. FreeBSD builds and manages the kernel memory using page tables and assigning privilege information to each user process [6]. We also believe that the KDRM can be implemented as a portability feature for FreeBSD.

8   Related Work

Running Kernel Protection: KASLR changes the kernel data and the virtual address of the kernel code to mitigate kernel memory corruption attacks [19]. Adelie proposes a method for extending KASLR to 64-bit and applying it to device drivers [18]. A method has also been proposed to apply KASLR to a guest OS from a virtual machine monitor [9].

Prevention Malicious Code Injection: As an attack prevention technique in the kernel, exclusive page frame ownership allows exclusive page allocation for the kernel and user processes [11]. KCoFI enables the kernel to apply control flow integrity (CFI), treating asynchronous processing as an exception and preventing incorrect code execution through code call order checking [2].

Table 5. Comparison of kernel data protection methods

Feature	KASLR [19]	KCoFI [2]	KDRM
Protection target	kernel code & data	kernel data	privilege information
Implementation	Memory layout randomization	Verifying control flow	Data relocation
Limitation	Kernel booting	Asynchronous	Relocation number

Kernel Attack Surface Reduction: As an attack surface minimization technique that removes attackable areas of the kernel, kRazor makes availability decisions on a per-kernel code basis during user process execution [12]. KASR places only the kernel code and data necessary for user process execution in memory space [20].

8.1   Comparison

Table 5 compares the proposed method with the previous studies [2, 19].

In particular, KASLR changes the virtual address used for the kernel data access and kernel code calls at each kernel boot to make attacks more difficult [19]. In contrast, the virtual address locations of kernel code and kernel data do not change during kernel startup. The virtual address of kernel code or kernel data can be identified by a side-channel attack and used for the attack [8]. The KDRM performs kernel data relocation by using multiple relocation-only pages (4KB). The KDRM can be applied to a running kernel, and in combination with KASLR, it can improve its resistance to attacks.

KCoFI runs the kernel on its architecture and can verify the call order of asynchronous processing [2]. CFI is effective in preventing illegal code calls.

In contrast, applying CFI to all kernel code calls in order increases the overhead. The KDRM features kernel data relocation and does not suppress attacks. Combined with CFI, the KDRM can prevent attacks when CFI is circumvented.

9 Conclusion

In this paper, we propose a KDRM that can relocate kernel data (e.g., privilege information) in the kernel memory to mitigate memory corruption attacks. The KDRM has multiple relocation-only pages, and privilege information is replicated to one of the randomly selected relocation-only pages. It ensures that allowing the placement of privilege information is changed dynamically and protected from privilege escalation. The KDRM can be used together with KASLR in the running kernel. In particular, identifying privilege information and privilege escalation attack is more challenging.

The evaluation results showed that privilege escalation attacks by user processes could be prevented. In the overhead evaluation, the kernel load when issuing system calls ranged from 102.88% to 149.67% with a kernel performance score of 2.50%. The attack difficulty evaluation of the kernel data relocation in KDRM indicates that this approach required more attack attempts than KASLR.

Acknowledgment. This work was partially supported by the Japan Society for the Promotion of Science (JSPS) KAKENHI Grant Number JP19H04109, JP22H03592, JP23K16882, and a contract of "Research and development on new generation cryptography for secure wireless communication services" among "Research and Development for Expansion of Radio Wave Resources (JPJ000254)". which was supported by the Ministry of Internal Affairs and Communications, Japan.

References

1. Chen, H., Mao, Y., Wang, X., Zhou, D., Zeldovich, N., Kaashoek, M.F.: Linux kernel vulnerabilities: state-of-the-art defenses and open problems. In: Proceedings of the Second Asia-Pacific Workshop on Systems. APSys 2011, Association for Computing Machinery, NY, USA (2011). https://doi.org/10.1145/2103799.2103805
2. Criswell, J., Dautenhahn, N., Adve, V.: Kcofi: Complete control-flow integrity for commodity operating system kernels. In: Proceedings of 2014 IEEE Symposium on Security and Privacy, pp. 292–307 (2014). https://doi.org/10.1109/SP.2014.26
3. Exploit Database: Nexus 5 android 5.0 - privilege escalation. https://www.exploit-db.com/exploits/35711/. Accessed 21 May 2019
4. Linux Foundation: The Linux kernel archives. https://www.kernel.org/ Accessed 10 June 2022
5. Linux Foundation: Randomize the address of the kernel image (KASLR). https://www.kernelconfig.io/config_randomize_base. Accessed 10 June 2022
6. FreeBSD: FreeBSD architecture handbook. https://www.freebsd.org/doc/en_US.ISO8859-1/books/arch-handbook/. Accessed 18 August 2019
7. grsecurity: super fun 2.6.30+/rhel5 2.6.18 local kernel exploit. https://grsecurity.net/spender/exploits/exploit2.txt. Accessed 21 May 2019

8. Gruss, D., Lipp, M., Schwarz, M., Fellner, R., Maurice, C., Mangard, S.: KASLR is dead: long live KASLR. In: Bodden, E., Payer, M., Athanasopoulos, E. (eds.) ESSoS 2017. LNCS, vol. 10379, pp. 161–176. Springer, Cham (2017). https://doi. org/10.1007/978-3-319-62105-0_11

9. Holmes, B., Waterman, J., Williams, D.: KASLR in the age of MicroVMs. In: Proceedings of the Seventeenth European Conference on Computer Systems, EuroSys 2022, pp. 149–165. Association for Computing Machinery, NY, USA (2022). https://doi.org/10.1145/3492321.3519578

10. Intel: Intel®64 and IA-32 architectures software developer's manual. https:// www.intel.com/content/www/us/en/developer/articles/technical/intel-sdm.html. Accessed 18 Aug 2021

11. Kemerlis, V.P., Polychronakis, M., Keromytis, A.D.: Ret2dir: rethinking kernel isolation. In: Proceedings of the 23rd USENIX Conference on Security Symposium, SEC 2014, pp. 957–972. USENIX Association, USA (2014). https://doi.org/10. 5555/2671225.2671286

12. Kurmus, A., Dechand, S., Kapitza, R.: Quantifiable run-time Kernel attack surface reduction. In: Dietrich, S. (ed.) DIMVA 2014. LNCS, vol. 8550, pp. 212–234. Springer, Cham (2014). https://doi.org/10.1007/978-3-319-08509-8_12

13. LWN.net: Kernel address space layout randomization. https://lwn.net/Articles/ 569635/. Accessed 12 May 2022

14. MITRE: Cve-2016-4997. https://cve.mitre.org/cgi-bin/cvename.cgi?name=CVE-2016-4997. Accessed 10 June 2019

15. MITRE: Cve-2016-9793. https://cve.mitre.org/cgi-bin/cvename.cgi?name=CVE-2016-9793. Accessed 10 June 2019

16. MITRE: Cve-2017-1000112.   https://cve.mitre.org/cgi-bin/cvename.cgi? name=CVE-2017-1000112. Accessed 10 June 2019

17. MITRE: Cve-2017-16995.   https://cve.mitre.org/cgi-bin/cvename.cgi? name=CVE-2017-16995. Accessed 10 June 2019

18. Nikolaev, R., Nadeem, H., Stone, C., Ravindran, B.: Adelie: continuous address space layout re-randomization for linux drivers. In: Proceedings of the 27th ACM International Conference on Architectural Support for Programming Languages and Operating Systems, ASPLOS 2022, pp. 483–498. Association for Computing Machinery, NY, USA (2022). https://doi.org/10.1145/3503222.3507779

19. Shacham, H., Page, M., Pfaff, B., Goh, E.J., Modadugu, N., Boneh, D.: On the effectiveness of address-space randomization. In: Proceedings of the 11th ACM Conference on Computer and Communications Security, CCS 2004, pp. 298–307. Association for Computing Machinery, NY, USA (2004). https://doi.org/10.1145/ 1030083.1030124

20. Zhang, Z., Cheng, Y., Nepal, S., Liu, D., Shen, Q., Rabhi, F.: KASR: a reliable and practical approach to attack surface reduction of commodity OS kernels. In: Bailey, M., Holz, T., Stamatogiannakis, M., Ioannidis, S. (eds.) RAID 2018. LNCS, vol. 11050, pp. 691–710. Springer, Cham (2018). https://doi.org/10.1007/978-3-030-00470-5_32

The Effectiveness of Transformer-Based Models for BEC Attack Detection

Amirah Almutairi[1,2]([envelope]) [ORCID], BooJoong Kang[1] [ORCID], and Nawfal Fadhel[1] [ORCID]

[1] School of Electronics and Computer Science, University of Southampton, Southampton, England, UK
{a.almutairi,b.kang,Nawfal}@soton.ac.uk
[2] Department of Computer Science, Shaqra University, Shaqra 11961, Saudi Arabia
amirah@su.edu.sa

Abstract. Business Email Compromise (BEC) attacks are a significant threat to organizations, with attackers using various tactics to acquire sensitive information and cause financial damage to target firms. These attacks are difficult to detect using existing email security systems, as approximately 60% of BEC attacks do not include explicit indicators such as attachments and links. Even state-of-the-art solutions using Natural Language Processing (NLP) rely heavily on such explicit indicators. This study proposes a transformer-based BEC detection method that can capture linguistic properties of emails so that could reduce the reliance on explicit indicators. Our method of combining BERT and BiLSTM offers the advantage of capturing both global context and local interdependence, resulting in a comprehensive and nuanced understanding of email text. In our experiment, the proposed method outperforms the state-of-the-art solutions, achieving a 0.99% accuracy and this highlights the potential of transformer-based models in detecting BEC attacks.

Keywords: Business Email Compromise BEC · Phishing · Email Security · Feature Engineering · Transformer · BERT · BiLSTM

1 Introduction

In today's digital age, emails are a crucial communication tool used in various fields, including business and education, due to their accessibility, convenience, and easy replicability. The number of worldwide email service users is expected to reach 4.48 billion by 2024, and over 347 billion global emails are predicted to be sent and received daily by 2023 [1]. However, despite their numerous advantages, emails also have drawbacks, including the prevalence of deceitful messages such as spam, phishing, and fake emails.

Phishing emails often appear as fraudulent emails from legitimate companies, such as banks or internet providers, that deceive the recipient into divulging sensitive information or taking action, such as changing passwords or disclosing login details. On the other hand, Business Email Compromise (BEC) attacks

S. Li et al. (Eds.): NSS 2023, LNCS 13983, pp. 77–90, 2023.
https://doi.org/10.1007/978-3-031-39828-5_5

involve an attacker impersonating someone within an organization, such as a supervisor or IT team member, to manipulate their targets into transferring money or sensitive information. These attacks can be highly effective, as even major companies like Google and Facebook have fallen victim to them. Thus, it is essential that individuals and organizations remain vigilant and take measures to protect themselves against these forms of cybercrime.

Business Email Compromise (BEC) attacks have become a significant concern for organizations due to the malicious financial damage they can cause by acquiring sensitive information related to executive accounts as stated by Ecclesie et al. [2]. Detecting BEC attacks is crucial for maintaining stability and confidence in digital communication among companies, especially since approximately 60% of BEC incidents do not use a link [3], making them difficult to detect using traditional email security systems.

The objective of this research is to proposes a transformer-based BEC detection method that can capture linguistic properties of emails so that could reduce the reliance on explicit indicators. Additionally, we aim to identify factors that could aid in identifying malicious attacks in email bodies without additional information about sources, links, or attachments. To achieve this goal, we will answer the following research question:

– How can transformer-based models be employed to detect BEC attacks in plain text emails, and what factors aid in their identification?

While solutions for this problem have been explored within the scope of NLP, the current state-of-the-art method heavily rely on explicit indicators of malicious messages, such as links or attachments (Maleki et al. 2019; Cidon et al. 2019) [4,5]. Our objective is to proposed a transformer-based models to detect BEC attacks in plain text emails, even without additional information about sources, links, or attachments, and to identify factors that aid in their identification. Our results demonstrate the effectiveness of Transformer models, beating both the baseline model and current state-of-the-art model with a 0.99% accuracy on Fraud datasets.

2   Background

Our model uses Bidirectional Encoder Representations from Transformers (BERT), and Long Short-Term Memory (LSTM). Therefore this section describes the general related information for the proposed methodology.

2.1   Bidirectional Encoder Representations from Transformers (BERT)

BERT is a pre-training technique for NLP based on a transformer model [6]. Unlike sequential directional models, the transformer encoder reads the entire word sequence at once, allowing the model to learn the context of words based on the sentence. BERT is designed to pre-train deep bidirectional representations from text by conditioning on both left and right contexts, and can be fine-tuned for a wide range of NLP tasks with only one additional output layer [7] as shown in Fig. 1. BERT is a plain text corpus-based transformer framework that employs pre-training and bidirectional, unsupervised language representation. Google started using BERT for English language search queries in October 2019 and adopted it for 70 languages in December 2019.

- BERT works bidirectionally, left-right or right-left, unlike other techniques, and provides extended performance and accuracy.
- BERT is pre-trained and uses an unlabelled, plain text corpus including the entire English Wikipedia. Masked Language Modelling and Next Sentence Prediction BERT tasks are used for NLP.
- BERT created the possibility of text classification in Python, like embeddings for our text documents.

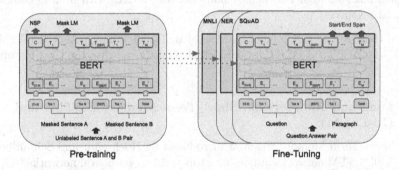

Fig. 1. Overall pre-training and fine-tuning procedures for BERT. [6]

Google uses BERT for its search engine, but it can be used for a variety of language tasks, like fine-tuning, questioning/answering, sentence classification, named entity recognition, sentence recognition and conversational response generation. BERT excels at Natural language understanding tasks like Polysemy and Coreference resolution, natural language inference, sentiment classification and word sense disambiguation. BERT is open source and is expected to introduce improvements in terms of higher accuracy and computation time requirements for different applications.

BERT also released the following pre-trained models:

- BERT-Base, Uncased: This refers to one of the two variants of the BERT model, which has 12 encoder layers, 768 hidden units, 12 attention heads, and 110 million parameters. It is called "uncased" because the model was trained on lowercase text, which allows it to be more robust to variations in capitalization.

- BERT-Large, Uncased: This model has 24 layers, 1024 hidden units, 16 attention heads, and a total of 340 million parameters.
- BERT-Base, Multilingual: Designed to handle multiple languages and has the following specifications: 104 languages, 12-layer, 768-hidden, 12-heads, and 110M parameters.
- BERT-Base, Chinese: a version of the BERT model designed for Chinese language understanding tasks. It consists of 12 layers, 768 hidden units, 12 attention heads, and 110 million parameters, and it supports both Simplified and Traditional Chinese.
- DistilBERT is a compressed version of BERT that uses fewer parameters and smaller computational resources while still achieving competitive results on various NLP tasks. It was introduced in 2019 by Sanh et al. [7]. and is designed to be faster and more lightweight than the original BERT model. The main idea behind DistilBERT is to leverage the knowledge distilled from the large BERT model and transfer it to a smaller model by using a knowledge distillation approach. DistilBERT has 40% fewer parameters than BERT-Base, which makes it easier to deploy and train on devices with limited computational resources.

and there are some Common models of BERT including patentBERT, Med-BERT, docBERT, G-BERT, and videoBERT, etc. as discussed by Rasmy et al. [8].

2.2 Long and Bidirectional Short-Term Memory (LSTM) and (Bi-LSTM)

Long Short-Term Memory was first introduced by Hochreiter and Schmidhuber in 1997 [9]. LSTM networks are built on top of recurrent neural networks (RNNs) and incorporate mechanisms to improve the storage of information from previous data, prolonging the propagation and influence of the current instance on future inputs. LSTMs are widely used in classification, time series analysis, and natural language processing tasks, given their versatility and robustness in maintaining context.

The three elements of the LSTM cell are commonly referred to as gates as illustrated in Fig. 2:

Input gate allows the cell to incorporate new information from the current input. Therefore, it determines which data will be stored in the memory cell and is dependent on the past output and current input.

Forget gate determines the need to retain or discard information from the previous time step. Therefore, it is responsible for determining how the memory cell is updated or reset.

Output gate updates information from the current time step to the next. Therefore, it decides which information will be passed to the next time step.

Bidirectional LSTM (Bi-LSTM) was first introduced by Schuster and Paliwal [11] Unlike LSTM which runs the input from future to the past, (Bi-LSTM) consists of two LSTM parts and uses the same elements but in different sequence.

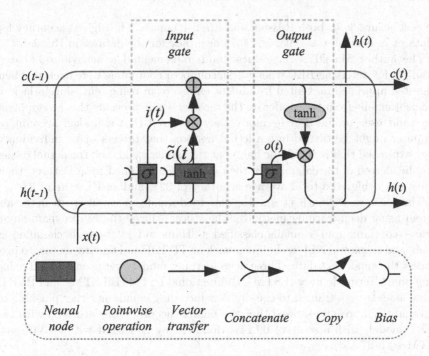

Fig. 2. The overall framework of the LSTM by Yong Yu et al. [10]

Forward LSTM runs input from the past to the future. While *Backward LSTM* run input from future to past. Then, the outputs of both LSTMs are concatenated to form the final output of the Bi-LSTM model. This design enables the model to analyze information from both the preceding and following context.

3   Related Works

Numerous studies have been performed to develop models that are capable of detecting malicious messages. However, most of them focus on the directional model, which does not consider the semantic meaning or context of the words, where input text reading is done sequentially or surrounding the words. Also, they depend heavily on explicit indicators of malicious messages but do not necessarily tackle the problem when such evidence is not available.

Vorobeva et al. [12] proposed a strategy for detecting BEC attacks based on an examination of the writing style in business email compromises and presented a functional model. The feature space included writing features such as words and three-gram phrases, as well as the day of the week and time of day the email was sent, its urgency, and its header features. Trials were conducted on datasets containing emails in Russian and English to determine the effectiveness of the BEC attack detection. The results showed that using word n-grams and Linear Support Vector Classification (LSVC) with a feature scaling algorithm produced the best accuracy for both Russian and English emails. The highest accuracy for a dataset in English was 0.95, and 0.75 accuracy for the dataset in Russian.

The author Maleki [4] introduced and implemented a behavioural- based paradigm for detecting BEC whenever accounts or computers were hacked. Their suggested approach prevented fraudulent emails from being sent, since a lack of sufficient emails from the sender on the receiver's side prevents the development of a valid user profile. Furthermore, they observed that a hacked account or computer might be turned into a lethal weapon that targets many individuals. They expressed that it should be halted at the sender's end, and the actual owner must be alerted of the calamity. In their experiment on the Enron Dataset, their framework achieved a total average accuracy of 92% and an F1 score of 93 %.

The authors Debnath et al. [13] aim to develop an email spam detection system using deep learning methods. The study utilized the Enron spam email dataset containing 3672 emails classified as Ham and 1499 emails classified as Spam, and employed NLP techniques, such as TF-IDF and text-to-vector, to pre-process the email text data. Three deep learning models were constructed using Long Short-Term Memory (LSTM), Bidirectional LSTM (BiLSTM), and BERT. These models were trained to classify new incoming emails as either phishing or legitimate. The results showed that the highest accuracy was achieved with the BERT model, with a score of 99.14%, followed by Bi-LSTM with 98.34% and LSTM with 97.15%.

The work by Xiao et al. [14] aims to detect phishing emails and spam by analysing textual content. The actual representation is done by TF-IDF (Term Frequency - Inverse Document Frequency) vector. To address a phishing email according to the attacker which is its source, a Bi-LSTM-Attention model with a self-trained word2vec model is proposed. The experiment took place with a dataset built over a random selection of 1200 safe emails, 1200 spam and 1800 phishing emails from the dataset (trec06p) public English corpus provided by TREC [15]. With the KNN model, the detection of both spam emails and phishing attacks was highly effective. In phishing detection, the achieved accuracy was 95.27% and the false positive rate was only 1.22%. For spam detection, the achieved accuracy was 94.53%, with a false positive rate as low as 2.58%. Based on different attack sources, phishing detection using the Bi-LSTM-Attention model achieved an accuracy of 91.51%.

Authors Cidon et al. [5] propose a two-stage approach to detect impersonation and avoid attacks of this kind. The setup relies on a divided task. The classifier first analyses metadata only (i.e., sender, receiver, CC and BCC fields) to detect impersonation emails by comparing previous behaviour and lists of reliable websites. Once this classifier raises the flag for a suspicious message, it is further analysed by a textual approach that individually processes title and body fields. The content classifier performs the task of detecting messages by employing an NLP text classifier and link detection. The textual content is represented using a counting TF-IDF model of unigrams and bigrams with 10,000 features. Links are defined as suspicious if they refer to a small or recent website or the sending entity is identified as an impersonator. With the two-stage prediction model, the impersonation model detection contributes substantially to the accuracy of the second stage (textual model). The link classifier achieved 97% precision and 96% recall with the random forest model. The text classification model achieved around 99% in precision and 97.5% in recall with the KNN classifier. It was possible to accurately determine most of the impersonation with the proposed system. It is notable that the attackers will constantly improvise their attacks and training models need regular upgrades/training to ensure maximum protection. By evaluating missed attacks, it was found that even small changes, such as the name of the sender and new patterns in the textual content could remain undetected in the system.

4 Proposed Model

BERT, one of the most popular transformer-based models, is an encoder stack of transformer structures that applies bidirectional training to language modelling developed by Devlin et al. [6]. BERT architectures have extensive feedforward networks and attention heads. They take a classification (CLS) token and a sequence of words as input. Each layer uses self-attention and passes the result through a feedforward network to the next encoder. The output corresponding to the CLS token can be used for classification tasks.

In this study, we use a pre-trained BERT_BiLSTM model to produce word embeddings from email texts. Our model uses BERT as a pre-trained language model for feature extraction, combined with BiLSTM, to enable the model to learn the context of words based on the sentence.

By combining BERT and BiLSTM, we can leverage the strengths of both models to provide a more comprehensive representation of the context of a word. BERT can capture the global context of a word, while BiLSTM can capture the local context of a word. This combination can help in detecting the most challenging phishing attacks Business Email Compromise (BEC) attacks, which rely on publicly available research and social engineering rather than actual malicious links and attachments.

In the following section, we will describe the experiments we conducted to evaluate the effectiveness of our approach.

5 Experiment

We will investigate the research question outlines in Sect. 1 using the following experiment protocol.

Step 1: Formulate the research hypothesis.
Step 2: Pre-process the dataset.
Step 3: Design the model.
Step 4: Evaluate the proposed model using traditional evaluation metrics.
Step 5: Compare our results against baseline models and current studies.

Step 6: Explore factors that aid in the identification of malicious attacks in plain email text.

We provide details on each step of the experiment protocol and discuss the rationale behind our choices. We also present the datasets used, the evaluation metrics, and the comparison methods. Finally, we analyze the results of our experiments and draw conclusions regarding the effectiveness of our proposed method.

5.1 Experimental Setup

The implementation was done in Python 3.9, and made use of the architectures implemented in PyTorch [16] and scikit-learn [17]. The pre-trained BERT embedding comes from the Hugging Face initiative [18].

For the transformer-based model for detection of BEC phishing attack emails and safe/legitimate emails, the dataset will be divided randomly into three parts; 70% of the dataset will be used for training the model, 10% will be used for validation and 20% will be selected for the testing.

Different proposed machine learning- and deep learning-based models will be tested and results will be evaluated to select the best performing model.

Step 1- Formulate the Experiment Hypothesis. This Experiment aims to study the following hypothesis:

In a scenario where there is no explicit indicator that mail is from an attacker, for example: BEC attacks, transformer machine learning based models can be used to classify messages from trustworthy sources and attackers accurately.

Our model addresses the gaps identified in recent studies by using a pre-trained language model, BERT, and BiLSTM for feature extraction. The combination of these models allows the model to learn the context of a word within a sentence, leveraging the strengths of BERT's ability to provide global context and BiLSTM's ability to provide local context. This approach is particularly useful for detecting Business Email Compromise (BEC) attacks, which rely on publicly available research and social engineering tactics rather than malicious links or attachments.

Step 2- Dataset Pre-processing. For our experiment, two datasets were used. The first one is the fraud email detection dataset [19]. This corpus contains 5,187 phishing emails and 6,742 reliable messages. The second dataset was first introduced on the Trec 2007 shared task [20], where participants had to build systems capable of determining the reliability of the messages. This dataset contains 50,199 phishing emails and 25,220 messages in the control group.

The dataset will be divided randomly into three parts; 70% of the dataset will be used for training the model, 10% will be used for validation and 20% will be selected for the testing. An automatic parser was used to extract only the body content of the message for the Trec dataset.

In contrast to prior works, the proposed method employs solely textual content to train and assess the efficacy of a natural language processing (NLP) model. The removal of supplementary metadata related to the sender, recipient, timestamp, and attachments is undertaken with the objective of creating a setting where detecting Business Email Compromise (BEC) is predicated not on metadata associated with the email medium, but rather on the linguistic content of the message. It is noteworthy that BEC is a type of phishing attack. The present scenario involves detecting BEC without any presence of malicious payloads and relying only on textual content. As such, employing a phishing dataset and eliminating malicious payloads is appropriate. By focusing on the language used in the email, rather than its metadata or attachments

Step 3- Design the Model. The proposed transform-based model shown in Fig. 3 uses a Bidirectional Encoder Representation from a variation of the regular BERT embedding model called DistilBERT by Sanh et al. [7]. The model uses pre-trained embeddings and is fine-tuned for the current task using an LSTM architecture. The LSTM layer is a bidirectional recurrent neural network layer (BiLSTM) with 50 neurons in the hidden layer. After the LSTM layer, a fully connected layer is applied with a softmax activation function.

The model starts by loading a pre-trained DistilBert model and storing its hidden size as a member variable. Then, the model creates a bidirectional LSTM layer with 50 hidden units The forward pass of the model starts with passing the input data through the DistilBert model to get the *last_hidden_state*. This is then permuted, packed, and passed through the LSTM layer to obtain the output hidden state, *output_hidden*. The output hidden state is then passed through a dropout layer, with a keep probability of 0.5 to prevent overfitting.

Finally, the output hidden state is passed through a fully connected linear layer with 2 units to get the binary classification prediction. The *softmax* function is then applied to the output to convert the predicted logits into a probability distribution over the two classes.

Each sentence was tokenized and limited to the first 150 BERT tokens, which helps reduce the input size while still maintaining a significant amount of context. To balance the memory constraints and training time, the model was trained with a batch size of 16 samples. We used AdamW optimizer with a learning rate of $2e^{-5}$ and a weighted cross-entropy loss function to account for the imbalanced nature of the dataset, where the number of legitimate emails is significantly higher than the number of phishing emails.

In this study, we trained the model with a maximum of 3 epochs and used a validation set to stop training early if necessary this helps prevent overfitting and ensures optimal generalization performance. Table 1 summarize the hyper parameters used.

To compare the results of the BERT-BiLSTM architecture, two additional baseline models were implemented. Both of them use a bag-of-words with weighted inverse frequency (TF-IDF) model as input data. The first one is

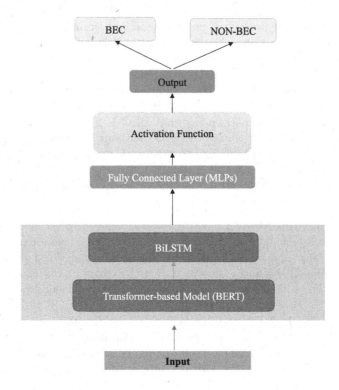

Fig. 3. The structure of BERT-BiLSTM model.

Table 1. Hyperparameters

Hyperparameter	Value
MAX_length	150
batch size	16
learning rate	$2e^{-5}$
epochs	3
hidden_dim	50

trained with an l2-regularized logistic regression as a classifier, and the second one is an Xgboost classifier. Table 2 summarizes the models.

In order to train the LogReg and Xgboost baseline models, the data was cleaned, removing stopwords, numbers, punctuation, math symbols and single letters. The same parser was used to extract the e-mail body from the Trec 2007 dataset. The input for the models will be a lower-case list of tokens in a sparse Tf-idf vector. There is no limit to vocabulary or minimum occurrence.

Table 2. Models

Model name	Method	Features
LogReg	Logistic regression	TF-IDF counts
Xgboost	Distributed gradient boosting	TF-IDF counts
BERT-BiLSTM	Long short-term memory network	DistilBERT embedding

Table 3. Phishing classification weighted average F1 results. (The best F1 score for each dataset is highlighted).

Model	Fraud mail			Trec07		
	Precision	Recall	F1	Precision	Recall	F1
LogReg	0.987	0.987	0.986	0.982	0.984	0.982
Xgboost	0.986	0.988	0.987	0.984	0.985	0.984
BERT	0.998	0.997	**0.998**	0.985	0.986	**0.986**

Step 4- Evaluate the Proposed Model by the Traditional Evaluation Metrics and Against the Baseline Model. In this step we evaluate the performance of the proposed model, we make use of a weighted f-measure for overall performance, as well as the analysis of the false positive rate with precision and false negative rate with recall metrics.

Table 3 summarizes the results of this exploratory experiment. In the case of the Fraud mail dataset (left side of Table 3), we observe that BERT is the overall best-performing alternative, obtaining a 1% improvement over the second best result. Xgboost performed second on this dataset; however, with a slight margin when compared with the logistic regression model.

When evaluating the performance over the Trec07 dataset (right side of Table 3), the BERT model still performed the best, but only with a small improvement over the Xgboost model, a relatively larger margin over the logistic regression one.

Step 5 - Compare Against the Current Studies. In this step, we compared the performance of our proposed model with an existing approach by Xiao et al. [14]. We chose this study for comparison because it also focused on analyzing textual content for phishing detection using the Fraud mail dataset. The authors used KNN and TF-IDF vector representation for their analysis, as well as a Bi-LSTM-Attention model with a self-trained word2vec model. By comparing the accuracy of our model with theirs, we can better evaluate its effectiveness in detecting BEC attacks. Table 4 shows the results of this comparison.

Step 6 - Explore the Factors that Aid in the Identification of Malicious Attacks as Plain Text Format. Furthermore, we explore the factors that aid in the identification of malicious attacks as plain email format, Fig. 4 which

Table 4. Accuracy Comparison with an Existing Approach

Model	Method	Dataset	Accuracy
KNN [14]	LSTM /TF-IDF	Fraud mail	0.94
(Proposed)	BiLSTM / DistilBERT	Fraud mail	**0.99**

presents the word-cloud plots from the 300 most important words to determine the class for the datasets fraud mail and trec07, respectively. The set of words is extracted from the initial TF-IDF model through univariate feature selection using ANOVA with F1 as the score function.

(a) Word cloud of the 300 most important words in the fraud mail dataset

(b) Word cloud of the 300 most important words in the trec06 dataset

Fig. 4. Word clouds of the most important words to determine the classes from datasets

When analysing the word clouds, it is possible to determine that certain messages are more likely to be an attack based on the content and what they aim to do with it. As expected, in Fig. 4a we can observe that the most important features are related to financial topics, which indicates they will be related to wire transactions. But also, it is notable that most of them address the request politely (e.g., the use of words *Mr.*, *please*, *dear*).

Similar behaviour can be found in Fig. 4b. However, this one is less dedicated to talking about financial topics. On the other hand, it is possible to find words that demonstrate the prevalence of links (e.g., *www*, *org*, *https*).

6   Discussion

The proposed model in this study demonstrates promising results in identifying Business Email Compromise (BEC) attacks, achieving an accuracy of 0.99. This is an improvement over the existing KNN approach used by Xiao et al. [14], which achieved an accuracy of 0.94. The comparison against this existing approach validates the effectiveness of our proposed model in detecting BEC attacks, which is crucial in mitigating financial losses and preventing fraud.

As for the most common ways to identify, the feature selection model as shown previously in Figs. 4a and 4b was able to identify the presence of prevalent patterns in both data sets. In this way, it is possible to identify that they will make constant use of language that refers to financial transactions, requests for help, and urgency, mention the organization itself and contains links to external sites. Those findings match with the previous features in the literature, but here the model could manage to identify them without our intervention.

7   Conclusions

In this study, we proposed a novel approach for detecting Business Email Compromise (BEC) attacks using a pre-trained DistilBERT deep learning model. Our proposed model achieved an impressive accuracy of 0.99 on the Fraud mail dataset, outperforming an existing approach that used KNN and TF-IDF vector representation. Our study also identified key factors that aid in the identification of malicious attacks, such as the presence of certain language and content patterns.

Our findings make a significant contribution to the field of email security, as they provide an effective and efficient approach for detecting BEC attacks, which are responsible for significant financial losses for individuals and organizations. Moreover, our study highlights the importance of considering language and content factors in the detection of phishing attacks. Specifically, we observed that polite language and financial topics were prevalent in the Fraud mail dataset, while the use of links was more common in the TREC07 dataset.

Moving forward, future research can explore the generalizability of our proposed model to other datasets and investigate the interpretability of the model's decisions. Additionally, integrating our model into existing email filtering systems can enhance their performance in detecting BEC attacks and prevent financial losses for individuals and organizations.

In summary, our proposed model offers a promising approach for detecting BEC attacks and advancing the field of email security. By identifying key factors that aid in the identification of malicious attacks, our study offers valuable insights that can be used to improve the performance of email filtering systems and prevent financial losses due to BEC attacks.

Acknowledgement. The authors would like to thank the Deanship of Scientific Research at Shaqra University and the Saudi Arabian Cultural Bureau in London (SACB) for allowing the research to be undertaken.

References

1. Inc statistics. Online industries most targeted by phishing attacks as of 1st quarter 2021 (2021)
2. Alessandro Ecclesie Agazzi. Business email compromise (BEC) and cyberpsychology. arXiv preprint arXiv:2007.02415 (2020)

3. Barracuda. Threat spotlight: Barracuda study of 3,000 attacks reveals BEC targets different departments (2018)
4. Maleki, N.: A behavioral based detection approach for business email compromises. PhD thesis, University of New Brunswick (2019)
5. Cidon, A., et al.: High precision detection of business email compromise. In: 28th USENIX Security Symposium (USENIX Security 19), pp. 1291–1307 (2019)
6. Devlin, J., Chang, M.W., Lee, K., Toutanova, K.: BERT: pre-training of deep bidirectional transformers for language understanding. arXiv preprint arXiv:1810.04805 (2018)
7. Sanh, V., Debut, L., Chaumond, J., Wolf, T.: DistilBERT, a distilled version of BERT: smaller, faster, cheaper and lighter. arXiv preprint arXiv:1910.01108 (2019)
8. Rasmy, L., Xiang, Y., Xie, Z., Tao, C., Zhi, D.: Med-BERT: pretrained contextualized embeddings on large-scale structured electronic health records for disease prediction. NPJ Digit. Med. 4(1), 86 (2021)
9. Hochreiter, S., Schmidhuber, J.: Long short-term memory. Neural Comput. 9(8), 1735–1780 (1997)
10. Yong, Yu., Si, X., Changhua, H., Zhang, J.: A review of recurrent neural networks: LSTM cells and network architectures. Neural Comput. 31(7), 1235–1270 (2019)
11. Schuster, M., Paliwal, K.K.: Bidirectional recurrent neural networks. IEEE Trans. Sign. Process. 45(11), 2673–2681 (1997)
12. Vorobeva, A., Khisaeva, G., Zakoldaev, D., Kotenko, I.: Detection of business email compromise attacks with writing style analysis. In: You, I., Kim, H., Youn, T.-Y., Palmieri, F., Kotenko, I. (eds.) MobiSec 2021. CCIS, vol. 1544, pp. 248–262. Springer, Singapore (2022). https://doi.org/10.1007/978-981-16-9576-6_18
13. Debnath, K., Kar, N.: Email spam detection using deep learning approach. In: 2022 International Conference on Machine Learning, Big Data, Cloud and Parallel Computing (COM-IT-CON), vol. 1, pp. 37–41. IEEE (2022)
14. Xiao, D., Jiang, M.: Malicious mail filtering and tracing system based on KNN and improved LSTM algorithm. In 2020 IEEE International Conference on Dependable, Autonomic and Secure Computing, International Conference on Pervasive Intelligence and Computing, International Conference on Cloud and Big Data Computing, International Conference on Cyber Science and Technology Congress (DASC/PiCom/CBDCom/CyberSciTech), pp. 222–229. IEEE (2020)
15. Bratko, A., Filipic, B., Zupan, B.: Towards practical ppm spam filtering: experiments for the TREC 2006 spam track. In: TREC, Citeseer (2006)
16. Paszke, A., et al.: Pytorch: an imperative style, high-performance deep learning library. In: Wallach, H., Larochelle, H., Beygelzimer, A., d'Alché-Buc, F., Fox, E., Garnett, R. (eds.) Advances in Neural Information Processing Systems vol. 32, pp. 8024–8035. Curran Associates Inc (2019)
17. Pedregosa, F., et al.: Scikit-learn: machine learning in Python. J. Mach. Learn. Res. 12, 2825–2830 (2011)
18. Wolf, T., et al.: Transformers: state-of-the-art natural language processing. In: Proceedings of the 2020 Conference on Empirical Methods in Natural Language Processing: System Demonstrations, pp. 38–45 (2020). Association for Computational Linguistics
19. Radev, D.: Clair collection of fraud email, ACL data and code repository. ADCR2008T001 (2008)
20. Macdonald, C., Ounis, I., Soboroff, I.: Overview of the TREC 2007 blog track. In: TREC vol. 7, pp. 31–43 (2007)

Blockchain

Resilience of Blockchain Overlay Networks

Aristodemos Paphitis[1](✉), Nicolas Kourtellis[2], and Michael Sirivianos[1]

[1] Cyprus University of Technology, Limassol, Cyprus
am.paphitis@edu.cut.ac.cy, michael.sirivianos@cut.ac.cy
[2] Telefonica Research, Barcelona, Spain
nicolas.kourtellis@telefonica.com

Abstract. Blockchain (BC) systems are highly distributed peer-to-peer networks that offer an alternative to centralized services and promise robustness to coordinated attacks. However, the resilience and overall security of a BC system rests heavily on the structural properties of its underlying peer-to-peer overlay. Despite their success, critical design aspects, connectivity properties, and interdependencies of BC overlay networks are still poorly understood. In this work, our aim was to fill this gap by analyzing the topological resilience of seven distinct BC networks.

In particular, we probed and crawled these BC networks for 28 days. We constructed, at frequent intervals, connectivity graphs for each BC network consisting of all potential connections between peers. We analyze the structural graph properties of these networks and their topological resilience. We show that by targeting fewer than 10 highly connected peers, major BCs such as Bitcoin can be partitioned into disconnected components. Finally, we uncover a hidden overlap between different BC networks, where certain peers participate in more than one BC network. Our findings have serious implications for the robustness of the overall ecosystem of the BC network.

Keywords: Blockchain · P2P Networks · Robustness

1 Introduction

The success of Bitcoin has resulted in the emergence of numerous blockchains and cryptocurrencies, with more than 20,000 cryptocurrencies in existence as of 2023. The distinctive features of blockchain technology have enhanced its visibility and are expected to disrupt various sectors that traditionally rely on trusted centralized third parties. Due to their ability to decentralize trust and improve asset management [12], numerous blockchain solutions have been proposed for a wide range of use cases, including healthcare, advertising, insurance, copyright protection, energy, cybersecurity, and government [5,13,14,62].

Blockchains (BC) rely on decentralized peer-to-peer (P2P) networks for their operation. Peers need to constantly maintain a local copy of all transactions and blocks, so the availability of the P2P overlay is essential for blockchain-data propagation. Generally, the security and resilience of networks depend on the structure of the underlying topology. Despite the significant amount of research on BC systems, the design and connectivity properties, as well as the interdependencies of BC networks, are not fully understood.

To develop secure and robust blockchain-based tools and infrastructure, it is crucial to examine the underlying P2P network of blockchains to identify potential limitations and vulnerabilities. Despite the security provided by proof-of-work consensus, attacks on the P2P network could weaken consensus in specific parts of the BC network. By analyzing and understanding the resilience of these networks, we can mitigate damage from both natural failures and targeted attacks.

Blockchains are already being used to process large amounts of money; considering their potential application in other aspects of everyday life, they become an attractive target for ill-intentioned attacks by malicious actors. Attackers can exploit network vulnerabilities to carry out various attacks on BC consensus and fairness [31]. Therefore, it is important to investigate whether small-scale attacks against a few nodes could provide attackers with a significant advantage.

Despite the rich literature on network resilience [2, 6, 42, 46], the research community has not yet investigated the robustness properties of blockchain networks. In this paper, our aim is to fill this gap by providing a first look at the resilience of seven distinct blockchain overlays. In particular, we are interested in the partition tolerance of these networks. We present and discuss the results of our analysis based on the connectivity graphs that we have collected. Our analysis focused on several key aspects of blockchain overlays, including their resilience against random failures and targeted attacks, their spatial centralization within Autonomous Systems, and their interdependencies. We first present the results of our analysis on the partition tolerance of blockchain overlays against random failures and targeted attacks, examining how these types of disruption can affect the stability and reliability of the network. Next, we delve into the issue of spatial centralization in Autonomous Systems and its impact on network resilience, exploring the concentration of nodes within the same AS and its impact on network stability. Finally, we discuss their interdependencies, examining the interconnections among blockchain overlays through common peers and links.

2   Background and Related Work

Although the Bitcoin and Ethereum overlay networks have been thoroughly studied, their resilience against attacks has not been adequately assessed. We believe that this omission in the literature is mainly due to a lack of accurate knowledge of the underlying topology.

2.1   Selected Overlay Networks

In this section, we provide background information on the blockchain networks under study. Seven networks were chosen, all of which are consistently included in the top 50 cryptocurrencies by market capitalization, according to [15] for the past few years. We list them alphabetically: Bitcoin, BitcoinCash, Dash, Dogecoin, Ethereum, Litecoin, and ZCash. With the exception of Ethereum, the aforementioned BCs are descendants of Bitcoin using very similar overlay implementations and node discovery protocols.

Bitcoin Overlay Network. In the Bitcoin overlay network, nodes communicate through non-TLS TCP connections to form an unstructured P2P network. Bitcoin's security heavily depends on the global consistent state of the BC, which relies on its Proof-of-Work based consensus protocol. The communication protocol is briefly documented in [22], but there is no formal specification. To understand its subtleties, we looked into previous studies [8,35,47] and Bitcoin's official source code [21] (reference client). When a node joins the network for the first time, it queries a set of DNS seeds that are hardcoded in the reference client. The response to this lookup query includes one or more IP addresses of full nodes that can accept new incoming connections. Once connected to the network, a node receives unsolicited `addr` messages from its connected peers that contain IP addresses of other peers in the network. In addition, the client can send to peers `getaddr` messages to gather additional peers. The reply to a `getaddr` message may contain up to 1000 peer addresses. All known addresses are maintained in an in-memory data structure managed by the address manager(`ADDRMAN`), and are periodically dumped to disk, in the `peers.dat` file. This allows the client to connect directly to those peers on subsequent starts without having to use DNS seeds. When node A initiates a connection with peer B, it is considered an *outbound* connection for A and an *inbound* for B. The default Bitcoin parameters dictate 8 outbound connections and up to 117 inbound.

Ethereum Overlay Network. Ethereum's network communication comprises three distinct protocols, described in Ethereum's official documentation [26]. Node discovery in Ethereum is based on the Kademlia routing algorithm, a distributed hash table (DHT) [44]. In Ethereum, each peer has a unique 512-bit node ID. A bitwise XOR is used to compute the distance between two Node IDs. Nodes maintain 256 buckets, each containing a number of entries. Each node assigns known peers to a bucket, according to the XOR distance from itself. To find peers, a new node first adds a hard-coded set of bootstrap node IDs to its routing table. Then sends to these bootstrapping nodes a `FIND_NODE` message that specifies a random target node ID. Each peer responds with a list of 16 nodes from its own routing table that are closest to the requested target. Subsequently, the node tries to establish a number of connections (typically between 25 and 50) with other peers in the network and performs the node discovery procedure continuously.

2.2   Related Work

Arguably, the aspects of the network layer of blockchain systems have received much less attention than security and consensus [31]. Dotan *et al.* [25] recognize that blockchain overlay networks have different requirements than traditional communication networks and observe that their fundamental design aspects are not well understood. Their work identifies differences and commonalities between blockchains and traditional networks and highlights open research challenges in network design for distributed decentralized systems.

Network measurements by Decker and Wattenhofer [18] have revealed that propagation delay is a critical parameter positively correlated with the appearance of blockchain forks. However, more recent studies indicate that Bitcoin's network infrastructure shows signs of improvement [27].

Gencer et al. where the first to point out that major cryptocurrencies face centralization issues [32]. A large fraction of reachable nodes are located in a handful of Autonomous Systems (AS). This opens the door for adversaries to launch network attacks at the Internet level by hijacking the BGP protocol [4]. Such attacks can isolate a large group of nodes from the rest of the network and introduce delays in message propagation. In fact, such attacks are becoming more sophisticated and are not easy to detect [55]. Additionally, less than five mining pools control the majority of hashing power. Furthermore, by combining knowledge of network topology and message distribution, researchers were able to identify highly influential nodes that have an advantage in block production and dissemination, strengthening centralization indications [7,24,28,33].

A large percentage of nodes that participate in the Bitcoin network are unreachable, making it difficult to accurately analyze their behavior and characteristics. However, previous research has shown that these unreachable nodes still play a significant role in the network. Wang and Pustogarov [58] found that a significant number of unreachable nodes propagate a large number of transactions and initiate a small number of connections to the reachable part of the network. The number of unreachable nodes is estimated to be between 10 and 100 times the number of reachable nodes [34]. These nodes have been found to have less secure wallets and initiate fewer connections to the reachable part of the network than the default bitcoin client. In general, understanding the behavior and characteristics of unreachable nodes in the Bitcoin network is important to improve our understanding of the network as a whole.

Numerous attack vectors, or methods that can compromise blockchain systems, have been proposed and analyzed in the literature [4,37,43,54,55,60]. Review articles have analyzed these attack vectors, highlighting how network attacks can be related to other types of attack and how the state of the network can facilitate the success of an attack. Such reviews [31] provide important information on the various ways networks can be targeted and the factors that can increase the probability of a successful attack. Understanding these attack vectors and their relationships to network conditions is crucial for developing effective defenses and countermeasures.

Accurate inference of the topology, or the arrangement and interconnection of nodes, in peer-to-peer (P2P) network overlays is a challenging problem that has yet to be fully solved. Although some research has successfully developed methodologies to accurately uncover the topology of Bitcoin and Ethereum networks [19,35,41,45,48], these approaches are often no longer applicable due to changes in the protocol or the official Bitcoin client [20,50,59]. Additionally, some of these methods [19,41] have an prohibitive cost to execute due to transaction fees imposed by the network. Furthermore, very few of these works present network metrics, which could provide insights into the characteristics and properties of the network. Recently, the study by Paphitis *et al.* [52] has shed more light on the structural properties of blockchain overlay networks. Their findings suggest that major blockchains exhibit dissimilar structural characteristics and show signs of vulnerability to malicious attacks due to the presence of highly central nodes. In this work, we are specifically investigating the topological robustness of such networks and their tolerance against partitioning due to random failures and targeted attacks. Moreover, we investigate whether their spatial centralization in various Autonomous Systems, and their hidden interdependencies, could further facilitate such attacks.

3   Methodology

In order to study the resilience of blockchain P2P overlays, information on the structure of the networks is needed. This section explains our main idea, which bypasses the need for an accurate topology mapping of the network. We prove that this idea is well founded and we proceed to describe the methods we used to collect and validate data.

Topology inference in blockchain overlays is a challenging problem that has not yet been solved. Our approach is to solve a simpler problem while still being able to measure the structural robustness of these networks. Instead of trying to accurately capture existing connections between online nodes, which is almost impossible due to the design of blockchain networks, we focus on collecting all *possible* connections that may exist over a period of time. A connection between two nodes is considered possible if one node includes the other in its list of known addresses. Using this strategy, we trade accuracy for completeness and are able to synthesize connectivity graphs that include the vast majority of potential links between nodes. This method also captures actual connections, that is, all active links between nodes. Our main aim is to identify structural deficiencies in the overlays, and we believe that if the synthesized graph of all possible connections can be partitioned, then the actual realized topology of the overlay is likely to be partitionable as well. In our data collection, we do not differentiate between mining nodes or full nodes. We view all nodes as important contributors to the health of the system and as vital in the dissemination of transactions and blocks. If most of these nodes were partitioned, the blocks would not propagate in the P2P network, thus preventing network synchronization.

The goal of our data collection process is to capture the contents of peer.dat of every reachable peer in the network. This consists of the peer's *view of the network*, which contains all available peers to which it can connect. This is easily achieved by repeatedly asking peers for addresses they know of. To discover the nodes (peers) of the overlay networks, we modified the crawler maintained by the popular site *bitnodes.io* to meet our needs [9,61]. We added features that enable: a) crawling multiple chains using distinct processes; b) storing the mapping of each node to its known-peers; c) and synchronizing the processes to dump the collected data for each blockchain at the same timestamp. Implementing an Ethereum crawler is substantially different since it uses a different protocol. The Ethereum crawler was built on the open source Trinity client [56] and all blockchain-related processing was disabled. We only implemented those parts of the protocols necessary to instantiate connections to Ethereum peers and participate in the discovery process.

3.1 Validation

A simple proof that the actual connection graph is not likely to be resilient when the synthesized one already is not, is provided here to further support our argument. As already described in the previous paragraphs, a synthesized graph G consists of all possible connections that could exist in the network. In this case, the actual graph R, which contains only the real links (active links between nodes), would be a spanning subgraph of G. A spanning subgraph is a subgraph that contains all the vertices (nodes) of the original graph but not all the edges (links). Our proposition is trivially proved considering Lemma 1 by Harary [36] which states the following: if R is a spanning subgraph of G, then the connectivity of R cannot be greater than the connectivity of G: $k(R) \leq k(G)$. That is, if G is disconnected i.e., $k(G) = 0$, then R is also disconnected. Thus, if the measured graph of possible connections can be partitioned by removing some nodes, then the actual graph will be partitioned as well.

Validation Against Controlled Monitor. To assess the viability of our goal, we set up an unmodified Bitcoin monitoring node using the official implementation [16]. We allowed the monitoring node to perform its initial bootstrap of the blockchain for one week. Subsequently, every ten minutes we retrieve the following information from the monitor: a) all inbound and outbound connections, b) a snapshot of the `peers.dat` file, and c) the `addr` reply to a `getaddr` probing message. We observe that by issuing enough `getaddr` messages, we are able to reconstruct the `peers.dat` file almost to its entirety.

During our validation period, the monitoring node created a total of 12,241 connections with other peers, 466 were outbound and 11,775 inbound. We observed 994 unique IP addresses, 368 corresponding to outbound connections, and 634 to inbound connections. Four of these addresses were in both sets. The crawler did not capture 444 of the 944 connected IP addresses. Looking at this weakness, we found that the missing IP addresses were not included in the `peers.dat` file. As expected, these were inbound connections from unreachable peers on the network. Further inspection revealed that most of these peers created short-lived connections that were dropped after the initial handshake. Only 30 of these peers (6% of inbound) created long-lasting connections of more than 40 min (a similar duration was used in [19]). Interestingly, the client version strings of these 30 nodes indicate that they were either network monitoring nodes (like `bitnodes.io`), experimental wallets, or client applications under development. We also observed a few client strings that have appeared in the past and were identified as non-contributing nodes [30] by the community. If we exclude these non-contributing peers, the total number of unique IP addresses that the monitoring node connected to is 570 and our crawler missed 10 of them. The ten missing nodes correspond to a percentage of 1.75%. Furthermore, we analyzed the messages sent from these missing nodes to the monitoring node and noticed that all these nodes were far behind on their blockchain. Their most recent block was several days behind the latest block observed by the monitor.

Validation Against External Data Sources. To further validate the coverage of our crawler against external data sources, we compared our results with the *DSN Bitcoin Monitoring* infrastructure in https://www.dsn.kastel.kit.edu/bitcoin, originally presented in [48]. Since the IP addresses of [48] are anonymized, we compare the number of reachable nodes we capture with the number of nodes scanned by the DSN Monitor. Counting only the reachable peers, we found that our crawler was able to retrieve a few hundred more nodes on a daily basis. Similarly, we compare the node counts with the historical data collected by a Bitcoin core developer [38] and the `bitnodes.io` crawler with similar results. We also note that although our data set is not very recent, comparing the number of peers collected to recent captures of the DSN Bitcoin Monitoring, we see that the size of the network has not changed significantly.

The previous paragraphs indicate that our method is adequate to create a network snapshot, capable of capturing all active connections that exist in the network, along with any potential connections that could be realized among the participating peers.

3.2 Datasets and Experiments

Using the methodology mentioned above, we crawled the selected BC networks from the datacenter of a European University. The monitoring server has an 8-core/3.2 GHz CPU, 64 GB RAM, and 2.1 TB of HDD storage. The crawling operations were carried out for a period of about one month (26/06-22/07/2020). Previous work [17,18,40,45] used a similar duration for their analyzes. At the end of the crawling period, we had collected 335 network snapshots for each BC network; 2345 graphs in total. The collected data set is available for review or reuse at [51]. Our ethical considerations are outlined in Appendix A.

We denote by C the set of the 7 BC networks crawled. At the end of every two hours period, we have seven different `edge` sets, one per BC $c \in C$. At the end of each day, all edge sets belonging to the same network are merged into a 24-h set. All sets are annotated with the date t of their crawl. Each set of edges corresponds to a graph, denoted S_c^t, representing a snapshot of the blockchain network c, on date t.

The following analysis uses the established procedure for the exploration of the resilience of a network [1,39]. The procedure starts by ranking the nodes by a network metric and subsequently removing the element in the network with the highest ranking. At each removal, the network is analyzed to calculate its remaining size and the number of connected components. The most common node-level network metrics used are node degree and betweenness centrality [2, 42].

4 Results

This section presents and discusses the results of the analysis performed on the synthesized graphs that were collected, focusing on several key aspects of BC overlays. The first aspect is the structural robustness of BC overlays to random failures and targeted attacks. The study examines the impact of these types of disruptions on the stability and reliability of the network. The next aspect is the issue of spatial centralization in Autonomous Systems and how it affects the network's resilience. This exploration includes an examination of the concentration of nodes within the same AS and how it impacts the network's stability. The study also investigates the interdependencies between BC networks, analyzing how these networks connected to other networks through peers and links.

4.1 Network Resilience to Attacks

This section answers the following question: To what extent are blockchain overlays prone to random failures and targeted attacks? We start this investigation by first describing the attack model. Then, we define three strategies that an attacker could employ to partition a BC network and evaluate the efficacy of each strategy. The practicality of the attack is beyond the scope of this work.

Attack Model. An adversary may have various incentives to attack a blockchain system. In this work, we specifically study attacks on the underlying topology of BC networks with the goal of impairing the main functions of the network. Specifically, we define the following two goals of an attacker:

1. Network partitioning: to force the overlay into two or more network partitions. A network partition is the decomposition of a network into independent subnets, so that no information flow between the partitions is possible due to the absence of links between nodes.
2. Disturb the information propagation mechanisms by introducing intolerable delays. Such delays can typically increase the time to reach consensus among all participants and create a split in the application layer of a BC system. In fact, propagation delays are known to be a key contributor to BC forks [18].

Such attacks would impair the main functions of a BC network, potentially causing a decrease in users' trust in the system. Attackers with external incentives would be highly motivated to carry out such attacks. To measure the effectiveness of each goal, we use the following three metrics: a) the size of the largest weakly connected component, b) the number of connected components, and c) the network diameter. To this end, we consider the following attack strategies:

1. Targeted attacks on unique nodes, based on a selected network metric. We test out-degree, betweenness centrality, and page-rank.
2. Random attacks using random node removal emulate failures that can occur in the network in a random fashion and are used as a baseline.
3. Attack minimum-cut edges, in order to partition the network by removing edges that are positioned in key places in the graph.

Targeted Node Attacks. The removal of a node simultaneously cuts all its adjacent links, therefore, it is more efficient for an attacker compared to the removal of targeted links. We focus on how to remove nodes in the most efficient way to minimize the number of node removals necessary to cause a disruption. A node can be removed from the network by various means, including DoS attacks. We follow a static procedure in the sense that each node is given a static priority of removal, based on a chosen metric. For example, when using the out-degree metric, the higher the degree, the greater the importance of the node to be attacked. After removing a node, the priorities are not recalculated. We remove only **reachable** nodes from the network one by one, following the given priority. After each removal, we calculate the size of the largest connected component and the approximate diameter of the resulting graph. We report the effectiveness of the three node ranking metrics (betweenness centrality, out-degree, and page-rank), and compare with the baseline random removal strategy. We performed the procedure described on all 24-h snapshots per BC. Due to the high number of graphs collected, we stopped execution after removing 12% of nodes per snapshot.

As can be seen in Fig. 1, in Bitcoin and Bitcoin Cash, the betweenness and out-degree strategies have roughly the same shape. The size of the largest connected component decreases significantly after the removal of only a few nodes. Further removal of nodes gradually shrinks the size to a threshold where the connected component abruptly falls to 1% of its initial size. This occurs after the removal of 6% and 4% of the nodes, respectively. Similar behavior has also been found on the Internet [42]. This finding may not seem very worrisome, since the reported percentages correspond to a few thousand nodes. However, closer inspection (shown in Fig. 3) of these two networks indicates that removal of the first five nodes reduces the size of the largest connected component by 60%, which is rather alarming. Unlike the size of the largest component, the diameter of the network starts to increase earlier in this process. This is more pronounced in Bitcoin Cash.

In Ethereum, the out-degree strategy is more potent. Unlike Bitcoin and Bitcoin Cash, the size of the largest component does not drop initially. After removing 2% of the nodes, the size gradually drops to a threshold, close to 5%, where its size abruptly drops to 1%. The diameter of the network starts to increase early, but not as quickly as in Bitcoin Cash.

When targeting high-betweenness nodes in Zcash, the largest component initially falls abruptly. Similarly to Bitcoin, the first removal of nodes reduces the largest component by 40%. When 4% of the nodes are removed, the largest

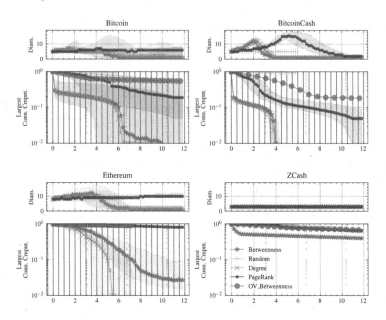

Fig. 1. Evolution of the approximate diameter (upper part) and size of largest weakly connected component (lower part) when the network in under targeted attack. The X-axis reports percentage of nodes removed. The lines correspond to the median value across all snapshots. The shaded area indicates values between 1st-3rd quartile. Orange x: Out-degree of unique nodes; Beige +: Random unique nodes; Green *: Betweenness of unique nodes; Red o: Betweenness of overlapping nodes; (Color figure online)

component drops to 50% of its initial size and then shrinks almost linearly. Targeting high out-degree nodes is less damaging in Zcash. More than 5% of the nodes must be removed to observe a 20% reduction in the largest component.

The number of connected components for Bitcoin, BitcoinCash, and Ethereum during the same experiment is plotted in Fig. 2. We cannot observe a notable rise in the number of components until the networks are significantly diminished.

Dash, Dogecoin, and Litecoin seem equally resilient to random and targeted attacks (plots omitted due to space limitations). The size of their largest component decreases linearly with the number of nodes removed, and their diameter is not significantly affected (Table 1).

4.2   Attack Minimum-Cut Edges

Targeting minimum cut edges does not have a significant effect in the networks' state and requires the removal (or disruption) of a considerable number of network links. To compute the minimum edge cuts, we used the algebraic connectivity of the derived graphs. The algebraic connectivity of a graph is defined as the second smallest eigenvalue of its Laplacian matrix L, $\lambda_2(L)$, and is a lower

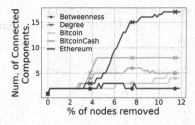

Fig. 2. Evolution of number of connected components during the same experiment as with Fig. 1

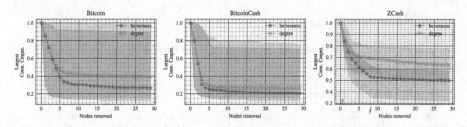

Fig. 3. Evolution of the largest weakly connected component when the network is under targeted attack. The difference with Fig. 1 is that this plot X-axis reports number of nodes removed. Orange x: Out-degree of unique nodes; Green *: Betweenness of unique nodes; (Color figure online)

bound on node/edge connectivity [29]. Since calculating the algebraic connectivity of a graph is computationally very expensive (i.e., more than 3 compute hours per snapshot), we analyzed one snapshot per network. Using the computed eigenvector, we count how many edges are required to be removed to split the network in two parts, and compute their sizes and ratio of the two subnets (cut-ratio, computed as largest subnet over the total). The results are presented in Table 2. Most cuts are highly unbalanced. Bitcoin Cash has an almost perfect cut, although a large fraction of edges have to be removed (6.5% of edges or 10k edges). Bitcoin and Zcash are somewhat affected, by removing less than 0.5% of their network edges. Overall, targeting minimum cut edges does not have a significant effect on the networks' state and would require the removal (or disruption) of a considerable number of edges connecting nodes.

4.3 Spatial Centralization of Blockchain Nodes

As already pointed out by previous works [4,54], BGP routing attacks can be mounted against Bitcoin by taking advantage of the fact that a high percentage of Bitcoin nodes reside in only a small number of Autonomous Systems (AS). We also verify this node centralization by mapping the collected IP address to ASes using the https://ip-api.com API. Furthermore, we were able to identify a single AS that hosts 20% of highly connected Bitcoin nodes in all timestamps, making it a strong candidate for such attacks. In more detail, we identify the

Table 1. Resilience of graphs to targeted node attacks. We report the number and percentage of nodes that, when removed, reduce the largest component to 0.5 and 0.01 of its initial size, respectively.

Network	Bitcoin	Bitcoin Cash	Dash	Dogecoin	Ethereum	Litecoin	Zcash
# of Nodes (50% reduction)	10	10	-	-	300	-	6
% of Nodes (99% reduction)	6.5%	4%	>12%	>12%	5.5%	>12%	>12%

Table 2. Resilience of synthesized graphs in edge and node removal when attacking minimum-cut edges.

	Bitcoin	Bitcoin Cash	Dash	Dogecoin	Ethereum	Litecoin	Zcash
Edges Removed	5545 (0.1%)	10603 (6.5%)	1451 (0.02%)	581 (0.44%)	2220 (2.71%)	544 (0.08%)	363 (0.33%)
Network Split	9964/ 43949	11367/ 11895	46/ 8556	11/ 1069	436/ 15345	37/ 6576	258/ 1231
Cut Ratio	0.815	0.511	0.995	0.990	0.972	0.994	0.827

100 highest connected nodes in each snapshot. We then look at the distribution of these nodes in ASes. Our results are summarized below.

1. 20% of the top Bitcoin nodes are located in a single AS.
2. A single AS hosts a significant number of highly connected nodes in all BCs (see Sect. 4.4).
3. Ethereum's top clients are spread over more than 550 ASes and have the most wide distribution. Bitcoin nodes are spread in 200 ASes, BitcoinCash, Dash, Dogecoin in 160 and Zcash and Litecoin in 65.

To measure the effect of targeted attacks against Autonomous Systems, we performed the following test. For each snapshot, we identified the top 10 ASes with the highest geometric mean of out-degree. Then we simulated the effect of an attack against these ASes by removing all collocated nodes. The results are plotted in Fig. 4. The blue dots correspond to the relative size of the largest connected component, on the left y-axis (median values across snapshots). The shaded area indicates values between the 1st and 3rd quartile. The yellow bars indicate the percentage of nodes removed (averaged) and correspond to the scale on the right y-axis.

Notably, these plots reveal the high centralization of BC nodes in the same Autonomous Systems, an observation made by previous works as well. Interest-

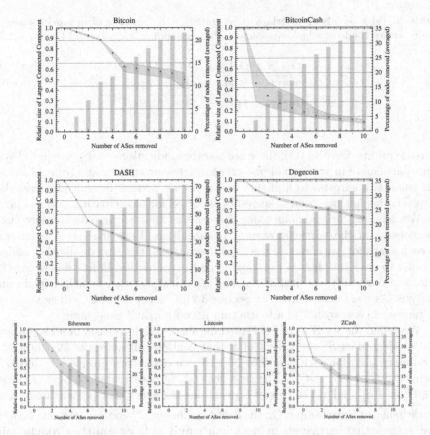

Fig. 4. Targeting selected ASed. X-axis reports number of ASes removed. The Y-axis on the left reports the size of the Largest Connected Component (blue dots). Right Y-axis reports the (average) percentage of nodes removed (yellow bars). (Color figure online)

ingly, all networks are sensitive to such attacks, mainly due to the centralization of nodes. This is true for DASH, Dogecoin, and Litecoin, where a single AS hosts 20% of each network's nodes. On the contrary, Bitcoin is less affected by this strategy (compared to attacking individual nodes), indicating that high-degree nodes are scattered in different ASes. Note that results may differ using a different selection strategy.

4.4   Dependency in Blockchain Overlays

In this section, we address the following questions: Are there network entities (peers, links) that participate in more than one BC network, concurrently? How do these common entities affect the resilience of overlay networks?

Chatzigiannis *et al.* [11] showed that miners can distribute their computational power over multiple pools and PoW cryptocurrencies to reduce risk and

Table 3. Edge and Node overlaps (aggregated). ON: number of networks where a\ unique entity (node or edge) was found to be overlapping, regardless of time

	$ON = 2$	$ON = 3$	$ON = 4$	$ON >= 5$
Nodes	34814	3909	1489	779
Edges	143577	11034	1958	222

increase profits. Despite [11], there are no other indications that peers in BC systems participate in more than one cryptocurrencies at the same time. It would not come as a surprise to find that end users are present in multiple networks, however, this has not been observed or reported for participating peers so far.

We define as *overlapping nodes* those nodes that participate in more than one network at the same timestamp. The intuition of our analysis is as follows. In each snapshot, we compare the set of *overlapping* nodes with all other nodes, in order to draw insights on *overlapping* nodes' properties. Before describing the details of our study, we outline our mathematical notation to help explain our analysis. As mentioned above (cf. Section 3.2), C is the set of BCs. The notation S_c^t represents a snapshot of a blockchain network c, at t timestamp.

We define the set $\mathbf{S}$ as our collected data set, which consists of all snapshots S_c^t. We denote as S^t the subset of $\mathbf{S}$ that contains all networks at timestamp t. Subsequently, for each snapshot $S_c^t \in S^t$ we define two groups, G_c^t and $G_c'^t$, such that $G_c^t = S_c^t - G_c'^t$. The first set, G_c^t, is constructed so that $\forall$ nodes $n \in G_c^t, n \notin S_{C\backslash c}^t$. That is, the set G_c^t contains the nodes that participate only in blockchain c at timestamp t. On the contrary, the set $G_c'^t$ contains the *overlapping nodes*; those that participate in blockchain c **and at least another blockchain** $c' \in C\backslash c$, at the same timestamp t.

A first approach to finding network overlaps is to look at our aggregated data set, $\mathbf{S}$, and count how many nodes and edges (i.e., pairs of endpoints), appear in more than one network, regardless of time. Table 3 shows the summary of these results. Evidently, there exists a significant number of network entities (both nodes and edges) that reside in more than one BC network.

A second step is to investigate whether overlapping entities occur frequently or sporadically over time. For this, we count all overlapping peers in each S_c^t. In Fig. 5 (left), for each BC network c, we plot the ratio of $|G_c'^t|$ over $|S_c^t|$, i.e., the number of overlapping peers in snapshot c over the total number of nodes in the snapshot. Our observations show that in all networks, there is a consistently high percentage of nodes that overlap and belong to more than one BC network. Based on this and previous results, we can conclude that there is significant overlap between BC overlays and that this overlap occurs consistently over time.

Attacking Overlapping Network Entities. To examine how overlapping nodes could impact the resilience of blockchain overlays to targeted attacks, we repeat the test of the previous Section (4.1) with a small variation. From each set $S_{c\in C}^t$, we remove all G_c^t sets. This new set, $S_{c\in C}'^t$, contains all nodes that participate in more than one network at the same timestamp. We then sort the unique elements of $S'^{t}_{c \in C}$ in descending order based on their maximum normalized betweenness centrality. Since a node can participate in more than one network, we sort the nodes based on the highest value they have across all networks at time t. We use the Min-Max method to normalize the betweenness centrality values for each snapshot. After sorting the nodes, we proceed to remove them from each snapshot S^{t}_{c} at the same time. The nodes are removed in the same order from all snapshots.

The results of targeting overlapping nodes first are plotted in Fig. 1 with red circles. The plot reports the average change in the largest connected component over all snapshots S^{t}_{c}. Clearly, this strategy is less effective compared to the strategies used earlier, which target the top central nodes within a specific network. However, it provides the benefit of attacking multiple networks simultaneously. An interesting finding is that Litecoin is more susceptible to this kind of attack compared to attacks focused on single BC node metrics (not shown in figure). This is partly explained by the fact that Litecoin has one of the highest percentages of overlapping nodes (see Fig. 5).

Closer inspection of the data at hand shows that an attacker is able to shrink the largest connected component of Bitcoin Cash, Bitcoin, Zcash, and Litecoin networks by 70%, 40%, 25% and 20% respectively. This demonstrates that by targeting overlapping nodes, a powerful adversary can still mount a successful partitioning attack in *4 different networks at the same time.*

Another effect of overlapping nodes is shown in the strategy described next. Similarly to the selection performed in Sect. 4.3, we calculated the geometric mean of the out-degree of all networks, for each AS, across all timestamps. That is, for each Autonomous System we took into consideration all nodes from all chains and calculated the geometric mean of their out-degree. We then remove each AS, simulating an attack against the AS, and calculate the effect on each network. Removal of an AS simultaneously removes all nodes (from all networks) that reside on that particular AS. The results of this selection strategy are plotted in Fig. 5. The significance of overlapping nodes is profound. A disruption in just 6 ASes could have considerable effects in five networks at the same time. In fact, ASes do not need to be broken down; as demonstrated by Apostolaki*et al.* [4] they could be manipulated by false BGP routing advertisements (BGP hijacks). Notably, a different selection strategy would produce different results.

5   Discussion

Our results suggest that BC overlay networks are robust against random failures but weak against targeted attacks, a known characteristic of scale-free networks [2]. This further suggests that BC overlay networks are not random, contrary to their intended design [18]. These results are in line with those obtained by Miller *et al.* [45] and Delgado *et al.* [19]. Our analysis supports the findings of Paphitis *et al.* [52], which suggest that larger BC networks are more susceptible to targeted attacks as a result of the presence of highly connected and centrally positioned peers.

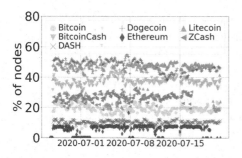
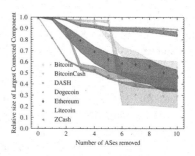

Fig. 5. *Left*: Percentage of nodes that were found in more than one BC network at the same timestamp. X-axis indicates the timestamp. *Right*: Size of the largest connected component of all networks when selected ASes are attacked.

Implications of Partitioning the Connectivity Graph. Peer-to-peer networks are known for their dynamic nature, allowing them to adapt to changing conditions. However, our research reveals that even this inherent dynamicity is insufficient in countering targeted attacks. The connectivity graphs we construct serve as representations of all potential connections that could exist in the actual network. Each edge in the connectivity graph signifies that two nodes are aware of each other's presence and have the ability to establish a connection.

Conversely, the absence of an edge in the connectivity graph indicates that two nodes are unaware of each other's existence and are highly unlikely to establish a connection. Partitioning of the connectivity graph has significant implications. Nodes within a specific partition not only become disconnected from other network partitions but also lack the knowledge required to establish links with nodes in different partitions. In essence, the nodes are confined to their own partition and remain unaware that a portion of the network has become disconnected.

Limitations. Measurement errors in network analysis are not infrequent [49] and our approach is not an exception. In fact, the proposed method introduces a number of false edges in the graph. Second, it is possible, albeit rare, that certain edges may be overlooked (see Sect. 3.1). To understand how much the calculated network properties are affected by these errors, we looked into related studies that investigate the effect of measurement errors in network data. In [52], we provide an in-depth analysis of these limitations and examine the impact of false-positive edges. Our findings suggest that the observed connectivity graphs demonstrate greater resilience compared to the actual connections in the real network.

Wang *et al.* [57] studied the effect of measurement errors on node-level network measures and found that networks are relatively robust to false positive edges. Booker [10] measures the effects of measurement errors on the attack vulnerability of networks. Similarly to [57], Booker also finds that false positive edges have the least impact on the effectiveness of random and targeted attacks.

From the same work, it is also evident that an error rate of 5% in missing links is acceptable, when analyzing the impact of different targeting strategies on the network structure. We believe that the error rate observed in our study is small enough to allow us to draw meaningful conclusions.

We readily admit that it is possible to miss connections from unreachable peers towards reachable peers. This resilience assessment relies on the assumption that these links constitute a small minority of all possible links. Our validation results in Sect. 3.1 support this assumption. This assumption is also supported by [34], which estimates an average degree of 9.8 for unreachable peers on the Bitcoin network. Our measurements estimate an average degree of 37 for unreachable peers. Furthermore, in [58] Wang and Pustogarov estimate that unreachable peers establish only 3.5 connections to the network, on average. Interestingly, they also find that such unreachable peers are not merely disposable nodes of the network. Instead, they are involved in the propagation of 43% of Bitcoin transactions. Our resilience study demonstrates that attacking a handful of key peers can disconnect a large number of unreachable peers and thus can severely affect message propagation in the network.

Moreover, transient disruptions of the network would increase the likelihood of forks and could facilitate attacks against consensus. DDoS attacks or BGP hijacks against a carefully selected AS could partition 10% to 50% nodes from a network, while a disruption in a handful of ASes has the potential to remove almost half of all BC nodes in most systems simultaneously.

6 Summary

Our results raise alarm about the resilience of the studied blockchains against partitioning and message propagation delay attacks. We demonstrate that by using our methodology, a deliberate and methodical attacker can uncover a small set of entities central to the topology and target them to substantially suppress message propagation in more than one BC network simultaneously. Importantly, all networks seem vulnerable to at least one type of attack strategy. This highlights the need to employ measures to enhance network robustness or employ open topology protocols, rather than relying on topology hiding techniques to secure the overlay network.

Acknowledgements. This project has received funding from the European Union's Horizon 2020 Research and Innovation program under the Marie Skłodowska-Curie INCOGNITO project (Grant Agreement No. 824015), CONCORDIA project (Grant Agreement No. 830927), SPATIAL project (Grant Agreement No. 101021808) and the Cyprus's Research and Innovation Foundation (Grant Agreement: COMPLEMENTARY/0916/0031). The authors bear the sole responsibility for the content presented in this paper, and any interpretations or conclusions drawn from it do not reflect the official position of the European Union nor the Research Innovation Foundation.

A   Ethics

In this work we followed standard ethical guidelines [3,23,53] for the collection and sharing of measurement data. We only collect and process publicly available data, make no attempt to deanonymize users or link people and/or organizations to their IP address. No personally identifiable information was collected.

While crawling the networks we only take part in the peer discovery mechanism of each network and gather IP addresses known to each node. Those addresses were only used to synthesize connectivity graphs on which our research was based. We did not try to identify any user by her IP address and no information was redistributed. In fact, our crawler created short lived connections to any discovered peer in the network and did not respond to any other requests except the expected initial handshake. We do not respond to any other messages or requests. In addition, we employed low bandwidth utilization to avoid resource exhaustion. Our measurements did not cause any disruption or exposure of the BC networks under study.

Our results unveil particular nodes whose targeting has the potential to disrupt the overlay's operation. To prevent misuse of this portion of the results, we do not publish the IP address of any node in our dataset. We instead replace the IP address with a persistent random identifier and we privately maintain a private map of IPs to random identifiers for verification and reproducibility purposes.

References

1. Albert, R., Barabási, A.L.: Statistical mechanics of complex networks. Rev. Mod. Phys. **74**, 47–97 (2002). https://doi.org/10.1103/RevModPhys.74.47, https://link.aps.org/doi/10.1103/RevModPhys.74.47
2. Albert, R., Jeong, H., Barabási, A.: Error and attack tolerance of complex networks. Nature **406**(6794), 378–382 (2000). https://doi.org/10.1038/35019019
3. Allman, M., Paxson, V.: Issues and etiquette concerning use of shared measurement data. In: IMC. ACM (2007)
4. Apostolaki, M., Zohar, A., Vanbever, L.: Hijacking bitcoin: routing attacks on cryptocurrencies. In: 2017 IEEE Symposium on Security and Privacy, S&P 2017. IEEE Computer Society (2017). https://doi.org/10.1109/SP.2017.29
5. Azaria, A., Ekblaw, A., Vieira, T., Lippman, A.: MedRec: using blockchain for medical data access and permission management. In: 2016 2nd International Conference on Open and Big Data (OBD) (2016). https://doi.org/10.1109/OBD.2016.11
6. Baumann, A., Fabian, B.: How robust is the internet? – insights from graph analysis. In: Lopez, J., Ray, I., Crispo, B. (eds.) CRiSIS 2014. LNCS, vol. 8924, pp. 247–254. Springer, Cham (2015). https://doi.org/10.1007/978-3-319-17127-2_18
7. Ben Mariem, S., Casas, P., Donnet, B.: Vivisecting blockchain p2p networks: unveiling the bitcoin IP network. In: ACM CoNEXT Student Workshop (2018)
8. Biryukov, A., Tikhomirov, S.: Deanonymization and linkability of cryptocurrency transactions based on network analysis. In: IEEE European Symposium on Security and Privacy (EuroS&P) (2019). https://doi.org/10.1109/EuroSP.2019.00022

9. bitnodes.io: Global bitcoin nodes distribution (2020). https://bitnodes.io
10. Booker, L.B.: The effects of observation errors on the attack vulnerability of complex networks: Technical report, Defense Technical Information Center, Fort Belvoir, VA (2012). https://doi.org/10.21236/ADA576235, http://www.dtic.mil/docs/citations/ADA576235
11. Chatzigiannis, P., Baldimtsi, F., Griva, I., Li, J.: Diversification across mining pools: optimal mining strategies under pow. J. Cybersecur. **8**(1), tyab027 (2022)
12. Chen, W., Xu, Z., Shi, S., Zhao, Y., Zhao, J.: A survey of blockchain applications in different domains. In: ICBTA, pp. 17–21. ACM (2018)
13. Chen, W., Xu, Z., Shi, S., Zhao, Y., Zhao, J.: A survey of blockchain applications in different domains. In: Proceedings of the 2018 International Conference on Blockchain Technology and Application. ICBTA 2018, Association for Computing Machinery, New York, NY, USA (2018). https://doi.org/10.1145/3301403.3301407
14. Christidis, K., Devetsikiotis, M.: Blockchains and smart contracts for the internet of things. IEEE Access **4**, 2292–2303 (2016). https://doi.org/10.1109/ACCESS.2016.2566339
15. CoinMarketCap: Coinmarketcap (2021). https://coinmarketcap.com
16. Core, B.: 0.20.1 release notes (2021)
17. Daniel, E., Rohrer, E., Tschorsch, F.: Map-z: exposing the Zcash network in times of transition. In: LCN. IEEE (2019)
18. Decker, C., Wattenhofer, R.: Information propagation in the bitcoin network. In: 13th IEEE International Conference on Peer-to-Peer Computing, IEEE P2P 2013. IEEE (2013). https://doi.org/10.1109/P2P.2013.6688704
19. Delgado-Segura, S., et al.: TxProbe: discovering bitcoin's network topology using orphan transactions. In: Goldberg, I., Moore, T. (eds.) FC 2019. LNCS, vol. 11598, pp. 550–566. Springer, Cham (2019). https://doi.org/10.1007/978-3-030-32101-7_32
20. Developers, B.C.: Bitcoin core 0.10.1 release notes (2015). https://github.com/bitcoin/bitcoin/blob/v0.10.1/doc/release-notes.md
21. Developers, B.C.: Bitcoin core integration/staging tree (2021). https://github.com/bitcoin/bitcoin
22. Developers, B.C.: Bitcoin p2p network (2021). https://developer.bitcoin.org/devguide/p2p_network.html
23. Dittrich, D., Kenneally, E., et al.: The menlo report: Ethical principles guiding information and communication technology research. Technical report US Department of Homeland Security (2012)
24. Donet Donet, J.A., Pérez-Solà, C., Herrera-Joancomartí, J.: The bitcoin P2P network. In: Böhme, R., Brenner, M., Moore, T., Smith, M. (eds.) FC 2014. LNCS, vol. 8438, pp. 87–102. Springer, Heidelberg (2014). https://doi.org/10.1007/978-3-662-44774-1_7
25. Dotan, M., Pignolet, Y.A., Schmid, S., Tochner, S., Zohar, A.: SOK: cryptocurrency networking context, state-of-the-art, challenges. In: Proceedings of the 15th International Conference on Availability, Reliability and Security. ARES 2020, ACM (2020). https://doi.org/10.1145/3407023.3407043
26. Ethereum: Ethereum peer-to-peer networking specifications (2014). https://github.com/ethereum/devp2p
27. Fechner, J., Chandrasekaran, B., Makkes, M.X.: Calibrating the performance and security of blockchains via information propagation delays: revisiting an old approach with a new perspective. Proceedings of the 37th ACM/SIGAPP Symposium on Applied Computing (2022)   ·

28. Feld, S., Schönfeld, M., Werner, M.: Analyzing the deployment of bitcoin's p2p network under an as-level perspective. Procedia Comput. Sci. **32**, 1121–1126 (2014). https://doi.org/10.1016/j.procs.2014.05.542, https://www.sciencedirect. com/science/article/pii/S187705091400742X, the 5th International Conference on Ambient Systems, Networks and Technologies (ANT-2014), the 4th International Conference on Sustainable Energy Information Technology (SEIT-2014)
29. Fiedler, M.: Algebraic connectivity of graphs. Czechoslovak Math. J. **23**(2), 298–305 (1973)
30. Forum, B.: UASF nodes wrongly reporting IP (2017). https://bitcointalk.org/index.php?topic=1954151.0
31. Franzoni, F., Daza, V.: SOK: network-level attacks on the bitcoin p2p network. IEEE Access **10**, 94924–94962 (2022). https://doi.org/10.1109/ACCESS.2022.3204387
32. Gencer, A.E., Basu, S., Eyal, I., van Renesse, R., Sirer, E.G.: Decentralization in bitcoin and ethereum networks. In: Meiklejohn, S., Sako, K. (eds.) FC 2018. LNCS, vol. 10957, pp. 439–457. Springer, Heidelberg (2018). https://doi.org/10.1007/978-3-662-58387-6_24
33. Gochhayat, S.P., Shetty, S.S., Mukkamala, R., Foytik, P.B., Kamhoua, G.A., Njilla, L.L.: Measuring decentrality in blockchain based systems. IEEE Access **8**, 178372–178390 (2020)
34. Grundmann, M., Amberg, H., Baumstark, M., Hartenstein, H.: Short paper: what peer announcements tell us about the size of the bitcoin P2P network. In: Eyal, I., Garay, J. (eds.) FC 2022. LNCS, vol. 13411, pp. 694–704. Springer, Cham (2022). https://doi.org/10.1007/978-3-031-18283-9_35
35. Grundmann, M., Neudecker, T., Hartenstein, H.: Exploiting transaction accumulation and double spends for topology inference in bitcoin. In: Zohar, A., et al. (eds.) FC 2018. LNCS, vol. 10958, pp. 113–126. Springer, Heidelberg (2019). https://doi.org/10.1007/978-3-662-58820-8_9
36. Harary, F.: The maximum connectivity of a graph. Proceedings Nat. Acad. Sci. U. S. Am. **48**(7), 1142–1146 (1962)
37. Heilman, E., Kendler, A., Zohar, A., Goldberg, S.: Eclipse attacks on bitcoin's peer-to-peer network. In: 24th USENIX Security Symposium (USENIX Security 15). USENIX Association (2015)
38. Jr, L.D.: Bitcoin historical node count (2022). https://luke.dashjr.org/programs/bitcoin/files/charts/historical.html
39. Kim, H., Anderson, R.J.: An experimental evaluation of robustness of networks. IEEE Syst. J. **7**, 179–188 (2013)
40. Kim, S.K., Ma, Z., Murali, S., Mason, J., Miller, A., Bailey, M.: Measuring ethereum network peers. In: IMC. ACM (2018)
41. Li, K., Tang, Y., Chen, J., Wang, Y., Liu, X.: Toposhot: uncovering Ethereum's network topology leveraging replacement transactions. In: Internet Measurement Conference, pp. 302–319. ACM (2021)
42. Magoni, D.: Tearing down the internet. IEEE J. Sel. Areas Commun. **21**(6), 949–960 (2003)
43. Marcus, Y., Heilman, E., Goldberg, S.: Low-resource eclipse attacks on ethereum's peer-to-peer network. IACR Cryptol. ePrint Arch. 2018 (2018). http://eprint.iacr.org/2018/236
44. Maymounkov, P., Mazières, D.: Kademlia: a peer-to-peer information system based on the XOR metric. In: Druschel, P., Kaashoek, F., Rowstron, A. (eds.) IPTPS 2002. LNCS, vol. 2429, pp. 53–65. Springer, Heidelberg (2002). https://doi.org/10.1007/3-540-45748-8_5

45. Miller, A., Litton, J., Pachulski, A., Gupta, N., Levin, D., Spring, N., Bhattachar-jee, B.: Discovering bitcoin's network topology and influential nodes. University of Maryland, Technical report (2015)
46. Muro, M.A.D., Valdez, L.D., Rêgo, H.H.A., Buldyrev, S.V., Stanley, H.E., Braun-stein, L.A.: Cascading failures in interdependent networks with multiple supply-demand links and functionality thresholds. Sci. Rep. **7**, 15059 (2017)
47. Neudecker, T.: Characterization of the bitcoin peer-to-peer network (2015–2018). Tech. Rep. 1, Karlsruher Institut für Technologie (KIT) (2019). https://doi.org/10.5445/IR/1000091933
48. Neudecker, T., Andelfinger, P., Hartenstein, H.: Timing analysis for inferring the topology of the bitcoin peer-to-peer network. In: UIC/ATC/ScalCom/CBDCom/IoP/SmartWorld. IEEE Computer Society (2016)
49. Newman, M.E.J.: Measurement errors in network data. ArXiv abs/1703.07376 (2017)
50. Nick, J.: Guessing bitcoin's p2p connections (2015). https://jonasnick.github.io/blog/2015/03/06/guessing-bitcoins-p2p-connections/
51. Paphitis, A., Kourtellis, N., Sirivianos, M.: Datasets for research on Resilience of Blockchain Overlay Networks. figshare. Dataset (2023). https://doi.org/10.6084/m9.figshare.23522919.v1
52. Paphitis, A., Kourtellis, N., Sirivianos, M.: Graph analysis of blockchain p2p over-lays and their security implications. In: Security and Privacy in Social Networks and Big Data. SocialSec 2023. LNCS, vol. 14097. Springer, Singapore (2023). https://doi.org/10.1007/978-981-99-5177-2_10
53. Rivers, C., Lewis, B.: Ethical research standards in a world of big data. F1000Research **3**, 38 (2014). https://doi.org/10.12688/f1000research.3-38.v2
54. Saad, M., Cook, V., Nguyen, L., Thai, M.T., Mohaisen, A.: Partitioning attacks on bitcoin: colliding space, time, and logic. In: 2019 IEEE 39th International Con-ference on Distributed Computing Systems (ICDCS) (2019). https://doi.org/10.1109/ICDCS.2019.00119
55. Tran, M., Choi, I., Moon, G.J., Vu, A.V., Kang, M.S.: A stealthier partitioning attack against bitcoin peer-to-peer network. In: 2020 IEEE Symposium on Security and Privacy (SP) (2020). https://doi.org/10.1109/SP40000.2020.00027
56. trinity.ethereum.org: The trinity Ethereum client (2021). https://trinity.ethereum.org
57. Wang, D.J., Shi, X., McFarland, D.A., Leskovec, J.: Measurement error in network data: a re-classification. Soc. Netw. **34**, 396–409 (2012)
58. Wang, L., Pustogarov, I.: Towards better understanding of bitcoin unreachable peers. CoRR abs/1709.06837 (2017)
59. Wuille, P.: Replace global trickle node with random delays (2022). https://github.com/bitcoin/bitcoin/pull/7125
60. Yang, J., Sun, G., Xiao, R., He, H.: Detectable, traceable, and manageable blockchain technologies BHE: an attack scheme against bitcoin p2p network. Wire-less Communications and Mobile Computing (2022)
61. Yeow, A.: Bitnodes network crawler (2021). https://github.com/ayeowch/bitnodes
62. Zyskind, G., Nathan, O., Pentland, A.S.: Decentralizing privacy: using blockchain to protect personal data. In: 2015 IEEE Security and Privacy Workshops (2015). https://doi.org/10.1109/SPW.2015.27

Provably Secure Blockchain Protocols from Distributed Proof-of-Deep-Learning

Xiangyu Su[1]($\boxtimes$)(iD), Mario Larangeira[1,2](iD), and Keisuke Tanaka[1](iD)

[1] Department of Mathematical and Computing Science, School of Computing,
Tokyo Institute of Technology, Tokyo-to Meguro-ku Oookayama 2-12-1 W8-55,
Tokyo, Japan
su.x.ab@m.titech.ac.jp, mario@c.titech.ac.jp, keisuke@is.titech.ac.jp
[2] Input Output Global, Singapore, Singapore
mario.larangeira@iohk.io

Abstract. Proof-of-useful-work (PoUW), an alternative to the widely used proof-of-work (PoW), aims to re-purpose the network's computing power. Namely, users evaluate meaningful computational problems, e.g., solving optimization problems, instead of computing numerous hash function values as in PoW. A recent approach utilizes the training process of deep learning as "useful work". However, these works lack security analysis when deploying them with blockchain-based protocols, let alone the informal and over-complicated system design. This work proposes a distributed proof-of-deep-learning (D-PoDL) scheme concerning PoUW's requirements. With a novel hash-traininßg-hash structure and model-referencing mechanism, our scheme is the first deep learning-based PoUW scheme that enables achieving better accuracy distributively. Next, we introduce a transformation from the D-PoDL scheme to a generic D-PoDL blockchain protocol which can be instantiated with two chain selection rules, i.e., the longest-chain rule and the weight-based blockchain framework (LatinCrypt' 21). This work is the first to provide formal proofs for deep learning-involved blockchain protocols concerning the robust ledger properties, i.e., chain growth, chain quality, and common prefix. Finally, we implement the D-PoDL scheme to discuss the effectiveness of our design.

Keywords: (Weight-based) blockchain protocols ·
Proof-of-useful-work · Distributed proof-of-deep-learning

1 Introduction

A promising new line of research is to consider the substitution of proof-of-work (PoW) with "useful work", *i.e.*, proof-of-useful-work (PoUW) [3], in dis-

This work was supported by the JST CREST under Grant JPMJCR14D6, through the JST OPERA, through the JSPS KAKENHI under Grant JP16H01705 and Grant JP17H01695, through the JST CREST Grant Number JPMJCR2113, through the JSPS KAKENHI JP21H04879 and JP21K11882.

S. Li et al. (Eds.): NSS 2023, LNCS 13983, pp. 114–136, 2023.
https://doi.org/10.1007/978-3-031-39828-5_7

tributed environments such as blockchain systems. This work focuses on the subset of these protocols, namely the *deep learning-based PoUW* schemes. First, we describe a brief but extensive survey of the research literature on deep learning-based schemes. The list is surprisingly short, considering the wide range of its applications. Our motivation is to formalize and extend these schemes so that we can achieve better use of computing power in blockchain-based protocols.

1.1 Background and Related Work

Recently, Chenli et al. [8] propose a PoUW scheme that utilizes the training process of deep learning tasks as useful work. To the best of our knowledge, there are only a handful of papers targeting the same problem [2,7,8,14–16]. We show a brief analysis to them in the following.

As a starting point, all these works involve task publishers who control the publication of deep learning tasks and miners who intend to solve the given tasks. Except for Proof-of-Learning (PoLe) [14], task publishers are forbidden to perform as miners under the assumption of limited computing power, whereas, PoLe [14] discards this impractical assumption by adding secure mapping layers during model training. However, this approach also prevents miners from collaborating, which violates our goal. A deep learning task consists of a description, a training dataset, a potential test dataset, and an accuracy target threshold. In Proof-of-Deep-Learning (PoDL) [8], Li et al.'s work [15] and PoLe [14], miners are required to train a model on the training dataset, and the model is verified according to the test dataset and test accuracy. This approach requires a strong synchronous network assumption because the task publisher has to publish the test dataset after miners produce their trained model. Otherwise, an adversary can directly train its model based on the test dataset.

DLchain [7] overcomes the strong synchronous assumption by removing the test dataset-based verification. Instead, it focuses on improving training accuracy. In order to verify a trained model efficiently, DLchain utilizes a merkle-tree-based verification [9] to check training history. Moreover, DLchain considers a similar goal to distribute PoDL, *i.e.*, achieving better accuracy distributively. They *partially* fulfill the goal with priorly determined "short-term targets" which are accuracy targets below the threshold. Miners can generate blocks once their models surpass a short-term accuracy target. However, considering only training accuracy may result in overfitting, and determined short-term targets can affect blockchain growth rate, which may weaken the security of the protocol [11].

CoinAI [2] is a descriptive work that proposes an outline for designing a deep learning-based PoUW and proof-of-storage scheme. The authors propose a "hash-to-architecture" mapping based on format context-free grammar. It maps a hash value to an initial deep learning model concerning model architectures, including hyper-parameters and initial learnable-parameters. The hash-to-architecture technique is vital for security since it prevents miners from grinding initial parameters. However, the security impacts are not clarified due to the lack of formality in [2]. Instead of proposing a PoUW-based blockchain protocol, Lihu et al. [7] aim at taking blockchain's security to enhance artificial intelligence systems. However, the protocol requires a dedicated blockchain structure and suffers from complicated system design. For example, participants must select their role before execution, and a unique type of participant called the supervisor needs to monitor all message history during the execution. Thus, their work cannot be integrated into any current blockchain-based protocols.

To sum up, none of these works can serve as a fully distributive deep learning task solver, which is more desirable in distributed environments. Another crucial problem is the lack of proper security analysis of the blockchain protocol. For example, only DLchain [7] provides security proof against double-spending attacks. However, a secure blockchain protocol should satisfy robust ledger properties, *i.e.*, the chain growth, chain quality, and common prefix. Therefore, our motivation for this work is to overcome the problems in the deep learning-based PoUW schemes mentioned above, *i.e.*, (1) to remove strong or impractical assumptions; (2) to *distribute* the computation of deep learning-based PoUW; (3) to provide concrete and thorough *security analysis* for blockchain protocols based on our extended scheme. Next, we further detail our work's significance.

1.2 Our Approach and Results

This work proposes a distributed proof-of-deep-learning (D-PoDL) scheme by extending deep learning-based PoUW schemes so that provers can work collaboratively on given tasks. Note that the term "distributed" in D-PoDL differs from distributed deep learning, *i.e.*, we do not require provers to perform a single training course together but let them train atop published pre-trained models.

Intuitively, D-PoDL provers train a model from a given deep learning task as their useful work. We propose a *"hash-training-hash"* structure to achieve adjustable difficulty while preventing provers from cherry-picking initial parameters (grinding attack) and pre-computing task instances (pre-computation resilience). As a result, the provers output a trained model with the corresponding accuracy and step number for D-PoDL verifiers to check. Another novelty of our scheme lies in how we handle intermediate models. Throughout the paper, an intermediate model, also called a pre-trained model, is a model "somewhat" trained yet failing to meet a given accuracy or security level. Instead of discarding such a model, we propose *"model-referencing"* that enables any prover to reference the pre-trained model. Hence, provers can start their training process atop the referenced model. Moreover, a referenced model will be rewarded so that even if the prover fails to meet the goals, it is incentivized to do more training iterations. We emphasize that this approach forms the distributed training process among provers, and such a design is never discussed in any previous work.

The second contribution is that we build a generic blockchain protocol based on our proposed D-PoDL scheme. We clarify the roles of participants: task publishers, miners, and external storage providers. Instead of assuming task publishers' inability to train models properly, we enable them to perform as miners while preventing them from pre-computing deep learning tasks with the hash-training-hash structure. Only Pole [14] shares the same property by embedding secure mapping layers into its training algorithm. Moreover, we make use of both training and test datasets. Concretely, miners (D-PoDL provers) extend the blockchain with models that have better *training* accuracy. In order to mitigate the overfitting problem while avoiding the strong synchronous network setting, we require miners to work on each deep learning task for multiple time slots. Hence, task publishers can evaluate the produced models with test dataset and select according to *test* accuracy. Since the training process is publicly verifiable, task publishers cannot take advantage by training directly on the test dataset. We will also discuss model verification and storage issues in Sect. 3.3 and Sect. 4.1.

Furthermore, the generic D-PoDL-based blockchain protocol is capable of two different chain selection rules: *i.e.*, the conventional "longest-chain rule" [11] and the "weight-based" framework [12,13]. The former requires honest miners to choose the longest branch as their chain whenever a fork occurs. In contrast, the weight-based framework assigns blocks with weights according to their quality. Hence, honest miners choose the branch with higher accumulated weight as their chain. Although the longest-chain rule can be considered a special case of the weight-based framework, we separate them into two concrete protocols and prove the robust ledger properties for each. Finally, we implement our D-PoDL scheme and compare it to existing schemes.

Table 1 compares our work and related works. Note that we omit CoinAI [2] due to its informality and Lihu et al.'s work [16] due to their different research focus. We also include a recent result on stochastic local search-based PoUW [10]. The difference between our work and the PoUW [10] is that we leverage deep learning characteristics, *e.g.*, verifiable training steps and test datasets, and derive a simple yet versatile protocol (*i.e.*, proven secure under different chain selection rules).

Table 1. Comparison with Previous Works

Protocols	Work Evaluation	Network Synchronicity	Publisher As Miner	*Distributed* Task Solver	Formal Security
Chenli et al. [8]	Test accuracy	Strong	X	X	X
Lan et al. [14]	Test accuracy	Strong	✓[1]	X	X
Li et al. [15]	Training accuracy	Bounded	X	X	X
Chenli et al. [7]	Training accuracy	Bounded	X	△[2]	△[3]
Fitzi et al. [10]	—[4]	Bounded	✓	✓	✓[5]
This work	Training and test	Bounded	✓	✓	✓[6]

Notes: (1) By secure mapping layers; (2) By pre-determined short-term targets; (3) Against double-spending attack; (4) Stochastic local search; (5) Under the longest-chain rule [11]; (6) Against robust ledger properties under the longest-chain rule [11] and the weight-based framework [12,13].

1.3   Paper Organization

The remainder is organized as follows. Section 2 reviews notations and the execution model of our blockchain protocol. The following two sections present our main contribution: blockchain protocols from distributed proof-of-deep-learning (D-PoDL). Concretely, Sect. 3 introduces the formal definition of D-PoDL scheme and explains our design choices based on PoUW requirements; Sect. 4 transforms the D-PoDL scheme into a generic blockchain protocol and presents two concrete protocols by instantiating the chain selection rule with the conventional longest-chain rule [11] and the weight-based framework [12,13]. We analyze the security of our concrete protocols regarding robust ledger properties in Sect. 5. Then, Sect. 6 provides an implementation of the D-PoDL scheme to compare with existing algorithms. Finally, Sect. 7 concludes this work.

2   Preliminaries

Throughout this paper, we use λ for the security parameter. For an integer $k \in \mathbb{N}$, $[k]$ denotes the set $\{1, \ldots, k\}$. Given a set X, $x \xleftarrow{\$} X$ denotes that x is randomly and uniformly sampled from X. For an algorithm Alg, $x \leftarrow \mathsf{Alg}$ denotes that x is assigned the output of an algorithm Alg on fresh randomness. Let Hash denote a collision-free hash function.

Moreover, we employ and modify the hash-to-architecture mapping mechanism from [2], which is based on the formal context-free grammar and is used to establish a surjective function between a hash value and a proper deep learning architecture setup. Denote the original hash-to-architecture mapping with HtoA^*, i.e., given a hash value h, $\mathsf{HtoA}^*(h) = (\mathsf{A}(\mathsf{hpp}), \mathsf{initLP})$ where $\mathsf{A}(\mathsf{hpp})$ is the architecture A concerning hyper-parameters hpp, and initLP denotes the initial learnable parameters. Our modification, denoted by HtoA, is to generate an additional random value from the hash, i.e., given a hash value $h = h_1 \| h_2$ and a hash function $\mathsf{Hash} : \{0,1\}^* \rightarrow \{0,1\}^\lambda$, we extract $r = \mathsf{Hash}(h_2)$ and run $\mathsf{HtoA}^*(h_1) = (\mathsf{A}(\mathsf{hpp}), \mathsf{initLP})$ so that the outputs of $\mathsf{HtoA}(h)$ is $(\mathsf{A}(\mathsf{hpp}), \mathsf{initLP}, r)$.

Protocol Execution Model. Protocol executions are modeled by the standard Interactive Turing Machines (ITM) approach [6]. A protocol refers to algorithms for a set of nodes (users) to interact with each other. All corrupted nodes are considered to be controlled by an adversary $\mathcal{A}$ who can read inputs and set outputs for these nodes. We present our protocol settings as follows.

Time and Network. We assume the protocol execution proceeds in rounds, which corresponds to the smallest unit of time of interest. The network is synchronous with a *known* bounded delay δ time on the delivery time, i.e., any message sent by an honest node in round r is guaranteed to arrive at all honest nodes until round $r + \delta$;

Corruptions. We allow the adversary to corrupt up to $\beta < \frac{1}{2}$ fraction of nodes before each round, *i.e.*, a corrupted node is under the adversary's complete control from the round. We also assume the adversary is rushing, *i.e.*, it receives honest users' messages first and decides the order of message delivery or whether to inject messages for each recipient.

3 The D-PoDL Scheme

As an extension of deep learning-based PoUW schemes, our D-PoDL scheme provides an interface for its provers to solve a deep learning task together. Like PoUW, a D-PoDL scheme involves two types of participants: provers and verifiers. On a given deep learning task, a prover intends to output a trained model, and claims the corresponding training accuracy and step number. Whereas, a verifier checks if the model matches the prover's claims and responds accordingly. This section presents the D-PoDL scheme in terms of requirements and syntax. We focus on a setting where provers work on a priorly given deep learning task with a designed target threshold. We clarify that the scheme focuses on solving the task and verifying the model. Discussions about task selection, block generation, and blockchain dynamics can be found in the protocol description in later sections, *i.e.*, Sect. 4 and Sect. 5.

D-PoDL Requirements. A D-PoDL scheme should satisfy the same security requirements [10] as the PoUW, *i.e.*, no-grinding, pre-computation resilience, and adjustable difficulty. Moreover, it should satisfy efficiency and usefulness requirements. The **requirements** are (1a) No-grinding: The adversary cannot cherry-pick hyper-parameters to gain training advantages, *i.e.*, less training steps with higher accuracy; (1b) Pre-computation resilience: The adversary cannot manufacture problem instances to train the model faster; (1c) Adjustable difficulty: The block difficulty (measured by training accuracy) can be adjusted to the computing power of the network; (2a) Efficient verification: The running time of the verification algorithm should be at most poly-logarithm of provers' training time; (2b) Measurable usefulness: The usefulness of a training process can be quantified and compared to each other.

3.1 Design Overview

Along with the two processes in a D-PoDL scheme, *i.e.*, solving a deep learning task and verifying the correctness of the solution, we propose a novel "hash-training-hash" structure for the solving process and utilize a widely used merkle-tree-based verification procedure [9] as a black-box for the verification process. Additionally, we propose a weighting algorithm to evaluate a weight function that quantifies a solution's usefulness. We describe the "hash-training-hash" structure briefly in this section. More details of our design choices can be found after the formal definition.

Intuitively, on a given deep learning task, we enable provers to initialize its solving algorithm with either a fresh or a pre-trained model from any prover, *i.e.*, for "model-referencing". The first hash requires provers to perform a proof-of-work (PoW) with threshold T_1, *i.e.*, a prover needs to find a nonce such that the hash value of the previous block, potentially a pre-trained model and the nonce is less than T_1. If the hash value passes the PoW check (less than T_1), the prover can map the hash value to an architecture with respect to hyper-parameters, (initial) learnable-parameters and a random seed with our modified hash-to-architecture algorithm. As introduced in Sect. 2, the architecture (with hyper-parameters) and learnable-parameters determine a deep learning model. The prover trains the model by updating learnable-parameters iteratively. The post-hash checks the output model against threshold T_2 to decide if the models are eligible for publishing. If the post-hash fails, the prover can return to the pre-hash or training process. The prover must perform more training iterations in both cases to generate a valid model.

3.2 Formal Syntax and Construction

A D-PoDL scheme involves a tuple of algorithms (Setup, Solve, Verify, Weight). Setup extracts a training dataset and a designed target threshold from a deep learning task. Solve consists of three sub-algorithms PreHash, Train, and PostHash. In general, PreHash determines the initial model, including its architecture, hyper-parameters, learnable-parameters, and a random seed. Train casts the training process and outputs a model with the corresponding accuracy and step number. Note that we do *NOT* restrict the training algorithm to provide generality for our design. Instead, as we will show in Sect. 5.1, we model it with an oracle due to its stochastic nature and model provers' computing power by their capability of oracle queries. Next, due to security concerns, PostHash returns a bit according to a hash proof. Verify verifies the trained model's validity concerning accuracy. Weight is available to both provers and verifiers, and it evaluates a weight function $w : \text{acc} \times T_{\text{acc}} \rightarrow \mathbb{R}$, which maps the model's accuracy and a priorly decided target threshold to a real value. We present the formal syntax and construction of the D-PoDL scheme as follows.

Construction 1 (D-PoDL Scheme). *Given the hash-to-architecture algorithm* HtoA$(\cdot)$ *from Sect. 2 and the weight function* $w : \text{acc} \times T_{\text{acc}} \rightarrow \mathbb{R}$, *the tuple algorithm of a D-PoDL scheme* (Setup, Solve, Verify, Weight) *works as follows:*

- Setup$(1^\lambda, \text{task})$ *takes as input the security parameter* λ *and the description of a deep learning task* task *from the task publisher.* Setup *extracts the public parameter* pp *and a pair of threshold* (T_1, T_2) *for security concerns from the system. It* parses *the task with a training dataset* D *and a target threshold* T_{acc}. Setup *outputs* (pp$, T_1, T_2, \text{D}, T_{\text{acc}})$. *We omit* pp *later for simplicity;*
- Solve$((T_1, \text{prevBK}, \text{refM}), (\text{D}, T_{\text{acc}}), T_2)$. *We divide* Solve *into three algorithms:* (PreHash, Train, PostHash).
  - PreHash$(T_1, \text{prevBK}, \text{refM})$ *takes as input* T_1, *a previous block* prevBK *and potentially a pre-trained model* refM. *It samples* nonce *such that*

$\mathsf{Hash}(\mathsf{prevBK}, \mathsf{refM}, \mathsf{nonce}) = h_1 \leq T_1$. *If* $\mathsf{refM} = \perp$, PreHash *runs* $\mathsf{HtoA}(h_1) = (\mathsf{A}(\mathsf{hpp}), \mathsf{lp}, r)$ *where* $\mathsf{A}(\mathsf{hpp})$ *denotes the architecture,* lp *denotes the learnable-parameters, and* r *denotes the random seed. It sets* $\mathsf{initM} = (\mathsf{A}(\mathsf{hpp}), \mathsf{lp})$; *Otherwise, It parses* $\mathsf{refM} = (\mathsf{A}(\mathsf{hpp}_{\mathsf{ref}}), \mathsf{lp}_{\mathsf{ref}})$ *and sets* $\mathsf{initM} \in \{\mathsf{refM}, (\mathsf{A}(\mathsf{hpp}), \mathsf{lp})\}$. *Then,* PreHash *returns* $(\mathsf{nonce}, \mathsf{initM}, r)$;

- Train$(\mathsf{D}, T_{\mathsf{acc}}, \mathsf{initM}, r)$ *takes as input the training dataset* D, *a target threshold* T_{acc}, *a initial model* initM *and a random seed* r. *It parses* $\mathsf{initM} = (\mathsf{A}(\mathsf{hpp}), \mathsf{lp})$ *and trains the model by updating learnable-parameters iteratively.* Train *returns* $\mathsf{M} = (\mathsf{A}(\mathsf{hpp}), \mathsf{lp}^*)$, *the corresponding training accuracy* $\mathsf{acc} \in [0, 1]$, *step number* S *and a list of checkpoints* $\mathsf{CPs} \triangleq \{(\mathsf{M}_i, \mathsf{acc}_i, S_i)\}$ *where each entry denotes an intermediate result of the training process;*

- PostHash$(T_2, \mathsf{M}, \mathsf{acc}, S)$ *takes as input* T_2 *and a model* M *with the corresponding accuracy* acc *and step number* S. *It computes* $\mathsf{Hash}(\mathsf{M}, \mathsf{acc}, S) = h_2$. *If* $h_2 \leq T_2$, PostHash *returns* 1; *Otherwise, it returns* 0.

Finally, Solve *outputs* $((\mathsf{refM}, \mathsf{nonce}, \mathsf{initM}, r), (\mathsf{M}, \mathsf{acc}, S), b)$ *where* $b \in \{0, 1\}$;

- Verify$((T_1, \mathsf{prevBK}, \mathsf{refM}, \mathsf{nonce}, \mathsf{initM}, r), (\mathsf{D}, T_{\mathsf{acc}}, \mathsf{M}, \mathsf{acc}, S, \mathsf{CPs}), (T_2, b))$ *checks:*

  - *If* $\mathsf{Hash}(\mathsf{prevBK}, \mathsf{refM}, \mathsf{nonce}) = h_1 \leq T_1$ *and if* initM *is derived correctly from* refM;
  - *If* M *is trained correctly from* initM *with* Train *according to* (S, CPs) *and if the corresponding accuracy* $\mathsf{acc}' = \mathsf{acc}$;
  - *Compute* $\mathsf{PostHash}(T_2, \mathsf{M}, \mathsf{acc}, S) = b'$ *and check if* $b' = b$.

  If the situations above are satisfied, Verify *outputs* 1; *Otherwise, it outputs* 0.
- Weight$(\mathsf{acc}, T_{\mathsf{acc}})$ *evaluates the weight function* w *and outputs* $\mathsf{w} \in \mathbb{R}$.

3.3 Design Choices Explanation

Here, we explain our construction choices with respect to the **requirements**.

Setting up Initial Models with Pre-hash. There are countless different architectures in deep learning, each with its characteristics and limitations. After selecting an appropriate architecture A, provers need to choose hyperparameters and initial learnable-parameters for the model, which may affect the speed and quality of the training process. Usually, hyper-parameters are not learnable, so provers must go through random sampling before obtaining a good set of hyper-parameters. However, we may open a gate for grinding attacks (**Requirement 1a**) if we offer provers the ability to choose hyper-parameters and initial learnable-parameters. An adversary may outperform honest users' training speed and quality by cherry-picking.

In order to mitigate this problem, we adopt the same approach as in Ofelimos [10]. Concretely, we rely on a PoW scheme with threshold T_1, which requires provers to sample a nonce nonce randomly and compute the hash of the previous block (prevBK), potentially a pre-trained model refM with the nonce such that $\mathsf{Hash}(\mathsf{prevBK}, \mathsf{refM}, \mathsf{nonce}) = h_1 \leq T_1$. The hash function's uniformity prevents provers from grinding hyper-parameters and learnable-parameters. Note that our T_1 should not be as hard as a stand-alone PoW, $e.g.$, the one in the Bitcoin system, because we intend to encourage provers to train models instead of solving PoW. Finally, if refM is empty, the prover needs to generate an initial model with $\mathsf{HtoA}(h_1) = (\mathsf{A}(\mathsf{hpp}), \mathsf{lp}, r)$ such that $\mathsf{initM} = (\mathsf{A}(\mathsf{hpp}), \mathsf{lp})$; Otherwise, the prover can either refer to the pre-trained model $\mathsf{refM} = (\mathsf{A}(\mathsf{hpp}_{\mathsf{ref}}), \mathsf{lp}_{\mathsf{ref}})$ or use the freshly generated hyper-parameters and the pre-trained learnable-parameters $(\mathsf{A}(\mathsf{hpp}), \mathsf{lp}_{\mathsf{ref}})$ as its initial model. In this case, the pre-hash enforces provers to establish links from their model to previous blocks and the referenced models. Such links are crucial to the security of model-referencing.

Model-Referencing and Pre-computation Resilience. An initial model can be sampled from HtoA or from a pre-trained model refM. The purpose of taking as input a pre-trained model is to enable provers to work atop any valid but not-good-enough model. Hence, we prevent their computing power from being wasted and form a distributed solver for given deep learning tasks. However, starting from a pre-trained model can shorten the prover's training iteration because these models may be only a few steps from reaching the accuracy target threshold. For example, an adversary may steal an honest prover's outputs $(\mathsf{M}_0, \mathsf{acc}_0, S_0)$ and produce a new model $\mathsf{M}_{\mathcal{A}}$ with accuracy $\mathsf{acc}_{\mathcal{A}} \geq T_{\mathsf{acc}} \geq \mathsf{acc}_0$ and a claimed step number $S_{\mathcal{A}}$. Such an attack violates pre-computation resilience (**Requirement 1b**) because the adversary achieves better accuracy while performing only $(S_{\mathcal{A}} - S_0)$ training steps.

In order to tackle this problem, we design a novel mechanism called "model-referencing". We require provers to make references if their models are trained based on another model. Otherwise, their models are regarded as invalid. The reference is $(\mathsf{prevBK}, \mathsf{refM}, \mathsf{nonce})$, which can be publicly verified with $\mathsf{Hash}(\mathsf{prevBK}, \mathsf{refM}, \mathsf{nonce}) \leq T_1$. Hence, model-referencing enables provers to train each others' models together for the same goal (surpassing the target threshold and post-hash check threshold) while preventing them from stealing others' models (by discarding those "use-without-reference" models). Furthermore, the provers should only reference the latest models, $i.e.$, if two pre-trained models share the same setup, provers should reference the model with higher accuracy and step number. With this setting, we also prevent provers from flooding the system with too many pre-trained models. Therefore, the mechanism inherently forms an additional "link" (like the hash link between blocks) that connects models, $i.e.$, a valid block must be linked to a previous block and a previous model. More details can be found in Sect. 4.1.

Adjusting Computation with Post-hash. One argument concerning the adjustable difficulty (**Requirement 1c**) is that training a model so that its accuracy surpasses the target threshold T_{acc} should be harder than finding a nonce to meet the PoW puzzle with threshold T_1. Otherwise, the computational difficulty is determined by the PoW rather than the training process, which violates the usefulness of our scheme. Hence, we propose a solution based on [5]'s approach, which requires the provers to perform *one* "post-hash" against a threshold T_2 to decide if their models are eligible for publishing. If a model fails the post-hash, the prover must revert to the pre-hash or training process. The threshold T_2 guarantees the overall security and usefulness level for our scheme, *e.g.*, to preserve the 10 min interval for block generation while enforcing provers' computation focus on model training instead of PoW. We will show the impact of the post-hash algorithm during our implementation of the D-PoDL scheme in Sect. 6.

Model Verification. In order to verify the outputs of a prover, a verifier needs to check three conditions: (1) If the nonce satisfies the PoW check with threshold T_1; (2) If the model has the claimed accuracy; (3) If the post-hash outputs a correct bit. In this section, we focus on verifying the model and its accuracy. A naive approach is to check the prover's model with the given training dataset. However, it takes as many iterations as the training algorithm, which violates the efficiency requirement (**Requirement 2a**).

We solve this problem by adopting the widely used merkle-tree-based verification [9] as a black box. This approach is also mentioned in the previous work [7]. Namely, provers are required to include several intermediate results as checkpoints into their training outputs and build a merkle-tree accordingly. Hence, verifiers only need to check the validity of these checkpoints. Given n checkpoints, the time complexity for verifiers can be reduced to $O(\mathsf{polylog}(n))$ at the cost of provers' space complexity being $O(\mathsf{poly}(n))$. Moreover, there is a trivial trade-off between the interval of two checkpoints and the granularity of the check. As pointed out by [7], the interval setting can be left to users in real-life applications and adjusted according to accuracy thresholds. However, since each checkpoint has the size of a model, we explain this in Sect. 4.1 with respect to external storage providers.

Measuring Usefulness. The D-PoDL scheme focuses on improving the models' training accuracy, whereas, the test accuracy is left for the protocol. Except for the conventional longest-chain-based blockchain protocols [11], we intend to build our D-PoDL scheme under a weight-based framework by [13]. In such a setting, blocks are assigned with weight, and the chain is selected based on the accumulated weight. We argue that the weight-based approach is natural for the D-PoDL scheme because accuracy can be regarded as a quantified measurement for usefulness (**Requirement 2b**). Moreover, we can generalize the weight-based approach to arbitrary PoUW schemes as long as their usefulness is measurable.

4   Our D-PoDL Blockchain Protocols

This section describes the transformation from our D-PoDL scheme to D-PoDL-based blockchain protocols. As mentioned in the execution model from Sect. 2, our protocol proceeds in rounds. Honest users may share a slightly different view of the round number. We further divide our protocol execution into time slots. Each time slot is associated with a deep learning task, and the time slot ends when a validly generated block is added to the blockchain. Thus, a time slot may include multiple rounds. Considering the workflow within a time slot, we propose a generic D-PoDL blockchain protocol design as in Fig. 1. Then, two concrete protocols are derived from the generic design by instantiating the chain selection rule with the longest-chain rule [11] and the weight-based framework [13]. Finally, we discuss the incentive model of our protocols.

4.1 Generic Protocol Workflow

The generic blockchain protocol involves three types of participants: task publishers, miners, and external storage providers. Task publishers handle deep learning tasks. Each task is associated with a dataset and desired accuracy thresholds. Task publishers first split the dataset into a training dataset and a test dataset. They publish the task description, the training dataset, and the corresponding desired training accuracy as the target threshold. Miners perform the protocol by generating and verifying blocks according to the D-PoDL scheme's instructions. Concerning the size of deep learning models and checkpoints (which are the same size as models), we employ the approach from [7] to prevent storage overhead, i.e., embedding only a downloadable link within the block and relying on external storage to store the whole model and checkpoints.

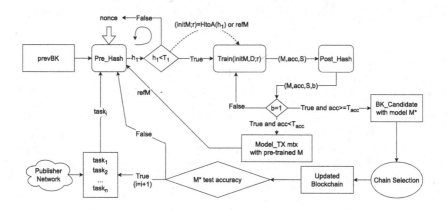

Fig. 1. Design of our Generic D-PoDL Blockchain Protocol

Task Publication. We start our generic D-PoDL blockchain protocol from the task publication mechanism. In order to keep the task publication as generic as possible, we consider a situation in which these publishers form a network to publish and decide the order of tasks. They aim to organize a distributed solver for deep learning tasks and can be benefited from receiving the solutions.

The only requirement is that the outputs of the publisher network should be an ordered list of deep learning tasks. We denote the output as $\{task_i\}_{i\in[n]}$ where $task_i$ spans over a period of ℓ_i time slots in $T_i = \{t_{i,j}\}_{j\in[\ell_i]}$.

Note that we do *NOT* separate task publishers from miners, *i.e.*, a task publisher can participate in the protocol as a miner and gain mining rewards. We argue that the task publisher cannot pre-compute the task to gain advantages over regular miners due to the pre-hash algorithm and the model-referencing mechanism. Without loss generality, let the current time slot be $t_{p,q}$, we consider an adversarial publisher who intends to pre-compute deep learning task $task_i$ where $i > p, q \in [\ell_p]$. Since $i > p$, without pre-trained models, the publisher has to train an initial model generated from HtoA, *i.e.*, to find nonce such that $Hash(prevBK, nonce) = h_1 \leq T_1$ where prevBK associates with slot $t_{i-1,\ell_{i-1}-1} \in T_{i-1}$ and compute initM from $HtoA(h_1)$. To find such a nonce requires the publisher to either predict the block in the future or find a collision in the hash function. Since the probabilities of both cases are negligible, the publisher cannot produce a trained or pre-trained model to pass the D-PoDL scheme's verification by pre-computing $task_k$.

Execution of D-PoDL Scheme. Now, we consider a deep learning task $task_i$ given to miners in time slot $t_{i,j}$ where $j \in [\ell_i]$. Each miner runs as a prover of the D-PoDL scheme. The Setup algorithm first extracts public parameters, a training dataset, and thresholds (T_1, T_2, T_{acc}). The miner then finds a nonce and initializes initM with PreHash; It runs the training course on the initial model with the randomness r to obtain a model M, the corresponding accuracy acc and step number S; PostHash tests the model according to T_2 and outputs a bit b. The miner outputs a tuple, including potentially a pre-trained model as the reference, a nonce, an initial model, a random training seed, a trained model with the corresponding accuracy and step number, and a post-hash check bit.

According to the post-hash check, the miner decides if its model is eligible for publishing. Moreover, for generality, we introduce a relation between the model accuracy and the target threshold as $\mathcal{R}(acc, T_{acc})$, which will be instantiated in concrete protocols. Hence, when $b = 1 \wedge \mathcal{R}(acc, T_{acc}) = 1$, the miner collects transactions from the mempool as in conventional blockchain protocols and generates a block candidate embedding the obtained model M; Otherwise, the miner generates a special *model-transaction* mtx for model-referencing, which contains the outputs of the Solve algorithm, *i.e.*, mtx = (prevBK, (refM, nonce, initM, r), (D, T_{acc}, M, acc, S, CPs), 1). mtx is published into the mempool as ordinary transactions. Any miner can reference the model M in the model-transaction mtx by including mtx in the miner's newly found block or model-transaction. That is, the miner takes as input refM$'$ = M for its Solve algorithm. Note that different miners can refer to the same model-transaction. We do not count this as "double-spending" since no ordinary (money-used) transaction is involved. Newly trained models still need to compete for acceptance. Moreover, miners can reference model-transactions recursively, *i.e.*, generating a model-transaction mtx$'$ with higher accuracy from mtx is acceptable. The only restriction here is that miners

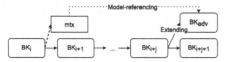 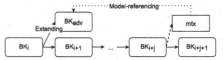

(a) The adversary intends to extend block bk_{i+j} by referencing an mtx that links to block bk_i.

(b) The adversary intends to extend block bk_i by referencing a model-transaction mtx that links to block bk_{i+j}.

Fig. 2. Intuition of Cross Time Slot Attacks

must reference the latest model-transaction, which embeds a pre-trained model with the highest accuracy observed so far. This prevents the adversary from releasing a large amount of model-transaction to DoS attack [17] the network.

Cross Time Slot Attacks and Restrictions on Step Number. We leave block selection (with respect to forks) to concrete protocols in Sect. 4.2. Here, we consider the whole period (a span of time slots) associated with a deep learning task. Once the blockchain gets updated, miners proceed to the next time slot. A task can span over multiple time slots so that the publisher network can check each selected model with the corresponding *test* dataset. This approach is to mitigate the trend toward overfitting models since miners are given only training datasets to overcome the strong synchronous network assumption.

However, this approach allows adversaries to reference models generated in different time slots from the block they extend. Given a fragment of the blockchain that associates with a deep learning task, we illustrate two attack strategies in Fig. 2a and 2b. Note that the adversary can also reference models embedded in blocks. We use model-transactions here for generality.

The first attack enables the adversary to extend the blockchain with fewer training steps while not violating model-referencing requirements. In the second attack, the adversary can produce a model with higher accuracy or weight using new information, *e.g.*, the model in mtx of Fig. 2b. This attack may subvert blockchain history if the adversary produces enough blocks to compete with the selected chain.

In order to tackle these problems, we restrict the training step number in published *blocks*. We introduce a lower bound of acceptable step number as S_{min} to control the selected blocks' step number during the period of a given task **task**. Denote the period with $T = \{t_i\}_{i \in [\ell]}$, and for each $i \in [\ell]$, we denote the selected model (in a block on the chain) with $M_i \in bk_i$ and the model's corresponding step number with S_i. Now, consider a block candidate bk embedding M_{bk} trying to extend bk_n with $n \in [\ell - 1]$. Let $M = (M'_j)_{j \in [k]}$ be M_{bk}'s recursively referenced model list. Each of these models is either embedded in a block or a model transaction that extends some blocks on the blockchain. Without loss of generality, we assume the first block being extended by one of these models in the period to be bk_m where $m \in [\ell - 1], m \leq n$. The **restriction** on M_{bk}'s step number S_{bk} is: $\sum_{j=0}^{k-1} S'_j + S_{bk} \geq \sum_{i=m}^{n-1} S_i + S_{min}$. Intuitively, the restriction requires that a newly generated block and its referred models have no less training steps than the steps on the main blockchain. It is reasonable in the sense that we require not only the accuracy of models/blocks, but also miners donating enough computing power (training steps). Moreover, our D-PoDL scheme enables us to leverage steps in model verification. The goal is to stabilize the block generation rate, and we will discuss this later in Sect. 5.2. Finally, miners repeat the above process when the publisher network proceeds to a new task.

4.2 Concrete Protocols

In this section, we instantiate the chain selection rule with the longest-chain rule from [11] and the weight-based framework from [13].

Longest-Chain-Based D-PoDL Blockchain. First, in the longest-chain-based protocol, we clarify the relation introduced above as: $\mathcal{R}(\text{acc}, T_{\text{acc}}) = 1$ if $\text{acc} \geq T_{\text{acc}}$. Hence, a model is eligible to be published as a block if $b = 1 \wedge \text{acc} \geq T_{\text{acc}}$. Otherwise, i.e., $\text{acc} < T_{\text{acc}}$, the model can be embedded in a model-transaction mtx and published to the mempool; if $b = 0$, the miner must continue training the model or resample the nonce for another initial model to be trained. By the longest-chain rule, miners of each time slot add blocks to the end of the longest blockchain they have observed and broadcast the chain to the network. Later, we will show that forks of the same length as the main chain can exist only with negligible probability by proving the robust ledger properties [11] for our longest-chain-based protocol.

Weighted-Based D-PoDL Blockchain. In the weight-based protocol, $\mathcal{R}(\text{acc}, T_{\text{acc}}) = 1$ for any pair of $(\text{acc}, T_{\text{acc}})$. The situation indicates that a miner can generate a block even if its deep learning model fails to surpass the target threshold. However, the number of blocks produced in a time slot can be overwhelming without proper filtering. Therefore, Kamp et al. [13] introduce a weight function to quantify the quality of blocks so that miners only choose the blockchain with the highest (accumulated) weight. Our weight function evaluates the embedded model according to $(\text{acc}, T_{\text{acc}})$ with the Weight algorithm. Instead of showing specific constructions, we will introduce two crucial properties for proving the security of the weight-based D-PoDL blockchain in the next section. With these properties, we show that forks with comparable weights as the main chain can only exist with negligible probability by proving the weight-based variant of robust ledger properties [13] for our weight-based protocol.

Discussion: Incentive Models. The incentive model is crucial to a practical protocol. We aim to reward miners according to their useful computation, *i.e.*, training
iterations. Moreover, our protocol differs from previous works in that miners can
reference model-transactions to generate another model-transaction, or a block,
without training models from the sketch. Models in model-transactions may
have inferior accuracy. However, they are crucial in forming the distributed deep
learning task solver. Hence, in order to incentivize miners to produce models,
we reward not only the miners who produce selected blocks but also the model-
transactions referenced by selected blocks. The rewards are given according to
the model accuracy and the step number. For example, let M be the selected
model, which is trained for S steps. Furthermore, let its recursively referenced
models set be $M = \{M_j\}_{j \in [k]}$, and each $j \in [k]$, M_j is trained for S_j steps.
Hence, M's miner receives $S/(\sum S_j + S)$ fraction of the total rewards, and each
M_j's miner receives $S_j/(\sum S_j + S)$ of the total rewards. Finally, we want to
clarify that incentive models may affect the assumptions on honest miners' fraction, which will further affect chain growth for robust ledgers [1]. However, this
work assumes honest miners' fractions directly. Hence, the incentive model in
this section will not change our security proofs.

5   Security Analysis

Our security analysis focuses on the period of one single deep learning task
because switching to a new task can be regarded as a mining difficulty shift in
the PoW-based protocols. However, extending the result to the whole blockchain
is easy if we assume the difficulty, represented by the accuracy target threshold,
is stable across different tasks. To clarify, the terms "model-transaction" and
"block" refer to the model embedded in the model-transaction or block.

Robust Ledger Properties. In this work, we focus on proving the robust ledger
properties, *i.e.*, the chain growth, chain quality, and common prefix, for our
concrete protocols. The definitions originate from [11]. We adopt the modified
version from [10] for the longest-chain-based protocol. The weight-based variant
can be found in the original paper [13].

Definition 1 (Robust ledger properties).

- *Chain Growth: For any honest miner with chain C at a round, the chain
  growth with parameter $\tau \in (0, 1]$ and $s \in \mathbb{N}$ states that for any portion of C
  spanning s consecutive rounds, the number of blocks in this portion is at least
  τs;*
- *Existential Chain Quality: For any honest miner with chain C at a round, the
  existential chain quality with parameter $s \in \mathbb{N}$ states that for any portion of C
  spanning s consecutive rounds, at least one honestly-generated block appears
  in this portion;*

– *Common Prefix: For any two honest miners with chains $\mathcal{C}_1, \mathcal{C}_2$ at round r_1, r_2 respectively, where $r_1 \leq r_2$, the common prefix with parameter $s \in \mathbb{N}$ indicates that $\mathcal{C}_1$ should be a prefix of $\mathcal{C}_2$ after removing the last s blocks.*

5.1 The Training Oracle

Our first step models the combination of training and post-hash process with a training oracle. Following [13]'s approach, we assume protocol participants can make at most one query to the training oracle in each round. This assumption is reasonable because a round is the smallest unit of time of interest in our protocol and corresponds to the time for evaluating the hash function over one training iteration on one miner's computing device. For a real-world miner with the computing power of more than one device, we model it as a collection of "one-query-per-round" participants.

In each round, a miner queries the oracle $\mathcal{O}_{\mathsf{Train}}$ with $(\mathsf{M}_{\mathsf{pre}}, \mathsf{acc}_{\mathsf{pre}}, S; r)$ where $\mathsf{M}_{\mathsf{pre}}$ denotes the pre-query model, $\mathsf{acc}_{\mathsf{pre}}$ and S denotes the corresponding training accuracy and step number, and r denotes the random seed for training. The oracle $\mathcal{O}_{\mathsf{Train}}$ first verifies the queried model and returns $\perp$ if the model is invalid. Otherwise, $\mathcal{O}_{\mathsf{Train}}$ performs one training iteration with r to obtain $(\mathsf{M}_{\mathsf{after}}, \mathsf{acc}_{\mathsf{after}}, S{+}1)$ where $\mathsf{M}_{\mathsf{after}}$ and $\mathsf{acc}_{\mathsf{after}}$ denote the model and training accuracy after query, respectively. It samples a random value $h_2 \leftarrow \{0,1\}^\lambda$ uniformly, where λ is the security parameter that indicates the length of the hash function output. $\mathcal{O}_{\mathsf{Train}}$ returns $(\mathsf{M}_{\mathsf{after}}, \mathsf{acc}_{\mathsf{after}}, S{+}1, h_2)$. Moreover, regarding queries with different random seeds (r) as different queries, $\mathcal{O}_{\mathsf{Train}}$ keeps a list of performed queries and replies to former queries according to the list.

The uniqueness of our model is that $\mathcal{O}_{\mathsf{Train}}$ performs one training iteration before sampling the random value. A query is said to be successful only if the output model satisfies: $h_2 \leq T_2 \wedge \mathcal{R}(\mathsf{acc}_{\mathsf{after}}, T_{\mathsf{acc}}) = 1$. Since h_2's distribution is defined to be uniform, we now consider the distribution of the output accuracy $\mathsf{acc}_{\mathsf{after}}$. Note that training accuracy usually grows faster before achieving a certain value. Like in [7], we name this value difficulty threshold, denoted by D_{acc}. Our model focuses on the training process after such a threshold. The reason is that, as explained in [4], increasing the training accuracy requires stochastic/random search after this threshold. Hence, we assume that if $\mathsf{acc}_{\mathsf{pre}} \geq D_{\mathsf{acc}}$, $\mathsf{acc}_{\mathsf{after}}$ follows an arbitrary distribution $\mathcal{D}$ over $\{\mathsf{acc} : \mathsf{acc} \geq D_{\mathsf{acc}}\}$ such that $f_1 \overset{\Delta}{=} \Pr[\mathsf{acc}_{\mathsf{after}} \geq T_{\mathsf{acc}} | \mathsf{acc}_{\mathsf{pre}} \geq D_{\mathsf{acc}}]$, *e.g.*, when $\mathcal{D}$ is uniform, $f_1 = \frac{1 - T_{\mathsf{acc}}}{1 - D_{\mathsf{acc}}}$. Otherwise, *i.e.*, $\mathsf{acc}_{\mathsf{pre}} < D_{\mathsf{acc}}$, we assume $\mathsf{acc}_{\mathsf{after}}$ increase be monotonically but unlikely to surpass T_{acc}, *i.e.*, less than ϵ, negligible of the security parameter λ. Therefore, we argue that the overall probability is $\Pr[\mathsf{acc}_{\mathsf{after}} \geq T_{\mathsf{acc}}] \geq \frac{1}{2} f_1$ because the number of training steps before reaching the difficulty threshold is much less than the step number afterward. The training oracle goes as follows.

Training Oracle $\mathcal{O}_{\mathsf{Train}}$

Let task be a deep learning task with dataset D and accuracy target threshold T_{acc}. The oracle $\mathcal{O}_{\mathsf{Train}}$ keeps a list $\mathbb{L}$ with performed queries. **On a query $(\mathsf{M}_{\mathsf{pre}}, \mathsf{acc}_{\mathsf{pre}}, S; r)$ from a miner in a round:**

- If $(\mathsf{M}_{\mathsf{pre}}, \mathsf{acc}_{\mathsf{pre}}, S; r)$ is invalid, *i.e.*, $\mathsf{M}_{\mathsf{pre}}$ has unmatched accuracy or step number, return $\bot$;
- If $(\mathsf{M}_{\mathsf{pre}}, \mathsf{acc}_{\mathsf{pre}}, S; r) \in \mathbb{L}$, return the reply entry $(\mathsf{M}_{\mathsf{after}}, \mathsf{acc}_{\mathsf{after}}, S+1)$ according to the list $\mathbb{L}$;
- Otherwise, run one training step $\mathsf{Train}(\mathsf{D}, T_{\mathsf{acc}}, \mathsf{M}_{\mathsf{pre}}, r) \rightarrow (\mathsf{M}_{\mathsf{after}}, \mathsf{acc}_{\mathsf{after}}, S+1)$ and sample $h_2 \leftarrow \{0,1\}^\lambda$ uniformly at random. Add $((\mathsf{M}_{\mathsf{pre}}, \mathsf{acc}_{\mathsf{pre}}, S; r), (\mathsf{M}_{\mathsf{after}}, \mathsf{acc}_{\mathsf{after}}, S+1, h_2))$ to $\mathbb{L}$ and return $(\mathsf{M}_{\mathsf{after}}, \mathsf{acc}_{\mathsf{after}}, S+1, h_2)$ to the miner.

We assume the distribution of $\mathsf{acc}_{\mathsf{after}}$ following the distribution $\mathcal{D}$ over $\{\mathsf{acc} : \mathsf{acc} \geq D_{\mathsf{acc}}\}$ such that $\Pr[\mathsf{acc}_{\mathsf{after}} \geq T_{\mathsf{acc}} | \mathsf{acc}_{\mathsf{pre}} \geq D_{\mathsf{acc}}] = f_1$, and $\Pr[\mathsf{acc}_{\mathsf{after}} \geq T_{\mathsf{acc}} | \mathsf{acc}_{\mathsf{pre}} < D_{\mathsf{acc}}] = \epsilon$ where ϵ is negligible of the security parameter λ.

5.2 Proving Ledger Properties

Consider the situation in which a deep learning task task_i spans over time slots $\mathsf{T}_i = \{t_{i,j}\}_{j \in [\ell]}$. We omit i in the following for simplicity. The hash function in the PreHash algorithm guarantees that a new block is never added between two existing blocks (insertions), the same block never occurs in two different positions (copies), and a block never extends a block that will be mined in later time slots (predictions).

The Longest-Chain-Based Protocol. A miner who outputs a block in slot t_j that meets the post-hash check, target accuracy, and step restriction has to perform at least S_j training steps, which is equivalent to S_j queries to $\mathcal{O}_{\mathsf{Train}}$. As miners, honest or adversarial, are bounded by the number of queries they can make in each round, they cannot generate too many blocks in any polynomial many consecutive rounds within the period T of task_i. Simultaneously, miners cannot generate too few blocks because the probability of at least one honest miner outputting a block is lower bounded by the success rate of the oracle.

Like [11], we define typical execution for the situation in which miners generate not too many nor too few blocks in polynomial many consecutive rounds of protocol execution. First, we consider three Boolean random variables X_r, Y_r, Z_{rpq}. If at round r an honest miner obtains an output from the oracle $\mathcal{O}_{\mathsf{Train}}$ that satisfies $h_2 \leq T_2 \wedge \mathcal{R}(\mathsf{acc}_{\mathsf{after}}, T_{\mathsf{acc}}) = 1$, then $X_r = 1$, otherwise $X_r = 0$. If at round r exactly one honest miner obtains such an output, then $Y_r = 1$, otherwise $Y_r = 0$. For the adversary, if at round r, the p-th corrupted miner's q-th query to the oracle $\mathcal{O}_{\mathsf{Train}}$ obtains such an output, then $Z_{rpq} = 1$, otherwise $Z_{rpq} = 0$. Hence, we define a variable $Z_r = \sum_p \sum_q Z_{rpq}$. For a set X of k consecutive rounds, we define $X(X) = \sum_{r \in X} X_r, Y(X) = \sum_{r \in X} Y_r, Z(X) = \sum_{r \in X} Z_r$.

Definition 2 $((\epsilon, k)$**-typical execution).** *Let* $\epsilon \in (0, 1)$ *and* $k \in \mathbb{N}$, *an execution is* (ϵ, k)-*typical if for any set* X *of at least* k *consecutive rounds within the period of a deep learning task, the following holds:*

- $(1 - \epsilon)\mathbb{E}[X(X)] < X(X) < (1 + \epsilon)\mathbb{E}[X(X)], (1 - \epsilon)\mathbb{E}[Y(X)] < Y(X);$
- $Z(X) < \mathbb{E}[S(X)] + \epsilon\mathbb{E}[X(X)].$

Theorem 1. *Assume the training oracle and at most* $\beta < \frac{1}{2}$ *corrupted miners each round, the longest-chain-based D-PoDL blockchain protocol satisfies the robust ledger properties (Definition 1).*

Proof. We first prove the following lemma.

Lemma 1. *An execution is* (ϵ, k)-*typical with probability* $1 - e^{-\Omega(\epsilon^2 kp)}$ *where* p *is the probability of at least one honest miner obtaining a model that satisfies* $h_2 \leq T_2 \wedge \mathsf{acc} \geq T_{\mathsf{acc}}$.

Let $\mathsf{acc}_{\mathsf{after}}$ be the input accuracy to $\mathcal{O}_{\mathsf{Train}}$ and D_{acc} be the difficulty threshold, according to our oracle description, the probability of the output accuracy $\mathsf{acc}_{\mathsf{after}}$ surpassing the target threshold T_{acc} in a query reply is:

$$
\begin{aligned}
\Pr[\mathsf{acc}_{\mathsf{after}} \geq T_{\mathsf{acc}}] &= \Pr[\mathsf{acc}_{\mathsf{after}} \geq T_{\mathsf{acc}} \wedge \mathsf{acc}_{\mathsf{pre}} \geq D_{\mathsf{acc}}] \\
&\quad + \Pr[\mathsf{acc}_{\mathsf{after}} \geq T_{\mathsf{acc}} \wedge \mathsf{acc}_{\mathsf{pre}} < D_{\mathsf{acc}}] \\
&\geq \Pr[\mathsf{acc}_{\mathsf{after}} \geq T_{\mathsf{acc}} | \mathsf{acc}_{\mathsf{pre}} \geq D_{\mathsf{acc}}] \cdot \Pr[\mathsf{acc}_{\mathsf{pre}} \geq D_{\mathsf{acc}}] \\
&= f_1 \cdot \Pr[\mathsf{acc}_{\mathsf{pre}} \geq D_{\mathsf{acc}}],
\end{aligned}
$$

For a query, we have $\Pr[\mathsf{acc}_{\mathsf{pre}} \geq D_{\mathsf{acc}}] \geq 1/2$, as we assumed training steps before reaching D_{acc}, which is less than the step number afterward. Thus, a miner who makes at least one query to $\mathcal{O}_{\mathsf{Train}}$ in a round obtains $\mathsf{acc}_{\mathsf{after}} \geq T_{\mathsf{acc}}$ from $\mathcal{O}_{\mathsf{Train}}$ with probability at least $\frac{1}{2} \cdot f_1$.

Let f_2 be the probability of at least one honest miner obtaining an h_2 from the training oracle $\mathcal{O}_{\mathsf{Train}}$ that satisfies $h_2 \leq T_2$ in a round. Because the output of the training algorithm is independent to the hash function, the probability of at least one honest miner obtaining a tuple $(\mathsf{M}_{\mathsf{after}}, \mathsf{acc}_{\mathsf{after}}, S{+}1, h_2)$ that satisfies $h_2 \leq T_2 \wedge \mathsf{acc}_{\mathsf{after}} \geq T_{\mathsf{acc}}$ should be at least $p \geq \frac{1}{2} \cdot f_1 \cdot f_2$ (and at most $p \leq f_2$).

Next, we analyze the probability of execution being typical. Note that the training oracle $\mathcal{O}_{\mathsf{Train}}$ takes queries with different training random seeds (r) as different queries. Moreover, a hash function, modeled as a random oracle, generates such random seeds in the pre-hash $\mathsf{PreHash}$ algorithm. Hence, the probability of two honest parties querying $\mathcal{O}_{\mathsf{Train}}$ with the same input in polynomial many rounds of execution is negligible of the security parameter λ. Such property enables us to condition the probability space on the event that no two honest parties query $\mathcal{O}_{\mathsf{Train}}$ with the same input in a polynomial many rounds of execution. In this space, the random variables X_r (and similarly Y_r and Z_{rpq}) are independent Bernoulli trials where each trail is successful with probability $\Theta(p)$ (as analyzed above). Hence, by the Chernoff bound, we prove the probability of an (ϵ, k)-typical execution is $1 - e^{-\Omega(\epsilon^2 kp)}$.

Directly from [11], we have the following lemma that parameterizes the chain growth, existential chain quality, and common prefix in a typical execution.

Lemma 2. *In an (ϵ, k)-typical execution, the chain growth property holds for parameter $\tau = (1-\epsilon)p$ and $s \geq k$, the existential chain quality property holds for parameter $s \geq 2kp$, and the common prefix property hold for parameter $s \geq 2kp$.*

Finally, by Lemma 1, we choose $k = \Omega(\log^2 \lambda)$ so that an execution fails to be typical with negligible probability of the security parameter λ. Therefore, we prove Theorem 1 with the parameters following Lemma 2.

The Weight-Based Protocol. One concern is that selecting models with inferior accuracy may accelerate the block generation rate because training such models requires fewer steps in each time slot. The block may not be adequately propagated to all honest miners before the next block is generated. To prevent so, we require the weight function to be appropriately bounded (with isolated-lower-bounds and upper-bounds, definitions can be found in [13]) so that the low block weight indicates low model accuracy and the low accuracy models are hard to be selected according to the weight function. Like the typical execution, we adopt model isolation (Definition 3) from [13] for the situation in which the round gap between any two models with sufficient accuracy is longer than the unknown network delay. Under the properly bounded weight functions, we further argue that our model-referencing mechanism cannot break model isolation. A miner has to perform enough training steps so that the total step number of its model, including all the referenced models, is no less than the total steps of the selected models (**Restriction**). Hence, the model-referencing mechanism offers no advantage to the miner in generating a model *faster*. Finally, we conclude the following theorem for the weight-based protocol.

Definition 3 (acc-Isolation). *Let M be the model embedded in the block mined in round r within the period of a deep learning task. M is left-isolated if M is generated by an honest miner, $\mathsf{acc_M} \geq \mathsf{acc}$, and there is no block on the left embedding a model with accuracy higher than acc in rounds $[r - \Delta, r]$ where Δ is the unknown network delay. M is isolated if M is generated by an honest miner, $\mathsf{acc_M} \geq \mathsf{acc}$, and there is no block embedding a model with accuracy higher than acc in rounds $[r - \Delta, r + \Delta]$.*

Theorem 2. *Assume the training oracle and at most $\beta < \frac{1}{2}$ corrupted miners each round, the weight-based D-PoDL blockchain protocol satisfies the weight-based robust ledger properties (Definition 1) if the weight function is isolated-lower-bounded and upper-bounded.*

Proof. It has been proven that a secure longest-chain-based blockchain protocol can be transformed into a secure weight-based protocol as long as the weight function is properly bounded [13]. We refer to their results and argue that our model-referencing mechanism will not break the proof.

First, for *chain growth*, the restrictions on training step number in Sect. 4.1 enable honest miners to have enough time for block propagation. Therefore, honest miners will have at least one chain that accumulates the weight from all left-isolated blocks. Assuming the weight function is left-isolated-lower-bounded, the probability of this accumulated weight being inferior to the lower bound is negligible to the security parameter. Next, for *chain quality*, the chain growth property guarantees that the chain will accumulate at least all left-isolated blocks' weights. Moreover, the adversary cannot generate left-isolated blocks fast enough because it has to perform enough training steps, and the total weight is upper bounded by the weight function. Finally, since model-referencing will not change block selection, *i.e.*, honest miners will only extend chains with sufficient weights by each round, *common prefix* preserves regardless of model-referencing.

6   Implementation of D-PoDL Scheme

This section shows a toy example for our D-PoDL scheme implementation. We compare the PoW scheme and the plain deep learning to our D-PoDL scheme with different sets of threshold parameters (T_1, T_2, T_{acc}). We utilize the MNIST dataset to implement deep learning-based schemes, *i.e.*, plain deep learning and our D-PoDL, and follow the original split of 60000 images for training and 10000 images for testing. Results can be found in Table 2.

Table 2. Experiment Results

Scheme/Algorithm	Average	Maximum	Minimum	Variance
PoW (2^{224})	433.37	1242.53	0.63	122336.11
Deep learning (0.97)	81.88	126.61	75.24	109.19
D-PoDL ($2^{240}, 2^{256}, 0.97$)	94.26	122.38	75.23	320.99
D-PoDL ($2^{244}, 2^{255}, 0.97$)	140.60	195.68	115.36	648.97

On MacBook Pro with 2.3GHz quad-core Intel Core i5 and 8GB of 2133MHz LPDDR3 onboard memory; Time consumption is presented in seconds and recorded for 20 attempts.

In the PoW implementation, we use a 256-bit hash function, *e.g.*, SHA-256, and set the difficulty to be $T = 2^{228}$, *i.e.*, to find a nonce with $\mathsf{Hash}(\mathsf{prevBK}, \mathsf{nonce}) < T$. Hence, the expected hash iteration is 2^{28}. Next, In the plain deep learning implementation, we set the batch size to 128, the learning rate to 0.001, and the target threshold to 0.97. Most models reach this threshold in 2 epochs, each including 387 training steps. Finally, in the two D-PoDL's Solve algorithm, we implement with $(T_1, T_2, T_{acc}) = (2^{240}, 2^{256}, 0.97)$ and $(2^{244}, 2^{255}, 0.97)$. For $T_2 = 2^{256}$, since the post-hash accepts all models, we use it to distinguish the impact of the pre-hash algorithm PreHash. The change in time comes from two factors: (1) Computation overhead from the hash function; (2) Training speed due to the different hyper-parameters. For the second D-PoDL implementation, the post-hash check significantly prolongs the average solving time despite the fact that we lower the pre-hash threshold T_1 to 2^{244}. The result indicates that the post-hash plays an important role in controlling the solution generation speed, which is the overall difficulty of the scheme.

Concerning variance values, we observe a big gap between deep learning-based schemes and the PoW scheme. The reason is that the stochastic gradient descent algorithm that optimizes the neural network has a more consistent convergence speed. In contrast, a well-behaving hash function in the PoW scheme should follow the uniform distribution with a high variance. However, low variance is not always preferable because the algorithm should involve enough stochasticity to prevent domination, *i.e.*, the miner with the most computing power generates all blocks. By comparing the variance value of the deep learning-based schemes, we notice that both pre-hash and post-hash algorithms involve randomness in the solving time, which can benefit the fairness among miners.

7   Conclusion

This paper extends the concept of deep learning-based proof-of-useful-work with distribution in solving the deep learning task. We then formalize the extended scheme as distributed proof-of-deep-learning (D-PoDL). Our novel designs, hash-training-hash, and model-referencing, enable users to train models distributively without suffering from grinding attacks and pre-computation attacks, which have not been achieved by any previous work. Next, a generic blockchain protocol is built atop the D-PoDL scheme alongside two concrete construction based on the longest-chain rule and the weight-based framework. We prove security for both concrete protocols in terms of robust ledger properties, which again is the first paper to achieve so. Finally, we implement the D-PoDL scheme to compare with PoW and deep learning-based schemes. We conclude that our D-PoDL fits in the middle point of these existing schemes with a more stabilized solution generation speed and enough randomness for fairness.

References

1. Badertscher, C., Garay, J., Maurer, U., Tschudi, D., Zikas, V.: But why does it work? a rational protocol design treatment of bitcoin. In: Nielsen, J.B., Rijmen, V. (eds.) EUROCRYPT 2018. LNCS, vol. 10821, pp. 34–65. Springer, Cham (2018). https://doi.org/10.1007/978-3-319-78375-8_2
2. Baldominos, A., Saez, Y.: Coin. AI: a proof-of-useful-work scheme for blockchain-based distributed deep learning. Entropy **21**(8), 723 (2019). https://doi.org/10.3390/e21080723
3. Ball, M., Rosen, A., Sabin, M., Vasudevan, P.N.: Proofs of work from worst-case assumptions. In: Shacham, H., Boldyreva, A. (eds.) CRYPTO 2018. LNCS, vol. 10991, pp. 789–819. Springer, Cham (2018). https://doi.org/10.1007/978-3-319-96884-1_26

4. Bergstra, J., Bengio, Y.: Random search for hyper-parameter optimization. J. Mach. Learn. Res. **13**, 281–305 (2012). http://dl.acm.org/citation.cfm?id=2188395

5. Blocki, J., Zhou, H.-S.: Designing proof of human-work puzzles for cryptocurrency and beyond. In: Hirt, M., Smith, A. (eds.) TCC 2016. LNCS, vol. 9986, pp. 517–546. Springer, Heidelberg (2016). https://doi.org/10.1007/978-3-662-53644-5_20

6. Canetti, R.: Universally composable security: a new paradigm for cryptographic protocols. In: 42nd Annual Symposium on Foundations of Computer Science, FOCS 2001, 14–17 October 2001, Las Vegas, Nevada, USA, pp. 136–145. IEEE Computer Society (2001). https://doi.org/10.1109/SFCS.2001.959888

7. Chenli, C., Li, B., Jung, T.: DLchain: blockchain with deep learning as proof-of-useful-work. In: Ferreira, J.E., Palanisamy, B., Ye, K., Kantamneni, S., Zhang, L.-J. (eds.) SERVICES 2020. LNCS, vol. 12411, pp. 43–60. Springer, Cham (2020). https://doi.org/10.1007/978-3-030-59595-1_4

8. Chenli, C., Li, B., Shi, Y., Jung, T.: Energy-recycling blockchain with proof-of-deep-learning. In: IEEE International Conference on Blockchain and Cryptocurrency, ICBC 2019, Seoul, Korea (South), 14–17 May 2019, pp. 19–23. IEEE (2019). https://doi.org/10.1109/BLOC.2019.8751419

9. Coelho, F.: An (almost) constant-effort solution-verification proof-of-work protocol based on Merkle trees. In: Vaudenay, S. (ed.) AFRICACRYPT 2008. LNCS, vol. 5023, pp. 80–93. Springer, Heidelberg (2008). https://doi.org/10.1007/978-3-540-68164-9_6

10. Fitzi, M., Kiayias, A., Panagiotakos, G., Russell, A.: Ofelimos: combinatorial optimization via proof-of-useful-work a provably secure blockchain protocol. In: Dodis, Y., Shrimpton, T. (eds.) CRYPTO 2022. Lecture Notes in Computer Science, vol. 13508, pp. 339–369. Springer, Cham (2022). https://doi.org/10.1007/978-3-031-15979-4_12

11. Garay, J., Kiayias, A., Leonardos, N.: The bitcoin backbone protocol: analysis and applications. In: Oswald, E., Fischlin, M. (eds.) EUROCRYPT 2015. LNCS, vol. 9057, pp. 281–310. Springer, Heidelberg (2015). https://doi.org/10.1007/978-3-662-46803-6_10

12. Garay, J.A., Kiayias, A., Leonardos, N., Panagiotakos, G.: Bootstrapping the blockchain, with applications to consensus and fast PKI setup. In: Abdalla, M., Dahab, R. (eds.) PKC 2018. LNCS, vol. 10770, pp. 465–495. Springer, Cham (2018). https://doi.org/10.1007/978-3-319-76581-5_16

13. Kamp, S.H., Magri, B., Matt, C., Nielsen, J.B., Thomsen, S.E., Tschudi, D.: Weight-based Nakamoto-style blockchains. In: Longa, P., Ràfols, C. (eds.) LATINCRYPT 2021. LNCS, vol. 12912, pp. 299–319. Springer, Cham (2021). https://doi.org/10.1007/978-3-030-88238-9_15

14. Lan, Y., Liu, Y., Li, B., Miao, C.: Proof of learning (pole): empowering machine learning with consensus building on blockchains (demo). In: Thirty-Fifth AAAI Conference on Artificial Intelligence, AAAI 2021, Thirty-Third Conference on Innovative Applications of Artificial Intelligence, IAAI 2021, The Eleventh Symposium on Educational Advances in Artificial Intelligence, EAAI 2021, Virtual Event, 2–9 February 2021, pp. 16063–16066. AAAI Press (2021). https://ojs.aaai.org/index.php/AAAI/article/view/18013

15. Li, B., Chenli, C., Xu, X., Jung, T., Shi, Y.: Exploiting computation power of blockchain for biomedical image segmentation. In: IEEE Conference on Computer Vision and Pattern Recognition Workshops, CVPR Workshops 2019, Long Beach, CA, USA, 16–20 June 2019, pp. 2802–2811. Computer Vision Foundation/IEEE (2019). https://doi.org/10.1109/CVPRW.2019.00339, http://

openaccess.thecvf.com/content_CVPRW_2019/html/BCMCVAI/Li_Exploiting_Computation_Power_of_Blockchain_for_Biomedical_Image_Segmentation_CVPRW_2019_paper.html

16. Lihu, A., Du, J., Barjaktarevic, I., Gerzanics, P., Harvilla, M.: A proof of useful work for artificial intelligence on the blockchain. CoRR abs/2001.09244 (2020). https://arxiv.org/abs/2001.09244

17. Pass, R., Shi, E.: Fruitchains: a fair blockchain. In: Schiller, E.M., Schwarzmann, A.A. (eds.) Proceedings of the ACM Symposium on Principles of Distributed Computing, PODC 2017, Washington, DC, USA, 25–27 July 2017, pp. 315–324. ACM (2017). https://doi.org/10.1145/3087801.3087809

Security Model for Privacy-Preserving Blockchain-Based Cryptocurrency Systems

Mayank Raikwar[1(✉)], Shuang Wu[2], and Kristian Gjøsteen[3]

[1] University of Oslo, Oslo, Norway
mayankr@ifi.uio.no
[2] DNV, Trondheim, Norway
Shuang.Wu@dnv.no
[3] Norwegian University of Science and Technology (NTNU), Trondheim, Norway
kristian.gjosteen@ntnu.no

Abstract. Privacy-preserving blockchain-based cryptocurrency systems have become quite popular as a way to provide confidential payments. These cryptocurrency systems differ in their designs, underlying cryptography, and confidentiality level. Some of these systems provide confidentiality for their users or transactions or both. There has been a thriving interest in constructing different privacy-preserving cryptocurrency systems with improved security and additional features. Nevertheless, many of these available systems lack security models which makes it hard to prove the security properties of these systems.

Despite the differences in the privacy notions of existing privacy-preserving cryptocurrency systems, in this paper, we present a first attempt to create a general framework for a privacy-preserving blockchain-based bank PBB. We present the security properties of this system and model the security experiments for each of the properties. Our PBB model can also work for bank-less cryptocurrency systems. Henceforth, we present a brief security analysis for one of the most notable privacy-preserving cryptocurrencies, Monero, using the security model of the PBB system. Our analysis proves that our PBB system can be easily used to formalise the security of other available privacy-preserving cryptocurrencies.

1 Introduction

Privacy-preserving blockchain-based cryptocurrency systems are financial systems that allow users to conduct cryptocurrency transactions. Similar to online banks, users can store their funds in cryptocurrencies, transfer cryptocurrencies between each other and withdraw their funds to fiat money. The privacy-preserving feature is that these financial activities are not completely transparent to the outsiders, in contrast to Bitcoin [16] and Ethereum [22] where

---

M. Raikwar and S. Wu—This work was done in part while the author was at NTNU, Norway.

S. Li et al. (Eds.): NSS 2023, LNCS 13983, pp. 137–152, 2023.
https://doi.org/10.1007/978-3-031-39828-5_8

transaction information is public. There are many constructions of privacy-preserving blockchain-based cryptocurrency systems [2,3,5,9–11,18,20], both in the literature and deployed. Even though these systems offer the same functionalities/services to the end-users, each of them has its own definitions and security claims, and some of them even lack security proofs despite being deployed. The diversity of the definitions and security models makes it hard to analyse and compare these protocols in general, resulting in less convincing security claims. There is therefore a need for a unified formal description and security model for these systems which we attempt to provide in this paper. The security model presented in the paper can be further matured by formal verification.

Giving a general definition and security model for privacy-preserving cryptocurrency systems is not a simple task since the systems vary in many aspects. Depending on the amount of information released to the public, these systems provide different levels of privacy which is captured by the security model. Some designs [3,7] provide confidential transactions where transfer values are hidden, but the identities of the senders and recipients are public. In anonymous cryptocurrencies such as Monero [20] and Zcash [18], the identities that are relevant to a certain transaction are hidden, but they still have a somewhat different form of anonymity. In addition to the differences in privacy levels, these systems also differ structurally from each other. They can generally be divided as: Layer 1 blockchain-based anonymous cryptocurrency like Monero, Zcash and Zether [3] and Layer 2 cryptocurrency like Pribank [7]. Pribank introduces a semi-trusted centralized bank operator above the blockchain which hides the sensitive information while relaying the users' transactions to the blockchain periodically.

Despite the above differentiation among the systems, we attempt to build a general model for privacy-preserving cryptocurrency systems. Firstly, we rename these systems as blockchain-based online banks, as the functionality and the services these systems provide are mostly identical to the traditional online bank system. Our model is capable of expressing the differences of privacy, and it captures the most essential functionality and properties of an online financial system (online bank) regardless of how they use the blockchain. We provide a security model that has two essential security properties: *Transaction Indistinguishability* (T-IND) and *Overdraft Safety*. Transaction indistinguishability captures the privacy features of an online bank, informally speaking, a transaction record on the blockchain does not reveal any information about the user's activity. Overdraft safety claims an honest user is always able to withdraw his/her full balance. This implies that no adversary can steal others' funds or withdraw more than it has.

The definition of transaction indistinguishability was first proposed by Zether without formalisation. There is a corresponding security definition in Zcash which is called *Ledger Indistinguishability* (L-IND). We prove that these two concepts are equivalent, but we believe that transaction indistinguishably is intuitively easier to use. In addition, we add a leakage function to the security experiment which controls the amount of information that is leaked to the adversary. By this leakage function, the model is able to express different privacy levels, i.e., from confidential transactions to completely anonymous transactions.

The proposed security model is built by following and modifying the security model of PriBank [7]. Our proposed model can also be employed to assess the security of bank-less cryptocurrency systems. We demonstrate the applicability and usability of our model by applying it to Monero as a case study.

1.1 Contribution

This paper presents a general definition and security model for the privacy-preserving blockchain-based online bank for cryptocurrencies. Our model can express different levels of privacy regardless of the structure of the systems. We prove that two privacy-related security definitions in the literature, *Transaction indistinguishability* and *Ledger Indistinguishability*, are equivalent. We also discuss the relationship among the definitions that are related to the integrity of the protocol, namely, *Balance* and *Overdraft Safety*. We give a general security model for a blockchain-based online bank system that has two essential properties: transaction indistinguishability and overdraft safety. We believe the proposed security notions are helpful to simplify and formalise the security analysis for privacy-preserving blockchain-based cryptocurrencies. We further analyse the security properties of anonymous cryptocurrency system Monero.

1.2 Related Work

There are many constructions of privacy-preserving blockchain based online banks for cryptocurrencies [2,3,5,9–11,18–20]. These systems are either built on top of an underlying blockchain or on top of a smart contract. The main goal of these systems are to provide privacy for their users and transactions. A detailed overview of can be found here [1]. These systems employ cryptographic primitives such as zero-knowledge proofs, ring signatures, or mixing techniques, and achieve a variety of different trade-offs with respect to privacy.

After the proposal of the Zcash [18] system, many follow-up [2,8,9,12,15,23] ledger-based constructions were proposed offering different meaningful privacy notions for cryptocurrency systems. Furthermore, the security model of these systems is based on the security model of Zcash. Systems such as Hawk [12], Zexe [2] and Z-Channel [23] provide on-chain privacy by performing high-frequency transactions (computation) off-chain. Hawk and Zexe employ zk-SNARK proof systems to generate privacy-preserving transactions. But neither system defines its security model and underlying properties. Z-Channel [23] is a micropayment system that adds multi-signature and time-lock functionalities to the Zcash. Z-Channel follows the security model of Zcash to prove its security guarantees.

Zcash inspired systems such as Lelantus [8], Spark [9] and a scheme by Mitani and Otsuka [15] provide on-chain privacy with additional usability features. Lelantus [8] is an anonymous payment system that ensures confidentiality, small proof size, and fast transaction verification. Spark [9] is a modification to the Lelantus that provides recipient privacy and opt-in transaction visibility to third parties. Mitani and Otsuka [15] constructed a Confidential and Auditable Payment (CAP) scheme. A CAP scheme uploads encrypted transactions to the ledger and also allows an authority to audit the transactions while keeping the transactions confidential. The security of all these on-chain privacy-enabled payment schemes is defined by following the security model of the Zcash system.

Privacy-preserving systems can also be built on top of smart contracts. Zether [3], zKay [19] and Kachina [10] are such systems built on Ethereum. These systems establish privacy-preserving smart contracts to provide confidential payment or confidential data. Zether [3] defines its security properties but does not provide formal security proofs which are essential to prove the security of an anonymous payment system. zKay [19] defines its privacy model by defining a language zKay for writing smart contracts with private data. Further, these contracts are transformed to be executable on Ethereum. zKay presents different security notions related to indistinguishability and privacy of data. However, the security proofs in zKay are informal and require more formalization.

Kachina [10] provides a unified security model based on the Universal Composition (UC) model to deploy privacy-preserving, general-purpose smart contracts. The security model of Kachina consists of complex proofs and does not capture properties, e.g., liveness. Kachina gives a proof sketch of Zcash but it is hard to justify whether Kachina actually manages to capture all the security properties through the UC-emulated Zcash contract. Hence, Kachina's security model cannot be used to assess the security of other privacy-preserving systems.

Another class of privacy-enabled systems is based on ring signature. The most notable one is Monero [20]. Using ring signatures Monero achieves anonymity of transacting parties. To achieve confidentiality, Monero uses confidential transactions together with a ring signature, referred to as Ring Confidential Transaction (RingCT). Although there has been a decent amount of work to explore the attacks on Monero [21], to the best of our knowledge only a recent work [4] formalises the security of Monero (published after the submission of this work).

There have been several attempts to analyze the security of RingCT, but due to the complexity of RingCT, most of them either provide informal proofs or miss the fundamental functionality. Moreover, Monero limits the ring size to only a few accounts. Therefore, to solve these issues, a new scheme, Omniring [13] was constructed that not only solves the above issues but also provides improved privacy without sacrificing performance. Omniring does provide a security model followed by rigorous proofs for its scheme but its model is quite complex and cannot be generalized to assess the security of other privacy-preserving systems.

Other works providing provable security notions are Quisquis [6] and an anonymous mixing scheme [14]. The security proofs in these schemes provide targeted security notions but it is not clear how these notions can be generalized.

The above described privacy-preserving systems define a number of security properties. A few main security properties can be (informally) described as:

- *Transaction Indistinguishability* Given two different transactions tx_0, tx_1 from an adversary $\mathcal{A}$, the ledger L records only one transaction tx_i where $i \in \{0, 1\}$, the adversary $\mathcal{A}$ cannot distinguish which transaction was recorded.
- *Ledger Indistinguishability* Given two different ledgers L_0, L_1 constructed by an adversary $\mathcal{A}$ using queries to two privacy-preserving system oracles, the adversary $\mathcal{A}$ cannot distinguish between L_0 and L_1.

- *Overdraft Safety* Given an adversary $\mathcal{A}$, an honest user can always spend (or withdraw) the funds that he rightfully owns.
- *Balance* No bounded adversary $\mathcal{A}$ can control more money than he minted or received.

Although there have been many constructions of privacy-preserving systems, as discussed above only a few systems define their security. This demonstrates a need to define a generic privacy-preserving blockchain-based cryptocurrency system and formalize its security. Therefore, we present a formal definition of a privacy-preserving blockchain-based bank system (PBB), followed by an analysis of essential security properties. We analyze the security of Monero system using our framework. Due to the expressiveness of our framework, our analysis can be further used to model the security of other structurally different systems having different levels of privacy such as Zcash, Dash [5], zKay [19], and Spark [9].

2   Privacy-Preserving Blockchain-Based Bank

Privacy-preserving cryptocurrency systems, despite different structures, aim to provide end-users services similar to an online bank. Based on this fact, we call these systems privacy-preserving blockchain-based online banks. In this section, we formally define this notion. In blockchain-based online banks, an entity always keeps two types of states: permanent state and temporary state. Permanent states are states that are already recorded on the blockchain, temporary states are states not recorded on the blockchain yet. We denote TempSt_x as temporary state and St_x as permanent state of an entity x (bank or a user).

We adapt the blockchain-based bank (BBank) defined in [7] and modify it to formally define a unified privacy-preserving blockchain-based bank (PBB). The BBank is a Layer 2 account-based ledger that works periodically in terms of epochs. Hence, the PBB is also based on an account-based model. However, our PBB system can also be used for the security analysis of UTXO-based systems.

Note: Depending on the concrete structure of a cryptocurrency system and its underlying ledger model, some algorithms in this definition can be eliminated.

Definition 1 (PBB). *A Privacy-preserving Blockchain-based Bank* **PBB** *is a tuple of algorithms* (Setup, KeyGen, EstablishBank, NewUser, Deposit, Withdraw, Pay, Commit, Contract) *with the following syntax and semantics*

- *The algorithm* Setup *takes input* 1^λ, *where* λ *is the security parameter and generates the public parameters* pp, *to be distributed off-chain. It also initialises a set* KeyList $\leftarrow \emptyset$.
- *The algorithm* KeyGen *takes the public parameters* pp *as input, and generates a key pair for a user* $(\mathsf{pk}_u, \mathsf{sk}_u)$ *or a bank* $(\mathsf{pk}_b, \mathsf{sk}_b)$.
- *The algorithm* EstablishBank *runs only once and establishes a bank. It takes the public parameters* pp *and a key pair* $(\mathsf{pk}_b, \mathsf{sk}_b)$ *of a bank as inputs, generates an initial state of the bank* TempSt_b *and a transaction* trans. *Once the transaction* trans *is accepted by the blockchain, the smart contract is launched.*
  (trans, TempSt_b) $\leftarrow$ EstablishBank($\mathsf{pk}_b, \mathsf{sk}_b, \mathsf{pp}$)

- *The algorithm* NewUser *is performed by a user to register on the smart contract but without any deposit for her account yet. It takes the public parameters* pp, *public key* pk_b *of the bank and the key pair* (pk_u, sk_u) *of a user as inputs, and outputs an initial state of the user* $TempSt_u$ *and a transaction* trans.
  $(trans, TempSt_u) \leftarrow NewUser(pk_b, pk_u, sk_u, pp)$

- *The protocol* Deposit *is run by the bank operator and a user to deposit money on the smart contract. It takes the public parameters* pp, *the key pairs and states of a user* pk_u, sk_u, St_u *and of a bank* pk_b, sk_b, St_b, *epoch counter* epoch, *deposit value* v *as inputs, outputs a transaction* trans *and temporary states of user and bank. Once the transaction* trans *get accepted by the smart contract, the user gets a commitment for her initial balance.*

$$(trans, TempSt_b, TempSt_u) \leftarrow Deposit(pk_b, sk_b, pk_u, sk_u, St_b, St_u, pp, v, epoch)$$

- *The algorithm* Withdraw *is performed by a registered user who wants to exit the bank. It takes the public parameter* pp, *the key pair* (pk_u, sk_u) *of a user, states of the user and the bank* St_u, St_b, *and the amount* v *of the user the bank holds at the epoch counter* epoch, *generates a transaction* trans *and updates the temporary states of this user and the bank.*
  $(trans, TempSt_b, TempSt_u) \leftarrow Withdraw(pk_u, sk_u, St_b, St_u, pp, v, epoch)$

- *The protocol* Pay *is run by the bank and a user (payer* p*) to send funds to other users. It takes the public key* pk_r *of the receiver* r, *the key pair* (pk_p, sk_p) *of the payer and* (pk_b, sk_b) *of the bank, the temporary states* $TempSt_p, TempSt_b$ *of the payer and the bank, the epoch counter* epoch *and the transferred amount* v′ *as inputs, and then it updates the temporary states of the payer and the bank.*

$$(TempSt_p', TempSt_b') \leftarrow Pay(pk_b, sk_b, pk_p, sk_p, pk_r, TempSt_p, TempSt_b, pp, v', epoch)$$

- *The algorithm* Commit *is performed by the bank at the end of each epoch* epoch. *It takes the key pair* (pk_b, sk_b), *and the states* $St_b, TempSt_b$ *of the bank as inputs and generates a transaction* trans *and updates the temporary state.*

$$(trans, TempSt_b') \leftarrow Commit(pk_b, sk_b, St_b, TempSt_b, epoch)$$

- *The algorithm* Contract *takes the public parameters* pp, *a transaction* trans, *all users' states* $\{St_u\}, \{TempSt_u\}$ *and bank states* $St_b, TempSt_b$ *as inputs and then updates all of them.*

$$(St_b', \{St_u'\}, TempSt_b', \{TempSt_u'\}) \leftarrow Contract(\{St_u\}, \{TempSt_u\}, St_b, TempSt_b, trans, pp)$$

3   Security Properties

In this section, we provide a brief description of security properties associated with the privacy-preserving blockchain-based online bank for cryptocurrencies. To define these properties, first, we define a notion of *Public Consistent* that

Q = (KeyGen)

1. Compute $(pk, sk) := KeyGen(pp)$
2. Add (pk, sk) to the key list KeyList
3. Output the public key pk

Q = (EstablishBank, pk_b, sk_b)

1. If (pk_b, sk_b) is not in KeyList, output $\perp$
2. Start a bank instance $(trans, TempSt_b)$ $\leftarrow$ EstablishBank(pk_b, sk_b, pp)
3. Store the key pair (pk_b, sk_b) and the temporary state $TempSt_b$ of the bank, initialise the epoch counter as 1
4. Output trans

Q = (NewUser, pk_u, sk_u)

1. If (pk_u, sk_u) is not in KeyList, output $\perp$
2. Compute $(trans, Tempst_u)$ $\leftarrow$ NewUser (pk_b, pk_u, sk_u, pp)
3. Store the key pair (pk_u, sk_u) and the temporary state $TempSt_u$ of the user
4. Output trans

Q = (Deposit, pk_u, v, epoch)

1. If $(pk_u, sk_u, TempSt_u)$ is not recorded, output $\perp$
2. Execute this instance of deposit protocol $(trans, TempSt_b, TempSt_u)$ $\leftarrow$ Deposit $(pk_b, sk_b, pk_u, sk_u, St_b, St_u, pp, v, epoch)$
3. Record the temporary states along with the transaction $(trans, TempSt_b, TempSt_u)$ if already not recorded
4. Output trans

Q = (Pay, pk_p, pk_r, v')

1. If pk_p or pk_r is not in the KeyList, output $\perp$
2. Execute this instance of the pay protocol for payer p and receiver r. $(TempSt_p', TempSt_b')$ $\leftarrow$ Pay$(pk_b, sk_b, pk_p, sk_p, pk_r, TempSt_p, TempSt_b, pp, v', epoch)$
3. Record and output the updated temporary states of the user and the bank $(TempSt_b', TempSt_u')$

Q = (Withdraw, pk_u, v)

1. Compute $(trans, TempSt_b, TempSt_u)$ $\leftarrow$ Withdraw$(pk_u, sk_u, St_b, St_u, pp, v, epoch)$
2. Output trans

Q = (Commit, epoch)

1. Compute $(trans, TempSt_b')$ $\leftarrow$ Commit $(pk_b, sk_b, St_b, TempSt_b, epoch)$
2. Output trans

Q = (Contract, trans)

1. Compute $(St_b', \{St_u'\}, TempSt_b', \{TempSt_u'\})$ $\leftarrow$ Contract$(\{St_u\}, \{TempSt_u\}, St_b, TempSt_b, trans, pp)$
2. Output $\{St_u'\}, St_b'$

Q = (Reveal, pk)

Output the secret key and the state of the user/bank who owns pk, i.e., output sk_u, St_u

Fig. 1. Query Description in Blockchain-based Bank Experiment

will be used in security proofs. Further, we give formal descriptions of the security properties in different ledger models. For the game-based security proofs, we describe the queries in Fig. 1 that an adversary can make in the security experiment. Our security definitions are based on this experiment.

Public Consistent: In our model, an adversary $\mathcal{A}$ will submit queries containing pairs of transactions. Public consistent applies restrictions for the queries that the adversary can make, with the goal being to prevent adversary from winning trivially. Informally, public consistent requires that the queries sent by an adversary $\mathcal{A}$ have transactions of matching type that are identical in terms of publicly-revealed information and the information related to addresses controlled by the adversary $\mathcal{A}$. Apart from public consistent, we also define a leakage function that captures the amount of information that leaked to the adversary for every query that the adversary makes.

Definition 2 (Leakage Function). *A leakage function* Leakage *maps a transaction to the query information leaked:* $\eta \leftarrow$ Leakage(**Q**)

Definition 3 (Public Consistent). *We require the query pairs* (**Q₀**, **Q₁**) *for* **Commit** *and* **Pay** *must be jointly consistent with respect to public information and* $\mathcal{A}$*'s view, namely:*

- *For all the users that the adversary controls (adversary has asked* **Reveal** *query for them), their states in the two banks should be consistent.*
- *If one of the queries* $\mathbf{Q}_0$ *and* $\mathbf{Q}_1$ *is not legitimate, the other query will not be proceeded by the experiment as well.*
- *The leaked information of* $\mathbf{Q}_0$ *and* $\mathbf{Q}_1$ *should be the same, i.e.,* Leakage($\mathbf{Q}_0$) = Leakage($\mathbf{Q}_1$).

3.1 Privacy

Privacy in a privacy-preserving blockchain-based online bank can refer to different meanings, ranging from the privacy of balance or identities of transacting parties to the privacy of transacting amount. Therefore, to capture these privacy requirements, two main security notions have been defined, transaction indistinguishability and ledger indistinguishability. Our preferred notion of transaction indistinguishability captures privacy at a basic level, where each transaction reveals no new information about transacting parties' activity. Ledger indistinguishability meanwhile captures the big picture where the ledger reveals no new information to an adversary beyond the publicly revealed information.

Ledger Indistinguishability. This property states that even in the presence of an adversary that can adaptively induce honest users to perform PBB operations, the ledger does not reveal any new information to the adversary except the publicly available information. Given two PBB scheme oracles $\mathsf{O}_0^{\mathsf{PBB}}$ and $\mathsf{O}_1^{\mathsf{PBB}}$, and two ledgers L_0 and L_1 constructed by a bounded adversary $\mathcal{A}$ using public consistent blockchain-bank queries to the two oracles, ledger indistinguishability implies that the adversary $\mathcal{A}$ cannot distinguish between L_0 and L_1.

Ledger indistinguishability is defined by an experiment L-IND, which involves a polynomial-time adversary $\mathcal{A}$ attempting to break a given PBB scheme. Given a PBB scheme Π, an adversary $\mathcal{A}$ and a challenger $\mathcal{C}$, the experiment L-IND($\Pi, \mathcal{A}$) proceeds as follows: First the challenger $\mathcal{C}$ samples a random bit b and initialises two PBB scheme oracles $\mathsf{O}_0^{\mathsf{PBB}}$ and $\mathsf{O}_1^{\mathsf{PBB}}$, maintaining ledgers L_0 and L_1. Throughout, the challenger $\mathcal{C}$ allows the adversary $\mathcal{A}$ to issue queries to $\mathsf{O}_0^{\mathsf{PBB}}$ and $\mathsf{O}_1^{\mathsf{PBB}}$, thus controlling the behaviour of honest parties on L_0 and L_1. Further, the challenger $\mathcal{C}$ provides the adversary $\mathcal{A}$ with the view of both ledgers, but in a randomized order: $\mathsf{L}_{\mathsf{Left}} := \mathsf{L}_b$ and $\mathsf{L}_{\mathsf{Right}} := \mathsf{L}_{1-b}$. The adversary's goal is to distinguish whether the view he sees corresponds to ($\mathsf{L}_{\mathsf{Left}}, \mathsf{L}_{\mathsf{Right}}$) = ($\mathsf{L}_0, \mathsf{L}_1$), i.e. $b = 0$, or to ($\mathsf{L}_{\mathsf{Left}}, \mathsf{L}_{\mathsf{Right}}$) = ($\mathsf{L}_1, \mathsf{L}_0$), i.e. $b = 1$. The formal description is here [18].

Transaction Indistinguishability. Transaction indistinguishability states that given two different queries of an adversary, only one of the two queries is processed and the ledger is updated with the corresponding transaction. Transaction indistinguishability states that the adversary cannot distinguish which query maps to the recorded transaction. Based on the leakage from the queries sent by the adversary to the ledger, this property can also indicate other notions of privacy such as confidential transactions or anonymity of the transacting parties.

Transaction indistinguishability is defined by an experiment T-IND, which involves a polynomial-time adversary $\mathcal{A}$ attempting to break a given PBB scheme. Given a PBB scheme Π and an adversary $\mathcal{A}$, the (probabilistic) experiment T-IND$(\Pi, \mathcal{A})$ proceeds as follows: The adversary $\mathcal{A}$ is allowed to send all the queries (defined in Fig. 1) except the reveal query for the secret key of the bank. In the challenge phase, first, the experiment randomly chooses $b \leftarrow \{0, 1\}$. The adversary is allowed to make multiple challenge queries. For each challenge query $\mathbf{Q} = \mathbf{Challenge}(\mathbf{Q_0}, \mathbf{Q_1})$ sent by the adversary $\mathcal{A}$, these two queries $\mathbf{Q_0}, \mathbf{Q_1}$ leak same information and the experiment only performs Q_b. At the end of the challenge phase, the adversary sends commit query $\mathbf{Q} = \mathbf{Commit}$ and receives the output trans$_b$. Finally, the adversary outputs a bit $b' \in \{0, 1\}$, and wins the game if $b' = b$. In this experiment T-IND, the queries sent by the adversary $\mathcal{A}$ during the challenge phase should also be public consistent.

3.2   Security

Following, we describe overdraft safety and balance properties and discuss the necessity to capture these in a privacy-preserving blockchain-based online bank.

Overdraft Safety. Informally, overdraft safety specifies that an honest user can withdraw all the balance that he owns in the blockchain. In UTXO based model, overdraft safety means that an honest user can always spend his unspent outputs inductively. In an account-based model, it means that an honest user can withdraw all the balance from his account (using smart contract). This security requirement prohibits an adversary to withdraw more than what it has since otherwise there must be an honest user who cannot withdraw all of his balance.

Experiment. Overdraft safety is defined by an experiment Overdraft, which involves a polynomial-time adversary $\mathcal{A}$ attempting to break a given PBB scheme. We now describe the Overdraft experiment for the PBB system. Given a PBB scheme Π and an adversary $\mathcal{A}$, the (probabilistic) experiment Overdraft$(\Pi, \mathcal{A})$ proceeds as the adversary is capable of sending all the queries in the experiment that we define in Fig. 1. In addition, if the system model involves a transaction relay entity, the adversary can send $\mathbf{Q} = \mathbf{Reveal}$ for the secret key and state of this entity. In the challenge epoch, the adversary wins if in a certain epoch, there is an honest user who tries and fails to withdraw all his balance within one epoch.

Balance. This property requires that no bounded adversary $\mathcal{A}$ can own more money than what he minted or received via payments from others. In other words, adversary $\mathcal{A}$ cannot spend more than what he owns. This property states that the total balance of honest users should not exceed the total balance of the system. In case of a UTXO-based system, an adversary $\mathcal{A}$ can spend more money (public unspent outputs) by directly putting a transaction on the ledger through pouring or by asking honest parties to create such transactions.

Experiment. The balance property is formalised by an experiment Balance, which involves a polynomial-time adversary $\mathcal{A}$ attempting to break a given PBB scheme. Given a PBB scheme Π and adversary $\mathcal{A}$, in the experiment Balance($\Pi, \mathcal{A}$), the adversary $\mathcal{A}$ adaptively interacts with a challenger $\mathcal{C}$ and produces a set of unspent coins. Given Addr as a set of honest user's addresses in ledger L, adversary $\mathcal{A}$ wins the game if the total value the adversary can spend or has spent already is greater than the value it has minted or received that means $v_{unspent} + v_{\mathcal{A} \longrightarrow \text{Addr}} > v_{mint} + v_{\text{Addr} \longrightarrow \mathcal{A}}$.

Note: Security properties such as transaction non-malleability, transaction unlinkability and transaction untraceablility are not covered in this work.

4   Relation Between T-IND and L-IND

4.1   Transaction Indistinguishability Implies Ledger Indistinguishability

Theorem 1. *If there exists an adversary $\mathcal{A}_{\text{T-IND}}$ that can win the T-IND experiment with advantage $\text{Adv}^{\text{PBB}}_{\mathcal{A}_{\text{T-IND}}}$ within runtime t, then there must be an adversary $\mathcal{B}_{\text{L-IND}}$ that can win the L-IND experiment with advantage $\text{Adv}^{\text{PBB}}_{\mathcal{B}_{\text{L-IND}}}$ within runtime essentially t such that*

$$\text{Adv}^{\text{PBB}}_{\mathcal{A}_{\text{T-IND}}} \leq 2\text{Adv}^{\text{PBB}}_{\mathcal{B}_{\text{L-IND}}}.$$

Proof. The proof is a game among a challenger $\mathcal{C}_{\text{L-IND}}$, an adversary $\mathcal{B}_{\text{L-IND}}$ and an adversary $\mathcal{A}_{\text{T-IND}}$. $\mathcal{B}_{\text{L-IND}}$ simulates a challenger $\mathcal{C}_{\text{T-IND}}$.

Initialisation. As described in the L-IND experiment, $\mathcal{C}_{\text{L-IND}}$ at the beginning samples a random bit b and initialises two **PBB** scheme oracles O_0^{PBB} and O_1^{PBB}, it provides adversary $\mathcal{B}_{\text{L-IND}}$ with two ledgers $(\mathsf{L}_{\text{Left}}, \mathsf{L}_{\text{Right}}) = (\mathsf{L}_b, \mathsf{L}_{1-b})$. $\mathcal{B}_{\text{L-IND}}$ is expected to distinguish the order of the ledgers.

Query Phase. When $\mathcal{C}_{\text{T-IND}}(\mathcal{B}_{\text{L-IND}})$ receives queries from $\mathcal{A}_{\text{T-IND}}$, $\mathcal{B}_{\text{L-IND}}$ forwards the queries (Q, Q) to O_0^{PBB} and O_1^{PBB} respectively. When the ledger L_{Left} gets updated by one round, denoted as $\mathsf{L}'_{\text{Left}}$, $\mathcal{C}_{\text{T-IND}}$ extracts the new transaction that is added in the last round, and forwards it back to $\mathcal{A}_{\text{T-IND}}$.

Challenge Phase. When $\mathcal{C}_{\text{T-IND}}(\mathcal{B}_{\text{L-IND}})$ receives two public consistent challenge queries Q_0, Q_1 from $\mathcal{A}_{\text{T-IND}}$, $\mathcal{C}_{\text{T-IND}}$ forwards queries (Q_0, Q_1) to oracles O_0^{PBB} and O_1^{PBB} respectively. When the ledger L_{Left} gets updated to $\mathsf{L}'_{\text{Left}}$, $\mathcal{C}_{\text{T-IND}}$ extracts the new transaction and returns it back to $\mathcal{A}_{\text{T-IND}}$.

Response Phase. If $\mathcal{A}_{\text{T-IND}}$ responds with 0, $\mathcal{B}_{\text{L-IND}}$ sets the view to be $(\mathsf{L}_{\text{Left}}, \mathsf{L}_{\text{Right}}) = (\mathsf{L}_0, \mathsf{L}_1)$, otherwise sets the view as $(\mathsf{L}_{\text{Left}}, \mathsf{L}_{\text{Right}}) = (\mathsf{L}_1, \mathsf{L}_0)$. Return the answer to $\mathcal{C}_{\text{L-IND}}$.

Analysis. The left ledger contains the transactions corresponding to L_b, so the transactions returned to $\mathcal{A}_{\text{T-IND}}$ always correspond to Q_b. It follows that the challenger $\mathcal{C}_{\text{L-IND}}$ and adversary $\mathcal{B}_{\text{L-IND}}$ always simulate the challenger $\mathcal{C}_{\text{T-IND}}$ with the random bit b. It follows that $\mathcal{B}_{\text{L-IND}}$ guesses the order of the ledgers correctly exactly as often as $\mathcal{A}_{\text{T-IND}}$ guesses its challenge bit correctly. The claim follows.

$\square$

4.2 Ledger Indistinguishability Implies Transaction Indistinguishability

In this section, we prove that ledger indistinguishability implies transaction indistinguishability. We first construct an adversary $\mathcal{A}_{\text{T-IND}}$ that only sends one challenge query from an adversary $\mathcal{A}_{\text{MultiT-IND}}$ that sends multiple (l_c) challenge queries. Then we prove that if there exists an adversary $\mathcal{B}_{\text{L-IND}}$ that can break ledger indistinguishability, there must be an adversary $\mathcal{A}_{\text{MultiT-IND}}$ can break transaction indistinguishability.

Lemma 1. *Let* T-IND_{l_c} *denote the transaction indistinguishability game in terms of* l_c *challenge queries, and* T-IND *denote the original transaction indistinguishability game in terms of one challenge query.*

If there exists an adversary $\mathcal{A}_{\text{T-IND}_{l_c}}$ *that can win* T-IND_{l_c} *game with advantage* $\text{Adv}^{\text{PBB}}_{\mathcal{A}_{\text{T-IND}_{l_c}}}$ *within run time* t, *there must be an adversary* $\mathcal{A}_{\text{T-IND}}$ *that can win* T-IND *game with advantage* $\text{Adv}^{\text{PBB}}_{\mathcal{A}_{\text{T-IND}}}$ *within run time essentially* t *such that*

$$\text{Adv}^{\text{PBB}}_{\mathcal{A}_{\text{T-IND}_{l_c}}} \leq l_c \text{Adv}^{\text{PBB}}_{\mathcal{A}_{\text{T-IND}}}.$$

This follows from a standard hybrid argument.

Theorem 2. *If there exists an adversary* $\mathcal{B}_{\text{L-IND}}$ *that can win the* L-IND *game with advantage* $\text{Adv}^{\text{PBB}}_{\mathcal{B}_{\text{L-IND}}}$ *within runtime* t, *then there exists an adversary* $\mathcal{A}_{\text{T-IND}_{l_c}}$ *that can win the* T-IND_{l_c} *game in terms of* l_c *challenge queries, with advantage* $\text{Adv}^{\text{PBB}}_{\mathcal{A}_{\text{T-IND}_{l_c}}}$ *and within runtime essentially* t *such that*

$$\text{Adv}^{\text{PBB}}_{\mathcal{B}_{\text{L-IND}}} \leq 2\text{Adv}^{\text{PBB}}_{\mathcal{A}_{\text{T-IND}_{l_c}}}.$$

Proof. We consider three hybrid games $\mathcal{H}_0$, $\mathcal{H}_1$ and $\mathcal{H}_2$ involving the adversary $\mathcal{B}_{\text{L-IND}}$, and two oracles O_0^{PBB} and O_1^{PBB}. The game constructs two ledgers L_0 and L_1 that the adversary is allowed to see. When the adversary makes a query (Q_0, Q_1), the game provides queries to the oracles and records their transactions on the appropriate ledger. The hybrid $\mathcal{H}_0$ gives the query Q_0 to O_0^{PBB} and Q_1 to O_1^{PBB}. The hybrid $\mathcal{H}_1$ gives the query Q_0 to both oracles. The hybrid $\mathcal{H}_2$ gives the query Q_1 to O_0^{PBB} and Q_0 to O_1^{PBB}. Denote by ϵ_i, $i \in \{0, 1, 2\}$, the probability that the adversary outputs 0 in hybrid $\mathcal{H}_i$.

We see that $\mathcal{H}_0$ behaves the same as the experiment L-IND with $b = 0$, while $\mathcal{H}_2$ behaves the same as the experiment L-IND with $b = 1$. Therefore,

$$\text{Adv}^{\text{PBB}}_{\mathcal{B}_{\text{L-IND}}} = |\epsilon_0 - \epsilon_2| \leq |\epsilon_0 - \epsilon_1| + |\epsilon_1 - \epsilon_2|.$$

Now we consider two adversaries $\mathcal{A}_0$ and $\mathcal{A}_1$ against T-IND. They run a copy of $\mathcal{B}_{\text{L-IND}}$ and an oracle O^{PBB}. They construct two ledgers L_0 and L_1 that the adversary $\mathcal{B}_{\text{L-IND}}$ is allowed to see. When $\mathcal{B}_{\text{L-IND}}$ makes a query (Q_0, Q_1), the adversaries make a query to their own challenge oracle, submit the query Q_0 to O^{PBB}, and update the ledgers. The adversary $\mathcal{A}_0$ makes the challenge query (Q_0, Q_1) and appends the result to L_1, appending the output of O^{PBB} to L_0. The adversary $\mathcal{A}_1$ makes the challenge query (Q_1, Q_0) and appends the result to L_0, appending the output of O^{PBB} to L_1. When $\mathcal{B}_{\text{L-IND}}$ outputs b', the adversaries $\mathcal{A}_0$ and $\mathcal{A}_1$ output b'. Note, the queries made by each adversary are public consistent.

Denote by $\delta_{i,\beta}$, $i \in \{0,1\}$, $\beta \in \{0,1\}$, the probability that the adversary $\mathcal{A}_{\text{L-IND}}$ outputs 0 when $\mathcal{A}_i$ interacts with a T-IND experiment with $b = \beta$. Then the advantage of $\mathcal{A}_i$ is $|\delta_{i,0} - \delta_{i,1}|$.

We see that the adversary $\mathcal{A}_0$ interacting with a T-IND experiment with $b = 1$ behaves exactly as the hybrid $\mathcal{H}_0$, so $\delta_{0,1} = \epsilon_0$. The adversary $\mathcal{A}_0$ interacting with a T-IND experiment with $b = 0$ behaves exactly as the adversary $\mathcal{A}_1$ interacting with a T-IND experiment with $b = 1$, which again behaves exactly as $\mathcal{H}_1$, so $\delta_{0,0} = \delta_{1,1} = \epsilon_1$. And the adversary $\mathcal{A}_1$ interacting with a T-IND experiment with $b = 0$ behaves exactly as the hybrid $\mathcal{H}_2$, so $\delta_{1,0} = \epsilon_2$.

Finally, we consider the adversary $\mathcal{A}_{\text{T-IND}_{l_c}}$. It samples $d \leftarrow^{\$} \{0,1\}$ and runs $\mathcal{A}_d$ and outputs its guess b'. Its advantage is the average advantage of $\mathcal{A}_0$ and $\mathcal{A}_1$. The claim follows. □

5   Security Analysis of Monero

Monero is a cryptocurrency based on CryptoNote protocol [17]. Monero uses ring signature to obfuscate a sender's address among other users' addresses. The value of a user's transaction is hidden by using the zero-knowledge protocol Bulletproof. The receiver's address is a one-time address that cannot be linked. By these techniques, Monero provides unlinkability among transactions to a certain extent, enabling the untraceable payment scheme. The idea of Monero is: An output set O (of size s) of public keys $(pk_1, pk_2, \ldots, pk_m)$ from the existing public keys of monero users $(U_1, U_2, \ldots, U_m)$ is chosen. A user U_k from the set O creates a ring signature σ on its transaction which can be verified by the set of public keys. The ring signature σ makes the signer U identity indistinguishable from the users of set O and hence provides the property of plausible deniability. We present Monero system (algorithms) according to our PBB system as follows.

- **Setup** The algorithm generates the public parameters pp.
- **KeyGen** The algorithm takes pp and generates the key pair for users.
- **Deposit/Mint** The algorithm is run by a miner to generate original coins (base coins) of value v. It takes pp, the ledger state St_{bc} (similar to St_b in PBB), and the key pairs of the miner u, outputs a new unspent transaction and update miner's temporary state.

$$(\text{trans}, \text{TempSt}_u) \leftarrow \text{Deposit}(pk_u, sk_u, St_{bc}, St_u, pp, v)$$

- **Pay** The protocol is run by a user (payer) p to send transactions to other users. It takes an anonymity set (a ring): a set of other irrelevant users' public keys, the size of the set n, the public key of the receiver r, the key pair of the payer, the state of the payer, an unspent transaction with amount v' and the ledger state St_{bc} as inputs, it outputs a transaction with its one time output address, and payer's temporary state.

$$(\text{trans}, \text{TempSt}'_p) \leftarrow \text{Pay}(pk_p, sk_p, pk_r, \{pk_i\}_{i=0}^{n-1}, St_p, St_{bc}, pp, v')$$

- **Contract** The algorithm takes the public parameters, a trans, the public state and all users' states as inputs and then updates all of them.

$$(St'_{bc}, \{St'_u\}) \leftarrow \text{Contract}(St_{bc}, \{St_u\}, \{\text{TempSt}_u\}, \text{trans}, pp)$$

Security Proof Sketch for Monero. Following we first describe the T-IND experiment customised to the algorithms of Monero, and further we define its leakage function to capture the privacy of Monero to give the security proofs.

Experiment. T-IND   Given a (candidate) PBB scheme Π, an adversary $\mathcal{A}$, and security parameter λ, the (probabilistic) experiment T-IND$(\Pi, \mathcal{A}, \lambda)$ proceeds as follows. In the query phase, the adversary is capable of sending queries for the Monero system to the experiment. In the challenge phase, the experiment randomly chooses $b \leftarrow \{0, 1\}$, adversary then sends a challenge query as $\mathbf{Q} = \mathbf{Challenge}(\mathbf{Q_0}, \mathbf{Q_1})$ where $\mathbf{Q_0}, \mathbf{Q_1}$ leak the some information and the experiment only performs Q_b. The adversary gets the output trans_b. At the end, the adversary outputs $b' \in \{0, 1\}$. The adversary wins the game if $b' = b$. During the challenge, the queries sent by the adversary need to be *Public Consistent*.

Leakage Function. The leakage function of Monero takes the total number N of available public keys that can be added into a ring signature , all these public keys $\{pk_i\}_{i=1}^N$, the size of the ring signature n, and a $\mathbf{Q} = (\text{Pay}, pk_p, pk_r, v)$ query as inputs, and outputs a set of public keys that is included in the ring signature.

$$\{pk\}_{j=1}^n \leftarrow \text{Leakage}(\mathbf{Q}, N, n, \{pk_i\}_{i=1}^N)$$

We adopt a game-hopping approach.

Experiment $\mathbf{Exp_0}$. The same as the T-IND experiment.

Experiment $\mathbf{Exp_1}$. The difference between $\mathbf{Exp_1}$ and $\mathbf{Exp_0}$ is that $\mathbf{Exp_1}$ does not use the sender's keys to generate the ring signature, instead, it uses a freshly generated public key in the ring to generate the ring signature on the output transaction. Due to a ring signature, an adversary is not able to distinguish which public key is the real signer, $\mathbf{Exp_1}$ is indistinguishable with $\mathbf{Exp_0}$.

Experiment $\mathbf{Exp_2}$. The experiment $\mathbf{Exp_2}$ modifies $\mathbf{Exp_1}$ by replacing the zero-knowledge proofs for balances by the simulated zero-knowledge proof using the Bulletproof SHVZK simulator. Because of the zero-knowledge property of zero-knowledge proof, the simulated proof reveals no information about the statement, i.e., the balances, thus $\mathbf{Exp_2}$ is indistinguishable with $\mathbf{Exp_1}$. Furthermore, the soundness property of zero-knowledge proof preserves the overdraft.

Experiment Exp$_3$. The **Exp$_3$** modifies **Exp$_2$** by replacing the one time address of the output with a randomly generated address, which is irrelevant to the receiver's public key. Therefore **Exp$_3$** is indistinguishable with **Exp$_2$**.

Balance + Overdraft Safety : Given the experiment Balance involving polynomial-time adversary $\mathcal{A}$ and challenger $\mathcal{C}$, the Monero scheme Π is Balance-secure, if

$$\Pr[\mathsf{Balance}(\Pi, \mathcal{A}) = 1] \leq \mathrm{negl}(\lambda)$$

We present a proof sketch for the above claim. Monero blockchain involves certain types of transaction assertions and for which a number of transaction-related knowledge proofs are implemented. In Monero, each user U has two pairs of private/public keys. The first key pair is the view key pair (k^v, K^v) that allows a user to view the transactions directed to him/her. The other pair is spend key pair (k^s, K^s) that allows the user to spend his/her coins. For each transaction tx, a sender first chooses a random number r and generates a One Time Address (OTA) K^o using r and the receiver's public keys (view and spend keys). The sender sends the K^o along with transaction public key PK_{tx} to the network. The transaction public key $PK_{tx} = rG$, where G is the base point in the elliptic curve. Further, the OTA is recorded in the blockchain.

We say the Monero ledger is balanced if the following conditions hold. In other words at anytime, it is possible to check any user's transaction history by verifying its incoming and outgoing transactions along with its unspent outputs.

- For each valid Pay transaction tx directed to a user U (receiver), U can always verify tx by creating a new OTA and by matching it with the OTA created by the sender. To prove the ownership of incoming transaction tx, the receiver U proves the knowledge of k^v in K^v and with the combination of transaction public key rG, proves the knowledge of $k^v * rG = rK^v$. A verifier having rK^v can check that the OTA is owned by the receiver's address.
- For each valid Pay transaction tx made by a user U (sender), U can verify tx by creating a valid key image for the owned output conditioning the key image has not appeared in the blockchain before. To prove this to a verifier, the sender U provides rK^v to the verifier and proves that it corresponds with the transaction public key rG and the receiver's address.
- For each valid address owned by a user U, the user can always verify to others that the provided address contains a minimum balance. To do that, the user creates key images for the unspent outputs conditioning the key images that have not appeared in the blockchain.

6   Conclusion

Privacy-preserving cryptocurrency systems should ensure the security properties of their systems. Despite having many such systems, there is no unified model to ensure or formalise the security of these systems. This paper attempts to create a general model referred to as a privacy-preserving blockchain-based bank that can be used to prove the security of privacy-preserving cryptocurrency systems. We presented the privacy properties of these systems and also the properties related to the integrity of these systems. Further, to show the usefulness of our model, we analysed the security of Monero system using our model. More details such as security analysis of Zcash, discussion of different security properties and their relationships with each other can be found in the full version of the paper.

References

1. Almashaqbeh, G., Solomon, R.: SoK: privacy-preserving computing in the blockchain era. Cryptology ePrint Archive, Report 2021/727 (2021). https://ia.cr/2021/727
2. Bowe, S., Chiesa, A., Green, M., Miers, I., Mishra, P., Wu, H.: ZEXE: enabling decentralized private computation. In: 2020 IEEE Symposium on Security and Privacy (SP), pp. 947–964 (2020). https://doi.org/10.1109/SP40000.2020.00050
3. Bünz, B., Agrawal, S., Zamani, M., Boneh, D.: Zether: towards privacy in a smart contract world. In: Bonneau, J., Heninger, N. (eds.) FC 2020. LNCS, vol. 12059, pp. 423–443. Springer, Cham (2020). https://doi.org/10.1007/978-3-030-51280-4_23
4. Cremers, C., Loss, J., Wagner, B.: A holistic security analysis of monero transactions. Cryptology ePrint Archive, Paper 2023/321 (2023). https://eprint.iacr.org/2023/321
5. Duffield, E., Diaz, D.: Dash: a privacy centric cryptocurrency (2015)
6. Fauzi, P., Meiklejohn, S., Mercer, R., Orlandi, C.: Quisquis: a new design for anonymous cryptocurrencies. In: Galbraith, S.D., Moriai, S. (eds.) ASIACRYPT 2019. LNCS, vol. 11921, pp. 649–678. Springer, Cham (2019). https://doi.org/10.1007/978-3-030-34578-5_23
7. Gjøsteen, K., Raikwar, M., Wu, S.: PriBank: confidential blockchain scaling using short commit-and-proof NIZK argument. In: Galbraith, S.D. (ed.) CT-RSA 2022. LNCS, vol. 13161, pp. 589–619. Springer, Cham (2022). https://doi.org/10.1007/978-3-030-95312-6_24
8. Jivanyan, A.: Lelantus: Towards confidentiality and anonymity of blockchain transactions from standard assumptions. IACR Cryptol. ePrint Arch. **2019**, 373 (2019)
9. Jivanyan, A., Feickert, A.: Lelantus spark: secure and flexible private transactions. Cryptology ePrint Archive (2021)
10. Kerber, T., Kiayias, A., Kohlweiss, M.: Kachina-foundations of private smart contracts. In: 2021 IEEE 34th Computer Security Foundations Symposium (CSF), pp. 1–16. IEEE (2021)
11. Kosba, A., Miller, A., Shi, E., Wen, Z., Papamanthou, C.: Hawk: the blockchain model of cryptography and privacy-preserving smart contracts. In: 2016 IEEE Symposium on Security and Privacy (SP), pp. 839–858 (2016). https://doi.org/10.1109/SP.2016.55
12. Kosba, A., Miller, A., Shi, E., Wen, Z., Papamanthou, C.: Hawk: The blockchain model of cryptography and privacy-preserving smart contracts. In: 2016 IEEE Symposium on Security and Privacy (SP), pp. 839–858. IEEE (2016)
13. Lai, R.W., Ronge, V., Ruffing, T., Schröder, D., Thyagarajan, S.A.K., Wang, J.: Omniring: scaling private payments without trusted setup. In: Proceedings of the 2019 ACM SIGSAC Conference on Computer and Communications Security, pp. 31–48 (2019)

14. Liang, M., Karantaidou, I., Baldimtsi, F., Gordon, S.D., Varia, M.: (ϵ, δ)-indistinguishable mixing for cryptocurrencies. Proc. Priv. Enhanc. Technol. **2022**(1), 49–74 (2021)
15. Mitani, T., Otsuka, A.: Confidential and auditable payments. In: Bernhard, M., et al. (eds.) FC 2020. LNCS, vol. 12063, pp. 466–480. Springer, Cham (2020). https://doi.org/10.1007/978-3-030-54455-3_33
16. Nakamoto, S.: Bitcoin: a peer-to-peer electronic cash system (2009). http://bitcoin.org/bitcoin.pdf
17. Saberhagen, N.V.: CryptoNote v 2.0 (2013). https://bytecoin.org/old/whitepaper.pdf
18. Sasson, E.B., et al.: Zerocash: decentralized anonymous payments from bitcoin. In: 2014 IEEE Symposium on Security and Privacy, pp. 459–474. IEEE (2014)
19. Steffen, S., Bichsel, B., Gersbach, M., Melchior, N., Tsankov, P., Vechev, M.: zkay: Specifying and enforcing data privacy in smart contracts. In: Proceedings of the 2019 ACM SIGSAC Conference on Computer and Communications Security, pp. 1759–1776 (2019)
20. The Monero Project: Monero (2014). https://web.getmonero.org
21. Wijaya, D.A., Liu, J., Steinfeld, R., Liu, D., Yuen, T.H.: Anonymity reduction attacks to monero. In: Guo, F., Huang, X., Yung, M. (eds.) Inscrypt 2018. LNCS, vol. 11449, pp. 86–100. Springer, Cham (2019). https://doi.org/10.1007/978-3-030-14234-6_5
22. Wood, G.: Ethereum: a secure decentralised generalised transaction ledger. Yellow Paper (2014)
23. Zhang, Y., Long, Y., Liu, Z., Liu, Z., Gu, D.: Z-channel: scalable and efficient scheme in zerocash. Comput. Secur. **86**, 112–131 (2019)

Cryptography and Privacy

Group Oriented Attribute-Based Encryption Scheme from Lattices with the Employment of Shamir's Secret Sharing Scheme

Maharage Nisansala Sevwandi Perera[1]([✉]) [iD], Toru Nakamura[2],
Takashi Matsunaka[1], Hiroyuki Yokoyama[1], and Kouichi Sakurai[3]

[1] Advanced Telecommunications Research Institute International, 2-2-2 Hikaridai,
Seika-cho, Soraku-gun, 619-0288 Kyoto, Japan
{perera.nisansala,ta-matsunaka,hr-yokoyama}@atr.jp
[2] KDDI Research, Inc., 2-1-15 Ohara, Fujimino, Saitama 356-0003, Japan
tr-nakamura@kddi.com
[3] Kyushu University, 744 Motooka Nishi-ku, Fukuoka 819-0395, Japan
sakurai@inf.kyushu-u.ac.jp

Abstract. This paper delivers a post-quantum construction for group-oriented attribute-based encryption (GO-ABE) using lattice-based cryptography. The GO-ABE scheme enables users from the same group to combine their attributes to satisfy a decryption policy without revealing their secret keys. GO-ABE is particularly useful when no single user can fulfill the decryption policy alone, but a group of users can satisfy it together. Li et al. introduced the idea of GO-ABE at NSS 2015, discussing its importance in accessing patient data during emergencies. However, since Li et al.'s scheme uses bilinear mappings, it is not secure against quantum attacks. To ensure security against quantum attacks, we construct the GO-ABE scheme using the post-quantum cryptographic primitive lattices, and employ Shamir's secret sharing scheme to meet the GO-ABE requirements.

Keywords: attribute-based encryption · group-oriented systems · privacy · lattice-based cryptography

1 Introduction

The traditional public key encryption (PKE) schemes allow a message-sending party to encrypt a message for a specific recipient only who can decrypt the ciphertext. However, PKE is only suitable when the recipient's identity is known to the sender, limiting its real-world applications. Attribute-based encryption (ABE) is a generalized form of PKE, which was first introduced by Sahai and Waters [55] at EUROCRYPT 2005. In their scheme, both ciphertexts and user private keys are constructed based on sets of attributes. A message sender encrypts the message with a specific attribute set (access policy) $\mathcal{W}$, while each user (receiver) has a decryption (private) key based on their possessing attribute set $\mathcal{S}$. A user can decrypt the ciphertext only when at least t (threshold value) posessing attributes match with the given policy $\mathcal{W}$. For instance, Alice encrypts a message using the attribute set A, B, C with a threshold value $t = 2$. Even though Bob possessing attributes A, B, can decrypt the message, Charles only having the attribute A, cannot access the message. Since attributes represent real-life characteristics like age, designation, and department, and the decryption party can be controlled via an access policy, ABE is more suitable for real-world applications than general PKE. Thus, ABE is used to provide secured and trusted cloud computing [6,60], controlled subscribed broadcasts, secured audit logs, and more.

The scheme of Sahai and Waters [55] satisfies the threshold access structure. In their work, they presented Fuzzy Identity-based Encryption (FIBE). Later, more works with constant size ciphertext [22,27,33], modifying user attributes [29], with multi-authority [41], and providing practical applications [14,38,43,45,53] were delivered using the threshold ABE technique. On the other hand, attribute-based encryption schemes can be seen as a generalization of identity-based encryption (IBE) [12,18,57,64]. Moreover, Goyal, Pandey, Sahai, and Waters [24] categorized ABE into two types, namely, Key-Policy Attribute-based Encryption (KP-ABE) and Ciphertext-Policy Attribute-based Encryption (CP-ABE).

In KP-ABE ([8,19,39,63,68]), each piece of data has attributes, i.e., a ciphertext is linked with a set of attributes, and a user private key is linked with a policy (an access tree). Thus the ciphertext can be decrypted only by satisfying the user access tree. KP-ABE is used when it is needed to decide which data can be accessed by a user. KP-ABE is widely used in applications like purchased (subscribe) broadcasting, structured organizations, and secure forensic analysis, which control data access. For instance, in a broadcasting channel, Alice can access data only what she has paid to watch. Goyal et al. [24] delivered the first KP-ABE scheme. Early presented KP-ABE schemes had a problem with ciphertext size. Solving that problem, Attrapadung et al. [8] submitted the first KP-ABE scheme that allows non-monotonic access structures and outputs constant-size ciphertexts. Then Li et al. [39] presented a decentralized KP-ABE scheme that does not require a trusted centralized party for setup. Moreover, their scheme outputs a constant-size ciphertext. On the other hand, Wang et al. [63] delivered an accountable authority KP-ABE scheme. In addition, many KP-ABE schemes were presented [38,69,70] to secure outsourced data in the cloud.

In CP-ABE ([10,17,20,21,35,36,49,52,65]), a message is encrypted with an access tree (policy) selected by the message sender, and a trusted authority produces private keys for users based on their attribute sets. Thus, only users whose possessing attributes meet the access policy can decrypt the message. CP-ABE controls who can access data. For instance, if attributes A, B, C are used to encrypt a text, then only a user who is possessing those attributes can decrypt the text. Bethencourt et al. [10] suggested the first CP-ABE scheme. After that, many CP-ABE schemes were presented, resolving security and scalable barriers. For instance, Cheung and Newport [17] proposed a provably secure CP-ABE scheme. Yu et al. [70] and Zhang et al. [71] discussed the essential issues of attribute revocation and user revocation in CP-ABE, respectively. Moreover, Emura et al. [21] delivered the CP-ABE scheme with constant-size ciphertexts, and Lewko and Waters [36] suggested decentralized authority for CP-ABE. CP-ABE is employed in applications more than KP-ABE because CP-ABE is more suitable in real-life applications [16,31,66,73] like data access in mobile Personal Health Record (PHR) systems [28,51] and IoT [44].

However, all the schemes mentioned above are in danger once quantum computers become a reality becasue those works are not constructed from quantum resists cryptographic primitives. Some IBE and ABE schemes were successfully realized using lattice-based cryptography [30]. Lattice-based cryptography seems to be the most promising alternative against quantum attacks [50]. For instance, in the work of presenting trapdoors on hard lattices [23], the authors delivered the construction of the lattice-based IBE scheme in the random model by using trapdoor functions. In the works of hierarchical IBE [2,3], the authors presented (H)IBE schemes in the standard model from lattices. Katsumata et al. [32] answered the security limitations of lattice-based (H)IBE, which supports the key revocation mechanism. In 2013, Xavier Boyen [13] suggested an attribute-based functional encryption scheme from lattices. Moreover, Yongtao Wang [62] presented a CP-ABE scheme in the standard model from lattices. Gür et al. [25] presented a software implementation of CP-ABE schemes from an efficient Gaussian sampling algorithm for trapdoor lattices. They provided an efficient Ring-LWE (Ring Learning with Errors) construction for CP-ABE schemes. Zhao et al. [72] also provided a revocable lattice-based CP-ABE from Ring-LWE. Recently, Yang et al. [67] presented a revocable and multi-authority CP-ABE scheme from Ring-LWE. Affum et al. [1] presented a different approach supporting the flexible expression of access policy in CP-ABE with the lattice-based construction.

In contrast to the CP-ABE schemes discussed earlier (which may or may not be safe against quantum attacks), Li et al. [37] proposed a new form of attribute-based encryption called Group-Oriented Attribute-Based Encryption (GO-ABE) in 2015. This scheme allows users in the same group to pool their attributes and private keys to generate a decryption key. If the union of attributes matches the access policy, then they can retrieve the message. GO-ABE appears advantageous in the setting of organizations, where two or more users' collaboration is required for decryption and in emergencies when no user alone possesses an attribute set that matches the access tree. The scheme guarantees that users from different groups cannot generate a valid decryption key by pooling their attributes, and it also ensures that no user reveals their private keys. However, the scheme is not quantum-safe because Li et al. [37] constructed the scheme using bilinear mappings. As Peter Shor [58] showed in 1997, these number-theoretic problems are vulnerable to quantum attacks. Therefore, as quantum computers may become a reality within next 30 years, cryptographic schemes relying on bilinear mappings will be in danger. Recently, research on quantum-safe constructions with post-quantum primitives has become a priority. In this paper, we deliver a lattice-based cryptography construction for the GO-ABE idea of Li et al. [37] that ensures the security of applications employing GO-ABE against quantum attacks.

1.1 Our Contribution

The motivation of this paper is to provide a quantum-safe construction for the GO-ABE scheme to use in real-world applications like PHR systems. Thus, we present the GO-ABE scheme from lattice-based cryptography, the post-quantum primitive. Even though the GO-ABE idea of Li et al. [37] was studied or utilized by many research works [26,40,48,61,66], especially in the aspect of allowing collaborative description, none of them were constructed using post-quantum cryptography. Thus, according to our knowledge, this paper presents the first quantum-safe GO-ABE scheme. GO-ABE scheme presented by Li et al. [37] is constructed from bilinear pairings. In GO-ABE, a single user (in case of possessing all the required attributes) or multiple users jointly (in case of required pooling of their attributes) can decrypt a ciphertext. The attribute pooling users should be from the same group. Moreover, they should not reveal their private keys. When constructing the GO-ABE scheme from lattices, the challenging point is satisfying the requirements; users should be from the same group and should not reveal their private keys. Validating the users from the same group is somewhat challenging because their identity is hidden. In group signature schemes, different techniques are used to validate the signer's group membership. For instance, in lattice-based group signature schemes [11,34,42], signers prove the validity of their signature using an underlying interactive zero-knowledge protocol without leaking any privacy-related information. Thus, if the verification process of the protocol is valid, the signature verifier is convinced about the validity of the signer. However, in the encryption scheme of GO-ABE, the member verification process is not applicable because GO-ABE requires collaboration to decrypt a ciphertext, and there is no verifier to check the validity of the collaborating users. Since there is no verification process to validate the collaborating users, GO-ABE satisfies the correction of the decryption process only if the users are from the same group. Otherwise, decryption fails. It seems challenging to reassure such a condition using only the techniques of existing lattice-based encryption schemes. Thus, to overcome the challenge, we employ Shamir's Secret Sharing (SSS) scheme and Lagrange interpolation formula as in the work of Agrawal et al. [5], the scheme fuzzy IBE from lattices. We intend to allow users from the same group to reconstruct a variable related to the group allowing them to satisfy the decryption of the given ciphertext and prove that they are from the same group. We borrow the construction idea from Agrawal's scheme. We share a public key into ℓ shares, where ℓ is the universal attribute size, and we generate the user private keys for each possessing attribute based on the group-related keys. In other words, a group has public and secret keys, and those keys are used for producing the secret keys of the user possessing attributes. Thus, unless the users from the same group collude, reconstruction of the decryption key that satisfies the shared public key is not possible. In conclusion, our lattice-based construction of GO-ABE enables users to ensure the requirement of being in the same group and correctly decrypt the given ciphertext by cooperating, while keeping their individual user secret keys private. The security of our construction is based on the hardness assumption of the learning with errors (LWE) problem and provides selective security in the security model.

1.2 Related Works

Our lattice-based construction is influenced by the work of Agrawal et al. [5] with the title 'Functional Encryption for Threshold Functions from Lattices'. Agrawal's scheme constructs a fuzzy IBE from the hardness of the LWE problem. They employed Shamir's $k - out - of - \ell$ secret-sharing scheme for the key extraction process. The idea of using the SSS scheme also appeared in the paper of Bendlin and Damgård [9], where the bounding size issue of the Lagrangian coefficient did not occur. However, in the case of Agrawal et al., [5], they face the bounding problem of the size of the Lagrangian coefficient, and they came up with the idea of clearing the denominator inspired by the work of Victor [59]. We follow the construction given by Agrawal et al. [5] when we provide GO-ABE from lattices. Thus our work also uses a constant D as in Agrawal's scheme [5]. We outline the construction given by Agrawal [5] to clear the denominators below.

The existing lattice-based IBE schemes [4, 15] encrypt a message bit $b \in \{0, 1\}$ as follows.

$$C_{id} = \mathsf{IBE.Enc}(id, b \in \{0,1\}) = (\mathbf{A}_{1,id_1}^T \mathbf{s} + \mathbf{e}_1, \ldots, \mathbf{A}_{\ell,id_\ell}^T \mathbf{s} + \mathbf{e}_\ell, \mathbf{u}^T \mathbf{s} + e' + b\lfloor q/2 \rfloor)$$

Herer, 2ℓ matrices $(\mathbf{A}_{1,0}, \mathbf{A}_{1,1}, \ldots, \mathbf{A}_{\ell,0}, \mathbf{A}_{\ell,1}) \in \mathbb{Z}_q^{n \times m}$ and vector $\mathbf{u} \in \mathbb{Z}_q^n = (\mathbf{u}_1, \ldots, \mathbf{u}_\ell - secret\,shares)$ are public parameters in a system with security parameter n, a small prime q, and $m \approx n \log q$. The vector $\mathbf{s} \in \mathbb{Z}_q^n$ and $smal\,error\,terms$ $\mathbf{e}_1, \ldots \mathbf{e}_\ell \in \mathbb{Z}^m$ and $e' \in \mathbb{Z}$ are selected for the encryption function. The decryption function shows that each component of $C_{id'}$ and secret key $\mathbf{SK}_{id} = (\mathbf{x}_1, \ldots, \mathbf{x}_\ell)$ gives a number approximately $\mathbf{u}_i^T \mathbf{s}$, such that

$$\mathbf{x}_i^T(\mathbf{A}_{i,id_i}^T \mathbf{s} + \mathbf{e}_i) = (\mathbf{A}_{i,id_i} \mathbf{x}_i)^T \mathbf{s} + \mathbf{x}_i^T \mathbf{e}_i = \mathbf{u}_i^T \mathbf{s} + \mathbf{x}_i^T \mathbf{e}_i \approx \mathbf{u}^T \mathbf{s}$$

Note that, $\mathbf{A}_{i,id_i} \mathbf{x}_i = \mathbf{u}_i$.

The correctness of lattice-based IBE schemes [4, 15] lies in bounding the decryption error terms $\mathbf{x}_i^T \mathbf{e}_i$. That is cummulative error term $e_i - \sum_{i=1}^k \mathbf{x}_i^T \mathbf{e}_i$ by $q/4$.

Instantiating the previous IBE schemes with $Shamir's\,secret\,sharing$ scheme, the new cumulative error term is given as $e_i - \sum_{i \in S}^k L_i \mathbf{x}_i^T \mathbf{e}_i$, where L_i are the fractional Lagrangian coefficients for reconstructing the secret and S is the subset of shares used in the reconstruction. Even though both numerator and denominator in L_i can be bounded as a fraction of integers, when presenting as an element in $\mathbb{Z}_q$ the value L_i is arbitrarily large. The idea of clearing the denominators prevents the large-value problem of L_i.

Let $D := (\ell!)^2$ be a sufficiently large constant, such that $DL_i \in \mathbb{Z}$ for all i. Multiplying noise vectors of the encryption function with D we get,

$$C_{id} = \mathsf{IBE.Enc}(id, b \in \{0,1\}) = (\mathbf{A}_{1,id_1}^T \mathbf{s} + D\mathbf{e}_1, \ldots, \mathbf{A}_{\ell,id_\ell}^T \mathbf{s} + D\mathbf{e}_\ell, \mathbf{u}^T \mathbf{s} + De' + b\lfloor q/2 \rfloor).$$

Thus, it is sufficient to bind the below for the correctness of the IBE scheme by $q/4$.

$$De_i - \sum_{i \in S}^{k} DL_i \mathbf{x}_i^T \mathbf{e}_i$$

Since DL_i is an integer bounded by D^2, it is enough to select noise vectors bounded by $q/4D\ell$ with overwhelming probability.

2   Preliminaries

In this section, we provide the notations we use in this paper, and briefly explain Shamir's Secret Sharing (SSS) Scheme. Then we provide definitions of lattices with the related algorithms. Moreover, we give the syntax of the traditional attribute-based encryption (ABE) scheme.

2.1   Notation

We symbolize matrices with upper-case bold letters and vectors with lower-case bold letters. For any integer $k \geq 1$, we show a set of integers $\{1, 2, \ldots, k\}$ by $[k]$. If S is a finite set, $|S|$ is its size. $S(k)$ represents its permutations of k elements and $b \leftarrow \mathcal{D}$ shows that b is sampled from a uniformly random distribution $\mathcal{D}$. The encoding function with full rank differences (FRD) $\mathcal{H} : \mathbb{Z}_q^n \to \mathbb{Z}_q^{n \times n}$ is taken as discussed by Agrawal et al. [2] paper.

2.2   Shamir's Secret Sharing Scheme [46,56]

Shamir's Secret Sharing, in short SSS, is used to secure a secret using the distributed method. A secret is partitioned into multiple parts and shared with different users, such that an individual share does not give any information about the secret. SSS is an algorithm in cryptography created by Adi Shamir [56]. The idea lies behind SSS is that for the given ℓ points we can find a polynomial equation with the degree $(\ell - 1)$. The Lagrangian coefficient is employed to control the reconstruction of the secret with a threshold value. For instance, a secret s can be reconstructed from k shares out of ℓ shares. Accordingly, no party alone can reconstruct the secret s, but k parties can.

Let ℓ-number of participants, $q \geq \ell + 1$ - a prime number, and s - the secret. Sharing algorithm:

1. Set ℓ distinct and select public parameters $x_1, x_2, \ldots, x_\ell \in \mathbb{Z}_q$ such that x_j for participant j, $1 \leq j \leq \ell$.
2. Select a $k-1$ degree random polynomial

$$f(x) = a_0 + a_1 x + \ldots + a_{k-1} x^{k-1} (\mod q)$$

, where $a_0 = s$ and $a_j \in \mathbb{Z}_q$, $(1 \leq j \leq k-1)$.
3. Compute shares $s_j = f(x), 1 \leq j \leq \ell$.

Reconstruction algorithm (based on the polynomial interpolation):

$$a(x) = \sum_{i=1}^{k} s_i \prod_{1 \leq j \leq = k, j \neq i} \frac{x - x_j}{x_i - x_j}$$

2.3 Lattices

Let q be a prime and $\mathbf{B} = [\mathbf{b}_1 | \cdots | \mathbf{b}_m] \in \mathbb{Z}_q^{r \times m}$ be linearly independent vectors in $\mathbb{Z}_q^r$. The r-dimensional lattice $\Lambda(\mathbf{B})$ for $\mathbf{B}$ is defined as

$$\Lambda(\mathbf{B}) = \{\mathbf{y} \in \mathbb{Z}^r \mid \mathbf{y} \equiv \mathbf{B}\mathbf{x} \mod q \text{ for some } \mathbf{x} \in \mathbb{Z}_q^m\},$$

which is the set of all linear combinations of columns of $\mathbf{B}$. The value m is the rank of $\mathbf{B}$.

We consider a discrete Gaussian distribution for a lattice. The Gaussian function centered in a vector $\mathbf{c}$ with parameter $s > 0$ is defined as $\rho_{s,\mathbf{c}}(\mathbf{x}) = e^{-\pi \|(\mathbf{x}-\mathbf{c})/s\|^2}$. The corresponding probability density function proportional to $\rho_{s,\mathbf{c}}$ is defined as $D_{s,\mathbf{c}}(\mathbf{x}) = \rho_{s,\mathbf{c}}(\mathbf{x})/s^n$ for all $\mathbf{x} \in \mathbb{R}^n$. With respect to a lattice Λ the discrete Gaussian distribution is defined as $D_{\Lambda,s,\mathbf{c}}(\mathbf{x}) = D_{s,\mathbf{c}}(\mathbf{x})/D_{s,\mathbf{c}}(\Lambda) = \rho_{s,\mathbf{c}}(\mathbf{x})/\rho_{s,\mathbf{c}}(\Lambda)$ for all $\mathbf{x} \in \Lambda$. Since $\mathbb{Z}^m$ is also a lattice, we can define a discrete Gaussian distribution for $\mathbb{Z}^m$. By $D_{\mathbb{Z}^m,\sigma}$, we denote the discrete Gaussian distribution for $\mathbb{Z}^m$ around the origin with the standard deviation σ.

Quantum computers can break the superposition principle where the quantum bits are perfectly aligned. Accordingly in future, the systems constructed from number theory and discrete logs are in danger. On the other hand, a lattice is multi-dimensional. Thus it is hard to find, for instance, the nearest point from the origin. Lattice-based cryptography is quantum resist because the computational problems on lattices are believed to be hard to solve, even for quantum computers. Among those computational problems, *Approximate Shortest Independent Vector Problem* $(SIVP_\gamma)$ is one of the most well-studied problems. LWE and SIS are two average-case $SIVP_\gamma$ problems that we employ in this paper.

Definition 1 (Approximate Shortest Independent Vectors Problem - $SIVP_\gamma$ [47]). *Given a basis $\boldsymbol{B}$ of an n-dimentional lattice $\mathcal{L} = \mathcal{L}(B)$, finding linearly independent vectors $s_1, \ldots, s_n$ is $SIVP_\gamma$ problem, where $\|s_i\| \leq \gamma(n) \cdot \lambda_n(\mathcal{L})$ for all i $(\lambda_n(\mathcal{L})$ is n-th successive minimum).*

Definition 2 (Learning With Errors (LWE)). *For integers $n, m \geq 1$, and $q \geq 2$, a vector $s \in \mathbb{Z}_q^n$, and the Gaussian error distribution χ, the distribution $A_{s,\chi}$ is obtained by sampling $a \in \mathbb{Z}_q^n$ and $e \leftarrow \chi$, and outputting the pair $(a, a^T \cdot s + e)$. LWE problem (decision-LWE problem) requires distinguishing LWE samples from truly random samples $\leftarrow \mathbb{Z}_q^n \times \mathbb{Z}_q$.*

For a prime power q, $b \geq \sqrt{n}\omega(\log n)$, and distribution χ, solving $LWE_{n,q,\chi}$ problem is at least as hard as solving $SIVP_\gamma$ *(Shortest Independent Vector Problem)*, where $\gamma = \tilde{\mathcal{O}}(nq/b)$ [23].

Since the LWE problem was defined [54], it has been extensively studied and used. In this paper, we use the decisional version of the LWE problem, which is defined in Definition 2.

Definition 3 (Small Integer Solution (SIS)). *Given uniformly random matrix $A \in \mathbb{Z}_q^{n \times m}$, find non-zero vector $x \in \mathbb{Z}^m$, such that $A \cdot x = 0 \mod q$ and $\|x\|_\infty \leq \beta$.*

For any m, $\beta = \mathsf{poly}(n)$, and $q > \sqrt{n}\beta$, solving $SIS_{n,m,q,\beta}$ problem with non-negligible probability is at least as hard as solving $SIVP_\gamma$ problem, for some $\gamma = \beta \cdot \tilde{\mathcal{O}}(\sqrt{nm})$ [23,42].

2.4 Lattice Related Algorithms

Lemma 1 (TrapGen[5,7]). *Let $n = n(\lambda)$, $q = q(\lambda)$, and $m = m(\lambda)$ be positive integers. For an odd integer $q \geq 2$ and $m = \lceil 5n \log q \rceil$ this algorithm outputs a matrix $\mathbf{A} \in \mathbb{Z}_q^{n \times m}$ and a basis $\mathbf{T_A} \in \mathbb{Z}_q^{m \times m}$ for $\Lambda_q^\perp(\mathbf{A})$ such that $\|\widetilde{\mathbf{T_A}}\| \leq O(\sqrt{n \log q})$ and $\|\mathbf{T_A}\| \leq O(n \log q)$ with all but negligible probability in n.*

Lemma 2 (SamplePre [23]). *On input a matrix $\mathbf{A} \in \mathbb{Z}_q^{n \times m}$, a trapdoor basis $\mathbf{R}$, a target image $\mathbf{u} \in \mathbb{Z}_q^n$, and the standard deviation $\sigma \geq \omega(\sqrt{\log m})$, the PPT algorithm $\mathsf{SamplePre}(\mathbf{A}, \mathbf{R}, \mathbf{u}, \sigma)$ outputs a sample $\mathbf{e} \in \mathbb{Z}^m$ from a distribution that is within negligible statistical distance of $D_{\Lambda_q^{\mathbf{u}}(A),\sigma}$.*

Lemma 3 (ExtBasis [15]). *ExtBasis is a PPT algorithm that takes a matrix $\mathbf{B} \in \mathbb{Z}_q^{n \times m'}$, whose first m columns span $\mathbb{Z}_q^n$, and a basis $\mathbf{T_A}$ of $\Lambda_q^\perp(\mathbf{A})$, where $\mathbf{A}$ is the left $n \times m$ sub-matrix of $\mathbf{B}$, as inputs, and outputs a basis $\mathbf{T_B}$ of $\Lambda_q^\perp(\mathbf{B})$ with $\|\widetilde{\mathbf{T_B}}\| \leq \|\widetilde{\mathbf{T_A}}\|$.*

2.5 Attribute-Based Encryption

Setup: This algorithm gets the security parameter λ as inputs, and generates a public parameter **PK** and a master secret key **MK**.

KeyGen: For a given public parameter **PK**, a master secret key **MK**, and an attribute set $\mathcal{S}$ for a user, this algorithm outputs a user private key **SK** associated with $\mathcal{S}$.

Encrypt: On input the public parameter **PK**, and an access tree (policy) $\mathcal{W}$, and a message M, this algorithm outputs a ciphertext C.

Decrypt: On input a user private key **SK** and a ciphertext C for a message M, if the user attribute set $\mathcal{S}$ can satisfy the given policy $\mathcal{W}$, this algorithm outputs the message M.

3 Group Oriented Attribute-Based Encryption (GO-ABE) Scheme

ABE schemes allow a user satisfying the decryption policy to read the message. Thus, no users colluding together can access the message. However, in many real-life scenarios, due to the orgnazation's structure, the encrypted data cannot be accessed individually by a single user alone. In many organizations and enterprises, some important data (files, documents, etc.) is shared among multiple users having responsibility to protect data. Those organizations require the multple users to collaborate to access data [66]. For instance, secured data (information, banknotes, or other resources) stored in a banking system (money safe/locker, data bank, or system) can be accessed by permitted authorities by collaborating. A single authority cannot access data. It is required $k-$number of authorities to join to open the data. The collaboration ensures the security of the data aginst illegal access.

Another requirement of user collaboration is the exceptional case of an emergency. In case of an emergency like accessing the Personal Health Records (PHR) of a patient stored in the cloud, if no user can satisfy the decryption policy, then the patient's life may be in danger. As a solution to this problem, Ming Li et al. [38] proposed a break-glass access method. Thus, when an emergency happens, the message-accessing party should contact the emergency department (ED), which provides temporary keys after validating the user and the emergency. However, considering a scenario where the message accessing party cannot contact ED, Li et al. [37] suggested the new ABE scheme, Group Oriented Attribute-Based Encryption (GO-ABE) Scheme.

In the GO-ABE scheme, the users belong to a specific group, and only users from the same group can combine their attributes to meet the access tree. For instance, when the decryption policy requires the user to satisfy two attributes A and B, the idea of GO-ABE allows two users with attributes A and B separately, from the same group to combine their attributes to generate the decryption key. However, no user will reveal their private keys. The following real-life example given in Li et al.'s paper [37] explains the requirement of user collaboration.

If the PHR owner Alice has heart and stomach problems, it is required a cardiologist and gastroenterologist to jointly diagnose her to give better treatment. That means it is required to satisfy the access policy (Cardiologist, Gastroenterologist, 2) to access her PHR. In a case, no individual doctor is satisfying both specialties; cardiology and gastroenterology, the system may put Alice's life in danger, if she is in an emergency. On the other hand, it is obvious that in a real-life situation, two or more doctors jointly diagnose complicated or serious patients. Therefore, it is rational to let doctors jointly decrypt the health records of patients in the cloud to treat them. However, since the doctors are from the same hospital, decrypting users should be from the same group g. The GO-ABE is proposed by Li et al. [37] addressing such kinds of emergencies.

3.1 GO-ABE

Definition 4 (GO-ABE). [37] *A group-oriented attribute-based encryption scheme is parameterized by a universal set of possible attributes* $\mathbb{A}$, *a space of group identities* $\mathbb{G} = g_1, g_2, \ldots, g_n$, *and a message space* $\mathbb{M}$, *and has the following algorithms.*

Setup: This randomized algorithm takes inputs as only the security parameter and outputs a public parameter **PK** and a master secret key **MK**.

Encryption: On input, a message $M \in \mathbb{M}$, the public parameter **PK**, and a set of attributes (access structure) $\mathcal{W}$, this algorithm outputs a ciphertext C for message M.

KeyGen: On input, an attribute set $\mathcal{S}$, a group id g, the master secret key **MK**, and the public parameter **PK**, this algorithm outputs a decryption key $\mathbf{SK}_{\mathcal{S}}^g$.

Decryption: On input, the ciphertext C, that was encrypted under a set of attributes $\mathcal{W}$, the public parameter **PK**, and a set of users from same group g, this algorithm pools the user attribute sets as $U = \mathcal{S}_1 \cup \mathcal{S}_2 \cup \ldots, \mathcal{S}_N$ to generate a decryption key $\mathbf{SK}_U^g$ and outputs the message M if $|\mathcal{W} \cap U| \geq t$, where t is the threshold value. Here N is the number of pooling users.

3.2 Security Definition: Selective-Set Model for GO-ABE

The selective set model game captures the indistinguishability of challenging ciphertext. The adversary's goal is to determine which of the two messages is encrypted.

Int: The adversary declares the attribute set $\mathcal{W}$ that he wishes to be challenged upon.

Setup: The challenger creates a public parameter **PK** and a master secret key **MK** executing Setup and sends **PK** to the adversary.

Phase 1: The adversary queries the private secret keys $\mathbf{SK}_{\mathcal{S}_i}^g$ for different attribute sets $\mathcal{S}_i$ with a group id $g \in \mathbb{G}$, where $|\mathcal{S}_i \cap \mathcal{W}| < t$ for all i queries.

At the end of Phase 1, $|U \cap \mathcal{W}| < t$, where $U = \mathcal{S}_1 \cup \mathcal{S}_2, \ldots, \mathcal{S}_N$ is the union of N attribute sets such that all are from the group g.

Challenge: The adversary sends two messages M_0 and M_1 whose lengths are the same. The challenger selects $b \leftarrow \{0, 1\}$ and encrypts M_b with $\mathcal{W}$. Then he passes the generated ciphertext C to the adversary.

Phase 2: Phase 1 is repeated with the same conditions.

Guess: The adversary outputs a guess b'.

The advantage of the adversary winning the game is $Pr[b' = b] - 1/2$.

Definition 5. *The GO-ABE scheme is secure in the Selective-set model of security if all polynomial time and adversaries have at most negligible advantage in the above Selective-set game.*

4   Lattice-Based Construction of GO-ABE Scheme

In this section, first, we delineate how we satisfy the requirements of GO-ABE while constructing the scheme from lattice-based cryptography. Recall that the GO-ABE scheme of Li et al. [37] required the users who are pooling together to be from the same group and not to reveal their private keys. The construction of GO-ABE from lattices is somewhat challenging to satisfy the requirements that only the users are from the same group can collude together and support the decryption without revealing the secret keys. We discuss this in the Subsect. 4.1. Then we provide the lattice-based construction of the GO-ABE scheme.

4.1   Description

GO-ABE required collaborating users to be from the same group and should be able to decrypt the given data. In Li et al.'s paper for the construction from bilinear mappings, a random $d - 1$ degree polynomial, $q_{g(x)}$ is taken for the group g, where each user should have polynomials with same valuation at point 0, that is $q_g(0) = y$. This ensures that the final decryption of each user's contribution satisfies y, i.e., users obtain decryption while proving they are from the same group. However, when constructing the GO-ABE scheme from lattices, we have to resolve this challenge. We came up with the idea of sharing a group-related public variable such that the collaboration of users satisfying matching attributes should be able to reconstruct it. We share the public vector $\mathbf{u}$, such that each universal attribute hold $\hat{\mathbf{u}}_i$ a piece of $\mathbf{u}$. In parallel, the user secret key for each possessing attribute is generated based on the group g ensuring that the user secret key for an attribute can satisfy the related piece of $\mathbf{u}$. That is $(\mathbf{A}_i \cdot (\mathbf{G}_d \cdot \mathbf{x}_i^d)) + \mathbf{g} = \hat{\mathbf{u}}_i$, where $\mathbf{A}_i$ is the public key of the relevant attribute, $\mathbf{G}_d$ is the public key of the user, and $\mathbf{x}_i^d$ is the secret key for the attribute that was generated based on the group id and user id. The vector $\mathbf{g}$ is a unique vector for the group. Thus, no outsider can collaborate with the group users to reconstruct $\mathbf{u}$. Below, we explain more about the lattice-based construction of GO-ABE.

Let $\mathbb{A}$ be the universal attribute set of size ℓ. Each attribute has a matrix $\mathbf{A}$, which is publicly available. Thus the public parameters $\mathbf{PK}$ consists of ℓ matrices $(\mathbf{A}_1, \ldots, \mathbf{A}_\ell)$ and a vector $\mathbf{u}$. The master secret key $\mathbf{MSK}$ consists of the trapdoors $(\mathbf{T}_1, \ldots, \mathbf{T}_\ell)$ corresponding to each matrix $\mathbf{A}_i$. The trapdoor $\mathbf{T}_i$ is used to derive secret key $\mathbf{x}_i$ using the Gaussian sampling algorithm. In our scheme, we take $g \in \mathbb{G}$ as the group id and each user id $d \in \mathbb{N}$. Each group has a uniformly random matrix $\mathbf{G} \in \mathbb{Z}_q^{m \times n}$ with related trapdoor $\mathbf{T}_G$ obtained from $\mathsf{TrapGen}(n, m, q)$, two other randomly selected matrices $\mathbf{G}_0, \mathbf{G}_1 \in \mathbb{Z}_q^{m \times n}$, and a uniformly random vector $\mathbf{g} \in \mathbb{Z}_q^n$. We set the group public key $\mathbf{GPK} = (\mathbf{G}, \mathbf{G}_0, \mathbf{G}_1, \mathbf{g})$. The secret key $\mathbf{T}_G$ for each group with id g is selected and stored such that only the authority with $\mathbf{MSK} = (\mathbf{T}_1, \ldots, \mathbf{T}_\ell)$ can access $\mathbf{T}_G$. Thus at the key generation for a set of attributes, only the authority can compute the secret keys relating to the group. First, using the SSS scheme, the authority shares the public key $\mathbf{u}$ into ℓ shares, where ℓ is the size of the universal attribute set. Next, based on the group and then based on the user id secret keys are computed for each user possessing an attribute. Since the secret keys are based on the group, only the same group of users can pool to regenerate or satisfy $\mathbf{u}$.

Satisfying the above requirements, we employ Shamir's k-out-of-ℓ secret sharing scheme. Inspired by the work of Agrawal et al. [5] to answer the issues of correctness and security challenges, fractional Lagrangian coefficients are used in reconstructing the public key $\mathbf{u}$. As a result, we take sufficiently large constant D as in Agrawal's work [5] to multiply with the noise vector when generating the ciphertext.

4.2   Construction of Algorithms

Let $\lambda \in \mathbb{Z}^+$ be a security parameter. Let $n = n(\lambda)$, $m = m(\lambda)$ be two positive integers and $q = q(\lambda)$ be a prime. Let $\sigma = \sigma(\lambda)$ be a Gaussian parameter. Let each group has an id g and has unique group public key $(\mathbf{GPK} = (\mathbf{G}, \mathbf{G}_0, \mathbf{G}_1, \mathbf{g}))$ and a secret key $(\mathbf{GSK} = \mathbf{T}_G)$ selected from $(\mathbf{G}, \mathbf{T}_G) \leftarrow \mathsf{TrapGen}(n, m, q)$ and $\mathbf{G}_0, \mathbf{G}_1 \in \mathbb{Z}_q^{m \times n}$, and $\mathbf{g} \in \mathbb{Z}_q^n$ randomly.

- $\mathsf{Setup}(1^\lambda)$: On input a security parameter λ, the algorithm outputs the public parameters $\mathbf{PK}$ and the master secret key $\mathbf{MSK}$.
  1. Obtain uniformly random matrices $\mathbf{A}_{i=1}^\ell \in \mathbb{Z}_q^{n \times m}$ and corresponding trapdoors $\mathbf{T}_{i=1}^\ell$ executing $\mathsf{TrapGen}(n, m, q)$ for all attributes in $\mathbb{A}$.
  2. Select uniformly random vector $\mathbf{u} \in \mathbb{Z}_q^n$.
  3. Output $\mathbf{PK} = (\{\mathbf{A}_i\}_{i \in [\ell]}, \mathbf{u})$ and $\mathbf{MSK} = \{\mathbf{T}_i\}_{i \in [\ell]}$.
- $\mathsf{Encrypt}(\mathbf{PK}, M, \mathcal{W})$: This algorithm takes the public parameter $\mathbf{PK}$, a message bit $M \in \{0, 1\} = b$, and a policy $\mathcal{W}$ with attribute size w, and outputs the ciphertext C as below.
  1. Let $D \overset{\mathrm{def}}{=} (\ell!)^2$.
  2. Select a uniformly random $\mathbf{s} \in \mathbb{Z}_q^n$, $\mathbf{e}_i \in \mathbb{Z}_q^m$ for $i \in [w]$, and $e' \in \mathbb{Z}_q$.
  3. Set $\mathbf{c}_1 = \mathbf{A}_i^T \mathbf{s} + D\mathbf{e}_i$ for $i \in [w]$, $\mathbf{c}_2 = \mathbf{u}^T \mathbf{s} + De' + b\lfloor q/2 \rfloor$.
  4. Output $C = (\mathbf{c}_1, \mathbf{c}_2)$.
- $\mathsf{KeyGen}(\mathbf{PK}, \mathbf{MSK}, g, \mathcal{S})$: On input the public parameter $\mathbf{PK}$, the master secret key $\mathbf{MSK}$, a group id g which the user belongs to, and a user id d with the possessing attribute set $\mathcal{S}$, this algorithm outputs private key (decryption key) $\mathbf{SK}_{\mathcal{S}}^g$ which consists of $\mathbf{sk}_i^{g,d}$ for each attribute $i \in \mathcal{S}$.
  1. Select the group public key $\mathbf{GPK} = (\mathbf{G}, \mathbf{G}_0, \mathbf{G}_1, \mathbf{g})$, and secret key $\mathbf{GSK} = \mathbf{T}_G$ related to the group id g.
  2. Select a fresh positive integer $d \in \mathbb{N}$ as the user id who is possessing $\mathcal{S}$.

3. Using Shamir secret sharing (SSS) scheme construct ℓ shares of vector $\mathbf{u} = (u_1, \ldots, u_n) \in \mathbb{Z}_q^n$ (applying SSS scheme for each co-ordinates of $\mathbf{u}$ independently). Be precise, for each $j \in [n]$ select a uniformly random polynomial $p_j \in \mathbb{Z}_q[x]$ of degree $k - 1$ such that $p_j(0) = u_j$. Here k is the threshold value. Construct the $j - th$ share vector $\hat{\mathbf{u}}_j = (\hat{u}_{j,1}, \ldots, \hat{u}_{j,n}) = (p_1(j), p_2(j), \ldots, p_n(j)) \in \mathbb{Z}_q^n$.
Calculate fractional Lagrangian coefficients L_j such that $\mathbf{u} = \sum_{j \in J} L_j \cdot \hat{\mathbf{u}}_j(\mod p)$. Note that for all $J \subset [\ell]$ such that $|J| \geq k$ [5].

4. For each attribute $i \in \mathcal{S}$, using $\mathsf{SamplePre}(\mathbf{A}_i, \mathbf{T}_i, \hat{\mathbf{u}}_i - \mathbf{g}, \sigma)$ get $\mathbf{v}_i \in \mathbb{Z}_q^m$ such that $\mathbf{A}_i \cdot \mathbf{v}_i = \hat{\mathbf{u}}_i - \mathbf{g}$.

5. For the user with id d compute $\mathbf{G}_d = [\mathbf{G}|\mathbf{G}_0 + d\mathbf{G}_1]\mathbb{Z}_q^{m \times 2n}$ and obtain a short basis $\mathbf{T}_d$ for the lattice $\Lambda^{\perp}(\mathbf{G}_d)$ executing $\mathsf{ExtBasis}(\mathbf{T}_G, \mathbf{G}_d)$.

6. Then for each attribute $i \in \mathcal{S}$ obtain $\mathbf{x}_i^d \leftarrow \mathsf{SamplePre}(\mathbf{G}_d, \mathbf{T}_d, \mathbf{v}_i, \sigma)$, such that $\mathbf{G}_d \cdot \mathbf{x}_i^d = \mathbf{v}_i$.
Note that, $(\mathbf{A}_i \cdot (\mathbf{G}_d \cdot \mathbf{x}_i^d)) + \mathbf{g} = \hat{\mathbf{u}}_i$.

7. Output $\mathbf{SK}_{\mathcal{S}}^g = ((\mathbf{x}_1^d, \ldots, \mathbf{x}_s^d), d)$, where $s = |\mathcal{S}|$.

- Decrypt($\mathbf{PK}, C, U^g$): On input the public parameter $\mathbf{PK}$, the ciphertext C, and the set of users U^g from the same group $\mathbb{G}$ with group id g, this algorithm executes as below and returns a message M if the attributes satisfy the decryption policy. That is , $|\mathcal{W} \cap U| \geq k$ and $U = S_1 \cup S_2 \cup \ldots \cup S_N$, where N is the number of pooling attribute sets (users). Note that the secret keys of users $\mathbf{SK}_{S_i}^g$ are only known to the owners.

1. Select an arbitrary subset $\mathcal{S}$ with size k of $\mathcal{W} \cap U$.
2. Each user computes $\mathbf{G}_d$ using his id d and publishes $\mathbf{y}_i = (\mathbf{G}_d \cdot \mathbf{x}_i)$ for $i \in [k]$.
3. The ciphertext can be decrypted as follows.
   - Calculate the fraction Lagrangian coefficients L_i; $\sum_{i \in [k]} L_i \mathbf{A}_i \mathbf{y}_i = \mathbf{u} \mod q$.
   - Compute $r \leftarrow \mathbf{c}_2 - ((k \times \mathbf{g})^T + \sum_{i \in [k]} L_i \mathbf{y}_i^T \mathbf{c}_1)(\mod q)$, where $\mathbf{g}$ is the unique key (part of the group public key) of the group with id g. View it as $r \in [-\lfloor q/2 \rfloor, \lfloor q/2 \rfloor) \subset \mathbb{Z}$.
   - If $|r| < q/4$, output 0, else output 1.

Figure 1 depicts the overall view of the lattice-based construction of the scheme.

Setup: Trusted Setup Party generates public parameters $\mathbf{PK}$ for all the other involving parties and master secret key $\mathbf{MSK}$ for the key generator.

Encrypt: Encrypting Party encrypts his message M with the selected access tree $\mathcal{W}$ and stores the ciphertext in the cloud or any other storing location.

KeyGen: Key Generator generates secret keys for individual users for their possessing attributes. For instance, he creates a secret key $\mathbf{SK}_{S1}^g$ for User 1 for the possessing attribute set $S1$.

Decrypt: Each user computes part of the decryption key which decrypts the given ciphertext. The part of the decryption key is produced based on the possessing attributes. For instance, User 1 with satisfying attributes $X_a \in S1$ generates

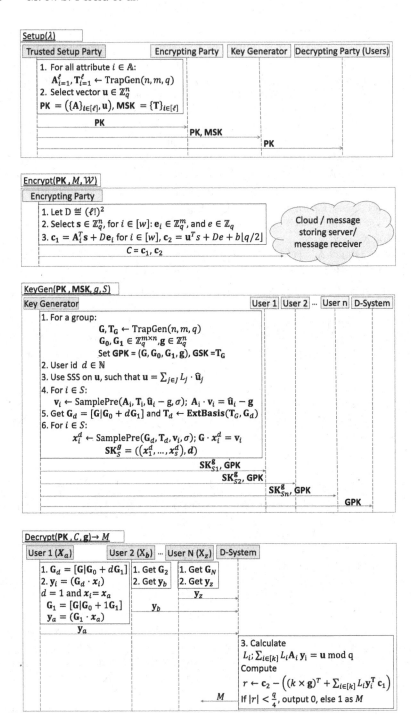

Fig. 1. Lattice-based construction of GO-ABE scheme

y_a share using the relevant secret key x_a. User 2 and other attribute-satisfying users follow the same two steps that were executed by User 1 but with their user id and secret keys for the matching attributes. Then they publish their shares to the decrypting system (D-system). D-System computes the final decryption key from the collected outputs of users and decrypts the ciphertext such that users can access it. Note that D-system may not be a centralized party, but an algorithm embedded in the decryption mechanism of the data location.

5   Analysis of the Scheme

This section shows the correctness and the indistinguishability of the lattice-based GO-ABE scheme.

5.1   Correctness

For the proof of the correctness of the decryption, we only need to consider the case $|J| \geq k$. Let L_j be the fractional Lagrangian coefficient as discussed before.

We compute the below to obtain the decryption of the ciphertext.

$r \leftarrow c_2 - ((k \times g)^T + \sum_{i \in [k]} L_i y_i^T c_1) \pmod{q}$.

Here,

$c_2 = u^T s + e + b\lfloor q/2 \rfloor$

k is the threshold value.

g is the group-related public key vector.

$y_i = (G_d \cdot x_i)$

$c_1 = A_i^T s + e_i$

Thus we can write,

$r \leftarrow c_2 - ((k \times g)^T + \sum_{i \in [k]} L_i y_i^T c_1)(\mod q)$ as

$r \leftarrow (u^T s + De + b\lfloor q/2 \rfloor) - ((k \times g)^T + (\sum_{i \in [k]} L_i (G_d \cdot x_i)^T A_i^T s + De_i))$.

In simple,

$r \leftarrow b\lfloor q/2 \rfloor + (u^T s - ((k \times g)^T + (\sum_{i \in [k]} L_i (G_d \cdot x_i A_i)^T s))) + (Dx - \sum_{i \in [k]} DL_i x_i^T e_i)(\mod q) \approx b\lfloor q/2 \rfloor$.

Here, $(Dx - \sum_{i \in [k]} DL_i x_i^T e_i) \approx 0$.

This proves the correctness of our scheme's construction.

The correctness of our scheme shown above is based on the SSS scheme and the correctness of Agrawal's scheme [5] we emphasize that the GO-ABE construction from lattices works properly only allowing users from the same group to collaborate to decrypt a given ciphertext without revealing their secret keys.

5.2   Security Proof

We show the lattice-based construction of GO-ABE provides ciphertext privacy in the Selective-Set model under the hardness of the LWE problem. Since our scheme is constructed using lattice-based cryptography, based on the hardness of the LWE problem our construction is secured. In other words, if an adversary can break the security of our scheme, then with the support of that adversary the LWE problem can be solved.

Theorem 1. *If there is an adversary $\mathcal{A}$ with advantage $\epsilon > 0$ against the selective-set model for the GO-ABE scheme, then there exists a PPT algorithm $\mathcal{B}$ that can solve the decision-LWE problem.*

Proof. The simulator $\mathcal{B}$ uses the adversary $\mathcal{A}$ to distinguish LWE oracle $\mathcal{O}$. First $\mathcal{B}$ queries the LWE oracle $\mathcal{O}$ for $(\ell m + 1)$ times and obtain LWE samples $(\mathbf{a}_k, b_k) \in \mathbb{Z}_q^n \times \mathbb{Z}_q$, where $k \in \{0, 1, 2, \ldots, m\}$. Then $\mathcal{B}$ proceeds as below. Take the public key $\mathbf{GPK} = (\mathbf{G}, \mathbf{G}_0, \mathbf{G}_1, \mathbf{g})$ and secret key $\mathbf{T}_G$ for each group with id g.

- **Init**: $\mathcal{A}$ announces the challenging access structure $\mathcal{W}^*$ to $\mathcal{B}$.
- **Setup**: $\mathcal{B}$ prepares the public keys as follows.
  1. Choose ℓ matrices $\hat{\mathbf{A}}_i$, $i \in [\ell]$ from LWE challenge as $\{(\mathbf{a}_0, b_0), (\mathbf{a}_i^1, b_i^1), (\mathbf{a}_i^2, b_i^2), \ldots, (\mathbf{a}_i^m, b_i^m)\}_{i \in [\ell]}$.
  2. Select ℓ matrices $\mathbf{A}_i$ and trapdoors $\mathbf{T}_i$ using TrapGen.
  3. Set vector $\mathbf{u}$ from LWE challenge $\mathbf{a}_0$.
  4. Give public parameters to $\mathcal{A}$.
- **Phase 1**: $\mathcal{B}$ answers each private key query for attribute set $\mathcal{S}$ as follows.
  1. Let $\mathcal{S} \cap \mathcal{W}^* := I \subset [\ell]$ and let $|I| = t < k$. (Assume first set of t attributes in $\mathcal{S}$ is equal to attributes in $\mathcal{W}^*$.
  2. Represents the shares of $\mathbf{u}$ as $\hat{\mathbf{u}}_i = \mathbf{u} + \mathbf{w}_1 i + \mathbf{w}_2 i^2 + \ldots + \mathbf{w}_{k-1} i^{k-1}$ where $\mathbf{w}_1, \ldots \mathbf{w}_{k-1}$ are vectors of length n each.
  3. For all $i \in [t]$ select $\mathbf{v}_i$ and set $\hat{\mathbf{u}}_i := (\mathbf{A}_i \mathbf{v}_i) + \mathbf{g}$.
  4. For all $[k-1-t]$ shares, that is for $\hat{\mathbf{u}}_{t+1}, \ldots, \hat{\mathbf{u}}_{k-1}$ determine values for $\mathbf{w}_1 \ldots \mathbf{w}_{k-1}$ such that all ℓ shares of $\hat{\mathbf{u}}_1, \ldots, \hat{\mathbf{u}}_\ell$ are determined.
  5. Invoke SamplePre$(\mathbf{A}_i, \mathbf{T}_j, \hat{\mathbf{u}}_j, \sigma)$ to find $\mathbf{v}_i$ such that $(\mathbf{A}_i \mathbf{v}_i) + \mathbf{g} = \hat{\mathbf{u}}_i$.
  6. Return $(\mathbf{v}_1, \ldots, \mathbf{v}_\ell)$.
- **Challenge**: $\mathcal{A}$ outputs challenge messages M_0 and M_1. The simulator $\mathcal{B}$ responds with a challenge ciphertext for $\mathcal{W}^*$ as follows.
  1. Let $c_1 = (Db_i^1, Db_i^2, \ldots, Db_i^m)$ for $i \in [\ell]$.
  2. Let $c_2 = D\mathbf{a}_0 + M_b \lfloor q/2 \rfloor$.
- **Phase 2**: The simulator repeats Phase 1 under the same conditions.
- **Guess**: The adversary $\mathcal{A}$ outputs a guess b'. If $b = b'$ then $\mathcal{A}$ wins the game.

The simulator $\mathcal{B}$ can use the adversary $\mathcal{A}$'s guess to determine an answer to the LWE problem.

Recall in the original construction of the lattice-based scheme the secret keys of attributes are computed based on the user id who are possessing the attributes. According to the construction (given in Sect. 4.2) $\mathbf{v}_i = \mathbf{G}_d \cdot \mathbf{x}_i^d$, where $\mathbf{G}_d = [\mathbf{G} | \mathbf{G}_0 + d\mathbf{G}_1]$ for the user d and $\mathbf{x}_i^d$ is the secret key of the attribute for that user. However, in the proof given above, we provide $\mathbf{v}$ as the secret key of the attribute, and no user id is used in the query. For the discussion of ciphertext privacy, it is not affected.

5.3   Further Discussion

In our scheme and the existing GO-ABE scheme, we have observed that each user shares their decrypted or collaborating output with others to compute the final decryption. We assume that the users communicate or send their results via a secure channel, so that nobody except the final decryption computing system can see each user's shared output, and nobody can trace it back to the original user. We assume the final computing system is a trusted party. We will need to provide a new security model that discusses user privacy against all other parties, in addition to proving the security of our scheme using the existing selective model. Moreover, in this paper, we prove our scheme's security using the existing selective model. It will not be enough when we discuss the security level of the final computing party. Thus, in the future, we need to provide a new security model discussing user privacy against all the other parties. Additionally, we have observed that in both our scheme and the existing GO-ABE scheme, users can pool their attributes even when there is no emergency. We believe that there should be some level of control based on the situation, and we will discuss these limitations in the future. However, the existing GO-ABE scheme with our constuction is more suitable for the applications that requires two or more user collaboartion because of the orgnization structure.

When we compare the efficiency of decryption in the GO-ABE scheme and other ABE schemes, we observe that the GO-ABE scheme's decryption is less efficient. In general ABE schemes, the attribute satisfying a single user involve in decryption, but in the GO-ABE scheme, two or more users and decrypting systems are involved. The decrypting system has to wait until all the user shares are recieved to generate the message. Moreover, other than decrypting process the users have to show that they are from the same group. Thus the construction given in this paper is somewhat less efficient compared to the general ABE schemes. However, the requirement of the GO-ABE scheme is reasonable to fulfill the real-world applications' requirements of collaborating users. The general ABE schemes cannot satisfy user collaboration for accessing data.

6   Conclusion

In this paper, we provided a construction of the GO-ABE scheme from lattices that supports users from the same group to pool their attributes anonymously (without revealing their secret keys) to satisfy a given access tree. Since we used lattice cryptography, our scheme is quantum resistant. The idea of GO-ABE seems advantageous in real-life applications, where multiple user collaboration is required to access data or applications like PHR systems to perform decryption, especially in emergencies. However, some limitations as shown in Sect. 5.3 need to discuss in the future to make GO-ABE more practical. This paper has answered the lack of security against quantum attacks in the GO-ABE schemes. We will discuss other limitations of GO-ABE in our future works.

References

1. Affum, E., Zhang, X., Wang, X.: Lattice CP-ABE scheme supporting reduced-OBDD structure. In: Bhatia, S.K., Tiwari, S., Ruidan, S., Trivedi, M.C., Mishra, K.K. (eds.) Advances in Computer, Communication and Computational Sciences. AISC, vol. 1158, pp. 131–142. Springer, Singapore (2021). https://doi.org/10.1007/978-981-15-4409-5_12

2. Agrawal, S., Boneh, D., Boyen, X.: Efficient lattice (H)IBE in the standard model. In: Gilbert, H. (ed.) EUROCRYPT 2010. LNCS, vol. 6110, pp. 553–572. Springer, Heidelberg (2010). https://doi.org/10.1007/978-3-642-13190-5_28

3. Agrawal, S., Boneh, D., Boyen, X.: Lattice basis delegation in fixed dimension and shorter-ciphertext hierarchical IBE. In: Rabin, T. (ed.) CRYPTO 2010. LNCS, vol. 6223, pp. 98–115. Springer, Heidelberg (2010). https://doi.org/10.1007/978-3-642-14623-7_6

4. Agrawal, S., Boyen, X.: Identity-based encryption from lattices in the standard model. Manuscript, 3 July 2009

5. Agrawal, S., Boyen, X., Vaikuntanathan, V., Voulgaris, P., Wee, H.: Functional encryption for threshold functions (or Fuzzy IBE) from lattices. In: Fischlin, M., Buchmann, J., Manulis, M. (eds.) PKC 2012. LNCS, vol. 7293, pp. 280–297. Springer, Heidelberg (2012). https://doi.org/10.1007/978-3-642-30057-8_17

6. Aluvalu, R., Uma Maheswari, V., Chennam, K.K., Shitharth, S.: Data security in cloud computing using ABE-based access control. Archit. Wirel. Netw. Solut. Secur. Issues 196, 47–61 (2021)

7. Alwen, J., Peikert, C.: Generating shorter bases for hard random lattices. Theory Comput. Syst. 48(3), 535–553 (2011)

8. Attrapadung, N., Libert, B., de Panafieu, E.: Expressive key-policy attribute-based encryption with constant-size ciphertexts. In: Catalano, D., Fazio, N., Gennaro, R., Nicolosi, A. (eds.) PKC 2011. LNCS, vol. 6571, pp. 90–108. Springer, Heidelberg (2011). https://doi.org/10.1007/978-3-642-19379-8_6

9. Bendlin, R., Damgård, I.: Threshold decryption and zero-knowledge proofs for lattice-based cryptosystems. In: Micciancio, D. (ed.) TCC 2010. LNCS, vol. 5978, pp. 201–218. Springer, Heidelberg (2010). https://doi.org/10.1007/978-3-642-11799-2_13

10. Bethencourt, J., Sahai, A., Waters, B.: Ciphertext-policy attribute-based encryption. In: SP 2007, pp. 321–334. IEEE (2007)

11. Beullens, W., Dobson, S., Katsumata, S., Lai, Y.F., Pintore, F.: Group signatures and more from isogenies and lattices: generic, simple, and efficient. Designs, Codes and Cryptography, pp. 1–60 (2023)

12. Boneh, D., Franklin, M.: Identity-based encryption from the Weil pairing. In: Kilian, J. (ed.) CRYPTO 2001. LNCS, vol. 2139, pp. 213–229. Springer, Heidelberg (2001). https://doi.org/10.1007/3-540-44647-8_13

13. Boyen, X.: Attribute-based functional encryption on lattices. In: Sahai, A. (ed.) TCC 2013. LNCS, vol. 7785, pp. 122–142. Springer, Heidelberg (2013). https://doi.org/10.1007/978-3-642-36594-2_8

14. Butnaru, A.I.: Attribute-based encryption for weighted threshold access structures. In: IC ECCO-2022. Technical University of Moldova (2022). https://doi.org/10.52326/ic-ecco.2022/SEC.03

15. Cash, D., Hofheinz, D., Kiltz, E., Peikert, C.: Bonsai trees, or how to delegate a lattice basis. J. Cryptol. 25(4), 601–639 (2012)

16. Cheng, R., Wu, K., Su, Y., Li, W., Cui, W., Tong, J.: An efficient ECC-based CP-ABE scheme for power IoT. Processes **9**(7), 1176 (2021)

17. Cheung, L., Newport, C.: Provably secure ciphertext policy ABE. In: CCS 2007, pp. 456–465 (2007)

18. Cocks, C.: An identity based encryption scheme based on quadratic residues. In: Honary, B. (ed.) Cryptography and Coding 2001. LNCS, vol. 2260, pp. 360–363. Springer, Heidelberg (2001). https://doi.org/10.1007/3-540-45325-3_32

19. Dai, W., et al.: Implementation and evaluation of a lattice-based key-policy ABE scheme. IEEE Trans. Inf. Forensics Secur. **13**(5), 1169–1184 (2017)

20. Das, S., Namasudra, S.: Macpabe: Multi-authority-based CP-ABE with efficient attribute revocation for IoT-enabled healthcare infrastructure. Int. J. Netw. Manag. **33**(3), e2200 (2023)

21. Emura, K., Miyaji, A., Nomura, A., Omote, K., Soshi, M.: A ciphertext-policy attribute-based encryption scheme with constant ciphertext length. In: Bao, F., Li, H., Wang, G. (eds.) ISPEC 2009. LNCS, vol. 5451, pp. 13–23. Springer, Heidelberg (2009). https://doi.org/10.1007/978-3-642-00843-6_2

22. Ge, A., Zhang, R., Chen, C., Ma, C., Zhang, Z.: Threshold ciphertext policy attribute-based encryption with constant size ciphertexts. In: Susilo, W., Mu, Y., Seberry, J. (eds.) ACISP 2012. LNCS, vol. 7372, pp. 336–349. Springer, Heidelberg (2012). https://doi.org/10.1007/978-3-642-31448-3_25

23. Gentry, C., Peikert, C., Vaikuntanathan, V.: Trapdoors for hard lattices and new cryptographic constructions. In: STOC 2008, pp. 197–206 (2008)

24. Goyal, V., Pandey, O., Sahai, A., Waters, B.: Attribute-based encryption for fine-grained access control of encrypted data. In: CCS 2006, pp. 89–98. ACM (2006)

25. Gür, K.D., Polyakov, Y., Rohloff, K., Ryan, G.W., Sajjadpour, H., Savaş, E.: Practical applications of improved gaussian sampling for trapdoor lattices. IEEE Trans. Comput. **68**(4), 570–584 (2018)

26. He, Y., et al.: An efficient ciphertext-policy attribute-based encryption scheme supporting collaborative decryption with blockchain. IEEE Internet Things J. **9**(4), 2722–2733 (2021)

27. Herranz, J., Laguillaumie, F., Ràfols, C.: Constant size ciphertexts in threshold attribute-based encryption. In: Nguyen, P.Q., Pointcheval, D. (eds.) PKC 2010. LNCS, vol. 6056, pp. 19–34. Springer, Heidelberg (2010). https://doi.org/10.1007/978-3-642-13013-7_2

28. Hong, H., Chen, D., Sun, Z.: A practical application of CP-ABE for mobile PHR system: a study on the user accountability. SpringerPlus **5**(1), 1320 (2016)

29. Ibraimi, L., Petkovic, M., Nikova, S., Hartel, P., Jonker, W.: Ciphertext-policy attribute-based threshold decryption with flexible delegation and revocation of user attributes (2009)

30. Jemihin, Z.B., Tan, S.F., Chung, G.C.: Attribute-based encryption in securing big data from post-quantum perspective: a survey. Cryptography **6**(3), 40 (2022)

31. Joshi, M., Joshi, K.P., Finin, T.: Delegated authorization framework for EHR services using attribute based encryption. IEEE Trans. Serv. Comput. **14**(6), 1612–1623 (2019)

32. Katsumata, S., Matsuda, T., Takayasu, A.: Lattice-based revocable (hierarchical) IBE with decryption key exposure resistance. Theor. Comput. Sci. **809**, 103–136 (2020)

33. Lai, J., Guo, F., Susilo, W., Jiang, P., Yang, G., Huang, X.: Generic conversions from CPA to CCA without ciphertext expansion for threshold ABE with constant-size ciphertexts. Inf. Sci. **613**, 966–981 (2022)

34. Langlois, A., Ling, S., Nguyen, K., Wang, H.: Lattice-based group signature scheme with verifier-local revocation. In: Krawczyk, H. (ed.) PKC 2014. LNCS, vol. 8383, pp. 345–361. Springer, Heidelberg (2014). https://doi.org/10.1007/978-3-642-54631-0_20

35. Lewko, A., Okamoto, T., Sahai, A., Takashima, K., Waters, B.: Fully secure functional encryption: attribute-based encryption and (hierarchical) inner product encryption. In: Gilbert, H. (ed.) EUROCRYPT 2010. LNCS, vol. 6110, pp. 62–91. Springer, Heidelberg (2010). https://doi.org/10.1007/978-3-642-13190-5_4

36. Lewko, A., Waters, B.: Decentralizing attribute-based encryption. In: Paterson, K.G. (ed.) EUROCRYPT 2011. LNCS, vol. 6632, pp. 568–588. Springer, Heidelberg (2011). https://doi.org/10.1007/978-3-642-20465-4_31

37. Li, M., Huang, X., Liu, J.K., Xu, L.: GO-ABE: group-oriented attribute-based encryption. In: Au, M.H., Carminati, B., Kuo, C.-C.J. (eds.) NSS 2014. LNCS, vol. 8792, pp. 260–270. Springer, Cham (2014). https://doi.org/10.1007/978-3-319-11698-3_20

38. Li, M., Yu, S., Zheng, Y., Ren, K., Lou, W.: Scalable and secure sharing of personal health records in cloud computing using attribute-based encryption. IEEE Trans. Parallel Distrib. Syst. **24**(1), 131–143 (2012)

39. Li, Q., Xiong, H., Zhang, F., Zeng, S., et al.: An expressive decentralizing KP-ABE scheme with constant-size ciphertext. IJ Netw. Secur. **15**(3), 161–170 (2013)

40. Li, Y., Zhang, Y., Liu, W., Ning, J., Zheng, D.: A collaborative access control scheme based on incentive mechanisms. In: Chen, X., Shen, J., Susilo, W. (eds.) Cyberspace Safety and Security. CSS 2022. LNCS, vol. 13547, pp. 48–55. Springer, Cham (2022). https://doi.org/10.1007/978-3-031-18067-5_4

41. Lin, H., Cao, Z., Liang, X., Shao, J.: Secure threshold multi authority attribute based encryption without a central authority. In: Chowdhury, D.R., Rijmen, V., Das, A. (eds.) INDOCRYPT 2008. LNCS, vol. 5365, pp. 426–436. Springer, Heidelberg (2008). https://doi.org/10.1007/978-3-540-89754-5_33

42. Ling, S., Nguyen, K., Wang, H.: Group signatures from lattices: simpler, tighter, shorter, ring-based. In: Katz, J. (ed.) PKC 2015. LNCS, vol. 9020, pp. 427–449. Springer, Heidelberg (2015). https://doi.org/10.1007/978-3-662-46447-2_19

43. Lu, Z., Guo, Y., Li, J., Jia, W., Lv, L., Shen, J.: Novel searchable attribute-based encryption for the internet of things. Wirel. Commun. Mob. Comput. **2022** (2022)

44. Moffat, S., Hammoudeh, M., Hegarty, R.: A survey on ciphertext-policy attribute-based encryption (CP-ABE) approaches to data security on mobile devices and its application to IoT. In: Proceedings of the International Conference on Future Networks and Distributed Systems (2017)

45. Nali, D., Adams, C.M., Miri, A.: Using threshold attribute-based encryption for practical biometric-based access control. IJ Netw. Secur. **1**(3), 173–182 (2005)

46. Olimid, R.F.: Setup in secret sharing schemes using random values. Secur. Commun. Netw. **9**(18), 6034–6041 (2016)

47. Peikert, C.: A decade of lattice cryptography. Found. Trends Theor. Comput. Sci. **10**(4), 283–424 (2016). https://doi.org/10.1561/0400000074

48. Perera, M.N.S., Nakamura, T., Hashimoto, M., Yokoyama, H., Cheng, C.M., Sakurai, K.: Decentralized and collaborative tracing for group signatures. In: Proceedings of the 2022 ACM on Asia Conference on Computer and Communications Security, pp. 1258–1260 (2022)

49. Porwal, S., Mittal, S.: A fully flexible key delegation mechanism with efficient fine-grained access control in CP-ABE. J. Ambient Intell. Humaniz. Comput. 1–20 (2022)

50. Process, N.P.S.: Lecture 08: Shamir secret sharing (introduction) (2022). https://csrc.nist.gov/News/2022/pqc-candidates-to-be-standardized-and-round-4

51. Pussewalage, H.S.G., Oleshchuk, V.: A delegatable attribute based encryption scheme for a collaborative e-health cloud. IEEE Trans. Serv. Comput. **16**(2), 787–801 (2022)

52. Ramu, G., Reddy, B.E., Jayanthi, A., Prasad, L.N.: Fine-grained access control of EHRs in cloud using CP-ABE with user revocation. Health Technol. **9**(4), 487–496 (2019)

53. Rasori, M., La Manna, M., Perazzo, P., Dini, G.: A survey on attribute-based encryption schemes suitable for the internet of things. IEEE Internet Things J. **9**(11), 8269–8290 (2022)

54. Regev, O.: New lattice-based cryptographic constructions. J. ACM (JACM) **51**(6), 899–942 (2004)

55. Sahai, A., Waters, B.: Fuzzy identity-based encryption. In: Cramer, R. (ed.) EURO-CRYPT 2005. LNCS, vol. 3494, pp. 457–473. Springer, Heidelberg (2005). https://doi.org/10.1007/11426639_27

56. Shamir, A.: How to share a secret. Commun. ACM **22**(11), 612–613 (1979)

57. Shamir, A.: Identity-based cryptosystems and signature schemes. In: Blakley, G.R., Chaum, D. (eds.) CRYPTO 1984. LNCS, vol. 196, pp. 47–53. Springer, Heidelberg (1985). https://doi.org/10.1007/3-540-39568-7_5

58. Shor, P.W.: Polynomial-time algorithms for prime factorization and discrete logarithms on a quantum computer. SIAM Review **41**(2), 303–332 (1999)

59. Shoup, V.: Practical threshold signatures. In: Preneel, B. (ed.) EUROCRYPT 2000. LNCS, vol. 1807, pp. 207–220. Springer, Heidelberg (2000). https://doi.org/10.1007/3-540-45539-6_15

60. Sun, P.J.: Privacy protection and data security in cloud computing: a survey, challenges, and solutions. IEEE Access **7**, 147420–147452 (2019)

61. Tao, X., Lin, C., Zhou, Q., Wang, Y., Liang, K., Li, Y.: Secure and efficient access of personal health record: a group-oriented ciphertext-policy attribute-based encryption. J. Chin. Inst. Eng. **42**(1), 80–86 (2019)

62. Wang, Y.: Lattice ciphertext policy attribute-based encryption in the standard model. IJ Netw. Secur. **16**(6), 444–451 (2014)

63. Wang, Y., Chen, K., Long, Y., Liu, Z.: Accountable authority key policy attribute-based encryption. Sci. China Inf. Sci. **55**(7), 1631–1638 (2012)

64. Waters, B.: Efficient identity-based encryption without random oracles. In: Cramer, R. (ed.) EUROCRYPT 2005. LNCS, vol. 3494, pp. 114–127. Springer, Heidelberg (2005). https://doi.org/10.1007/11426639_7

65. Waters, B.: Ciphertext-policy attribute-based encryption: an expressive, efficient, and provably secure realization. In: Catalano, D., Fazio, N., Gennaro, R., Nicolosi, A. (eds.) PKC 2011. LNCS, vol. 6571, pp. 53–70. Springer, Heidelberg (2011). https://doi.org/10.1007/978-3-642-19379-8_4

66. Xue, Y., Xue, K., Gai, N., Hong, J., Wei, D.S., Hong, P.: An attribute-based controlled collaborative access control scheme for public cloud storage. IEEE Trans. Inf. Forensics Secur. **14**(11), 2927–2942 (2019)

67. Yang, Y., Sun, J., Liu, Z., Qiao, Y.: Practical revocable and multi-authority CP-ABE scheme from RLWE for cloud computing. J. Inf. Secur. Appl. **65**, 103108 (2022)

68. Yin, H., Xiong, Y., Zhang, J., Ou, L., Liao, S., Qin, Z.: A key-policy searchable attribute-based encryption scheme for efficient keyword search and fine-grained access control over encrypted data. Electronics **8**(3), 265 (2019)

69. Yu, S., Wang, C., Ren, K., Lou, W.: Achieving secure, scalable, and fine-grained data access control in cloud computing. In: 2010 Proceedings IEEE INFOCOM, pp. 1–9. IEEE (2010)
70. Yu, S., Wang, C., Ren, K., Lou, W.: Attribute based data sharing with attribute revocation. In: ASIACCS 2010, pp. 261–270. ACM (2010)
71. Zhang, R., Li, J., Lu, Y., Han, J., Zhang, Y.: Key escrow-free attribute based encryption with user revocation. Inf. Sci. **600**, 59–72 (2022)
72. Zhao, S., Jiang, R., Bhargava, B.: RL-ABE: a revocable lattice attribute based encryption scheme based on R-LWE problem in cloud storage. IEEE Trans. Serv. Comput. **15**(2), 1026–1035 (2020)
73. Zhao, Y., Zhang, X., Xie, X., Ding, Y., Kumar, S.: A verifiable hidden policy CP-ABE with decryption testing scheme and its application in VANET. Trans. Emerg. Telecommun. Technol. **33**(5), e3785 (2022)

New LDP Approach Using VAE

Andres Hernandez-Matamoros$^{(\boxtimes)}$ [iD] and Hiroaki Kikuchi [iD]

Meiji University, 4-21-1 Nakano, Nakano-ku, Tokyo 164-8525, Japan
{matamoros,kikn}@meiji.ac.jp
https://www.kikn.fms.meiji.ac.jp

Abstract. Local Differential Privacy allows individuals to share their personal data without compromising their privacy. In traditional data collection and analysis methods, sensitive information such as names, addresses, and other identifying details may be included, making it easy to link the data to a specific individual. On the other hand, Local Differential Privacy enables data to be collected and analyzed in a way that safeguards individual privacy. This makes it possible for people to participate in data collection and analysis without the fear of being identified. While Local Differential Privacy approaches have been proposed for releasing privacy-preserving databases with statistical approximations, they have limitations when dealing with k-dimensional distribution estimations. To address this issue, we propose a solution that guarantees Local Differential Privacy based on the latent space of a Variational AutoEncoder (VAE), which is used to recover the original distribution. We tested our proposal on four real and open datasets with different characteristics, including the number of users, the number of attributes, and their cardinality. The proposed solution outperforms the well-known approach, LoPub. Our work can reduce the average variant distance by the LoPub algorithm from 0.6 to 0.1. These results suggest that the VAE can serve as a useful tool for privacy-preserving data. The source code used in this paper can be downloaded from the following link https://github.com/phdmatamoros/New-LDP-approach-using-VAE.

Keywords: Local Differential Privacy · Latent Space · VAE

1 Introduction

Our everyday activities involve sharing personal information with various services, such as online streaming, food delivery, social media, and filling out application forms. These services store our data on their central servers to obtain insights into their user base or train machine learning models. In recent years, the emergence of Differential Privacy [2], also known as Central Differential Privacy (CDP), aims to release databases for statistical analysis of sensitive individual data while preserving user privacy. One drawback of CDP is that users send their data without protection, entrusting it to the central server.

To address this issue, Local Differential Privacy (LDP) was introduced, where users only trust themselves. LDP is a technique that involves encoding and

© The Author(s), under exclusive license to Springer Nature Switzerland AG 2023
S. Li et al. (Eds.): NSS 2023, LNCS 13983, pp. 177–191, 2023.
https://doi.org/10.1007/978-3-031-39828-5_10

introducing random noise to users' data before sending it to the central server, allowing the central server to compute the distribution of the users' information. By using this approach, it is possible to protect sensitive data while still allowing it to be used for research or other purposes. LDP is also important in situations where privacy is legally mandated, such as in the European Union's General Data Protection Regulation or the California Consumer Privacy Act.

Ren et al. proposed LoPub [3], in which users encode their data using Bloom filters and perturb the encoded data using the Randomize Response (RR) algorithm [10]. The perturbed-encoded data is then transmitted to the central server, which estimates the multi-dimensional joint distribution using the LASSO algorithm [6] and the Expectation Maximization algorithm [7]. While LoPub demonstrates good performance in datasets with low multi-dimensional joint distributions, it encounters issues with low data utility when the number of attributes is high or the cardinality of an attribute is large.

In LDP, both cardinality and attributes have an impact on the data utility and accuracy of the estimated joint distribution. Firstly, cardinality refers to the number of distinct elements in an attribute. In high-dimensional data with a large number of attributes and high cardinality, LDP approaches may experience a reduction in data utility, resulting in compromised estimation accuracy. This occurs because the introduced noise can make it challenging to identify correlations and patterns, leading to inaccurate estimates.

Secondly, highly correlated attributes can also pose challenges in LDP. When attributes exhibit strong correlations, introducing noise to one attribute can cause the noise to propagate to other attributes, leading to a further decline in data utility. This propagation of noise makes it difficult to accurately estimate joint probability distributions. To mitigate the spread of noise across attributes, Mina [1] made an assumption that the features in the dataset are both independent and categorical. Based on this assumption, a framework was developed that incorporates feature selection to generate a synthetic dataset.

We propose leveraging the latent space of a Variational Auto-Encoder (VAE) [18] within LDP to enhance privacy-preserving data analysis. VAEs have been successfully utilized in various domains and applications [16]. By incorporating the VAE's latent space, which captures meaningful representations of the data, we can improve the utility and accuracy of LDP in scenarios with a high number of attributes or large attribute cardinalities. The VAE acts as a denoising and reconstructing tool, enabling precise estimation of joint probability distributions. This approach offers a more effective and privacy-preserving solution compared to traditional LDP methods, especially in complex, high-dimensional datasets.

To evaluate the performance of our VAE based approach in comparison to a baseline method introduced by Ren [3], we conducted experiments on four publicly available datasets featuring varying numbers of users and cardinalities. Our approach follows the data encoding and perturbation method proposed by [3], but with the incorporation of VAE on the central server. Table 1 highlights the distinctions between the [3] method and our proposed approach. The key contributions of this paper can be summarized as follows:

- We propose a novel LDP approach that utilizes a VAE on the central server to estimate joint probability distributions. In our approach, we use a VAE to learn a latent representation of the data that is shared across all parties. This allows us to estimate the joint probability distribution of the data.
- We explore the impact of attribute cardinality on the reconstruction error during VAE training. We find that as the attribute cardinality increases, the reconstruction error also increases. This is because it becomes more difficult for the VAE to learn a latent representation that is able to capture the diversity of the data.
- We compare our proposed approach to [3], a baseline algorithm for LDP. We find that our proposed approach outperforms [3] in terms of accuracy with same privacy budget.
- We demonstrate the effectiveness of VAE in estimating the joint probability distribution through experiments on four diverse datasets. We find that VAE is able to accurately estimate the joint probability distribution of the data in all four datasets.

Table 1. Difference between LoPub and ours

	LoPub [3]	Ours
User	Hash F. Randomize Response	Hash F. Randomize Response
Central Server	LASSO regression	Latent space (VAE)

The paper is structured as follows: Sect. 2 presents the preliminaries, Sect. 3 describes our proposed approach, and the paper concludes with the Experiments and Conclusion sections.

2 Preliminaries

2.1 Generalizing the Problem

In LDP approaches, the users encode and perturb their data before share their information with a central server. By doing this, the users preserve their anonymity. In this work, we follow the user steps proposed by LoPub [3]. We generalize the LDP problem; a dataset U with N users could be represented as $U = \{u^1, u^2, u^3, ..., u^N\}$.

The users have the same number of attributes k, and each attribute has a specific domain. Thinking about the nth user has a k-dimensional vector $(u_1^n, u_2^n, u_3^n, ..., u_k^n)$, the domain of each attribute $j \in \{1, ..., k\}$ is denoted $\Omega_j = \{\omega_i^1, ..., \omega_i^{|\Omega_j|}\}$. The cardinality $|\Omega_j|$ means the number of elements in the attribute j.

2.2   Local Differential Privacy (LDP)

LDP proposes that for any user n, a randomization mechanism Ψ satisfies ϵ-LDP if and only if for any two records u^n, w^n, and for any outputs $\tilde{u_\tau} \in \text{Range}(\Psi)$, the probability computed over Ψ's and $\epsilon > 0$; privacy budget holds

$$Pr[\Psi(u^n) = \tilde{u_\tau}] \le e^\epsilon Pr[\Psi(w^n) = \tilde{u_\tau}] \tag{1}$$

On Eq. (1), we can figure how important is the privacy budget. A smaller ϵ means stronger privacy protection, and viceversa.

2.3   Privacy Analysis

User privacy is preserved by claiming the privacy of local randomizers, which all user run on data records separately. Local perturbation of a specific attribute value can achieve ϵ-LDP, where $\epsilon = 2h \ln \frac{2-f}{f}$, with h being the number of hash functions in the Bloom filter [9] and f the flip bit probability. Based on the sequential composition theorem [14], the local transformation of a k-dimensional data record achieves ϵ-LDP, where:

$$\epsilon = 2kh \ln \frac{2-f}{f},$$

with k being the number of attributes in the original data. Because all users perform the same transformation independently, the above ϵ-LDP guarantee applies to all distributed users.

2.4   Lopub Scheme

The LDP approach relies on the participation of two components: users and a central server. In this work, we utilize the algorithm proposed by Ren [3] to encode and perturb users' data. Our proposal involves replacing the LASSO and EM algorithms with VAE in the central server.

User. This section explains how users encode and perturb their data, an approach consisting of two main steps:

- Encoding user information. The user input is represented using a Bloom filter (BF) $\mathcal{H}$, a technique used to test whether an element is a member of a set; it is a probabilistic data structure proposed by Bloom [9]. To encode each u_j^n, the user incorporates BF using a set $\mathcal{H}_j$ of hash functions that are designed for U_j, where U_j is the jth attribute of U. Specifically, the user applies h_j hash functions $\mathcal{H}_{j,1}, \ldots, \mathcal{H}_{j,h_j}$ from $\mathcal{H}_j$ to map u_j^n to a length-m_j bit string s_j^n, where m_j is the length of the BF. Therefore, u_j^n is inserted into a length m_j bit BF using h_j hash functions from $\mathcal{H}_j$, represented as $H_j(\omega)$, where

$s_j^n[b]$ denotes the bth bit of the bit string s_j^n. The length of BF m_j for U_j is computed as:

$$m_j = \frac{\ln \frac{1}{p}}{\ln 2^2}|\Omega_j|, \tag{2}$$

where $|\Omega_j|$ is the cardinality of the attribute U_j and p is the false positive probability; in our experiments we set $p = 0.022$.

- Perturbing the data. Randomized Response (RR) is a method proposed by Warner [10] that allows interviewee to give their answers while maintaining confidentiality. Randomly whether the question is to be answered truthfully is unknown to the interviewer. RR is applied after encoding each step, where each bit $s_j^n[b]$ $(b = 1, 2, \ldots, m_j)$ is randomly flipped using the following rule:

$$\hat{s}_j^i = \begin{cases} s_j^n \text{ with probability of } 1 - f, \\ 1 \text{ with probability of } f/2, \\ 0 \text{ with probability of } f/2 \end{cases} \tag{3}$$

Where $f \in [0, 1]$ is the probability of flipping a bit randomly. Once the randomized BF s_j^n is obtained, the nth user combines s_1^i through s_k^n to create a bit vector $(s_1^n||...||s_k^n)$, which consists of $(\sum_{j=1}^{k} m_j)$ bits. This resultant vector is transmitted to the server.

Central Server. After users encode and perturb their data, they send their data to the central server, which receives the distribution of users with random noise added by RR. For each bit b in each attribute j, the central server counts the number of frequencies of the perturbed value $\hat{s}_j^i$ as $\hat{y}_j[b] = \sum_{i=1}^{N} \hat{s}_j^i[b]$. Next, the original count $y_j[b]$ is estimated as

$$y[b] = \frac{\hat{y}[b] - \frac{fN}{2}}{1 - f},$$

where after the original count is computed, the candidate bit matrix is created using a candidate set of Bloom filters $\mathcal{H}$, as $M = [\mathcal{H}_1(\Omega_1) \times \mathcal{H}_2(\Omega_2) \times \cdots \times \mathcal{H}_d(\Omega_d)]$, where d is the number of attributes. As we illustrate, the block diagram in Fig. 1 reviews how it works from the previous steps applied by the central server and gives an example with $k = 2$-way, estimating the distribution of two attributes in the following steps. To estimate the distribution from the noise data using a regression technique, $y = M\beta$. LASSO, is a linear regression technique that performs regularization order to improve prediction accuracy; it was introduced by [8]. If the reader wants to read more about the whole process, please refer to [3].

3   Proposed Scheme

3.1   VAE Preliminaries

Auto-Encoders (AE) were introduced by Hinton in 1986 [17]. They are designed to encode input data into an essential representation and then decode it back

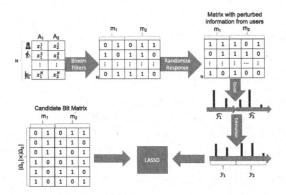

Fig. 1. Central server block diagram proposed by [3] computing the joint distributions of two attributes for N users.

to create a reconstructed input that is as similar as possible to the original input. AE consists of two parts: the encoder and the decoder. The input to the encoder is the data Γ. The output of the encoder is called Y, which is the reduced representation of Γ in a latent space. Next, the decoder is adjusted to reconstruct the data Γ. Finally, the decoder reconstructs the original data Γ from Y by minimizing the Euclidean distance between Γ and Γ'.

Later, in 2013, Kingma proposed a variation of AE called Variational Auto-Encoder (VAE) [18]. The main difference between AE and VAE is that the encoder in AE outputs latent vectors, whereas VAE imposes a constraint on this latent distribution, forcing it to be a normal distribution. VAE has two main stages: training and testing. In the training stage of VAE, a reconstruction error function $RE(\Gamma, \Gamma')$ is defined as follows:

$$RE\left(\Gamma, \Gamma'\right) = \sqrt{\sum \left(\Gamma - \Gamma'\right)^2} + MMD(V, Sample_z), \qquad (4)$$

where V is the output of VAE's encoder and $Sample_z$ is drawn from $\mathcal{N}(0,1)$, the Maximum Mean Discrepancy (MMD) distance measures the distance between the feature maps of two probability distributions. A smaller distance suggests that the two distributions are more alike.

3.2   VAE Model

Training. During the training step, the Algorithm 1 is applied to synthesizing two datasets.

– X contains the encoded information of each attribute.
– X' is X after being perturbed using RR.

Using these datasets, our model trains to create a latent space for each attribute available in the dataset. VAE is trained on two datasets: a perturbed dataset X' and a non-perturbed dataset X, where $RR(X) = X'$ (Fig. 2). These

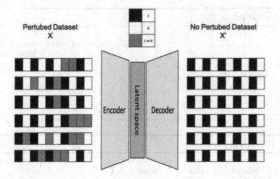

Fig. 2. How train VAE.

Algorithm 1. Creating Datasets

Require: j^{th} attribute   ▷ Attribute on Dataset
Require: $t = 1000$ ▷ Perturbed times
Require: $X_j = [\ ]$ ▷ No perturbed
Require: $X'_j = [\ ]$ ▷ Perturbed
Require: $L_j = [\ ]$ ▷ Attributes Label
Require: f ▷ Flip Bit Probability
  for *element* in j **do**
    $\mathcal{H}_j$ ▷ The Bloom filters on j^{th} attribute
    for *each* $p = 1, 2, ..., t$ **do**
      $X_j \leftarrow [X_j, \mathcal{H}_j(element)]$ ▷ Append
      $X'_j \leftarrow [X'_j, RR(\mathcal{H}_j(element), f)]$ ▷ Append
      $L_j \leftarrow [L_j, element]$ ▷ Append
    end for
  end for
  return X_j, X'_j, L_j

---

datasets are created by the central server using the method described in Algorithm 1. For this experiment, the central server creates one thousand artificial users per attribute in both X and X' datasets. The datasets are then split into training and validation sets with a ratio of 90% and 10%, respectively.

The Algorithm 2 invokes Algorithms 1 and 3. Given a specific value of f, Algorithm 1 uses it to create datasets X and X' for each attribute. Algorithm 3 is used to train the VAE. A summary of the VAE is available in Appendix A.1. In Algorithm 3, a simplified algorithm for training the VAE is presented. For further details on how to train the VAE, please refer to [11].

The outputs of Algorithm 2 are the encoder E_j and the latent space Y_j for attribute j. The latent space models the cardinality for each element in the attribute. Examples of a $2D$ latent space for the "Marital Status" and "Sex" attributes in the Adult dataset are shown in Fig. 5. In our experiments, we set the latent space as $4D$.

Latent Space Evaluation. Once the model has been trained on synthetic datasets, it is evaluated using real datasets. To achieve this, the records of perturbed data are transformed into the latent space by the VAE encoder. Sub-

Algorithm 2. Main algorithm

Require: $t = 1000$ ▷ Perturbed times
Require: k ▷ Number of attributes on the original dataset
Require: f ▷ Flip Bit Probability Value
  for each j=1,..., k **do**
    $X_j, X_j', L_j \leftarrow Creating\ Datasets(j, f, t)$ ▷ Algorithm 1
    $E_j, V_j \leftarrow TrainingVAE(X_j, X_j')$ ▷ Algorithm 3
  end for
  return E_j, V_j, L_j

Algorithm 3. Training VAE

Require: X_j, X_j' ▷ Created by Algorithm 1
Require: Encoder of VAE please refer to Appendix A.1
Require: Decoder of VAE please refer to Appendix A.1
Require: epochs=1000
Require: Optimizer Adam, lr=0.0001
  $patience = 0$
  for each $epoch = 1$,..., epochs **do**
    $Y_j \leftarrow Encoder_j(X_j')$
    $W_j \leftarrow Decoder_j(Y_j)$
    $Re_j \leftarrow RE(X_j, W_j)$ ▷ Eq. 4
    Using lr update internal parameters of VAE
    $Re_{epoch} \leftarrow$ average of Re_j
    if $Re_{epoch} \geq Re_{epoch-1}$ **then**
      $patience \leftarrow patience + 1$
    end if
    if patience=16 **then**
      finish training
    end if
  end for
  return $Encoder_j, Y_j$

---

sequently, the approach calculates the Euclidean distance between the user's coordinates and the latent space created during the training step for a specific attribute.

For simplicity, the latent space Y_j which belongs to the jth attribute using f value will be represented as Y in the following expressions. Y is a matrix with s rows and d columns, where s is the number of elements of latent space and d is the dimension of the latent space. In our experiments the dimension of latent space d is four and the number of elements of latent space s is $900|\Omega_j|$ for each jth attribute.

$$Y = \begin{bmatrix} Y_{1,1}, Y_{1,2}, ..., Y_{1,d} \\ Y_{2,1}, Y_{2,2}, ..., Y_{2,d} \\ Y_{3,1}, Y_{3,2}, ..., Y_{3,d} \\ ... \\ Y_{s,1}, Y_{s,2}, ..., Y_{s,d} \end{bmatrix}$$

The latent space evaluation consists of two steps, as shown in Fig. 3;

- The first step is performed by the encoder E_j, which transforms i^{th} user's record into the latent space. E_j outputs a vector V of size d, where each component V_i corresponds to a dimension in the latent space.

$$E_j(i^{th} \text{ user's record}) = (V_1, ..., V_d)$$

- We compare the vector V with the latent space Y_j, which was computed during the training stage. Our proposed method involves computing the Euclidean distance between V and each row in the matrix Y_j. By identifying the index of the row that exhibits the closest similarity to V, we evaluate this index in L_j which is created using Algorithm 1, to determine the potential element in the attribute.

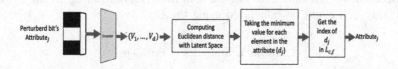

Fig. 3. Latent Space Evaluation.

Algorithm 4. Inference Attribute

Require: E_i, Y_i, L_i
Require: $D = [\ ]$ ▷ Recovered Dataset
Require: fpb
  for each $u = 1, 2, ..., Users$ **do**
    for each j=1,...,k **do**
      $V \leftarrow E_j(j)$ ▷ Transforming V into Latent Space
      $d_j = dis(V, Y_j)$ ▷ Computing Euclidean distance
      $j^* = argmin(d_j)$
      $D(u, j) \leftarrow L_j(j^*)$
    end for
  end for
  return D

After Algorithm 4 finishes, we obtain D, where each row represents an anonymous user and each column represents a possible attribute. This matrix can be used to estimate the joint distribution of the original dataset. To calculate the joint probability distribution of two or more attributes for the users in D, follow these steps:

- Calculate the total number of users in the D.
- Count the frequency of each combination of attribute values for the users of interest. It is the joint frequency distribution.
- Divide the joint frequency of each combination by the number of users to obtain the joint probability of that combination.

4   Experiments

4.1   Experimental Method

We tested our approach on four open datasets from different areas. The Nursery dataset [15] was originally created in the 1980s s to evaluate applications for nursery schools in Europe. The NHANES dataset [12] was used in the PWS Cup 2021 [13] to provide anonymized healthcare data. The Adult dataset [4] is one of the most popular datasets used to measure the performance of CDP and LDP approaches. The Bank dataset [5] contains information about marketing campaigns. Table 2 summarizes the datasets, showing the number of users, attributes, their cardinality, and their size after encoding.

The default parameters for our approach are as follows: we use $h = 5$ hash functions for all four datasets. The value of m varies depending on the dataset's cardinality and could be calculated using the Eq. 2.

Table 2. Statistics of Datasets

Dataset	Users	Attributes	Cardinality		m	
			min	max	min	max
Adult	45223	8	2	16	8	64
Bank	45212	10	2	12	8	47
Nursery	12960	9	2	5	8	20
NHANES	4190	5	2	6	8	23

4.2 Results

VAE Reconstruction Error (RE). We evaluated the Reconstruction Error (RE) during the training stage of the VAE using Eq. 4. The results are presented in Figs. 4(a)–(b). Figure 4(a) displays the results for the Adult dataset, where the attribute $marital - status$ exhibits a lower reconstruction error compared to the attribute sex. A comparison between their latent spaces is depicted in Figs. 5(a) and (b). For simplicity, the latent spaces are shown in 2D, although 4D were used in the experiments.

Figure 4(b) shows the results for the NHANES dataset, with the attribute *Education* having a lower RE than the others. The attribute Qm demonstrates the highest reconstruction error.

Joint Probability. We randomly selected k-way joint probabilities of attributes one hundred times. To analyze the joint distributions, we used the Average Variance Distance (AVD) metric to quantify the difference between the real and computed data. The AVD distance, as used by [3], is defined as follows:

$$AVD = \frac{1}{2} \sum_{\omega \in \Omega} |P(\omega) - Q(\omega)|. \tag{5}$$

Figures 6(a)–(d) show the results of VAE and LASSO using color and grayscale, respectively. The x-axis corresponds to the AVD distance, while the y-axis shows the algorithms with a flip bit probability $f = 0.5$. LASSO regression,

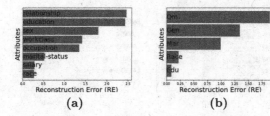

Fig. 4. Reconstruction Error with $f = 0.5$ **(a)** Adult, **(b)** NHANES Datasets.

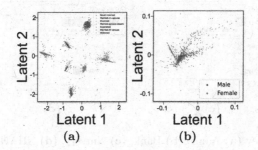

Fig. 5. Latent Space for Adult dataset with $f = 0.1$ on training stage **(a)** Marital Status, **(b)** Sex Attributes.

proposed by [3], was used to recover the original distribution in LDP schemes. In summary, the comparison of LASSO and VAE models on different datasets revealed interesting insights. In the NHANES dataset, LASSO struggled to capture complex patterns, as indicated by increasing AVD distances with higher values of k-way. On the other hand, VAE consistently outperformed LASSO, suggesting its ability to effectively capture latent representations and reproduce patterns in the NHANES dataset.

Similarly, on the Adults dataset, LASSO exhibited decreasing predictive accuracy with higher model complexity, while VAE consistently outperformed LASSO with lower AVD distances. This indicates that VAE's capacity to capture latent representations and generate data is advantageous for the Adults dataset.

The Nursery dataset posed challenges for LASSO, as it struggled to accurately predict values with higher values of k-way. In contrast, VAE significantly outperformed LASSO on the Nursery dataset, indicating its superior ability to capture complex relationships and reproduce values accurately.

The Bank dataset showed relatively good performance for LASSO, with low AVD distances across all values of k-way. VAE slightly outperformed LASSO, indicating its capability to capture and reproduce underlying patterns in the Bank dataset.

In summary, VAE consistently outperformed LASSO in terms of AVD distances across different datasets and values of k-way. VAE's ability to capture latent representations and generate data allows it to capture complex patterns and relationships better, resulting in improved predictive accuracy.

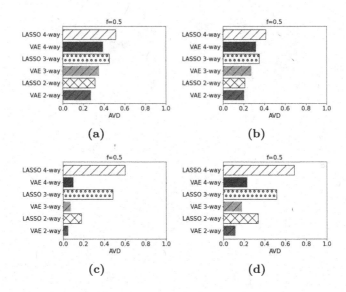

Fig. 6. Accuracy **(a)** Adult, **(b)** Bank, **(c)** Nursery, **(d)** NHANES Datasets.

Figures 7(a)–(d) display the results of VAE and LASSO with $f = 0.5$ when varying the number of users N. The dotted line represents the results of Lasso, while the solid line represents the results of VAE. The blue color represents the results of k-way=2, yellow represents k-way=3, and green represents k-way=4. Then, we discuss the performance for each dataset

In the Adult dataset shown in Fig. 7(a), VAE performs better than LASSO for all values of k-way when $N > 15000$. In the case where k-way is two and $N < 15000$, LASSO and VAE have similar performance. However, when $N = 5000$, LASSO shows better performance than our approach, but the difference between the two is minimal.

In the Bank dataset shown in Fig. 7(b), VAE outperforms LASSO for k-way equal to four when $N > 10000$. For k-way equal to three and $N > 15000$, VAE also outperforms LASSO. However, for k-way equal to two, VAE performs better when $N < 30000$, after which LASSO and VAE exhibit similar performance.

In the Nursery dataset shown in Fig. 7(c), VAE outperforms LASSO for k-way={3,4}, regardless of the number of users. For k-way=2 and $N > 3000$, VAE also outperforms LASSO.

Finally, in NHANES dataset, VAE outperforms LASSO for k-way={2, 3, 4}, regardless of the number of users.

The difference in AVD values across the Dataset is related to the cardinality of the attributes. For instance, the Nursery dataset has more attributes than the Adult dataset, but the Adult dataset exhibits the maximum cardinality, as shown in Table 2. The experimental results demonstrate that VAE outperforms LASSO for all four datasets analyzed in this paper when the number of users is greater than half the size of the original dataset.

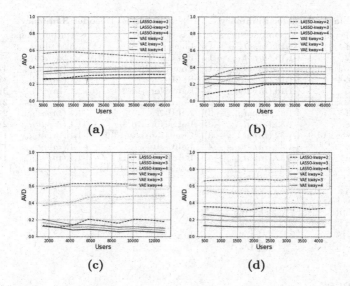

Fig. 7. Accuracy versus N users with $f = 0.5$ (a) Adult, (b) Bank, (c) Nursery, (d) NHANES Datasets.

5   Conclusions

In conclusion, this work proposes the use of the latent space of a VAE in the central server of the LDP scheme to calculate the joint probability. The approach is tested on real datasets with varying numbers of users and attribute cardinalities using a single VAE model. The results show that VAE outperforms LASSO regression, as it allows each attribute to have its own independent latent space, preventing noise from one attribute from affecting others. The AVD of VAE exhibits stable behavior across different numbers of users, indicating that the LDP model using VAE can be applied to extract information from datasets that increase over time. Future work includes investigating the relationship between attribute cardinality and corresponding latent space to develop an improved VAE model, which could be used to create synthetic datasets by computing correlations between attributes.

Acknowledgements. This work was supported by JST, CREST Grant Number JPMJCR21M1, Japan.

A   Appendix

A.1   VAE's Summary

This appendix provides an overview of the VAE architecture. For more detailed information on these concepts, please refer to [11].

Table A. Encoder Summary

Layer(Type)	Output Shape
Conv1d-1	$[-1,16,(input_{dim}-1)]$
ReLU-2	$[-1,16,(input_{dim}-1)]$
BatchNorm1d-3	$[-1,16,(input_{dim}-1)]$
Conv1d-4	$[-1,16,(input_{dim}-2)]$
ReLU-5	$[-1,16,(input_{dim}-2)]$
BatchNorm1d-6	$[-1,16,(input_{dim}-2)]$
Conv1d-7	$[-1,32,(input_{dim}-3)]$
ReLU-8	$[-1,32,(input_{dim}-3)]$
BatchNorm1d-9	$[-1,32,(input_{dim}-3)]$
Conv1d-10	$[-1,32,(input_{dim}-4)]$
ReLU-11	$[-1,32,(input_{dim}-4)]$
BatchNorm1d-12	$[-1,32,(input_{dim}-4)]$
Linear-13	$[-1,64]$
ReLU-14	$[-1,64]$
BatchNorm1d-15	$[-1,64]$
Linear-16	$[-1,16]$
ReLU-17	$[-1,16]$
Linear-18	$[-1,4]$
Linear-19	$[-1,4]$

Table B. Decoder Summary

Layer(Type)	Output Shape
Linear-1	$[-1,1,32\text{x}(input_{dim}-4)]$
ReLU-2	$[-1,1,32\text{x}(input_{dim}-4)]$
ConvTranspose1d-3	$[-1,1,(input_{dim}-4)]$
ReLU-4	$[-1,1,(input_{dim}-3)]$
BatchNorm1d-5	$[-1,1,(input_{dim}-3)]$
ConvTranspose1d-6	$[-1,1,(input_{dim}-2)]$
ReLU-7	$[-1,1,(input_{dim}-2)]$
BatchNorm1d-8	$[-1,1,(input_{dim}-2)]$
ConvTranspose1d-9	$[-1,1,(input_{dim}-1)]$
ReLU-10	$[-1,1,(input_{dim}-1)]$
BatchNorm1d-11	$[-1,1,(input_{dim}-1)]$
ConvTranspose1d-12	$[-1,1,input_{dim}]$

References

1. Alishahi, M., Moghtadaiee, V., Navidan, H.: Add noise to remove noise: local differential privacy for feature selection. Comput. Secur. **123**, 102934 (2022). https://doi.org/10.1016/j.cose.2022.102934. ISSN: 0167-4048

2. Dwork, C., Roth, A.: The algorithmic foundations of differential privacy. Found. Trends Theoret. Comput. Sci. **9**(3–4), 211–407 (2014)

3. Ren, X., et al.: *LoPub*: high-dimensional crowdsourced data publication with local differential privacy. IEEE Trans. Inf. Forensics Secur. **13**, 2151–2166 (2018). https://doi.org/10.1109/TIFS.2018.2812146

4. Adult: UCI Machine Learning Repository (1996)

5. Moro, S., Rita, P., Cortez, P.: Bank Marketing. In: UCI Machine Learning Repository (2012)

6. Zou, H., Hastie, T., Tibshirani, R.: On the "degrees of freedom" of the lasso, Institute of Mathematical Statistics, 35, The Annals of Statistics

7. Dempster, A.P., Laird, N.M., Rubin, D.B.: Maximum likelihood from incomplete data via the EM algorithm. J. Roy. Statist. Soc.: Ser. **39**, 1–22 (1977)

8. Santosa, F., Symes, W.W.: Linear inversion of band-limited reflection seismograms. SIAM J. Sci. Statist. Comput. **7**(4), 1307–1330 (1986). https://doi.org/10.1137/0907087

9. Bloom, B.H.: Space/time trade-offs in hash coding with allowable errors. Commun. ACM **13**(7), 422–426 (1970)

10. Warner, S.L.: Randomized response: a survey technique for eliminating evasive answer bias. J. Am. Statist. Assoc. **60**, 63–69 (1965)

11. Alzubaidi, L., Zhang, J., Humaidi, A.J., et al.: Review of deep learning: concepts, CNN architectures, challenges, applications, future directions. J Big Data **8**, 53 (2021). https://doi.org/10.1186/s40537-021-00444-8

12. Kikuchi, H.: PWS Cup: Data Anonymization Competition 'Diabetes' (2021). https://github.com/kikn88/pwscup2021. Accessed 10 May 2023

13. PWS: PWS (2021). https://www.iwsec.org/pws/2021/cup21.html. Accessed 10 May 2023

14. McSherry, F.D.: Privacy integrated queries: an extensible platform for privacy-preserving data analysis. In: Proceedings of the ACM SIGMOD, pp. 19–30 (2009)
15. Rajkovic, V.: Nursery, UCI Machine Learning Repository (1997)
16. Bengio, Y., Yao, L., Alain, G., Vincent, P.: Generalized denoising auto-encoders as generative models. In: Advances in Neural Information Processing Systems (2013)
17. Rumelhart, D.E., Hinton, G.E., Williams, R.J. : Learning internal representations by error propagation. In: Parallel Distributed Processing: Explorations in the Microstructure of Cognition: Foundations, pp. 318–362. MIT Press (1987)
18. Diederik, P.: Kingma. Auto-Encoding Variational Bayes, ICLR, Max Welling (2014)

Machine Learning

Privacy-Preserving Federated Learning with Hierarchical Clustering to Improve Training on Non-IID Data

Songwei Luo[1]([✉]) [iD], Shaojing Fu[1]([✉]) [iD], Yuchuan Luo[1] [iD], Lin Liu[1] [iD],
Yanxiang Deng[1] [iD], and Shixiong Wang[2]

[1] College of Computer, National University of Defense Technology, Changsha, China
{luosongwei20,fushaojing,luoyuchuan09,liulin16,
dengyanxiang20}@nudt.edu.cn
[2] Academy of Military Sciences, Beijing, China

Abstract. Federated learning (FL), as a privacy-enhanced distributed machine learning paradigm, has achieved tremendous success in solving the data silo problem. However, data heterogeneity (Non-IID data) between parties (data owners) poses challenges for the vanilla federated learning aggregation approach (FedAvg), including more interaction rounds and lower accuracy of the global model. To address this challenge, some works make improvements based on FedAvg. However, most of these works do not consider the privacy protection of gradients, which would leak private data information about the parties involved in the training. To protect parties' privacy and enhance the FL training on Non-IID data at the same time, in this paper, we present PPFL+HC, an efficient, private FL framework. Our PPFL+HC follows the state-of-the-art Non-IID FL method (FL+HC IJCNN'20), which presents a modification to FL by introducing a hierarchical clustering step to separate clusters of parties by the similarity of their local gradients, adapting it to the privacy-preserving context. We design a series of secure cryptographic protocols to ensure the privacy of parties. Specifically, first, we use additive secret sharing to protect local gradients and global gradients privacy, while using pseudorandom generation techniques to reduce half the communication overhead. Second, we design a secure and efficient Euclidean distance computation and Manhattan distance computation protocol to accelerate the secure hierarchical clustering process. Finally, to improve the computational efficiency of the clustering process, we perform randomized gradient cropping to reduce the computational overhead while ensuring the accuracy of clustering. Moreover, experiments conducted on two real-world datasets demonstrate that our PPFL+HC achieves secure and efficient FL training for Non-IID data.

Keywords: Federated Learning · Privacy-preserving · Non-IID Data · 2PC

S. Li et al. (Eds.): NSS 2023, LNCS 13983, pp. 195–216, 2023.
https://doi.org/10.1007/978-3-031-39828-5_11

1   Introduction

Federated learning (FL) [23] is a novel distributed machine learning framework that empowers privacy-conscious participants to train jointly, and has been applied in real-world scenarios, such as Google's mobile keyboard prediction [13], intelligent medical diagnosis [7] and treatment systems to protect patient's privacy [19], and WeBank's credit risk prediction [5]. Roughly speaking, FL completes the joint training of participants (e.g. mobile users) via aggregating local updates (e.g., gradients) under the coordination of a service provider (e.g. aggregation server), while keeping the private datasets of participants local. Despite these advantages, works [9,10,41] have shown that FL still suffers from privacy threats, e.g., the service provider can infer private information (e.g., sensitive data of participants) from the uploaded gradients, which violates data protection regulations, such as General Data Protection Regulation (GDPR) [34]. Meanwhile, heterogeneous data, i.e., non-independent and identically distributed data (Non-IID data) poses challenges to FL [33,38,39]. Concretely, in the real-world FL scenarios, it is common that the private data of participants do not conform to independent and identically distributed (IID) settings, which negatively affects the performance of the global model in vanilla FL.

To address the privacy leakage problem of gradients in FL, many secure aggregation schemes [1,6,12,22] based on cryptographic protocols are proposed for enhancing the security of vanilla FL. For example, several schemes [1,22] use homomorphic encryption (HE) to encrypt local gradients and perform aggregation without decryption, so the service provider cannot compromise the private data of parties. Besides, some works [6,12] utilize secure multi-party computation (MPC) to achieve privacy protection for gradients, since MPC can perform arbitrary function evaluations without revealing participants' inputs. On the other hand, to improve the performance of FL on Non-IID data, several works [4,8,11,21] based on FedAvg [23] have been proposed. For instance, work [21] fine-tunes the local training process, i.e., adds a regularization term in the objective function, to reduce the weight divergence between the different participants.

Although there are many efforts to address the privacy leakage problem as well as the data heterogeneity problem, most of them consider these two components separately. Many solutions to address privacy leakage do not apply to Non-IID scenarios, while many solutions that work to improve the performance of FL on Non-IID data do not consider the privacy protection of the gradients, and they tend to collect local gradients of participants directly. Some schemes [26,35,40] based on differential privacy consider both aspects, but the noise added to gradients can negatively affect the global model accuracy.

In this paper, we implement privacy-preserving FL with hierarchical clustering (PPFL+HC), an accurate, efficient, and Non-IID compatible FL framework. Our framework is based on the state-of-the-art Non-IID compatible FL framework, FL+HC [4], and adapts it to the privacy-preserving context to achieve full privacy protection, which includes the parties' local gradients privacy, as well as the global gradients privacy after aggregation. We are committed to achieving an efficient and high-precision privacy-preserving hierarchical clustering (HC) process. Specifically, we design secure algorithms to calculate the inter-gradient distance on Secure 2-Party Computation (2PC). We perform random cropping of gradients with high dimensions to reduce computational and communication overheads while ensuring clustering accuracy. Meanwhile, we use pseudo-random generations (PRGs) [36] to achieve privacy protection for global gradients without boosting additional communication overhead. In summary, our contributions are as follows:

- We propose an FL scheme that simultaneously preserves gradients (including local gradients and global gradients) privacy and is compatible with Non-IID scenarios.
- We elaborate several protocols for secure distance computation on the secret shared gradients to achieve accurate, private, and effective hierarchical clustering.
- Experiments on real-world datasets and comprehensible security analysis show that our scheme achieves strong privacy preservation while improving training on FL with Non-IID data.

2   Related Work

FL on Non-IID Data: The classical FL aggregation algorithm FedAvg [23] is based on the assumption of independent identical distribution (IID) of the data, and the performance of the global model is affected by the weight divergence when the data distribution is non-independent identical distribution (Non-IID). To address this challenge, there are three main types of solutions, including data sharing [33,38,39], local training fine-tuning [8,21] and clustering-based approaches [4,11,37]. Zhao et al. [39] propose sharing a global dataset between participants for reducing weight divergence between participants. However, it relies heavily on the quality of the shared dataset and compromises data privacy, violating the original purpose of FL. Li et al. [21] propose a local training fine-tuning approach (adding a regularisation term to the local optimization) to reduce the weight divergence and thus improve the performance of the global model. However, both of the above approaches train a single joint model, which is difficult to perform well across all participants simultaneously at Non-IID settings. Therefore some FL schemes based on clustering are proposed. Briggs et al. [4] propose an FL with hierarchical clustering (FL+HC) setting. Hierarchical clustering of gradients is performed at a specific round, and then participants in the same cluster are allowed to train collaboratively. Yeganeh et al. [37] also introduce a FL scheme based on Hierarchical clustering, which uses meta-learning to improve the personalization of the participants' models. Sattler et al. [30] present clustered FL (CFL), a novel federated multitask learning (FMTL) framework, which exploits geometric properties of the FL loss surface to group the client population into clusters with jointly trainable data distributions. Huang et al. [15] propose FedAMP, a new method employing federated attentive message passing to facilitate similar clients to collaborate more, exploring a novel idea of facilitating pairwise collaborations between clients with similar data. Nevertheless, none of the above schemes consider the privacy-preserving of gradients, so they have privacy issues.

Privacy-Preserving FL: Uploading gradients in plaintext violates user privacy due to the aggregation server could infer the raw data of participants through data reconstruction attacks [10,41] and membership inference attacks [24]. To protect user privacy, some FL frameworks have been proposed, mainly based on the following three cryptographic techniques, Differential Privacy (DP) [32], Secure 2-Party Computation (2PC) [6,12], Homomorphic Encryption (HE) [22]. Shokri et al. [32] first proposed a privacy-preserving FL framework, which is implemented by selectively sharing small subsets of model parameters and perturbing them by exploiting the DP mechanism. However, this scheme has to make a trade-off between accuracy and privacy. Hao et al. [12] and Dong et al. [6] send additional secret sharing values of gradients to two servers, and then use custom 2PC protocols for secure aggregation. All operations are performed under secret shared values, so no gradient privacy is compromised. Liu et al. [22] perform homomorphic encryption on gradients before uploading to the aggregation server, and they protect the privacy of intermediate results by adding random masks. However, none of the above privacy-preserving FL methods considers the Non-IID settings in FL, which is common in the real world. To accommodate Non-IID settings in FL, Zhou et al. [40] propose a secure and privacy-preserving machine learning method (PPML-Omics) by designing a decentralized version of the DP FL algorithm. Xiong et al. [35] propose the 2DP-FL scheme, which uses DP approach to add noise to both the local model and the global model. Noble et al. [26] use DP to modify SCAFFOLD and propose the DP-SCAFFOLD scheme, which is dedicated to solving the problem of degraded model training performance due to the introduction of noise. The above DP FL schemes compromise on data availability and can only provide a certain degree of privacy protection for gradients. At the same time such type of schemes inevitably affect the performance of the original algorithm due to the addition of noise.

3   Preliminaries

3.1   Effect of Non-IID Data in FL

In real FL scenarios, Non-IID data among participants is commonly encountered, which can have a large impact on FedAvg [17,20]. Specifically, the data distribution between participants is inconsistent, e.g., $\mathcal{P}_i \neq \mathcal{P}_j$, which causes the local objective of party P_i to be inconsistent with party P_j. Thus, there exists a *drift* in the local updates [18]. Eventually, the converged global model has much worse accuracy than in the IID scenarios. The following are some typical Non-IID settings [17]:

- **Feature distribution skew:** The $\mathcal{P}_i(x)$ (party P_i's feature distribution) varies between participants, which is the case where the input features are not evenly distributed between participants.

- **Label distribution skew:** The $\mathcal{P}_i(y)$ (party P_i's label distribution) varies between participants, which is the case where the data labels are not evenly distributed between participants.
- **Concept shift (same features, different label):** The $\mathcal{P}_i(y \mid x)$ conditional distribution varies between participants. In this case, different labels are assigned for the same features across participants. For example, participant P_i labels all cat images as 'cat', but client p_j labels all cat images as 'dog'.

3.2 FL+HC

FL+HC is committed to addressing the challenge of Non-IID data in FL and proposes a modified FL framework based on hierarchical clustering (HC). Specifically, FL+HC introduces a clustering step at communication round t during the FL procedure. Before the clustering step, FL+HC behaves the same as FedAvg. When the clustering round t comes, FL+HC performs HC based on the similarity between the gradients of all participants, and divides the participants into different clusters based on the clustering results. In subsequent rounds, participants in the same cluster are considered to have the same objective, and each cluster collaboratively generates a global model as FedAvg. Thus, each cluster has a global model that is independent of other clusters. As Fig. 1 shows, participants with different objectives are divided into different clusters after HC and then aggregated to generate different global models.

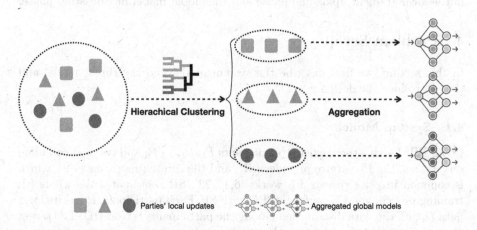

Fig. 1. Brief Introduction of FL+HC.

3.3 Cryptographic Primitives

Secret Sharing Schemes. In this paper, we use 2-out-of-2 additive secret sharing schemes [31] over different rings. The two specific rings that we consider are the field $\mathbb{Z}_2$ and the ring $\mathbb{Z}_p$, where $p = 2^l$ ($l = 32$, typically), the former is also knowns as boolean secret sharing. In boolean secret sharing, we denote the boolean shares of $x \in \mathbb{Z}_2$ as $\langle x \rangle_0^B$ and $\langle x \rangle_1^B$, which satisfies $x = \langle x \rangle_0^B \oplus \langle x \rangle_0^B$. To additively share $x \in \mathbb{Z}_p$, we indicate an additive secret sharing of x as a pair of $(\langle x \rangle_0, \langle x \rangle_1) = (r, x - r) \in \mathbb{Z}_p^2$, where r is sampled randomly over $\mathbb{Z}_p$. By using the 2PC protocols [28,29], arithmetic operations can be performed on shared values without reconstruction.

Secure Two-Party Computation Functions. For performing secure two-party computation (2PC) functions over shared values, we introduce several functions [28] that are used in our PPFL+HC:

- *Signed value multiplication* ($\mathcal{F}_{SMul}$): The SMul functionality ($\mathcal{F}_{SMul}$), takes as input $\langle x \rangle$ and $\langle y \rangle$ and outputs $\langle z \rangle$ such that $z = x \times y$.
- *Multiplexer* ($\mathcal{F}_{MUX}$): The MUX functionality ($\mathcal{F}_{MUX}$), takes as input $\langle x \rangle^B$ and $\langle y \rangle$ and outputs $\langle z \rangle$ such that $z = y$ if $x = 1$ and $z = 0$ otherwise.
- *DRelu* ($\mathcal{F}_{DRelu}$): The DRelu functionality ($\mathcal{F}_{DRelu}$), takes as input $\langle x \rangle$ and outputs $\langle z \rangle^B$ such that $z = 1$ if $x \geq 0$ otherwise $z = 0$.

Pseudorandom Generator. A Pseudorandom Generator (PRG) [36] could generate a long pseudorandom string with a uniformly random seed. The secure of PRG ensures that the output of the generator is indistinguishable from the uniform distribution in polynomial time, as long as the seed is hidden from the adversary. PRG is applied in our PPFL+HC to cut the communication to half in the local gradient uploading phase and the global model broadcasting phase.

4   Problem Setup

In this section, we first describe the system model and the threat model and then introduce the design goals.

4.1   System Model

In our PPFL+HC, there exist n participants $P_1, P_2, ..., P_n$ and two non-colluding servers, i.e., the FL service provider (SP) and the computing server (CS), which is common in prior private FL works [6,12,22]. SP coordinates the whole FL training process and CS performs 2PC with SP. Each participant P has its local data $\mathcal{D}$, and the data distribution among the participants is Non-IID. The target of participant P is to combine other participants with the same objective (participants with similar data distribution) and train a global model with improved performance. Figure 2 shows the system model of our PPFL+HC, which contains three steps at each iteration. Specifically, at step I, SP broadcasts the corresponding global model to each participant P. Then in step II, each party P trains the local model and sends the encrypted local updates to SP. Finally, in step III, SP and CS perform private aggregation of local updates with HC results by using custom 2PC protocols.

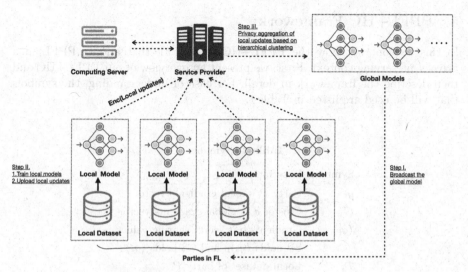

Fig. 2. System model of PPFL+HC.

4.2 Threat Model

In our PPFL+HC, we consider the servers (SP and CS) as honest-but-curious, which means that SP and CS will strictly follow the private secure aggregation protocols but try to passively infer private data information of FL parties. Besides, we assume that SP and CS will not be complicit, so it is secure to upload the gradients in a 2-out-of-2 secret sharing manner to SP and CS. This setting is reasonable and also consistent with the real-world FL system [25]. Namely, for maintaining a good reputation to provide more FL services, the servers (e.g., Google and Amazon) prefer to follow protocols rather than collude to obtain private information of parties.

4.3 Design Goals

In Our PPFL+HC, we are committed to improving FL's privacy-preserving ability on gradients and the accuracy of joint training on Non-IID data at the same time. Specifically, our design goals are as follows:

– **Privacy protection:** We aim to achieve full privacy protection of the gradients, which includes the local gradients uploaded by the parties, and the global gradients after aggregation.
– **Accuracy on Non-IID data:** When encountering the Non-IID data in FL, we aim to improve the test accuracy of the global model with the designed secure HC process.
– **Efficient 2PC protocols:** We carefully design the 2PC protocols to minimize the complexity of computation and communication while ensuring the correct gradients clustering and aggregation results.

5   PPFL+HC Framework

In this section, we show the PPFL+HC framework that adopts PPFL in a privacy-preserving context. First, we present an overview of our PPFL+HC and then describe the framework in detail. For ease of understanding, the symbols that will be used are listed in Table 1.

Table 1. Symbols

Symbols	Description
g_i	Party P_i's local gradients vector
G_x	Cluster c_x's global gradients vector
$\langle g_i \rangle$	Gradients g_i's secret sharing values SP holds $\langle g_i \rangle_0$ and CS holds $\langle g_i \rangle_1$
$\mathcal{D}_i$	Local dataset of party P_i
$EDis$	Euclidean distance
$MDis$	Manhattan distance

5.1   Overview

In the upload phase of the gradients, consistent with SecureFL [12], our PPFL+HC reduces the communication overhead by half by having participants send only a secret sharing of the gradient to SP, while another shared share of the gradient is generated by PRGs with the same random seeds that are negotiated between the participants and CS. In the gradients' aggregation phase, SP and CS follow our privacy-preserving HC algorithm to obtain the clustering results in the HC round. Then the SP and CS collaborate to complete the aggregation of local gradients based on the clustering results (If before the HC round, all parties are treated as a cluster). Finally, SP and CS complete the broadcast of global gradients while protecting the global gradients' privacy.

5.2   Details of PPFL+HC Framework

Phase 1: The Initialization Phase
This phase is called once for the entire protocol. By using the Diffie-Hellman key agreement protocol [14], each participant P_i establishes a private seed key k_i^{seed} with CS. The k_i^{seed} is applied in the upload and broadcast phases of the gradients, allowing CS and P_i to generate the same vector of random numbers non-interactively using PRGs, the details are shown in Phase 2 and Phase 4 below.

Phase 2: The Gradients' Generation and Encoding Phase
This phase describes how participant P_i generates the secret sharing of gradients g_i, which includes $\langle g_i \rangle_0$ for SP and $\langle g_i \rangle_1$ for CS.

First, the participant P_i updates the local model using the obtained global gradient and then trains the local data $\mathcal{D}_i$ to obtain the local gradient $\overline{g_i}$, the original floating-point gradient vector. We then map $\overline{g_i}$ onto the ring Z_p ($p = 2^l$, l denotes bit width) using fixed-point encoding. For float value v, our fixed-point encoding operation is as follows:

$$Encode(v) = \lfloor 2^s \times v \rfloor \bmod p,$$

where $\lfloor v \rfloor$ denotes the largest integer less than or equal to v and s indicates the precision of fixed-point number. Then we obtain g_i over Z_p by performing

$$g_i = Encode(\overline{g_i})$$

where function $Encode$ is carried out element-wise.

Then, participant P_i samples random vector r_i over Z_p using PRGs on k_i^{seed} and sends $\langle g_i \rangle_0 = g_i - r_i$ to SP. To improve communication efficiency, CS uses PRGs to obtain sharing $\langle g_i \rangle_1 = r_i$ non-interactively, where r_i is sampled by using PRGs with k_i^{seed}.

Phase 3: Secure Hierarchical Clustering of Gradients

This phase will complete the hierarchical clustering of gradients without revealing the plain text of gradients. We provide secure Euclidean distance (SED) calculation and secure Manhattan distance (SMD) calculation algorithms to support the calculation of mutual distances between gradients, and can be paired with different inter-cluster distance calculation methods (avg, min or max) to perform secure hierarchical clustering (SHC)of gradients.

In the rounds prior to the HC round, we treat all participants involved in the training as a cluster (act as FedAvg), and if it comes to the HC round, we execute the secure hierarchical clustering algorithm we designed once to update the clustering results. Hierarchical clustering can be divided into two steps, the first step is to calculate the distance between any two gradients (Euclidean distance or Manhattan distance), and the second step is to perform the clustering process based on the obtained distance matrix and related parameters such as distance thresholds to obtain the clustering results, the details of the specific privacy-preserving hierarchical clustering are described as follows.

To calculate the above distance matrix, we devise secure Euclidean distance (SED) and secure Manhattan distance (SMD) calculations, based on 2PC. For SED, we adopt $\mathcal{F}_{SMul}$ in [28] to perform signed secret sharing multiplication. The details of SED are shown at Algorithm 1. For SMD, we use $\mathcal{F}_{DRelu}$ and $\mathcal{F}_{MUX}$ in [28] to obtain the positive values and negative values separately. The details of SMD are displayed at Algorithm 2.

Remark 1. In both our SED and SMD protocols, the final results ($\langle EDis \rangle$ and $\langle MDis \rangle$) are reconstructed from shared values to plaintexts (*EDis* and *MDis*), we believe that this reconstruction of distance information does not violate the user's data privacy. Existing privacy inference schemes [10, 24, 41] need to obtain the global model and the user gradients information. Our PPFL+HC achieves

---

Algorithm 1. Secure Euclidean Distance
$\text{SED}(\langle g_i \rangle, \langle g_j \rangle) \rightarrow EDis$

Input: SP holds $\langle g_i \rangle_0$ and $\langle g_j \rangle_0$, CS holds $\langle g_i \rangle_1$ and $\langle g_j \rangle_1$. $\mathcal{F}_{\text{SMul}}$ are adopted from [28].

Output: Euclidean distance $EDis$ between g_i and g_j

1: SP sets $\langle z \rangle_0 = \langle g_i \rangle_0 - \langle g_j \rangle_0$.
2: CS sets $\langle z \rangle_1 = \langle g_i \rangle_1 - \langle g_j \rangle_1$.
3: **for** $i \in 1$ **to** m **do**   ▷ m is the dimension of g_i
4:    SP and CS invoke an instance of $\mathcal{F}_{\text{SMul}}$, in which SPs input is $\langle z \rangle_0[i]$ and CSs input is $\langle z \rangle_1[i]$. After that SP and CS learn result of multiplication $\langle d \rangle_0[i]$ and $\langle d \rangle_1[i]$, respectively.
5: **end for**
6: SP sets $\langle EDis^2 \rangle_0 = \sum_{i=1}^{m} \langle d \rangle_0[i]$.
7: CS sets $\langle EDis^2 \rangle_1 = \sum_{i=1}^{m} \langle d \rangle_1[i]$.
8: CS sends $\langle EDis^2 \rangle_1$ to SP, SP reconstructs $EDis^2 = \langle EDis^2 \rangle_0 + \langle EDis^2 \rangle_1$ and gets $EDis$.
9: **return** Eucliean distance $EDis$ at SP.

Algorithm 2. Secure Manhattan Distance
$\text{SMD}(\langle g_i \rangle, \langle g_j \rangle) \rightarrow MDis$

Input: SP holds $\langle g_i \rangle_0$ and $\langle g_j \rangle_0$, CS holds $\langle g_i \rangle_1$ and $\langle g_j \rangle_1$. $\mathcal{F}_{\text{DRelu}}$ and $\mathcal{F}_{\text{MUX}}$ are adopted from [28].

Output: Manhattan distance $MDis$ between g_i and g_j

1: SP sets $\langle z \rangle_0 = \langle g_i \rangle_0 - \langle g_j \rangle_0$
2: CS sets $\langle z \rangle_1 = \langle g_i \rangle_1 - \langle g_j \rangle_1$
3: SP and CS invoke $\mathcal{F}_{\text{DRelu}}$ with input $\langle z \rangle$ to learn output $\langle y \rangle^B$
4: SP and CS set $\langle \tilde{y} \rangle_0^B = \langle y \rangle_0^B$ and $\langle \tilde{y} \rangle_1^B = \langle y \rangle_1^B \oplus 1$, respectively.
5: SP and CS invoke $\mathcal{F}_{\text{MUX}}$ with input $\langle z \rangle$ and $\langle y \rangle^B$ to learn the positive values $\langle d_p \rangle$
6: SP and CS invoke $\mathcal{F}_{\text{MUX}}$ with input $\langle z \rangle$ and $\langle \tilde{y} \rangle^B$ to learn the negative values $\langle d_n \rangle$
7: SP sets $\langle MDis \rangle_0 = \sum_{i=1}^{m} \langle d_p \rangle_0[i] - \sum_{i=1}^{m} \langle d_n \rangle_0[i]$ ▷ m is the dimension of g_i
8: CS sets $\langle MDis \rangle_1 = \sum_{i=1}^{m} \langle d_p \rangle_1[i] - \sum_{i=1}^{m} \langle d_n \rangle_1[i]$
9: CS sends $\langle MDis \rangle_1$ to SP and SP reconstructs $MDis = \langle MDis \rangle_0 + \langle MDis \rangle_1$.
10: **return** Manhattan distance $MDis$ at SP.

---

the confidentiality of the global model parameters from SP and CS, thus SP cannot generate virtual gradients based on the global model. Secondly, the distance information between gradients obtained by SP does not reveal any specific information of the gradients, including the magnitude and direction of gradients as well as the positive and negative of individual elements, so SP cannot construct the optimization objective based on real gradients. In summary, the reconstruction of distance information does not violate the data privacy of users.

Based on the above secure distance metric algorithms (SED and SMD), the next step is to complete the secure HC of gradients. Considering that the distance information between the gradients does not leak the original data information (see REMARK 1), we reconstruct the above distance matrix into plain text before performing the subsequent clustering process. Due to the high dimensionality of $\langle g_i \rangle$, the overhead of using all dimensions of $\langle g_i \rangle$ to calculate the distance is too much, so we randomly crop the party's gradients with a retention proportion. Note that we choose the same dimension for all gradients. The experiments show that random dimensionality reduction has little effect on the clustering accuracy while improving 2PC protocols' efficiency significantly. The details are described in Algorithm 3.

Algorithm 3. Secure Hierarchical Clustering of Gradients
$\text{SHC}(\{\langle g_1 \rangle, \langle g_2 \rangle, ..., \langle g_n \rangle\}) \rightarrow \{c_1, c_2, ..., c_l\}$

Input: SP and CS hold $\{\langle g_1 \rangle, \langle g_2 \rangle, ..., \langle g_n \rangle\}$ ▷ n is the number of parties
Output: l clusters $\{c_1, c_2, ..., c_l\}$
1: SP and CS perform random dimensionality reduction with $\{\langle g_1 \rangle, \langle g_2 \rangle, ..., \langle g_n \rangle\}$, and then obtain: $\{\langle \dot{g}_1 \rangle, \langle \dot{g}_2 \rangle, ..., \langle \dot{g}_n \rangle\}$
2: **for** $i \leftarrow 1$ **to** n **do**
3:     **for** $j \leftarrow 1$ **to** n **do**
4:         SP and CS invoke $Dis_{ij} \leftarrow \text{SMD}(\langle \dot{g}_i \rangle, \langle \dot{g}_j \rangle)$ (or $\text{SED}(\langle \dot{g}_i \rangle, \langle \dot{g}_j \rangle)$), then SP holds Dis_{ij}
5:     **end for**
6: **end for**

7: $\{c_1, c_2, ..., c_l\} \leftarrow \text{CLUSTERING}(\begin{bmatrix} Dis_{1,1} & Dis_{1,2} & \cdots & Dis_{1,n} \\ Dis_{2,1} & Dis_{2,2} & \cdots & Dis_{2,n} \\ \vdots & \vdots & \ddots & \vdots \\ Dis_{n,1} & Dis_{n,2} & \cdots & Dis_{n,n} \end{bmatrix})$ ▷ Hierarchical
clustering results based on a precomputed distance matrix

Phase 4: Gradients' Aggregation and Broadcast
After obtaining the clustering results, we perform a linear aggregation of the participants in each cluster to obtain the global gradients. Specifically, for $c_x \in \{c1, c2, ..., c_l\}$, SP and CS calculate as follows:

$$\langle G_x \rangle = \frac{\sum_{j \in c_x} \langle g_j \rangle}{n_x}$$

where n_x denotes the number of participants in cluster c_x.

To ensure the privacy of $\langle G_x \rangle$, instead of letting SP and CS reconstruct G_x directly, we design a secure global gradients broadcast (SGB) algorithm. The details are shown in Algorithm 4.

6   Security Analysis

The purpose of this scheme is to protect the privacy of the local data of the participants and the privacy of the global gradient after aggregation. This section

---

Algorithm 4. Secure Global Gradients Broadcast
$SGB(\langle G_x \rangle) \rightarrow G_x$

Input: SP and CS hold party P_i's global gradients $\langle G_x \rangle$.
Output: Party P_i gets the corresponding global gradients G_x
1: P_i and CS generates $r_i' = \mathrm{PRG}(k_i^{seed})$ with the same dimension as G_x ▷ Identical k_i^{seed} guarantee the consistency of r_i' in P_i and CS
2: CS masks $\langle G_x \rangle_1$ as follows: $\widehat{\langle G_x \rangle}_1 = \langle G_x \rangle_1 + r_i'$
3: CS sends $\widehat{\langle G_x \rangle}_1$ to SP, then SP reconstructs masked global gradients $\widehat{G_x}$ as follows: $\widehat{G_x} = \langle G_x \rangle_0 + \widehat{\langle G_x \rangle}_1$
4: SP sends $\widehat{G_x}$ to P_i, then P_i unmask the global gradients as follow: $G_x = \widehat{G_x} - r_i'$

---

analyzes the security of the secure computing protocols SED, SMD, SHC , and SGB, where the adversaries are the semi-honest servers (SP and CS).

To justify this scheme, this section defines security under the semi-honest model, as shown in Definition 1 and two lemmas, i.e., Lemma 1 and Lemma 2.

Definition 1. (Security under the semi-honest model [3]). *We say a protocol is secure if there exists a probabilistic polynomial-time simulator S that can generate a view for the adversary A in the real world and the view is computationally indistinguishable from its real view.*

Lemma 1. *A protocol is perfectly simulated if all its sub-protocols are perfectly simulated [2].*

Lemma 2. *If a random element r is uniformly distributed on $\mathcal{Z}_p$ and independent from any variable $x \in \mathcal{Z}_p$, then $r \pm x$ is also uniformly random and independent from x [3].*

Next, We analyze the security of the protocols as follows:

Theorem 1. *The SED protocol proposed is secure under the semi-honest model.*

Proof.
In the SED protocol, the SP obtains the real view as $\{\langle z \rangle_0, \langle d \rangle_0, \langle EDis^2 \rangle_0\}$, where $\langle z \rangle_0$ is obtained by subtracting independent shared values, and according to Lemma 2, $\langle z \rangle_0$ is randomly and uniformly distributed. $\langle d \rangle_0$ is obtained from the SP and CS by invoking $\mathcal{F}_{SMul}$ with input $\langle z \rangle$, and the security of $\mathcal{F}_{SMul}$ is proved in [28]. $\langle EDis^2 \rangle_0$ is obtained by summing the vectors $\langle d \rangle_0$ over the internal elements with random uniform distribution, and by Lemma 2 it follows that $\langle EDis^2 \rangle_0$ is also randomly and uniformly distributed, so based on Lemma 1, it is impossible for SP to distinguish in polynomial time between the real view and the simulated view generated by the simulator S. Similarly, for the real view held by CS $\{\langle z \rangle_1, \langle d \rangle_1, \langle EDis^2 \rangle_1\}$, it cannot be distinguished from the randomly generated simulated view, so the SED protocol is secure under the semi-honest model.

Theorem 2. *The SMD protocol proposed is secure under the semi-honest model.*

Proof. In the SMD protocol, the SP gets the real view as

$$\{\langle z \rangle_0, \langle y \rangle_0^B, \langle \widetilde{y} \rangle_0^B, \langle d_p \rangle_0, \langle d_n \rangle_0\},$$

where $\langle z \rangle_0$ is randomly and uniformly distributed by the Proof 6, and $\langle y \rangle_0^B$ is obtained by calling the function $\mathcal{F}_{\mathrm{MUX}}$ jointly by SP and CS, and the security of $\mathcal{F}_{\mathrm{MUX}}$ has been proved by [28]. $\langle \widetilde{y} \rangle_0^B$ is the opposite of $\langle y \rangle_0^B$ since $\langle y \rangle_0^B$ is randomly and uniformly distributed, so $\langle \widetilde{y} \rangle_0^B$ is also randomly and uniformly distributed. Both $\langle d_p \rangle_0$ and $\langle d_n \rangle_0$ are the result of SP and CS running protocol $\mathcal{F}_{\mathrm{MUX}}$, whose security has been proved in the [28], and in summary, combined with Lemma 1, SP in polynomial time cannot distinguish between the real view and the simulated view generated by the simulator $\mathcal{S}$. Similarly, for the real view received by CS $\{\langle z \rangle_1, \langle y \rangle_1^B, \langle \widetilde{y} \rangle_1^B, \langle d_p \rangle_1, \langle d_n \rangle_1\}$, it is also indistinguishable from the randomly generated simulated view, so the SMD protocol under the semi-honest model is secure.

Theorem 3. *The SHC protocol proposed is secure under the semi-honest model.*

Proof. The SHC protocol proposed is built on top of the SED and SMD protocols, and since the security of the SED and SMD protocols under the semi-honest model has been proved (see Proof 6 and Proof 6), the SHC protocol is also secure under the semi-honest model according to Lemma 1.

Theorem 4. *The SGB protocol proposed is secure under the semi-honest model.*

Proof. In the SGB protocol, the SP receives a true view of $\{\langle \widehat{G_x} \rangle_1, \widehat{G_x}\}$, where $\langle \widehat{G_x} \rangle_1$ is obtained by summing the shared values and the random vector, and $\widehat{G_x}$ is obtained by summing the shared values and the perturbed shared values, which are randomly and uniformly distributed according to Lemma 2, so the real view received by SP is indistinguishable from the simulator $\mathcal{S}$ randomly generated. The real view obtained by the CS is $\{\langle G_x \rangle_1, r_i, \langle \widehat{G_x} \rangle_1\}$, where $\langle G_x \rangle_1$ is the shared values, r_i is the generated random vector, all are randomly and uniformly distributed, and $\langle \widehat{G_x} \rangle_1 = \langle G_x \rangle_1 + r_i$ is also randomly and uniformly distributed by Lemma 2, so neither SP nor CS can distinguish the real view from the simulated view generated by the simulator $\mathcal{S}$, and thus the SGB protocol is safe under the semi-honest model.

7   Evaluation

In this section, we demonstrate the improvement of Non-IID data training and analyze the performance of 2PC protocols in PPFL+HC by conducting a series of comparative experiments with real-world datasets. All our experiments are executed on a custom server with the configuration of Ubuntu 20.04, Intel(R) Core(TM) i9-10980XE CPU @ 3.00 GHz CPU and 64 GB RAM. The parties and servers are simulated with separate processes. The local model training in parties is implemented using PyTorch [27], the 2PC protocols on is implemented in C++, and the communication between entries is implemented using gRPC.

7.1   Experiment Setup

Datasets and Model Architectures: To evaluate the performance of the PPFL+HC, we chose two classic image classification datasets, (i) MNIST dataset, including $60,000$ handwritten digit pictures with a size of 28×28, and $10,000$ test samples, (ii) CIFAR-10 dataset, containing $60,000$ color images in total and $50,000$ of them is used for training and the other $10,000$ is used for testing. These images are divided into 10 categories with the size of 32×32 and each category has $6,000$ images. The model structure of the MNIST classification task has a two-layer fully connected network, and the parameter settings of each layer are 724×100 and 100×10 in sequence respectively, for a total of about $80K$ parameters. For the CIFAR-10 image classification task, we use a simple model architecture in the TensorFlow tutorial online[1] which consists of three convolutional layers followed by two fully connected layers, for a total of about $123K$ parameters.

Non-IID Settings: (i) Pathological Non-IID (as described in [23]), which partitions the data such that parties receive digits corresponding to only 2 labels. For example, the first party might receive 300 examples labeled as 2 and 300 examples labeled as 7. Subsequent parties might receive different labels. Again all parties have 600 examples to perform local learning on. In this setting, we test how the FL model performs with label distribution skew, as $\mathcal{P}(y)$ varies across parties. (ii) Label-swapped Non-IID (described in [30]), which first shuffles the data and then partitions the data into four groups. For each group, two digit labels are swapped. For example, one group might swap all digits labeled as 3 to 9 and vice versa. Each group is then evenly distributed to 25 parties, resulting in 100 parties each with 600 training examples. This way, the parties naturally form 4 clusters and allow us to test FL's ability to train models in the presence of concept shift ($\mathcal{P}(y \mid x)$ varies between parties).

Hyper-parameters: For each experiment, we set the batch size of training to 2^7, the momentum of SGD to 0.9, and the initial learning rate to 0.1. Moreover, in each FL round, the server aggregates all the uploaded gradients by parties. The scale s in fixed-point encoding is set to 6 and the ring $\mathbb{Z}_p$'s size p is set to 2^{32}.

7.2   Experiment Results

Accuracy Evaluation. Many factors affect the accuracy of the global model, including the capacity of the model, the quality and quantity of parties' data, the number of training rounds, etc. We focus on testing the improvement of training quality of PPFL+HC in the Non-IID setting. We thus conduct experiments on how the number of rounds before clustering, i.e., HC round affects the global model's test accuracy. Note that the model architecture for the CIFAR-10 classification task is relatively simple, which results in relatively low accuracy.

---

[1] web URL: https://www.tensorflow.org/tutorials/images/cnn?hl=en.

However, we only focus on the improvement compared to FedAvg on Non-IID data training.

Impact of the different Non-IID settings: Figure 3 demonstrates the impact of different datasets (MNIST and CIFAR-10) with different Non-IID settings (Pathological Non-IID and Label-swapped Non-IID), the impact of different HC rounds on the joint training accuracy. Table 2 and 3 show the comparison of the post round of HC and the final round with FedAvg in terms of accuracy We observe that the test accuracy for all scenarios has a significant increase (1.04–1.57× FedAvg) in the final round. Nearly all scenarios achieve an accuracy improvement in the post round of HC, with the CIFAR-10 in the Pathological Non-IID setting has the largest increase in test accuracy (5.0× FedAvg). This indicates that our secure hierarchical clustering process can classify participants well, allowing participants with similar gradients to train collaboratively and avoiding the influence of participants with inconsistent objectives, thus improving the global test accuracy.

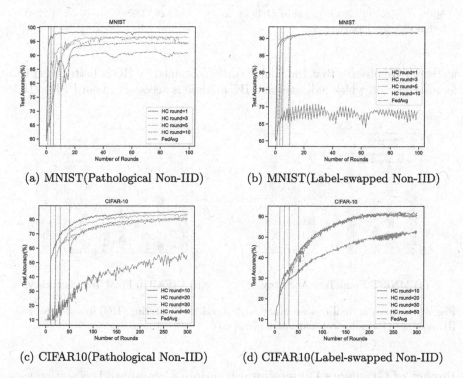

(a) MNIST(Pathological Non-IID)   (b) MNIST(Label-swapped Non-IID)

(c) CIFAR10(Pathological Non-IID)   (d) CIFAR10(Label-swapped Non-IID)

Fig. 3. Impact of different Non-IID settings and different HC rounds on test accuracy, In Figs. (a) (b), The MNIST dataset is used to evaluate. In Figs. (c) (d), The CIFAR-10 dataset is used to evaluate.

Comparing with Random Clustering: Figure 4 shows the final accuracy comparison using Hierarchical Clustering (HC) and Random Clustering (RC)

Table 2. MNIST Key Round Accuracy

MNIST (Pathological Non-IID)			MNIST (Label-swapped Non-IID)		
HC round	Post round of HC	Final round	HC round	Post round of HC	Final round
1	92.68 (1.4×)*	98.28 (1.08×)	1	87.42 (1.42×)	91.63 (1.36×)
3	88.21 (1.28×)	94.79 (1.04×)	3	87.83 (1.35×)	91.65 (1.36×)
5	82.52 (1.09×)	96.54 (1.06×)	5	88.37 (1.35×)	91.61 (1.36×)
10	77.00 (0.87×)	94.54 (1.04×)	10	89.58 (1.28×)	91.67 (1.36×)

Table 3. CIFAR10 Key Round Accuracy

CIFAR10 (Pathological Non-IID)			CIFAR10 (Label-swapped Non-IID)		
Hc round	Post round of HC	Final round	HC round	Post round of HC	Final round
10	50.21 (5×)	85.54 (1.57×)	10	24.0 (1.13×)	60.32 (1.15×)
20	36.76 (2.88×)	80.12 (1.47×)	20	29.76 (1.12×)	60.09 (1.15×)
30	53.14 (2.59×)	83.37 (1.53×)	30	32.17 (1.07×)	60.67 (1.16×)
50	58.39 (2.28×)	81.01 (1.49×)	50	35.26 (1.07×)	61.56 (1.17×)

* (1.4x) Means 1.4x FedAvg.

methods. We observe that the final accuracy obtained by HC is better than RC for all scenarios, which indicates that HC method is necessary in our PPFL+HC.

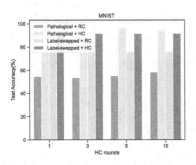
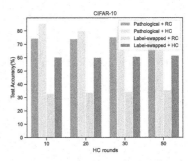

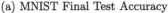

(a) MNIST Final Test Accuracy   (b) CIFAR10 Final Test Accuracy

Fig. 4. Comparing final test accuracy with Random Clustering (RC) in different Non-IID settings (Pathological and Label-swapped)

Impact of Gradients Dimensional Random Cropping. This section uses the Adjusted Rand Index (ARI) [16] as a measure of the clustering results. ARI provides regularized output which ranges from −1 to 1. In the Label-swapped Non-IID setting, the data held by participants have distinct category features (four categories), thus we choose to compare the effects of different factors on the HC results in this scenario. Firstly, we explore the effect of different dimensional retention proportion in dimensional random cropping, and then compare the effect of two metrics on the HC results.

Impact of Dimensional Retention Proportion: Table 4 shows the effect of the retention proportion of gradient dimensionality in the random cropping of gradient on the HC results under different HC rounds. From Table 4, we can see that the gradients generated by the MNIST dataset can be fully consistent with the true clustering results under different HC rounds and different retention proportions, indicating that the dimensional random cropping does not affect its clustering accuracy. As for CIFAR-10, the ARI is higher with larger retention proportion and larger HC rounds. And the ARI is relatively low when the retention proportion is 0.1% (the dimension is 122) and the HC round is small. In summary, the gradient random cropping method proposed in this paper, under the premise of controlling the retention proportion and the HC round, basically does not have a negative impact on the clustering accuracy.

Table 4. Different Gradients Dimensional Retention Proportions' ARI

MNIST ARI					CIFAR-10 ARI				
HC round	Retention Proportion				HC round	Retention Proportion			
	100%	10%	1%	0.1%		100%	10%	1%	0.1%
1	1.0	1.0	1.0	1.0	10	1.0	1.0	0.59	0.47
3	1.0	1.0	1.0	1.0	20	1.0	1.0	0.92	0.71
5	1.0	1.0	1.0	1.0	30	1.0	1.0	0.97	0.97
10	1.0	1.0	1.0	1.0	50	1.0	1.0	1.0	0.97

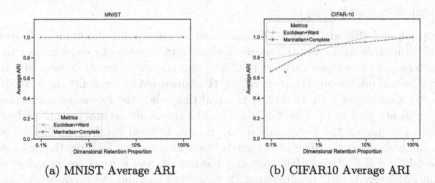

(a) MNIST Average ARI   (b) CIFAR10 Average ARI

Fig. 5. Different dimensional retention proportions' average ARI

Impact of Different Metrics: The distance metrics between gradients, such as SED and SMD, can be combined with other hyperparameters to accomplish SHC. In this section, The inter-cluster distance metric strategy paired with the Euclidean distance is Ward Linkage, while the Manhattan distance is paired with Complete Linkage. Figure 5 shows the effect of these two metrics on the

HC results (measured as the average ARI of different HC rounds) at different retention proportions. As can be seen in Fig. 5, the MNIST dataset performs well with both metrics, matching the true classification results perfectly. As for the CIFAR-10 dataset, the average ARI difference between two metrics is small, and both gradually approach a perfect match as the retention proportion increases. In summary, the two metrics do not differ much in the clustering performance for the gradients, and both can complete the clustering with high accuracy at the appropriate retention proportion.

The Efficiency of PPFL+HC. Our PPFL+HC performance bottleneck lies in the computation of the mutual distance between all gradients (using SED or SMD), which has a complexity of $O(n^2 \times d)$ for n participants, each with gradient dimension d. Then we test the communication cost and execution time of the distance matrix calculation separately.

Impact of the Different Number of Parties: In Figs. 6a and 6b we fix the input dimension as 795 (1%Retention proportion of MNIST gradients dimension) and observe the change in communication cost and execution time by varying the number of parties, we find that there is a significant increase in both communication cost and time overhead as the number of parties increases. Considering that HC is performed only once during the training process, and combined with the efficiency improvement brought by the dimensional random cropping, the complexity can be practical even if the number of participants increases. Comparing the different distance measures (SED or SMD), it can be seen that using SMD results in an 8.93× improvement in communication overhead and a 1.11–1.44× improvement in execution time over using SED. The performance advantage of the SMD Algorithm 2 comes from the lightweight building block (without secure multiplication operations).

Impact of Different Input Dimensions: To reduce the communication cost and computational cost of the secure distance matrix without compromising the clustering accuracy, we perform random cropping on gradients before HC. In Figs. 6c and 6d, we progressively reduce the dimension of gradients (from 79510 to 79). Combining with Table 4, it is found that when the retention proportion of gradients goes to 1% (795 for MNIST), the clustering accuracy is guaranteed while minimizing the computation and communication overhead. This is due to the high dimensionality of the gradients, which retains features that can be identified by HC after random cropping. For the different metrics, we also observe that SMD versus SED results in a 4.78–8.93× less communication overhead and a 1.33-1.77× less execution time overhead.

Combining with the efficiency test and clustering metrics test, there is little difference in the clustering metrics when using SED or SMD for HC, but SMD has a significant advantage in efficiency, so it is recommended to use SMD as the distance metric for SHC.

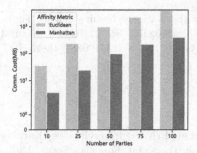

(a) Communication cost over the different numbers of parties.

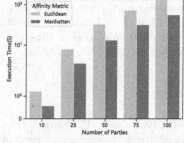

(b) Execution time over the different numbers of parties.

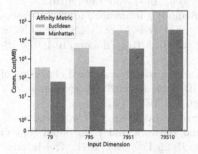

(c) Communication cost over the different numbers of input dimension.

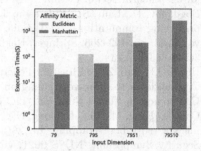

(d) Execution time over the different numbers of input dimension.

Fig. 6. Communication Cost and Execution Time of PPFL+HC's secure distance matrix of gradients with different affinity metrics, In Figs. (a) (b), the number of input dimensions is fixed as 795. In Figs. (c) (d), the number of parties is fixed as 100.

8   Conclusion

In this paper, we introduce PPFL+HC, a novel FL framework that achieves full privacy protection of gradients and high accuracy over Non-IID data at the same time. PPFL+HC designs efficient cryptographic protocols to implement secure hierarchical clustering over 2PC. Moreover, we evaluate our PPFL+HC on two real-world datasets over two classic Non-IID settings, to justify our claim.

The main downside is that PPFL+HC adapts the scheme of FL+HC to the privacy-preserving context, and so PPFL+HC inherits some constraints of the scheme, which includes the performance of the global model is more dependent on the accuracy of the clustering results. An additional limitation is that our framework requires two non-colluding servers. Reducing to a single-server setting requires more elaborate secret protocol construction and may also introduce efficiency bottlenecks. We leave the resolutions of these limitations for future works.

Acknowledgment. This work is supported by the National Nature Science Foundation of China (No. 62102429, No. 62072466, No. 62102430, No. 62102440), Natural Science Foundation of Hunan Province, China (Grant No. 2021JJ40688), the NUDT Grants (No. ZK19-38, No. ZK22-50).

References

1. Aono, Y., Hayashi, T., Wang, L., Moriai, S., et al.: Privacy-preserving deep learning via additively homomorphic encryption. IEEE Trans. Inf. Forensics Secur. **13**(5), 1333–1345 (2017)
2. Bi, R., Chen, Q., Xiong, J., Liu, X.: Design method of secure computing protocol for deep neural network. Chin. J. Netw. Inf. Secur. **6**(4), 130–139 (2020)
3. Bogdanov, D., Laur, S., Willemson, J.: Sharemind: a framework for fast privacy-preserving computations. In: Jajodia, S., Lopez, J. (eds.) ESORICS 2008. LNCS, vol. 5283, pp. 192–206. Springer, Heidelberg (2008). https://doi.org/10.1007/978-3-540-88313-5_13
4. Briggs, C., Fan, Z., Andras, P.: Federated learning with hierarchical clustering of local updates to improve training on non-IID data. In: 2020 International Joint Conference on Neural Networks (IJCNN), pp. 1–9. IEEE (2020)
5. Cao, X., Fang, M., Liu, J., Gong, N.Z.: FLTrust: byzantine-robust federated learning via trust bootstrapping. In: 28th Annual Network and Distributed System Security Symposium, NDSS 2021, virtually, 21–25 February 2021. The Internet Society (2021). https://www.ndss-symposium.org/ndss-paper/fltrust-byzantine-robust-federated-learning-via-trust-bootstrapping/
6. Dong, Y., Chen, X., Li, K., Wang, D., Zeng, S.: FLOD: oblivious defender for private byzantine-robust federated learning with dishonest-majority. In: Bertino, E., Shulman, H., Waidner, M. (eds.) ESORICS 2021, Part I. LNCS, vol. 12972, pp. 497–518. Springer, Cham (2021). https://doi.org/10.1007/978-3-030-88418-5_24
7. Erickson, B.J., Korfiatis, P., Akkus, Z., Kline, T.L.: Machine learning for medical imaging. Radiographics **37**(2), 505–515 (2017)
8. Gao, L., Fu, H., Li, L., Chen, Y., Xu, M., Xu, C.Z.: FedDC: federated learning with non-IID data via local drift decoupling and correction. In: Proceedings of the IEEE/CVF Conference on Computer Vision and Pattern Recognition, pp. 10112–10121 (2022)
9. Gao, W., Guo, S., Zhang, T., Qiu, H., Wen, Y., Liu, Y.: Privacy-preserving collaborative learning with automatic transformation search. In: Proceedings of the IEEE/CVF Conference on Computer Vision and Pattern Recognition, pp. 114–123 (2021)
10. Geiping, J., Bauermeister, H., Dröge, H., Moeller, M.: Inverting gradients-how easy is it to break privacy in federated learning? Adv. Neural. Inf. Process. Syst. **33**, 16937–16947 (2020)
11. Ghosh, A., Chung, J., Yin, D., Ramchandran, K.: An efficient framework for clustered federated learning. Adv. Neural. Inf. Process. Syst. **33**, 19586–19597 (2020)
12. Hao, M., Li, H., Xu, G., Chen, H., Zhang, T.: Efficient, private and robust federated learning. In: Annual Computer Security Applications Conference, pp. 45–60 (2021)
13. Hard, A., et al.: Federated learning for mobile keyboard prediction. arXiv preprint arXiv:1811.03604 (2018)
14. Hellman, M.: New directions in cryptography. IEEE Trans. Inf. Theory **22**(6), 644–654 (1976)

15. Huang, Y., et al.: Personalized cross-silo federated learning on non-IID data. In: Proceedings of the AAAI Conference on Artificial Intelligence, vol. 35, pp. 7865–7873 (2021)
16. Hubert, L., Arabie, P.: Comparing partitions. J. Classif. $2(1)$, 193–218 (1985)
17. Kairouz, P., et al.: Advances and open problems in federated learning. Found. Trends® Mach. Learn. $14(1-2)$, 1–210 (2021)
18. Kaissis, G.A., Makowski, M.R., Rückert, D., Braren, R.F.: Secure, privacy-preserving and federated machine learning in medical imaging. Nat. Mach. Intell. $2(6)$, 305–311 (2020)
19. Li, B., Wu, Y., Song, J., Lu, R., Li, T., Zhao, L.: DeepFed: federated deep learning for intrusion detection in industrial cyber-physical systems. IEEE Trans. Industr. Inf. $17(8)$, 5615–5624 (2020)
20. Li, Q., et al.: A survey on federated learning systems: vision, hype and reality for data privacy and protection. IEEE Trans. Knowl. Data Eng. (2021)
21. Li, T., Sahu, A.K., Zaheer, M., Sanjabi, M., Talwalkar, A., Smith, V.: Federated optimization in heterogeneous networks. Proc. Mach. Learn. Syst. 2, 429–450 (2020)
22. Liu, X., Li, H., Xu, G., Chen, Z., Huang, X., Lu, R.: Privacy-enhanced federated learning against poisoning adversaries. IEEE Trans. Inf. Forensics Secur. 16, 4574–4588 (2021)
23. McMahan, B., Moore, E., Ramage, D., Hampson, S., y Arcas, B.A.: Communication-efficient learning of deep networks from decentralized data. In: Artificial Intelligence and Statistics, pp. 1273–1282. PMLR (2017)
24. Nasr, M., Shokri, R., Houmansadr, A.: Comprehensive privacy analysis of deep learning: passive and active white-box inference attacks against centralized and federated learning. In: 2019 IEEE Symposium on Security and Privacy (SP), pp. 739–753. IEEE (2019)
25. Nguyen, T.D., et al.: {FLAME}: taming backdoors in federated learning. In: 31st USENIX Security Symposium (USENIX Security 2022), pp. 1415–1432 (2022)
26. Noble, M., Bellet, A., Dieuleveut, A.: Differentially private federated learning on heterogeneous data. In: International Conference on Artificial Intelligence and Statistics, pp. 10110–10145. PMLR (2022)
27. Paszke, A., et al.: PyTorch: an imperative style, high-performance deep learning library. Advances Neural Inf. Process. Syst. 32 (2019)
28. Rathee, D., et al.: SIRNN: a math library for secure RNN inference. In: 2021 IEEE Symposium on Security and Privacy (SP), pp. 1003–1020. IEEE (2021)
29. Rathee, D., et al.: CrypTflow2: practical 2-party secure inference. In: Proceedings of the 2020 ACM SIGSAC Conference on Computer and Communications Security, pp. 325–342 (2020)
30. Sattler, F., Müller, K.R., Samek, W.: Clustered federated learning: model-agnostic distributed multitask optimization under privacy constraints. IEEE Trans. Neural Netw. Learn. Syst. $32(8)$, 3710–3722 (2021). https://doi.org/10.1109/TNNLS.2020.3015958
31. Shamir, A.: How to share a secret. Commun. ACM $22(11)$, 612–613 (1979)
32. Shokri, R., Shmatikov, V.: Privacy-preserving deep learning. In: Proceedings of the 22nd ACM SIGSAC Conference on Computer and Communications Security, pp. 1310–1321 (2015)
33. Tuor, T., Wang, S., Ko, B.J., Liu, C., Leung, K.K.: Overcoming noisy and irrelevant data in federated learning. In: 2020 25th International Conference on Pattern Recognition (ICPR), pp. 5020–5027. IEEE (2021)

34. Voigt, P., Von dem Bussche, A.: The eu general data protection regulation (GDPR). A Practical Guide, 1st edn., vol. 10, no. 3152676, p. 10–5555. Springer, Cham (2017)
35. Xiong, Z., Cai, Z., Takabi, D., Li, W.: Privacy threat and defense for federated learning with non-IID data in AIoT. IEEE Trans. Industr. Inf. 18(2), 1310–1321 (2021)
36. Yao, A.C.: Theory and application of trapdoor functions. In: 23rd Annual Symposium on Foundations of Computer Science (SFCS 1982), pp. 80–91. IEEE (1982)
37. Yeganeh, Y., Farshad, A., Boschmann, J., Gaus, R., Frantzen, M., Navab, N.: Adaptive personlization in federated learning for highly non-IID Data. arXiv preprint arXiv:2207.03448 (2022)
38. Yoshida, N., Nishio, T., Morikura, M., Yamamoto, K., Yonetani, R.: Hybrid-FL: cooperative learning mechanism using non-IID data in wireless networks. arXiv preprint arXiv:1905.07210 (2019)
39. Zhao, Y., Li, M., Lai, L., Suda, N., Civin, D., Chandra, V.: Federated learning with non-IID data. arXiv preprint arXiv:1806.00582 (2018)
40. Zhou, J., et al.: PPML-omics: a privacy-preserving federated machine learning system protects patients' privacy from omic data. bioRxiv, pp. 2022–03 (2022)
41. Zhu, L., Liu, Z., Han, S.: Deep leakage from gradients. Adv. Neural Inf. Process. Syst. 32 (2019)

RRML: Privacy Preserving Machine Learning Based on Random Response Technology

Jia Wang[1]([✉])(iD), Shiqing He[2], and Qiuzhen Lin[1]

[1] Shenzhen University, 3688 Nanhai Avenue, Shenzhen, Guangdong, China
{jia.wang,qiuzhlin}@szu.edu.cn
[2] Shangqiu University, No. 66, Beihai East Road, Shangqiu, Henan, China

Abstract. Machine learning algorithms are proven to be vulnerable to model inversion and membership inference attacks, which raises much privacy concerns for its applications in sensitive scenarios. Typically, the state-of-the-art privacy preserving machine learning methods tend to provide privacy protection guarantee at the cost of losing data utility. This inevitably causes degradation of the model performance, especially for those tasks who are trained using small data sets. Therefore, optimizations on the trade-offs between individual privacy and data utility become a critical issue in machine learning. In this work, we proposed a privacy preserving machine learning algorithm RRML (Random Response Machine Learning) by combining the random response mechanism with the semi-supervised teachers-student learning way, and give the privacy analysis. Extensive experiments have been conducted to validate the effectiveness of RRML in addressing the above mentioned problem. The experimental results confirmed its superiority in balancing data utility and privacy against the state-of-the-art privacy preserving machine learning algorithms, especially in small data scenarios.

Keywords: Privacy preserving · Machine Learning · Random response

1 Instruction

Constructively combined with the advances of computational and analytical methods, data-driven learning models burst the full power of massive flux of data [7], which leads to new insights in terms of, inter alia, healthcare treatment [5,11,21,25], finance [16], the Internet of Things [13], automation and robotics [29]. However, as the popularity of machine learning continues to increase, security issues have become particularly prominent. Recent works [4,17,27] demonstrated that machine learning algorithms suffer from malicious privacy attacks. As shown in Fig. 1, despite of data collection, privacy leakage could also happen in processes such as model training and the prediction stage. Song *et al.* [24] indicated that the learning model may unintentionally memorize the training data, which makes it possible for the adversaries to extract sensitive information of the deep learning participants. [20,23] showed that the traditional data-to-model training task is not a one-way process. Even if the model training service

© The Author(s), under exclusive license to Springer Nature Switzerland AG 2023
S. Li et al. (Eds.): NSS 2023, LNCS 13983, pp. 217–234, 2023.
https://doi.org/10.1007/978-3-031-39828-5_12

provider is trusted, an attacker can still obtain relevant information about the model or data in its usage, by applying attacks such as membership inference, model inversion, or model parameter extraction. In fact, due to the statistically driven nature of the learning algorithm, the training process tends to encode data patterns as model parameters. Once the decoder is successfully constructed, even if the model parameters are not explicitly shared, the source domain statistics can still be recovered in the reverse direction [8,19].

In membership inference attacks, an attacker tries to determine whether the data of a specific person exists in the training data set of the target model. Nasr *et al.* [14] assumed that the attacker could use the structure and parameter knowledge of the neural network model to perform membership inference attack. They firstly proposed a layered attack method, which took the output and gradient information of each layer of the neural network as the input characteristics of the attack model, and input them to several full-connection layers and convolutional layers respectively to construct the attack model. The accuracy rate of white-box attack reached 75.1% on the CIFAR dataset. Hayes *et al.* [9] firstly applied member inference attack using a generative adversarial network, with the generative model as the target model. Model inversion attacks attempt to infer some or all of the attribute values of a certain target data in the training set through the output of the model. When an attacker adopts a passive attack method and performs model backwards without intervening in the model training process, the basic idea is to find the input that makes a certain type of output most likely to the observed one. Fredrikson *et al.* [8] also proposed a model inversion attack that applies more models and obtained better attacking performance. Authors in [10] launched a model push attack on the deep learning model in a white box scenario to restore the user's face data. Wang *et al.* [31] proposed white box model backward attack, assuming the central server who calculates the participants' average gradient as the attacker. It also designed a multi-task generative adversarial model as the attack model, which successfully restored the images in the training set of a participant. Song *et al.* [24] envisioned the following attack scenario: the data owner obtains the algorithm code of the model from the model provider, and then runs it on his own data set. Assuming that the model provider is a potential attacker, he is designing the algorithm When the training algorithm is slightly modified, the specific training data you want can be obtained during the release stage of the model. Model parameter extraction refers to an attack in which when the target model parameters are not disclosed, the attacker knows part of the model structure information and label information, and tries to obtain the model parameters by accessing the target model. Authors in [3] proposed and extended the model extraction method for equation solving, and discussed the occasions where only the output labels are accessible with the target model.

As to the defense techniques, data anonymization [26], homomorphic encryption [2] and differential privacy are most commonly used. Data anonymization intends to protect privacy by removing personally identifiable information from the collected raw data. Algorithms in this category work efficiently in protecting data from identity disclosure and linking attacks. However, they could not resist machine learning privacy attacks. Homomorphic encryption methods allow one to perform certain types of computation on the encrypted data without knowing its contents. Although homomorphic encryption provides promising privacy protection guarantee for machine learning tasks, there are still few design challenges exist in its practical application in scenarios like neural networks, mainly in terms of limitations in supported operation types, operator data types, computation complexity as well as efficiency.

Differential Privacy (DP) [6] is widely acknowledged as a mathematically rigorous privacy definition. Countermeasures [12,18] constructed on this concept provide insights into the design of privacy preserving machine learning approaches. In [18], Papernot *et al.* proposed a practical differential private machine learning algorithm, namely Private Aggregation of Teacher Ensembles (PATE), which ensures security of the training data against model inversion and membership inference attacks. PATE works in a collaborative learning fashion. Data segregation is firstly applied to independently train multiple teacher models. Coupled with a noisy aggregation mechanisms for teacher ensembles, a general consensus is then learned to train a student model in a query-answer way. Since no underlying data or parameter is accessed by the student model, privacy guarantee could be achieved intuitively.

However, Many research works [12,15] have made their attempt to provide better privacy-utility trade-offs under PATE infrastructure, either by applying new noisy aggregation mechanism or new student learning methodology. However, the data segregation may still cause undesirable performance loss of the learned model. For instance, if the number of teacher models is not large enough, even a small amount of noise will cause the model accuracy drop drastically, mainly due to the sensitivity of the voting mechanism. On the other hand, these algorithms all assume the existence of a trusted training service provider, which not always hold.

Wang *et al.* [30] formally proved that randomized response technique provides better statistical utility preservation compared with the standard Laplace mechanism (output perturbation) in data collection scenarios, especially when the privacy budget is very limited. Inspired by [30], we propose a local differential private machine learning algorithm based on randomized response (dubbed RRML) mechanism and conduct privacy analysis on it. Extensive experiments have been conducted and the results show the superiority of our algorithm to PATE in preserving privacy of machine learning while ensuring the accuracy, especially when there are strict privacy requirements and the training data is relatively small. Meanwhile, RRML adds disturbances locally, and privacy protection can be achieved even if the third party is not trusted.

Contributions of this work are listed as follows:

1. A differential private classification method based on randomized response perturbed aggregation teacher ensembles (RRML) is proposed. In contrast with standard Laplace noise mechanism which directly uses noised statistical results to train a student model, RRML utilizes maximum likelihood estimate to approximate the real aggregated teacher ensembles. It's proved both

formally and empirically that RRML obtains better utility while applied in private data classification tasks, especially when the privacy budget is small.

2. In the case of small data learning scenarios, RRML still guarantees a relatively high prediction accuracy. We confirmed this through extensive experiments on a real COVID-19 dataset, which contains 349 COVID-19 CT images from 216 patients and 463 non-COVID-19 CT images. The results show that the proposed scheme provides a privacy guarantee of $\varepsilon \leq 1.5$ with a COVID-19 prediction accuracy drop of 0.03, in contrast of 0.11 for PATE under the same privacy budget.

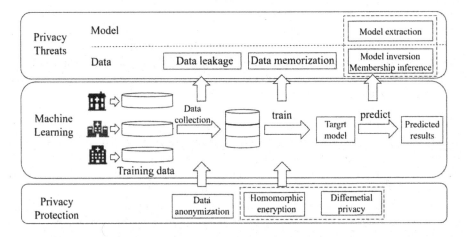

Fig. 1. Privacy risks and protection schemes in machine learning.

The rest of this paper is organized as follows. Section 2 briefs some relative background knowledge. Section 3.1 presents the proposed RRML algorithm and its privacy analysis. Section 4 gives the empirical results and the analysis. Section 5 concludes the paper.

2   Related Work

In this section, we focus on the background knowledge used in the proposed RRML framework, including differential privacy, moment accounting as well as the privacy calculation method. Then we introduce the random perturbation technology and differential private machine learning algorithms.

2.1   Differential Privacy

A randomized algorithm $\mathcal{A} : D \rightarrow R$ satisfies ϵ-differentially privacy $((\epsilon, \delta)$-DP) if for any given adjacent datasets $d, d' \in D$ $(|d \mathrel{\Delta} d'| \leq 1)$ and any output subset $S \subseteq R$, it holds that

$$\Pr[\mathcal{A}(d) \in S] \le e^{\varepsilon} \Pr[\mathcal{A}(d') \in S] + \delta, \tag{1}$$

where ε and δ are two non-negative real numbers and $\Pr[.]$ denotes the probability.

2.2 Moment Accountant

Moment accountant (MA) is a method used to estimate the privacy loss. It's firstly proposed in [1]. The basic idea is as follows. For an output $o \in R$, the privacy loss at o is defined as:

$$c(o; \mathcal{A}, aux, d, d') \triangleq \log \frac{\Pr[\mathcal{A}(aux, d) = o]}{\Pr[\mathcal{A}(aux, d') = o]},$$

where aux denotes an auxiliary input, the privacy loss random variable is defined as $c(\mathcal{A}(d); \mathcal{A}, aux, d, d')$. MA could be calculated by:

$$\alpha_{\mathcal{A}}(\lambda) \triangleq \max_{aux, d, d'} \alpha_{\mathcal{A}}(\lambda; aux, d, d'),$$

where $\alpha_{\mathcal{A}}(\lambda; aux, d, d') \triangleq \log \mathbb{E}[\exp(\lambda C(\mathcal{A}, aux, d, d'))]$ is the moment generation function of the privacy loss random variable. The following properties of the moments accountant are proved in [1].

Theorem 1 (Composability). *Suppose that a mechanism $\mathcal{A}$ consists of a sequence of adaptive mechanisms $\mathcal{A}_1, ... \mathcal{A}_k$, where $\mathcal{A}_i : \prod_{j=1}^{i-1} R_j \times D \to R_i$, then for any output sequence $o_1, o_2, ..., o_{k-1}$ and any λ, there is:*

$$\alpha_{\mathcal{A}}(\lambda; d, d') = \sum_{i=1}^{k} \alpha_{\mathcal{A}_i}(\lambda; o_1, ..., o_{i-1}, d, d').$$

where $\alpha_{\mathcal{A}}$ is conditioned on $\mathcal{A}_i$'s output being o_i for $i < k$.

Theorem 2 (Tail Bound). *For any $\varepsilon > 0$, the mechanism $\mathcal{A}$ is (ε, δ)-DP and*

$$\delta = \min_{\lambda} \exp(\alpha_{\mathcal{A}}(\lambda) - \lambda \varepsilon). \tag{2}$$

2.3 Random Perturbation

Randomized response is firstly proposed by Warner to eliminate bias in surveys which may involve sensitive individual information. Instead of outsourcing obfuscated answers or datasets to the curator, it responds randomly, *i.e.*, the respondents have plausible deniability. Hence randomized response mechanism can intuitively prevent the private individual data from being disclosed before its collection and provides local privacy. Meanwhile, the curator can still conduct statistical analysis on the collected randomized data. A toy example is given as follows.

Suppose there are n respondents taking the AIDS questionnaire and each responds the true answer of the question "Are you an AIDS patient?" with a probability p. Let the number of people who answered "yes" be denoted as n_1, and the number of people who answered "no" be denoted by n_2. Obviously $n_2 = n - n_1$. Assume the real prevalent rate of AIDS is π, there are

$$\Pr(X_i = yes) = \pi p + (1 - \pi)(1 - p),$$
$$\Pr(X_i = no) = (1 - \pi)p + \pi(1 - p).$$

Obviously, the above statistical ratio is not an unbiased estimate of π. Upon the construction of the likelihood function

$$L = [\pi p + (1 - p)(1 - \pi)]^{n_1}[(1 - \pi)p + \pi(1 - p)]^{n - n_1}, \tag{3}$$

the maximum likelihood estimate for π can be calculated as

$$\hat{\pi} = \frac{p - 1}{2p - 1} + \frac{n_1}{(2p - 1)\,n}. \tag{4}$$

Let N represents the corrected statistical estimate of the number of people with AIDS and

$$N = \hat{\pi} \times n = \frac{p - 1}{2p - 1}n + \frac{n_1}{2p - 1}. \tag{5}$$

To ensure that it meets ε-localized differential privacy, the privacy budget ε is set to:

$$\varepsilon = \ln\frac{p}{1 - p} \tag{6}$$

where the disturbance probability $p \in (0, 1)$ and $e^\varepsilon > 0$. We extend it to a sensitive polychotomous attribute with $t\,(t \geq 2)$ mutually exclusive and exhaustive classes. The corresponding unknown proportions to be estimated are denoted as $\pi_1, ...\pi_t$, the randomization device is such that an individual belonging to the v-th category $(v = 1, ...t)$, reports a random value u $(u = 1, ...t)$ with probability p_{uv} and $\sum_{u=1}^{t} p_{uv} = 1$ for all $v = 1, ...t$.

The matrix $P = \{p_{uv}\}$ is called the design matrix, where the sum of each column in P is 1:

$$P = \begin{pmatrix} p_{11} & \cdots & p_{1t} \\ \vdots & \ddots & \vdots \\ p_{t1} & \cdots & p_{tt} \end{pmatrix} \tag{7}$$

The probability λ_u of the (randomized) response u is given as:

$$\lambda_u = \sum_{v=1}^{t} p_{uv}\pi_v \tag{8}$$

In order to maximize the sum of the diagonal elements, the design matrix for randomized response $P = \{P_{uv}\}$ should be in the following form:

$$p_{uv} = \begin{cases} \frac{e^\varepsilon}{t - 1 + e^\varepsilon}, & u = v \\ \frac{1}{t - 1 + e^\varepsilon}, & u \neq v \end{cases} \tag{9}$$

where p_{uv} represents the elements of the design matrix, $\mathbf{u}$ represents the disturbance label, $\mathbf{v}$ is the output label, e stands for the natural constant, and $t \geq 2$ denotes the label, ε demonstrates the privacy budget. And obviously when $t = 2$, we have $\varepsilon = ln\frac{P}{1-P}$, where P represents the probability that the scrambled label is the same as the output label.

3   Local Differentially Private Machine Learning Algorithm Based on Randomized Response Mechanism

PATE in [18] proposed to divide the private training set into multiple independent data groups, and use each group to train a teacher model. Then the inference results of all the teacher models are aggregated to teach a student model in the query-answer manner. It provides precise privacy guarantee on the training data, independent of the learning algorithms adopted. However, there are still several issues to be addressed to enhance its practicality, including the following two aspects.

1) PATE as well as its variants require disjoint training data for a large number of teacher models to compensate the introduced Laplace noises for the privacy preserving guarantee. Meanwhile, the data partitioning way is of much impact on the prediction accuracy. To achieve differential privacy, they proposed to add Laplace noise to the voting results before releasing it to the student model. Since the perturbation is conducted directly on the queried results, PATE-G and its variants may cause inevitable significant degradation on the learning accuracy, $i.,e$, the trade-off between accuracy and privacy is highly dependent on the number of teacher models. As the number of teacher models increase in an ensemble, the accuracy deceases, especially for learning tasks in small data scenarios.
2) PATE as well as its variants require the exist of a third trusted data center to train an ensemble of the teacher models and then use it to supervise the training of a student model.

[30] proved that random perturbations are more efficient in achieving differential privacy compared with Laplacian mechanism, especially when the privacy budget is relatively small. To maximize the utility of the data while providing rigorous local differential privacy, this paper proposes a randomized response based machine learning algorithm RRML. It combines the random perturbation mechanism with the general teacher-student training framework.

In order to address these limitations of PATE mentioned in Sect. 2, we propose the RRML framework, which combines the semi-supervised teachers-student learning way with random response based local differential privacy. The privacy analysis demonstrates its superiority in obtaining better statistical utility preservation, compared with private machine learning algorithms like PATE and its variants.

3.1   Differential Privacy Based on Randomized Response Mechanism

Instead of adding Laplace-distributed noises into the data, the random response mechanism achieves data privacy protection by injecting probabilistic disturbances locally.

The Realization Principle of Differential Privacy Based on Randomized Response Mechanism. First, let's observe the settings in Differential Privacy in PATE. Similar to the user uploading data to the server, the server performs a data analysis algorithm that satisfies differential privacy on the data, and obtains the machine learning model for its own use or release for human use. For foreign attackers who have obtained machine learning models, they cannot make reliable inferences about individual data. It is assumed here that the server is reliable and the user's raw data is available on the server. The setting of Local Differential Privacy assumes that this server is not trusted by us, and requires users to add noise before uploading data, so that the server cannot obtain effective information about individual users.

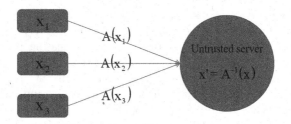

Fig. 2. Local Differential Privacy.

As shown in Fig. 2, Algorithm A satisfies local differential privacy, where $\forall t \in Range\,(A)$, $\frac{Pr[A(X_1=t)]}{Pr[A(X_2=t)]} \leq e^{\varepsilon}$, The individual user encrypts the data and then uploads it to the server. The server restores the user information through a certain method (may be agreed with the user in advance) so that it can understand the trend on the entire data set. The current Local Differential Privacy is mostly based on the random response mentioned in Chap. 2. Random response can make managers get distorted individual information, but can get an estimate of real information on this information.

Application of Random Response Differential Privacy in Two Classification. Now we only consider a two-category problem. There is a transition matrix, like:

$$P = \begin{pmatrix} P_{00} & P_{01} \\ P_{10} & P_{11} \end{pmatrix}, P_{uv} = P\,[y_i = v | X_i = u]\,(u, v \in [0, 1]) \tag{10}$$

where X_i is the true value, Y_i is a random output value. Generally, there are $P_{00} = P_{11}$. The server expects to construct the original distribution after collecting all noisy data, where the original distribution of $0(1)$ is $\pi_0(\pi_1)$, the observed distribution is $\lambda_0(\lambda_1)$, then there is:

$$\hat{\pi}_b = \frac{P_{bb} - 1}{2P_{bb} - 1} + \frac{\lambda_b}{2P_{bb} - 1} \tag{11}$$

Then construct a probability transition matrix that is satisfied with differential privacy, which has:

$$P = \begin{pmatrix} \frac{e^\varepsilon}{1+e^\varepsilon} & \frac{1}{1+e^\varepsilon} \\ \frac{1}{1+e^\varepsilon} & \frac{e^\varepsilon}{1+e^\varepsilon} \end{pmatrix}, \tag{12}$$

where P satisfy $\varepsilon - DP$, this form proved to be the best DP-randomized response under a single two-category. ("best" means that the restored estimate has a smaller variance). The Laplace Mechanism used in PATE is also the most common noise addition method for differential privacy. Here is the following form, first add a Laplace Noise, and then round to $\lambda_0(\lambda_1)$:

$$y_i = \begin{cases} 0, & if \ x_i + Lap\,(1/\varepsilon) < 0.5. \\ 1, & if \ x_i + Lap\,(1/\varepsilon) \geq 0.5. \end{cases} \tag{13}$$

$$P = \begin{pmatrix} 1 - \frac{1}{2}e^{-\frac{\varepsilon}{2}} & \frac{1}{2}e^{-\frac{\varepsilon}{2}} \\ \frac{1}{2}e^{-\frac{\varepsilon}{2}} & 1 - \frac{1}{2}e^{-\frac{\varepsilon}{2}} \end{pmatrix}. \tag{14}$$

In fact, LM can be regarded as a special random response, In the comparison of Mean Squared Error/Variance two types of indicators, RR is better than LM. It can be found here that exactly $\frac{P_{00}}{P_{11}}$ in RR is e^ε, and $\frac{P_{00}}{P_{11}}$ in LM is less than e^ε. It can be considered that the rounding and truncation after adding Laplace noise provides further privacy protection, thereby increasing the error.

Application of Random Response Differential Privacy in Multi-classification. Now it is extended to the category attribute categorical attribute with t values. The direct extension to the above RR and LM is:

$$P_{uv} = \begin{cases} \frac{e^\varepsilon}{t-1+e^\varepsilon}, & if \ u = v. \\ \frac{1}{t-1+e^\varepsilon}, & if \ u \neq v. \end{cases} \tag{15}$$

$$P_{uv} = \begin{cases} F_{v,\frac{\varepsilon}{t-1}}\,(1.5), & if \ u = 1. \\ 1 - F_{v,\frac{\varepsilon}{t-1}}\,(1.5), & if \ u = t. \\ F_{v,\frac{\varepsilon}{t-1}}\,(u+0.5) - F_{v,\frac{\varepsilon}{t-1}}\,(u-0.5), & otherwise. \end{cases} \tag{16}$$

where $F_{v,\frac{\varepsilon}{t-1}}\,(1.5)$ is a cumulative distribution function that satisfies the Laplace distribution with a mean of v, a variance of $2\lambda^2$, and $\lambda = (t-1)/\varepsilon$. Compared with the sensitive attribute LDL in YesiWell dataset [30], for the reconstruction of the two methods on the original data distribution, it can be seen that RR performs better than that of LM.

3.2   The Basic Infrastructure of RRML

From Sect. 3.1, we find that random response based differential privacy can achieve better privacy utility tradeoff than Laplace noising based differential privacy, and it allows applications with untrustworthy third-parties. Inspired by this observation, we propose to improve the teacher consensus mechanism in PATE, and establish a teacher consensus aggregation learning mechanism based on random response differential privacy, which is referred to as the RRML mechanism.

As depicted in Fig. 3, in RRML, each teacher model is trained on an independent data group of the privacy dataset. In contrast with PATE-G, the teachers output the predicted results for the queried input x in a randomized-response way.

Suppose there're totally n teachers trained independently. Let the originally predicted label on input x of the i-th ($i \in \{1, 2, ...n\}$) teacher model be denoted as $f_i(x)$, suppose $f_i(x) = v$, where $v \in \{1, 2, ...n\}$. Disrupt $f_i(x)$ and obtain $f'_i(x)$ and let $f'_i(x) = u$, where $u \in \{1, 2, ...n\}$. Denote $P_{uv} = \left\{ f_i(x) = v, \hat{f}_i(x) = u \right\}$, where $\hat{\lambda}$ represents the proportion of disturbed labels in all labels. For example, $\hat{\lambda}_u$ represents the percentage of the u-th label $\mathbf{u}v$ in all labels in the scrambled label. Let the number of the u-th tag $\mathbf{u}$ in the disturbed tag $f'_i(x)$ is $n'_u(x)$, then $\hat{\lambda}_u = \frac{n'_u(x)}{n}$. Count the number of each label in the disturbed label and the total n labels to get $\hat{\lambda}$. Define $\lambda = (\lambda_1, \ldots, \lambda_t)^T, \pi = (\pi_1, \ldots, \pi_t)^T$, we have:

$$\lambda = p\pi, \tag{17}$$

where λ represents the proportion of the scrambled label in all labels, π represents the unbiased estimate of the label count of the scrambled label, and $p = \{p_{uv}\}$, represents the design matrix.

In the data collection scenario, compared with the standard Laplace mechanism, the random response technique can provide better statistical utility, especially when the privacy budget is very limited. In order to maximize the sum of diagonal elements, the random response design matrix $p = \{p_{uv}\}$ should be in Eq. (9).

Therefore, there is $\pi = p^{-1}\lambda$. It should be noted that there is no sample size here. For a simple random sample replaced with n, $\hat{\lambda}$ is a vector of sample proportions corresponding to λ. For example, λ represents the proportion of the disturbed label in all labels, of course, $\hat{\lambda}_u$ means the sample proportion of the disturbed label u among all disturbed labels. Then suppose that the design matrix p is non-singular, $\hat{\pi}$ represents the unbiased estimator of the label count, because according to the above derivation, $\pi = p^{-1}\lambda$, then there is $\hat{\pi} = p^{-1}\hat{\lambda}$, then the label of each label The unbiased estimator corresponding to the count is:

$$\hat{n}_j(x) = \hat{\pi} \times n = p^{-1}\hat{\lambda}n. \tag{18}$$

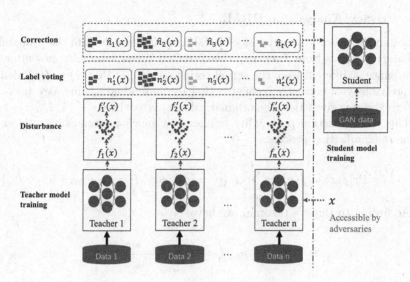

Fig. 3. The proposed RRML Algorithm

Specifically, each label corresponds to a $\hat{n}_j(x)$, where $\hat{n}_j(x)$ is an unbiased estimator of $n_j(x)$, that is to say, although $n_j(x)$ and $n'_j(x)$ are disturbed The difference between $\hat{n}_j(x)$ and $n_j(x)$ is small after correction.

Since the output label needs to be scrambled to ensure privacy, and the scrambled label obtained by the scrambled has a large difference with the output label, the scrambled label needs to be corrected to obtain the estimated label, so that the difference between the estimated label and the output label is small, So that the estimated labels and queries can be used as data sets. The estimated label is determined according to the unbiased estimator, and the label when the unbiased estimator takes the maximum value is used as the estimated label. Specifically, the estimated label is:

$$\hat{f}(x) = \arg\max_j\{\hat{n}_j(x)\},$$

where, $\hat{f}(x)$ represents the estimated label, and argargmax(ŭ) represents the variable value when the objective function is maximized. Specifically, the label corresponding to the maximum value of $\hat{n}_j(x)$ is used as the estimated label, that is to say, the unbiased estimator of the label count corresponding to each label, the label count The maximum value of the unbiased estimator, the label is the estimated label, and the difference between $\hat{n}_j(x)$ and $n_j(x)$ obtained after disturbance and correction is small, then the label is estimated The accuracy is also higher.

3.3   Privacy Analysis on RRML

To obtain the overall privacy loss of RRML, we firstly calculate the probability of that $\hat{f}(x)$ differs from $f(x)$, i.e., the corrected voting label obtained after the disturbance is different from the actual voting result. Let $\Pr[\hat{f}(x) = f(x)]$ denote the probability of correctly reconstructing the individual's value as v from the perturbed data, given that the original value x_i is v where $v \in \{1, 2, ...n\}$.

This reconstruction probability implies how much information is preserved in the randomization process:

$$\Pr[\hat{f}(x) = f(x)] = \sum_{u=1}^{t} P\left(y_i = u | x_i = u\right) P\left(\hat{x}_i = v | y_i = u\right) \tag{19}$$

According to Bayes's theorem, we have:

$$\Pr[\hat{f}(x) = f(x)] = \sum_{u=1}^{t} \frac{p_{uv}^2 \bullet \pi_v}{\lambda_u} \tag{20}$$

We denote this failure probability as q and obviously $q = 1 - \Pr[\hat{f}(x) = f(x)]$, q could be further derived as:

$$q = 1 - \sum_{j=0,1} \left(\frac{p^2 \lambda_j}{p\lambda_j + (1-p)(1-\lambda_j)} + \frac{(1-p)^2 \lambda_j}{(1-p)\lambda_j + p(1-\lambda_j)} \right). \tag{21}$$

Then we utilize moment accountant to tighten the total privacy budget for multiple queries and it's proven in [18] that the following theorem holds.

Theorem 3 (MA). *Let $\mathcal{A}$ be a randomized algorithm which satisfies ε-DP, where $\varepsilon, l \geq 0$, for any two adjacent databases d, d', there's*

$$\alpha_{\mathcal{A}}(l) \leq \log(1-q)(\frac{1-q}{1-e^\varepsilon q})^l + qe^{\varepsilon l}. \tag{22}$$

The total privacy budget ϵ_{total} is bounded by Theorem 2. Details of the proposed RRML scheme and the computation of ϵ_{total} are presented in Algorithm 1.

4   Experimental Results and Analysis

We use the MNIST and SVHN datasets to verify the effectiveness of RRML, and then compare its performance with the PATE framework. Our MNIST model stacks two convolutional layers with max-pooling and one fully connected layer with ReLUs. When trained on the MNIST dataset, the non-privacy-preserving model obtains a test accuracy of 99.18%. For SVHN, we add two hidden layers. The non-private model achieves a test accuracy of 92.8%. In this paper, we are more interested in comparing the private student model's performance with the non-privacy-preserving model as well as the state-of-art privacy-preserving machine learning algorithms trained on the same dataset, under different privacy-preserving guarantees. Finally, in order to further verify the effectiveness of RRML in practical medical scenarios, we conducted experiments on the COVID-CT-Dataset. The COVID-CT-Dataset contains 349 COVID-19 CT images from 216 patients and 463 non-COVID-19 CTs.

Experiment 1: The test accuracy of the proposed RRML algorithm on MNIST and SVHN. Figure 4 illustrates the test accuracy of the proposed RRML scheme under different settings in terms of disturbance probability and the number of teacher models (n). As shown in the figure, when $n = 100$, better results can be achieved by the student model. While $n = 10$, the performance of the model is more susceptible to be affected by the probability of disturbance. For $n = 250$, each teacher model is allocated less data, which leads to an overall decrease in accuracy. It can also be observed that the greater the probability of disturbance is, the smaller the privacy budget will be. When $n = 100$ and $p = 0.1$, the accuracy of MNIST can reach 98.03% and SVHN can reach 89%.

Algorithm 1. RRML algorithm

Input: teacher models' training data set D_t, query dataset T, student models' training dataset, a Learner
Other Parameter: number of teachers n, disturbance probability p, the number of iterations N, moment number m
Output: ε, accuracy, precision, recall, AUC, F-measure

1: Let $t = 0$.
2: **while** $t < N$ **do**
3:    Divide D_t into n disjoint data subsets (X_i, Y_i), and train n classifiers f_i, where $i \in 1, 2, ..., n$;
4:    Input $x \in T$, each teacher model calculate a label $f_i(x)$ and suggest a randomly disturbed label $f_i'(x)$ with disturbance probability of p;
5:    Calculate the proportion for each label:
      $\lambda = p\pi$;
6:    Count the voting results:
      $\hat{n}_j(x) = \hat{\pi} \times n = p^{-1}\hat{\lambda}n$;
7:    Correct the voting results:
      $\hat{f}(x) = \arg\max_j\{\hat{n}_j(x)\}$;
8:    Using the Learner to train the student model on database $\left(x, \hat{f}(x)\right)$ and evaluate its performance, output its accuracy, precision, recall, F-measure, AUC;
9:    Estimate the privacy loss of each query using Eq. (9);
10:   Calculate failure probability q using Eq. (21);
11:   Calculate moment accountant l_m at m randomly selected moment using Eq. (22);

12:   Calculate the total privacy loss:
      $\varepsilon_{total} = \min\left(\frac{\alpha - \log(\delta)}{l_m}\right)$
13: **end while**
14: **return** ε, Accuracy, precision, recall, F-measure, AUC

Table 1. Test accuracy comparison of RRML and other privacy-preserving machine learning algorithms

Dataset	Aggregator	Queries	ε	Accuracy	
				Student	Baseline
MNIST	PATE	1000	8.03	98.1	99.2
	DSSGD	/	10	99.17	
	ARDEN	/	5	98.16	
	PATE-G	286	1.97	98.5	
	RRML	**128**	**1.22**	**98.9**	
SVHN	PATE	1000	8.19	90.7	92.8
	DSSGD	/	10	92.99	
	ARDEN	/	5	90.02	
	PATE-G	3098	4.96	91.6	
	RRML	**640**	**4.01**	**90.84**	

Experiment 2: Performance comparison of RRML and Other frames. PATE utilizes Laplace noising scheme to disturb the teachers' voting results, while PATE-G [17] adopts GAN to further reduce privacy budget. The DSSGD algorithm [22] also uses the Laplacian noising mechanism on the selected gradients before it's uploaded or distributed by the participants or the service provider. The noise depends on the budget and the sensitivity level of each parameter gradient. ARDEN is a new mechanism for perturbing and transforming local data based on the differential privacy mechanism proposed in [28]. RRML uses randomized response technique as the disturbance mechanism. As depicted in Table 1, RRML achieved the best performance, considering the privacy-preserving guarantee level as well as the test accuracy. Random disturbance means to add disturbance when each teacher model predicts. When the number of teacher models increases to a certain degree (not very large), the influence of the probability of disturbance can be kept within a certain range. For example, when $n = 100$ and $n = 200$, the performance of RRML based models are very close. However, PATE adds disturbance to the statistical results of the total n teacher models. The n of PATE is required to be large enough to tolerate the added noise. For example, performance of PATE while $n = 200$ is obviously better than that of $n = 100$.

Therefore, it can be concluded that the random response can achieve high accuracy when the teacher model is not too large, especially in small data training scenarios. In order to further understand this favorable feature, we conducted experiments on a small dataset COVID-CT-Dataset, which has higher privacy preserving requirements.

Experiment 3: Comparison of model accuracy loss based on RRML and PATE on the COVID-CT-Dataset. As demonstrated in Fig. 5, The blue line represents the training accuracy of the student model based on the RRML

Table 2. Performance comparison on Covid-CT-Dataset of RRML and PATE-G with ϵ fixed at 10.

Scenarios	Accuracy	Precision	Recall	F-measure	AUC
Baseline	0.84	0.77	0.98	0.96	0.88
PATE-G	0.71	0.64	0.93	0.76	0.77
RRML	**0.76**	**0.70**	**0.91**	**0.80**	**0.82**

framework, and the red line represents the training accuracy of the student model based on the PATE framework. A larger ϵ means a smaller interference probability or noise that can be added to the training frame and consequently higher accuracy that can be achieved. At the same time we can see that when the value of ϵ is very small, the accuracy loss based on the RRML framework is much smaller than that of PATE, due to the difference between the two noising mechanism.

Experiment 4: Comparison of the data statistical utility of Laplace noising scheme and random response disturbance. As demonstrated in Fig. 6, the green line represents the percentage of correct labels after the teacher models' voting. The blue line indicates the proportion of correct labels after adding Laplace noise to the number of votes. We can see that the overall random perturbation is closer to the green line, especially when the privacy budget is small, the overall error is relatively small. When the ϵ of the blue line is less than 2.5, there is a high probability of outputting wrong results. Figure 7 shows the predicted results of 100 queries when the number of teacher models are 3, 5, and 7, and the ordinate represents the number of queries with correct predicted results. The green line represents the prediction result of the original model, and the red line represents the prediction result with the random response mechanisim. The blue line represents the prediction result after adding noise. It can be seen that due to insufficient training data, as the number of teacher models increases, the number of correctly predicted labels gradually decreases, but the performance of random response is obviously better than the Laplacian noising method, especially when the number of teacher models is relatively small. Since the purpose of adding noise is to obtain strict privacy protection, there must be a sufficient number of teachers to guarantee the learning performance. In small data training scenarios, without a large number of teacher models, the overall data utility will be greatly reduced. Occasions where privacy is a main concern.

Experiment 5: Performance comparison on Covid-CT-Dataset of RRML and PATE-G with ϵ fixed at 10. As demonstrated in Table 2, compared with the PATE-G framework, RRML framework obtains higher precision with the same privacy guarantee.

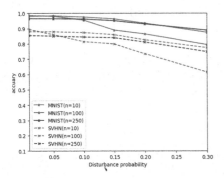

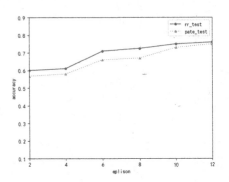

Fig. 4. Test accuracy of MNIST and SVHN under different disturbance probabilities and teachers' numbers.

Fig. 5. Comparison of model accuracy loss based on RRML and PATE the COVID-CT-Dataset under different privacy budgets.

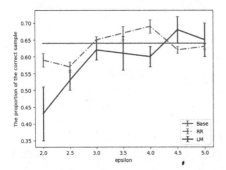

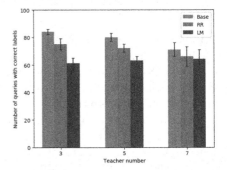

Fig. 6. Comparison of model accuracy loss based on RRML and PATE the COVID-CT-Dataset under different privacy budgets

Fig. 7. Comparison of model accuracy loss based on RRML and PATE the COVID-CT-Dataset under different privacy budgets

5   Conclusions

This work proposes a randomized response based privacy preserving machine learning algorithm RRML, in order to address data privacy-utility trade-off issues existed in machine learning. Intensive experiments have been conducted to evaluate the performance of the proposed RRML algorithm. Experimental results show that randomized response based disturbance provides better data privacy-utility trade-off than Laplace noising mechanism, especially when the amount of data is small, $e.g.$, COVID-19 data, or the privacy budget is tight, $e.g.$, $\epsilon \leq 1.5$.

Acknowledgements. This work was supported in part by the National Nature Science Foundation of China under Grant No. 6197226, the Natural Science Foundation of Guangdong Province under Grant No. 2021A1515011153, and the Shenzhen Science and Technology Innovation Commission under Grant No. 20200805142159001, No. JCYJ20220531103401003.

References

1. Abadi, M., et al.: Deep learning with differential privacy. In: Proceedings of the 2016 ACM SIGSAC Conference on Computer and Communications Security, pp. 308–318. ACM (2016)
2. Aono, Y., Hayashi, T., Wang, L., Moriai, S., et al.: Privacy-preserving deep learning via additively homomorphic encryption. IEEE Trans. Inf. Forensics Secur. **13**(5), 1333–1345 (2017)
3. Ateniese, G., Mancini, L.V., Spognardi, A., Villani, A., Vitali, D., Felici, G.: Hacking smart machines with smarter ones: how to extract meaningful data from machine learning classifiers. Int. J. Secur. Netw. **10**(3), 137 (2015)
4. Carlini, N., Liu, C., Erlingsson, Ú., Kos, J., Song, D.: The secret sharer: evaluating and testing unintended memorization in neural networks. In: 28th USENIX Security Symposium (USENIX Security 2019), pp. 267–284 (2019)
5. Che, Z., Purushotham, S., Cho, K., Sontag, D., Liu, Y.: Recurrent neural networks for multivariate time series with missing values. Sci. Rep. **8**(1), 1–12 (2018)
6. Dwork, C.: Differential privacy. In: Bugliesi, M., Preneel, B., Sassone, V., Wegener, I. (eds.) ICALP 2006. LNCS, vol. 4052, pp. 1–12. Springer, Heidelberg (2006). https://doi.org/10.1007/11787006_1
7. Esteva, A., et al.: A guide to deep learning in healthcare. Nat. Med. **25**(1), 24–29 (2019)
8. Fredrikson, M., Jha, S., Ristenpart, T.: Model inversion attacks that exploit confidence information and basic countermeasures. In: Proceedings of the 22nd ACM SIGSAC Conference on Computer and Communications Security, pp. 1322–1333. ACM (2015)
9. Hayes, J., Melis, L., Danezis, G., De Cristofaro, E.: LOGAN: evaluating information leakage of generative models using generative adversarial networks. arXiv preprint arXiv:1705.07663 (2017)
10. Hitaj, B., Ateniese, G., Perez-Cruz, F.: Deep models under the GAN: information leakage from collaborative deep learning. In: Proceedings of the 2017 ACM SIGSAC Conference on Computer and Communications Security, pp. 603–618 (2017)
11. Liu, J., Zhang, Z., Razavian, N.: Deep EHR: chronic disease prediction using medical notes. arXiv preprint: arXiv:1808.04928 (2018)
12. Long, Y., Lin, S., Yang, Z., Gunter, C.A., Li, B.: Scalable differentially private generative student model via pate. arXiv preprint arXiv:1906.09338 (2019)
13. Mahdavinejad, M.S., Rezvan, M., Barekatain, M., Adibi, P., Barnaghi, P., Sheth, A.P.: Machine learning for internet of things data analysis: a survey. Digit. Commun. Netw. **4**(3), 161–175 (2018)
14. Nasr, M., Shokri, R., Houmansadr, A.: Comprehensive privacy analysis of deep learning: passive and active white-box inference attacks against centralized and federated learning. In: 2019 IEEE Symposium on Security and Privacy (SP), pp. 739–753. IEEE (2019)
15. Nicolas, P., Shuang, S., Ilya, M., Ananth, R., Kunal, T., Úlfar, E.: Scalable private learning with pate. arXiv preprint arXiv:1802.08908 (2018)
16. Ozbayoglu, A.M., Gudelek, M.U., Sezer, O.B.: Deep learning for financial applications: a survey. Appl. Soft Comput. 106384 (2020)
17. Papernot, N.: A marauder's map of security and privacy in machine learning. arXiv preprint arXiv:1811.01134 (2018)
18. Papernot, N., Abadi, M., Erlingsson, U., Goodfellow, I., Talwar, K.: Semi-supervised knowledge transfer for deep learning from private training data. arXiv preprint arXiv:1610.05755 (2016)

19. Phong, L.T., Aono, Y., Hayashi, T., Wang, L., Moriai, S.: Privacy-preserving deep learning: revisited and enhanced. In: Batten, L., Kim, D.S., Zhang, X., Li, G. (eds.) ATIS 2017. CCIS, vol. 719, pp. 100–110. Springer, Singapore (2017). https://doi.org/10.1007/978-981-10-5421-1_9

20. Pyrgelis, A., Troncoso, C., De Cristofaro, E.: Knock knock, who's there? Membership inference on aggregate location data. arXiv preprint arXiv:1708.06145 (2017)

21. Rajkomar, A., et al.: Scalable and accurate deep learning with electronic health records. NPJ Digit. Med. **1**(1), 1–10 (2018)

22. Shokri, R., Shmatikov, V.: Privacy-preserving deep learning. In: ACM Conference on Computer and Communications Security (CCS) (2015)

23. Shokri, R., Stronati, M., Song, C., Shmatikov, V.: Membership inference attacks against machine learning models. In: 2017 IEEE Symposium on Security and Privacy (SP), pp. 3–18. IEEE (2017)

24. Song, C., Ristenpart, T., Shmatikov, V.: Machine learning models that remember too much. In: Proceedings of the 2017 ACM SIGSAC Conference on Computer and Communications Security, pp. 587–601 (2017)

25. Suresh, H., Hunt, N., Johnson, A., Celi, L.A., Szolovits, P., Ghassemi, M.: Clinical intervention prediction and understanding with deep neural networks. In: Machine Learning for Healthcare Conference, pp. 322–337. PMLR (2017)

26. Tai, C.H., Tseng, P.J., Yu, P.S., Chen, M.S.: Identity protection in sequential releases of dynamic networks. IEEE Trans. Knowl. Data Eng. **26**(3), 635–651 (2014)

27. Veale, M., Binns, R., Edwards, L.: Algorithms that remember: model inversion attacks and data protection law. Philos. Trans. R. Soc. A: Math. Phys. Eng. Sci. **376**(2133), 20180083 (2018)

28. Wang, J., Zhang, J., Bao, W., Zhu, X., Cao, B., Yu, P.S.: Not just privacy: improving performance of private deep learning in mobile cloud. In: Proceedings of the 24th ACM SIGKDD International Conference on Knowledge Discovery & Data Mining, KDD 2018, pp. 2407–2416. Association for Computing Machinery, New York (2018). https://doi.org/10.1145/3219819.3220106

29. Wang, W., Siau, K.: Artificial intelligence, machine learning, automation, robotics, future of work and future of humanity: a review and research agenda. J. Database Manag. (JDM) **30**(1), 61–79 (2019)

30. Wang, Y., Wu, X., Hu, D.: Using randomized response for differential privacy preserving data collection. In: EDBT/ICDT Workshops, vol. 1558 (2016)

31. Wang, Z., Song, M., Zhang, Z., Song, Y., Wang, Q., Qi, H.: Beyond inferring class representatives: user-level privacy leakage from federated learning. In: IEEE Conference on Computer Communications, IEEE INFOCOM 2019, pp. 2512–2520. IEEE (2019)

SPoiL: Sybil-Based Untargeted Data Poisoning Attacks in Federated Learning

Zhuotao Lian, Chen Zhang, Kaixi Nan, and Chunhua Su[⊠]

Department of Computer Science and Engineering, The University of Aizu,
Aizuwakamatsu, Japan
chsu@u-aizu.ac.jp

Abstract. Federated learning is widely used in mobile computing, the Internet of Things, and other scenarios due to its distributed and privacy-preserving nature. It allows mobile devices to train machine learning models collaboratively without sharing their local private data. However, during the model aggregation phase, federated learning is vulnerable to poisoning attacks carried out by malicious users. Furthermore, due to the heterogeneity of network status, communication conditions, hardware, and other factors, users are at high risk of offline, which allows attackers to fake virtual participants and increase the damage of poisoning. Unlike existing work, we focus on the more general case of untargeted poisoning attacks. In this paper, we propose novel sybil-based untargeted data poisoning attacks in federated learning (SPoiL), in which malicious users corrupt the performance of the global model by modifying the training data and increasing the probability of poisoning by virtualizing several sybil nodes. Finally, we validate the superiority of our attack approach through experiments across the commonly used datasets.

Keywords: Federated learning · Poisoning attacks · Sybil · Distributed learning

1 Introduction

Federated learning has emerged as a prominent distributed machine learning paradigm that enables collaboration among data owners without the need to share sensitive data. It allows each participant to train a local model using their private data and then aggregate the models' parameters to create a global model. This approach has found applications in various domains, including finance, recommendation systems, and healthcare, due to its privacy-preserving nature and compliance with data privacy regulations [13]. One of the key advantages of federated learning is its ability to facilitate collaboration between distrustful clients, such as competing banks or mobile phone users [14]. By enabling collaboration without compromising data privacy, federated learning allows competitors to benefit from shared insights and advancements while preserving their business interests and privacy. For example, banks can collectively train credit

S. Li et al. (Eds.): NSS 2023, LNCS 13983, pp. 235–248, 2023.
https://doi.org/10.1007/978-3-031-39828-5_13

models, and medical institutions can collaborate on disease diagnosis models, which would be challenging using traditional machine learning methods with gathered sensitive data.

Despite the privacy protection mechanisms in federated learning, it is susceptible to poisoning attacks due to the lack of direct access to training data. Poisoning attacks refer to the fact that a subset of participants in a federated learning system, which we call compromised clients, can be owned or controlled by a malicious user, and thus can artificially interfere with the local training of the node and thus further interfere with the effectiveness of the global model. Data poisoning attempts to make the model learn such patterns with incorrectly associated labels by modifying the data used for model training, thereby affecting the integrity and availability, which in turn affects the training performance [11].

Furthermore, federated learning participants exhibit high heterogeneity in multiple aspects. Firstly, the collected data among participants is often heterogeneous, including variations in data volume, label distributions, and data quality. This heterogeneity, commonly referred to as non-independent and identically distributed (non-IID) data, has been a focus of research, particularly regarding label distribution imbalances [6,18,19]. Secondly, heterogeneity exists in terms of hardware capabilities and device configurations [16]. Differences in CPU, GPU, memory, and network environments introduce variations in participant capabilities. Additionally, the dynamic and intermittent nature of participant involvement in the training process increases the risk of offline scenarios, creating opportunities for adversaries to exploit vulnerabilities [8]. In such scenarios, sybil-based attacks become viable, allowing malicious users to create multiple virtual nodes and assume fake identities, enabling more malicious users to participate in the training and parameter aggregation process, thereby amplifying the impact of data poisoning.

While there are limited studies focusing on sybil-based untargeted poisoning attacks, untargeted attacks are more prevalent and practical in real-world scenarios. Through our inductive analysis, we have identified untargeted attacks as having higher prevalence and research value. Therefore, this paper aims to propose a novel sybil-based untargeted poisoning attack method that leverages virtual node forgery by malicious users and manipulates local training data to undermine the performance of the global model.

In summary, our contributions are as follows:

- An overview of poisoning attacks in federated learning systems is provided, emphasizing the importance of untargeted attacks within a broader context.
- We explore sybil-based untargeted data poisoning attacks, in which malicious users further enhance the harm of poisoning by virtualizing sybils.
- Simulation experiments are conducted to evaluate the impact of key factors on attack performance, including the proportion of malicious users, the number of Sybil nodes, and the ratio of poisoned data. And we presented a comprehensive analysis based on the experimental results.

2   Background

2.1   Federated Learning (FL)

Federated Learning (FL) is a distributed approach to machine learning that allows large-scale training on devices with decentralized data while preserving the privacy of sensitive data held by device owners [10]. FL brings the machine learning model to the endpoint, rather than transferring data to a central server for local collection and training [1]. This decentralized paradigm enables collaboration among data stakeholders while protecting the privacy of customers and organizations [2]. In domains like financial payment, FL plays a crucial role in ensuring personal privacy and complying with institutional or corporate data security requirements. For instance, platforms like Jingdong Lending leverage FL to collaborate with financial institutions and assess the credit risk of users, effectively addressing the challenge of "data silo" under legal regulations [2].

2.2   Targeted Poisoning Attacks in FL

Poisoning Attack is an attack in which a malicious participant injects malicious information into the training data or uploaded model parameters to disrupt the accuracy of federal learning [3]. There are two types of Poisoning Attacks: Data Poisoning Attacks and Model Poisoning Attacks [17].

Poisoning attacks are malicious attempts by participants to inject harmful information into the training data or uploaded model parameters, with the intention of disrupting the accuracy of federated learning [3]. In terms of the targets of poisoning attacks, they can be classified into two categories: data poisoning attacks and model poisoning attacks [17].

- Data Poisoning Attacks refer to malicious participants modifying the labels or features of their local training data to make them inconsistent with the global data distribution, thus affecting the accuracy and robustness of the global model. Examples of data poisoning attacks include label flipping and feature transformation.
- Model poisoning attacks in federated learning involve participants manipulating the shared global model's weights and injecting malicious elements through unauthorized modifications, aiming to compromise the model's integrity and performance and undermine the effectiveness of the global model [20]. These attacks exploit participants' control over the model updates and training strategies to evade detection and

Poisoning attacks can be categorized into three types as illustrated in Table 1 based on their goals: targeted attacks, untargeted attacks, and backdoor attacks [15]. Targeted attacks aim to manipulate the model's behavior to generate specific incorrect predictions. Untargeted attacks focus on diminishing the overall accuracy and robustness of the model without specific target objectives. Backdoor attacks involve inserting a concealed trigger into the model to manipulate

Table 1. Poisoning Attacks in Federated Learning.

Type of Attack	Goal
Targeted Attack	Misclassify the target class of data
Untarget Attack	Misclassify all classes of data from the distribution
Backdoor Attack	Misclassify data with trigger patterns

its behavior when a specific trigger condition is met. In the context mentioned, the focus is specifically on untargeted attacks.

Untargeted attacks in federated learning aim to disrupt the performance of models without specific target objectives, such as by introducing random noise or labels that degrade the model's generalization ability [12], as illustrated in Fig. 1. These attacks are challenging to detect because the attacker's goal is to reduce the overall accuracy of the model, and the service provider does not predefine the expected overall accuracy. This makes it harder to identify the presence of untargeted poisoning attacks.

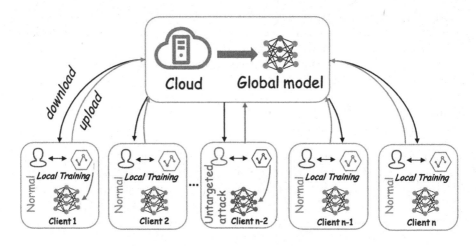

Fig. 1. Example diagram of Untargeted Attacks.

2.3   Sybil Attacks in FL

Sybil attack is a term used to describe the act of adversaries creating multiple virtual identities, accounts, or nodes in order to disrupt the balance of a global system [5]. Interestingly, sybil attacks share many similarities with distributed poisoning attacks. For instance, both attacks involve controlling or utilizing multiple clients to interfere with the global model. However, the sybil attack could be primarily carried out by a single adversary, while the distributed poisoning attack is usually a coordinated effort involving multiple adversaries [4]. In the

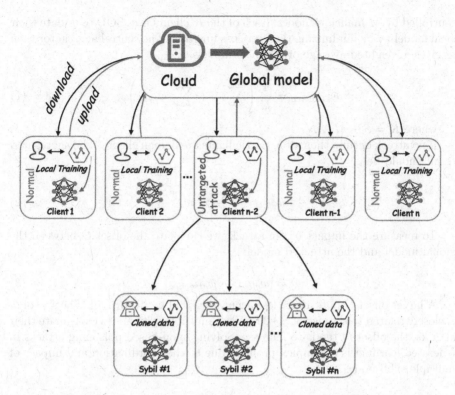

Fig. 2. Sybil-based Untargeted Attacks. Sybil attacks often interfere with the global model in federated learning by constructing fake identities, and may even be coordinated among Sybils.

context of untargeted attacks, sybil attacks, compared to traditional distributed attacks, have the advantage of leveraging the relationship between malicious nodes and Sybil nodes to further maximize the impact of the attack on the global model. Additionally, s sybil nodes can theoretically be created in larger numbers and are more susceptible to control under a coordinated attack strategy. This makes sybil attacks more potent in terms of their potential impact on the system (Fig.2).

A sybil-based poisoning attack represents an evolved form of distributed poisoning attacks. Due to the inherent difficulty in identifying the existence and number of sybil nodes, detecting such attacks becomes more challenging. Moreover, sybil attacks are more destructive in nature, as they allow for coordinated efforts to maximize the impact of the attack, even in the absence of specific target objectives. For instance, a malicious user can monitor the success of the attack on the controlled sybil nodes, facilitating convenient adjustments to specific attack parameters.

This mathematical representation illustrates the scenario in federated learning where there are K participants, including N benign clients and S sybil clients controlled by M malicious nodes. Each of the K clients uses SGD to update their local model w_i by minimizing the local loss function. The central aggregator then receives a weighted average of the local models.

$$w_{attacked} = \frac{1}{K} \left(\sum_i^N w_i + \sum_i^{S+M} w_{i+N} \right) \tag{1}$$

where $K = S + M + N$.

If no attack occurs, then all K participants are benign clients. The aggregated result should be:

$$w_{global} = \frac{1}{K} \sum_{i=1}^K w_i \tag{2}$$

To measure the impact of the attack, we calculate the offset O between the global model and the attacked model:

$$O = |w_{global} - w_{attacked}| \tag{3}$$

A larger offset O indicates a less accurate global model overall. The size of O is closely related to the size of $S+M$. When multiple sybil nodes coordinate their attacks, the offset O tends to increase. Solving sybil-based poisoning attacks in federated learning is a complex problem due to the coordination and impact of multiple sybil nodes.

3   Design of SPoiL

In this part, we first introduce the threat model of SPoiL, including the adversary's ability, knowledge, etc., and then further, we give the algorithm description.

In this section, we begin by presenting the threat model of SPoiL, which includes the objective, knowledge, and capabilities of the adversary. We then proceed to provide a detailed description of the algorithm.

3.1   Threat Model

Adversary's Objective. In SPoiL, the adversaries aim to cause misclassification of any test input without targeting a specific class. The objective of the attack is indiscriminate, and the specific incorrect class label assigned to the misclassified sample is not a concern for the attacker.

Adversary's Knowledge. We assume that the adversary has complete access to the global model information. This assumption is reasonable in federated learning since the global model is shared among all participants. Additionally, this assumption is necessary as the adversary will create virtual nodes to train on the poisoned data. Regarding data access, we assume that the adversary can only access the local initial data of compromised users.

Adversary's Capabilities. In SPoiL, we consider a more generalized assumption where the adversary can only modify local data to perform data poisoning attacks, indirectly influencing the global model. For model poisoning attacks, it is unrealistic to expect the adversary to directly manipulate the updated data uploaded by users by bypassing the security protocols. This assumption is not practical in large-scale federated learning systems.

3.2 Algorithms

In this section, we give a generalized algorithm representation of SPoiL. Then we explain the design of the algorithm in detail from the perspectives of the user and the server.

Algorithm 1. SPoiL

1: **Input:**Initial global model $w(t)$, Learning rate η, Loss function L
2: **Output:**$w(t+1)$
3: //$User$-$side$
4: **for** Honest users $i = 1$ to h **do**
5:     $w_i(t) \leftarrow LocalTraining(w(t), D_i)$
6: **end for**
7: **for** Malicious users $j = 1$ to m **do**
8:     Modify local data D_j;   ▷ Construct the poisoning dataset
9:     $w_j(t) \leftarrow LocalTraining(w(t), D_j)$
10:     Virtualize s sybil users;
11:     **for** Sybil users $k = 1$ to s **do**
12:         $w_k(t) \leftarrow LocalTraining(w(t), D_j)$ ▷ Sybil users will inherit the dataset
13:     **end for**
14: **end for**
15: //$Sever$-$side$
16: Sever will aggregate the local models
17: Randomly select n from $h + m + m * s$ users   ▷ $n \le h + m + m * s$
18: $w(t+1) \leftarrow GlobalAggregation(w_i(t), |D_i|)$
19: return $w(t+1)$;

In the considered federated learning scenario, a classic user-server architecture is employed. Users participate in collaborative training to develop a global model. Initially, each user performs local training using their local data. The updated local models are then uploaded to the server. The server conducts aggregation operations to generate a new global model, which is subsequently broadcasted to all users. This iterative process continues for multiple epochs until the model converges or the predetermined number of communication rounds is reached.

It is important to note that data poisoning occurs during specific rounds, which is referred to as static poisoning. If the poisoned data is not repaired afterward, allowing for long-term attacks, the attack becomes persistent.

Additionally, if data poisoning is performed in multiple rounds with different techniques, it can be considered a dynamic poisoning attack. In this paper, we primarily focus on a typical static poisoning approach.

User-Side. In this system, there are different types of users, including honest users, malicious users, and sybil users, collectively forming the participant pool of federated learning.

During round t, each user initializes their local model with the latest model $w(t)$ generated by the server. Honest users employ gradient descent to train their local models on their respective local data and update them accordingly.

Malicious users, on the other hand, start by modifying their local data. In this context, we consider the construction of a poisoned dataset using label flipping. Since our focus is on untargeted attacks, random incorrect labels are assigned to the original training samples. Of course, other methods of data modification can also be applicable to our system.

Subsequently, malicious users create multiple sybil users, as depicted in line 10 of the algorithm. We assume that each malicious user is capable of creating s sybil users. The value of s depends on the capabilities of the malicious users, algorithm constraints, and other factors. It should not be excessively large, as an excessively large value may expose the attack. The sybil users inherit the poisoned data from the original malicious users. Both malicious users and sybil users train poisoning models using the poisoned data.

Server-Side. In the server-side process, after the local training is finished, the server performs parameter aggregation using the popular FedAvg algorithm. The server begins by randomly selecting n users from the user pool and proceeds to compute a weighted average of their respective local models. It's worth noting that in this context, we simplify the aggregation process by using simple averaging, as many existing works also adopt this approach. The intention here is to focus on the attack methods without utilizing weight-related mechanisms.

4   Simulation Experiments

In this section, we aim to validate the effectiveness of our attack by conducting experiments on the task of fake news identification. We begin by presenting the details of our experimental settings, including the hardware and software configurations used. Next, we describe the chosen data sets that we employed in our experiments. Moreover, we elaborate on the models selected for our analysis, providing insights into their architecture and training methodology. Finally, we present a comprehensive analysis of the experimental results, highlighting the impact of our attack on the performance of the fake news identification models.

4.1 Settings

We conducted our distributed virtual experiments on a single machine running Ubuntu 18.04. The machine was equipped with 32GB of RAM and an Nvidia GTX 3070 GPU, which provided the necessary computational resources for our experiments.

Kaggle Fake News Dataset. In this study, we selected the Kaggle fake news dataset [7] for our experiments. The dataset consists of five attributes: "ID," "Title," "Text," "Author," and "Label." For our experiments, we focused on two attributes: "Text" and "Label," which were used to train our model. The training dataset (train.csv) contained 20,800 records. To preprocess the text data, we followed the approach described in [9]. After preprocessing, we trained our neural network model on the preprocessed dataset.

Neural Network Model. Our neural network model consisted of three hidden layers, totaling 163,570 trainable parameters. The activation function used for the first three dense layers was Rectified Linear Unit (ReLU), while the activation function for the last layer was softmax. These choices of activation functions helped in capturing complex patterns and making predictions based on the learned representations.

4.2 Results

We clarify that the malicious users mentioned do not include sybil users. We specifically state that each malicious user, along with their created sybil users, shares the same local data. The experimental setup involves a total of 20 users participating in the training process, with 20 epochs of training conducted. For each round, 10 users are randomly selected. For each experiment, we performed five repetitions and obtained the average results.

The dataset is evenly partitioned among the participants, ensuring that each user has 800 local data items. The malicious users carry out two operations as part of their attacks. Firstly, they create several sybil users who can share local data and collaborate in subsequent attacks. Secondly, they execute label-flipping attacks on the training data. Once the data is poisoned, the impact on the training process persists throughout. These attack strategies employed by malicious users result in a continuous and persistent impact on the training process, undermining the integrity and reliability of the trained model. Based on our experiments, we obtained the following results regarding the impact of the propotion of malicious users, sybil users, and poisoned data.

Number of Malicious Users. We conducted poison attacks initiated by the malicious users in the 9th epoch, where they randomly flipped the corresponding labels of the training data. We tested different scenarios with varying proportions of malicious users: 0%, 5%, 10%, and 20%.

The confusion matrix of the trained model, depicting the classification results, is presented in Fig. 3. A darker color along the main diagonal in the matrix indicates higher accuracy. Here are our observations: When the proportion of malicious users reaches 20%, the model becomes almost unusable. The classification accuracy rates for real and false information are 25.6% and 10.4% respectively. As the number of malicious users decreases to around 10%, which aligns with assumptions made in many existing works, the classification accuracy rate for false information improves to 79.8%. This rate surpasses the 50% accuracy of random selection in binary classification. The best performance is achieved when there are no malicious users present, resulting in a classification accuracy rate of 89.67%. These findings highlight the significant impact of the proportion of malicious users on the attack's effectiveness. The presence of even a small proportion of malicious users can lead to a considerable decrease in classification accuracy.

Number of Sybils Created by Each Malicious User. Next, we investigated the influence of the number of sybils each malicious user can create on the model. In this scenario, we considered a general case where 10% of the users are malicious. We used s in Fig. 4 to represent the number of sybil users created by each malicious user. We visualized the changes in accuracy and loss over the training epochs. The term "Attack" indicates the time when the attack begins.

From Fig. 4a, we can make two observations. Firstly, it is clear that the attack has a direct and significant impact on the model's accuracy and loss. Upon initiating the attack, the model's accuracy decreases by approximately 14%, 11%, 5%, and 0.6% for s = 4, 3, 2, and 1, respectively. This indicates that a higher number of sybil users leads to a greater impact on the global model, even when using the same local training data. As anticipated, the effect on the loss is also considerable. Secondly, since the poisoned data is not rectified, the influence of malicious users on the model's training persists for a long time. Even if the majority of users are benign, the presence of malicious users still hampers the performace of the model.

The Proportion of Poisoned Data and the Number of Sybils. Finally, we investigated the combined impact of the number of Sybil users created, denoted as "s," and the proportion of poisoned data, denoted as "P_d," on the model's accuracy. We used a surface plot in Fig. 5 to visually represent the experimental results. The deepest blue region in the plot corresponds to the lowest accuracy, indicating that higher values of P_d and a larger number of s result in a more pronounced negative impact on the model.

Furthermore, we observed that the decrease in accuracy is not linear but rather exhibits a gradual acceleration as P_d and s change. This observation provides inspiration and raises considerations for our future work, particularly in the design of defenses that can achieve better results while minimizing costs.

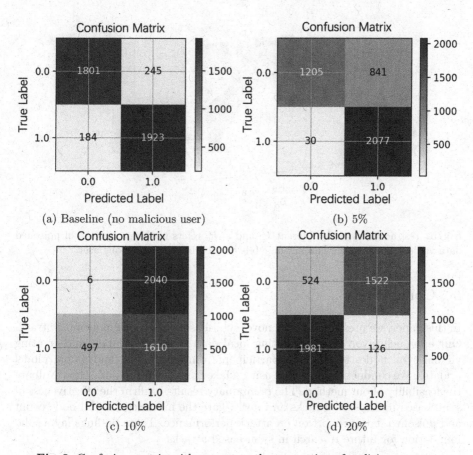

Fig. 3. Confusion matrix with respect to the proportion of malicious users.

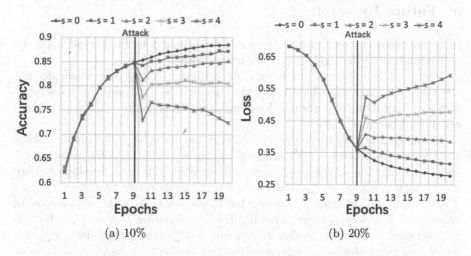

Fig. 4. Accuracy versus epochs with respect to the number of sybils.

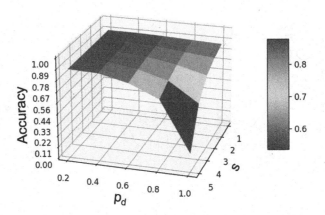

Fig. 5. Test accuracy with different P_d and s. P_d refers to the proportion of poisoned data while s refers to the number of sybils created by each malicious user.

5   Conclusion

In this paper, we present SPoiL, a novel sybil-based untargeted poisoning attack. Our approach involves manipulating local data by flipping labels and creating virtual sybil nodes to simulate participants during training and global model updates. We conduct experiments using a fake news detection dataset to evaluate the feasibility of our method. The preliminary results confirm the effectiveness of sybil-based untargeted attacks and investigate the influence of sybil node count and poisoned data proportion on attack performance. These findings lay a solid foundation for future research in sybil-based attacks.

6   Future Research

In future research, several directions can be explored to further advance the understanding and mitigation of sybil-based attacks.

Firstly, it is important to investigate the effectiveness of existing defense mechanisms against sybil-based attacks. This includes analyzing the vulnerabilities and limitations of current defense methods when confronted with sophisticated sybil-based strategies.

Secondly, studying the impact of synergy among sybil nodes on the attack effectiveness is crucial. Understanding how coordinated actions among sybil nodes enhance the attack potency can provide insights into developing more robust defense strategies that can disrupt such collaborative efforts.

Moreover, an intriguing direction for future research is the exploration of sybil-based backdoor attacks. This involves investigating how sybil nodes can be leveraged to implant hidden triggers or manipulate the model's behavior under specific conditions. Understanding the mechanisms and implications of such attacks can provide valuable insights for the development of effective countermeasures to mitigate the impact of these stealthy and potentially devastating attacks.

Overall, future research should focus on enhancing the understanding of sybil-based attacks, developing robust defense mechanisms, and investigating the various aspects of sybil node collaboration and backdoor attacks. By addressing these aspects, we can enhance the security and resilience of federated learning systems against sybil-based threats.

Acknowledgment. This work was partially supported by JSPS Grant-in-Aid for Scientific Research (C) 23K11103 and NEC C&C Foundation under Grants for Researchers.

References

1. Bonawitz, K., et al.: Towards federated learning at scale: system design. Proc. Mach. Learn. Syst. **1**, 374–388 (2019). https://proceedings.mlsys.org/paper/2019/hash/bd686fd640be98efaae0091fa301e613-Abstract.html
2. Bonawitz, K., et al.: Practical secure aggregation for privacy-preserving machine learning. In: Proceedings of the 2017 ACM SIGSAC Conference on Computer and Communications Security, CCS 2017, pp. 1175–1191. Association for Computing Machinery, New York, NY, USA (2017). https://doi.org/10.1145/3133956.3133982
3. Cao, D., Chang, S., Lin, Z., Liu, G., Sun, D.: Understanding distributed poisoning attack in federated learning. In: 2019 IEEE 25th International Conference on Parallel and Distributed Systems (ICPADS), pp. 233–239. IEEE (2019). https://doi.org/10.1109/ICPADS47876.2019.00042
4. Cao, D., Chang, S., Lin, Z., Liu, G., Sun, D.: Understanding distributed poisoning attack in federated learning. In: 2019 IEEE 25th International Conference on Parallel and Distributed Systems (ICPADS), pp. 233–239 (2019). https://doi.org/10.1109/ICPADS47876.2019.00042
5. Douceur, J.R.: The Sybil attack. In: Druschel, P., Kaashoek, F., Rowstron, A. (eds.) IPTPS 2002. LNCS, vol. 2429, pp. 251–260. Springer, Heidelberg (2002). https://doi.org/10.1007/3-540-45748-8_24
6. Jamali-Rad, H., Abdizadeh, M., Singh, A.: Federated learning with taskonomy for non-IID data. IEEE Trans. Neural Netw. Learn. Syst., 1–12 (2022). https://doi.org/10.1109/TNNLS.2022.3152581
7. Kaggle fake news dataset. https://www.kaggle.com/competitions/fake-news/data
8. Kourtellis, N., Katevas, K., Perino, D.: Flaas: federated learning as a service. In: Proceedings of the 1st Workshop on Distributed Machine Learning, DistributedML 2020, pp. 7–13. Association for Computing Machinery, New York, NY, USA (2020). https://doi.org/10.1145/3426745.3431337
9. Krešňáková, V.M., Sarnovský, M., Butka, P.: Deep learning methods for fake news detection. In: 2019 IEEE 19th International Symposium on Computational Intelligence and Informatics and 7th IEEE International Conference on Recent Achievements in Mechatronics, Automation, Computer Sciences and Robotics (CINTI-MACRo), pp. 000143–000148 (2019). https://doi.org/10.1109/CINTI-MACRo49179.2019.9105317

10. McMahan, B., Ramage, D.: Federated Learning: Collaborative Machine Learning without Centralized Training Data (2017). https://ai.googleblog.com/2017/04/federated-learning-collaborative.html

11. Nuding, F., Mayer, R.: Data poisoning in sequential and parallel federated learning. In: Proceedings of the 2022 ACM on International Workshop on Security and Privacy Analytics, IWSPA 2022, pp. 24–34. Association for Computing Machinery, New York, NY, USA (2022). https://doi.org/10.1145/3510548.3519372

12. Sagar, S., Li, C.S., Loke, S.W., Choi, J.: Poisoning attacks and defenses in federated learning: a survey. arXiv (Jan 2023). https://doi.org/10.48550/arXiv.2301.05795

13. Sharma, P.K., Park, J.H., Cho, K.: Blockchain and federated learning-based distributed computing defence framework for sustainable society. Sustain. Cities Soc. **59**, 102220 (2020)

14. Shejwalkar, V., Houmansadr, A., Kairouz, P., Ramage, D.: Back to the drawing board: a critical evaluation of poisoning attacks on production federated learning. In: 2022 IEEE Symposium on Security and Privacy (SP), pp. 1354–1371 (2022). https://doi.org/10.1109/SP46214.2022.9833647

15. Shejwalkar, V., Houmansadr, A., Kairouz, P., Ramage, D.: Back to the drawing board: a critical evaluation of poisoning attacks on production federated learning. In: 2022 IEEE Symposium on Security and Privacy (SP), pp. 1354–1371. IEEE (2022). https://doi.org/10.1109/SP46214.2022.9833647

16. Tahir, M., Ali, M.I.: On the performance of federated learning algorithms for IoT. IoT **3**(2), 273–284 (2022)

17. Tolpegin, V., Truex, S., Gursoy, M.E., Liu, L.: Data poisoning attacks against federated learning systems. In: Chen, L., Li, N., Liang, K., Schneider, S. (eds.) ESORICS 2020. LNCS, vol. 12308, pp. 480–501. Springer, Cham (2020). https://doi.org/10.1007/978-3-030-58951-6_24

18. Wang, H., Kaplan, Z., Niu, D., Li, B.: Optimizing federated learning on non-IID data with reinforcement learning. In: IEEE INFOCOM 2020-IEEE Conference on Computer Communications, pp. 1698–1707. IEEE (2020)

19. Zhao, Y., Li, M., Lai, L., Suda, N., Civin, D., Chandra, V.: Federated learning with non-IID data. arXiv preprint arXiv:1806.00582 (2018)

20. Zhou, X., Xu, M., Wu, Y., Zheng, N.: Deep model poisoning attack on federated learning. Future Internet **13**(3), 73 (2021). https://doi.org/10.3390/fi13030073, https://www.mdpi.com/1999-5903/13/3/73

Agnostic Label-Only Membership Inference Attack

Anna Monreale[2] , Francesca Naretto[1,2(✉)] , and Simone Rizzo[2]

[1] Scuola Normale Superiore, Pisa, Italy
francesca.naretto@sns.it
[2] University of Pisa, Pisa, Italy
anna.monreale@unipi.it, s.rizzo14@studenti.unipi.it

Abstract. In recent years we are witnessing the diffusion of AI systems based on powerful Machine Learning models which find application in many critical contexts such as medicine and financial market. In such contexts, it is important to design *Trustworthy* AI systems while guaranteeing privacy protection. However, some attacks on the privacy of Machine Learning models have been designed to show the threats of exposing such models. Membership Inference is one of the simplest privacy threats faced by Machine Learning models. It is based on the assumption that an adversary, observing the confidence of the model prediction, can infer whether a particular record was used for training the classifier. A variant, called Label-Only attack, exploits the adversary's knowledge of the training data statistics to infer the record membership without accessing the confidence score of the prediction. In this paper, we propose a variant of the Label-Only attack, called ALOA, which estimates the prediction confidence exploiting a mechanism that is completely *agnostic* to the input data distributions. In fact, it requires neither statistical knowledge of the data nor the type of variables. Experimental results show better performance of our attack with respect to the competitors.

1 Introduction

The increasing prevalence of smart technology in our daily lives, including self-learning and automated decision-making systems, can be attributed to advancements in Machine Learning (ML) [3,9]. ML algorithms are utilized in applications such as Gmail's spam filtering and YouTube's video recommendations, enhancing their functionality. However, along with the benefits, ML also brings potential vulnerabilities that attackers can exploit for malicious purposes, jeopardizing system reliability.

One notable privacy attack, introduced by Shokri et al. in 2017 [13], and subsequent variants like the Label-Only Membership Inference Attack [2], aim to distinguish between records used during the training phase of an ML model and those that were not, operating under different assumptions. These attacks pose risks to privacy and confidentiality. The reconstruction of training data can

S. Li et al. (Eds.): NSS 2023, LNCS 13983, pp. 249–264, 2023.
https://doi.org/10.1007/978-3-031-39828-5_14

potentially conflict with trade secrets, as some training data may derive from successful corporate experiences, providing competitive advantages. Consequently, organizations holding such data are reluctant to disclose it to competitors.

In this paper, we present ALOA, an improved variant of LABELONLY, which achieves high performance and stable prediction metrics. Unlike LABELONLY, ALOA calculates a data-agnostic robustness score without exploiting knowledge of the training data's feature distribution. This score determines membership. The experimental results highlight that our attack allows for better stability and an enhanced performance, up to 3 percentage points, in terms of accuracy in predicting the records membership. Even if this enhancement may seem small, for the privacy setting this is extremely risky since it means that the adversary may have a higher probability of re-identifying people in the dataset. In addition, we relax the assumption that the attacker needs a dataset following the same distribution as the original training dataset, making the attack easier to perform with respect to the competitors.

The remaining of the paper is organized as follows. Section 2 discusses prior works related to our; Sect. 3 introduces some preliminary notions useful for understanding the details of our attack. In Sect. 4 we describe how to learn and apply ALOA while in Sect. 5, we present the experimental results on its performance. Lastly, Sect. 6 concludes the paper.

2   Related Work

In this Section, we contextualize our work concerning the current literature. The issue of privacy has been addressed in several fields to assess the privacy risk and/or protect information systems from the dangerous disclosure of sensitive information. Disclosure of sensitive information may derive from accessing directly data [15] or accessing ML models [1,5,13]. Indeed, ML models learn from data, and even if the data are not exposed but simply used during the training, querying the model may still leak sensitive information about the people in the training dataset. In the context of data privacy, the first goal is to assess the privacy risk of the users represented in a dataset by using a *privacy risk assessment* methodology. Then, depending on the results of this assessment, a *privacy protection* technique on the data or the ML model can be applied to protect the users from malicious adversaries. Such protection techniques are based on well-defined privacy models, such as randomization, differential privacy, and k-anonymity [4,12,15], and transform data/ML models in such a way to guarantee certain thresholds on the risk of privacy leaks. In this paper, we focus on the research topic of privacy risk assessment, Therefore, in the following, we discuss the literature in this context. The process of assessing privacy risks can be applied to either data or ML models. Pratesi et al. [11] proposed PRUDEnce, a framework enabling a systematic assessment of empirical privacy risk concerning specific privacy attacks on data. In practice, it simulates an adversary that, for each individual, possesses the knowledge to maximize the privacy risk of that individual. To this end, the framework generates all the possible background knowledge that the adversary may know and assesses the risk with respect to the worst. Similar approaches have been studied in various works over the past few years to detect privacy attacks against ML models. Shokri et al. [13] proposed the Membership Inference Attack (MIA) with the aim is to infer the membership of a given record to the training set of a classification model. Fredrikson et al. [5, 6] designed the so-called reconstruction attacks, where the attacker's objective is to reconstruct one or more training samples and their respective training labels. Another type of attack is the property inference attack [7], which extracts unintentionally learned information not explicitly encoded as features in the model. For instance, property inference attacks can uncover information such as the gender ratio in the training data set. Such attacks can be used in tandem with MIA or reconstruction attacks to enhance the adversary's knowledge. Recently, Choquette-Choo et al. [2] proposed a variant of the original Membership Inference Attack called LABELONLY attack, in which some of the assumptions of Shokri's attack are relaxed. In particular, MIA needs the probability vector for inferring the membership of a record while LABELONLY exploits only the hard labels. In our paper, we present ALOA, a variant of the LABELONLY attack, which is completely agnostic.

3   Background

Before providing the details of our privacy attack against classification models, in this Section we introduce some basic notions that are fundamental for understanding the details of our approach.

Classifier. A classifier, is a function $b : \mathcal{X}^{(m)} \rightarrow \mathcal{Y}$ which maps instances (tuples) x from a feature space $\mathcal{X}^{(m)}$ with m input features to a decision y in a target space $\mathcal{Y}$ of size $L = |\mathcal{Y}|$, i.e., y can assume one of the L different labels ($L = 2$ is binary classification). We use $f(x) = y$ to denote the decision y taken by b we denote by $\overline{y}_b$ the probability vector of size L in which the sum of all the values is one. An instance x consists of a set of m attribute-value pairs (a_i, v_i), where a_i is a feature (or attribute) and v_i is a value from the domain of a_i. The domain of a feature can be continuous or categorical. We assume a classifier is available as a function that can be queried at will.

Membership Inference Attack (Mia). Shokri et al. [13] assume that a ML algorithm is used to train a classifier b that captures the relationship between data records and their labels. To attack b trained on D_b^{train}, MIA defines an attack model $A(\cdot)$: it is a ML model able to discern if a record was part of the training dataset D_b^{train} or not. Note that, D_b^{train} is composed by $(x^i, y_o^i)_b$, where y_o^i is the true labels associated to x_b^i. In practice, the attack $A(\cdot)$ is a binary classifier that predicts IN if the record was part of the training set or OUT otherwise. $A(\cdot)$ is trained on a dataset D_a^{train}: $(x^i, y^i)_a$, where each x_a^i is composed by the label predicted by the classifier b for a record under analysis and its probability vector $\overline{y^i}$ of length L obtained by querying a shadow model $s^i(\cdot)$ mimicking b; while y_a^i is the correct membership label and that can be IN or

OUT. The attack model $A(\cdot)$ is a voting model composed of L ML models: one for each output class of the classifier model under attack. The key factor in this attack is the knowledge of the probability vector: given how the probabilities in $\overline{y}_b$ are distributed around the true value of the record, the attack model computes the membership probability $\Pr\{(x, y) \in D_b^{train}\}$, which is the probability that x belongs to the IN class, i.e. it is part of the training set. To obtain the dataset $(x^i, y^i)_a$, on which the MIA model $A(\cdot)$ is trained, the authors used *shadow models*. In the original paper, the authors assume a black-box setting in which there is no knowledge about the type of classifier to be attacked or the training dataset used to train it. In the following, we use the term black-box model to indicate the classifier to be attacked. To overcome the limitation of absence of knowledge on data and model, they employed a set of k shadow models $s^i(\cdot)$: ML models trained to mimic the decisions of the black-box model $b(\cdot)$ we would like to attack. These shadow models are trained on D_s^{train}: $(x^i, y^i)_s$, in which x_s^i has the same format and similar distribution w.r.t. to the dataset employed to train the black-box model X, while y_s^i is the predicted class obtained querying the black-box model $b(\cdot)$. After the training, we know which record was part of the training dataset (class IN) for each shadow model and which was part of the test one (class OUT). Hence, we can exploit this information to create a supervised training dataset for training the attack model $A(\cdot)$, which is D_a^{train}.

The datasets employed for training the shadow models are disjoint from the unknown dataset used to train the black-box model. Shokri et al. [13] tested different kinds of training data for the shadow models: (i) a *random* dataset, with randomly generated records labeled querying the black-box model; (ii) a *statistical* one, with synthetic data generated exploiting the original statistical distribution; (iii) a *noise* one, in which the attacker knows a noisy portion of data from the same distribution of the original training dataset. The different data for shadow models allow for privacy attacks of different strengths.

Label-Only Membership Inference Attack (LabelOnly). Choquette-Choo et al. [2] design a variant of MIA which relaxes some requirements of the original attack. Given a black-box model b, LABELONLY $A_{LO}(\cdot)$ targets it by exploiting only the hard labels, i.e. the output predictions of the model under analysis. Hence, the probability vector $\overline{y}^i$, employed by MIA, is not exploited in LABELONLY. It develops a procedure that derives the robustness of a model to perturbations and uses it as a proxy for model confidence in its predictions. The basic intuition is that records which exhibit high robustness belong to the training dataset. $A_{LO}(\cdot)$ exploits a dataset D_s^{train} for training only one shadow model $s(\cdot)$, i.e., a ML model mimicking the decision of black-box model b. The dataset D_s^{train}: $(x^i, y^i)_s$ is composed of records with the same format and similar distribution w.r.t. to the dataset for training the black-box b, and is labeled by the predicted class obtained querying b. With the shadow model, we know which records were part of the training dataset (IN) of the shadow model and which was part of the test (OUT). For each tuple x_s^i the algorithm generates a set of records resulting from its perturbation and labels the generated records using the trained shadow model. Analyzing the percentage of generated records

---

Algorithm 1: ALOA $(b, D_s, p_{min}, p_{max}, k, n)$

Input : b - classifier,
$\qquad\quad D_s$ - dataset for training the shadow models,
$\qquad\quad p_{min}, p_{max}$ - perturbation percentage range,
$\qquad\quad k$- number of neighbours to be generated

Output: $threshold_{split}$ - split threshold found for the dataset D_s

1 $\{D_{s^1}, \ldots, D_{s^k}\} \leftarrow RandomSample(D_s, k)$
2 $S \leftarrow \emptyset; D \leftarrow \emptyset; Scores \leftarrow \emptyset$
3 **for** $i \in \{1, \ldots, k\}$ **do**
4 $\quad D_{s^i}^{\mathrm{train}}, D_{s^i}^{\mathrm{test}} = split\_train\_test(D_{s^i})$
5 $\quad S \leftarrow S \cup train\_shadow(D_{s^i}^{\mathrm{train}})$
6 $\quad D_{s^i}^{\mathrm{IN}} \leftarrow$ Assign the IN label to each record in $D_{s^i}^{\mathrm{train}}$
7 $\quad D_{s^i}^{\mathrm{OUT}} \leftarrow$ Assign the OUT label to each record in $D_{s^i}^{\mathrm{test}}$
8 $\quad D \leftarrow D \cup D_{s^i}^{\mathrm{IN}} \cup D_{s^i}^{\mathrm{OUT}}$
9 **for** $x^i \in D$ **do**
10 $\quad N_x^i \leftarrow Noisy\_Neighborhood\_Generation(x^i, p_{min}, p_{max}, n)$
11 $\quad rScore_{x^i} \leftarrow Robustness\_Score(N_x^i, S, b(x^i))$
12 $\quad Scores \leftarrow Scores \cup rScore_{x^i}$
13 $threshold_{split} \leftarrow Iterative\_Thresholding(D, Scores)$
14 **return** $threshold_{split}$

---

having the same predicted class of x_s^i, the algorithm computes the robustness score of the black-box with respect to the x_s^i classification. Then, the attack uses an iterative thresholding procedure on the robustness scores, assigned to each record of the training an testing dataset of the shadow model, to find a threshold on the scores to separate the records between IN and OUT. The attack will use this threshold for classifying new records as part of the training of the black-box or not.

4   Agnostic Label-Only Membership Inference Attack

In this paper, we present ALOA (*Agnostic Label-Only* membership inference *Attack*), which is a variant of LABELONLY attack, presented in Sect. 3. The LABELONLY attack assumes the statistical distributions and the domain of the features in training data. This knowledge is exploited for applying a perturbation to each feature tailored to its type and its statistical distribution. We propose a variant completely *agnostic* with respect to the training data and the type of classifier to be attacked.

Threat Model. The objective of this kind of attack is to determine whether or not a given data record belongs to the training dataset of a specific classification model. To conduct an attack, the adversary can exploit specific prior knowledge that can be accessed. In this paper we assume an adversary having black-box access to the classifier b.: the adversary can only query the model to obtain a prediction and, as in [2], the model only returns hard labels to queries.

The adversary does not know the model architecture, e.g., the type of classifier. The adversary knows the total number of classes, the class labels, and the input format. To perform ALOA we do not need to know distributions of the original training dataset, nor during the training of the shadow model, nor in the perturbation mechanism, in contrast to LABELONLY.

Learning ALOA. Given a black-box b, trained on D_b^{train}, ALOA targets it by exploiting only the hard labels, e.g. $b(x) = \hat{y}$, and deriving a robustness score by an agnostic data perturbation. This score enables ALOA to determine if a record x belongs to the training data D_b^{train} of the black-box model under attack. The algorithm's pseudo-code is reported in Algorithm 1. The process to create ALOA model requires as input a dataset D_s: $(x^i, y^i)_s$ in which x_s^i has the same format of training data of b and y_s^i is the predicted class obtained querying the black-box model b. Given the agnostic nature of ALOA, it does not rely on any assumptions about D_s, which may include a completely random dataset.

After querying the black-box model for labeling each x_s^i, ALOA splits the dataset D_s into training and testing datasets, obtaining D_s^{train} and D_s^{test} respectively, and then it trains one or more shadow models, $s^i(\cdot)$ on sub-samples of D_s^{train} (lines 6–7). The goal is to mimic the behavior of b, by also knowing which records are part of the training set and which are not. In particular, as reported in Algorithm 1, ALOA constructs a dataset D, where assigns the label IN to each record in the training data of the shadow models and the label OUT to those belonging to their test data (lines 8–10).

At this point, ALOA performs its core process: the *agnostic perturbation* of the data used for training and testing a given shadow model (line 12, Algorithm 1). We call this procedure *Noisy Neighborhood Generation* and we report its pseudo-code in Algorithm 2. For each data record x_s^i of the shadow dataset D_s, it generates a neighborhood of n records obtained perturbing the values of its attributes. Since the goal is to perturb each data record in their local vicinity without using any knowledge of the dataset's domain or attributes distribution, making the algorithm completely domain agnostic, our perturbation mechanism adds noise values to each attribute of the record under analysis. Given an instance x_s^i composed by m attribute-value pairs (a_j, v_j), to generate the noise value for perturbing v_j ALOA adds or subtracts to v_j a noise values $\nu = p \times v_j$ (lines 10–14, Algorithm 2). The value p is a percentage randomly generated from a uniform distribution in the range $[p_{min}, p_{max}]$ (line 5, Algorithm 2). The noise value ν is added or subtracted with a probability equal to 50% (i.e., following a Bernoulli process).

After this perturbation, ALOA computes for each record in the shadow dataset the *robustness score* to estimate the confidence of the shadow model s in predicting the record label (line 13, Algorithm 1). This score is formally defined as follows:

$$rScore_{x_s^i}(N_{x_s^i}) = \begin{cases} 0 & \text{if } s(x_s^i) \neq b(x_s^i) \\ \dfrac{\sum_{x' \in N_{x_s^i}} F(s(x'), s(x_s^i))}{|N_{x_s^i}|} & \text{otherwise} \end{cases} \quad (1)$$

Algorithm 2: Noisy_Neighborhood_Generation(x, p_{min}, p_{max}, n)

Input : x - a record composed by m attribute-value pairs (a_j, v_j),
$\quad\quad\quad p_{min}$, p_{max} - perturbation percentage range,
$\quad\quad\quad n$ - number of neighbours to be generated
Output: N_x - Set of new generated records

1 $N_x \leftarrow \emptyset$
2 **for** $t \in \{1, \ldots, n\}$ **do**
3 $\quad$ $x' \leftarrow x$
4 $\quad$ **for** $j \in \{1, \ldots, |x'|\}$ **do**
5 $\quad\quad$ $p \leftarrow randomNumber(p_{min}, p_{max})$
6 $\quad\quad$ **if** $v_j == 0$ **then**
7 $\quad\quad\quad$ $v_j == randomNumber()$
8
9 $\quad\quad$ **else**
10 $\quad\quad\quad$ $\nu \leftarrow v_j \times p$
11 $\quad\quad\quad$ **if** $randomBoolean() == True$ **then**
12 $\quad\quad\quad\quad$ $v_j \leftarrow v_j + \nu$
13 $\quad\quad\quad$ **else**
14 $\quad\quad\quad\quad$ $v_j \leftarrow v_j - \nu$
15 $\quad$ $N_x \leftarrow N_x \cup \{x'\}$
16 **return** N_x

---

where $F(s(x'), s(x^i))$ is a function returning 0 in case the shadow model predicts a label for the neighbor x', which is not coherent with the label predicted for x^i. In other words, if the shadow model is faithful to the black-box model on x^i, the robustness score on this record is computed as the fraction of perturbed records having coherent labels with x^i. This score has values in the range $[0, 1]$: values close to 1 mean that the classifier is robust to perturbations, thus the model is confident in predicting the record, while values close to zero register low confidence of the classifier in the prediction, indeed, in this case several neighbors have the opposite class label to the record under analysis, meaning that the model is unsure of the prediction since it is very close to the boundary.

Once each record of the shadow dataset has its robustness score, we get a dataset where for each record x_s^i we have its score $rScore_{x_s^i}$ and the label IN, in case x_s^i belongs to the training dataset of the shadow model, or OUT if it belongs to the test dataset. Using the iterative thresholding procedure, ALOA finds the threshold value on the score that optimizes the accuracy in separating records with class label IN and OUT (line 15, Algorithm 1).

ALOA Application. Once ALOA has been trained, an adversary can use it to determine whether a given record belongs to the training dataset of the black-box model b or not. Given a record x, having the same shape as the records D_b^{train} on which the black-box was trained, our attack performs the following steps:

1. ALOA applies the Noisy Neighborhood Generation procedure, presented in Algorithm 2, to the record x. The result is a set of synthetic neighbors N_x which are perturbed through our agnostic procedure;
2. Exploiting the neighborhood N_x, ALOA computes the Robustness Score $rScore$ of the record x applying Eq. (1);
3. The best threshold value $threshold_{split}$, found during the training of ALOA, is used to discern whether the record x is part of the training set or not: if $rScore \geq threshold_{best}$ then it will be predicted as part of the training set, otherwise not.

5   Experiments

In this Section, we report the results obtained testing ALOA attack, presented in Sect. 4 the code developed is in Python 3.8 and publicly available [10]. We present the experiments as follows: we present the datasets used and their pre-processing (Sect. 5); then, we describe the trained black-box models on which we tested the validity of our attack (Sect. 5). Lastly, in Sect. 5.1 we present the results of ALOA attacks to all the ML models, comparing the performance with respect to the original MIA and LABELONLY attack, and discussing the privacy risk of each of them.

Datasets. We use three classification datasets, each with different characteristics.

We utilize the ADULT dataset, a benchmark dataset of $48,842$ records and 15 numerical or categorical variables. It has information about employees, such as job, capital loss, marital status, etc. The labels are "$\leq$50K" or "$>$50K," referred to as Class 0 and 1 respectively. They indicate whether the individual's annual income will be above or below $50,000$. Next, we exploit the BANK dataset, which contains information about bank's customers. It has $150,000$ records and 10 numerical variables. The objective is to classify individuals as either good or bad creditors. Finally, we include the SYNTH dataset, which is a synthetic dataset generated using a Gaussian mixture model. It has $30,000$ records and 30 numerical variables, with 15 classes. We chose this dataset to address the multiclass classification problem and to evaluate the attack's behavior in a controlled environment through synthetic data.

For ADULT, we handled null values by removing them exploiting a Pearson correlation analysis among the variables ($\geq 80\%$ correlation were dropped). For the categorical variables, we applied a one-hot encoding technique. For the BANK dataset, null values were also eliminated, and a correlation analysis was performed. Regarding the SYNTH dataset, since it was synthetically generated, we did not perform any pre-processing procedures.

Following the pre-processing stage, we partitioned each dataset into two subsets: (i) 70% of the original dataset (D_b) was utilized for training and testing the black-box models, and (ii) the remaining 30% of the pre-processed data (D_s) was designated for training the attack models.

Black-Boxes. Given each pre-processed dataset D_b, we split it into D_b^{train} (70% of it) and D_b^{test} (30% of it). We use D_b^{train} for training the black-box models. The ML models selected are described in the following:

1. Decision Tree (DT), selected for its simplicity, but prone to overfitting and to noise data;
2. Random Forest (RF), an ensemble model composed of multiple decision trees, with better performance with respect to the DT;
3. Neural Network (NN), a feed-forward network with some hidden layers, varying from 1 to 3, depending on the data in input;

For all the models we trained two variants: *regularized*, with very good performance and with a good level of generalization; and *overfitted* on purpose, specific to the input training dataset and with poor generalization capabilities. This choice resides in the fact that it has been proved that MIA leads to higher privacy risk when attacking overfitted models ([14, 16]). For this reason, we also want to evaluate how privacy exposure changes concerning the level of overfitting of black-boxes. We report the classification performance of these models in Table 1[1]. The results reported in this table show that all the black-box models have an overall good performance, with comparable performance for the RF and NN models, and a slightly worse prediction performance for the DT, as expected. The model performance reported in the table also shows a different behavior of the *regularized* models w.r.t. the *overfitted* ones.

Table 1. Prediction performance of the black-box models for all the dataset. We report the Accuracy both for the train and test sets to appreciate the difference in performance in generalization capability for the *generalized* and *overfitted* models. We achieve good performance for all the models presented.

Data	Metric	DT	DT-O	RF	RF-O	NN	NN-O
ADULT	TR Acc	0.84	1	0.84	1	0.83	1
	TS Acc	0.81	0.78	0.82	0.85	0.82	0.79
SYNTH	TR Acc	0.78	1	0.81	1	0.78	0.97
	TS Acc	0.77	0.69	0.79	0.78	0.78	0.70
BANK	TR Acc	0.84	1	0.98	1	0.93	1
	TS Acc	0.61	0.59	0.87	0.89	0.92	0.90

---

[1] The results reported refer to the best set of hyperparameters determined by a grid search. The results were validated with a 3 fold cross-validation.

5.1   Evaluation of ALOA and Comparison Against Competitors

In this Section, we present the privacy threats obtained by applying ALOA, LABELONLY and the original MIA to the trained black-boxes. In order to train all the attacks, we need to have the shadow dataset D_s having the same format as the data used for training the black-box model. We employed two variants of this dataset, denoted as D_s^{stat} and D_s^{rand}, in our experiments. The former was designed to have the same statistical distribution as the original training dataset, whereas the latter was generated randomly. We used D_s^{stat} for learning the LABELONLY attack because the procedure described in [2] requires training the shadow models on a dataset with similar distributions to those of the training data of the black box, and it also exploits the distribution knowledge in the computation of the robustness score. Although ALOA does not require the use of D_s^{stat}, as it is agnostic to the training data distributions, we conducted experiments with both D_s^{stat} and D_s^{rand} to evaluate the effectiveness of ALOA and having a more complete comparison with LABELONLY. To ensure a clear understanding of the performance of the attack, we have balanced the D_s used for creating the attack models: having 50% of the rows of class IN and 50% of class OUT. This setting is the same used in [2] to clearly compare our proposal and the attacks in the literature. Indeed, the balanced setting enables the possibility to compare the attack performance based on accuracy that, in this case, cannot be influenced by the under or over-representation of one class with respect to the others. In this way, if the attack has more than 50%

The results of the attacks are reported in Table 2 for ADULT, BANK and SYNTH. ALOA was run three times for each black-box, with $n = 1000$ perturbations for each record of D_s (the same n is used for the training of LABELONLY attack), p_{min} and p_{max} set to[2]0.10 and 0.50 respectively, and a Bernoulli probability $p = 0.50$ for adding or subtracting the noise value. MIA was created with 8 shadow models and NN as final attack models. For LABELONLY we applied the same hyper-parameters as in the work [2]: $n = 1000$ perturbations, with a Bernoulli flip probability of 0.60% and a Gaussian noise with $\sigma = 0.04$. We remark that MIA and LABELONLY were tested on the D_s^{stat} due to the assumptions needed, while ALOA was tested both on D_s^{stat} and on D_s^{rand}.

Regarding ADULT dataset, MIA and LABELONLY attacks performance is coherent with the one presented in their original papers. For the MIA, overall the attack against *regularized* models is not effective, apart from the decision tree with 51% of accuracy. On the other hand, the *overfitted* models are easily attacked, in particular RF-O and NN-O. However, the attack on the DT-O is not posing a privacy threat. This result may be due to the poor prediction performance of the DT-O for ADULT. In fact, the overall accuracy of the model is 48%, suggesting that the model is not able to learn patterns in the data. Hence, the attack cannot have sufficient information from the confidence. By looking at the LABELONLY attack, it is ineffective for all the *regularized* models, while it poses

---

[2] This range adjusts the level of perturbation of the data, it is a parameter of the attack, after some observations shown in Fig. 1 we felt that a range between 0.10 and 0.50 is sufficient to have a good estimate of the robustness of the points.

privacy threats for all the *overfitted* ones. Analyzing ALOA in both experimental settings, we have the same performance as LABELONLY on the *overfitted* models with 54% DT, 55% RF, 60% NN. Instead, by looking at the *regularized* models, we have in general better performance: the attack has gained 1–3% points in the attack compared to LABELONLY. With ALOA based on D_s^{stat} we are always better than LABELONLY except for the regularized NN, for which we have the same performance. Hence, for ADULT ALOA poses the worst privacy threats both for the *overfitted* and *regularized* models. Among the ML models, the attack shows more privacy leakage for the RF and NN. This finding is reasonable because, as highlighted in prior works, more complex models learn more information.

For BANK dataset, the results are in line with the ones described for ADULT, even if overall they are slightly lower. Interestingly, the improvement in terms of privacy threats posed by ALOA is more significant for the RF-O model (+3%) and lower for the NN-O one (+1%). This result may be due to the different structure of this dataset: it is composed of only a few numerical variables.

In SYNTH dataset we can better appreciate the effectiveness of ALOA: the trend is again that the attacks undermine the privacy more in the case of *overfitted* models, while *regularized* ones remain in danger, but with a lower privacy risk. Both ALOA and LABELONLY have better privacy threats with respect to MIA. However, ALOA in both settings shows better or comparable performance with respect to LABELONLY with an improvement for RF-O and NN-O. Comparing the two experimental settings of ALOA, our results indicate that the performance of our attack is generically consistent for both D_s^{stat} and D_s^{rand}, showing at most a discrepancy of 1% in accuracy. More importantly, they also demonstrate that even if our attack is assuming an adversary with weaker knowledge with respect to LABELONLY, we achieve higher or comparable privacy risks. These findings have significant implications for privacy protection in ML models.

Overall, the experiments show that ALOA poses a worrying privacy risk, especially if the model is overfitted. The more complex a model is, the easier it is to overfit and experience higher privacy leakage. Comparing ALOA against the LABELONLY attack, we note that for the *overfitted* models we have comparable or better performance. This behavior may be the result of the agnostic perturbation we perform, which is independent of the distributions of the input variables, and hence ALOA is not affected by the slight changes in the data. We remark that this property is valid for both cases where we use D_s^{stat} and D_s^{rand} since the perturbation mechanism always remains agnostic. Regarding ALOA against the original MIA, the performances of our method are overall better with the exception of RF-O. For this model, in fact, the accuracies of the MIA attack are always higher w.r.t. both LABELONLY and ALOA, highlighting that in the case of overfitted RF the added knowledge of the prediction probability has a greater impact in this setting. However, for the regularized RF and NN, instead, MIA shows higher accuracy and precision for the IN class but an extremely low recall and hence F-1 score, showing that this attack is unstable.

ALOA performed overall better than the LABELONLY, with an improvement up to 3%. It is a significant improvement in the context of privacy assessment, where every gain in performance can shed light on the privacy leakage of a model. ALOA is more stable and the perturbation we performed is data agnostic, without knowledge of the distribution of the features. Importantly, our attack showed better results in attacking regularized models compared to others.

Table 2. Results of the attacks on the three datasets for all the black-box models selected. In bold are highlighted the highest privacy risks. We remark that for the MIA and LABELONLY we exploit the statistical dataset D_s^{stat}, while ALOA was tested both on the D_s^{stat} and on the D_s^{rand}, showing that it is completely agnostic w.r.t. the data and a good stability. ALOA is the one with the highest privacy threats overall, showing a good stability since for all the datasets we achieve similar performance.

Attack	Model	ADULT P_{IN}	R_{IN}	$F1_{IN}$	Acc	BANK P_{IN}	R_{IN}	$F1_{IN}$	Acc	SYNTH P_{IN}	R_{IN}	$F1_{IN}$	Acc
MIA$_{D_s^{stat}}$	DT	0.51	0.53	0.52	0.51	0.50	0.58	0.54	0.51	0.49	0.51	0.50	0.49
	DT-O	0.48	0.62	0.55	0.48	0.49	0.49	0.49	0.49	0.51	0.47	0.49	0.51
	RF	0.45	0.27	0.34	0.47	0.53	0.16	0.24	0.51	0.73	0.04	0.08	0.51
	RF-O	0.59	0.68	0.63	**0.61**	0.67	0.60	0.63	**0.65**	0.90	0.86	**0.88**	**0.88**
	NN	0.53	0.04	0.08	0.50	0.45	0.03	0.06	0.50	0.52	0.30	0.38	0.51
	NN-O	0.55	0.94	0.69	**0.59**	0.53	0.85	0.65	0.54	0.58	0.59	0.58	0.58
LabelOnly$_{D_s^{stat}}$	DT	0.50	0.62	0.55	0.50	0.51	0.79	0.62	0.51	0.58	0.84	0.69	0.62
	DT-O	0.52	0.85	0.65	**0.54**	0.59	0.98	0.74	0.65	0.63	1.00	0.77	**0.70**
	RF	0.51	0.78	0.62	0.51	0.50	0.76	0.61	0.51	0.54	0.94	0.68	**0.57**
	RF-O	0.53	0.83	0.65	0.55	0.55	0.84	0.66	0.57	0.56	1.00	0.72	0.61
	NN	0.50	0.55	0.53	0.50	0.50	0.70	0.58	0.50	0.51	0.91	0.65	0.51
	NN-O	0.56	1.00	0.71	0.60	0.59	0.80	0.68	0.63	0.54	1.00	0.70	0.57
ALOA$_{D_s^{stat}}$	DT	0.51	0.81	0.63	0.52	0.51	0.80	0.62	**0.51**	0.58	0.84	0.69	**0.62**
	DT-O	0.53	0.86	0.65	**0.54**	0.59	1.00	0.74	**0.66**	0.63	1.00	0.77	**0.70**
	RF	0.52	0.51	0.52	**0.52**	0.51	1.00	0.67	**0.52**	0.54	0.83	0.66	**0.57**
	RF-O	0.54	0.65	0.59	0.55	0.56	0.98	0.71	**0.60**	0.58	0.96	0.72	0.63
	NN	0.53	0.49	0.51	**0.53**	0.50	0.76	0.60	0.49	0.51	0.89	0.65	**0.52**
	NN-O	0.56	1.00	0.72	**0.60**	0.58	0.98	0.73	**0.64**	0.55	1.00	0.71	**0.59**
ALOA$_{D_s^{rand}}$	DT	0.52	0.83	0.64	**0.53**	0.49	0.66	0.56	0.49	0.59	0.81	0.68	**0.62**
	DT-O	0.53	0.86	0.65	**0.54**	0.59	0.95	0.73	0.64	0.63	0.95	0.76	**0.70**
	RF	0.51	0.44	0.47	**0.52**	0.49	0.71	0.58	0.48	0.54	0.97	0.69	**0.57**
	RF-O	0.55	0.66	0.59	0.55	0.56	1	0.72	**0.60**	0.57	0.98	0.72	0.62
	NN	0.50	0.64	0.56	0.50	0.50	0.68	0.58	0.51	0.51	0.91	0.66	**0.52**
	NN-O	0.56	1	0.72	**0.60**	0.60	0.84	0.70	**0.64**	0.54	1	0.70	0.58

Comparison Between Regularized and Overfitted Models. Recently, several works have empirically shown that if the model being attacked is overfitted, the attack will be much more damaging to the users of the training set [14,16]. For this reason, we study the behavior of both models that generalize well and those that are overfitting. From the results in Table 2, all the *overfitted* models exhibit a higher degree of privacy leakage than regularized models, as evidenced in all three datasets, particularly in the third one. This dataset highlights the vulnerability of models that are not properly regularized and exhibit a gap between training and test accuracy. As outlined in [8], the gap between training and test accuracy is directly proportional to the efficacy of the accuracy of an attack - the larger the gap, the more effective the attack. To better analyze this aspect, we took advantage of the SYNTH dataset, which allows for a controlled study in which ML models achieve excellent performance and it is easy to overfit ML models. In Fig. 1, it is possible to examine the difference in the performance of ALOA for NN and NN-O trained on the SYNTH dataset. In particular, we present a box plot on the robustness score which shows that the *overfitted* model exhibits a larger difference between the average IN and OUT robustness scores, which could potentially enable an attacker to distinguish between the two classes more easily. In this way, we empirically prove the existing link between model overfitting and privacy risk and the train-test gap [8].

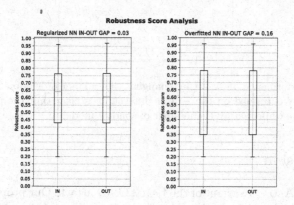

Fig. 1. These two box plots show the robustness score behaviour for *overfitted* and *regularized* NN on SYNTH. It is possible to see that the *overfitted* exhibits a larger difference between the average IN and OUT robustness scores, which could enable an attacker to distinguish between the two classes more easily. This confirms the existing link between model overfitting and privacy risk and the train-test gap [8]. On the other hand, the *regularized* displayed a smaller gap between the two classes, hence separating the two classes is more difficult.

Analysis on the Number of Shadow Models. There are many conflicting opinions in the literature about the use of shadow models, i.e., models that mimic the behavior of the original black box. In fact, in the first publication of MIA [13] the authors used a large number of shadow models, but in LABELONLY [2] only one shadow model is used. In our paper, we present the results with only one shadow model after having analyzed the effectiveness of using different shadow models, and our results highlight that for ALOA one or k models does not lead to any improvement. This behavior can be seen in Fig. 2, in which the performance of the attack on ADULT is the same whether using only one or 10 shadow models. Given this finding, our experiments were conducted with just one shadow model for time constraints.

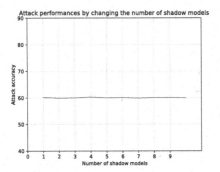

Fig. 2. The performance of ALOA by changing the number of shadow models from 1 to 10 for the NN-O trained on the ADULT dataset. It is clear that the performance of the attack are not affected by the number of shadow models.

6   Conclusion

We presented ALOA, a variant of the LABELONLY attack. Our proposed attack is completely data agnostic, both in the shadow model training and in the perturbation mechanism. In particular, the perturbation does not exploit knowledge of the statistical distributions and domains of the features in the training data. Our results demonstrate that ALOA outperforms the traditional LABELONLY attack with an improvement of up to 3% in terms of attack accuracy, although it assumes an adversary with weaker prior knowledge. This improvement is significant in the context of privacy assessment, where every gain in performance can provide valuable, sensitive insights into the people represented in the data. The agnostic nature of our attack raises concerns regarding privacy protection, as it can be executed without any specific assumptions. Moreover, ALOA exhibits excellent stability in terms of prediction performance, outperforming standard MIA and other attacks when targeting regularized models. In summary, ALOA offers a robust and effective approach for assessing the privacy of ML models.

Acknowledgments. This work is supported by the European Union - Horizon 2020 Program under the scheme "INFRAIA-01-2018-2019 - Integrating Activities for Advanced Communities", Grant Agreement n.871042, "SoBigData++: European Integrated Infrastructure for Social Mining and Big Data Analytics" (http://www.sobigdata.eu/), TAILOR (G.A. 952215) and HumanE-AI-Net (G.A. 952026).

A   Appendix: Machine Learning Models Hyper-parameters

DecisionTree. Parameters for DT and DT-O in Table 3 (Scikit-learn library).

Table 3. Best hyper parameter setting for DT and DT-O for each dataset.

	ADULT				BANK				SYNTH			
Model	Criterion	Max depth	Max feat	Min split	Criterion	Max depth	Max feat	Min split	Criterion	Max depth	Max feat	Min split
DT	Entropy	80	Auto	30	Entropy	20	5	50	Gini	13	Best	2
DT-O	Entropy	None	Auto	20	Entropy	None	Auto	20	Gini	None	Auto	20

RandomForest. Parameters for RF and RF-O in Table 4 (Scikit-learn library).

Table 4. Best set of hyper parameters for the RF and RF-O for each dataset.

	ADULT						BANK						SYNTH					
Model	Criterion	Max depth	Max feat	Min split	Boostrap	Estimators	Criterion	Max depth	Max feat	Min split	Boostrap	Estimators	Criterion	Max depth	Max feat	Min split	Boostrap	Estimators
RF	Gini	500	Auto	50	False	100	Gini	100	5	5	True	350	Gini	500	Auto	10	False	100
RF-O	Gini	False	Sqrt	2	True	100	Gini	False	Sqrt	2	True	100	Gini	False	Sqrt	2	True	100

NeuralNetwork. Parameters in Table 5 (TensorFlow). The layers are Dense (ADULT 256 nodes for NN and 300 for NN-O; BANK and SYNTH 300 neurons). Hidden layers *tanh*, output layers *softmax*.

Table 5. Hyper parameters selected for the NN and NN-O models.

	ADULT							BANK							SYNTH						
Model	Layers	Dropout	Loss	Optim	Learning rate	Epochs	Batch	Layers	Dropout	Loss	Optim	Learning rate	Epochs	Batch	Layers	Dropout	Loss	Optim	Learning rate	Epochs	Batch
NN	2	0.10	SCC	Adam	0.005	10	512	2	0.30	SCC	Adam	0.001	30	512	2	0.30	SCC	Adam	0.001	30	512
NN-O	6	None	SCC	Adam	0.001	250	512	6	None	SCC	Adam	0.001	250	512	6	None	SCC	Adam	0.001	250	512

References

1. Al-Rubaie, M., Chang, J.M.: Privacy-preserving machine learning: threats and solutions. IEEE Secur. Priv. **17**(2), 49–58 (2019)
2. Choquette-Choo, C.A., Tramer, F., Carlini, N., Papernot, N.: Label-only membership inference attacks. In: Proceedings of the 38th International Conference on Machine Learning (2021)
3. Dada, E.G., Bassi, J.S., Chiroma, H., Abdulhamid, S.M., Adetunmbi, A.O., Ajibuwa, O.E.: Machine learning for email spam filtering: review, approaches and open research problems. Heliyon (2019)
4. Dwork, C., et al.: Calibrating noise to sensitivity in private data analysis. In: TCC 2006, pp. 265–284 (2006)
5. Fredrikson, M., Jha, S., Ristenpart, T.: Model inversion attacks that exploit confidence information and basic countermeasures. In: Proceedings of the 22nd ACM SIGSAC Conference on Computer and Communications Security, CCS 2015 (2015)
6. Fredrikson, M., Lantz, E., Jha, S., Lin, S., Page, D., Ristenpart, T.: Privacy in pharmacogenetics: an end-to-end case study of personalized warfarin dosing. In: Proceedings of the 23rd USENIX Conference on Security Symposium, SEC 2014 (2014)

7. Ganju, K., Wang, Q., Yang, W., Gunter, C.A., Borisov, N.: Property inference attacks on fully connected neural networks using permutation invariant representations. In: Proceedings of the 2018 ACM SIGSAC Conference on Computer and Communications Security, CCS 2018 (2018)

8. Hardt, M., Recht, B., Singer, Y.: Train faster, generalize better: stability of stochastic gradient descent. CoRR (2015)

9. Mwinyi, I.H., Narman, H.S., Fang, K.C., Yoo, W.S.: Predictive self-learning content recommendation system for multimedia contents. In: 2018 Wireless Telecommunications Symposium (WTS) (2018)

10. Naretto, F., Monreale, A., Rizzo, S.: Datasets for research on Agnostic Label-Only Membership Inference Attack (2023). https://doi.org/10.6084/m9.figshare.23559921.v1

11. Pratesi, F., Monreale, A., Trasarti, R., Giannotti, F., Pedreschi, D., Yanagihara, T.: PRUDEnce: a system for assessing privacy risk vs utility in data sharing ecosystems. Trans. Data Priv. **11**(2), 139–167 (2018)

12. Samarati, P., Sweeney, L.: Generalizing data to provide anonymity when disclosing information. In: ACM (1998)

13. Shokri, R., Stronati, M., Song, C., Shmatikov, V.: Membership inference attacks against machine learning models. In: IEEE Symposium on Security and Privacy, pp. 3–18. IEEE Computer Society (2017)

14. Song, L., Shokri, R., Mittal, P.: Membership inference attacks against adversarially robust deep learning models. In: 2019 IEEE Security and Privacy Workshops (SPW) (2019)

15. Torra, V.: Data Privacy: Foundations, 1st edn. New Developments and the Big Data Challenge. Springer Publishing Company, Incorporated (2017)

16. Yeom, S., Giacomelli, I., Fredrikson, M., Jha, S.: Privacy risk in machine learning: analyzing the connection to overfitting. In: 2018 IEEE 31st Computer Security Foundations Symposium (CSF) (2018)

ppAURORA: Privacy Preserving Area Under Receiver Operating Characteristic and Precision-Recall Curves

Ali Burak Ünal[1,3(✉)] [iD], Nico Pfeifer[2,3] [iD], and Mete Akgün[1,3] [iD]

[1] Medical Data Privacy Preserving Machine Learning (MDPPML),
University of Tübingen, Tübingen, Germany
[2] Methods in Medical Informatics, University of Tübingen, Tübingen, Germany
[3] Institute for Bioinformatics and Medical Informatics (IBMI),
University of Tübingen, Tübingen, Germany
{ali-burak.uenal,nico.pfeifer,mete.akguen}@uni-tuebingen.de

Abstract. Computing an area under the curve (AUC) as a performance measure to compare the quality of different machine learning models is one of the final steps of many research projects. Many of these methods are trained on privacy-sensitive data and there are several different approaches like ϵ-differential privacy, federated learning and cryptography if the datasets cannot be shared or used jointly at one place for training and/or testing. In this setting, it can also be a problem to compute the global AUC, since the labels might also contain privacy-sensitive information. There have been approaches based on ϵ-differential privacy to address this problem, but to the best of our knowledge, no exact privacy preserving solution has been introduced. In this paper, we propose an MPC-based solution, called ppAURORA, with private merging of individually sorted lists from multiple sources to compute the exact AUC as one could obtain on the pooled original test samples. With ppAURORA, the computation of the exact area under precision-recall and receiver operating characteristic curves is possible even when ties between prediction confidence values exist. We use ppAURORA to evaluate two different models predicting acute myeloid leukemia therapy response and heart disease, respectively. We also assess its scalability via synthetic data experiments. All these experiments show that we efficiently and privately compute the exact same AUC with both evaluation metrics as one can obtain on the pooled test samples in plaintext according to the semi-honest adversary setting.

Keywords: Privacy preserving AUC · ROC curve · PR curve · MPC

1 Introduction

Recently, privacy preserving machine learning studies aimed at protecting sensitive information during training and/or testing of a model in scenarios where data is distributed between different sources and cannot be shared in plaintext

[3, 7, 8, 12, 13, 15, 17, 18]. However, privacy protection in the computation of the area under curve (AUC), which is one of the most preferred methods to compare different machine learning models with binary outcome, has not been addressed sufficiently. There are several differential privacy based approaches in the literature for computing the receiver operating characteristic (ROC) curve [2, 5, 6]. Briefly, they aim to protect the privacy of the data by introducing noise into the computation so that one cannot obtain the original data used in the computation. However, due to the nature of differential privacy, the resulting AUC is different from the one which could be obtained using non-perturbed prediction confidence values (PCVs) when noise is added to the PCVs [16]. For the precision-recall (PR) curve, there even exists no such studies in the literature. As a general statement, private computation of the exact AUC has never been addressed before to the best of our knowledge.

In this paper, we propose a 3-party computation based privacy preserving area under receiver operating characteristic and precision-recall curves (ppAURORA). For this purpose, we use CECILIA [17] offering several efficient privacy preserving operations. The most important missing operation of it is division. To address the necessity of an efficient, private and secure computation of the exact AUC, we adapt the division operation of SecureNN [18]. Since the building blocks of CECILIA require less communication rounds than SecureNN, we implemented the division operation of SecureNN using the building blocks of CECILIA. Using ppAURORA, we compute the area under the PR curve (AUPR) and ROC curve (AUROC). We address two different cases of ROC curve in ppAURORA by two different versions of AUROC computation. The first one is designed for the computation of the exact AUC using PCVs with no tie. In case of a tie of PCVs of samples from different classes, this version just approximates the metric based on the order of the samples, having a problem when values of both axes of ROC curve plot change at the same time. To compute the exact AUC even in case of a tie, we introduce the second version of AUROC with a slightly higher communication cost than the first approach. Along with the privacy of the resulting AUC, since the labels are also kept secret during the whole computation, both versions are capable of protecting the information of the number of samples belonging to the classes from all participants of the computation. Otherwise, such information could have been used to obtain the order of the labels of the PCVs [19]. Furthermore, since we do not provide the data sources with the ROC curve, they cannot regenerate the underlying true data. Therefore, both versions are secure against such attacks [11]. We used the with-tie version of AUROC computation to compute the AUPR since the values of both axes can change at the same time even if there is no tie. To the best of our knowledge, ppAURORA is the first study for the privacy preserving AUPR computation.

2 Motivation

ppAURORA can enable collaborative privacy preserving evaluation of a binary model. Especially when there are parties with insufficient test samples, even if these parties obtain the collaboratively trained model, they cannot reliably evaluate the predictions of this model on their test samples. The result of AUC on such a small set of test samples could vary significantly as shown in Fig. 1, making the reliability of the model evaluation questionable.

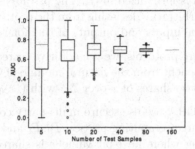

Fig. 1. AUROC for varying number of test samples from the all dataset

To demonstrate ppAURORA's contribute to the community more, let us imagine a scenario where a model is trained collaboratively using MPC framework [7,13,18], federated learning framework [9] or any other privacy preserving training method. Once the model is obtained, the participating parties can perform predictions on the model using their test samples to evaluate it. However, the parties with fewer data cannot reliably determine the performance of the model. Instead of individual evaluation of the model that could lead to incorrect assessment of the model's performance, they can use ppAURORA to evaluate it collaboratively and obtain the result of this evaluation as if it was performed on the pooled test samples of the parties without sacrificing the privacy of neither the labels nor the predictions of the samples.

3 Preliminaries

Security Model: In this study, we aim to protect the privacy of the PCVs and the labels of the samples from parties, the ranking of these samples in the globally sorted list and the resulting AUC. We prove the full security of our solution (i.e., privacy and correctness) in the presence of semi-honest adversaries that follow the protocol specification, but try to learn information from the execution of the protocol. We consider a scenario where a semi-honest adversary corrupts a single server and an arbitrary number of data owners in the simulation paradigm [4,10] where two worlds are defined: the real world where parties run the protocol without any trusted party, and the ideal world where parties make the computation through a trusted party. Security is modeled as the view of an adversary called a simulator S in the ideal world, who cannot be distinguished from the view of an adversary A in the real world. The universal composability framework [4] introduces an adversarial entity called environment Z, which gives inputs to all parties and reads outputs from them. The environment is used in modeling the security of end-to-end protocols where several secure protocols are used arbitrarily. Security here is modeled as *no environment can distinguish if it interacts with the real world and the adversary $\mathcal{A}$ or the ideal world and the simulator $\mathcal{S}$*. We also provide privacy in the presence of a malicious adversary corrupting any single server, which is formalized in [1]. The privacy is formalized by saying that a malicious party arbitrarily deviating from the protocol description, cannot learn anything about the inputs and outputs of the honest parties.

Notations: In our secure protocols, we use additive secret sharing over the ring $\mathbb{Z}_K$ where $K = 2^{64}$ to benefit from the natural modulo of CPUs of most modern computers. We denote two shares of x over $\mathbb{Z}_K$ with $(\langle x \rangle_0, \langle x \rangle_1)$.

CECILIA: In ppAURORA, we use secure multi-party computation framework CECILIA, which has three computing parties, P_0, P_1 and P_2, and uses 2-out-of-2 additive secret sharing where an ℓ-bit value x is shared additively in a ring among P_0 and P_1 as the sum of two values. For ℓ-bit secret sharing of x, we have $\langle x \rangle_0 + \langle x \rangle_1 \equiv x \mod L$ where P_i knows only $\langle x \rangle_i$ and $i \in \{0, 1\}$. All arithmetic operations are performed in the ring $\mathbb{Z}_L$.

3.1   Area Under Curve

One of the most common ways summarizing the plot-based model evaluation metrics is area under curve (AUC). It calculates the area under the curve of a plot-based model such as ROC curve and the PR curve.

Area Under ROC Curve (AUROC): The ROC curve takes the sensitivity and the specificity of a binary classifier into account by plotting the false positive rate (FPR) on the x-axis and the true positive rate (TPR) on the y-axis. AUC summarizes this plot by measuring the area between the line and the x-axis, which is the area under the ROC curve (AUROC). Let M be the number of test samples, $V \in [0, 1]^M$ contain the sorted PCVs of test samples in descending order, $T \in [0, 1]^M$ and $F \in [0, 1]^M$ contain the corresponding TPR and FPR values, respectively, where the threshold for entry i is set to $V[i]$, and $T[0] = F[0] = 0$. In case there is no tie in V, the privacy-friendly AUROC computation is as follows:

$$AUROC = \sum_{i=1}^{M} \left(T[i] \cdot (F[i] - F[i-1]) \right) \tag{1}$$

This formula just approximates the exact AUROC in case of a tie in V depending on samples' order. As an extreme example, let V have 10 samples with the same PCV. Let the first 5 samples have label 1 and the last 5 samples have label 0. Such a setting outputs $AUROC = 1$ via Eq. 1. In the reverse order, however, it gives $AUROC = 0$. To define an accurate formula for the AUROC in case of such a tie condition, let ξ be the vector of indices in ascending order where the PCV of the sample at that index and the preceding one are different for $0 < |\xi| \leq M$ where $|\xi|$ denotes the size of the vector. Assuming that $\xi[0] = 0$, the computation of AUROC in case of a tie can be done as follows:

$$AUROC = \sum_{i=1}^{|\xi|} \Big(T[\xi[i-1]] \cdot (F[\xi[i]] - F[\xi[i-1]]) + \qquad\qquad (2)$$
$$\frac{(T[\xi[i]] - T[\xi[i-1]]) \cdot (F[\xi[i]] - F[\xi[i-1]])}{2} \Big)$$

As Eq. 2 indicates, one only needs TPR and FPR values on the points where the PCV changes to obtain the exact AUROC. We will benefit from this observation in the privacy preserving AUROC computation when there is a tie condition in the PCVs.

Area Under PR Curve (AUPR): The PR curve evaluates binary models by plotting recall on the x-axis and precision on the y-axis and summarizes it by measuring the area under the PR curve (AUPR). It is generally preferred over AUROC for problems with class imbalances. Since both precision and recall can change at the same time even without a tie, we measure the area by using the Eq. 2 where T becomes the precision and F becomes the recall.

4   ppAURORA

In this section, we give the description of our protocol for ppAURORA where we have data owners that outsource their PCVs and the ground truth labels in secret shared form and three non-colluding servers that perform 3-party computation on secret shared PCVs to compute the AUC. The data sources start the protocol by outsourcing the labels and the predictions of their test samples to the servers. Afterward, the servers perform the desired calculation privately. Finally, they send the shares of the result back to the data sources. The communication between all parties is performed over a secure channel (e.g., TLS).

Outsourcing: At the start of ppAURORA, each data owner H_i has a list of PCVs and corresponding ground truth labels for $i \in \{1, \ldots, n\}$. Then, each data owner H_i sorts its whole list L_i according to PCVs in descending order, divides it into two additive shares L_{i_0} and L_{i_1}, and sends them to P_0 and P_1, respectively. We refer to P_0 and P_1 as *proxies*.

Sorting: After the outsourcing phase, P_0 and P_1 obtain the shares of individually sorted lists of PCVs of the data owners. The proxies need to merge individually sorted lists pairwise until they obtain the global sorted list of PCVs. This can be considered as the leaves of a binary tree merging into the root node, which is, in our case, the global sorted list. Due to the high complexity of privacy preserving sorting, we decided to make the sorting parametric to adjust the trade-off between privacy and practicality. Let $\delta = 2a + 1$ be this parameter determining the number of PCVs that will be added to the global sorted list in each iteration for $a \in \mathbb{N}$, and L_{i_k} and L_{j_k} be the shares of two individually sorted lists of PCVs in P_ks for $k \bullet \in \{0, 1\}$ and $|L_i| \geq |L_j|$ where $|.|$ is the size operator. First, the proxies privately compare the lists elementwise. They use the results of the comparison in MUXs to privately exchange the shares of PCVs in each pair, if the PCV in L_j is larger than the PCV in L_i. In the first MUX, they input the share in L_{i_k} to MUX first and then the share in L_{j_k} along with the share of the result of the comparison to select the larger of the PCVs. They move the results of the MUX to L_{i_k}. In the second MUX, they reverse the order to select the smaller of the PCVs and move it to L_{j_k}. We call this stage *shuffling*. Then, they move the top PCV of L_{i_k} to the merged list of PCVs. If $\delta \neq 1$, then they continue comparing the top PCVs in the lists and moving the largest of them to the merged list. Once they move δ PCVs to the merged list, they shuffle the lists again, and if $|L_{j_k}| > |L_{i_k}|$, then they switch the lists. Until finishing up the PCVs in L_{i_k}, the proxies follow shuffling-moving cycle.

By shuffling, we increase the number of candidates for a specific position and, naturally, lower the chance of matching a PCV in the individually sorted lists to a PCV in the merged list. The highest chance of matching is 50%, leading to a very low chance of guessing the matching of whole PCVs in the list. In sorting, δ must be an odd number to make sure that shuffling always leads to an increment in the number of candidates. An even value of δ may cause ineffective shuffling during the sorting. Although $\delta = 1$ provides the utmost privacy, which means that the chance of guessing the matching of the whole PCVs is 1 over the number of all possible merging of those two individually sorted lists, the execution time of sorting can be relatively high. For $\delta \neq 1$, the execution time can be low but the number of possible matching of PCVs in the individually sorted list to the merged list decreases in parallel to the increment of δ. As a guideline on the choice of δ, one can decide it based on how much privacy loss any matching could cause on the specific task. In case of $\delta \neq 1$ and $|L_{j_k}| = 1$ at some point in the sorting, the sorting continues as if it had just started with $\delta = 1$ to make sure that the worst case scenario for guessing the matching can be secured. More details of the sorting phase are in the Appendix.

Division (DIV): For the exact AUC, we need a division operation which is not offered by CECILIA. Therefore, we adapted the division operation from SecureNN [18]. However, we use the building blocks of CECILIA to implement the division operation since they have less communication round complexities than SecureNN. DIV uses long division to find the quotient. Although DIV of SecureNN is rather a normalization operation, requiring the denominator to be larger than the nominator, it is still useful for the exact AUC computation. In both AUROC and AUPR, the denomitors and nominators of the division operations satisfy this requirement.

4.1   Secure Computation of AUROC

Once P_0 and P_1 obtain the global sorted list of PCVs, they calculate the AUROC based on this list using one of the versions of AUROC depending on whether there exists a tie in the list.

input : $\langle L \rangle_i = (\{\langle con_1 \rangle_i, \langle label_1 \rangle_i\}, ..., \{\langle con_M \rangle_i, \langle label_M \rangle_i\})$, $\langle L \rangle_i$ is a share of the global sorted list of PCVs, and labels

1 For each $i \in \{0, 1\}$, P_i executes Steps 2-11
2 $\langle TP \rangle_i \leftarrow 0$, $\langle P \rangle_i \leftarrow 0$, $\langle pFP \rangle_i \leftarrow 0$, $\langle N \rangle_i \leftarrow 0$
3 **foreach** *item* $\langle t \rangle \in \langle L \rangle$ **do**
4 $\quad$ $\langle TP \rangle_i \leftarrow \langle TP \rangle_i + \langle t.label \rangle_i$
5 $\quad$ $\langle P \rangle_i \leftarrow \langle P \rangle_i + i$
6 $\quad$ $\langle FP \rangle_i \leftarrow \langle P \rangle_i - \langle TP \rangle_i$
7 $\quad$ $\langle A \rangle_i \leftarrow \mathsf{MUL}(\langle TP \rangle_i, \langle FP \rangle_i - \langle pFP \rangle_i)$
8 $\quad$ $\langle N \rangle_i \leftarrow \langle N \rangle_i + \langle A \rangle_i$
9 $\quad$ $\langle pFP \rangle_i \leftarrow \langle FP \rangle_i$
10 $\langle D \rangle_i \leftarrow \mathsf{MUL}(\langle TP \rangle_i, \langle FP \rangle_i)$
11 $\langle ROC \rangle_i \leftarrow \mathsf{DIV}(\langle N \rangle_i, \langle D \rangle_i)$

Algorithm 1: Secure AUROC computation without ties

input : $\langle L \rangle_i = (\{\langle con_1 \rangle_i, \langle label_1 \rangle_i\}, , ..., \{\langle con_M \rangle_i, \langle label_M \rangle_i\})$, $\langle L \rangle_i$ is a share of the global sorted list of PCVs, and labels

1 For each $i \in \{0, 1\}$, P_i executes Steps 2-14
2 $\langle TP \rangle_i \leftarrow 0$, $\langle P \rangle_i \leftarrow 0$, $\langle pFP \rangle_i \leftarrow 0$, $\langle pTP \rangle_i \leftarrow 0$, $\langle N_1 \rangle_i \leftarrow 0$, $\langle N_2 \rangle_i \leftarrow 0$
3 **foreach** *item* $\langle t \rangle_i \in \langle L \rangle_i$ **do**
4 $\quad$ $\langle TP \rangle_i \leftarrow \langle TP \rangle_i + \langle t.label \rangle_i$
5 $\quad$ $\langle P \rangle_i \leftarrow \langle P \rangle_i + i$
6 $\quad$ $\langle FP \rangle_i \leftarrow \langle P \rangle_i - \langle TP \rangle_i$
7 $\quad$ $\langle A \rangle_i \leftarrow \mathsf{MUL}([\langle pTP \rangle_i, \langle TP \rangle_i - \langle pTP \rangle_i], [\langle FP \rangle_i - \langle pFP \rangle_i, \langle FP \rangle_i - \langle pFP \rangle_i])$
8 $\quad$ $\langle A \rangle_i \leftarrow \mathsf{MUL}(\langle A \rangle_i, [\langle t.con \rangle_i, \langle t.con \rangle_i])$
9 $\quad$ $\langle N_1 \rangle_i \leftarrow \langle N_1 \rangle_i + \langle A[0] \rangle_i$
10 $\quad$ $\langle N_2 \rangle_i \leftarrow \langle N_2 \rangle_i + \langle A[1] \rangle_i$
11 $\quad$ $[\langle pre\_FP \rangle_i, \langle pre\_TP \rangle_i] \leftarrow \mathsf{MUX}([\langle pFP \rangle_i, \langle pTP \rangle_i], [\langle FP \rangle_i, \langle TP \rangle_i],$
$\quad$ $[\langle t.con \rangle_i, \langle t.con \rangle_i])$
12 $\langle N \rangle_i \leftarrow 2 \cdot \langle N_1 \rangle_i + \langle N_2 \rangle_i$
13 $\langle D \rangle_i \leftarrow 2 \cdot \mathsf{MUL}(\langle TP \rangle_i, \langle FP \rangle_i)$
14 $\langle ROC \rangle_i \leftarrow \mathsf{DIV}(\langle N \rangle_i, \langle D \rangle_i)$

Algorithm 2: Secure AUROC computation with tie

Secure AUROC Computation without Ties: In Algorithm 1, we compute the AUROC as shown in Eq. 1 by assuming that there is no tie in the sorted list of PCVs. At the end of the secure computation, the shares of numerator N and denominator D are computed. Since N is always greater than or equal to D, we can use the division of SecureNN to obtain $AUROC = N/D$. With the help of high numeric value precision of the results, most of the machine learning algorithms yield different PCVs for samples. Therefore, this version of computing the AUROC is applicable to most machine learning tasks. However, in case of a tie between samples from two classes in the PCVs, it does not guarantee the exact AUROC. Depending on the order of the samples, it approximates the score. To have a more accurate AUROC, we propose another version of AUROC computation with a slightly higher communication cost in the next section.

Secure AUROC Computation with Ties: To detect ties in the list of PCVs, P_0 and P_1 compute the difference between each PCV and its following PCV. P_0 computes the modular additive inverse of its shares. The proxies apply a common random permutation to the bits of each share in the list to prevent P_2 from learning the non-zero relative differences. They also permute the list of shares using a common random permutation to shuffle the order of the real

---

input : $\langle C \rangle_i = (\langle con_1 \rangle_i, ..., \langle con_M \rangle_i)$, $\langle C \rangle_i$ is a share of the global sorted list of PCVs, M is the number of PCVs

1 P_0 and P_1 hold a common random permutation π for M items
2 P_0 and P_1 hold a list of common random values R
3 P_0 and P_1 hold a list of common random permutation σ for ℓ items
4 For each $i \in \{0, 1\}$, P_i executes Steps 5-13
5 **for** $j \leftarrow 1$ **to** $M - 1$ **do**
6 $\quad \langle C[j] \rangle_i \leftarrow (\langle C[j] \rangle_i - \langle C[j+1] \rangle_i)$
7 $\quad$ **if** $i = 0$ **then**
8 $\quad\quad \mid \quad \langle C[j] \rangle_i = K - \langle C[j] \rangle_i$
9 $\quad \langle C[j] \rangle_i = \langle C[j] \rangle_i \oplus R[j]$
10 $\quad \langle C[j] \rangle_i = \sigma_j (\langle C[j] \rangle_i)$
11 $\langle D \rangle_i = \pi(\langle C \rangle_i)$
12 Insert arbitrary number of dummy zero and non-zero values to randomly chosen locations in $\langle D \rangle_i$
13 P_i sends $\langle D \rangle_i$ to P_2
14 P_2 reconstructs D by computing $\langle D \rangle_0 \oplus \langle D \rangle_1$
15 **foreach** *item* $\langle d \rangle \in \langle D \rangle$ **do**
16 $\quad$ **if** $d > 0$ **then**
17 $\quad\quad \mid \quad d \leftarrow 1$

18 P_2 creates new shares of D, denoted by $\langle D \rangle_0$ and $\langle D \rangle_1$, and sends them to P_0 and P_1, respectively.
19 For each $i \in \{0, 1\}$, P_i executes Steps 18-21
20 Remove dummy zero and non-zero values from $\langle D \rangle_i$
21 $\langle C \rangle_i = \pi^{-1}(\langle D \rangle_i)$
22 **for** $j \leftarrow 1$ **to** $M - 1$ **do**
23 $\quad \langle L[j].con \rangle_i \leftarrow \langle C[j] \rangle_i$
24 $\langle L[M].con \rangle_i \leftarrow i$

Algorithm 3: Secure detection of ties

---

test samples. Then, they send the list of shares to P_2. P_2 XORes two shares and maps the result to one, if it is greater than zero and zero otherwise. Then, proxies privately map PCVs to zero if they equal to their previous PCV and one otherwise. This phase is depicted in Algorithm 3. In Algorithm 2, P_0 and P_1 use these mappings to take only the PCVs which are different from their subsequent PCV into account in the computation of the AUROC based on Eq. 2. In Algorithm 2, DIV adapted from SecureNN can be used since the numerator is always less than or equal to the denominator, as in the AUROC computation.

4.2 Secure AUPR Computation

As in the AUROC with tie computation, P_0 and P_1 map a PCV in the global sorted list to 0 if it equals the previous PCV and 1 otherwise via Algorithm 3. Then, we use Eq. 2 to calculate AUPR as shown in Algorithm 4. The most significant difference of AUPR from AUROC with tie computation is that the denominator of each precision value is different in the AUPR calculation. Thus, we need to compute the precision for each iteration in advance, requiring a vectorized division operation before iterating the list of PCVs mapped to one.

---

input : $\langle L \rangle_i = (\{\langle con_1 \rangle_i, \langle label_1 \rangle_i\}, ..., \{\langle con_M \rangle_i, \langle label_M \rangle_i\})$, $\langle L \rangle_i$ is a share of the
global sorted list of PCVs, and labels
1 P_0 and P_1 hold a common random permutation π for M items
2 For each $i \in \{0, 1\}$, P_i executes Steps 3-19
3 $\langle TP[0] \rangle_i \leftarrow 0$, $\langle RC[0] \rangle_i \leftarrow 0$, $\langle pPC \rangle_i \leftarrow i$, $\langle pRC \rangle_i \leftarrow 0$, $\langle N_1 \rangle_i \leftarrow 0$, $\langle N_2 \rangle_i \leftarrow 0$
4 for $j \leftarrow 1$ to M do
5 $\quad$ $\langle TP[j] \rangle_i \leftarrow \langle TP[j-1] \rangle_i + \langle L[j].label \rangle_i$
6 $\quad$ $\langle RC[j] \rangle_i \leftarrow \langle RC[j-1] \rangle_i + i$

7 $\langle T\_TP \rangle_i = \pi(\langle TP \rangle_i)$
8 $\langle T\_RC \rangle_i = \pi(\langle RC \rangle_i)$
9 $\langle T\_PC \rangle_i \leftarrow \mathsf{DIV}(\langle T\_TP \rangle_i, \langle T\_RC \rangle_i)$
10 $\langle PC \rangle_i = \pi'(\langle T\_PC \rangle_i)$
11 for $j \leftarrow 1$ to M do
12 $\quad$ $\langle A \rangle_i \leftarrow \mathsf{MUL}([\langle pPC \rangle_i \langle RC[j] \rangle_i - \langle pRC \rangle_i], [\langle RC[j] \rangle_i - \langle pRC \rangle_i, \langle PC[j] \rangle_i - \langle pPC \rangle_i])$

13 $\quad$ $\langle A \rangle_i \leftarrow \mathsf{MUL}(\langle A \rangle_i, [\langle L[j].con \rangle_i, \langle L[j].con \rangle_i])$
14 $\quad$ $\langle N_1 \rangle_i \leftarrow \langle N_1 \rangle_i + \langle A[0] \rangle_i$
15 $\quad$ $\langle N_2 \rangle_i \leftarrow \langle N_2 \rangle_i + \langle A[1] \rangle_i$
16 $\quad$ $[\langle pPC \rangle_i, \langle pRC \rangle_i] \leftarrow$
$\quad$ $\mathsf{MUX}([\langle pPC \rangle_i, \langle pRC \rangle_i], [\langle PC[j] \rangle_i, \langle RC[j] \rangle_i],$
$\quad$ $[\langle L[j].con \rangle_i, \langle L[j].con \rangle_i])$

17 $\langle N \rangle_i \leftarrow 2 \cdot \langle N_2 \rangle_i$
18 $\langle D \rangle_i \leftarrow 2 \cdot \langle TP[M] \rangle_i$
19 $\langle PRC \rangle_i \leftarrow \mathsf{DIV}(\langle N \rangle_i, \langle D \rangle_i)$

Algorithm 4: Secure AUPR computation

---

5 Security Analysis

In this section, we provide semi-honest simulation-based security proofs for the computations of ppAURORA based on the security of CECILIA's building blocks.

Lemma 1. *The protocol in Algorithm 1 securely computes AUROC in the $(\mathcal{F}_{\mathsf{MUL}}, \mathcal{F}_{\mathsf{DIV}})$ hybrid model.*

Proof. In the protocol, we separately calculate the numerator N and the denominator D of the AUROC, which can be expressed as $AUROC = \frac{N}{D}$. Let us first focus on the computation of D. It is equal to the multiplication of the number of samples with label 1 by the number of samples with label 0. In the end, we have the number of samples with label 1 in TP and calculate the number of samples with label 0 by $P - TP$. Then, the computation of D is simply the multiplication of these two values. To compute N, we used Eq. 1. We have already shown the denominator part of it. For the numerator part, we need to multiply the current TP by the change in FP and sum up these multiplication results. $\langle A \rangle \leftarrow \mathsf{MUL}(\langle TP \rangle, \langle FP \rangle - \langle pFP \rangle)$ computes the contribution of the current sample on the denominator and we accumulate all the contributions in N, which is the numerator part of Eq. 1. Therefore, we can conclude that we correctly compute the AUROC.

Next, we prove the security of our protocol. P_i where $i \in \{0, 1\}$ sees $\{\langle A \rangle\}_{j \in M}$, $\langle D \rangle$ and $\langle ROC \rangle$, which are fresh shares of these values. Thus the view of P_i is perfectly simulatable with uniformly random values.

Lemma 2. *The protocol in Algorithm 3 securely marks the location of ties in the list of prediction confidences.*

Proof. For the correctness of our protocol, we need to prove that for each index j in L, $L[j].con = 0$ if $(C[j] - C[j+1]) = 0$, $L[j].con = 1$, otherwise. We first calculate the difference of successive items in C. Assume we have two additive shares $(\langle a \rangle_0, \langle a \rangle_1)$ of a over the ring $\mathbb{Z}_K$. If $a = 0$, then $(K - \langle a \rangle_0) \oplus \langle a \rangle_1 = 0$ and if $a \neq 0$, then $(K - \langle a \rangle_0) \oplus \langle a \rangle_1 \neq 0$ where $K - \langle a \rangle_0$ is the additive modular inverse of $\langle a \rangle_0$. We use this fact in our protocol. P_0 computes the additive inverse of each item $\langle c \rangle_0$ in $\langle C \rangle_0$ which is denoted by $\langle c \rangle_0'$, XORes $\langle c \rangle_0'$ with a common random number in R, which is denoted by $\langle c \rangle_0''$ and permutes the bits of $\langle c \rangle_0''$ with a common permutation σ which is denoted by $\langle c \rangle_0'''$. P_1 XORes each item $\langle c \rangle_1$ in $\langle C \rangle_1$ with a common random number in R which is denoted by $\langle c \rangle_1''$ and permutes the bits of $\langle c \rangle_1''$ with a common permutation σ which is denoted by $\langle c \rangle_1'''$. P_i where $i \in \{0,1\}$ permutes values in $\langle C \rangle_i'''$ by a common random permutation π which is denoted by $\langle D \rangle_i$. After receiving $\langle D \rangle_0$ and $\langle D \rangle_1$, P_2 maps each item d of D to 0 if $\langle d \rangle_0' \oplus \langle d \rangle_1 = 0$ which means $\langle d \rangle_0 + \langle d \rangle_1 = 0$ and maps 1 if $\langle d \rangle_0' \oplus \langle d \rangle_1 \neq 0$ which means $\langle d \rangle_0 + \langle d \rangle_1 \neq 0$. After receiving a new share of D from P_2, P_i where $i \in \{0,1\}$ removes dummy values and permutes remaining values by π^{-1}. Therefore, our protocol correctly maps items of C to 0 or 1.

We next prove the security of our protocol. P_i where $i \in \{0,1\}$ calculates the difference of successive prediction values. The view of P_2 is D, which includes real and dummy zero values. P_i XORes each item of $\langle C \rangle_i$ with fresh boolean shares of zero, applies a random permutation to bits of each item of $\langle C \rangle_i$, applies a random permutation π to $\langle C \rangle_i$ and add dummy zero and non-zero values. Thus the differences, the positions of the differences, and the distribution of the differences are completely random. The number of zero and non-zero values are not known to P_2 due to dummy values. With common random permutations $\sigma_{j \in M}$ and common random values $R[j], j \in M$, each item in C is hidden. Thus P_2 can not infer anything about real values in C. Furthermore, the number of repeating predictions is not known to P_2 due to the random permutation π.

Lemma 3. *The protocol in Algorithm 2 securely computes AUROC in ($\mathcal{F}_{\mathsf{MUL}}$, $\mathcal{F}_{\mathsf{MUX}}$, $\mathcal{F}_{\mathsf{DIV}}$) hybrid model.*

Proof. To compute the AUROC in case of a tie, we use Eq. 2, of which we calculate the numerator and the denominator separately. The calculation of the denominator D is the same as Lemma 1. The computation of the numerator N has two different components, which are N_1 and N_2. N_1, more precisely the numerator of $T[i-1] * (F[i] - F[i-1])$, is similar to the no-tie version of privacy preserving AUROC computation. This part corresponds to the rectangle areas in the ROC curve. The decision of adding this area A to the cumulative area N_1 is made based on the result of the multiplication of A by $L.con$. $L.con = 1$ indicates if the sample is one of the points of prediction confidence change, 0 otherwise. If it is 0, then A becomes 0 and there is no contribution to N_1. If it is 1, then we add A to N_1. On the other hand, N_2, which is the numerator of

$(T[i] - T[i-1]) * (F[i] - F[i-1])$, accumulates the triangular areas. We compute the possible contribution of the current sample to N_2. In case this sample is not one of the points that the prediction confidence changes, which is determined by $L.con$, then the value of A is set to 0. If it is, then A remains the same. Finally, A is added to N_2. Since there is a division by 2 in the second part of Eq. 2, we multiply N_1 by 2 to make them have common denominator. Then, we sum N_1 and N_2 to obtain N. To have the term 2 in the common denominator, we multiply D by 2. As a result, we correctly compute the denominator and the nominator of the AUROC.

Next, we prove the security of our protocol. P_i where $i \in \{0, 1\}$ sees $\{\langle A \rangle\}_{j \in M}$, $\{\langle pFP \rangle\}_{j \in M}$, $\{\langle pTP \rangle\}_{j \in M}$, $\langle D \rangle$ and $\langle ROC \rangle$, which are fresh shares of them. Thus the view of P_i is perfectly simulatable with uniformly random values.

Lemma 4. *The protocol in Algorithm 4 securely computes AUPR in ($\mathcal{F}_{\mathsf{MUL}}$, $\mathcal{F}_{\mathsf{MUX}}$, $\mathcal{F}_{\mathsf{DIV}}$) hybrid model.*

Proof. To compute the AUPR, we use Eq. 2 of which we calculate the numerator and the denominator separately. We nearly perform the same computation with the AUROC with tie computation. The main difference is that we need to perform a division to calculate each precision value because denominators of each precision value are different. The rest of the computation is the same with the computation in Algorithm 2. The readers can follow the proof of Lemma 3.

Next, we prove the security of our protocol. P_i where $i \in \{0, 1\}$ sees $\{\langle T\_PC \rangle\}_{j \in M}$, $\{\langle A \rangle\}_{j \in M}$, $\{\langle pPC \rangle\}_{j \in M}$, $\{\langle pRC \rangle\}_{j \in M}$ and $\langle PRC \rangle$, which are fresh shares of them. Thus the view of P_i is perfectly simulatable with uniformly random values.

Lemma 5. *The sorting protocol in Sect. 4 securely merges two sorted lists in ($\mathcal{F}_{\mathsf{CMP}}$, $\mathcal{F}_{\mathsf{MUX}}$) hybrid model.*

Proof. First, we prove the correctness of our merge sorting of lists L_1 and L_2. In the merging of L_1 and L_2, the corresponding values are first compared using CMP operation. The larger values are placed in L_1 and the smaller values are placed in L_2, after MUX operation is called twice. This process is called *shuffling* because it shuffles the corresponding values in the two lists. After the shuffling, we know that the largest element of the two lists is the top element of L_1. Thus, it is moved to the global sorted list L_3. On the next step, the top elements of L_1 and L_2 are compared with CMP method. The comparison result is reconstructed by P_0 and P_1 and the top element of L_1 or L_2 is moved to L_3 based on the result of CMP. The selection operation also gives the largest element of L_1 and L_2 because L_1 and L_2 are sorted. We show that shuffling and selection operations give the largest element of two sorted lists. This ensures that our merge sort algorithm that only uses these operations correctly merges two sorted lists privately.

Next, we prove the security of our merge sort algorithm in which CMP and MUX are called. CMP outputs fresh shares of comparison of corresponding values in L_1 and L_2. Shares of these comparison results are used in MUX that generates fresh shares of the corresponding values. Thus, P_0 and P_1 cannot precisely map

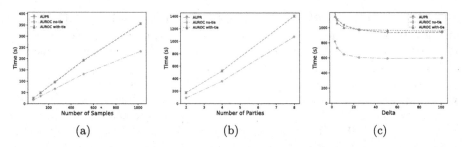

Fig. 2. The scalability of ppAURORA to varying (a) number of samples, (b) number of parties and (c) δ where the other parameters are fixed

these values to the values in L_1 and L_2. In the selection operation, CMP is called and its reconstructed output is used to select. P_0 and P_1 are still unable to map the values added to L_3 to the values in L_1 and L_2 precisely since at least one shuffling operation took place before these repeated selection operations. Shuffling and $\delta - 1$ selection operations are performed repeatedly until the L_1 is empty. After each shuffling operation, the fresh share of the larger corresponding values in L_1 and the fresh share of the smaller corresponding values in L_2 are stored. The view of P_0 and P_1 are perfectly simulatable with random values due to the shuffling process performed at regular intervals.

To prevent the usage of unshuffled values in some cases, the following rules are followed in the execution of the merge protocol. If there are two lists that do not have the same length, the longer list is chosen as L_1. If the δ is greater than the length of the L_2 list, it is set to the largest odd value smaller or equal to the length of L_2 so that the unshuffled values that L_1 may have are not used in selection processes. If the length of L_2 is reduced to 1 at some point in the sorting, the δ is set to 1. Thus L_2 will have 1 element until the end of the merge and shuffling is done before each selection. After moving δ values to the sorted list, if the length of L_2 is greater than the length of L_1, we switch the list.

5.1 Privacy Against Malicious Adversaries

Araki et al. [1] defined a privacy notion against malicious adversaries in the client-server setting where the servers performing secure computation on the shares of the inputs to produce the shares of the outputs do not see the plain inputs and outputs of the clients, which is very similar to our setting. In our framework, two parties exchange a seed to generate common random values between them. Two parties randomize their shares using these random values, which are unknown to the third party. It is very easy to add fresh shares of zero to outputs of two parties with common random values shared between them. In our algorithms, we do not state the randomization of outputs with fresh shares of zero. Thus, our framework provides privacy against a malicious party by relying on the security of a seed shared between two honest parties.

6   Results

Dataset: We used the Acute Myeloid Leukemia (AML) dataset[1] and the UCI Heart Disease dataset[2] for the correctness analysis of ppAURORA. AML dataset is from the submission of the team *Snail*, which has the lowest score, in the first subchallenge of the DREAM Challenge [14] and has 191 samples, among which 136 patients have complete remission. UCI Heart Disease test set has 54 samples with binary outcome. Moreover, we aimed to analyze the scalability of ppAURORA for different settings. For this purpose, we generated a synthetic dataset with no restriction other than having the PCVs from $[0, 1]$.

Experimental Setup: We conducted our experiments on LAN and WAN settings. In the LAN, we ran the experiments with 0.18 ms round trip time (RTT). In the WAN, we simulated the network connection with 10 ms RTT.

Correctness Analysis: We conducted the correctness analysis on the LAN setting. To assess the correctness of AUROC with tie, we computed the AUROC of the predictions on the AML dataset by ppAURORA, yielding $AUROC = 0.693$ which is the same the result obtained without privacy on the DREAM Challenge dataset. For the correctness of AUROC with no-tie of ppAURORA, we randomly picked one of the samples in tie condition in DREAM Challenge dataset and generated a subset of the samples with no tie. We got the same AUROC with no-tie version of AUROC of ppAURORA as the non-private computation. We directly used the UCI dataset in AUROC with no-tie since it does not have any tie condition. The result, which is $AUROC = 0.927$, is the same for both private and non-private computation. Besides, we verified that ppAURORA computes the same AUPR as for the non-private computation for both the DREAM Challenge and the UCI dataset, which are $AUPR = 0.844$ and $AUPR = 0.893$, respectively. These results indicate that ppAURORA can privately compute the exact same AUC as one could obtain on the pooled test samples.

Scalability Analysis: We evaluated the scalability of no-tie and with-tie versions of AUROC and AUPR of ppAURORA to the number of samples $M \in \{64, 128, 256, 512, 1024\}$ with $\delta = 1$ and 3 data sources. The results showed that ppAURORA scales almost quadratically in terms of both communication costs among all parties and the execution time of the computation. We also analyzed the performance of all computations of ppAURORA on a varying number of data sources. We fixed $\delta = 1$ and the number of samples in each data sources to 1000, and we experimented with D data sources where $D \in \{2, 4, 8\}$. ppAURORA scales around quadratically to the number of data sources. We also analyzed the effect of $\delta \in \{3, 5, 11, 25, 51, 101\}$ by fixing D to 8 and M in each data source to 1000. The execution time displays a logarithmic decrease for increasing δ. In all analyses, since the dominating factor is sorting, the execution times of the computations are close to each other. Additionally, our analysis showed that LAN is 12 to 14 times faster than WAN on average due to the high

---

[1] https://www.synapse.org/#!Synapse:syn2700200.

[2] https://archive.ics.uci.edu/ml/datasets/heart+disease.

Table 1. The results of AUPR computation with ppAURORA where D is the number of data sources and M is the number of samples in one data source. UNB, i.e. unbalanced sample distribution, is $\{12, 18, 32, 58, 107, 258, 507, 1008\}$.

D × M	δ	Communication Costs (MB)				Time (sec)
		P_1	P_2	Helper	Total	
3 × 64	1	1.96	1.3	1.13	4.39	24.41
3 × 128	1	6.61	4.14	3.97	14.72	48.05
3 × 256	1	24.44	15.23	15.06	54.73	95.65
3 × 512	1	93.23	58.44	58.26	209.93	191.55
3 × 1024	1	359.67	226.62	226.41	812.7	355.32
2 × 1000	1	125.05	78.37	78.19	281.61	174.16
4 × 1000	1	726.44	458.81	458.57	1643.82	523.39
8 × 1000	1	3355.74	2125.91	2125.51	7607.16	1404.22
8 × 1000	3	1692.85	1069.58	1069.25	3831.68	1194.08
8 × 1000	5	1137.91	717.45	717.15	2572.51	1105.46
8 × 1000	11	583.02	365.36	365.08	1313.46	1032.29
8 × 1000	25	284.22	175.76	175.5	635.48	972.0
8 × 1000	51	156.23	94.54	94.29	345.06	935.65
8 × 1000	101	93.59	54.79	54.53	202.91	940.07
8 × UNB	1	130.48	81.82	81.6	293.9	379.99

round trip time of WAN, which is approximately 10 ms. Even with such a scaling factor, ppAURORA can be deployed in real life scenarios if the alternative is a more time-consuming approval process required for gathering all data in one place still protecting the privacy of data. Figure 2 and Table 1 display the results.

7   Conclusion

In this work, we presented an efficient and exact solution based on a secure 3-party computation framework to compute AUC of the ROC and PR curves privately even when there exist ties in the PCVs. We benefited from the built-in building blocks of CECILIA and adapted the division operation of SecureNN to compute the exact AUC. ppAURORA is secure against passive adversaries in the honest majority setting. We demonstrated that ppAURORA can compute correctly and privately the exact AUC that one could obtain on the pooled plaintext test samples, and ppAURORA scales quadratically to the number of both parties and samples. In future work, we will further optimize the sorting phase in terms of both privacy and efficiency.

Acknowledgement. This study is supported by the DFG Cluster of Excellence "Machine Learning - New Perspectives for Science", EXC 2064/1, project number 390727645 and the German Ministry of Research and Education (BMBF), project number 01ZZ2010.

References

1. Araki, T., Furukawa, J., Lindell, Y., Nof, A., Ohara, K.: High-throughput semi-honest secure three-party computation with an honest majority. In: Proceedings of the 2016 ACM SIGSAC Conference on Computer and Communications Security, pp. 805–817 (2016)
2. Boyd, K., Lantz, E., Page, D.: Differential privacy for classifier evaluation. In: Proceedings of the 8th ACM Workshop on Artificial Intelligence and Security, pp. 15–23 (2015)
3. Byali, M., Chaudhari, H., Patra, A., Suresh, A.: Flash: fast and robust framework for privacy-preserving machine learning. Proc. Priv. Enh. Technol. **2020**(2), 459–480 (2020)
4. Canetti, R.: Universally composable security: A new paradigm for cryptographic protocols. In: 42nd Annual Symposium on Foundations of Computer Science, FOCS 2001, 14–17 October 2001, Las Vegas, Nevada, USA, pp. 136–145. IEEE Computer Society (2001). https://doi.org/10.1109/SFCS.2001.959888
5. Chaudhuri, K., Vinterbo, S.A.: A stability-based validation procedure for differentially private machine learning. In: Advances in Neural Information Processing Systems, pp. 2652–2660 (2013)
6. Chen, Y., Machanavajjhala, A., Reiter, J.P., Barrientos, A.F.: Differentially private regression diagnostics. In: ICDM, pp. 81–90 (2016)
7. Damgård, I., Escudero, D., Frederiksen, T., Keller, M., Scholl, P., Volgushev, N.: New primitives for actively-secure MPC over rings with applications to private machine learning. In: 2019 IEEE Symposium on Security and Privacy (SP), pp. 1102–1120. IEEE (2019)
8. Juvekar, C., Vaikuntanathan, V., Chandrakasan, A.: {GAZELLE}: a low latency framework for secure neural network inference. In: 27th {USENIX} Security Symposium ({USENIX} Security 2018), pp. 1651–1669 (2018)
9. Li, B., Wu, Y., Song, J., Lu, R., Li, T., Zhao, L.: Deepfed: federated deep learning for intrusion detection in industrial cyber-physical systems. IEEE Trans. Industr. Inf. **17**(8), 5615–5624 (2020)
10. Lindell, Y.: How to simulate it – a tutorial on the simulation proof technique. In: Lindell, Y. (ed.) Tutorials on the Foundations of Cryptography. ISC, pp. 277–346. Springer, Cham (2017). https://doi.org/10.1007/978-3-319-57048-8_6
11. Matthews, G.J., Harel, O.: An examination of data confidentiality and disclosure issues related to publication of empirical ROC curves. Acad. Radiol. **20**(7), 889–896 (2013)
12. Mohassel, P., Rindal, P.: ABY3: a mixed protocol framework for machine learning. In: Proceedings of the 2018 ACM SIGSAC Conference on Computer and Communications Security, pp. 35–52 (2018)

13. Mohassel, P., Zhang, Y.: Secureml: a system for scalable privacy-preserving machine learning. In: 2017 IEEE Symposium on Security and Privacy (SP), pp. 19–38. IEEE (2017)
14. Noren, D.P., et al.: A crowdsourcing approach to developing and assessing prediction algorithms for AML prognosis. PLoS Comput. Biol. **12**(6), e1004890 (2016)
15. Patra, A., Suresh, A.: BLAZE: blazing fast privacy-preserving machine learning. In: 27th Annual Network and Distributed System Security Symposium, NDSS 2020, San Diego, California, USA, 23–26 February 2020. The Internet Society (2020)
16. Sun, J., Yang, X., Yao, Y., Xie, J., Wu, D., Wang, C.: Differentially private AUC computation in vertical federated learning. arXiv preprint arXiv:2205.12412 (2022)
17. Ünal, A.B., Akgün, M., Pfeifer, N.: CECILIA: comprehensive secure machine learning framework. CoRR abs/2202.03023 (2022). https://arxiv.org/abs/2202.03023
18. Wagh, S., Gupta, D., Chandran, N.: SecureNN: efficient and private neural network training. IACR Cryptology ePrint Archive, vol. 2018, p. 442 (2018)
19. Whitehill, J.: How does knowledge of the AUC constrain the set of possible ground-truth labelings? In: Proceedings of the AAAI Conference on Artificial Intelligence, vol. 33, pp. 5425–5432 (2019)

Security Through Hardware

Modular Polynomial Multiplication Using RSA/ECC Coprocessor

Aurélien Greuet[1]([⊠]) [iD], Simon Montoya[1,2] [iD], and Clémence Vermeersch[1]

[1] IDEMIA, Cryptography and Security Labs, Courbevoie, France
{aurelien.greuet,simon.montoya,clemence.vermeersch}@idemia.com
[2] LIX, INRIA, CNRS, École Polytechnique, Institut Polytechnique de Paris, Palaiseau, France
simon.montoya@lix.polytechnique.fr

Abstract. Modular polynomial multiplication is a core and costly operation of ideal lattice-based schemes. In the context of embedded devices, previous works transform the polynomial multiplication to an integer one using Kronecker substitution. Thanks to this transformation, existing coprocessors which handle large-integer operations can be re-purposed to speed-up lattice-based cryptography. In a nutshell, the Kronecker substitution transforms by evaluation the polynomials to integers, multiplies it with an integer multiplication and gets back to a polynomial result using a radix conversion. The previous work focused on optimization of the integer multiplication using coprocessors. In this work, we pursue the seminal research by optimizing the evaluation, radix conversion and the modular reductions modulo q with today's RSA/ECC coprocessor. In particular we show that with a coprocessor handling addition/subtraction, (modular) multiplication, shift and logical AND on large integers, the whole modular polynomial multiplication can be computed. The efficiency of our modular polynomial multiplication depends on the component specification and on the cryptosystem parameters set. Hence, we assess our algorithm on a chip for several lattice-based schemes, which are finalists of the NIST standardization. Moreover, we compare our modular polynomial multiplication with other polynomial multiplication techniques.

Keywords: Post-Quantum Lattice-based Cryptography · Modular Polynomial Multiplication · Embedded devices

1 Introduction

In the next few years, a quantum computer powerful enough to run Shor's algorithm [19] could emerge. Such a computer can break the entire cryptography based on the hardness of integer factorization and discrete logarithm like RSA or Elliptic Curve Cryptography (ECC). Due to this potential threat, national agencies started to study new proposals (e.g. [7]) and initiated standardization of quantum safe algorithms [9,16]. The most followed standardization by the

S. Li et al. (Eds.): NSS 2023, LNCS 13983, pp. 283–304, 2023.
https://doi.org/10.1007/978-3-031-39828-5_16

community is the one of the National Institute of Standards and Technology (NIST), which was launched in 2016 [16]. This standardization aims to bring together an important part of the community to determine future Key Encapsulation Mechanisms (KEMs) and signatures standards. In 2020, the third round of this standardization started with seven finalists remaining, including four KEMs and three signatures. Among these seven finalists, five are based on lattice or assimilated problems [17]. In July 2022, NIST published the four algorithms selected for standardization [1]. Three of them are related with lattices. Hence, the international community around post-quantum cryptography is very likely to include lattice-based standards. Therefore, optimizing and ensuring practical security of these cryptosystems is an important area of research.

Post-quantum cryptography will be deployed on embedded devices like smartcards. Today on a smartcard, the amount of RAM or the CPU frequency are very limited: less than 60 kB of RAM and less than 100 MHz. Therefore, implementing efficient cryptosystems in these constrained environments is a real challenge. In order to speed-up the cryptographic algorithms, these devices may embed additional hardware coprocessors for symmetric and asymmetric cryptographic computations. Moreover, these coprocessors can provide additional security features as hardware and software security against faults and side-channel leakage. Most of the asymmetric coprocessors currently deployed are designed for the ECC or RSA schemes and not for lattice-based cryptosystems. However, the underlying arithmetic of these cryptosystems can be tweaked with the purpose of using an arithmetic close to the one used on RSA/ECC schemes. Therefore, re-purposing such asymmetric coprocessors is interesting to optimize lattice-based schemes and to facilitate the transition in the post-quantum world. Indeed, the easier the transition, the more it will be used and deployed.

Motivations and Previous Works. Lattice-based cryptography is believed to be a promising direction to provide efficient and secure post-quantum algorithms. One of the main operation in these schemes is *modular polynomial multiplication*. Research has been conducted in the way of optimizing the polynomial multiplication operation using specific software instructions or by designing a specific hardware. However, most of the polynomial multiplication optimization are intended to ARM-Cortex M4, or less frequently to ARM-Cortex M3 CPU architecture. The ARM CPU is powerful and has a larger panel of interesting assembly instruction. However, embedded systems generally don't have such a powerful CPU and base their cryptographic efficiency on the additional coprocessor.

Moreover, the transition period should rely on *hybrid cryptography* which is the combination of a post-quantum algorithm and a classical one. Hence, such cryptography is both secure against quantum attacks, thanks to the post-quantum part, and secure against classical attacks, with at least the same security level as a pure classical crypto algorithm. Several governmental agencies (NIST, ANSSI, BSI) recommend and will impose in a few years the use of hybrid cryptography for long term security certification [3,7]. In this context, re-purposing the current asymmetric coprocessors to optimize the modular polynomial multiplication is of interest in terms of costs, ease of deployment and to propose optimization for a wide range of components.

The seminal work of Albrecht *et al.* in [2] re-purposes a RSA/ECC coprocessor to optimize polynomial multiplication on Kyber algorithm. To do so, they use techniques introduced in [13] which transform polynomial multiplication to an integer one using the Kronecker substitution [14]. Afterwards, another work in [20] adapts the previous technique on Saber algorithm.

The work of *Bos et al.* in [6] introduced `Kronecker+`, a generalization of the Kronecker substitution used by Albrecht *et al.* in [2]. This generalization allows trade-off between number of integer multiplications, size of the integers and the number of polynomial evaluations. Depending on the component and coprocessor specifications, `Kronecker+` allows a faster polynomial multiplication than Kronecker substitution.

In [12], the authors provide a variant of the Kronecker substitution and an adaptation of the schoolbook multiplication to perform hardware polynomial multiplication. Depending on the RSA/ECC coprocessor specifications, one of these algorithms can outperform the classical Kronecker substitution.

Our Contribution. This work aims to perform modular polynomial multiplication in $R_{q,\delta} = \mathbb{Z}_q[X]/(X^N + \delta)$ using a RSA/ECC coprocessor, where $\delta \in \{-1, 1\}$. These rings are the most used by the lattice-based in the NIST standardization.

The contemporary asymmetric coprocessor can perform integer operations and not polynomial ones. As we have seen previously, most techniques to repurpose current coprocessor to optimize polynomial multiplication on embedded devices are based on the Kronecker substitution. In $R_{q,\delta}$ this substitution can be summarized in four steps:

1. Convert polynomials in $R_{q,\delta}$ to integers in $\mathbb{N}$ of bit size `bitsize`. When polynomials have coefficients with a negative representation, this conversion requires additional operations.
2. Modular integer multiplication mod $2^{\texttt{bitsize}} + \delta$ of the obtained integers.
3. Convert back integer multiplication result to a polynomial in $\mathbb{Z}[X]/(X^N + \delta)$. Like Step 1, if the initial polynomials have coefficients with a negative representation this conversion requires additional operations.
4. Reduce the coefficients modulo q to have result over $R_{q,\delta}$.

All the previous works re-purpose the coprocessor only to optimize Step 2. All the other steps are implemented in software without the use of coprocessor.

In this work for most of the previous steps, we describe algorithms which allow to re-purpose existing coprocessor. Our work focuses on two mains contributions:

- Handle negative evaluation and radix conversion using RSA/ECC coprocessor (Steps 1 and 3).
- Perform modular reduction of the coefficients modulo q with a RSA/ECC coprocessor (Step 4).

These improvements are possible only if the coprocessor can handle the following integer operations: addition/subtraction, bitwise AND, logical shift, multiplication and modular multiplication. Except the logical AND operation, most of current asymmetric coprocessors handle these operations. The logical AND is less common on the current RSA/ECC coprocessor. However adding this operation to an existing architecture is easier and cheaper than designing a new one for polynomial multiplication.

Organization. In Sect. 2 we introduce notations which we use in the rest of the paper. In Sect. 2.3 we present how to perform a polynomial multiplication in $\mathbb{N}[X]$ using the *Kronecker substitution*. Afterwards, in Sect. 3 we explain how to use the coprocessor instructions to perform the *Kronecker substitution* evaluation and radix conversation, since the polynomials are in $R_{q,\delta} = \mathbb{Z}_q[X]/(X^N + \delta)$, where $\delta \in \{-1, 1\}$. In Sect. 4 we describe modular reductions modulo q using coprocessor instructions. Finally, in Sect. 5 we present the results of our practical implementations of our algorithms on several lattice-based finalists.

2   Background

RSA/ECC Coprocessor. The RSA/ECC coprocessor are designed to speed-up RSA or elliptic curves cryptosystems. To do so, these components provide a range of integer operations. In this work, we assume that we have access to a component which can perform, at least, addition/subtraction, bitwise AND, logical shift, multiplication and modular multiplication operations.

2.1   Element Representation

Integers Representation. Let $a \in \mathbb{N}$ such that $0 \le a < 2^\ell$. In the following, we say that a is represented over ℓ bits to mean that a is stored in a machine buffer of ℓ bits.

Let $b \in \mathbb{Z}$ such that $-2^{\ell'-1} < b < 2^{\ell'-1}$. Let $\tilde{b}$ be the two's complement representation of b over ℓ' bits, defined by $\tilde{b} = 2^{\ell'} + b \mod 2^{\ell'} \in \mathbb{N}$. In the following, we say that b is represented over ℓ' bits to mean that the two's complement representation of b is stored in a machine buffer of ℓ' bits.

Let r be a $N\ell$-bit natural number. We denote by r_i the i-th digit of r in base 2^ℓ. In other words, $r = \sum_{i=0}^{N-1} r_i 2^{i\ell}$ with $0 \le r_i < 2^\ell$. We use the following notation $r = (r_0, r_1, \ldots, r_{N-1})_\ell$.

Polynomial Representation. Let $F(X) = f_0 + f_1 X + \ldots + f_{N-1} X^{N-1} \in \mathbb{Z}[X]$ of degree at most $N - 1$. Let $\tilde{f}_i$ be a two's complement representation of f_i.

- Array representation: the usual machine representation of $F(X)$ is an array where the i-th item is $\tilde{f}_i$. To ease the reading, we denote in the following, f_i or $f[i]$ the coefficient associated to the i-th item. Moreover, unless otherwise specified, a polynomial is represented as an array.

– Packed integer representation: $F(X)$ is represented as the concatenation of all the $\tilde{f}_i$ into a buffer $f = \tilde{f}_{N-1}|\ldots|\tilde{f}_1|\tilde{f}_0 \in \mathbb{N}$.

In this work, this representation is used to represent polynomials into a natural number. Afterwards, the polynomial arithmetic is carried out with operations on this natural number.

2.2 Notations

Rings. Let $q \in \mathbb{N}$, $\delta \in \{-1, 1\}$ and $R_{q,\delta} = \frac{\mathbb{Z}_q[X]}{(X^N+\delta)}$. $F(X) \in R_{q,\delta}$ is represented as a polynomial of degree at most $N-1$ with coefficients in $\{0, \ldots, q-1\}$. $R_{q,\delta}^-$ denotes the elements of $R_{q,\delta}$ represented by a polynomial of degree at most $N-1$ with coefficients in $\{-\frac{q}{2}-1, \ldots, \frac{q}{2}\}$.

Integer Operations. In the sequel, the algorithms are described using the following notations. Their purpose is to clarify the size of the manipulated operands.

– **add**(a,b,bitlen) (resp. **sub**(a,b,bitlen)): addition (resp. subtraction) between a and b. The values a and b are represented over bitlen bits.
– **lshift**(a,k,bitlen) (resp. **rshift**(a,k,bitlen)): left (resp. right) shift $a << k$ (resp. $a >> k$) over bitlen bits.
– **and**(a,b,bitlen): bitwise logical AND $a\&b$ over bitlen bits.
– **mult**(a,b,bitlen$_a$,bitlen$_b$): integer multiplication $a \times b$ where a (resp. b) is represented on bitlen$_a$ (resp. bitlen$_b$) bits.
– **modMult**(a,b,bitlen$_a$,bitlen$_b$,p): modular multiplication $a \times b \bmod p$ where a (resp. b) is represented on bitlen$_a$ (resp. bitlen$_b$) bits.

Concatenation. Let $(\ell, k, N) \in \mathbb{N}^3$ with $\ell \leq k$ and $m \in \mathbb{N}$ represented over ℓ bits. Define **concat**(m, k, N) $= \sum_{j=0}^{N-1} m2^{jk} \in \mathbb{N}$, that represents m on k bits and concatenates this new representation N times.

Example 1. Let $m = 1$. Then **concat**($m, 8, 3$) $= $ 0x10101.

Integer to Polynomial. Let $(\ell, k, N) \in \mathbb{N}^3$, $\ell > k$ and $F(X) = f_0 + \ldots + f_{N-1}X^{N-1} \in \mathbb{Z}[X]$. For all i, let $\tilde{f}_i$ be the two's complement representation of f_i over k bits. We define $f = \mathbf{polyToN}(F(X), k, \ell) = \sum_{i=0}^{N-1} \tilde{f}_i 2^{i\ell} \in \mathbb{N}$.

Polynomial to Integer. Let $g = (g_0, g_1, \ldots, g_{N-1})_\ell \in \mathbb{N}$ a $N\ell$-bit number. We define $G(X) = \mathbf{NtoPoly}(g, \ell) = \sum_{i=0}^{N-1} g_i X^i$. $G(X)$ lies in $\mathbb{N}[X]$ and has degree at most $N-1$.

Example 2. Let $F(X) = f_2 X^2 + f_1 X + f_0 = 2X^2 + 4X - 2$. Let $\tilde{f}_0 = $ 0xE, $\tilde{f}_1 = $ 0x4, $\tilde{f}_2 = $ 0x2, be representations of all f_i over 4 bits. Then, $f = \mathbf{polyToN}(F(X), 4, 8) = $ 0x02040E and $\mathbf{NtoPoly}(f, 8) = 2X^2 + 4X + 14$

2.3 Multiplication in $\mathbb{N}[X]$ Using Kronecker Substitution

The Kronecker substitution was first introduced in [14]. We give here the main steps of this substitution. The idea of this substitution is to transform a polynomial multiplication to an integer one by evaluating the polynomials and get back to the result using a radix conversion. In the context of embedded devices, this transformation is of interest to perform polynomial multiplication by using the RSA/ECC coprocessor. Indeed, such coprocessor handles multiplication on integers. In this section we assume that our polynomials are defined over $\mathbb{N}[X]$.

Kronecker Substitution. The Kronecker substitution multiplies two polynomials $F(X)$ and $G(X)$ using an integer multiplication. This substitution can be summarized in three steps (see Appendix A for examples illustrating these steps):

1. Evaluation of $F(X)$ and $G(X)$ at 2^ℓ. The value ℓ is chosen such that all the coefficients after the polynomial multiplication are lower than 2^ℓ.
2. Integer multiplication $r = F\left(2^\ell\right) G\left(2^\ell\right), r \in \mathbb{N}$.
3. Get back to polynomial $R(X) \in \mathbb{N}[X]$ using radix conversion on r.

Evaluation. The first step of the Kronecker substitution is the polynomial evaluation at 2^ℓ. Since $F(X)$ has coefficients in $\mathbb{N}$ represented over k bits:

$$\text{EVALUATION}_{\geq 0}(F(X), k, \ell) := F\left(2^\ell\right) = \textbf{polyToN}(F(X), k, \ell) \qquad (1)$$

Evaluation Point. Let $R(X) = F(X)G(X)$ where $F(X), G(X) \in \mathbb{N}[X]$ of degree at most $N - 1$. The evaluation point 2^ℓ is chosen such that for all $i \leq 2(N - 1)$:

$$r_i \leq N \max_{j \in \{0, \ldots, N-1\}} (f_j) \max_{j \in \{0, \ldots, N-1\}} (g_j) < 2^\ell$$

By the fact that all the coefficients are non-negative, this evaluation is only a representation of all the f_i over ℓ bits. Then in an implementation, the evaluation does not require arithmetic operations.

Radix Conversion. Radix conversion aims to transform an integer into a polynomial. Let $f = (f_0, \ldots, f_{N-1})_\ell \in \mathbb{N}$, then:

$$F(X) = f_0 + \ldots + f_{N-1}X^{N-1} := \text{RADIXCONV}_{\geq 0}(f) = \textbf{NtoPoly}(f, \ell) \qquad (2)$$

The radix conversion converts a packed integer representation to an array one. Like the evaluation algorithm, in an implementation, the radix conversion does not require arithmetic operation.

3   Multiplication in $R_{q,\delta}$ Using Kronecker Substitution

In the previous section we perform polynomial multiplication as an integer one with polynomials in $\mathbb{N}[X]$. However, in lattice-based schemes some polynomials have coefficients in $\{-\mu, \mu\}$ for a small $\mu \in \mathbb{N}$. Moreover, the reduction modulo $X^N + 1$ can also bring negative coefficients. Then in this section we focus on polynomial multiplication in $R_{q,\delta} = \mathbb{Z}_q[X]/(X^N + \delta)$. In $R_{q,\delta}$, the polynomial multiplication using Kronecker substitution is achieved as follows:

- Evaluation of polynomials considering negative coefficients.
- Integer multiplication modulo $2^{N\ell} + \delta$. The modular reduction ensures that after radix conversion the polynomial result is reduced modulo $X^N + \delta$.
- Radix conversion to obtain a polynomial in $\mathbb{Z}[X]/(X^N + \delta)$.
- Reduction modulo q of the polynomial coefficients.

Previous works [2,6,12] achieve the evaluation and the radix conversion with negative coefficients using array representations. In this section we describe a way to realize these algorithms where polynomial are represented as packed integer. The main advantage of this representation is that it allows the use of existing coprocessor.

3.1   Evaluation with Negative Coefficients

Our goal is to perform polynomial multiplication over $R_{q,\delta}$ with at least one input in $R_{q,\delta}^-$. Such a polynomial can be transformed to a polynomial in $R_{q,\delta}$ by adding q to its negative coefficients. However, since δ is small, these coefficients would be close to q. This implies a larger evaluation point for the Kronecker substitution, leading to operations on larger integers (see [12]). Then for the sake of efficiency it is relevant to work with polynomials in $R_{q,\delta}^-$.

Let $F(X) = f_0 + f_1 X + \ldots + f_{N-1} X^{N-1} \in R_{q,\delta}^-$ and $\tilde{f}_i$ be the two's complement representation over k bits of f_i.

Our goal is to evaluate $F(X)$ at 2^ℓ where $\ell > k$, then for $i = 0$ to $N - 1$:

- If $f_i \geq 0$, then we only have to represent it on ℓ bits (as in Sect. 2).
- If $f_i < 0$, then we have to represent it with a two's complement over ℓ bits and propagate a borrow to the next coefficient. To obtain a two's complement representation from k bits to ℓ bits, we compute:

$$\tilde{f}_i + (2^\ell - 2^k) = 2^k + f_i + (2^\ell - 2^k) = 2^\ell + f_i$$

Algorithm 1 computes the two's complement representation of the polynomial evaluation when the coefficients are in $\mathbb{Z}$. This evaluation is done using arithmetic operations on a packed integers representation. To do so, we first represent the polynomial coefficients into a packed integer form, as defined in Eq. 1. Afterwards, we use arithmetic operations in order to convert the two complement's representation from k to ℓ bits and to propagate the required borrows.

An example to illustrate Algorithm 1 execution is given in Appendix B.

Algorithm 1. EVALUATION

Input: $F(X) \in R_{q,\delta}^{-}$, $k, \ell \in \mathbb{N}$ where $\ell > k$.

Output: $\tilde{f} \in \mathbb{N}$ the two's complement representation of $F\left(2^{\ell}\right) \mod 2^{N\ell}$

1: mask ← **concat**$(1, \ell, N)$ //Precomputed
2: $\tilde{f}$ ← **polyToN**$(F(X), k, \ell)$
3: neg ← **rshift**$(\tilde{f}, k-1, N\ell)$
4: neg ← **and**$(\text{neg}, \text{mask}, N\ell)$ // Detect negative coefficients
5: tmp ← **mult**$(\text{neg}, 2^{\ell} - 2^{k}, N\ell, 32)$
6: $\tilde{f}$ ← **add**$(\tilde{f}, \text{tmp}, N\ell)$ // Two's complement representation of each coeff over
                                                                                    ℓ bits

7: neg ← **lshift**$(\text{neg}, \ell, N\ell)$
8: $\tilde{f}$ ← **sub**$(\tilde{f}, \text{neg}, N\ell)$ // Borrow propagation
9: **return** $\tilde{f}$

Remark 1. The value mask is always the same for a fixed scheme. Then, this integer can be precomputed and stored in Non-Volatile Memory (NVM).

Remark 2. The EVALUATION (Algorithm 1) returns the two's complement representation of $F\left(2^{\ell}\right) \mod 2^{N\ell}$. If $F\left(2^{\ell}\right) \geq 0$, then the returned value is equal to $F\left(2^{\ell}\right)$. Otherwise, the returned value is not equal to $F\left(2^{\ell}\right)$. This case occurs when the latest non-zero coefficient of $F(X)$ is negative.

To obtain the expected result after the Kronecker Substitution, the last case requires additional operations before the radix conversion. These additional operations are described in Sect. 3.2.

3.2   Radix Conversion with Negative Coefficient Representation

As mentioned in [2,12], the radix conversion has to be adapted since some coefficients have negative representations. Two issues arise with the negative coefficients:

1. The evaluation and the integer multiplication propagate borrow between the polynomial coefficients.
2. The negative evaluation algorithm returns the two's complement representation over $N\ell$ bits.

Borrow Between the Coefficients. The evaluation converts a polynomial to a packed integers representation. In the following of the Kronecker substitution, the obtained natural numbers are manipulated regardless the original polynomial structure. Therefore, borrows can be propagated between the coefficients. However in order to retrieve the expected polynomial result, the radix conversion must compensate the propagated borrows by propagating back carries.

Let $\tilde{r} = (\tilde{r}_0, \tilde{r}_1, \ldots, \tilde{r}_{N-1})_\ell \in \mathbb{N}$ be the integer that we want to convert to a polynomial, where for all i, $\tilde{r}_i$ is a two's complement representation over ℓ bits of an integer $-2^{\ell-1} < r_i < 2^{\ell-1}$. In order to propagate back the carries, we transform the negative coefficients to non-negative ones by adding a multiple of our modulus q: maxValue. More precisely, maxValue is the smallest multiple of q such that for all i, $-\text{maxValue} \leq r_i < \text{maxValue}$. Moreover with the parameters that we use in Sect. 5, we have $\text{maxValue} < 2^{\ell-1}$. Then, by adding maxValue we got:

- If $r_i < 0$, then $2^\ell \leq \tilde{r}_i + \text{maxValue} = 2^\ell + r_i + \text{maxValue} < 2^{\ell+1}$. Therefore a carry is propagated to $\tilde{r}_{i+1}$.
- If $r_i \geq 0$, then $\tilde{r}_i + \text{maxValue} = r_i + \text{maxValue} < 2^\ell$.

After adding maxValue, the values r_i are considered as natural numbers represented over ℓ bits. Then, the expected polynomial is obtained by using the radix conversion algorithm defined in Eq. 2 on $\tilde{r}$.

This negative to non-negative conversion is possible because the polynomial multiplication is done over $R_{q,\delta}$. Indeed after reduction modulo q, the added value maxValue is equal to 0.

Two's Complement Representation of the Evaluated Polynomial. The second issue is due to the two's complement representation of the evaluated polynomial.

Let $F(X) = f_0 + \ldots + f_{N-1}X^{N-1} \in R_{q,\delta}^-$ of degree $N-1$ and $\ell \in \mathbb{N}$. Then Algorithm 1 returns the integer $f \leftarrow \text{EVALUATION}(F(X), k, \ell)$, that is the two's complement representation of $F(2^\ell) \mod 2^{N\ell}$. Two cases are to be distinguished:

- $f_{N-1} > 0$, then $f = F(2^\ell) \in \mathbb{N}$.
- $f_{N-1} < 0$, then $f = 2^{N\ell} + F(2^\ell)$ is the two's complement of $F(2^\ell) \mod 2^{N\ell}$.

Only the second case will lead to a wrong result after the modular multiplication. Indeed, let $g \in \mathbb{N}$ and $f = 2^{N\ell} + F(2^\ell)$ we got:

$$r \mod (2^{N\ell} + \delta) = fg \mod (2^{N\ell} + \delta) = 2^{N\ell}g + F(2^\ell)g \mod (2^{N\ell} + \delta)$$
$$\neq F(2^\ell)g \mod (2^{N\ell} + \delta)$$

Then depending on δ, we must add or subtract g to r before radix conversion:

- $\delta = 1 : 2^{N\ell}g \mod (2^{N\ell} + 1) = -g \mod (2^{N\ell} + 1)$, then

$$r + g \mod (2^{N\ell} + 1) = F(2^\ell)g \mod (2^{N\ell} + 1)$$

- $\delta = -1 : 2^{N\ell}g \mod (2^{N\ell} - 1) = g \mod (2^{N\ell} - 1)$, then

$$r - g \mod (2^{N\ell} - 1) = F(2^\ell)g \mod (2^{N\ell} - 1)$$

Previously, we supposed that at most one polynomial can have negative coefficients. In case of lattice-based schemes, this is always the case.

Algorithm 2. RADIXCONV

Input: $r, g, \mathtt{maxValue} \in \mathbb{N}$, and $\mathtt{sign} \in \{0, 1\}$
Output: $R(X) \in \mathbb{N}[X]/(X^N + \delta)$
 1: $\mathtt{max} \leftarrow \mathbf{concat}(\mathtt{maxValue}, \ell, N)$ //Can be precomputed
 2: **if** $\mathtt{sign}$ eq 1 **then**
 3:     **if** δ eq 1 **then** $r \leftarrow \mathbf{add}(r, g, N\ell)$ // To handle negative last coeff
 4:     **else** $r \leftarrow \mathbf{sub}(r, g, N\ell)$
 5: **else**
 6:     **if** δ eq 1 **then** $\mathtt{dummy} \leftarrow \mathbf{add}(r, g, N\ell)$ // For isochrony
 7:     **else** $\mathtt{dummy} \leftarrow \mathbf{sub}(r, g, N\ell)$
 8: **end if**
 9: $r \leftarrow \mathbf{add}(r, \mathtt{max}, N\ell)$ // Add $\mathtt{maxValue}$ to each coefficient
10: $R(X) \leftarrow \text{RADIXCONV}_{\geq 0}(r)$

3.3 Multiplication in $R_{q,\delta}$ Using Coprocessor

Sections 3.1 and 3.2 are used to obtain a polynomial multiplication algorithm in $R_{q,\delta}$ using, mainly, a packed integer representation. More precisely, except for the modular reductions modulo q, the operations are done using this representation. All operations performed on the packed integers representation can be achieved with coprocessor as defined in Sect. 2.

The Polynomial Multiplication in $R_{q,\delta}$ algorithm is described in Algorithm 3. In the following section we determine how to perform modular reductions modulo q using packed integers representation.

Algorithm 3. POLYNOMIAL MULTIPLICATION IN $R_{q,\delta}$

Input: $(F(X), G(X)) \in (R_{q,\delta}^-, R_{q,\delta})$ of degree $N - 1$. Let $k, \ell, q \in \mathbb{N}$ where $\ell > k$, and
    $\mathtt{maxValue}$ defined as above.
Output: $R(X) = F(X)G(X) \in R_{q,\delta}$
 1: $f \leftarrow \text{EVALUATION}(F(X), k, \ell)$
 2: $G\left(2^\ell\right) \leftarrow \text{EVALUATION}_{\geq 0}(G(X), k, \ell)$
 3: $r \leftarrow \mathbf{modMult}(f, G\left(2^\ell\right), N\ell, N\ell, 2^{N\ell} + \delta)$
 4: $b \leftarrow \mathbf{sign}(F[N-1])$ // if $F_{N-1} < 0$ then $b = 1$, otherwise $b = 0$.
 5: $R(X) \leftarrow \text{RADIXCONV}(r, G\left(2^\ell\right), \mathtt{maxValue}, b)$
 6: $R(X) \leftarrow R(X) \bmod q$ // Any modular reduction
 7: **return** $R(X)$

---

4 Reducing Coefficients Modulo q

In this section we show how to perform reduction modulo q using packed integers representation. As mentioned previously, such representation allows to repurpose existing RSA/ECC coprocessor.

Let $r = (r_0, \ldots, r_{N-1})_\ell \in \mathbb{N}$. In our context, r is obtained after polynomial evaluation and modular integer multiplication. Moreover, each r_i is such that for all i, $0 \le r_i < 2\texttt{maxValue}$ like in Sect. 3.2.

In the following we denote by *simultaneous reduction* the process of reducing all the $r_i \mod q$ by performing operations on r.

4.1 Power-of-Two Modulus

Some lattice-based schemes, like NTRU [8] and Saber [10], use a power-of-two modulus. In this context, the simultaneous reduction is simply achieved with the following logical AND: $r \,\&\, \textbf{concat}(q-1, \ell, N)$.

4.2 Prime Modulus

In this section we adapt the Barrett reduction, introduced in [4], to perform simultaneous reduction.

The main idea is to precompute an approximation of a division and use it to perform modular reduction. Let $\alpha, \beta \in \mathbb{Z}$ and $a \in \mathbb{N}$ be an integer to reduce modulo $q \in \mathbb{N}$ of bit-length k. Barrett reduction precomputes $m = \left\lfloor \frac{2^{k+\alpha}}{q} \right\rfloor$ and computes $a' = a - [((a >> (k+\beta)) \cdot m) >> (\alpha - \beta)]\, q$.

Note that when $\alpha = \beta$, it becomes $a' = a - [a >> (k+\beta)] \cdot m \cdot q$, so that only one shift and one multiplication is performed ($m \cdot q$ is precomputed).

The result a' is equal to $a \mod q + tq$ where $0 \le t < \left\lfloor \frac{a}{q} \right\rfloor$. Note that a better bound on t can be obtained, depending on α and β. Further details on the Barrett algorithms are given in [15].

Algorithm 4 describes the simultaneous Barrett reduction, where logical ANDs are use to avoid overflow of coefficient $i+1$ on coefficient i after a shift.

Algorithm 4. SIMULT. BARRETT$_{\alpha,\beta}$

Input: $r = (r_0, \ldots, r_{N-1})_\ell \in \mathbb{N}$. Let $q \in \mathbb{N}$ of bit-length k and $m = \left\lfloor \frac{2^{k+\alpha}}{q} \right\rfloor$.

Output: $r' = (r'_0, \ldots, r'_{N-1})_\ell \in \mathbb{N}$, all r_i are reduced with BARRETT reduction

1: $\texttt{mask} \leftarrow \textbf{concat}(2^{\ell-\alpha+\beta} - 1, \ell, N)$ // Can be precomputed
2: $\texttt{mask}' \leftarrow \textbf{concat}(2^{\ell-k-\beta} - 1, \ell, N)$ // Can be precomputed
3: $\texttt{tmp} \leftarrow \textbf{rshift}(r, k + \beta, N\ell)$
4: $\texttt{tmp} \leftarrow \textbf{and}(\texttt{tmp}, \texttt{mask}', N\ell)$
5: $\texttt{tmp} \leftarrow \textbf{mult}(\texttt{tmp}, m, N\ell, 32)$ // Mult between a word and a large integer
6: $\texttt{tmp} \leftarrow \textbf{rshift}(\texttt{tmp}, \alpha - \beta, N\ell)$
7: $\texttt{tmp} \leftarrow \textbf{and}(\texttt{tmp}, \texttt{mask}, N\ell)$
8: $\texttt{tmp} \leftarrow \textbf{mult}(\texttt{tmp}, q, N\ell, 32)$ // Mult between a word and a large integer
9: $r' \leftarrow \textbf{sub}(r, \texttt{tmp}, N\ell)$
10: **return** r'

Final Reduction. Using the simultaneous Barrett Algorithm 4, the returned result $r' = (r'_0, \ldots, r'_{N-1})_\ell \in \mathbb{N}$ is such that, for all i, $r'_i = r_i \mod q + t_i q$. With the parameters sets that we use in Sect. 5, for all i, $t_i \in \{0, 1, 2\}$.

Let k and c such that $q = 2^k - c$. Then $r'_i \geq 2q$ if and only if $r'_i + 2c$ has its $(k+1)$-th bit equal to one. This fact is used in Algorithm 5 to detect and subtract q to coefficients $\geq 2q$ in a packed integers representation.

After using the Algorithm 5, the r''_i are bounded by $2q$. In that case, this algorithm can be adapted replacing $2c$ by c (line 1) and $k + 1$ by k (line 3). It follows that q is subtracted from each $r''_i \geq q$. Afterwards, each r''_i is necessary lower than q.

Algorithm 5. SIMULT. CONDITIONAL SUBTRACTION

Input: $r' = (r'_0, \ldots, r'_{N-1})_\ell$ with all $0 \leq r'_i < 3q$, where $q = 2^k - c$, $\ell, N \in \mathbb{N}$.

Output: $r'' = (r''_0, \ldots, r''_{N-1})_\ell$ with all $0 \leq r''_i < 2q$

1: $(\texttt{C}, \texttt{mask}) \leftarrow (\textbf{concat}(2c, \ell, N), \textbf{concat}(1, \ell, N))$ //Can be precomputed
2: $\texttt{tmp} \leftarrow \textbf{add}(r', \texttt{C}, N\ell)$ //Raised the $k + 1$-th bit in each coeff
3: $\texttt{tmp} \leftarrow \textbf{rshift}(\texttt{tmp}, k + 1, N\ell)$ // Move the $k + 1$-th bit to position 0 in each coeff
4: $\texttt{tmp} \leftarrow \textbf{and}(\texttt{tmp}, \texttt{mask}, N\ell)$ // Detect the coeff $\geq 2q$
5: $\texttt{tmp} \leftarrow \textbf{mult}(\texttt{tmp}, q, N\ell, 32)$ // Mult between a word and a large integer
6: $r'' \leftarrow \textbf{sub}(r', \texttt{tmp}, N\ell)$ // Subtract q to each coeff $\geq 2q$
7: **return** r''

4.3 Modular Polynomial Multiplication Using Coprocessor

Algorithm 6 performs polynomial multiplication in $R_{q,\delta}$ using operations on packed integers representation. All operations performed on this representation can be achieved with coprocessor as defined in Sect. 2.

Algorithm 6. MODULAR POLYNOMIAL MULTIPLICATION

Input: $(F(X), G(X)) \in (R_{q,\delta}^-, R_{q,\delta})$ of degree $N - 1$. Let $k, \ell, q \in \mathbb{N}$ where $\ell > k$, and maxValue defined as above.

Output: $R(X) = F(X)G(X) \in R_{q,\delta}$

1: max ← concat(maxValue, ℓ, N)   // Precomputed
2: $(f, G(2^\ell)) \leftarrow (\text{EVALUATION}(F(X), \ell), \text{EVALUATION}_{\geq 0}(G(X), \ell))$
3: $r \leftarrow \text{modMult}(f, G(2^\ell), N\ell, N\ell, 2^{N\ell} \pm \delta)$
4: $b \leftarrow \text{sign}(f[N - 1])$
5: **if** b eq 1 **then**
6:    **if** δ eq 1 **then** $r \leftarrow \text{sub}(r, G(2^\ell), N\ell)$ // To handle negative last coeff
7:    **else** $r \leftarrow \text{add}(r, G(2^\ell), N\ell)$
8: **else**
9:    **if** δ eq 1 **then** dummy ← $\text{sub}(r, G(2^\ell), N\ell)$ // For isochrony
10:    **else** dummy ← $\text{add}(r, G(2^\ell), N\ell)$
11: **end if**
12: $r \leftarrow \text{add}(r, \text{max}, N\ell)$ //Negative to non negative representation for all r_i'
13: **if** q eq 2^k **then**
14:    mask' ← concat($2^k - 1, \ell, N$)
15:    $r \leftarrow \text{and}(r, \text{mask}', N\ell)$
16: **else**
17:    $r \leftarrow$ SIMULT. BARRETT(r)
18:    $r \leftarrow$ SIMULT. COND. SUB.(r, ℓ, N) Can be applied twice if some $r_i \geq 2q$
19: **end if**
20: $R(X) \leftarrow \text{RADIXCONV}_{\geq 0}(r)$
21: **return** $R(X)$

The MODULAR POLYNOMIAL MULTIPLICATION Algorithm 6 works as follows:

1. Line 2: Polynomial evaluations defined in Eq. 1 and Algorithm 1.
2. Line 3: Modular integer multiplication modulo $2^{N\ell} + \delta$ of the evaluated polynomials.
3. Line 4 to 11: Handle the two's complement representation of the evaluated polynomial; see Sect. 3.2.
4. Line 12: Convert the negative representation to non negative one; see Sect. 3.2. This operation allows to perform simultaneous reduction mod q and radix conversion.
5. Line 13 to 19: Perform simultaneous reduction mod q. This ensures that the polynomial result has coefficients reduced mod q.
6. Line 20: Radix conversion defined in Eq. 2 to obtain a polynomial result.

5   Applications and Results

In this section, after some preliminaries, we present the component on which we perform our experiments and the results obtained by implementing the Modular Polynomial Multiplication (MPM), see Algorithm 6, and another polynomial multiplication depending of the evaluated scheme. The evaluated lattice-based algorithms are Kyber, NTRU, and Saber. Results for Dilithium, that need additional tweaks to be competitive on our target, are given in Appendix C.

5.1   Background

NTT. NTT is an algorithm allowing to perform fast polynomial multiplication in $R_{q,1}$ [18]. Given a and $b \in R_{q,1}$, $a \times b$ is computed as $\mathrm{NTT}^{-1}(\mathrm{NTT}(a) \circ \mathrm{NTT}(b))$, where $\circ$ is the coefficient-wise multiplication.

Theoretically, NTT has the best asymptotic complexity for multiplication in $R_{q,1}$. However, in constrained environments (e.g. smart cards), devices may have dedicated hardware to perform fast large-integer arithmetic. In this context, NTT can be outperformed by an algorithm relying on integer arithmetic, even if its theoretical complexity is worse than NTT.

Evaluation Point. In our context the Karatsuba subdivision requires to increase the size of the evaluation point by 1 bit at each subdivision. It is due to the computation $(f_I + f_S)(g_I + g_S)$. Indeed, this computation is performed on integers of length twice as small but with values twice as large.

In the following results, the evaluation point is chosen to take into account the negative coefficients and the Karatsuba subdivisions.

Polynomial Distribution. The following polynomial multiplications are performed between a polynomial $G(X) \in R_{q,\delta}$ and $F(X) \in R_{q,\delta}^-$. More precisely, the coefficients of $G(X)$ are sampled uniformly in $\{0, \dots, q-1\}$ and the coefficients of $F(X)$ are sampled in a distribution $\mathcal{D}_\sigma$. Using a distribution $\mathcal{D}_\sigma$, the coefficients are represented in $\{-\sigma, \dots, 0, \dots, \sigma\}$.

Masked Secret Polynomial. Most of the time the polynomial using the distribution $\mathcal{D}_\sigma$ is the secret polynomial. In some use cases, an embedded implementation must be strongly secured against side-channel attacks. One way to do this is to mask the secret data. To do so, we split the sensitive data into shares $x = x_1 + x_2$ mod q, where x_1, x_2 belongs to $\{0, \dots, q-1\}$, and then we process the operations on each share separately. In our context the value q is much larger than the secret distribution. Therefore, that implies we will manipulate larger secret data and then it increases the evaluation point. For some assessments, in order to consider this security requirement, we suppose that the polynomial $F(X)$ is defined over $R_{q,\delta}$ and its coefficients are sampled uniformly in $\{0, \dots, q-1\}$. In the following results, we denote this case by $\mathcal{U}_q$ distribution.

In the following results, we only specify the distribution of $F(X)$.

Target. Assessments are done on a smart card component using a 32-bit architecture. In the following we refer to this device as Component A. Due to intellectual properties reasons, the component name or a detailed description cannot be given. Then, we only give the main characteristics of Component A:

- Standard 32-bit instructions: add, sub, shifts, bitwise and, bitwise xor, bitwise or, etc. Each logical or arithmetic instruction is executed in 1 cycle. Data transfert from and to memory takes 2 cycles.
- No CPU multiplication, no CPU division.
- A coprocessor which handles bitwise AND, addition, modular addition, subtraction, modular subtraction, shifts, integer multiplication and modular Montgomery multiplication.

  To perform one operation, its opcode and the size and address of each operand are given to the coprocessor. It takes 15 cycles regardless of the operation or the size of the operands.

  Bitwise AND, addition, modular addition, subtraction, modular subtraction and shifts are executed in roughly $s/2$ cycles, where s is the number of 32-bit words of the largest operand.

  Integer multiplication and modular Montgomery multiplication are done in roughly $s_1 \cdot s_2/4$ cycles, where s_1 and s_2 are the size of operands in words.

Except for the bitwise AND, these operations are standard on such a coprocessor. The bitwise AND is less common but easy to add to a standard design.

The following results take into account a complete modular reduction. Moreover like the previous works [2,6,12,20], we assume that the inputs are already in the appropriate machine representation. This implies that the inputs are in:

- Polynomial representation for NTT, Karatsuba and schoolbook polynomial multiplication.
- Packed integers representation for the MPM algorithm.

5.2 Results

Kyber. Kyber [5] is a lattice-based KEM, selected by the NIST for standardization. The polynomial ring defined in Kyber is $R_{q,1} = \mathbb{Z}_q[X]/(X^N + 1)$, where $q = 3329$ and $N = 256$. The polynomial multiplication used in the specification is the NTT algorithm. In this context, we have implemented two polynomial multiplications:

- A NTT multiplication. It is adapted from the reference implementation, in order to use the hardware Montgomery multiplication. Tables of roots of unity have been recomputed to handle the Montgomery arithmetic with $R = 2^{32}$, the smallest handled by the coprocessor, instead of $R = 2^{16}$. In addition, the multiplication followed by a Montgomery reduction is replaced by a call to the coprocessor Montgomery multiplication. In Table 1 we present timings from the NTT's implementation.

Table 1. Kyber NTT cycles on Component A

	NTT	Pointwise	NTT^{-1}
Cycles	98k	40k	106k

- The modular polynomial multiplication (MPM) described in Algorithm 6. For this algorithm we consider two distributions for the polynomial $F(X)$:
  - $\mathcal{D}_3$. In this case the modular reduction modulo q is done using `Simult.Barrett`$_{11,0}$. In order to completely reduce the coefficients we perform 2 final subtractions using the technique described in Sect. 4.2.
  - $\mathcal{U}_q$. In this case the modular reduction modulo q is done using `Simult. Barrett`$_{10,10}$ and then an application of `Simult. Barrett`$_{13,-2}$. Afterwards, a final subtraction is performed using the technique described in Sect. 4.2.

In Table 2, we give the ℓ such that the evaluation point is 2^ℓ, the maximum value to convert negative coefficients to non-negative ones, the subdivision used and the number of cycles for MPM algorithms.

Table 2. Parameters and cost of one multiplication in $R_{q,1}$ for Kyber parameters

Distribution	ℓ	maxValue	Subdivision	Cycles MPM
$\mathcal{D}_3$	23	$3qn$	None	50k
$\mathcal{U}_q$	34	$q^2 n$	2 calls to Karatsuba	67k

Comparison. The previous results take into account one execution of MPM algorithm and each NTT routine. In order to compare NTT and MPM algorithms, we must not only compare `pointwise` routine with MPM algorithm. Indeed, we must also take into account calls to the NTT and NTT^{-1} routines. Then, in order to compare the two polynomial multiplication methods we must determine how many times each algorithm is called.

Table 3 describes the number of calls to NTT, `pointwise` multiplication and NTT^{-1} during the Key Generation, Encrypt and Decrypt routines. The number of calls depends on the Kyber's security parameters which are $k = 2/3/4$. Note that the number of pointwise matches the number of MPM calls.

Table 3. Number of call to NTT routines in Kyber

	NTT	Pointwise/MPM	NTT^{-1}
Key Gen.	$2k$	k^2	0
Encrypt	k	$k^2 + k$	$k + 1$
Decrypt	k	k	1

In order to fairly compare NTT and MPM algorithms we use:

- The official specification of Kyber for the NTT algorithm. The private and public keys are stored in the NTT domain.
- A tweaked version of Kyber for the MPM algorithm. The private and public keys are not stored in the NTT domain. Therefore, we do not need to apply NTT^{-1} to perform MPM algorithm.

The MPM algorithm is called with the $\mathcal{U}_q$ distribution parameters (Table 4).

Table 4. Cycle count for all multiplications in Kyber for the $\mathcal{U}_q$ distribution parameters

	Total cycles NTT	Total cycles MPM	Ratio (NTT/MPM)
Key Gen. $k = 2$	552k	**268k**	2
Encrypt $k = 2$	754k	**402k**	1.9
Decrypt $k = 2$	382k	**134k**	2.9
Key Gen. $k = 3$	948k	**603k**	1.6
Encrypt $k = 3$	1198k	**804k**	1.5
Decrypt $k = 3$	520k	**201k**	2.6
Key Gen. $k = 4$	1424k	**1072k**	1.3
Encaps $k = 4$	1722k	**1340k**	1.3
Decrypt $k = 4$	658k	**268k**	2.5

Saber and NTRU

Saber. Saber [10] is a lattice-based KEM finalist of the NIST standardization. The polynomial ring used in Saber is $R_{q,1} = \mathbb{Z}_q[X]/(X^N + 1)$, where $N = 256$ and $q = 8192 = 2^{13}$. In this work we consider two distributions for $F(X)$:

- $\mathcal{D}_5$. Other distributions are used in Saber. However we only describe the worst one for the MPM algorithm.
- $\mathcal{U}_q$.

Since the modulus is a power of two, the reductions are achieved using a bitwise AND with the appropriate mask.

NTRU. NTRU [8] is also a KEM finalist of the NIST competition. The polynomial ring used in NTRU is $R_{q,-1} = \frac{\mathbb{Z}_q[X]}{(X^N - 1)}$. The modulus q and the value N depends on the security parameters. In this work we only consider NTRU HPS 1 parameters, where $N = 509$ and $q = 2048 = 2^{11}$.

The value of N does not allow to easily make subdivisions. To overcome this issue, we work on polynomials with $\tilde{N} = 512$ coefficients where the latest coefficients are equal to 0.

In this work, we consider only a $\mathcal{U}_q$ distribution. Since q is a power of two, the modular reductions are performed with a bitwise AND.

Comparison. The Saber and NTRU MPM algorithms are compared with the polynomial multiplication used in their reference implementations.

- Saber: A combination of a 4-way Toom-Cook and Karatsuba algorithms.
- NTRU: A schoolbook multiplication.

The polynomial multiplication of the reference implementations are achieved with the 32 bits coprocessor multiplication. The Table 5 describes the obtained results on Component A.

Table 5. Parameters and cost of one multiplication in $R_{q,\delta}$ for Saber and NTRU parameters

Distribution	ℓ	maxValue	Subdivision	Cycl.MPM	Cycl. ref.
Saber					
$\mathcal{D}_5$	25	$5qn$	None	47k	1405k
$\mathcal{U}_q$	36	q^2n	2 calls to Karatsuba	61k	1405k
NTRU					
$\mathcal{U}_q$	34	q^2n	3 calls to Karatsuba	173k	17256k

6 Conclusion

We pursue the previous works that optimize lattice-based schemes, by re-purposing today's RSA/ECC coprocessor. We propose an algorithm, MPM, that performs modular polynomial multiplication using coprocessor instructions. It handles modular reductions and negative coefficients during polynomial multiplication.

We assess in practice the MPM algorithm for some NIST lattice-based finalists. This assessment is done on a component that bases the asymmetric cryptographic efficiency on its RSA/ECC coprocessor. The MPM algorithm is compared to software polynomial multiplications, as NTT or Karatsuba. On this component, MPM algorithm brings a significant speed-up.

Hence, re-purposing standard asymmetric coprocessor to speed-up lattice-based cryptography is of interest, especially in a context of hybrid deployment.

Acknowledgements. We would like to thank the reviewers for the valuable comments and suggestions, which helped us in improving the quality of the article.

A   Examples for Section 2.3

Example 3 (Evaluation). Let $F(X) = 2X^2 + X + 3$ then, $F(2^8) = \text{0x020103} = \text{EVALUATION}_{\geq 0}(F(X), 2, 8)$

Example 4 (Radix Conversion). Let $f = \text{0x020103}$. Then $F(X) = 2X^2 + X + 3 = \text{RADIXCONV}_{\geq 0}(f)$.

Example 5 (Kronecker Multiplication). Let $F(X) = 2X^2 + X + 3$ and $G(X) = X^2 + 1$. Then,

$$F(2^8) = \text{0x020103} = \text{EVALUATION}_{\geq 0}(F(X), 2, 8)$$
$$G(2^8) = \text{0x010001} = \text{EVALUATION}_{\geq 0}(G(X), 2, 8)$$

Then evaluations are multiplied: $r = F(2^8)G(2^8) = \text{0x201050103}$. Finally, we get $R(X) = \text{RADIXCONV}_{\geq 0}(r) = 2X^4 + X^3 + 5X^2 + X + 3$.

B   Example for Sect. 3.1

Example 6 (Evaluation with Negative Coefficients). Let $F(X) = 3X^2 - 2X + 2$, where all the coefficients are encoded with a two's complement representation over $k = 4$ bits. Let $N = 3$ and $\ell = 8$. The expected result is $F(2^8) = \text{0x02FE02}$. This is obtained with EVALUATION$(F(X), k, \ell)$:

1. mask $\leftarrow$ **concat**$(1, 8, 3) = \text{0x010101}$
2. $\tilde{f} \leftarrow$ **polyToN**$(F(X), 4, 8) = \text{0x030E02}$
3. neg $\leftarrow$ **rshift**$(\tilde{f}, 4 - 1, 3 \times 8) = \text{0x0061C0}$
4. neg $\leftarrow$ **and**(neg, mask, 3×8) $= \text{0x000100}$
5. tmp $\leftarrow$ **mult**(neg, $2^8 - 2^4, 3 \times 8, 32$) $= \text{0x00F000}$
6. $\tilde{f} \leftarrow$ **add**$(\tilde{f}, \text{tmp}, 3 \times 8) = \text{0x03FE02}$
7. neg $\leftarrow$ **lshift**(neg, $8, 3 \times 8$) $= \text{0x010000}$
8. $F(2^8) \leftarrow$ **sub**$(\tilde{f}, \text{neg}, 3 \times 8) = \text{0x02FE02}$

C   Results for Dilithium

Dilithium [11] is a lattice-based signature, selected by the NIST for standardization. The polynomial ring defined in Dilithium is $R_{q,1} = \mathbb{Z}_q[X]/(X^N + 1)$, where $q = 8380417$ and $N = 256$. Like Kyber, the specification specified the use of NTT polynomial multiplication. Therefore, we have implemented two polynomial multiplications:

- A NTT multiplication. To this end, we adapt the reference implementation. Tables of roots of unity are recomputed to get non-negative values and multiplications followed by a Montgomery reduction in the reference code are replaced by a call to the hardware Montgomery multiplication (Table 6).

Table 6. Dilithium NTT cycles on Component A

	NTT	Pointwise	NTT^{-1}
Cycles	114k	15k	128k

- MPM algorithm. Two distributions for polynomial coefficients are considered:
    - $\mathcal{D}_1$. The polynomial sampled in this distribution is always not sensitive to side-channel attacks. Therefore, we never need to mask it. The modular reduction modulo q is done by calling SIMULT. QUOTIENT APPROXIMATION REDUCTION with $J'_\ell = \{23\}$ and a final subtraction is performed using the technique described in Sect. 4.2.
    - $\mathcal{U}_q$. The modular reduction modulo q is done by calling SIMULT. QUOTIENT APPROXIMATION REDUCTION algorithm with $J'_\ell = \{23, 33\}$ and afterwards by calling it twice with $J'_\ell = \{23\}$. A final subtraction is performed using the technique described in Sect. 4.2.

Many other distributions are used in Dilithium. For the sake of clarity, we describe only the worst ones for MPM algorithm (Table 7).

Table 7. Parameters and cost of one multiplication in $R_{q,1}$ for Dilithium parameters

Distribution	ℓ	maxValue	Subdivision	Cycles MPM
$\mathcal{D}_1$	32	$60q$	None	48k
$\mathcal{U}_q$	57	q^2n	3 calls to Karatsuba	146k

Comparison. Like Kyber, not every NTT-based multiplication uses all the three algorithms NTT, pointwise and NTT^{-1}.

Table 8 presents the number of calls to NTT, pointwise multiplication and NTT^{-1} depending on the Dilithium's security parameters which are $(k,l) = (4,4)/(6,5)/(8,7)$. In this operation count we suppose that during the sign algorithm there is no rejection sampling. Note that the number of pointwise matches the number of MPM calls. The pointwise operations in boldface correspond to the polynomial multiplication with one polynomial in $\mathcal{D}_1$.

Table 8. Number of call to NTT routines in Dilithium

	NTT	Pointwise/MPM	NTT^{-1}
Key Gen.	l	lk	k
Sign	$2l + 2k + 1$	$lk + l + \mathbf{2k}$	$l + 3k$
Verify	$l + k + 1$	$lk + \mathbf{k}$	k

Like Kyber, in order to compare fairly NTT and MPM algorithms we use:

- The official specification of Dilithium for the NTT algorithm. The public key is stored in the NTT domain.
- A tweaked version of Dilithium for the MPM algorithm. The public keys is not stored in the NTT domain. Therefore, we do not need to apply NTT^{-1} to perform MPM algorithm.

Moreover, for the MPM algorithm, the multiplication in boldface implies a polynomial sampled in $\mathcal{D}_1$ and the other ones are performed with a polynomial sampled in a $\mathcal{U}_q$ distribution.

Table 9. Cycle count for all multiplications in Dilithium for the $\mathcal{U}_q$ distribution parameters

	Total cycles NTT	Total cycles MPM	Ratio (NTT/MPM)
Key Gen. $(k,l) = (4,4)$	**1208k**	2336k	0.5
Sign $(k,l) = (4,4)$	4406k	**2912k**	1.5
Verify $(k,l) = (4,4)$	**1838k**	2528k	0.7
Key Gen. $(k,l) = (6,5)$	**1788k**	4380k	0.4
Sign $(k,l) = (6,5)$	6271k	**5196k**	1.2
Verify $(k,l) = (6,5)$	**2676k**	4668k	0.6
Key Gen. $(k,l) = (8,7)$	**2662k**	8176k	0.3
Sign $(k,l) = (8,7)$	**8687k**	9280k	0.9
Verify $(k,l) = (8,7)$	**3808k**	8560k	0.4

In this context, MPM algorithm is almost less efficient than NTT. However, we can combine NTT and MPM algorithms to obtain a faster Sign and Verify routines. Indeed, one can perform the multiplication which implies a polynomial sampled $\mathcal{D}_1$ using the MPM algorithm and the others multiplication using NTT algorithm. By combining these two multiplications, we avoid a lot of NTT and NTT^{-1} transformation which ensures an efficient polynomial multiplication. Moreover, this combination is achieved without changing the Dilithium specification.

In Table 10 the ratio is between the best algorithm in Table 9 (result in bold face) over the combination of NTT and MPM algorithms.

Table 10. Cycle count for all multiplications in Dilithium using the $\mathcal{U}_q$ and $\mathcal{D}_1$ distribution parameters

	Best in Table 9	Total cycles NTT + MPM	Ratio
Sign $(k,l) = (4,4)$	2912k	**1784k**	1.6
Verify $(k,l) = (4,4)$	1838k	**1400k**	1.3
Sign $(k,l) = (6,5)$	5196k	**2604k**	2
Verify $(k,l) = (6,5)$	2676k	**2076k**	1.3
Sign $(k,l) = (8,7)$	8687k	**3766k**	2.3
Verify $(k,l) = (8,7)$	3808k	**3046k**	1.25

References

1. Alagic, G., et al.: Status report on the third round of the NIST post-quantum cryptography standardization process. Technical report, National Institute of Standards and Technology (2022). https://doi.org/10.6028/NIST.IR.8413
2. Albrecht, M.R., Hanser, C., Hoeller, A., Pöppelmann, T., Virdia, F., Wallner, A.: Implementing RLWE-based schemes using an RSA co-processor. IACR Trans. Cryptograph. Hardw. Embed. Syst. 169–208 (2019). https://doi.org/10.13154/tches.v2019.i1.169-208
3. ANSSI: Technical position paper - ANSSI views on the Post-Quantum Cryptography transition. https://www.ssi.gouv.fr/publication/anssi-views-on-the-post-quantum-cryptography-transition/
4. Barrett, P.: Implementing the Rivest Shamir and Adleman public key encryption algorithm on a standard digital signal processor. In: Odlyzko, A.M. (ed.) CRYPTO 1986. LNCS, vol. 263, pp. 311–323. Springer, Heidelberg (1987). https://doi.org/10.1007/3-540-47721-7_24
5. Bos, J., et al.: CRYSTALS - Kyber: a CCA-Secure module-lattice-based KEM. In: 2018 IEEE European Symposium on Security and Privacy (EuroS&P), pp. 353–367 (2018). https://doi.org/10.1109/EuroSP.2018.00032
6. Bos, J.W., Renes, J., van Vredendaal, C.: Post-quantum cryptography with contemporary co-processors. USENIX (2021). https://www.usenix.org/system/files/sec22summer_bos.pdf
7. BSI: Migration zu Post-Quanten-Kryptografie - Handlungsempfehlungen des BSI. https://www.bsi.bund.de/SharedDocs/Downloads/DE/BSI/Krypto/Post-Quanten-Kryptografie.pdf

8. Chen, C., et al.: NTRU (2020). https://ntru.org/
9. Chinese Association For Cryptography Research: National Cryptographic Algorithm Design Competition (2018). https://www.cacrnet.org.cn/site/content/838.html
10. D'Anvers, J.-P., Karmakar, A., Sinha Roy, S., Vercauteren, F.: Saber: module-LWR based key exchange, CPA-secure encryption and CCA-secure KEM. In: Joux, A., Nitaj, A., Rachidi, T. (eds.) AFRICACRYPT 2018. LNCS, vol. 10831, pp. 282–305. Springer, Cham (2018). https://doi.org/10.1007/978-3-319-89339-6_16
11. Ducas, L., et al.: CRYSTALS-Dilithium: a lattice-based digital signature scheme. IACR Trans. Cryptograph. Hardw. Embed. Syst. **2018**(1), 238–268 (2018). https://doi.org/10.13154/tches.v2018.i1.238-268
12. Greuet, A., Montoya, S., Renault, G.: On using RSA/ECC coprocessor for ideal lattice-based key exchange. In: Bhasin, S., De Santis, F. (eds.) COSADE 2021. LNCS, vol. 12910, pp. 205–227. Springer, Cham (2021). https://doi.org/10.1007/978-3-030-89915-8_10
13. Harvey, D.: Faster polynomial multiplication via multipoint Kronecker substitution. J. Symb. Comput. **44**(10), 1502–1510 (2009). https://doi.org/10.1016/j.jsc.2009.05.004
14. Kronecker, L.: Grundzüge einer arithmetischen theorie der algebraischen grössen. (abdruck einer festschrift zu herrn e. e. kummers doctor-jubiläum, 10. september 1881.). J. für die reine angewandte Math. **92**, 1–122 (1882)
15. Menezes, A.J., Van Oorschot, P.C., Vanstone, S.A.: Handbook of Applied Cryptography. CRC Press, Boca Raton (2018)
16. Moody, D.: Post-quantum cryptography NIST's plan for the future (2016). https://csrc.nist.gov/CSRC/media/Projects/Post-Quantum-Cryptography/documents/pqcrypto-2016-presentation.pdf
17. Moody, D., et al.: Status report on the second round of the NIST post-quantum cryptography standardization process. Technical report, National Institute of Standards and Technology (2020). https://doi.org/10.6028/NIST.IR.8309
18. Nussbaumer, H.J.: Number theoretic transforms. In: Nussbaumer, H.J. (ed.) Fast Fourier Transform and Convolution Algorithms. Springer Series in Information Sciences, vol. 2, pp. 211–240. Springer, Heidelberg (1982). https://doi.org/10.1007/978-3-642-81897-4_8
19. Shor, P.W.: Polynomial-time algorithms for prime factorization and discrete logarithms on a quantum computer. SIAM J. Comput. **26**(5), 1484–1509 (1997). https://doi.org/10.1137/S0097539795293172
20. Wang, B., Gu, X., Yang, Y.: Saber on ESP32. In: Conti, M., Zhou, J., Casalicchio, E., Spognardi, A. (eds.) ACNS 2020. LNCS, vol. 12146, pp. 421–440. Springer, Cham (2020). https://doi.org/10.1007/978-3-030-57808-4_21

T3E: A Practical Solution to Trusted Time in Secure Enclaves

Gilang Mentari Hamidy$^{(\boxtimes)}$, Pieter Philippaerts , and Wouter Joosen

imec-DistriNet, KU Leuven, Leuven, Belgium
{gilang.hamidy,pieter.philippaerts,wouter.joosen}@kuleuven.be

Abstract. Time is used in secure systems to validate security properties. Consequently, it is vital to protect the integrity of time information. Intel SGX enables building secure applications inside a Trusted Execution Environment (TEE), called an *enclave*, isolated from the untrusted OS. However, accessing time information from the enclave remains challenging as the OS controls the system time. Previous versions of the SGX SDK provided the `sgx_get_trusted_time` function as an alternative to OS time. However, Intel removed the API in 2020, without providing an alternative. This paper examines trusted time challenges in SGX and presents TPM-based Trusted Time Extensions (T3E), a novel solution that builds on readily available hardware. T3E leverages TPM functionality to provide trusted time services in enclaves while protecting against common attacks. It offers better time granularity and lower latency than Intel's `sgx_get_trusted_time` implementation. Unlike related work, it does not rely on deprecated features or hardware/firmware modifications.

Keywords: Intel SGX · Trusted Time · Trusted Execution Environment

1 Introduction

Time information is essential in computer systems as it represents the frame of reference for events occurring in the real world. Specifically, in computer security, time is essential to implement secure validation operations, such as checking the lifetime of cryptographic keys, or timing out sessions for sensitive operations. A prominent example is checking the validity of a digital certificate, which requires time information to check whether the certificate is not expired when being used.

Applications running in a Trusted Execution Environment (TEE), such as Intel SGX, also need access to time information [2]. SGX allows third-party vendors to build their own trusted applications for their specific purposes. It introduces the concept of an *enclave*, which provides total isolation of the software running inside it. Developers build their applications using a traditional software development approach, by leveraging existing toolchains and application libraries.

© The Author(s), under exclusive license to Springer Nature Switzerland AG 2023
S. Li et al. (Eds.): NSS 2023, LNCS 13983, pp. 305–326, 2023.
https://doi.org/10.1007/978-3-031-39828-5_17

While SGX provides a Trusted Runtime (TRTS) for the trusted application, it has a main limitation: it does not provide support for operating system services. According to the SGX threat model, the operating system is untrusted. Therefore, trusted applications must explicitly express their desire to access any OS-related functions in their code through an *OCALL*, i.e., a call from the trusted application to the untrusted domain. The trusted application must treat information obtained from the untrusted domain with caution as it may have been tampered with to attack the trusted app.

Time is usually managed centrally by the operating system. Applications can use the time services that are provided by the OS to request the current time or measure time differences. As the operating system is untrusted in the SGX threat model, trusted applications cannot rely on conventional time services. Intel previously provided an API in their TRTS called `sgx_get_trusted_time` that acted as a secure alternative to regular time services. Yet, the `sgx_get_trusted_time` function was removed circa 2020 from the Intel SGX SDK 2.8 release for Linux, leaving enclaves with no secure option to get time information.

In this paper, we present TPM-based Trusted Time Extensions (T3E) as a solution to the trusted time problem in SGX. T3E combines Trusted Platform Module (TPM) hardware, which is readily available, with SGX to guarantee that the time is reliable from a point when it was securely provisioned. It can be used as a replacement for Intel's `sgx_get_trusted_time` function but offers a higher granularity, better performance, and a comparable degree of security. In contrast to related work, it does not rely on hardware or firmware modifications.

Section 2 provides a background on Intel SGX, Trusted Platform Modules, and Sect. 3 explores related work. We outline the design of our proposed T3E system in Sect. 4, and evaluate the security of our design in Sect. 5. Section 6 focuses on the implementation of the T3E system and presents benchmark results. Finally, Sect. 7 concludes the paper, summarizing our findings.

2   Background

This section gives an overview of the two main technologies used in T3E: TPM and SGX. Despite the fact that both TPM an SGX are TEE technologies, they both play a very different role. Therefore, it is common for a machine to support both SGX and TPM.

2.1   Intel SGX

Intel introduced Software Guard eXtensions (SGX, [13,19]) in 2013 as a novel technique to establish a Trusted Execution Environment (TEE) in user space, called a *secure enclave*. It provides user programs with a way to instantiate an isolated code and data region, which offers confidentiality, integrity, and authenticity. An enclave enables a program to have two different domains: the trusted part, where the processor enforces certain security guarantees, and the untrusted part, which is the regular code. SGX protects enclaves from external adversaries, including a malicious operating system on which the program executes. Since its debut, SGX has been incorporated into many consumer and server-grade processors.

SGX protects confidentiality by isolating the memory region used by the enclave in the *processor reserved memory*. This hardware-based enforcement protects an enclave's private data to be only accessible by itself. Meanwhile, the authenticity of an enclave is protected through an attestation mechanism, which uses a hardware-based private key as the root of trust. Finally, an enclave signature protects the integrity of an enclave. The processor checks the signature when loading the enclave into memory. Therefore, any modifications to the enclave code can be detected, and the processor will refuse to execute it.

2.2 Trusted Platform Module

A Trusted Platform Module (TPM) is a security device that enables computing platforms to establish trust. A TPM device provides essential cryptographic operations to perform integrity measurements, key storage and reporting [5]. It is isolated from the primary system, which ensures the trustworthiness of its cryptographic operations. TPM devices are commonly used as a root of trust in a secure system. Every TPM device must comply with the TPM specification [23], which defines the features that must be present, as well as the interface to access these features. However, the actual implementation of the device can vary.

The most common implementation of a TPM is via a discrete TPM chip. This low-powered device with limited computing power is connected to the processor via a hardware bus. Although it is dedicated to processing TPM requests, its throughput remains low. Firmware TPMs (fTPM, [7,20]) are TPMs that are implemented in firmware and use the main processor to handle cryptographic calculations. While they might theoretically be more prone to tampering, they offer much-improved performance, allow updates of the firmware code, and often support additional functionality beyond the use cases of a TPM. To enable an unlimited number of virtual machines to access TPM services, a hypervisor can create a virtual TPM (vTPM, [6]). vTPMs are software implementations that emulate the behavior of a regular TPM and are protected by the hypervisor's hardware boundaries.

2.3 Trusted Time Sources in Intel SGX

According to the threat model for SGX, the trusted code must treat all information obtained from outside of the enclave as untrusted unless the trust can be established through, for example, attestation. Meanwhile, the SGX instruction set does not provide programming primitives for system operations and services, such as access to a real-time clock. Hence, enclaves have to rely on external sources by performing an OCALL.

Early iterations of the SGX SDK provided a trusted service called the Platform Service Enclave (PSE, [15]), which offers services that are natively unavailable in the SGX instruction set. The PSE ran as a separate enclave to which the application enclave could establish a secure connection through local attestation. The PSE was the gateway for the application enclave to access Intel's *Converged Security and Management Engine* (CSME). CSME provided several trusted services, including a trusted time service and a monotonic counter service, which were made available to the application enclave via the PSE.

The Linux SGX SDK provided an API function to access the PSE services called `sgx_get_trusted_time` to obtain trusted time from the CSME. However, Intel removed this API in early 2020[1] from the SDK and eventually removed the PSE entirely. The removal of the PSE and its related services break all applications that rely on those services. Intel has not issued an official statement regarding the reason of the removal[2], and they provide no clear alternative.

Earlier research results rely on the existence of the `sgx_get_trusted_time` API in SGX [3,10,18,24,27,28]. Without a secure alternative to this deprecated function, it is unclear what the impact is on these previously published results. Other research based on SGX opts to utilize time from untrusted sources, such as the OS [26]. In this case, the time information is considered untrusted and may not be suitable to be used as part of a security primitive.

One straightforward approach to solve the trusted time problem is to call an external time service, such as an NTPSec server, whenever trusted time is needed. While this approach could work for some scenarios, it has some notable drawbacks. It will have a (much) higher latency, thus rendering it less effective in scenarios characterized by high loads. Moreover, the attack surface of a network-based channel is much larger compared to locally-sourced time information.

3   Related Work

Due to the availability of the `sgx_get_trusted_time` function in the SGX SDK, accessing trusted time inside enclaves has not been a major research topic in the past. Nonetheless, prior work exists where the authors aimed to replace the `sgx_get_trusted_time` function with solutions that offer better security properties or better performance characteristics.

Anwar et al. [4] discussed the importance and challenges of trusted time in a trusted application. In their follow-up research, they propose TimeSeal [3] as a solution to secure time-based primitives. TimeSeal offers a high-resolution clock by interpolating the trusted low-resolution clock through a trusted counting thread which counts the subticks per low-resolution trusted tick. Unfortunately, TimeSeal relies on SGX's `sgx_get_trusted_time` function, which renders this solution unusable in the current iteration of the SGX SDK.

---

[1] Removed as of Intel SGX SDK for Linux version 2.8 (https://github.com/intel/linux-sgx/releases/tag/sgx_2.8).

[2] A post on the Intel Developer Forum by a moderator suggests that the reason of the removal might be linked to the fact that the CSME is not available on server platforms, and due to licensing issues. https://community.intel.com/t5/Intel-Software-Guard-Extensions/The-delay-attack-towards-the-trusted-time/m-p/1343497.

Alder et al. [1] proposed a solution for a high-resolution timer inside an SGX enclave in combination with their Secure-Function-as-a-Service (S-FaaS) proposal as a cloud-based confidential computing platform. S-FaaS requires a trusted timer to reliably measure the resource usage that both the platform owner and user can trust.

S-FaaS adapted the approach proposed by Chen et al. [9] to create a reference clock inside an SGX enclave. The proposed solution uses a separate counter thread and uses the behavior of the Intel Transactional Synchronization Extension (TSX) that allows the enclave to detect an asynchronous exit event, which may interrupt the counter thread. While the S-FaaS solution may guarantee strict lower-bound timing, the time measurement is tied to processor clock speed rather than the actual real-world tick. It relies on Intel TSX to detect malicious attempts to manipulate the time measurement, but TSX has recently been disabled by Intel to mitigate a transient execution attack [16].

Liang et al. [17] proposed a trusted time service for SGX enclaves by creating a trusted channel between the hardware timer and the SGX enclave. This is achieved by implementing a custom handler for the System Management Interrupt (SMI) handler. This approach requires the system firmware to be updated, which Liang et al. evaluated by modifying the SMI handler for SeaBIOS, an open-source implementation of an x86 BIOS. The trusted channel implemented in the SMI handler allows SGX enclaves to obtain authenticated information from the hardware timer. However, this approach can be considered too intrusive for regular use as it requires modifying the firmware of commodity hardware.

Appendix A presents a more-detailed comparison of the related works with respect to each other and T3E. Unlike other solutions, T3E does not depend on uncommon or deprecated APIs, does not require custom hardware modifications, and does not rely on modified firmware, making T3E generally applicable.

4   Design

T3E is an open-source[3] secure time service for the Intel SGX platform. It relies on the TPM as the trusted time source and builds a trusted path between the TPM and the enclave. T3E leverages the specialized characteristics of the SGX and TPM trusted execution environments. It takes into account that the TPM is not designed to run user software and that the current version of SGX does not provide a viable trusted time source for software that requires it. Our goal is to provide applications with trusted time information even under high system load.

4.1   The TPM as a Time Source

While it is possible to utilize an external time service to provide time services to a trusted application, it is highly desirable to source the trusted time information

---

[3] https://github.com/DistriNet/T3E.

as close as possible to the running program. An external time authority, such as a trusted NTP server, adds additional latency that may reduce the system's performance and dependability. It also does not protect against delay attacks as the network packet still has to pass through the untrusted operating system. For this reason, we consider the TPM as the best choice available to support a trusted time service in an Intel SGX environment, which can provide a considerable performance benefit while preserving the trustworthiness of the time information.

The TPM provides a trusted time source independent from the machine's hardware clock. It tracks two separate counters: the *time* and the *clock*. The time is a value that contains the time in milliseconds since the TPM has been powered on. Meanwhile, the clock counts the milliseconds since the TPM epoch, i.e., when the TPM was powered on and initialized for the first time. While TPM time is ephemeral, the TPM records its clock periodically in non-volatile memory (NVRAM). The TPM provides a security guarantee that its clock is monotonously increasing.

The monotonic clock is primarily used by the TPM to perform the time-stamping required for attestation and authorization [8]. In addition to that, external users may request the TPM to produce attested time, in which external users can validate the authenticity of the time information from the TPM device.

4.2   Overview of T3E

The trust model in Fig. 1 shows all the components in the T3E architecture. The T3E component represents the implementation of the time service. It is located in the secure enclave, together with the code of the client application that uses the time service. The T3E component obtains the time information from the TPM, which is transmitted via an untrusted channel between the enclave and the TPM. The time information is validated by verifying it with the TPM chain of trust, which allows third parties to identify a genuine TPM device and attest and verify TPM-generated data using public key cryptography.

A TPM device possesses an *Endorsement Key* (EK) that is provisioned by the manufacturer. The EK is signed by the TPM manufacturer and acts as a certificate authority in the TPM public key infrastructure. The EK, however, cannot be used to sign data. Consequently, the TPM must derive a signing key from the EK, which is called the *Attestation Key* (AK). The AK can be used to sign information from the TPM.

T3E validates the authenticity of the time data from the TPM and stores it inside the protected enclave. The client application code, which resides in the same enclave, fully trusts the T3E library and its time information. T3E effectively acts as a trust proxy between the TPM and the client code and increases the availability of time data by caching it.

The TPM driver resides in the OS and is untrusted from the viewpoint of the enclave. Since confidentiality is not required in this trust model, the T3E and TPM are not required to establish an encrypted channel. Trust is established by attesting the TPM device to T3E during the provisioning phase.

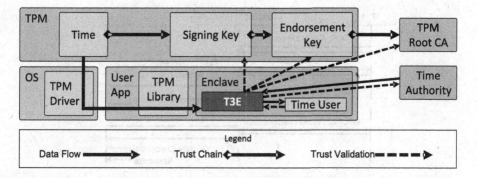

Fig. 1. Trust model for the T3E system. Components with a green background belong to the trusted domain. Components with a red background are untrusted. (Color figure online)

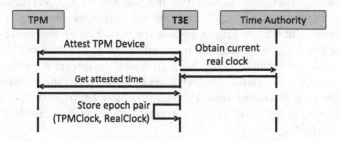

Fig. 2. TPM provisioning steps

Initialization of T3E requires access to an external time authority, for example, a trusted NTPSec server. The time authority does not have to be fast and will only be used sporadically to resynchronize.

4.3 Provisioning the Time Service

During the initialization process of the enclave, the T3E framework is required to be provisioned with credentials to access the TPM. Furthermore, T3E must receive the initial time information from an external trusted real-world clock as presented in Fig. 2.

The first step is to establish trust between T3E and the TPM by using a TPM attestation procedure. The steps of the attestation procedure are outlined in Fig. 3. The TPM device produces an attestation key that T3E can use to validate the data it receives from the TPM. It also generates a credential, which serves as proof that the TPM owns the endorsement key, thus proving that it is indeed a genuine device.

The TPM attestation procedure involves an untrusted party that may see the public key that is transferred between the TPM and T3E. However, only the TPM can produce the correct attestation information, which requires access to the private parts of the EK and the AK.

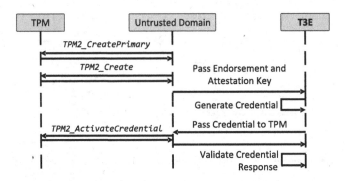

Fig. 3. TPM attestation steps

T3E needs to securely obtain the manufacturer's CA certificate for the attestation to work correctly. T3E should not automatically trust a certificate obtained from an untrusted source, such as the operating system certificate store. A simple approach is to attach the root certificate to the enclave binary, which is equivalent to certificate pinning. SGX provides the integrity assurance by validating the enclave's signature before launch. A more advanced approach is to transmit the root certificate from the manufacturer's infrastructure, as done in remote attestation protocols. The implementation of such a protocol is beyond the scope of this paper.

After verifying the TPM device, the next step is to obtain the current real-world time to serve as the epoch for T3E. An eligible trusted time source can be a trusted NTPSec server, which provides authenticated time information. Alternatively, an operator with direct access to the machine can manually provision the epoch time as part of the provisioning process.

The real-world clock epoch is paired with the first timestamp obtained from the TPM, thus constructing the epoch pair used by T3E. T3E uses this epoch pair to calculate the current time information by simply computing the elapsed time between the TPM time epoch and the current TPM time, and adding the elapsed time to the real clock epoch, resulting in the current real-world clock time. Pairing the TPM epoch with the real-world clock epoch is necessary because the TPM does not track real-world time. Instead, its time epoch starts when the TPM is initialized or started.

4.4 Refreshing the Internal Clock

T3E advances its internal clock by reading the TPM time periodically. The implementation can optimistically request the TPM time as often as possible and without delay. This ensures that the cache always contains the most recent time information. Algorithm 1 shows the ClockTick function to advance the internal clock of T3E. An infinite loop requests the current time from the TPM and processes the result.

Algorithm 1. Advance the internal clock when new time information is received from the TPM

Ensure: $epoch_{TPM} \neq \emptyset, epoch_{Clock} \neq \emptyset$
  $time \leftarrow \emptyset$
  procedure CLOCKTICK
  repeat
    $nonce \leftarrow$ GETRANDOM
    $timeMsg \leftarrow$ OCALL_GETTIME($nonce$)
    if VERIFYSIG($timeMsg.sig, tpmAK, nonce$)
  then
    $tpmtime \leftarrow timeMsg.time$
    else
    ERROR
    end if
    $time \leftarrow (tpmtime - epoch_{TPM}) + epoch_{Clock}$
  until terminates
  end procedure

Algorithm 2. The pseudo-code implementation of the GetTrustedTime function

Ensure: $time \neq \emptyset, c_{max} \neq \emptyset$
  $time_{thread} \leftarrow \emptyset$
  $c_{thread} \leftarrow \emptyset$
  procedure GETTRUSTEDTIME
    while $c_{thread} \geq c_{max} \wedge time_{thread} = time$
  do
    SLEEP
  end while
  if $time > time_{thread}$ **then**
    $time_{thread} \leftarrow time$
    $c_{thread} \leftarrow 0$
  end if
  $c_{thread} \leftarrow c_{thread} + 1$
  return $time_{thread}$
  end procedure

The `ClockTick` function calls the `TPM2_GetTime` function to obtain verified time information. To ensure the freshness of the time request, a random nonce is passed to the TPM and included in the signed time information. After successfully verifying the signature, the time information is updated. T3E calculates the delta between the TPM epoch and the current time, which gives the number of milliseconds since the previous synchronization with the time authority. Then, the epoch of the real-world clock is added to calculate the real-world time. This algorithm is implemented in a separate logical thread. It continuously updates the current time and stores it in enclave memory.

While the time is reported in milliseconds, the actual granularity of the time information is determined by the latency of the requests to the TPM. Depending on the type of TPM used, this latency can range from tens of milliseconds to hundreds of milliseconds, which is still an improvement over Intel's `sgx_get_trusted_time` with second granularity.

4.5 Processing Trusted Time Requests

Retrieving the current time information from the TPM quickly becomes a bottleneck, due to the latency introduced by the TPM. For this reason, T3E caches the information received from the TPM and allows a client application to reuse the same information multiple times.

Under normal circumstances, time information is received at regular intervals from the TPM. However, as the attacker has full access to the operating system and the TPM driver, they could delay or completely block time information from reaching T3E. In the absence of a trusted internal clock within the SGX environment, it is impossible to accurately measure the interval between two TPM messages.

To address this issue, T3E enforces a security policy that sets a maximum use count on cached time information before requiring a refreshed time value from the TPM. When a counter reaches a specific threshold, requests to T3E will block until a fresh message with time information has been received from the TPM. Whenever a new message from the TPM arrives, the use count is reset to 0.

The maximum use count is not uniform across different hardware configurations or workloads. The following formula can be used to calculate the use count limit:

$$c_{max} = \frac{\bar{t}_{tpm\_interval}}{\bar{t}_{usertime}}$$

where $\bar{t}_{tpm\_interval}$ is the average latency of the GetTPMTime function, and $\bar{t}_{usertime}$ is the average duration between time requests made by the client code.

The average latency and the average duration between time requests should be measured by benchmarking the enclave code on a target machine. Therefore, it is preferable to perform the measurement during the provisioning process, in order for T3E to enforce the policy throughout the unattended processing afterward.

To maximize the throughput on a multi-core processor, T3E evaluates the maximum use count on a thread-specific basis. Multiple enclave threads requesting time data in parallel should not disproportionately affect the freshness of the cached time information. The maximum number of threads in the enclave is defined by the enclave developer and stored in the enclave manifest. Intel recommends not to exceed the number of processor cores.

Algorithm 2 presents the GetTrustedTime procedure as it is implemented in T3E. The procedure blocks the call when the use count, stored in c_{thread}, has exceeded c_{max} and no new time information, stored in the global variable *time*, has been received.

4.6   Reprovisioning Time from the Time Authority

T3E uses the trusted time authority (e.g., a trusted external NTPSec server) to periodically resynchronize the time epoch. This is necessary to avoid clock drift—a normal phenomenon that occurs between any two clocks. Resynchronization also serves as a mitigation against delay attacks where the attacker tries to secretly manipulate the progression of time (cf. Sect. 5.5). The periodicity of the resynchronization can be configured by the enclave owner and is expressed in a multiple of TPM ticks. T3E will expect an answer from the time authority in a timely manner. If it receives no response within a configurable number of TPM ticks, the processing of time requests by the client application will be suspended.

5   Security Evaluation

Attackers may try to manipulate the time information in a trusted system to gain an advantage. For a time service to be trusted, it must be able to guarantee the integrity of the time information or be able to detect any attempt to influence the returned time within certain reasonable bounds. In this section, we define the requirements of a secure time service and evaluate the T3E framework. Appendix A further evaluates and compares the related works, presented in Sect. 3, with respect to the security requirements that are presented in this section.

5.1 Requirement 1: The Time Source Must Be Authentic

A trusted time service is built around a time source that is trusted. Many different time sources may be available on a system (e.g., OS time, SW timers [22], TSC [14], HPET [12], PTP [25], TPM [5]), but most do not protect the integrity of the time information. Because the SGX threat model assumes a strong attacker with full control over the operating system, the time source must be able to resist any attempt to manipulate the returned time information, even by privileged users.

T3E uses two time sources: an initial real-world time source during the provisioning phase and the TPM time. T3E defines two practical ways to provision the initial time source. Automatic provisioning is supported by using an NTPSec server. Protocols such as NTS [11] support authenticated and integrity-protected access to a time service. Alternatively, T3E can be provisioned manually by the owner of the enclave.

The TPM provides time information that can be attested. The enclave can verify the authenticity of the TPM device and can agree on a key to validate the time data. This trust model also prevents man-in-the-middle attacks where the adversary tries to impersonate the TPM device or otherwise forge time information. An adversary can never access the attestation or endorsement keys, as they are kept inside the TPM. T3E validates the signature on the timing information it receives from the TPM (cf. Algorithm 1). If the signature is invalid, the information is discarded.

5.2 Requirement 2: Time Information Cannot Be Replayed

The time information returned by the trusted time service must be monotonously increasing. An adversary may try to trick the time service into returning old time information by intercepting and replaying messages from the trusted time source. This would effectively revert the clock to an earlier time and repeat the time that has passed. A trusted time service must detect and mitigate replay attacks.

The ClockTick function (cf. Algorithm 1) uses a random nonce to request time information from the TPM. The nonce ensures freshness and avoids replay attacks. The nonce is generated inside the protection boundaries of the enclave, and cannot be guessed or otherwise deduced by an attacker.

5.3 Requirement 3: Time Cannot Be Sped Up

A reliable time source must provide a stable and consistent progression of time, synchronously with the real-world clock. An adversary may try to advance the clock to expedite an event that should not have yet occurred. A trusted time service must be resilient against artificial time progression.

For an attacker to be able to speed up time, they must be able to forge messages from the TPM and manipulate the reported time information. However, the signatures on the time information messages protect them from being tampered with. The attacker cannot falsify the signature because the associated private keys are securely stored inside the TPM.

An attacker can try to influence the clock frequency of the TPM to adjust the speed of the reported time, or may attack the TPM chip directly by trying to inject faults or retrieve secret keys through side channels. However, TPM chips are specifically designed to defend against these types of attacks, and any successful attack should be considered a design flaw of the TPM and not a weakness in the T3E architecture.

5.4   Requirement 4: Time Cannot Be Paused or Slowed Down

Due to the absence of a trusted time source that is directly accessible from within an enclave, the time service must communicate with an external trusted time source. Communication between the enclave and the external time source can be intercepted by the OS and an attacker may choose to block certain messages indefinitely, thus causing time to slow down or stand still. While this problem can only be fully solved on an architectural level, the time service must have mitigations in place against this type of attack.

When the TPM provides new time information, the attacker could delay the message from reaching the enclave. Because the enclave does not have direct access to a trusted time source, it cannot accurately measure the latency of the TPM messages and detect the delay. While a comprehensive solution would involve changing part of the processor architecture, only Intel is in a position to effectuate this.

T3E mitigates delay attacks by enforcing a maximum use count after receiving time information from the TPM. This forces the attacker to regularly allow new time measurements to reach the enclave, or T3E would refuse to hand out time information, blocking the client program in the enclave.

Delaying TPM messages will also increase the frequency with which the maximum use count is reached by the client program. This can serve as an early indication that a resynchronization with the trusted time anchor from the external time oracle is necessary.

5.5   Attack Scenarios

To evaluate the effectiveness of T3E, we discuss four potential strategies that an attacker may use and discuss how they impact T3E.

Introducing Delays: An adversary may introduce arbitrary delays between T3E and the TPM. Figure 4 shows the normal operation of T3E, and Fig. 5 shows the attack, where each tick is delayed and arrives later than expected.

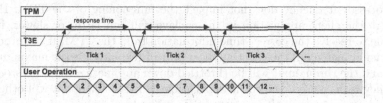

Fig. 4. The normal operation of T3E

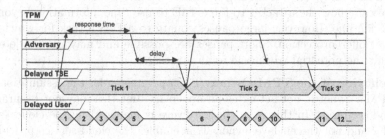

Fig. 5. The behavior of T3E in a delay attack

If the enclave was provisioned with the appropriate maximum use count, T3E would hit the limit around the time the next tick should have been received and block the client application until fresh time information has arrived. If the attacker delays the ticks for long periods, the client application will be denied service by T3E. Like SGX, T3E does not protect against DoS attacks. If the attacker delays the ticks for only a short period, the difference between the actual time and the time reported by T3E is small, limiting the effectiveness of the attack. The periodic resynchronization with an external trusted time source further mitigates this attack. Note that the delay does not accumulate over multiple ticks because T3E only sends the request for the next tick after receiving the previous one. To maintain a false sense of time, the attacker must delay all communication between T3E and the TPM. If the attack stops, T3E will automatically revert to the real time.

Precaching Results: An adversary may request attested time information from the TPM, cache the results, and slowly feed T3E with outdated time information. This would slow down the time from the perspective of T3E, and could over time result in a large clock drift between the T3E time and the actual time. T3E counters this threat by adding a random nonce to each TPM `GetTime` request, which is included in the signature. As the attacker cannot know which random nonce T3E will use for a request, they cannot proactively request time information from the TPM that will be accepted by T3E.

Changing the CPU Frequency: An adversary may attempt to change the CPU frequency to process requests at a faster or slower rate to create the illusion in the enclave that time is sped up or slowed down. However, changing the processor frequency does not impact the functioning of the TPM. Hence, although the client application in the enclave will run faster or slower, it will continue to receive the correct time information from the TPM. If the processor frequency is increased, the client application will regularly hit the maximum use count and the throughput will be throttled down automatically. If the processor frequency is decreased, the client application will run slower but will otherwise see no impact with respect to trusted time requests.

Scheduling Attacks: An adversary has full control over the scheduler in the OS and may arbitrarily interrupt or pause the execution of T3E. Pausing the enclave can allow the attacker to force T3E to use time information beyond its normal lifetime. However, large pauses equate to a DoS attack for which T3E does not offer protection. Short pauses are possible and may not be detected, but limit the potential advantage to an attacker.

Misbehavior of the TPM Owner: T3E operates under the assumption that the TPM's owner is not acting as an adversary, but this may not be practical in cloud scenarios. In this case, the hardware is managed by the cloud service provider and not the enclave owner. This enables the cloud service provider to use the TPM owner authorization password to move the clock forward. T3E can mitigate this type of attack by comparing the time received from the TPM with the time received in the previous tick. If the difference is suddenly larger than expected (because an adversary has moved the clock forward), T3E can trigger a resynchronization with the external time source. If the attacker only advances the time of the TPM slightly, T3E may not detect the modification. However, the advantage for the attacker would be small, and the modification will be neutralized during the next periodic resynchronization with the external time source.

Microarchitectural and Rollback Attacks on SGX: Previous research [21] has leveraged different types of microarchitectural attacks against SGX enclaves. These attacks allow adversaries to recover secret data from within the bounds of the enclave. However, as T3E does not process any secret data, microarchitectural attacks are not directly applicable to T3E. In enclave rollback attacks [18], an attacker violates the integrity of a protected enclave state by replaying old persistently stored data. This type of attack also does not apply to T3E, because T3E does not store persistent data. Instead, whenever the enclave is reinitialized, it resynchronizes the time with the external trusted time source and stores all its data in volatile memory.

6   Implementation and Analysis

We implemented the T3E framework in C++ using the Intel SGX SDK[4] v2.17 and the TPM2 Software Stack (TSS)[5] v3.2. Most of the TPM2 library runs as

---

[4] https://www.intel.com/content/www/us/en/developer/tools/software-guard-extensions/get-started.html.

[5] https://github.com/tpm2-software/tpm2-tss.

Table 1. Machine specification for the experiments

	Machine 1	Machine 2	Machine 3
Processor	Core i7 10700	Xeon Platinum 8480+	Celeron J4025
Base Freq.	2.9 GHz	2.0 GHz	2.0 GHz
SGX Ver.	1	2	2
TPM Type	Discrete	fTPM	fTPM
TPM Model	Infineon SLB9670	Intel PTT	Intel PTT

Table 2. Measurement results for the different signature schemes (in milliseconds)

	RSASSA-PKCS1			RSASSA-PSS			ECDSA		
	Avg	Min	Max	Avg	Min	Max	Avg	Min	Max
Machine 1	396	391	401	402	398	415	280	278	297
Machine 2	83	82	92	85	84	95	30	29	37
Machine 3	231	227	291	231	229	254	138	136	190

part of the untrusted code outside of the enclave. However, to guarantee the integrity and confidentiality of the attestation protocol between the TPM and T3E, the attestation challenge generation algorithm and the signature verification scheme were ported into the enclave and are a part of the trusted domain. We conducted the experiment on three different machines, as outlined in Table 1. The experimental application is compiled using Clang/LLVM 14.

For the analysis, we use the RDTSC instruction to measure the internal timing of T3E. In the SGX 1 machine, which cannot call RDTSC inside the enclave, we execute the instruction in the untrusted code via an OCALL and subtract the average overhead caused by the enclave transition from the result.

6.1 Microbenchmark Results

We evaluated three signature schemes for signing the time information received from the TPM2_GetTime command in our TPM device: two RSA-based signatures schemes and one elliptic-curve signature scheme. Our test application invokes TPM2_GetTime from an enclave via an OCALL, and verifies the signed time information internally in the trusted domain. This corresponds to the inner workings of the ClockTick function (Algorithm 1). The enclave obtains the time information repeatedly for 60 s.

The results of these measurements are presented in Table 2. The numbers in the table represent the duration of the GetTPMTime function, measured in milliseconds and derived from the time date received from the TPM. In T3E terminology, this corresponds to the tick count of the system. The measurements show that ECDSA performs almost 30% faster than the RSA-based signature schemes.

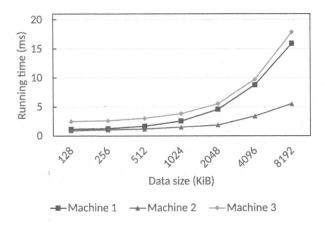

Fig. 6. Timing results for timestamping data of various input sizes

Our experiment also presents the performance potential of fTPM solutions, which provide more frequent ticks and thus have a higher time granularity than the discrete TPM solution. Using ECDSA on Machine 2's fTPM, the T3E framework can retrieve fresh time information every 30ms. This is a $33\times$ improvement over the 1-second granularity of Intel's `sgx_get_trusted_time` implementation. It also translates to a shorter tick interval, which improves security by reducing the attack potential of an adversary to abuse the use count by launching a delay attack.

6.2   Macrobenchmark Using OpenSSL

To evaluate T3E in a realistic use case of trusted time, we implemented *Timestamping Authority* (TSA, [29]) functionality inside the enclave. The implementation uses OpenSSL's timestamp components, where the enclave performs data measurement and generates a signed timestamp along with the hash of the data that can be verified using the TSA verification mechanism.

Our experiment uses exponentially increasing input data size to observe the execution time growth over the input data. We specifically measure the execution time of the timestamp query and reply process. Additional administrative operations, such as loading keys and certificates, are excluded from the measurement.

We can calculate the machine throughput by dividing the microbenchmark timing results from Table 2 and the macrobenchmark result in Fig. 6. The throughput value can become the baseline from which to calculate the maximum use count for the trusted time. A throughput n can be interpreted as follows: within a single tick (i.e., the granularity of the T3E clock), n time information requests are sent to T3E.

Since the throughput n depends on the data size that has to be processed, it is also important to build an accurate profile of the average input for the actual application. If the expected throughput is estimated too low, the T3E framework

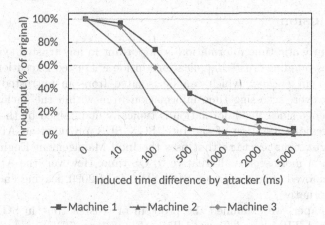

Fig. 7. Effect of delay and scheduling attacks on throughput

might use a maximum use count that is too low and some time requests may be blocked. If the expected throughput is estimated too high, the maximum use count will never be reached, giving an attacker some extra leeway to perform a delay attack.

6.3   Impact of Attacks on Throughput

As discussed in Sect. 5.5, an attacker can use a delay attack or scheduling attack to introduce small slowdowns in the reported time. Using the results from Table 2, we can calculate the effect these slowdowns have on the system's throughput.

Consider t_{tick} the tick interval (i.e., the average time between two TPM messages) and d the delay that is induced by an attacker through a delay or scheduling attack. Because of the delay, fewer TPM messages will reach T3E in a given time frame, causing T3E to hit the maximum use count c_{max} and throttle down the time requests. We can calculate this effect on the throughput τ as follows:

$$\tau = \frac{t_{tick}}{t_{tick} + d}$$

Figure 7 plots the results of this calculation for the three test systems and different delays. The impact of the tick interval on the effectiveness of the attack is clearly visible: with only a minimal delay of 10ms, Machine 2 (with the shortest tick interval) loses 25% of its original throughput. For the same delay, Machine 1 only loses 3.4% throughput. Hence, frequent ticks do not only increase the time granularity, but also improve the protection against attacks.

When the delay is increased, the throughput plummets. Delaying the time by 1 s reduces the throughput of the systems to 3%–22% of the original throughput. This change in system behavior would be immediately visible to external monitoring tools.

7 Conclusion

Access to authentic time information is important in any trusted system. Intel SGX enables building trusted applications inside a Trusted Execution Environment, called an *enclave*, which can be isolated from an untrusted operating system. However, accessing time information from within the enclave poses a major challenge since this information is typically maintained by the untrusted OS. The previous iteration of the Intel SGX SDK provided an API function called sgx_get_trusted_time that uses the Intel Management Engine technology stack as a more secure alternative to OS time. However, the API function has been removed from the Linux SGX SDK as of 2020, leaving enclaves with no good alternative.

In this paper, we examined the problem of trusted time in SGX enclaves and presented TPM-based Trusted Time Extensions (T3E), a novel solution that builds on readily available hardware components. T3E leverages TPM 2.0 functionality to provide trusted time services in enclaves, while also protecting against common attacks. It offers better time granularity and lower latency than Intel's sgx_get_trusted_time implementation. Unlike related work, it does not rely on deprecated features or hardware/firmware modifications.

Acknowledgements. This research is partially funded by the Research Fund KU Leuven, and by the Flemish Research Program Cybersecurity. The authors thank all reviewers, who provided constructive feedback to improve our paper. In addition, the first author would like to also thank Dody Suhendra from Sandhiguna for triggering the discussion leading to this research question.

A   Appendix:·Comparison with Related Solutions

The features of T3E are comparable to the related works presented in Sect. 3. However, T3E can be implemented without requiring intrusive changes to hardware or software. It does not rely on deprecated infrastructure or APIs and does not require modifications to commodity hardware such as custom-made firmware. T3E is an alternative for the deprecated sgx_get_trusted_time function, offering better security guarantees and a higher clock granularity.

T3E builds on the security properties of the TPM and SGX to ensure the clock's monotonicity and authenticity. A trusted channel is set up between the TPM and the enclave. This approach is similar to the TimeSeal solution, where the time information originates from the PSE.

To mitigate delay attacks, T3E maintains a maximum use count for each set of time information received from the TPM. While TimeSeal considered a scheduling delay, it did not consider the possibility of the entire application thread being suspended, pausing the time progression altogether. S-FaaS can detect the pause attack, but it cannot determine the duration of the delay, making it impossible to use it as a reliable tick source for a clock. TrustedClock does not have this issue because the tick generator is completely isolated from the untrusted OS. However, a powerful adversary can still suspend the enclave

Table 3. Comparison of T3E and related solutions for trusted time in SGX.

Solution	Tick Granularity	Time Unit	Uses PSE	H/W Changes
sgx_get_trusted_time	1 s	Timepoint	•	–
TimeSeal [3]	~100 ms	Timepoint	•	–
S-FaaS [1]	ns	Duration	–	–
TrustedClock [17]	~1 ms	Timepoint	–	•
T3E	30~300 ms	Timepoint	–	–

Table 4. Security evaluation of T3E and related solutions for trusted time in SGX, with regard to the security requirements in Sect. 5

Requirement 1	Requirement 2	Requirement 3	Requirement 4
Intel SGX PSE (sgx_get_trusted_time)			
Uses Intel's (deprecated) PSE, protected against privileged adversaries, to update the clock value inside the trusted domain	Guaranteed to be monotonically increasing, inherited from its underlying hardware (Intel CSME)	The operating system does not have access to the clock configuration, which prevents tampering to accelerate the clock	The hardware runs independently from the main processor, however, the time information passes through the OS and has no mitigations against delay attacks
TimeSeal [3]			
Uses Intel's (deprecated) PSE, and in addition, calculates the subtick interpolation inside the trusted domain	Inherits PSE guarantees and the interpolated subtick is also designed to be monotonically increasing	Inherits the properties of the PSE time source that prevents accelerating the clock	Faces similar delay attack as SGX PSE, however, TimeSeal detects these delays via separate counter threads and corrects it via interpolation
S-FaaS [1]			
The software timer and its state resides within the trusted domain	The software timer is designed to be monotonically increasing	The software timer may be sped up by overclocking the processor	Can detect if the software timer is being paused, but unable to determine the pause duration, and not immune to processor clock changes
TrustedClock [17]			
Uses a hardware timer that cannot be modified by a privileged attacker	Monotonically increasing derived from the hardware timer specification	The hardware clock runs independently of the OS. The OS cannot influence the behavior of the time source, including delaying its messages, as it runs in a higher privilege level (System Management Mode)	
T3E			
Combines the authenticated hardware timer from the TPM and a software counter inside the trusted domain	Monotonically increasing derived from the TPM clock specification	The TPM clock can only be manually changed using the owner authorization secret, and T3E can detect the irregular tick that may be caused by an adversary	TPM clock runs independently from the OS, and a software counter limits the maximum use count of time information, and periodically resynchronizes with an external trusted time authority

execution right before the trusted time is used, allowing TOCTTOU (Time-of-Check to Time-of-Use) attacks. We summarize our comparison in Table 3 and Table 4.

References

1. Alder, F., Asokan, N., Kurnikov, A., Paverd, A., Steiner, M.: S-FaaS: trustworthy and accountable function-as-a-service using Intel SGX. In: Proceedings of the 2019 ACM SIGSAC Conference on Cloud Computing Security Workshop, CCSW 2019, pp. 185–199. Association for Computing Machinery, New York (2019). https://doi.org/10.1145/3338466.3358916
2. Alder, F., Scopelliti, G., Bulck, J.V., Mühlberg, J.T.: About time: on the challenges of temporal guarantees in untrusted environments. In: Proceedings of the 6th Workshop on System Software for Trusted Execution (SysTEX 2023) (2023)
3. Anwar, F.M., Garcia, L., Han, X., Srivastava, M.: Securing time in untrusted operating systems with TimeSeal. In: 2019 IEEE Real-Time Systems Symposium (RTSS), pp. 80–92 (2019). https://doi.org/10.1109/RTSS46320.2019.00018
4. Anwar, F.M., Srivastava, M.: Applications and challenges in securing time. In: 12th USENIX Workshop on Cyber Security Experimentation and Test (CSET 2019), Santa Clara, CA. USENIX Association (2019). https://www.usenix.org/conference/cset19/presentation/anwar
5. Arthur, W., Challener, D., Goldman, K.: A Practical Guide to TPM 2.0: Using the New Trusted Platform Module in the New Age of Security. Springer, Cham (2015). https://doi.org/10.1007/978-1-4302-6584-9
6. Berger, S., Caceres, R., Goldman, K.A., Perez, R., Sailer, R., van Doorn, L.: vTPM: virtualizing the trusted platform module. In: 15th USENIX Security Symposium (USENIX Security 2006), Vancouver, B.C., Canada. USENIX Association (2006). https://www.usenix.org/conference/15th-usenix-security-symposium/vtpm-virtualizing-trusted-platform-module
7. Boubakri, M., Chiatante, F., Zouari, B.: Towards a firmware TPM on RISC-V. In: 2021 Design, Automation & Test in Europe Conference & Exhibition (DATE), pp. 647–650. IEEE (2021). https://doi.org/10.23919/DATE51398.2021.9474152
8. Chen, L., et al.: Trusted Computing Platforms: TPM2.0 in Context. Springer, Cham (2015). https://doi.org/10.1007/978-3-319-08744-3
9. Chen, S., Zhang, X., Reiter, M.K., Zhang, Y.: Detecting privileged side-channel attacks in shielded execution with Déjà Vu. In: Proceedings of the 2017 ACM on Asia Conference on Computer and Communications Security, ASIA CCS 2017, pp. 7–18. Association for Computing Machinery, New York (2017). https://doi.org/10.1145/3052973.3053007
10. Dang, H., Dinh, A., Chang, E.C., Ooi, B.C.: Chain of trust: can trusted hardware help scaling blockchains. arXiv preprint arXiv:1804.00399 (2018)
11. Franke, D.F., et al.: Network Time Security for the Network Time Protocol. RFC 8915 (2020). https://www.rfc-editor.org/info/rfc8915
12. Intel: IA-PC HPET (High Precision Event Timers) Specification. Intel (2004). https://www.intel.com/content/dam/www/public/us/en/documents/technical-specifications/software-developers-hpet-spec-1-0a.pdf
13. Intel: Intel® Software Guard Extensions Programming Reference (2014). https://www.intel.com/content/dam/develop/external/us/en/documents/329298-002-629101.pdf
14. Intel: Intel® 64 and IA-32 Architectures Software Developer's Manual, chap. 39, pp. 13–14. Intel (2016). https://www.intel.com/content/dam/www/public/us/en/documents/manuals/64-ia-32-architectures-software-developer-vol-3d-part-4-manual.pdf

15. Intel: Trusted Time and Monotonic Counters with Intel® Software Guard Extensions Platform Services (2017). https://community.intel.com/legacyfs/online/drupal_files/managed/1b/a2/Intel-SGX-Platform-Services.pdf

16. Intel: Intel® Transactional Synchronization Extension (Intel® TSX) Disable Update for Selected Processors (2022). https://cdrdv2.intel.com/v1/dl/getContent/643557

17. Liang, H., Li, M.: Bring the missing jigsaw back: trustedclock for SGX enclaves. In: Proceedings of the 11th European Workshop on Systems Security, EuroSec 2018. Association for Computing Machinery, New York (2018). https://doi.org/10.1145/3193111.3193119

18. Matetic, S., et al.: ROTE: rollback Protection for Trusted Execution. In: 26th USENIX Security Symposium (USENIX Security 2017), pp. 1289–1306 (2017). https://www.usenix.org/conference/usenixsecurity17/technical-sessions/presentation/matetic

19. McKeen, F., et al.: Innovative instructions and software model for isolated execution. In: Proceedings of the 2nd International Workshop on Hardware and Architectural Support for Security and Privacy, HASP 2013. Association for Computing Machinery, New York (2013). https://doi.org/10.1145/2487726.2488368

20. Raj, H., et al.: fTPM: a software-only implementation of a TPM chip. In: 25th USENIX Security Symposium (USENIX Security 2016), pp. 841–856 (2016). https://www.usenix.org/system/files/conference/usenixsecurity16/sec16_paper_raj.pdf

21. Schwarz, M., Gruss, D.: How trusted execution environments fuel research on microarchitectural attacks. IEEE Secur. Priv. 18(5), 18–27 (2020). https://doi.org/10.1109/MSEC.2020.2993896

22. Schwarz, M., Weiser, S., Gruss, D., Maurice, C., Mangard, S.: Malware guard extension: using SGX to conceal cache attacks. In: Polychronakis, M., Meier, M. (eds.) DIMVA 2017. LNCS, vol. 10327, pp. 3–24. Springer, Cham (2017). https://doi.org/10.1007/978-3-319-60876-1_1

23. The Trusted Computing Group: ISO/IEC 11889-1:2015 - Information Technology - Trusted Platform Module (2015). https://www.iso.org/standard/66510.html

24. Tople, S., Park, S., Kang, M.S., Saxena, P.: VERICOUNT: verifiable resource accounting using hardware and software isolation. In: Preneel, B., Vercauteren, F. (eds.) ACNS 2018. LNCS, vol. 10892, pp. 657–677. Springer, Cham (2018). https://doi.org/10.1007/978-3-319-93387-0_34

25. Trach, B., Krohmer, A., Gregor, F., Arnautov, S., Bhatotia, P., Fetzer, C.: ShieldBox: secure middleboxes using shielded execution. In: Proceedings of the Symposium on SDN Research, SOSR 2018. Association for Computing Machinery, New York (2018). https://doi.org/10.1145/3185467.3185469

26. Tsai, C.C., Porter, D.E., Vij, M.: Graphene-SGX: a practical library OS for unmodified applications on SGX. In: 2017 USENIX Annual Technical Conference (USENIX ATC 2017), pp. 645–658 (2017). https://www.usenix.org/conference/atc17/technical-sessions/presentation/tsai

27. Wang, H., Chen, G., Zhang, Y., Lin, Z.: Multi-certificate attacks against proof-of-elapsed-time and their countermeasures. In: Network and Distributed System Security Symposium, NDSS 2022 (2022). https://www.ndss-symposium.org/ndss-paper/auto-draft-253/

28. Zhang, F., Cecchetti, E., Croman, K., Juels, A., Shi, E.: Town crier: an authenticated data feed for smart contracts. In: Proceedings of the 2016 ACM SIGSAC Conference on Computer and Communications Security, CCS 2016, pp. 270–282. Association for Computing Machinery, New York (2016). https://doi.org/10.1145/2976749.2978326

29. Zuccherato, R., et al.: Internet X.509 Public Key Infrastructure Time-Stamp Protocol (TSP). RFC 3161 (2001). https://doi.org/10.17487/RFC3161. https://www.rfc-editor.org/info/rfc3161

Decentralized SGX-Based Cloud Key Management

Yunusa Simpa Abdulsalam[1(✉)], Jaouhara Bouamama[1(✉)], Yahya Benkaouz[2], and Mustapha Hedabou[1]

[1] College of Computing, Mohammed VI Polytechnic University, Benguerir, Morocco
{abdulsalam.yunusa,jaouhara.bouamama,mustapha.hedabou}@um6p.ma
[2] Computer Science Department, Faculty of Sciences, Mohammed V University in Rabat, Rabat, Morocco
yahya.benkaouz@fsr.um5.ac.ma

Abstract. The adoption of cloud computing is expanding at an astonishing pace for personal and professional usage. The high computational power and storage capacity have created a preference for traditional on-premise service provisioning. However, security remains the primary issue when dealing with the cloud paradigm. Encryption schemes have been considered a straightforward approach to protecting sensitive data. Yet, several key management schemes are vulnerable to various threats that weaken the long-term efficiency of the encryption scheme. This paper proposes MultiSGX-KMS, an efficient and secure cloud key management scheme. The suggested scheme aims to protect exchanged user keys while ensuring fault tolerance using secret sharing and trusted execution environments. In addition, the encryption keys are deployed in the SGX instance in the cloud while being fully controlled by the end user. The scheme is robust against proactive attacks and mitigates against a computationally bounded attacker without assuming a possible hardware attack on an SGX enclave. The proposed scheme presents a limited overhead of 0.1% for a file size of 50 MB compared to the traditional approach. The overhead further decreases proportionally as file sizes increase.

Keywords: key Management · Intel SGX · Secret Sharing Schemes

1 Introduction

In recent times, cloud application systems have been highly rated due to their effective storage capacity and availability. This is because outsourcing information reduces data management and storage bottlenecks, which lowers costs [7]. In most cloud settings, cloud service providers have partial or full control over key management functions, including highly sensitive cryptographic keys [16]. Therefore, organizations face challenges in migrating to public cloud systems due to the lack of efficient key user-centric management solutions. To protect cryptographic keys, several approaches have been proposed in the literature [4,15,21,23], including software and hardware solutions. However, these approaches have limitations in terms of performance, scalability, and on-demand self-service.

Trusted Execution Environments (TEEs) are secure areas in central processing units that were developed to provide a safe, isolated environment for executing secret codes [24]. Popular technologies like ARM TrustZone [3] and Intel Software Guard Extensions (SGX) [1] utilize TEEs to isolate sensitive code from untrusted access. However, Intel SGX is preferred over the ARM TrustZone because it operates over one CPU, which can have multiple secure environments running over untrusted software [20]. Although SGX enclaves offer protection against various attacks, their use necessitates careful application refactoring into trusted and untrusted environments to achieve the desired security and privacy goals. This paper proposes a cloud key management system that can be leveraged to solve problems of authentication, integrity, confidentiality, and a single SGX point of failure. The proposed scheme is based on a redefined Trusted Execution Environment. The solution allows the secure execution of an on-premise software key management system on the cloud providers for keeping control over sensitive keys. The proposed scheme splits and distributes a cryptographic key over multiple trusted execution environments (SGX instances) to enhance security for encryption keys. The proposed protocol offers confidentiality without commitment schemes, reducing the heavy computational power required for generating and reconstructing secret shares. Additionally, the approach provides proactive confidentiality and integrity through the generation of shares distributed to each SGX, which are encrypted within SGX_i using a unique seal key $SGX_{i_{key}}$. This approach provides mitigation against computationally bounded attackers without relying on the assumption of a possible hardware attack on an SGX enclave. The major contributions of this work are summarized as follows:

1. We design MultiSGX-KMS, a scalable cloud-based key management scheme.
2. We present a security analysis of the suggested scheme.
3. We validate the efficiency of our scheme with implementation and evaluation.

The remainder of this paper is organized as follows: Section 2 presents the preliminaries on Intel SGX as an efficient TEE technology and the different secret-sharing schemes in the literature. Section 3 provides a literature review on SGX for data security. Section 4 presents an overview of the considered system and adversarial models. Section 5 presents the suggested MultiSGX-KMS scheme. Section 6 presents the security analysis. Section 7 shows the experimental results and discusses the takeaways, the advantages and the limitations of the suggested system. Finally, Sect. 8 concludes and provides direction for future works.

2   Preliminaries

This section presents the building blocks used in the proposed MultiSGX-KMS scheme. Mainly, we present the Intel SGX and the secret sharing scheme.

2.1 Intel SGX

Intel SGX is a technology that enables high-level protection of secrets against all non-authorized access, including operating systems and hypervisors. SGX uses *enclave* to allocate hardware-protected memory where data and code reside. The enclave code can be invoked only via special instructions such as ECALL and OCALL. The ECALL instruction is a call to a predefined function inside the enclave from the application. The OCALL allows an enclave to invoke a predefined function in the application.

Furthermore, Intel SGX provides dedicated attestation and sealing mechanisms to build a secure model. To this end, two different keys are associated with the enclave: a report key to verify the signature of the enclave and a seal key to encrypt sensitive data outside the enclave. Generally, a *software attestation* aims to convince a challenger that the software is trustworthy and runs on the same platform. Accordingly, an enclave can prove its identity to another enclave on the same platform or remotely. These processes are identified as *Local Attestation* and *Remote Attestation*.

As shown in Fig. 1, the service provider requests attestation from the enclave. The enclave generates a signed REPORT. This REPORT is sent to the quoting enclave. This step is a local attestation between two enclaves on the same platform. The quoting enclave is responsible for converting a local REPORT to a QUOTE verifiable by the service provider. The QUOTE is generated by signing the REPORT with the private key of the enclave, then, forwarded to the service provider. Finally, the service provider verifies the QUOTE via Intel Attestation Service, a public web service operated by Intel that proves the trustworthiness of QUOTES [5].

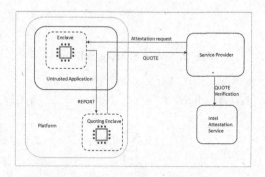

Fig. 1. Remote Attestation Flow

2.2 Secret Sharing Schemes

Secret Sharing Schemes (SSS) refer to methods by which a party divides a secret into multiple shares distributed amongst a group of parties. The secret is shared such that only authorized subsets of parties can reconstruct the secret. The secret is reconstructed if at least t participants present their shares. The knowledge of $t-1$ or fewer shares leaves the secret s undetermined. These schemes are called the (t, n)–threshold scheme (Fig. 2). Such schemes represent a building block in several solutions for multiple purposes, such as *Distributed polling* [9] and *Private data aggregation* [8]. Several schemes have been suggested in the literature, such as Shamir's scheme [25], Blakley et al. [11] and Asmuth et al. [6]. Shamir's scheme is one of the earliest and most studied schemes. It is based on the idea that: from a set of t points, a unique polynomial of degree $t-1$ passes through the t points.

Hence, given t points in the 2-dimensional plane $(x_1, y_1), (x_2, y_2), \ldots, (x_t, y_t)$, with distinct x_i's, there is only one polynomial $p(x) = a_0 + a_1 x + a_2 x^2 + \cdots + a_{t-1} x^{t-1}$ of degree $t-1$ such that $p(x_i) = y_i$ for all i. In order to create the shares, according to Shamir's scheme, the user chooses a random polynomial of degree $t-1$ in which the secret is the first coefficient, $p(0) = s$. Then, n random points are chosen from the curve. The coordinates of these points represent the shares to be given to the different parties. Thus, the n shares are $s_i = p(i)$ with $i \neq 0$. Given t distinct shares, the secret is recovered based on the Lagrange interpolation in Eqs. 1 and 2.

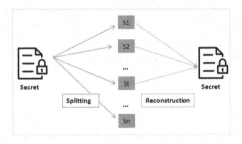

Fig. 2. Secret Sharing Scheme

Given $(x_1, y_1), \ldots, (x_t, y_t)$, where, $x_i \neq x_j : f(x) := \sum_{j=1}^{t} y_j l_j(x)$

$$f(x) := \sum_{j=1}^{t} y_j l_j(x) \tag{1}$$

$$l_j(x) := \prod_{\substack{1 \leq m \leq t \\ m \neq j}} \frac{x - x_m}{x_j - x_m} \tag{2}$$

3   Related Works

Intel SGX is widely used to protect sensitive data and has been evaluated to some extent to provide hardware protection to many potential cloud actors [14].

Several approaches have been proposed in the literature by using the tamper-resistant nature of Intel SGX. EnclaveCache [17] provided privacy and data confidentiality by leveraging the Intel SGX. Their multi-tenant key-value cache ensured the security of a distinct encryption key for cryptographic operations guarded by SGX enclaves. EnclaveDB [22] provided a less sophisticated approach to key management (Intel SGX enclaves) that guaranteed integrity, data freshness, and confidentiality by managing and associating encryption keys for data columns that represent sensitive information. KMSGX [12] proposed an efficient and secure model allowing on-premise software key management securely on the cloud provider side. RansomClave [10], a cryptographic key management scheme using enclaves, provided enhanced encryption, key generation, and release phases of enclave-ransomware. SecureKeeper [13] reduced the complexity of a key management scheme by creating a non-interactive enclave for confidentiality and integrity. Unfortunately, independent enclaves still use the same secret key to encrypt and decrypt users' data.

Highlighted works in the literature [10,12–14,17,22] propose an approach that seals the secret key within a single SGX appliance. Their approach lacks flexible authentication, verification, and scalability. Also, these approaches can easily be faulted by a compromised or failed appliance. Thus, there is a high tendency to lose the secret key alongside its encrypted sensitive data. Table 1 shows a comparison of the different approaches in the literature. Our suggested design MultiSGX-KMS aims to build a multi-trusted execution environment that guarantees secure cryptographic keys while in transit and at rest. Also, the scheme provides a secure verification of each SGX in the computation process while ensuring secret key availability.

Table 1. Related works summary

Approach	Confidentiality	Integrity	Authentication	Single Point of Failure	Scalability
Traditional Approach	×	×	✓	×	×
KMSGX [12]	×	✓	✓	×	×
EnclaveDB [22]	✓	✓	✓	×	×
RansomClave [10]	✓	✓	✓	×	×
EnclaveCache [17]	✓	✓	✓	×	×
SecureKeeper [13]	✓	✓	✓	×	×
MultiSGX-KMS	✓	✓	✓	✓	✓

4 System Model and Adversarial Model

This section presents the system model for the suggested cloud-based key management scheme. As well as the security and adversarial model. The system's protocol notations and definitions are presented in Table 2.

4.1 System Model

The proposed scheme is configured and runs on the cloud side by the end user which, involves two entities, the Key Management System (KMS) and n virtual appliances.

- Key Management System (KMS) on-premise responsible for key generation, splitting, and distribution of shares among the participants.
- n Virtual SGX appliance running on the cloud side, executing sensitive codes within its enclaves.

Table 2. Notations and definitions

Notation	Definition
n	Number of SGX appliances
ID_{SGX_i}	SGX unique identifier
t	Threshold for key reconstruction
M_{sKey}	Master Key
KMS_{key}	Cloud key management system key
SGX_{ikey}	SGX's unique seal key
$\mathbb{Q}$	Attestation request
σ	Enclave's signature for the service provider
ρ	Enclave's signature confirmation for the KMS
φ	Encrypted shares
ϕ	Encrypted KMS key

The system model is divided into four phases as shown in the Fig. 3.

- Attestation: The KMS initiates a communication with the n SGX appliances to create secure channels. Using, the SGX remote attestation, the KMS can verify the trustworthiness of the appliances and exchange a channel session key with each SGX.
- Key generation: The KMS on-premise generates an encryption key to protect sensitive data.
- Key Sharing/Reconstruction: The encryption key is split using a $(t, n)-$threshold secret sharing scheme. Where, each share is encrypted and transmitted to an SGX appliance using its session key. The reconstruction phase requires that at least t SGX appliances send their shares to the KMS.
- Sealing/Unsealing: After receiving the shares, each appliance decrypts its share with the session key. Then, each share is encrypted with a hardware key (seal key) by creating a stamp known only to the actual enclave. The unsealing phase is done in reverse.

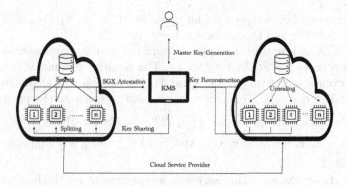

Fig. 3. System model

4.2 Adversarial Model

The proposed system model is designed to enable the secure generation, distribution, and storage of encryption keys. An authorized user is assumed to be trustworthy and can generate encryption keys with an enabled KMS. The model considers multiple SGX running in the cloud for secret sharing with a distrusted virtual cloud service provider. The key integrity of SGX enclave instances is ensured by Intel's standard assumption of providing isolation for SGX enclave [1]. However, an adversary may attempt to steal cryptographic keys by exploiting vulnerabilities, such as compromising the integrity and verification of each SGX instance. This can be achieved through a faulty SGX because SGX instances are prone to failure or denial of service availability. Here, the cloud service provider is considered honest and curious [14]. The proposed model considers concrete scenarios where an adversary can generate shares for enclave verification and contribute to the key reconstruction process. Likewise, an attacker can create an adversarial enclave that contributes to the initialization process. The security analysis of the proposed scheme goes by the standard assumptions of a secret sharing protocol that an intruder can not compromise more than $t - 1$ SGX appliance.

5 The MultiSGX-KMS Scheme

This section presents the proposed cloud key management system and the underlying protocol. The designed protocol is further grouped into different algorithms, as shown in Sect. 5.2

5.1 MultiSGX-KMS Protocols Definition

The proposed design consists of the following protocols.

Initialization: all SGX appliances are initialized by the KMS. A secure communication channel is set up between the KMS and SGX before starting any secret sharing. Let n represents all available SGX, $SGX_1, \cdots, SGX_n$ with a unique identifier as ID_{SGX_i} for $i = 1, \cdots, n$.

Key Generation: takes as input the required security parameter to generate respective keys for $SGX_1, \cdots, SGX_n$. The security parameter is computed from a cyclic group with generator g and prime order p. The algorithm outputs a secret key $\alpha \xleftarrow[\in_R]{} \mathbb{Z}_p$. This secret key is used to generate the preshared key g^α. Then the KMS generates $g^{\alpha\beta_1}, g^{\alpha\beta_2} \cdots g^{\alpha\beta_n}$ for all $\beta_i \xleftarrow[\in_R]{} \mathbb{Z}_p$. Finally, $M_{sKey} \xleftarrow[\in_R]{} \mathbb{Z}_p$ is the Master Key. And, $SGX_{i_{key}} \xleftarrow[\in_R]{} \mathbb{Z}_p$ is a unique seal key for every SGX_i.

Attestation: the algorithm serves as a replacement for the heavy computational power of a traditional commitment. In this protocol, an enclave proves its identity to maintain the integrity.

1. KMS generates a private key as $\alpha \xleftarrow[\in_R]{} \mathbb{Z}_p$, and a corresponding public key as g^α.
2. Enclave generates a private key as $\beta_i \xleftarrow[\in_R]{} \mathbb{Z}_p$, and a corresponding public key as g^{β_i}.
3. The KMS and each enclave establish a session key $g^{\alpha\beta_i}$
4. KMS sends an attestation request $\mathbb{Q}$ stamped with his public key as $(\mathbb{Q}_i)^{g^\alpha}$.
5. Enclaves creates a signature (σ) of the stamped request $(\mathbb{Q}_i)^{g^\alpha}$ to be verified by the service provider. For each SGX_i the signature is generated as follows:
$$\sigma_i = sign\left(SGX_{i_{key}}, \mathbb{Q}_i \parallel ID_{SGX_i}\right).$$
6. KMS receives a signed confirmation (ρ) from each enclave using their established private key as follows $\rho_i = sign\left(\beta_i, \sigma_i \parallel ID_{SGX_i}\right)$.
7. KMS performs the verification of ρ by performing the following function:
$$Verify(g^{\beta_i}, \rho_i \parallel ID_{SGX_i}) \stackrel{?}{=} True$$

Share Generation: is initialized by the KMS if previous verification is correct:

1. KMS generates the master key M_{sKey} to be shared among SGX_i and determines the threshold t necessary for the reconstruction phase.
2. Define a polynomial of degree $t - 1$ as $f(x) = a_0 + a_1 x + \cdots + a_{t-1} x^{t-1}$, such that $M_{sKey} = a_0$ where
$$a_1, \cdots, a_{t-1} \xleftarrow[\in_R]{} \mathbb{Z}_p$$
3. Compute n shares as $(x_1, f(x_1)), ..., (x_n, f(x_n))$ for each $SGX_i, i = 1, \cdots n$
4. Encrypt the shares $(x_i, f(x_i))$ using the KMS key as
$$\varphi_i = Enc\left(KMS_{key}, (x_i, f(x_i))\right)$$
then, encrypt the KMS key using the shared key as
$$\phi_i = Enc\left(g^{\alpha\beta_i}, KMS_{key}\right)$$

5. Send the tuple (φ_i, ϕ_i) to each SGX_i, $i = 1, \cdots n$
6. SGX_i receives the tuple (φ_i, ϕ_i) and creates a stamp using its unique seal key, for integrity check and future retrieval: $(\varphi_i, \phi_i)^{SGX_{i_{key}}}$.

Share Reconstruction: the algorithm is performed by the KMS, initiated by the user for sensitive data recovery. The protocol is performed as follows.

1. KMS sends t reconstruction requests $(\mathbb{R})_{i \in t}^{g^\alpha}$ stamped with the KMS public key to avoid impersonation.
2. Each SGX_i, $i = 1, \cdots, n$ processes the request by retrieving

$$(\varphi_i, \phi_i)^{SGX_{i_{key}}}$$

3. Each SGX_i, $i = 1, \cdots n$ sends $(x_i, f(x_i))_{i \in t}^{g^{\alpha \beta_i}}$ and ρ_i to the KMS.
4. KMS apply the following check: $Verify(g^{\beta_i}, \sigma_i \parallel ID_{SGX_i}) \overset{?}{=} True$, if check is valid KMS requests another share from $SGX_{j \neq i}$
5. KMS reconstruct the polynomial $f(x)$ using t shares. The Polynomial $f(x)$ is constructed using Newton Divided Differences Interpolating.

5.2 MultiSGX-KMS Algorithms

The proposed solution is grouped into three algorithms: Initialization, Download, and Upload.

1. **Initialization**: Algorithm 1 depicts the initialization algorithm for chosen appliances, the exchange of session keys and the generation of encryption keys.

Algorithm 1 Initialization

1: **Attestation**
2: **Input:** n Number of SGX Appliances
3: KMS chooses a generator g in a finite cyclic group G
4: KMS generates random α
5: KMS sends g^α to SGX_i
6: SGX_i generates β_i
7: SGX_i sends $QUOTE(g^{\beta_i})$ to KMS
8: **Output:** $SK_i := g^{\alpha \beta_i}$ session key between KMS and SGX_i
9: **Key Generation**
10: generate M_{sKey}
11: **Output:** M_{sKey} : encryption key

---

2. **Download**: Algorithm 2 depicts the download algorithm, which consists of unsealing the shares using the same specific seal key and send the shares to the KMS through the dedicated secure channel. When receiving the threshold number of shares the reconstruction can be done using Newton divided differences interpolation.

Algorithm 2 Download

1: **Unsealing**
2: **Input:** SGX_{iKey} (SGX_i's sealing key)
3: Unseal $(x_i, f(x_i))$ with $SGX_{i_{key}}$
4: **Output:** send $< (x_i, f(x_i)) >_{KMS_{key}}$ to SGX_i
5: **Input:** t threshold number, $(x_i, f(x_i))$ for $i \geq t$
6: Apply Newton Divided differences:
7: $f(x) = f(x_0) + (x - x_0)f[x_0, x_1] + ... + (x - x_0)...(x - x_t)f[x_0, .., x_t]$
8: **Output:** M_{sKey} Encryption key

---

3. **Upload:** Algorithm 3 depicts the upload algorithm which consists of splitting and sharing each part of the key to the specific appliance. Then, each appliance seals the share to an external storage using a seal key.

Algorithm 3 Upload

1: **Split Key.**
2: **Input:** t threshold number, M_{sKey} encryption key
3: KMS generates random $a_1 \cdots a_{t-1}$
4: KMS computes $f(x) = a_0, a_1 x \cdots a_{t-1} x^{t-1}$, where $a_0 = M_{sKey}$
5: KMS generates n shares $(x_1, f(x_1)) \cdots (x_n, f(x_n))$
6: **Output:** n shares: $(x_1, f(x_1)) \cdots (x_n, f(x_n))$
7: **Distribute Shares.**
8: **Input:** SK_i (SGX_i's session key), $(x_i, f(x_i))$, KMS_{key}
9: Using SK_i as the key in the exchange protocol, Encrypt KMS_{key}
10: Encrypt shares with KMS_{key}
11: **Output:** send $< (x_i, f(x_i)) >_{KMS_{key}}$ to SGX_i
12: **Sealing.**
13: **Input:** SGX_{iKey} (SGX_i's sealing key)
14: Decrypt $< (x_i, f(x_i)) >_{KMS_{key}}$ using the shared key SK_i for exchanging KMS_{key}
15: Seal $(x_i, f(x_i))$ with $SGX_{i_{key}}$

---

6 Security Analysis

In the adversary model, we assume that communication between the user and the cloud is secured through standard IT channels. However, an active attacker may have high privileges within the cloud, where all system software is considered malicious, including the operating system and hypervisor. Therefore, the adversary's goal is to retrieve the user's secret key to learn its sensitive data. On the other hand, it is also assumed that an attacker cannot perform any hardware attacks on the SGX appliances [18,19], and side channel attacks are out of the scope of this study for future recommendations. Additionally, we assume that the SGX as a TEE offers a complete secure private computations within its enclaves.

Thus, the security of the proposed scheme is analyzed using Theorems 1 and 2, going by the standard assumptions defined as follows:

1. Let the Discrete Logarithm (DL) problem in the presence of probabilistic polynomial time adversary $\mathbb{A}$ be defined as $Adv_{DL}[\mathbb{A}, a]$, where $DL = g^a$. Then, $Pr[DL = 1] \leq \texttt{negligible}$.
2. Let the Decisional Diffie Hellman (DDH) problem in the presence of probabilistic polynomial time adversary $\mathbb{A}$ be defined as $Adv_{DDH}[\mathbb{A}, a, b]$, where $DDH = g^{ab}$. Then, $Pr[DDH = 1] \leq \texttt{negligible}$.
3. A function $\varepsilon(\cdot) : N \rightarrow R^+$ is called $\texttt{negligible}$ if for all $n > 0$ there exists p_0 such that $\texttt{negligible} < \frac{1}{p^n}$ for all $p > p_0$.

Theorem 1. *The M_{sKey} cannot be learned with the presence of an adversary $\mathbb{A}$ except with an advantage of $Adv_{SS}[\mathbb{A}, M_{sKey}] < \varepsilon$.*

The semantic security is defined by an advantage (Adv_{SS}) on M_{sKey} for the adversary to obtain given a key in key space $\kappa \leftarrow [0, 1]^{128}$, according to Lemma 1.

Lemma 1. *Let $\prod$ represent the proposed cloud key management scheme. Then $\prod$ with key space $\kappa \leftarrow [0, 1]^{128}$ is termed secure if and only if Theorem 1 holds for every $M_{sKey} \in \kappa$*

Proof. Assume an adversary $\mathbb{A}$, and for an instance of **Share Reconstruction** t is the threshold required for a successful recovery of M_{sKey}. Then, the requested shares for reconstruction must be at least t for the polynomial $f(x)$ to be fully reconstructed. The first case of $\mathbb{A}$ is to provide a single rogue share $(x_1', f'(x_1))$, then, trivially $Pr[F(X) = f(x) | (X_i, F(X_i)) = (x_i, f(x_i))] < \varepsilon$ since there are t shares needed to reconstruct $f(x)$ and $Pr[(x_0', f'(x_0)) = (x_i, f(x_i))] < \varepsilon$, given $a_1, a_2 \cdots a_{t-1} \underset{\in_R}{\leftarrow} \mathbb{Z}_p$. The non trivial situation will be for an adversary to provide all t shares necessary to reconstruct $f(x)$. The probability of reconstructing polynomials $f(x)$ with shares $(x_i, f(x_i))_{i \geq t}$ for $a_0 = M_{sKey}$ is shown below.

$$Pr[f(x) | (x_i, f(x_i))] = \frac{Pr[(x_i, f(x_i)) | f(x)] \cdot Pr[f(x)]}{Pr[(x_i, f(x_i))]}$$
$$= \frac{Pr[(x_i, f(x_i)) | f(x)] \cdot Pr[f(x)]}{\sum_{f'(x_i) \in F(X_i)} Pr[(x_i, f(x_i)) | f'(x)] \cdot Pr[f'(x)]}$$

Let $\partial = Pr[(x_i, f(x_i)) | f(x)]$, then

$$Pr[f(x) | (x_i, f(x_i))] = \frac{\partial \cdot Pr[f(x)]}{\sum_{f'(x_i) \in F(X_i)} \partial \cdot Pr[f'(x)]}$$
$$= \frac{Pr[f(x)]}{\sum_{f'(x_i) \in F(X_i)} Pr[f'(x)]} = Pr[f(x)]$$
$$= Pr[f(x)] \Rightarrow Pr[a_0 = M_{sKey}] < \frac{1}{2^{128}} < \epsilon$$

This implies that $Pr[F(X) = f(x) | (X_i, F(X_i)) = (x_i, f(x_i))] = Pr[F(X) = f(x)]$. Therefore, $\prod$ is secure, recall that $M_{sKey} \in \kappa \leftarrow [0, 1]^{128}$.

Theorem 2. *The integrity of every verified $SGX_1, SGX_2 \cdots SGX_n$ is without forgery, even in the presence of software impersonation.*

Lemma 2. *The proposed cloud key management scheme $\prod$ guarantees availability and integrity, if and only if Theorem 2 holds.*

Proof. Before initializing the shares, the KMS has to verify that a signature $\rho_i = sign\left(\beta_i, \rho_i \parallel ID_{SGX_i}\right)$ is valid for a particular SGX for every attestation sequence. Additionally, the enclaves proves its integrity before sending a signature to the KMS by verifying $\sigma_i = sign\left(SGX_{i_{key}}, \mathbb{Q}_i \parallel ID_{SGX_i}\right)$ for an attestation request from the KMS. This process can only be correctly verified with the $SGX_{i_{key}}$ since $\sigma_i = sign\left(SGX_{i_{key}}, \mathbb{Q}_i \parallel ID_{SGX_i}\right)$. To ensure the correctness of $Verify(g^{\beta_i}, \rho_i \parallel ID_{SGX_i}) \overset{?}{=} true$, the KMS retrieves the public key of the intended SGX and the private key used for signing. In fact, the session key cannot be retrieved by an adversary according to standard assumptions of Discrete Logarithm and Decisional Diffie-Hellman problems.

According to Theorem 1, we claim that the confidentiality of generated shares is maintained in the presence of an active attacker since each share $(x_i, f(x_i))$ is processed inside a secure SGX enclave. However, to maintain the integrity of generated shares in the presence of a rogue SGX, each $(x_i, f(x_i))$ is signed using $SGX_{i_{key}}$ by the intended SGX. Consider an active adversary $\mathbb{A}$ that participates in the shares reconstruction with shares $(x_1', f'(x_1))$. A trivial way of retrieving the secret key by the KMS is to reconstruct all shares in the presence of the adversary $\mathbb{A}$ as $f'(x) := \sum_{j=1}^{t} y_j' l_j'(x)$ and $l_j'(x) := \prod_{\substack{1 \le m \le t \\ m \ne j}} \frac{x - x_m'}{x_j - x_m}$. This implies that $f(x) \ne f'(x)$, since $l_j(x) \ne l_j'(x)$ and therefore $a_0 \ne a_0'$, meaning that M_{sKey} will not be retrieved. The proposed scheme offers a moderate and yet achievable solution by running only the `Attestation` part of the protocol, which is independent of the entire protocol, to re-ensure the integrity of SGX_i for all $i = 1, 2, 3 \cdots n$.

7   Experimental Results

The scheme was evaluated on Intel i5-8259U processors simulating multiple virtual appliances hosted in Ubuntu 18.04 LTS 64bit running the SGX driver, SDK, and platform software version 2.9.1. PyKMIP version 0.10.0 [2] is a Python implementation of the key management interoperability protocol: It was used to illustrate the key management system on-premise. A KMIP server was responsible for generating, deleting, and encrypting secret data on behalf of the user. The tests were performed over several files: 10 MB, 20 MB, 50 MB, 100 MB, 200 MB, and 500 MB, using different (n, t) values for secret sharing: (n = 3, t = 2), (n = 5, t = 3), (n = 7, t = 4). The distribution of the time performance for Algorithms 1, 2, and 3 includes the cryptographic primitives (i.e. key generation, encryption, and secret sharing), as well as duration via the remote attestation and sealing included in the Intel SGX as illustrated in Fig. 4.

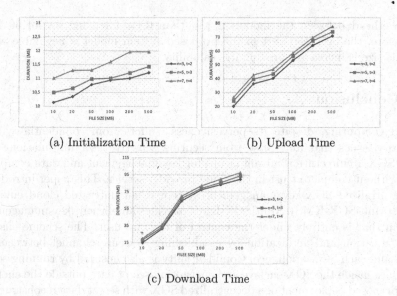

(a) Initialization Time   (b) Upload Time

(c) Download Time

Fig. 4. MultiSGX-KMS duration

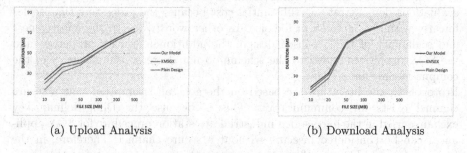

(a) Upload Analysis   (b) Download Analysis

Fig. 5. MultiSGX-KMS overhead

The performance of the proposed scheme was measured within the three phases and using different (n, t) parameters. Afterward, we compared it with [12] where only one SGX appliance was used. Also, we compared the system model with a plain design in which no cryptography algorithm and SGX primitives were included.

The experimental results show that the time required for model initialization scales linearly for all document sizes with varied secret-sharing system choices. Similarly, upload and download times scale linearly with file size, with minimal overhead between parameters. Furthermore, the comparison experiments between our model, KMSGX [12], and plain design show that the added security properties of key splitting/ reconstruction, encryption/decryption, and sealing/unsealing in both the upload and download phases did not significantly degrade the performance of the proposed model. Figures 5a and 5b shows that the overhead between the models is less than 0.1% for a file size of 50 MB. Therefore, the overhead cost of the proposed system model is negligible when the file size is increased, proving its scalability.

8   Conclusion

Cloud computing, despite its pervasiveness, suffers from confidentiality and integrity issues that may arise from securing sensitive user information. The Intel SGX architecture is advantageous for key management and data computation without complete trust in the cloud provider service. This paper introduces a decentralized SGX-key management system in an untrusted cloud environment (MultiSGX-KMS). MultiSGX-KMS provides an efficient key management system that is entirely under the control of the end user. The scheme ensures authentication and verification by establishing a secure channel between the KMS and each SGX appliance. Confidentiality is also ensured by running sensitive data inside the SGX enclave and encrypting secret data outside the enclave. The proposed deployment of a decentralized SGX with secret data reconstruction ensures that users' sensitive data is always available, removing the bottleneck of a single SGX failure, breakdown, or sabotage. The scheme's experimental evaluations demonstrate no substantial cost because the processing time scales linearly with the increase in file size. In other words, due to the effectiveness and scalability of the proposed design, the additional security properties and the SGX primitives added to the scheme do not decrease the efficiency of the computational time.

Protocols in the literature are based on the general assumption that a secure channel exists for communication. This is because the Diffie-Helman key exchange used in the hard-coded industrial attestation procedure for SGX appliances can be considered insecure without a secure channel. Therefore, in the future, we would like to address the insecurity that might exist using the above basic ad-hoc approach. We will also like to explore mitigations against cache and page-fault side-channel attacks for SGX deployed in the cloud. Also, to apply the same approach that will support multi-cloud requirements while preserving privacy.

References

1. Intel software guard extensions. https://www.intel.com
2. Python implementation of the key management interoperability protocol
3. Security technology-building a secure system using trustzone technology, ARM technical white paper (2009)
4. Amazon, cloudhsm (2015). http://www.amazon.com/
5. Anati, I., Gueron, S., Johnson, S., Scarlata, V.: Innovative technology for CPU based attestation and sealing. In: Proceedings of the 2nd International Workshop on Hardware and Architectural Support for Security and Privacy, vol. 13. ACM New York, NY, USA (2013)

6. Asmuth, C., Bloom, J.: A modular approach to key safeguarding. IEEE Trans. Inf. Theory **29**(2), 208–210 (1983)
7. Azougaghe, A., Oualhaj, O.A., Hedabou, M., Belkasmi, M., Kobbane, A.: Many-to-one matching game towards secure virtual machines migration in cloud computing. In: 2016 International Conference on Advanced Communication Systems and Information Security (ACOSIS), pp. 1–7. IEEE (2016)
8. Benkaouz, Y., Erradi, M.: A distributed protocol for privacy preserving aggregation with non-permanent participants. Computing **97**(9), 893–912 (2015)
9. Benkaouz, Y., Guerraoui, R., Erradi, M., Huc, F.: A distributed polling with probabilistic privacy. In: 2013 IEEE 32nd International Symposium on Reliable Distributed Systems, pp. 41–50. IEEE (2013)
10. Bhudia, A., O'Keeffe, D., Sgandurra, D., Hurley-Smith, D.: RansomClave: ransomware key management using SGX. In: The 16th International Conference on Availability, Reliability and Security, pp. 1–10 (2021)
11. Blakley, G.R.: Safeguarding cryptographic keys. In: Managing Requirements Knowledge, International Workshop on, pp. 313–313. IEEE Computer Society (1979)
12. Bouamama, J., Hedabou, M., Erradi, M.: Cloud key management using trusted execution environment. In: 18th International Conference on Security and Cryptography, pp. 10–16 (2021)
13. Brenner, S., et al.: SecureKeeper: confidential zookeeper using intel SGX. In: Proceedings of the 17th International Middleware Conference, pp. 1–13 (2016)
14. Brorsson, J., Bideh, P.N., Nilsson, A., Hell, M.: On the suitability of using SGX for secure key storage in the cloud. In: Gritzalis, S., Weippl, E.R., Kotsis, G., Tjoa, A.M., Khalil, I. (eds.) TrustBus 2020. LNCS, vol. 12395, pp. 32–47. Springer, Cham (2020). https://doi.org/10.1007/978-3-030-58986-8_3
15. Chakrabarti, S., Baker, B., Vij, M.: Intel SGX enabled key manager service with openstack barbican. arXiv preprint arXiv:1712.07694 (2017)
16. Chandramouli, R., Iorga, M., Chokhani, S.: Cryptographic key management issues and challenges in cloud services. Secure Cloud Comput. 1–30 (2014)
17. Chen, L., Li, J., Ma, R., Guan, H., Jacobsen, H.A.: EnclaveCache: a secure and scalable key-value cache in multi-tenant clouds using intel SGX. In: Proceedings of the 20th International Middleware Conference, pp. 14–27 (2019)
18. Kocher, P., et al.: Spectre attacks: exploiting speculative execution. In: 2019 IEEE Symposium on Security and Privacy (SP), pp. 1–19. IEEE (2019)
19. Lipp, M., et al.: Meltdown: reading kernel memory from user space. In: 27th USENIX Security Symposium (USENIX Security 18), pp. 973–990 (2018)
20. Mukhtar, M.A., Bhatti, M.K., Gogniat, G.: Architectures for security: a comparative analysis of hardware security features in intel SGX and ARM TrustZone. In: 2019 2nd International Conference on Communication, Computing and Digital systems (C-CODE), pp. 299–304. IEEE (2019)
21. Phegade, V., Schrater, J., Kumar, A., Kashyap, A.: Self-defending key management service with intel® software guard extensions (2017)
22. Priebe, C., Vaswani, K., Costa, M.: EnclaveDB: a secure database using SGX. In: 2018 IEEE Symposium on Security and Privacy (SP), pp. 264–278. IEEE (2018)
23. Rosen, A.: Analysis of the porticor homomorphic key management protocol. Porticor Cloud Security (2012)
24. Sabt, M., Achemlal, M., Bouabdallah, A.: Trusted execution environment: what it is, and what it is not. In: 2015 IEEE Trustcom/BigDataSE/ISPA. vol. 1, pp. 57–64. IEEE (2015)
25. Shamir, A.: How to share a secret. Commun. ACM **22**(11), 612–613 (1979)

Security in the Wild

Spying on the Spy: Security Analysis of Hidden Cameras

Samuel Herodotou$^{(\boxtimes)}$ and Feng Hao

Warwick University, Coventry CV4 7AL, UK
{samuel.herodotou,feng.hao}@warwick.ac.uk

Abstract. Hidden cameras, also called spy cameras, are surveillance tools commonly used to spy on people without their knowledge. Whilst previous studies largely focused on investigating the detection of such a camera and the privacy implications, the security of the camera itself has received limited attention. Compared with ordinary IP cameras, spy cameras are normally sold in bulk at cheap prices and are ubiquitously deployed in hidden places within homes and workplaces. A security compromise of these cameras can have severe consequences. In this paper, we analyse a generic IP camera module, which has been packaged and re-branded for sale by several spy camera vendors. The module is controlled by mobile phone apps available on iOS and Android. By analysing the Android app and the traffic data, we reverse-engineered the security design of the whole system, including the module's Linux OS environment, the file structure, the authentication mechanism, the session management, and the communication with a remote server. Serious vulnerabilities have been identified in every component. Combined together, these vulnerabilities allow an adversary to take complete control of a spy camera from anywhere over the Internet, enabling arbitrary code execution. This is possible even if the camera is behind a firewall. All that an adversary needs to launch an attack is the camera's serial number, which users sometimes unknowingly share in online reviews. We responsibly disclosed our findings to the manufacturer. Whilst the manufacturer acknowledged our work, they showed no intention to fix the problems. Patching or recalling the affected cameras is infeasible due to complexities in the supply chain. However, it is prudent to assume that bad actors have already been exploiting these flaws. We provide details of the identified vulnerabilities in order to raise public awareness, especially on the grave danger of disclosing a spy camera's serial number.

Keywords: Internet of Things · Security · Vulnerability · IP Camera · Spy Camera

1 Introduction and Motivation

Hidden cameras, also known as spy cameras, are digital cameras hidden or disguised as part of common objects, and are generally deployed with the goal to conduct surveillance on people without their knowledge [24]. Although there are legitimate use cases for such cameras (e.g., lawful surveillance on suspects),

© The Author(s), under exclusive license to Springer Nature Switzerland AG 2023
S. Li et al. (Eds.): NSS 2023, LNCS 13983, pp. 345–362, 2023.
https://doi.org/10.1007/978-3-031-39828-5_19

they can also be misused to spy on people unscrupulously. It has been reported that many Airbnbs (1 in 19 in Singapore) have hidden cameras installed, but only 17% of Airbnb providers specify where these cameras are located [8]. Hidden cameras are also frequently installed by parents at homes to monitor the activities of nannies and often the children themselves [9].

The ubiquitous presence of hidden cameras installed in private spaces within homes and workplaces to monitor people without their knowledge clearly raises many privacy concerns. This has motivated many researchers to investigate the detection of such cameras, e.g., via a smartphone's time-of-flight sensors [20], a stimulating-and-probing technique [16], the analysis of thermal emissions [24], the RF (radio frequency) signal characteristics [6,21], the Wi-Fi data fluctuations [3–5,7,13,14,19], and the camera's electromagnetic emanations [17].

However, the security of the hidden camera itself has received limited attention. So far, only a few researchers have investigated this subject. Abdalla et al. show that many cameras use default passwords and the communications are unencrypted [1]. Ling et al. reveal that it is possible to perform an online brute-force attack to uncover the camera's password when the password is only four-digits long [15]. They further show that if the MAC address of the camera is known, it is possible to spoof the camera. Biondi et al. demonstrate that when an attacker is in the same Wi-Fi network as the IP camera, they can eavesdrop on the video data [2]. Although these studies provide useful insights, their analysis is not systematic, and the identified vulnerabilities tend to have a limited impact. Some of the attacks will not work if the attacker is not in the same network as the camera or if the user changes the default password.

This paper presents a thorough and systematic analysis of a generic IP camera module, which after repackaging and re-branding, has been built into several best-selling hidden cameras available on Amazon. The camera modules under investigation were purchased at around $30 each. Some of these hidden cameras are integrated into household objects such as alarm clocks, and are typically sold on Amazon in the range of $50–120. The camera module is controlled by mobile phone apps that are freely available on iOS and Android. One example is the *LookCam* app, which has over half a million downloads on Google Play alone. However, there are also other apps that work with the same type of module but are branded by different vendors. Security designs for the camera module and the app are not officially published.

By decompiling the *LookCam* Android app and analysing the camera's traffic data, we were able to reverse-engineer the entire security design of the camera system. This includes the Linux operating system (OS) environment on the module, the file structure in the firmware, the authentication mechanism, the session management, and the remote communication with servers in the cloud. Security flaws have been identified in all these areas, and are detailed in Sect. 3.

Our contributions are summarised below.

– Based on publicly available hardware modules and mobile applications, we have reverse-engineered the security design of a generic hidden camera system. This design does not represent all hidden cameras in the market but is believed to be fairly common among commercial products.

- Based on the reverse-engineered security design, we have identified categorical flaws and presented proof-of-concept attacks accordingly. These flaws allow an adversary to perform remote code execution on a camera from anywhere in the world with the mere knowledge of the camera's serial number.
- Based on the findings, we propose mitigation measures and good practices for designing more secure camera systems in the future.

Ethics and Responsible Disclosure. The camera modules being analysed were purchased and owned by the authors. Proof-of-concept attacks were demonstrated against these devices only without affecting other IP cameras in use. We responsibly disclosed the findings to the manufacturer. Whilst the manufacturer acknowledged our work, they showed no intention to fix the problems, mainly because patching/recalling these modules is infeasible due to complexities in the supply chain. On the other hand, the public needs to be informed of the risk of using hidden cameras, especially since users sometimes share serial numbers of the purchased cameras in online reviews. One CVE (Common Vulnerabilities and Exposures) has already been assigned (*CVE-2023-30400*), and others are also under review at the time of writing. The following sections will detail the vulnerabilities with the manufacturer's name anonymised.

2 Hardware and Supply Chain

The generic camera module under analysis is a portable, thumb-sized device that can be powered with a battery or micro-USB. It works completely standalone, supporting live video streaming and Wi-Fi connectivity out-of-the-box. Optionally, a Micro SD card can be inserted to enable video recordings. Figure 1 shows a photograph of the camera module.

The device is designed to connect with a companion app, which is developed by vendors under different brands. The app analysed in this investigation is called *LookCam*. Its features include live streaming, remote configuration, and downloading previously recorded footage.

The modules in question originate from a prominent firm in the electronics industry, referred to hereafter as *the manufacturer*. This manufacturer specialises in the production of camera modules and CCTV (closed-circuit television) equipment, and according to publicly available information online, exports $5–10 million worth of product yearly, with their main markets in Europe, America and Asia.

In terms of the supply chain, this manufacturer acts as the OEM (original equipment manufacturer). The modules are sold in bulk to other vendors, which are then packaged and re-branded. The final products are released to consumers in online stores such as *Amazon*. After the generic camera modules are sold in bulk, even the manufacturer cannot track where these modules are distributed to third-party sellers at multiple retail levels. The complexities in the supply chain have profound security implications since if there is a security flaw in the generic module, it is virtually impossible to patch or recall the affected products.

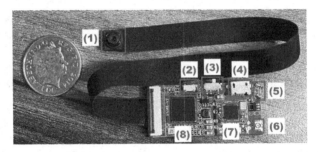

Fig. 1. The Camera Module. (1) Micro camera. (2) Reset button. (3) Power switch.
(4) Micro-USB port. (5) Power pins (battery). (6) Wi-Fi antenna. (7) Wi-Fi module.
(8) Central Processing Unit.

This manufacturer also partners with two other companies in producing the
camera modules. One is a leading integrated circuit manufacturer. They produce
the system-on-chip, which is a core component of the camera module, providing an embedded-Linux operating system and drivers to support an IP camera
product. The other company specialises in providing a peer-to-peer networking
system, which is a software component of the camera module responsible for
facilitating remote connections to the cameras. Serious flaws have been discovered in these components as well. According to public information available on
the company's website, the peer-to-peer networking system has been adopted by
over 50 million IoT devices.

3   Investigation

This section describes the testbed setup, the reverse-engineering process, and
the vulnerabilities identified with proof-of-concept attacks.

3.1   Pairing the Device

To pair a camera with the mobile app, there are multiple approaches. When no
network is configured (e.g., if reset to factory settings), the device hosts its own
hotspot network which the user can connect to. Once connected, the *LookCam*
app can automatically pair by listening for packets sent by the device (which
contain its serial number). Alternatively, a user can add a device that is already
connected to the internet by supplying its serial number to the app. It is common
for these devices to include a sticker or QR code which contains the serial. When
connecting via the app, the user will be prompted to enter a password to gain
access. All devices are configured with a default password of 123456.

3.2   Testbed Setup

To facilitate an investigation of the network services running on the device, it
is necessary to construct a network sandbox to intercept all relevant communications. This was achieved by connecting an external wireless network adapter

(*Alfa-Network AWUS036NHA*) to a *Kali Linux* virtual machine. By using the *hostapd* tool, a custom Wi-Fi hotspot was created with the adaptor. Configuring the camera module to connect to this network would then enable all communications to be intercepted using a packet-sniffing tool such as *Wireshark*. By using an additional network adaptor to create the hotspot, the built-in network adaptor of the Kali machine could be used to bridge an Internet connection to the hotspot, enabling all external traffic to be intercepted (e.g., communications with peer-to-peer servers). See Fig. 2 for a diagram of the structure. This testbed was set up only for reverse-engineering the security design of the camera system. For attacking the system, the adversary does not need to be in the same Wi-Fi network as the camera; the attack can be launched from anywhere on the Internet.

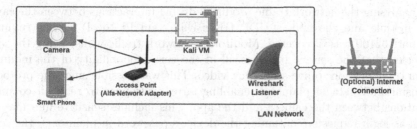

Fig. 2. Architecture of the network sandbox used to intercept traffic

3.3   Mobile Application Analysis

Without knowledge of the camera's security design, the reverse-engineering process started with analysing the controlling app, in particular, the *LookCam* Android app that is publicly available in Google Play. Decompiling the *Look-Cam* Android application with *Jadx* enabled its source code to be analysed. From an initial scan, it was discovered that the core of the networking functionality is implemented within a C-library named `libPPCS_API.so`. Investigating this library required disassembly in *Ghidra*, and is discussed later in this paper.

Additionally, a *secret* logging feature was discovered in the `AboutActivity.java` file. This file controls how users can interact with the 'About' page in the app. The code reveals that, if a user holds down the 'LookCam' logo for a few seconds, a menu is revealed that allows the user to export a debug log. Other applications were also discovered to include this functionality. This log contains output from all the components of the application, including the C-libraries that communicate directly with the camera. This log output provided vital information on how the phone communicates with the camera module, and revealed a JSON (JavaScript Object Notation) command system in use. Listing 1 provides a portion of the output, revealing the structure of a login command sent to the camera.

```
LookCam[28765:1775458] Connect Success!! SessionID=34
LookCam[28765:1775458] will login with session 34
LookCam[28765:1775519] mediaDataRecThread going...
LookCam[28765:1775458] send json {
    cmd = LoginDev;
    pwd = 123456;
}
```

Listing 1. Log output revealing a JSON-style command system in use

3.4 Unencrypted Communications

By analysing the network traffic produced during interactions between the camera module and the app, a UDP (User Datagram Protocol) service running on port 32100 was discovered. Monitoring network traffic whilst using the app revealed that the service provides all of the core functionality of the module, from configuration to live-streaming video. This was possible since the protocol transmits all data in plaintext, enabling an eavesdropper to read all communications between the camera and the app. This includes sensitive information such as login requests (containing the device's password in plaintext), the contents of configuration commands, and live video footage. Once the attacker has intercepted the device's password, they can gain full access to the camera via the mobile application as if they were a legitimate user. However, exploiting this flaw is not easy as it requires the adversary to be a man-in-the-middle (MITM) between the camera and the phone. However, this MITM requirement no longer becomes a constraint when exploiting vulnerabilities in the camera's peer-to-peer and command systems, enabling the camera to be controlled from anywhere on the Internet. These vulnerabilities are discussed in the following sections.

3.5 Vulnerable Command System

Many flaws were discovered in the JSON command system, used by the app to interact with the camera. A custom client was developed to mimic the actions of the mobile phone app, which enabled custom JSON payloads to be sent that could exploit potential vulnerabilities in the implementation of the command handlers.

Bypassing Authentication. To begin, an analysis of communications between the camera and the app revealed that the camera's password is included in every request made by the app. This is included in plaintext under the pwd field in the JSON body. Not only does this increase the probability of an eavesdropper capturing the device's password, but highlights a lack of session management in use by the system. Listing 2 demonstrates the standard format used by all commands sent by the app.

```
{
    "cmd": "[Command name]",
    "pwd": "[Device password]",
    "...": "...",
}
```

Listing 2. JSON structure of commands

When sending an incorrect value for the `pwd` field, one would expect the camera to reject the command completely. However, using the custom client to send malformed commands with the `pwd` field omitted revealed that the camera makes no attempt to verify the supplied credentials. This shows that the user's password authentication is performed client-side in the app, and not on the camera. Although the `LoginDev` command is sent to the camera to verify the supplied password, this command simply verifies the correctness of the password without updating the state of the system or establishing a session. This makes it possible for an attacker to gain full access to the camera without knowing the password by using a custom client, similar to the one developed in this investigation. Alternatively, using dynamic instrumentation tools such as *Frida* makes it possible to disable the code responsible for performing the client-sided check. The `loginDevice` function within `LuPPCSSession.java` was successfully hooked and overwritten to bypass this check. This eliminates the need for an adversary to develop a custom app from scratch to bypass the authentication system. Thus, by adding any known serial number to the *LookCam* app with this custom code enabled, an attacker can gain full access to a target camera without being on the same network or being a MITM.

Reading Configuration Values. Given that full access can be granted without knowing the password, an attacker no longer needs to perform a man-in-the-middle attack and rely on user-interaction for sensitive information to be obtained. This information can be requested directly, as the device cannot distinguish an attacker from a legitimate user. The `GetDevInfo` command can be sent, which is then responded with sensitive information such as the user's Wi-Fi credentials, as shown in Fig. 3. The transmission of the Wi-Fi credentials to the app appears totally unnecessary, which demonstrates a lack of security-consciousness from the manufacturer in the security design.

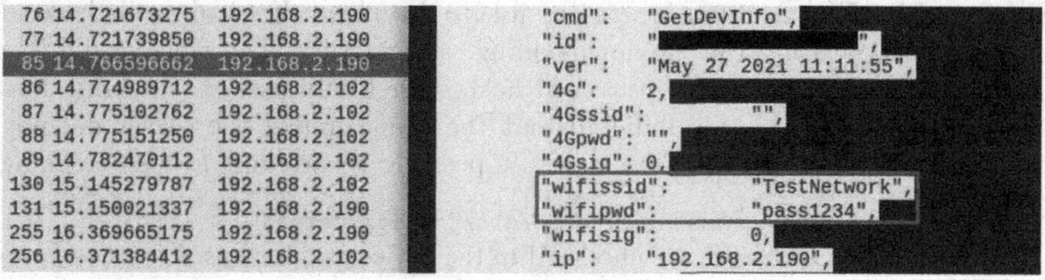

Fig. 3. Extracting Wi-Fi credentials in Wireshark

Live Streaming. By imitating the requests the application makes when requesting a live-stream, an attacker can access live-footage from a target camera without the user's interaction. Many of these cameras also include microphones, enabling audio to be captured too. Even the installer of the camera may not be aware that the spy camera can be spied on by random people on the Internet. This clearly aggravates privacy concerns about these hidden cameras.

Arbitrary File Downloading. The camera module offers a file-downloading command to facilitate the remote retrieval of historic footage. A vulnerability was discovered in the file-download command handler that enables attackers to download arbitrary files present on the system. See Listing 3 for an example file-download request.

```
{
    "cmd": "DownloadFile",
    "pwd": "123456",
    "patch": "/mnt/CYC_DV/20220708@111673.mp4",
    "pos": 0
}
```

Listing 3. Example file download request

By sending modified requests with a custom client that was designed to mimic the *LookCam* app, it was possible to send *any file path* under the `patch` parameter. The camera immediately responds with a series of UDP packets containing the contents of the file. No attempt was made by the manufacturer to sandbox the file system or ensure file paths are within the recording directory. This makes it possible to download any file on the device, as long as the path is known. Recalling that this can be performed without the user's password, the scope in which an attacker can extract data is no longer limited by what information the network service is designed to share. For example, the file `/etc/jffs2/.devpsd` was discovered, which stores the user's password in plaintext.[1] The lack of encryption in this file makes it possible for an attacker to effortlessly obtain this information. This breach of confidentiality could pave the way for further malicious activities, as the password may be reused on other systems.

Shadow File Extraction. It was possible to download the shadow file located in `/etc/shadow` using the file-downloading vulnerability. The shadow file is a protected file that stores the password hashes for Linux users.[2] Not only does the ability to read this file indicate that the user running the server daemon has superuser privileges; it also makes it possible to attempt a hash-cracking

---

[1] In some newer devices, this is stored in `/etc/config/.devpsd`.

[2] We note that these hashes are unrelated to the device password used by the app to authenticate users. They are instead part of the internal Linux environment.

attack on the *root* password set by the manufacturer. The password was hashed using the insecure *MD5 Crypt* algorithm, making it more vulnerable to cracking attacks compared to modern hashing algorithms [18]. Despite this, it was not feasible to crack the password after an aggressive combination of dictionary and brute-force attacks lasting over a month. This shows that the root password set by the manufacturer is a long and complex string. However, taking control of the device does not require knowing the root password, as this can be achieved by exploiting command-injection vulnerabilities. Furthermore, through the command-injection attack, the root password can be modified to an arbitrary one, hence effectively bypassing the root password authentication. Details of this are discussed later in this paper.

3.6   Firmware Extraction

The existence of the file-downloading vulnerability made it possible for the entire file system to be extracted for further examination. By analysing the `/proc/mounts` file, three files were discovered which, if downloaded, could be used to rebuild the entire file system. This solved the blind file-downloading limitation, as all files could be downloaded at once without having to know (or fuzz) specific paths. Table 1 provides further details of these files.

Table 1. File systems mounted by the device

Path	Type	Contents
`/dev/mtdblock5`	jffs2	Stores user data, such as configuration values. Mounted at `/etc/jffs2`[a].
`/dev/mtdblock6`	Squashfs	Read-only partition for the `/usr` directory. Stores vendor-specific binaries and scripts, such as startup scripts and the core server application.
`/dev/root`	Squashfs	Stores remaining files that belong in the root folder (`/`). Includes the Linux kernel and built-in executables

[a] In some newer devices, this area is mounted at `/etc/config`.

Having access to the file system made it possible to discover and analyse additional files on the device. This included custom programs such as `/usr/bin/anyka_ipc`, the daemon responsible for the UDP service.

3.7   Remote Code Execution

Analysis of the file system and start-up procedure revealed a chain of bash scripts that are executed on boot, as seen in Fig. 4. Some of these scripts contain command-injection vulnerabilities that enable an attacker to perform remote code execution on a target device with superuser privileges.

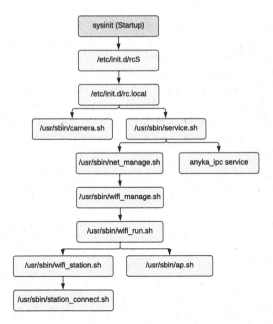

Fig. 4. Chain of processes and scripts called on startup

Vulnerable code has been discovered in modules with software versions as recent as November 2022. A lack of remote updating functionality found in these modules means that it is impossible for patches to be pushed by the manufacturer. An example includes `station_connect.sh`, a script responsible for connecting the camera to a user-configured Wi-Fi network. Listing 4 contains a vulnerable excerpt from the script.

```
SSID=\'\"$GSSID\"\'
PSK=\'\"$GPSK\"\'
...
sh -c "wpa_cli -iwlan0 set_network $NET_ID ssid $SSID"
...
sh -c "wpa_cli -iwlan0 set_network $NET_ID psk $PSK"
```

Listing 4. Vulnerable code in `station_connect.sh`

The script makes multiple calls to the command 'sh -c', which instructs the shell to interpret any following string as a shell command. The variables `$GSSID` and `$GPSK` originate from the camera's configuration settings (the network name and password), making them directly modifiable by the user, and also an attacker. The danger present is that the user-supplied values are being passed directly into the command, making it possible for a crafted payload to execute arbitrary commands. A weak attempt was made by the manufacturer to prevent this from occurring, however. These values are initially read and parsed in another script, `wifi_station.sh`, before being sent to `station_connect.sh`. The inputs are weakly sanitised with an `awk` script (see Listing 5) that performs the following operations, according to the `awk` reference [11]:

– Removes all double quotes
– Removes leading whitespace
– Removes any occurrences of the semicolon (;) character, and any following characters on the same line

```
BEGIN {FS="="}/[wireless]/{a=1} a==1 &&
$1~/^ssid/{
    gsub(/\"/,"",$2);
    gsub(/\;.*/, "", $2);
    gsub(/^[[:blank:]]*/,"",$2);
    print $2
}
```

Listing 5. Script to read and sanitise the configuration value for the Wi-Fi SSID

The removal of the semicolon character (and anything after) is a clear attempt to prevent command-chaining. However, not all cases were considered, since additional chaining operators using the ampersand (`&&`) and pipe (`||`) symbols are never filtered out, which can be used to achieve a similar result. Additionally, the inputs are surrounded with pairs of single and double quotes (see lines 1 and 2 in Listing 4), in an attempt to ensure the input is interpreted as a string instead of being executed. These techniques, although potentially thwarting a naive command-injection attempt, proved futile since the source code could be viewed. By surrounding the payload with a pair of single quotes, it was possible to break out of the string and achieve code execution.

To perform the attack, an `OpenWifi` command is sent to the device to update the Wi-Fi settings with the embedded payload. When this is sent, the camera updates its configuration file with the inputs and reboots. On boot, `station_connect.sh` is executed, triggering the attacker's code via the call to 'sh -c'. A slight barrier to the attack is that the `OpenWifi` command only supports a maximum length of 32 characters for the SSID and password fields. Recall that the file `/etc/jffs2/.devpsd` was previously discovered to store the device's password in plaintext. By updating the password to be the contents of a desired script, the password file can be used as a temporary storage mechanism for the payload. The input in the `OpenWifi` command can then be shortened to execute the contents of this file with the command 'source /etc/jffs2/.devpsd'.

Thus, a more sophisticated attack involves sending two commands. The first updates the camera's password to a payload of choice (Listing 6), whilst the second updates the Wi-Fi configuration so that the payload is executed on the next boot (Listing 7). It should be noted that no user interaction is required to perform this attack.

```
{
    "cmd": "ModifyPwd",
    "newpwd": $payload, // desired payload
    "pwd": ""
}
```

Listing 6. Command to update the device's password

```
{
    "cmd": "OpenWifi",
    "sid": $ssid, // user's SSID
    "wifiPwd": "'&&source /etc/jffs2/.devpsd '",
    "state": 1
}
```

Listing 7. Payload sent to exploit the command-injection vulnerability in `station_connect.sh`

Since the exploit requires an attacker to update the camera's network configuration, this attack has the side-effect of disconnecting the camera from the Internet, preventing an attacker from sending further commands. This can be resolved by rolling back the credentials after code execution is established. The shell code in Listing 8 can be added to the payload to restore the original configuration and reconnect to the Internet. Additionally, the password file can be reinstated to its original value to make the attack much harder to detect. By ignoring this step, however, a denial-of-service attack is achieved, since updating the password file is equivalent to changing the password. With the device's password being set to the contents of an arbitrary script, the user will no longer be able to connect to their device via the *LookCam* app.

```
sed -i 's/^password.*=.*/password = [OLD PASSWORD]/'
 ↪ /etc/jffs2/anyka_cfg.ini
reboot
```

Listing 8. Shell code to reinstate the previous Wi-Fi password

Searching for the vulnerable code segments discovered via *Github Code Search* [10] and *Sourcegraph* [22] revealed that the scripts originate from the *AK3918* microcontroller software development kit (SDK). Consequently, the command-execution vulnerability is not restricted to the specific modules in this investigation, but potentially to many other products that incorporate the same SDK (or derivatives).

3.8 Persistent Access

With the ability to perform code execution, an adversary can perform more sophisticated attacks to persist this access, such as installing a malicious start-up script that exposes a reverse shell. These attacks are immune to the device's 'reset' button, as resetting the device only restores the factory configuration file whilst leaving the rest of the filesystem unaffected. In a large-scale attack, this could lead to the formation of a botnet, enabling considerable attacks such as distributed denial of service, botnet mining and mass surveillance. A vulnerable section of code located in `service.sh` (see Listing 9) exposes debug functionality left behind by the manufacturer, making it possible to install a custom start-up script. The code looks for a script located in `/mnt/usbnet/product_test`, and if present, executes it on every boot. Additionally, `Telnet` and FTP (File Transfer Protocol) daemons are started, exposing additional entry points to the camera.

```
if test -d /mnt/usbnet ;then # Checks if the directory exists
        FACTORY_TEST=1
...
if [ $FACTORY_TEST = 1 ]; then
    /usr/bin/tcpsvd 0 21 ftpd -w / -t 600 & # Start FTP
    telnetd & # Start Telnet
    echo "start product test."
    /mnt/usbnet/product_test & # Execute the start-up script
...
```

Listing 9. Vulnerable debug functionality left behind in `service.sh`

An adversary can insert an additional command into the start-up script to change the vendor-set root password to an arbitrary one, as shown in Listing 10. This effectively bypasses the root password originally set by the vendor and enables the adversary to authenticate themselves to the `Telnet` and FTP services which were previously protected by this root password.

```
echo -e "1234\n1234" | passwd root
```

Listing 10. Changing the vendor-set root password to '1234' by exploiting the exposed start-up script

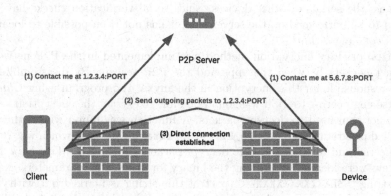

Fig. 5. UDP hole punching procedure

3.9   Insecure Peer-to-Peer System

To facilitate remote connections to the cameras outside of the user's local network, the peer-to-peer (P2P) system is utilised. Although it offers convenience by enabling users to access their cameras from anywhere in the world, exposing devices to the Internet creates the opportunity for the previously discussed vulnerabilities to be exploited remotely.

The P2P system uses a proprietary security protocol and is inherently insecure. The main role of this P2P network is to provide clients with a direct IP connection to the requested device without requiring complex network configuration changes. To achieve this, a technique called *UDP hole-punching* [12] is employed. This method makes it possible for the camera to traverse the NAT (Network Address Translation) system in place within the user's network, essentially performing a port-forward operation without requiring manual changes to the router's settings. It abuses the fact that in many networks, when an outgoing request to a server is made, a temporary NAT rule is created to enable the response to be received. By constantly firing out packets to the client, a 'hole' in the NAT table is left open, allowing the app to connect directly to the camera. Figure 5 shows the steps involved in UDP hole punching. The procedure works as follows:

1. Both the app and the camera inform centralised peer-to-peer server(s) of their IP addresses and listener ports.
2. Given that both the phone app and the camera are online, the camera sends outgoing packets to the phone's IP and port to open a NAT hole.
3. Once the NAT hole is open, the app can connect directly to the camera.

Each camera is assigned a unique serial number for identification. When an app wishes to connect to a camera, it sends a request to the peer-to-peer server with the respective serial number. Figure 6 depicts the serial number format in further detail. Each serial consists of a vendor prefix, an ID number, and a check code (there are 1 million IDs for each prefix; a vendor can license multiple prefixes to support more devices). The check code is used as an attempt to prevent serial numbers from being enumerated, making it difficult for attackers to guess the serials of other devices. Since serial verification checks have been found to be performed on the server side, it has not been possible to locate the check-code algorithm.

A proprietary encryption method was implemented in the P2P network to protect packets between the apps and the P2P servers. By disassembling the code responsible for this encryption in the `anyka_ipc` program using *Ghidra* (a reverse-engineering tool), it was found possible to extract the encryption key and the algorithm used to decrypt packets. A function was found within the disassembled program called `cs2p2p_P2P_Proprietary_Decrypt`, which was reverse-engineered and rewritten in C to decrypt packets captured in *Wireshark*. Multiple keys were located by probing the binary for encryption parameters. Namely, the string '`SSDXXXXXXXXXXXXk.`' (part of this string is marked out with 'X') is used as a global symmetric key to encrypt and decrypt packets. An additional

Prefix   **Device ID**   **Check Code**

Fig. 6. Format of the serial numbers used to identify devices

256-byte key was discovered that is incorporated as an additional parameter to the encryption/decryption functions. These keys are hard-coded into the binary and are the same for all cameras of the same type. They are also present in the `libPPCS_API.so` library included in the mobile app, as it also communicates with the peer-to-peer system.

With the ability to communicate with the P2P servers, an attacker can request the IP addresses of cameras, enabling a direct connection to be made. It is important to note that this vulnerability does not only apply to the cameras in question, but to any IoT device using this network to facilitate P2P connections. This makes it possible for vulnerabilities present in the spy cameras and also other IoT devices to be exploited remotely, since no authentication is required to gain a direct IP connection. This raises concerns surrounding potentially many more products in the IoT space.

To sum up, these generic hidden camera modules have exhibited considerable defects in their various components, involving multiple companies in the supply chain. The network service running on each camera to support the mobile apps contains several vulnerabilities that enable attackers to bypass the authentication system and extract sensitive information. The insecure configuration scripts included as part of the microcontroller SDK make the cameras vulnerable to command-injection attacks. Poor system configuration enables the command injection attacks to be performed with superuser privileges. A flawed encryption system in use by the peer-to-peer system enables attackers to impersonate legitimate users, exposing IoT devices to the Internet and allowing attacks to be performed on an international scale, to potentially many millions of devices.

4   Mitigation Measures

To protect these cameras, a complete overhaul of the system would be necessary. This is due to the numerous vulnerabilities present in all of their components. Despite several attempts to bring these issues to the attention of the responsible parties, many refused to respond or cooperate whilst others expressed no interest. The lack of success in identifying remote updating functionality in the system suggests that any mitigation attempt through patching would be infeasible nevertheless. A list of remedial actions has been compiled below to address each of the identified vulnerabilities for the future development of IP cameras:

1. **Verbose debug logging** – Strip out debug messages in the production build of the controlling app.
2. **Unencrypted communications** – Implement Transport Layer Security (TLS) to protect traffic in-transit.

3. **Authentication loophole** – Issue a token on successful login and verify the presence of a valid token in the subsequent requests.

4. **Unencrypted password storage** – Store a salted hash of the user's password instead of storing it in plaintext.

5. **Arbitrary file downloading** – Associate each video file with an identifier and have an internal database mapping identifiers to file paths. With this method, a user only inputs an identifier instead of a path. Thus, the input is not directly incorporated into the path, avoiding directory traversal.

6. **Unnecessary exposure of sensitive information** – Avoid printing sensitive information such as Wi-Fi credentials in command responses, e.g., GetDevInfo.

7. **Poor access control** – Create a non-privileged Linux user to run the application server. Modify file/directory permissions to protect privileged information.

8. **Outdated password hashing algorithm** – Ensure password hashes for all users are using a modern algorithm such as *bcrypt* [18].

9. **Command injection** – Modify shell scripts to correctly sanitise user input. Alternatively, rewrite the functionality in another language such as C to mitigate the risk of command injection.

10. **Flawed encryption in P2P network** – Implement a TLS layer to protect traffic in-transit.

11. **Device impersonation** – Adopt a secure enrolment process to register a camera with the app, e.g., based on Thread [23], to create end-to-end secure channels between the camera and the controlling app without having to trust any peer-to-peer servers.

5   Future Work

It has been demonstrated how attackers can perform remote code execution on an arbitrary spy camera with only the knowledge of its serial number. The proprietary check-code algorithm used to verify serial numbers serves as the sole defence against device enumeration, which could lead to the formation of a botnet of potentially millions of vulnerable devices. Serial enumeration does not only impact the hidden cameras investigated in this paper, but also any type of IoT device connected to the P2P network. Recalling that over 50 million IoT devices are estimated to be using this system, the possible impact here can be much greater. Flaws in the design of the network and its encryption protocol make it possible to gain a direct IP connection to arbitrary devices without supplying any credentials. Further exploits could be possible based on the designs of these devices. A possible route to cracking the check-code algorithm would be to purchase a copy of the P2P server software from the manufacturer (which costs around $1,000), so one has access to the source code of the server software including the implementation of the check-code algorithm. With the knowledge of the check-code algorithm, an attacker may extend the reported attacks to an arbitrary IoT device with a valid device ID in the P2P network, including not only IP cameras but also IP-based smart locks, doorbells, bulbs, light switches, speakers and so on. We leave this to future study.

6   Conclusion

A systematic investigation of the security of IP-based hidden cameras has been conducted, revealing a broad range of vulnerabilities. These vulnerabilities allow a remote attacker, with the mere knowledge of the camera's serial number, to take complete control of the camera even if the camera is within an internal network behind a firewall. Proof-of-concept attacks have been demonstrated to eavesdrop on the audio and video streams, retrieve any recorded video stored on the camera module along with other sensitive information (such as the Wi-Fi passwords of the user's home network), and run a reverse shell script on the camera device (by abusing the password update function and specifying the reverse shell as part of the input to that function), thus turning the camera into a platform to attack other nodes in the home network or as part of a botnet. These attacks are not just limited to hidden cameras; they are generally applicable to IoT devices that follow a similar security design. Countermeasures are proposed to contain these attacks. However, patching or recalling the affected cameras is infeasible given the existing designs of these products and the complexities of the supply chain. Manufacturers are urged to pay more attention to security and get it right at the start, as failures can cause unintended, severe, and long-lasting consequences, especially when retrospective fixes are impossible. In the meantime, the public should be informed of the security issues of a hidden camera, especially about the danger of sharing a camera's serial number with others. Even if a user diligently does not share the serial number, we caution that an attacker may already know it, e.g., by enumeration, or reading the product information in the supply chain. To ultimately address the vulnerabilities identified in this paper, we call for open, peer-reviewed and standardised security designs, which are currently lacking for hidden cameras and similar IoT products.

Acknowledgements. The second author is supported by Royal Society (ICA\R1\180226) and EPSRC (EP/T014784/1).

References

1. Abdalla, P.A., Varol, C.: Testing IoT security: the case study of an IP camera. In: 2020 8th International Symposium on Digital Forensics and Security (ISDFS), pp. 1–5. IEEE (2020)
2. Biondi, P., Bognanni, S., Bella, G.: Vulnerability assessment and penetration testing on IP camera. In: 8th International Conference on Internet of Things: Systems, Management and Security (IOTSMS), pp. 1–8. IEEE (2021)
3. Chaudhary, P.R., Narasimhan, A., Maiti, R.R.: Demystifying video traffic from IoT (spy) camera using undecrypted network traffic. In: Proceedings of the Twelfth ACM Conference on Data and Application Security and Privacy, pp. 361–363 (2022)
4. Cheng, Y., Ji, X., Lu, T., Xu, W.: DeWiCam: detecting hidden wireless cameras via smartphones. In: Proceedings of the 2018 on Asia Conference on Computer and Communications Security, pp. 1–13 (2018)

5. Cheng, Y., Ji, X., Lu, T., Xu, W.: On detecting hidden wireless cameras: a traffic pattern-based approach. IEEE Trans. Mob. Comput. **19**(4), 907–921 (2019)
6. Cunningham, R., Tan, W.L.: Detection and localization of hidden Wi-Fi cameras. In: 2022 27th Asia Pacific Conference on Communications (APCC), pp. 12–17. IEEE (2022)
7. Dao, D., Salman, M., Noh, Y.: DeepDeSpy: a deep learning-based wireless spy camera detection system. IEEE Access **9**, 145486–145497 (2021)
8. Janssen, D.: Many Airbnbs have cameras installed, especially in the US, Canada and Singapore. https://vpnoverview.com/news/camera-presence-airbnb-accommodations/. Accessed 09 Mar 2023
9. Laljee, F.: Using a nanny cam in the home. https://www.kidsitter.co.uk/blog/using-nanny-cam-in-the-home/. Accessed 09 Mar 2023
10. Github: Github Code Search. https://github.com/features/code-search. Accessed 04 Mar 2023
11. GNU: The GNU Awk User's Guide. https://www.gnu.org/software/gawk/manual/gawk.html. Accessed 04 Mar 2023
12. Halkes, G., Pouwelse, J.: UDP NAT and firewall puncturing in the wild. In: Domingo-Pascual, J., Manzoni, P., Palazzo, S., Pont, A., Scoglio, C. (eds.) NETWORKING 2011. LNCS, vol. 6641, pp. 1–12. Springer, Heidelberg (2011). https://doi.org/10.1007/978-3-642-20798-3_1
13. Heo, J., et al.: Are there wireless hidden cameras spying on me? In: Proceedings of the 38th Annual Computer Security Applications Conference, pp. 714–726 (2022)
14. Lee, J., Seo, S., Yang, T., Park, S.: Ai-aided hidden camera detection and localization based on raw IoT network traffic. In: 2022 IEEE 47th Conference on Local Computer Networks (LCN), pp. 315–318. IEEE (2022)
15. Ling, Z., Liu, K., Xu, Y., Jin, Y., Fu, X.: An end-to-end view of IoT security and privacy. In: IEEE Global Communications Conference (GLOBECOM), pp. 1–7. IEEE (2017)
16. Liu, T., Liu, Z., Huang, J., Tan, R., Tan, Z.: Detecting wireless spy cameras via stimulating and probing. In: Proceedings of the 16th Annual International Conference on Mobile Systems, Applications, and Services, pp. 243–255 (2018)
17. Liu, Z., et al.: CamRadar: hidden camera detection leveraging amplitude-modulated sensor images embedded in electromagnetic emanations. Proc. ACM Interact. Mob. Wear. Ubiquit. Technol. **6**(4), 1–25 (2023)
18. Provos, N., Mazieres, D.: A future-adaptable password scheme. In: USENIX Annual Technical Conference, FREENIX Track, vol. 1999, pp. 81–91 (1999)
19. Salman, M., Dao, N., Lee, U., Noh, Y.: CSI: DeSpy: enabling effortless spy camera detection via passive sensing of user activities and bitrate variations. Proc. ACM Interact. Mob. Wear. Ubiquit. Technol. **6**(2), 1–27 (2022)
20. Sami, S., Tan, S.R.X., Sun, B., Han, J.: LAPD: hidden spy camera detection using smartphone time-of-flight sensors. In: Proceedings of the 19th ACM Conference on Embedded Networked Sensor Systems, pp. 288–301 (2021)
21. Sindhu, K., Subhashini, R., Gowri, S., Vimali, J.: A women safety portable hidden camera detector and jammer. In: 2018 3rd International Conference on Communication and Electronics Systems (ICCES), pp. 1187–1189. IEEE (2018)
22. Sourcegraph: Sourcegraph. https://sourcegraph.com. Accessed 04 Mar 2023
23. Thread Group: Thread specification. https://www.threadgroup.org/support#specifications. Accessed 09 Mar 2023
24. Yu, Z., Li, Z., Chang, Y., Fong, S., Liu, J., Zhang, N.: HeatDeCam: detecting hidden spy cameras via thermal emissions. In: Proceedings of the 2022 ACM SIGSAC Conference on Computer and Communications Security, pp. 3107–3120 (2022)

Security Analysis of Mobile Point-of-Sale Terminals

Mahshid Mehr Nezhad[(⊠)], Elliot Laidlaw, and Feng Hao

Department of Computer Science, University of Warwick, Coventry, UK
{Mahshid.Mehr-Nezhad,Elliot.Laidlaw,Feng.Hao}@warwick.ac.uk

Abstract. The increasing prevalence of Card Present (CP) transactions has driven the growth of mobile Point-of-Sale (mPoS) terminals. These compact, wireless, and low-cost terminals allow merchants to process transactions conveniently by utilizing a mobile phone. In this paper, we analyze the security implications of mPoS terminals with a focus to study the merchants' mobile phones as a key component in the mPoS ecosystem. Our examination covers the security aspects of the mobile phone's communication with the mPoS terminal and the payment provider server, and also the security risks in the mobile phone application itself. We perform an eavesdropping attack to reveal the cryptographic keys in the BLE (Bluetooth Low Energy) communication between the mPoS terminal and the merchant phone, execute a man-in-the-middle (MITM) attack to tamper with the mPoS terminal messages transmitted between the mPoS terminal and the payment provider server, and reverse engineer the mobile phone application to disable the security features that are controlled by the mobile phone.

Keywords: EMV · Payment Systems · Contactless Payment · mPoS Terminals

1 Introduction

Card Present (CP) transactions, also known as face-to-face (F2F) transactions, are growing in popularity as consumers increasingly use credit and debit cards for purchases [8], in contrast to Card Not Present (CNP) transactions. CP transactions are performed when the card is physically present, typically at a Point-of-Sale (PoS) terminal, while CNP transactions occur when neither the cardholder nor the credit card is physically present at the time of the transaction [28]. The focus of this paper is CP transactions.

Traditionally, PoS terminals have been used to process CP transactions. These terminals are typically large, fixed devices that are found in retail stores and other locations where goods and services are sold. They are connected to a payment processor through a wired or wireless network. However, with the growing demand for more flexible and cost-effective payment solutions, mobile PoS (mPoS) terminals have emerged as an alternative to traditional PoS terminals

© The Author(s), under exclusive license to Springer Nature Switzerland AG 2023
S. Li et al. (Eds.): NSS 2023, LNCS 13983, pp. 363–384, 2023.
https://doi.org/10.1007/978-3-031-39828-5_20

due to their flexibility and affordability, especially for small businesses. Examples are Sumup [29], Square [27], and iZettle [14]. These terminals are small, compact, low-cost, wireless and easy to configure, requiring a few simple steps. They are equipped to accept various payment methods such as debit/credit/prepaid cards with magnetic strips or embedded chips, contactless payments through mobile wallets, QR codes, and/or cash and checks [9]. They offer the ability for anyone with a bank account to establish their own payment terminal, mostly without requiring a business account or a fixed contract.

Although they provide convenience for merchants and customers, they raise potential risks that can be exploited for malicious purposes. This can include holding an mPoS terminal near a victim's payment device (credit/debit card or Near Field Communication (NFC)-enabled devices such as smartphones or wearable devices (e,g, smartwatches) without their knowledge, in conjunction with other emulation hardware, to perform malicious activities. An example of such exploitation is using these mPoS terminals in a man-in-the-middle (MITM) attack setup, as shown in [22], which bypasses the lock screen on mobile phones as a method of cardholder verification when a Visa card is utilized on Apple Pay with transit mode enabled. Furthermore, studies conducted by researchers at ETH Zurich have revealed various methods for bypassing the Personal Identification Number (PIN) on contactless cards during transactions above the contactless limit, including PIN bypass on Visa cards [3] and on Mastercard cards [4,5] by using an mPoS terminal with emulators. Another example is the mPoS-based passive attack (also known as digital pick-pocketing), which effectively combines all the required emulation components in a relay attack in a single mPoS terminal for a fraudulent merchant to perform passive relay attacks in order to steal money from users via contactless transactions without their knowledge [17].

The management of these terminals is usually done with a mobile device such as a mobile phone or tablet which plays a crucial role in various aspects of the transaction process, including the establishment of a Bluetooth connection with the mPoS terminal, the connection to the payment provider server over the internet, and the installation of an application on the device to manage the mPoS terminal. In this paper, the potential security risks and vulnerabilities of mPoS terminals are analyzed with a focus on the involvement of mobile phones in their management, which is owned by the merchant. Specifically, the security aspects of the communication between the mobile phone and the mPoS terminal, the communication between the mobile phone and the payment provider server, and the mobile phone application itself are examined. The security of the Bluetooth Low Energy (BLE) communication between the mobile phone and the mPoS terminal is analyzed, and methods for revealing the cryptographic keys used in this communication are explored. Furthermore, a MITM attack is performed to demonstrate the vulnerability of the communication between the mobile phone and the payment provider server. Additionally, the feasibility of reverse engineering the mobile phone application code is shown, and the modification of the security features of the mPoS terminals controlled by the mobile phone is demonstrated. We summarize our contributions as follows:

- Performing an eavesdropping attack on the BLE communication between the mobile phone and the mPoS terminal to extract the cryptographic keys used for communication;
- Performing a MITM attack between the mobile phone and the payment server to intercept and tamper with the messages to be displayed on the terminal;
- Demonstrating the feasibility of reverse engineering the mobile phone application code and the alteration of the security features of the mPoS terminals that are controlled by the mobile phone.

This paper employs the terms *card reader*, *terminal*, and *mPoS terminal* interchangeably. The rest of the paper is organized as follows. In Sect. 2, we provide the background and the related work on studying the mPoS terminals vulnerabilities. Section 3 explains encryption security, with a focus on the BLE communication between the mPoS terminal and the mobile phone. Section 4 explains network security, with a focus on the security vulnerabilities of the HTTP communication between the mobile phone and the payment server. In Sect. 5, we investigate the mobile application installed on the mobile phone and demonstrate the feasibility of bypassing the security features, followed by a discussion in Sect. 6. Finally, we conclude the paper in Sect. 7.

2   Background and Related Work

The installation of an mPoS terminal requires a series of straightforward steps. These steps include purchasing the device, which can vary in price based on its features (with options starting as low as £19), registering for an online account (usually done via the vendor website), installing the corresponding application on the merchant's mobile phone, pairing the phone with the terminal, and finally, making transactions.

The ecosystem of mPoS terminals and their communication with various entities in transactions are depicted in Fig. 1. The mPoS terminal is operated by a mobile phone, owned by the merchant. The merchant downloads an application on their mobile phone and uses it to connect to the mPoS terminal. This enables the merchant to initiate and request payments. When the payment is sent from the merchant's mobile phone to the mPoS terminal, the user is ready to pay.

As shown in Fig. 1, the user has the option to make a payment transaction through either a contactless or chip-and-PIN method by tapping, inserting, or swiping their payment device against the mPoS terminal (1). The payment is then transmitted from the mPoS terminal to the merchant's mobile phone through Bluetooth communication (2). The transaction information is then transmitted from the merchant's mobile phone to the payment provider server for authorization (3). The payment provider, in turn, communicates with the acquirer bank to verify the transaction details and ensure its security and accuracy (4). The acquirer verifies the authenticity of the customer's payment card and checks the available funds with the payment network (5), which communicates with the card issuer (6). Upon receiving approval from the card issuer,

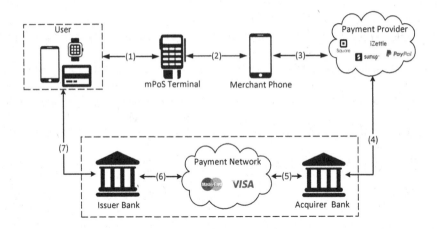

Fig. 1. Mobile Point-of-Sale (mPoS) Terminals Ecosystem

the customer's account is charged, and the customer is notified (7). The merchant's account is credited, and the notification is propagated all the way back to the merchant's mobile phone.

The mPoS terminals have been the subject of security studies in the past decade. One of the first studies, by Frisby et al. [10] in 2012, investigated the smartphone-based PoS systems that consist of a software application combined with an audio-jack magnetic stripe reader (AMSR) on a smartphone. The study focused on mPoS systems that relied on a smartphone, incorporating an AMSR and a corresponding application running on an Android smartphone. The security assessment concluded that any application running on the smartphone could potentially disable the magnetic stripe reader and obtain confidential cryptographic keys. However, the architecture of mPoS terminals has since evolved, and the current study is not centred around AMSR but shifts the focus from audio-jack magnetic stripe smartphone-based PoS systems to mPoS terminals that are controlled via smartphones.

A subsequent study on mPoS terminals is by Mellen et al. [18] where they demonstrated potential attack vectors for Square [27] mPoS terminals, both in the software and hardware. In software, their research found security weaknesses in the old Square terminals, which were later deprecated, and discovered vulnerabilities in the encrypted Square reader S4 model and Square registration application, which have since been addressed. In the hardware, the researchers discovered that the Square Reader devices used a chip for point-of-swipe encryption, but were able to bypass the encryption by jumping the connection from the magnetic head reader to the headphone jack input or by crushing the encryption chip. The attack tool, called Swordphish, was developed to record unencrypted swipes and transmit the credit card information to an external server.

In another study published in [15], the security of mPoS terminals, with a specific emphasis on the Miura [30] Shuttle chip-and-PIN reader, was thoroughly investigated. The researchers demonstrated the capability of performing arbitrary code execution as a root user on the device, utilizing both the USB and Bluetooth interfaces. Additionally, they exhibited how they could gain root access to the terminal via the chip-and-PIN mode, thereby manipulating the display and keyboard of the device to elicit the entry of the user's PIN, by changing the displayed message to "Try Again" and downgrading to magnetic stripe (magstripe) mode. However, this vulnerability was remediated by 2014.

In 2018, researchers in [11] conducted a follow-up investigation, exploiting a vulnerability that existed at that time through the Bluetooth interface. It was found that the SumUp [29] terminal transmitted commands in plaintext over Bluetooth, thereby allowing for the sending of arbitrary commands and tampering of amounts, following the reverse engineering of the terminal's characteristics and functions. As a result, researchers were able to perform a similar attack vector as outlined in [15], by manipulating the displayed messages to prompt the user to swipe their card, with a message that reads "Please Swipe Card". Our subsequent analysis of transaction data collected from SumUp terminals, however, revealed that the vulnerability had been addressed by the vendor, with the implementation of encryption for all messages. More details will be provided in Sect. 3. Thus, the demonstrated attack vector is no longer viable, as a successful attacker would require knowledge of the encryption key to send valid messages to the card reader through Bluetooth communication. The researchers also explored the manipulation of amounts in magstripe mode transactions, through the forcing of card swiping. Finally, the study highlights the use of a tamper detection circuit in the tested terminals, which would render the device inoperable in the event of attempted tampering.

Having previously addressed vulnerabilities from various angles on different mPoS terminals, in this paper, we explore the mPoS terminal ecosystem from a novel standpoint, examining the capacity of merchant's mobile phones to initiate attacks as it is a crucial part of the mPoS ecosystem. This study involves a comprehensive analysis of the mobile application and the communication protocols between the mPoS terminal, merchant phone, and payment provider server. The aim of the analysis is to identify and examine security weaknesses at various layers, in order to provide insights into the mitigation of associated risks. The results of our analysis will be presented in the subsequent sections of this paper.

3   Encryption Security

The deployment of an mPoS terminal requires the establishment of a wireless communication channel with the merchant's device, typically a mobile phone which is owned by the merchant. Bluetooth Low Energy (BLE) is a widely used technology for this purpose. The merchant first pairs an mPoS terminal with their mobile phone and uses that established communication link to send and receive transactions to/from the mPoS terminal. However, it is critical to consider the security implications of this communication channel, as exploitation of vulnerabilities can result in extracting the cryptographic keys. As previously stated, the attack vector described in [11] is no longer viable; our analysis of Bluetooth traffic contradicts the findings in [11], where certain commands sent to the SumUp terminal were discovered in plaintext. Subsequent security improvements made to the SumUp platform have made both packet analysis and arbitrary command execution more challenging since all the packets on the BLE communication are encrypted now.

To carry out the arbitrary command execution attack, an attacker would need knowledge of the encryption key in order to send valid messages to the mPoS terminal through Bluetooth communication. In this section, we first provide background information on BLE communication with a focus on the pairing session and then demonstrate how it is possible to capture the cryptographic keys of the BLE communication by exploiting existing vulnerabilities in the pairing session between the mPoS terminal and the merchant's mobile phone.

3.1   BLE Communication

The BLE protocol stack is comprised of three main architectural layers: the Controller, Host, and Application. The Host Controller Interface (HCI) serves as a bridge between the Host and Controller. The Security Manager Protocol (SMP) located in the Host layer is of particular importance in this context, as it is responsible for establishing secure connections and facilitating secure data exchange between devices. SMP outlines the procedures for pairing, authentication, and encryption of links between devices. During the pairing process, keys are generated for encrypting links and shared through a key distribution protocol for future connections and verification of data. The two devices involved in pairing are differentiated as the initiating device and the responding device. In the context of this paper, the initiating device is the merchant's mobile phone and the responding device is the mPoS terminal.

Based on the BLE specification [26], the SMP carries out pairing in three phases: phase 1, phase 2, and phase 3. In phase 1, the devices engage in a Pairing Feature Exchange using the SMP Pairing Request and Pairing Response commands. During this exchange, information such as Input/Output (I/O) capability, Out-of-Band (OOB) data flags, Bonding flags, MITM protection and Secure Connection (SC) requirements are shared between the devices. The Key Press (KP) flag is only relevant in the Passkey Entry protocol and is ignored in other protocols. Based on this information, both devices determine their I/O capabilities and select the appropriate pairing mechanism for use in the next phase of the pairing process, according to the mapping table specified in the BLE specification.

In phase 2 of the pairing process, the devices utilize the information exchanged in the Pairing Feature Exchange to determine the suitable pairing mechanism, either Low Energy Legacy (LE Legacy) pairing or Secure Connection (SC) pairing. In **LE Legacy** pairing, the devices exchange a Temporary Key (TK) and use it to create a Short Term Key (STK) which is used to encrypt the connection. If the I/O capabilities of a device, either the initiating or responding device, has a display capability, then it will display a randomly generated passkey value between "000000" and "999999". The other device should have an input capability like a keyboard so a user can input the value displayed for the TK. If the I/O capabilities of both the initiating and responding devices do not have display capabilities but only have a keyboard, the user needs to guarantee that the TKs between the initiating and responding devices are the same. This is a special case for Passkey Entry. After the generation of the TK, it is then combined with two random numbers to produce the STK; *Mrand* for the initiating device, *Srand* for the responding device. The *Mconfirm* and *Sconfirm* are 128-bit confirmation values that can be calculated using the confirm value generation function *c1*. The detail for this function is out of the scope of this research and can be found in Bluetooth Specification [26]. The security of this process depends greatly on the pairing method used to exchange the TK. In Legacy Pairing, the pairing method can be Just Works, Out of Band (OOB), or Passkey. In Just Works, the TK is set to zero. In OOB, the TK is exchanged using a different wireless technology such as NFC. In Passkey, the TK is a 6-digit number that is passed between the devices by the user.

In LE **Secure Connection**, instead of using a TK and STK, LE Secure Connections use a single Long Term Key (LTK) to encrypt the connection. This LTK is generated and exchanged using the Elliptic Curve Diffie Hellman (ECDH) protocol. In addition to supporting the pairing methods in the LE Legacy, it also supports the Numeric Comparison pairing method. It is similar to Just Works but adds another step at the end. Once the devices confirm that the confirmation values match, then both devices will independently generate a final 6-digit confirmation value using nonces. They both then display their calculated values to the user and the user manually checks both values match and confirms the connection.

In phase 3, the devices use the secure communication channel established in the previous phase to share the LTKs which will be used for link encryption. Each LTK is a 128-bit random number that may be generated along with a 16-bit Encrypted Diversifier (EDIV) and 64-bit Random Number (Rand) by both the slave and master device. The exact function of EDIV and Rand keys may vary depending on the implementation of the BLE protocol, but they are typically used to identify or derive the LTK for future connections. In order to conserve energy and storage, the slave device may not retain these values, leaving the responsibility of encrypting future communications to the master device, which in this case is the smartphone.

3.2   Eavesdropping to Extract Cryptographic Keys

The attacker, who may be a malicious merchant or an eavesdropper, can extract the cryptographic keys by capturing the pairing session between the mPoS terminal and the merchant's mobile phone. These keys are then used to carry out various attacks. Malicious merchants can capture their phone's pairing session with their terminal during the initial BLE communication setup to obtain the cryptographic keys. These keys can then be utilized to access future transaction data exchanged between the phone and the terminal. An eavesdropper can also sniff the established BLE communication to compromise the encryption.

As demonstrated in [24], the attacker can exploit the vulnerability of the BLE communication by jamming the connection, which forces the master and slave to reconnect and establish a new pairing session. During this process, the eavesdropper can inject appropriate control packets to initiate a key renegotiation to obtain the keys. Our proposed model takes advantage of the vulnerability present in the BLE communication between the merchant's phone and the mPoS terminal without requiring physical access to the mPoS terminal.

Eavesdropping: There are two primary methods for eavesdropping on BLE traffic: using the HCI Snoop Log on the merchant's mobile phone and using over-the-air Bluetooth sniffers. The HCI Snoop Log approach involves capturing and analyzing the HCI data packets on the merchant's Android phone, which can provide detailed information about the BLE communication between the phone and other devices. The over-the-air Bluetooth sniffers, on the other hand, capture BLE communication in the air by using specialized hardware and software. This approach is useful for monitoring and analyzing the Bluetooth traffic between multiple devices over a larger area. Both of these approaches have their own advantages and disadvantages and it depends on the specific requirements of the task and the environment in which it is being performed.

The utilization of HCI snoop logs, which requires the *Developers Options* setting to be enabled on the Android phone, offers several advantages. Firstly, the HCI snoop log is immune to missing packets during the capture process, which is a prevalent issue with over-the-air Bluetooth sniffers. Secondly, as the HCI protocol is situated above the Link Layer (LL) in the Bluetooth protocol stack, the contents of all packets are already decrypted by the LL. This results in a more straightforward analysis of the packets, as they are not impacted by the encryption performed by the LL. However, it has a limitation for some of the mPoS terminals, such as Square [27], that is equipped with the ability to recognize whether Developer Options are enabled on the smartphone, thereby disabling any transactions during this period. As a result, over-the-air Bluetooth sniffers would be a better choice for these mPoS terminals. We used the combination of HCI Snoop Log and Bluefruit BLE sniffer [1] to eavesdrop on the pairing session of the mPoS terminal's BLE communication with an Android phone.

We used Pixel6 as our phone and tested SumUp Air and Square mPoS terminals to capture their pairing session with the phone. The pairing session of the Square [27] terminal is very similar to the SumUp [29] terminal. Hence, for our proof-of-concept, we show the pairing session for a SumUp terminal in Fig. 2, with detailed Pairing Request and Pairing Response shown in Table 1.

Extracting Cryptographic Keys: The pairing request, as depicted in Fig. 2, is initiated by the smartphone and details the desired parameters for the BLE connection. This includes the type of pairing, the I/O capabilities of both devices (the keyboard and display), the request for bonding for future connections, and the demand for a secure connection with MITM protection. The Max Encryption Size field of the request is set to 16, and the Initiator Key Distribution and Responder Key Distribution fields specify that all of the encryption keys

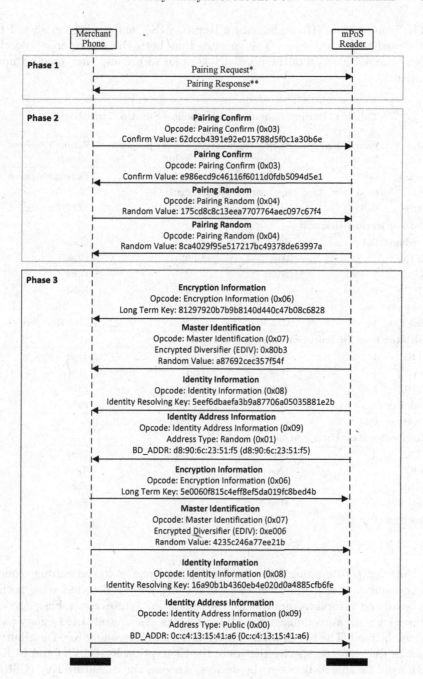

Fig. 2. Pairing Session- SumUp Card Reader

(LTK, Identity Key (IRK), Signature Key (CSRK), and Link Key) should be distributed to both devices. This ensures that both the smartphone and the mPoS terminal have all of the necessary keys for secure and encrypted communication.

Table 1. Pairing Request and Response- SumUp Card Reader

Field	Pairing Request Value	Pairing Request Meaning	Pairing Response Value	Pairing Response Meaning
Code	0x01	Pairing Request	0x02	Pairing Response
I/O	0x04	Keyboard/Display	0x03	No I/O
OOB	0x00	NOT Present	0x00	NOT Present
Authentication Request				
Bonding	0x1	Bonding	0x1	Bonding
MITM	1	True	0	False
SC	1	True	0	False
KP	0	False	0	False
Reserved	0x0	–	0x0	–
Max Enc	16	Max Enc. Size	16	Max Enc. Size
Initiator Key Distribution				
LTK	1	True	1	True
IRK	1	True	1	True
CSRK	1	True	0	False
Link Key	1	True	0	False
Reserved	0x0	–	0x0	–
Responder Key Distribution				
LTK	1	True	1	True
IRK	1	True	1	True
CSRK	1	True	0	False
Link Key	1	True	0	False
Reserved	0x0	–	0x0	–

However, the response from the SumUp card reader to the pairing request is surprising in that it indicates a lack of I/O capabilities despite having both a keyboard and a display. Additionally, the respondent refuses to establish a secure connection and protection against MITM attacks. As a result, **LE Legacy** pairing will be used. The Initiator Key Distribution and Responder Key Distribution fields in the response specify that only the Encryption Key (LTK) and Id Key (IRK) will be shared between the devices, whereas the Signature Key (CSRK) and Link Key will not be exchanged.

It is determined from the mapping of I/O capabilities to the key generation method in the BLE specification (as specified in Table 2.8 of the Bluetooth Core Specification v5.3 [26]) that, given the initiator has a keyboard and display and the responder claims to have no input or output capabilities, the *Just Works-Unauthenticated* key generation method will be employed. The utilization of the Just Works pairing method results in the generation of the TK and STK. The Just Works STK generation method provides no protection against eavesdropping or MITM attacks during the pairing process. Both devices set the TK value utilized in the authentication mechanism to **zero**, leading to a lack of protection against such attacks. The STK is not explicitly shared between the devices, rather the participating devices share random values and calculate the STK individually.

Due to the lack of utilization of the mPoS terminal's keyboard and display for a secure pairing method, the attacker can have access to the distributed keys in phase 3, as shown in Fig. 2. The access to security keys used in a LE Legacy pairing session by an attacker grants them the ability to eavesdrop on the data being transmitted between the two devices. This is because these keys are used to encrypt and secure communication, and having access to them would enable the attacker to decrypt the data and have access to it. For instance, if the attacker possesses the LTK, they could use it to encrypt the data exchanged between the two devices, allowing them to intercept and manipulate the data. Crackle [23] is one of the tools that can be used for this purpose. With the "Decrypt with LTK" feature, crackle uses a user-supplied LTK to decrypt communications between a master and slave.

Not utilizing the I/O capabilities for secure pairing is not common practice across all mPoS terminals. The examination of the SumUp Air mPoS terminal in this study revealed that it does not employ such mechanisms, in contrast to other terminals like iZettle, which do incorporate secure pairing techniques. Specifically, iZettle's method involves the presentation of a numerical value on the terminal's display, which the user must then confirm as matching the corresponding value on their paired device [13].

4 Network Security

The implementation of a mobile application on a smartphone connected to an mPoS terminal requires interaction with servers of the payment service providers through the Internet. In this section, we investigate the analysis of decrypted Hypertext Transfer Protocol Secure (HTTPS) packets and the feasibility of modifying these packets. The subsequent sections present the specifics of our intercepted network traffic, followed by a demonstration of a tampering attack on this traffic, serving as proof of concept for MITM attacks.

4.1 HTTPS Interception

The merchant's mobile phone uses HTTPS packets to communicate with payment providers over the Internet. This protocol employs Transport Layer Security (TLS) to encrypt network traffic. In order to gain access to the contents of these packets, a MITM attack is employed using a proxy server. The proxy server is able to intercept and decrypt the HTTPS packets, as the smartphone establishes a secure connection with it, believing it to be the intended recipient of the network traffic. The proxy server subsequently forwards the packets to the payment server. Details of communication over the course of a transaction for a SumUp terminal can be seen in Fig. 3. As shown in this figure, a transaction begins with a Checkout Request from the merchant's mobile phone, which requests the appropriate resources to display in the application during the transaction from the payment server. Other information in this request includes the currency, transaction amount, location and mPoS terminal device information, which is sent to the SumUp device for logging and handling purposes. For example, the transaction will fail and the sequence will end if the battery level of the terminal is too low. Continuing from the Checkout Request is a Transaction Request, where the beginning of the transaction is requested from a payment endpoint within SumUp's payment server. This is also the point at which the merchant's mobile phone begins to act as a proxy for communications between the terminal and payment server, which exchange messages without the SumUp application's influence. After this response to the transaction request, we then see four or five request-response pairs to and from the payment endpoint, depending on the payment method (chip-and-PIN or contactless). After successful payment, the transaction ends with a response from the payment endpoint and a value *stop*. The SumUp application processes this action to end the transaction and reject any other responses from the terminal. The transaction officially ends when the merchant phone sends two messages to the terminal on behalf of the payment server, signalling a successful closure of the transaction.

In our attack scenario, the Mitmproxy tool [19] is utilized as the proxy server on a desktop computer to perform a MITM attack between the SumUp application and the payment server. This tool is designed as an interactive, SSL/TLS-capable intercepting proxy for HTTP/1, HTTP/2, and web sockets, as it allows the attacker to monitor, capture and alter connections in real time. On the smartphone, a manual proxy configuration is set up, with the local IPv4 address being used as the server address and 8080 as the port. The Mitmproxy's Certificate Authority (CA) is then installed on the smartphone.

When an application establishes an HTTPS connection, it verifies the legitimacy of the server's certificate through comparison with the trusted system certificate authorities listed in the Android operating system. The list of CA is fixed and secure, but some applications may choose to implement their own custom certificate validation process, known as "Certificate Pinning". We bypass this process by using the Apk-mitm [20] tool. This is accomplished through the application of a series of steps, including 1) decoding the APK file with Apktool (more details in Sect. 5), 2) replacing the application's network security configuration to allow user-added certificates, 3) modifying the source code to disable various certificate pinning implementations, 4) encoding the patched APK file with Apktool, and finally, 5) signing the patched APK file with Uber-apk-signer [21]. The application of the Apk-mitm to the extracted SumUp APK file results in the creation of a modified version of the app. This modified app

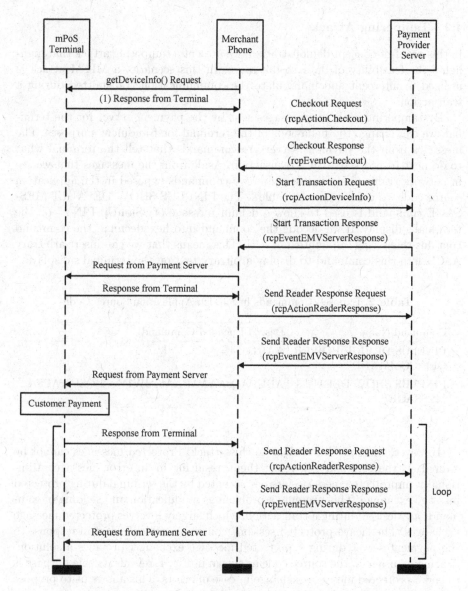

Fig. 3. Sequence Diagram of the Exchanged Messages

now trusts the Mitmproxy certificate, which is added to Android's built-in list of trusted system certificate authorities, allowing for the interception of traffic sent to SumUp's payment provider servers.

4.2   Tampering Attack

In this proof-of-concept demonstration, we present a tampering attack that highlights the feasibility of data modification. In this scenario, a MITM attack is utilized to intercept and manipulate the communication transmitted during a transaction.

By tampering with the messages sent by the payment server for the terminal, we can change the behaviour of the terminal for fraudulent purposes. The messages from the payment server are commands that tell the terminal what to do next to proceed with a transaction. Aside from the messages that we see in network traffic analysis, there are two commands exposed in the application source code, as can be seen in Table 2. The PINPLUS SHOW DEFAULT MESSAGE command is used to show a default message of "SumUp PIN+" on the terminal's display. If we decode the command into hexadecimal, the command contains this string in plaintext ASCII. This means that we can insert arbitrary ASCII into this command to display arbitrary text on the terminal's display.

Table 2. Exposed Commands in SumUp Application Source Code

Command Name	Base64-Encoded Command
PINPLUS DEVICE POWER OFF COMMAND	AAIBAQ4=
PINPLUS SHOW DEFAULT MESSAGE	ABUBAQsAAAABAAtTdW1VcCBQSU4rAP8A

However, there are limitations to this attack. Protected messages cannot be altered, as the terminal will reject them, resulting in an error message. Additionally, unprotected messages are not accepted by the terminal during protected message exchange. This presents a problem as modification and sending of commands are desired during a transaction, which largely involves protected message exchanges. The "leave_protected_session" command, which is sent in response to the payment server during a protected message exchange, provides a solution. Tracing its usage in the source code as shown in Fig. 4, reveals its sole purpose is to end a protected message exchange in case of errors. This allows us to propose an attack on the SumUp terminal by exploiting the ability to exit a protected message exchange at any point during a transaction.

The ability to leave a protected message exchange at any point in a transaction allows us to propose an attack on the SumUp terminal. At the end of a normal transaction, the payment server will send two commands to the terminal to inform it that the transaction was successful. In our attack, we replace these two commands to trick the terminal into displaying that the payment method was declined. First, we use the "leave_protected_session" command sent earlier in the transaction to exit the protected message exchange, allowing us to send an unprotected command. This is followed by the PINPLUS SHOW DEFAULT

```
@Override
public void onError(i.t.n.a.c.b bar, @Nullable List<j> list, h
    hVar) {
    String str = "onError event received. error code: " + hVar;
    if ((hVar == i.t.n.a.d.b.NOT_ALLOWED ||
    hVar == i.t.n.a.d.b. INVALID_SEQUENCE_NUMBER_IN_PROTECTED
        _MODE && ReaderCoreManager
    ReaderCoreManager.this.leave_Protected_Mode();
    }

    else {
        WReaderModuleCoreState.getBus().m(new
            CardReaderErrorEvent(bar, ReaderCoreManager.this.
            isReadyToTransmit(), list));
    }
}
```

Fig. 4. Usage of Leaving a Protected Session in the SumUp's Application Source Code

MESSAGE command that has been modified to display the text "Declined" on the terminal's display. The result of this attack is a successful transaction with the terminal displaying that the transaction was not successful. This is shown in Fig. 5. This vulnerability could be part of a social engineering attack and multiple transactions could be carried out.

5   Software Security

The security of mPoS terminals can be analyzed through the reverse engineering of their code. Reverse engineering refers to the systematic examination of the code of a software program to comprehend its functioning, identify its vulnerabilities, and potentially modify it. In this section, we demonstrate the viability of reverse engineering the code of mPoS terminals mobile applications. In particular, we employ an Android smartphone to analyze the source code and demonstrate the capability of modifying the behaviour of the mPoS terminal through the alteration of the mobile application code. In our case study, we use the SumUp Air mPoS terminal and the Android mobile application. To this end, we outline the procedures involved in the reverse engineering process and present the results of our case study. Our findings underscore the significance of adopting secure code development and deployment practices for mPoS technology to prevent potential security threats.

Fig. 5. Tampering Attack on Transaction Messages

5.1   Reverse Engineering

The Android applications are primarily written in Java and are stored as Android packages in the Android Package Kit (APK) file format, which is essentially zip files that encompass resources and assembled Java code. The process of reverse engineering the APK files on Android phones includes several steps: decompiling, making modifications, re-compiling, and signing the APK to be used on Android phones. We use the APK of the SumUp application and decompiled using two methods, Apktool [20] and a standard Java decompiler [7]. The first tool produces Smali code, while the second produces Java code. We use two different tools as they are complementary. Smali code is more difficult to read, therefore we use Java code to understand the application code and identify the vulnerable parts that can be exploited, apply the changes in the relevant part of the Smali code and use it to rebuild and sign the code. To do this, we reverse the decompiling process by rebuilding and signing the APK. The APK was rebuilt using Apk-mitm [25], which uses Apktool to encode the patched APK file and the Uber-apk-signer [21] tool to sign and verify the APK.

5.2   Software Modification Attack

As outlined in Sect. 4.1, modification of the code can circumvent the Certificate Pinning mechanism,. thereby allowing the attacker to execute MITM and tampering attacks on the communication between the merchant's mobile phone and the server of the service provider. Here, we demonstrate another software modification attack, showcasing how this vulnerability can be exploited to neutralize an additional security feature: *beep sound*.

The process of performing a contactless payment on an mPoS terminal is often accompanied by an audible beep sound as a security feature, which alerts the user to the transaction taking place. This serves as a notification to the user regarding the ongoing transaction and is essential in the prevention of relay attacks. However, a study of the SumUp Air card reader application showed that it is possible to compromise this security feature through modification of the app software.

The analysis of the code revealed that the volume of the beep sound is controlled by the *PlaySoundEffect* method within the *AudioManagers* class. By modifying this method, it is possible to completely control the sound and disable this security feature. In addition, the keyboard input sound made by the SumUp app can also be muted through modification of the code. This involved removing all function declarations and calls related to the *PlaySoundEffect* method from the code base. The recompilation and installation of the modified application showed that the sound is no longer played when keyboard inputs are used during the charge creation process. This highlights the vulnerability of the application to modification and raises concerns about the potential for malicious actors to manipulate the app and compromise the security protocols designed to protect customers. This finding underscores the importance of employing more secure solutions to ensure the safety of user transactions. Relying solely on an audible beep sound as a security feature is insufficient and poses a significant risk to users.

6   Discussion

6.1   Ethical Disclosures

The present study was performed within a controlled setting. The authors purchased commercially available mPoS terminals and used their own bank accounts to demonstrate the proof-of-concept attacks. Our research primarily focused on the SumUp Air mPoS terminal. We have shared our findings with the vendor for their review and feedback. We are currently in discussions with them to further address these issues.

6.2   Mitigating the Vulnerabilities

During our study, we have identified possible solutions for the security issues of mPoS terminals. These solutions include secure pairing methods for encryption security, code obscuring [32], anti-tampering (AT) [6], and abuse detection [2] techniques for traffic security and application code protection. In future research, we plan to study these potential solutions further and evaluate the feasibility and effectiveness of these countermeasures in addressing the identified security issues.

6.3   Tap-to-Phone Technology

The next generation of acceptance terminals, like Tap-to-Phone [31] (also known as Tap-to-Pay [16]), offers potential solutions to the security risks and vulnerabilities associated with mPoS terminals. This technology utilizes Near Field Communication (NFC), allowing merchants to accept contactless payments through their mobile devices. On the other hand, contactless payments have seen a significant increase in popularity in the UK, accounting for over a quarter of all payments made, with mobile payments playing a significant role in this growth. The trend towards contactless payment methods continues to grow, as the spending limit in the UK has increased progressively over the years, reaching £100 in 2021 [12]. Tap-to-Phone technology provides a more convenient and cost-effective solution to accepting these increasingly contactless payments without the need for a dedicated mPoS terminal. However, new systems are still susceptible to security risks, which require further research.

7   Conclusion

This paper analyzes the security implications of mobile Point-of-Sale (mPoS) terminals and their relationship with merchant's mobile phones as a key component of the mPoS system. The security aspects of communication between the (merchant's) mobile phone and the mPoS terminal, the mobile phone and the payment server, and also the security risks in the mobile phone application itself are examined. An eavesdropping attack is performed to reveal cryptographic keys in the BLE communication, a man-in-the-middle (MITM) attack is performed to tamper with mPoS terminal messages, and the mobile phone application is reverse engineered to alter the security features of the mPoS terminals controlled by the mobile phone.

Future research directions for this study include examining other mPoS terminals for their security vulnerabilities and investigating potential solutions to the attacks and vulnerabilities identified in this study. These steps will contribute to a more comprehensive understanding of the security landscape of mPoS terminals and aid in the development of effective security measures to mitigate the risks.

Acknowledgements. The third author is supported by Royal Society (ICA\R1\ 180226) and EPSRC (EP/T014784/1).

A   Appendix

(See Table 3).

Table 3. List of Acronyms

Acronym	Stands For	Description
APK	Android Package Kit	The file format for applications used on the Android operating system (OS)
AT	Anti Tampering	A security approach that hampers or prevents the reverse engineering or modification of the software or application
AMSR	Audio-jack Magnetic Stripe Reader	A device that plugs into the audio jack of a smartphone or tablet and reads the magnetic stripe on a credit or debit card for mobile payment processing
BLE	Bluetooth Low Energy	A power-efficient variant of the classic Bluetooth technology, used for connecting and exchanging data between devices over short distances
CA	Certificate Authority	An entity that stores, signs, and issues digital certificates
CNP	Card Not Present	A payment term for transactions where the cardholder does not physically present the card to the merchant (like online purchases)
CP	Card Present	A payment term for transactions where the card is physically swiped, inserted, or tapped at a payment terminal
CSRK	Signature Key	Encryption Key used in BLE Protocol
ECDH	Elliptic Curve Diffie Hellman	A key agreement protocol that allows two parties, each having an elliptic-curve public-private key pair, to establish a shared secret over an insecure channel
EDIV	Encrypted Diversifier	A 16-bit stored value used to identify the LTK distributed during LE legacy pairing
F2F	Face to Face	A payment term for transactions where the payment device is physically present
HCI	Host Controller Interface	A standardized communication interface in BLE that provides a layer for transmitting and receiving data between the host and the controller
HTTP	Hypertext Transfer Protocol	The secure version of HTTP
HTTPS	Hypertext Transfer Protocol Secure	A protocol used for communication between a web server and a client
I/O	Input/Output	The capabilities of the devices to enter (input) or display (output) information
IRK	Identity Key	Encryption Key used in BLE Protocol
KP	Key Press	The notifications sent between devices to indicate when a key on one device is pressed during the passkey entry pairing method

(*continued*)

Table 3. (*continued*)

Acronym	Stands For	Description
LE Legacy	Low Energy Legacy	A method of pairing devices in Bluetooth Low Energy (BLE) prior to the introduction of Secure Connections, which provides a lower level of security compared to Secure Connections
LL	Link Layer	A layer in Bluetooth protocol stack responsible for managing the connection and communication between Bluetooth devices
LTK	Long Term Key	Encryption Key used in BLE Protocol
MITM	Man-in-the-middle	A type of cyber attack where a malicious actor intercepts and possibly alters the communication between two parties without their knowledge
mPoS	Mobile Point-of-Sale	Similar to PoS, but smaller compact PoS terminals that are portable and are usually managed by a smartphone (merchant's phone)
NFC	Near Field Communication	A wireless communication technology allowing data exchange between devices in close proximity
OOB	Out-of-band	A method for sharing pairing information using an external channel, separate from the standard BLE channel
PIN	Personal Identification Number	A numerical code used in payment cards providing a layer of security by verifying the user's identity
PoS	Point-of-Sale	A device used by merchants to accept card payments
SMP	Security Manager Protocol	The protocol responsible for pairing and key distribution between devices
SC	Secure Connection	A protocol that authenticates two Bluetooth devices and derives a shared secret key between them
STK	Short Term Key	Encryption Key used in BLE Protocol
TK	Temporary Key	Encryption Key used in BLE Protocol
TLS	Transport Layer Security	A cryptographic protocol that provides secure communication between devices on Internet communications

References

1. Adafruit. Adafruit Bluefruit BLE Sniffer. https://www.adafruit.com/product/2269. Accessed 10 May 2022
2. Android. Safetynet attestation API. https://developer.android.com/training/safetynet/attestation. Accessed 12 Mar 2023
3. Basin, D., Sasse, R., Toro-Pozo, J.: The EMV standard: break, fix, verify. In: 2021 IEEE Symposium on Security and Privacy (SP), Los Alamitos, CA, USA, pp. 1766–1781. IEEE Computer Society (2021)
4. Basin, D., Sasse, R., Toro-Pozo, J.: Card brand mixup attack: bypassing the PIN in non-visa cards by using them for visa transactions. In: 30th USENIX Security Symposium (USENIX Security 2021), pp. 179–194. USENIX Association (2021)

5. Basin, D., Schaller, P., Toro-Pozo, J.: Inducing authentication failures to bypass credit card PINs. In: 32rd USENIX Security Symposium (USENIX Security) (2023)
6. Berlato, S., Ceccato, M.: A large-scale study on the adoption of anti-debugging and anti-tampering protections in Android apps. J. Inf. Secur. Appl. **52**, 102463 (2020)
7. Java Decompiler. Java online decompiler. http://www.javadecompilers.com/apk. Accessed 13 May 2022
8. EMVCo. Worldwide EMV deployment statistics. https://www.emvco.com/about-us/worldwide-emv-deployment-statistics/. Accessed 11 Jan 2023
9. Forbes. What is POS and how does it work? https://www.forbes.com/advisor/in/banking/what-is-pos-and-how-does-it-work/. Accessed 11 Jan 2023
10. Frisby, W., Moench, B., Recht, B., Ristenpart, T.: Security analysis of smartphone point-of-sale systems. In: WOOT, pp. 22–33 (2012)
11. Galloway, L.-A., Yunusov, T.: For the love of money: finding and exploiting vulnerabilities in mobile point of sales systems. https://leigh-annegalloway.com/for-the-love-of-money/. Accessed 11 Jan 2023
12. United Kingdom Government. 2021 budget plan. https://www.gov.uk/government/publications/budget-2021-documents. Accessed 01 June 2021
13. iZettle. In-app pairing guide. https://developer.zettle.com/docs/ios-sdk/user-guides/manage-in-app-pairing. Accessed 12 Mar 2023
14. iZettle. iZettle card reader. https://www.izettle.com/. Accessed 11 Jan 2023
15. MWR Labs. Mission mpossible: Mobile card payment security. https://www.youtube.com/watch?v=iwOP1hoVJEE. Accessed 11 Jan 2023
16. Mastercard. Mastercard tap to pay on iPhone. https://partner.visa.com/site/programs/visa-ready/tap-to-phone.html. Accessed 11 Jan 2023
17. Nezhad, M.M., Hao, F.: OPay: an orientation-based contactless payment solution against passive attacks. In: Annual Computer Security Applications Conference, pp. 375–384 (2021)
18. Mellen, A., Moore, J., Losev, A.: Mobile Point of Scam: Attacking the Square Reader. Black Hat, USA (2015)
19. Mitmproxy. How mitmproxy works. https://docs.mitmproxy.org/stable/concepts-howmitmproxyworks/. Accessed 11 Jan 2023
20. Patrickfav. APK tool-a tool for reverse engineering Android APK files. https://ibotpeaches.github.io/Apktool/. Accessed 13 May 2022
21. Patrickfav. Uber APK signer. https://github.com/patrickfav/uber-apk-signer. Accessed 13 May 2022
22. Radu, A.-I., Chothia, T., Newton, C.J.P., Boureanu, I., Chen, L.: Practical EMV relay protection. In: 2022 IEEE Symposium on Security and Privacy (SP), pp. 1737–1756 (2022)
23. Ryan, M.: Crackle. https://github.com/mikeryan/crackle. Accessed 24 May 2022
24. Ryan, M.: Bluetooth: with low energy comes low security. In: 7th USENIX Workshop on Offensive Technologies (WOOT 2013) (2013)
25. shroudedcode. apk-mitm. https://github.com/shroudedcode/apk-mitm. Accessed 13 May 2022
26. Bluetooth SIG. Bluetooth core specification, v5.2. https://www.bluetooth.com/specifications/specs/core-specification-5-2/. Accessed 9 May 2022
27. Square. Square card reader. https://squareup.com/gb/en. Accessed 11 Jan 2023
28. Square. What is a card-not-present (CNP) transaction and why does it cost more. https://squareup.com/gb/en/townsquare/what-is-a-card-not-present-transaction. Accessed 11 Jan 2023

29. Sumup. Sumup card reader. https://www.sumup.com/en-gb/. Accessed 11 Jan 2023
30. Miura Systems. Miura card reader. https://www.miurasystems.com/. Accessed 11 Jan 2023
31. Visa. Visa tap to phone. https://partner.visa.com/site/programs/visa-ready/tap-to-phone.html. Accessed 11 Jan 2023
32. Wermke, D., Huaman, N., Acar, Y., Reaves, B., Traynor, P., Fahl, S.: A large scale investigation of obfuscation use in Google Play. In: Proceedings of the 34th Annual Computer Security Applications Conference, pp. 222–235 (2018)

On the Design of a Misinformation
Widget (MsW) Against Cloaked Science

David Arroyo[1] , Sara Degli-Esposti[2(✉)] , Alberto Gómez-Espés[1],
Santiago Palmero-Muñoz[1], and Luis Pérez-Miguel[1]

[1] Institute of Physics and Information Technologies "Leonardo Torres Quevedo"
(ITEFI), Spanish National Research Council (CSIC), Madrid, Spain
`david.arroyo@csic.es`
[2] Institute of Philosophy, Spanish National Research Council (CSIC), Madrid, Spain
`sara.degli.esposti@csic.es`

Abstract. Amongst all types of fabricated information travelling on
open social networks, scientific disinformation, or *cloaked science*, is both
insidious and challenging to be investigated. Here we present the design
of the TRESCA misinformation widget (MsW), which is both a methodology and a toolbox for investigating disinformation operations leveraging scientific communications. In developing MsW we adopt a human-in-charge approach to AI: the automated tools included in MsW REST API
are meant to support, not to substitute or undermine, users' decision-making capacity. On the journey toward information verification, MsW
AI toolbox helps users test both the veracity of claims and the reliability of sources. While the toolbox integrates open source intelligence
solutions, MsW methodology fosters users' critical thinking.

Keywords: Disinformation · Cloaked science · Verification ·
Infodemics · Fake News

1 Introduction

The pandemic has exacerbated the risk that misleading scientific communications can harm public and individual health. The hoax about the benefits of
bleach-based alcohol against SARS-COV-2 caused the hospitalization of hundreds of people and deaths in some countries [6]. Emphasis about the origin of
the pandemic in Wuhan (China) and claims that SARS-COV-2 was human-made
triggered hate speech against Asian people on Twitter [23].

Supporters of the theory of SARS-COV-2 being a bioweapon developed in
a Chinese laboratory used as evidence two scientific reports sponsored by the
Rule of Law Society in September 2020 and authored by Dr Li-Meng Yan. The
preprints supposedly contained scientific evidence that SARS-CoV-2 had been
deliberately engineered. Despite the scientific claims being discredited by the
scientific community [16], Dr Yan's story appeared credible to some mainstream

S. Li et al. (Eds.): NSS 2023, LNCS 13983, pp. 385–396, 2023.
https://doi.org/10.1007/978-3-031-39828-5_21

American news media that described her as a whistle-blower. Her theory was even endorsed by former US president Donald Trump and his administration [3].

Media expert Dr. Joan Donovan considers the Yan reports an example of *cloaked science* [10]. Cloaked science refers to the use of scientific jargon and procedures to hide political, ideological, or financial interests under the appearance of legitimate scientific research. Cloaked science follows within the vast range of strategies used in disinformation campaigns or information operations. In line with previous investigations in the context of national security [9], we distinguish dis- from mis-information. Disinformation is deliberately false or misleading information that spreads for political gain or economic profit. It can include information meant at discrediting a specific target (individual, group, movement, or political party) or fabricated or contextualized information meant to support conspiracy thinking, democratic disaffection or even protests or uprising part of undeclared belligerent actions by foreign powers known as *hybrid threats*. Misinformation, in contrast, refers to information whose inaccuracy is unintentional and whose spread is not promoted by malicious agents through an orchestrated strategy.

The problem of attribution is key to establishing whether the events we are observing are part of a disinformation campaign or not. Attribution is a task that always requires indepth knowledge and insight about the motivations and strategy of an attacker. This is the reason why we adopt a human-in-charge (HIC) approach to the investigation of cloaked science. Political responsibility No fully-automated tool shall assume the political responsibility of identifying who is the enemy in the context of national security. To ensure human intelligence and artificial intelligence complement each other, a space for soft skills and non-quantifiable information needs to be preserved in the decision-making process. This is the reason why MsW gives users the initial and final word in the process of verification and envision the entire process as recursive and subject to adaptation and change.

In the digital ecosystem it is worryingly easy to convert someone into an expert and give them tools to amplify their voice. The rise in the number of articles published before peer-review (preprints), the presence of retracted scientific articles, and the proliferation of predatory scientific journals contribute to the weaponisation of science. The crisis of the peer-review system and the "publish or perish" mainstream culture can make science increasingly vulnerable to disinformation. Furthermore, the complexity of science and its numerous controversies create the conditions for fabricating scientific falsehoods starting from half-true arguments exploiting rumours and psychological biases. Self-proclaimed experts can reach large audiences by mixing pseudo-scientific information and conspiracy theories. In March 2021 the *Center for Countering Digital Hate* identified twelve influential anti-vaxxers producing high volumes of content against COVID19 vaccines and distributing this false information to a considerable large numbers of followers [7].

Fighting disinformation is a priority for society and national security. In 2016, the European Commission adopted a Joint Framework to foster the resilience to countering hybrid threats in cooperation with NATO, while in 2018, it issued a Communication titled "Tackling online disinformation: a European approach", followed in 2021 by a Code of Practice on Disinformation, which has been signed by digital platforms (Facebook, Google, Mozilla, Twitter, Microsoft, and Tik-Tok) and trade associations.

Despite these efforts, there is still a lack of "solutions (especially automated ones) that can mitigate the ease that existing online infrastructures allow adversaries to engage in deceptive content creation and dissemination" [19]. We respond to this call by presenting a methodological contribution that includes a *modus operandi* and a toolbox developed as part of the activities of H2020 project TRESCA and called Misinformation Widget, or MsW.

In the rest of the article, we present the methodology, then the MsW API REST logic and functionalities. We discuss how to apply the methodology while discussing a hypothetical case based on actual research performed by the authors. In the conclusion we discuss limitations and future directions for research.

2 Blending Human and Machine Intelligence: Human-in-Charge Approach to the Investigation of Cloaked Science

On 19 May 2021 the Spanish fact-checking agency Newtral disputed the accuracy of a text circulating on WhatsApp saying that in India only people who were vaccinated were getting infected. The text misquoted an excerpt from an interview with Spanish doctor Amaia Foces, who lives in New Delhi. Was this story the product of poor quality journalism or was it part of an orchestrated cloaked science operation?

In the investigation of scientific misinformation we need to assess both claim veracity and source credibility. There are tools we can use to assess the credibility of the source of a claim by analysing the degree of expertise and trustworthiness of individuals and institutions alike (e.g. ORCID). There are also solutions available to fact-check scientific claims. An example is *CORD-19 Claim Verification demo* [21], which is a solution that can be used to assess the veracity of claims in scientific articles. Thus, we argue that at the time of investigating controversial scientific claims we need to treat the veracity of claims and the credibility of sources as complementary things. Assessing authors' reputation and credentials can be applied as a predictor of content veracity and can also be used to establish authors' motivations and worldview.

The methodology presented below and the logic of the toolbox are based on this basic assumption: the recursive relationship between claim veracity and source credibility and the need for users' constant engagement and critical thinking to reach a conclusion about whether the events they are observing are instances of simple misinformation or can follow within the category of scientific disinformation. As disinformation investigation requires attribution, which demands an evaluation of malicious agents' intentions, we need to rely on human intelligence especially at the time of assessing inter-state coordination and state-backed information operations [22].

3   MsW Methodology

The basic assumption behind MsW methodology is the interconnection between claims and sources.

By *claim* we mean a statement about reality that can appear in a scientific outlet, but also in a newspaper, a blog, or a social media. In the specific case of scientific claims the distinction between inreach and outreach communication activities is useful to classify the format of the communication: the claim can appear in scientific outlets or conference proceedings (inreach activity), or in newspaper articles, blog posts, memes or videos (outreach activity).

By *source* we mean the author of a claim, but also the publisher of the newspaper where the claim appears, or any other individual or relevant entity spreading the claim. MsW methodology includes various steps for verifying the accuracy of claims and the credibility of sources. These steps include various verification tasks that could be performed with the support of MsW toolbox; the methodology also includes reflections meant to help users leverage their ability to think critically.

MsW methodology underlines the active role users need to play not only to distinguish true from false information, but also to perform attribution, that is, to establish if we are facing simple misinformation or we are dealing with disinformation. Thus, in the design of MsW methodology and toolbox, we have adopted a *human-in-charge* (HIC) approach. HIC is a variation of the *human-in-the-loop machine learning* (HITL-ML) approach [8] that not only requires human-machine interaction, but also the assignment of clear responsibility to humans during the decision-making process. The result is the partial automation of the investigative process, which is expected to reduce the risk of making mistakes that may undermine public trust in the scientific enterprise. We can consider HIC an approach to Explainable AI (XAI) that introduces multiple points of human verification and control. Clearly this approach is costly and, thus, mostly suitable in the investigation of politically sensible cases.

Below we present the critical questions and actions that inform the investigative journey of MsW methodology with the support of solutions integrated in MsW toolbox. The journey is organised around three moves: assess, verify and estimate or AVE.

1. **First move - Assess the credibility of the source.**
   Where does the post come from? Is the source real and credible? What do we know about the intentions, interests, worldview of the source?
   (a) Verify the credentials, *curriculum vitae* and reputation of sources that claim to be experts or official authorities.
      - MsW toolbox integrates functionalities to search authors' social profiles in OSN and also scientists' profiles on DBPedia, Google Scholar or e-thesis online services (such as EthOS in the UK or Teseo in Spain).
   (b) Check for partisan bias, that is for a specific worldview the source might be reproducing.

- In case of news outlets, MsW toolbox helps users assess outlet ideological bias based on Media Bias Fact Check.
- For scientific articles, check if the journal appears in
Beall's list of potential predatory journals and publishers or if it is a
preprint that has not been peer-reviewed yet.

(c) In the case of social media, check if the source authoring or sharing the
claim are bots rather than real people.

- MsW toolbox relies on the Botometer to assess the likelihood of a
Twitter account being a bot [20].

(d) Be aware of your own psychological and social biases.

- Pay attention to sociopsychological dynamics associated with group
identity and ingroup-outgroup communication strategies.
- If the person who shares the post is not the author, but a family
member or friend, do not trust their judgement simply because their
are similar or close to you.

2. **Second move - Verify the veracity of the claim.**
What type of evidence or research supports the claim? Do I know enough to
express an informed opinion?

(a) Verify that the headline matches the content, that is if the title of the
article reflects the story written in it.

- Use the clickbait functionality available in MsW toolbox [13,14].

(b) Check whether a reputable fact-checking organisation or official authority
has already verified the claim.

- From MsW toolbox send a query to Skeptics Stack Exchange,
Google Fact Check or other national fact-checkers websites.
- In the case of a scientific publication, from MsW toolbox verify if the
claim appears in a retracted publication on Retraction Watch.

(c) Verify that the source is not re-posting old stories claiming they are timely
and relevant after taking the information or image out of context.

- From MsW toolbox perform a reverse image search with
Google Image or Yandex Image to find out the true origin of the pic-
ture [15].
- From MsW toolbox check whether a quote has been misreported
based on Wikiquote API and other similar resources such as
Quotations Page.

3. **Third move - Estimate if the claim can trigger collective action.**
Is the claim about a politically controversial scientific issues? Does the claim
produce strong emotional reactions? Does the claim create distrust or division
between social groups?

(a) If the claim makes people feel really excited or angry it might be an
attempt to trigger a collective response by increasing polarisation, division, and distrust between different social groups.

- Use MsW toolbox to perform a sentiment analysis of the content of
the claim while also looking for the presence of satire [18].

– Double-check claims that area ssociated with discourses that try to: undermine the integrity of the election system; spread hate and division based on misogyny, racism, antisemitism, Islamophobia, and homophobia; denigrate immigrants; promote conspiracies about global networks of power; include a call to a violent or extreme response.

(b) Beware of claims presented in an unbalanced way and that emphasise specific aspects hiding others and disregarding the complexity and subtleties of broader issues.

– Use the controversy measure functionality in MsW [4] to address whether a topic is being talked about in a separated manner according to the keywords used by the communities discussing it.

4   MsW REST API

In line with the methodology presented, MsW toolbox (shown in Fig. 1) and REST API includes external and internal tools for dealing with the evaluation of both claim accuracy and source credibility. All functionalities return outputs that can be downloaded in JSON format.

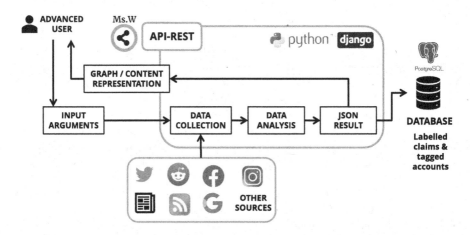

Fig. 1. MsW API REST for advanced users

Internal tools have been developed by the research team: the clickbait algorithm is based on [11], while the sentiment analysis associated with the response to a post is based on [18]; authorship identification is based on [12].

External tools leverage open-source intelligence (OSINT), which refers to the analysis of publicly available information that may come from media such as newspapers, television and websites and that can help establish the identity, reputation and network of supporters and detractors of an argument or a user account. Social bots play an important role in disinformation campaigns [2]: between January and April 2020 bots promoting anti-Asian hate speech were highly vocal and hateful (compared to non-bot users) and comprised 10.4 percent of hateful users on Twitter [23]. To control for bot presence, MsW Toolbox includes the Botometer and other similar tools for bots and trolls detection [1]. The toolbox also includes blacklists such as *Stop Funding Misinformation*, Iffy+ and the dataset compiled by [5] to identify malicious accounts (Fig. 2).

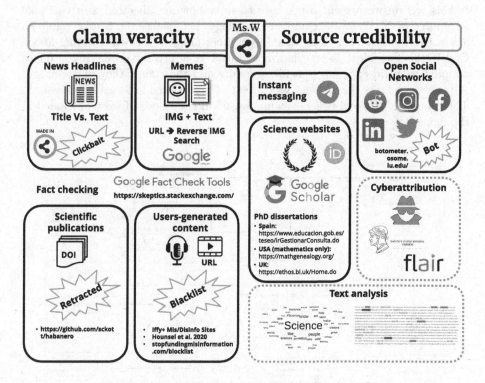

Fig. 2. An overview of MsW toolbox and methodology

An example of how MsW methodology and tools can be used to monitor malicious accounts and contents across platforms such as Twitter and Telegram is described in [15].

4.1   MsW Users' Profiles and Access Privileges

MsW REST API envisions three types of users: a super-user or system administrator (admin), an advanced user and a basic user. The admin has all privileges and has complete access to the system. The admin can create users' profiles and let them access the REST API. The advanced user accesses the REST API directly and has writing privileges: they can upload RSS feeds from their favourite news outlets, add definitions to the glossary, and upload labelled datasets. Basic users only have reading privileges and access the REST API through MsW frontend.

5   Presenting MsW Methodology and Toolbox with a Use Case

In this section we present a use case to show how an advanced user can take advantage of MsW toolbox and methodology. Let us assume a user wants to assess the veracity of a claim made in a tweet about a scientific finding about COVID19. The ideal tweet shown in Fig. 3 is a privacy-preserving artefact adopted to avoid exposing specific accounts and the claims they endorse; still the tweet preserves the format and content of tweets used in a real investigation. The content of the real tweets is summarised in the clouds of words included in the figure.

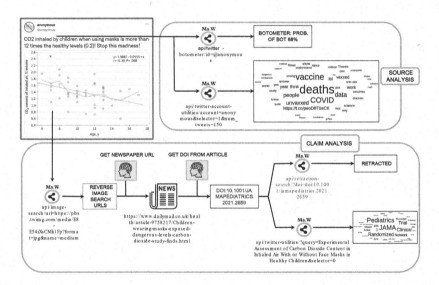

Fig. 3. Using MsW toolbox and methodology to investigate fabricated scientific claims

Following MsW methodology, we start from assessing the credibility of the source by, for example, evaluating whether the account promoting the claim is a bot. The advanced user calls the Botometer endpoint and obtains as a result a 68% chance of the Twitter account being a bot (taking into account that 28% of accounts with a bot score above 1.1 are labeled as humans by the Botometer).

To better understand the worldview of the source, the user then obtains from MsW REST API a wordcloud of the last 150 tweets the account published (in Fig. 3 Twitter handles are removed to protect users' identities). Words appearing in the cloud show that the account has been vocal about COVID19 vaccine. Focusing now on the claim made in the post, the advanced user decides to run, on the endpoint, a reverse image search. From all returned URLs that may include the image, the user selects a URL from a newspaper article where she finds the scientific article, which is the true origin of the image.

As the news article provides the DOI of the scientific article, the user calls the retraction endpoint to confirm whether or not the scientific article was accepted or retracted. Afterwards, the user requests from the endpoint a wordcloud of the tweets that contain the title of the scientific article in order to obtain aggregated information about it. Besides content specific expressions such as "clinical trial", the word "retracted" is also visible in the results with the name of the scientist authoring the piece.

This information is especially relevant as it helps the user identify other accounts talking about the retracted scientific article. MsW includes tools for performing complex network analysis facilitating the study of the community of supporters and opponents emerging around a controversial scientific claim. In the use case here discussed this analysis was performed but was not included in the article to preserve accounts' privacy. The identification of the community enables he user to label new data. Once it has been obtained the list of similar suspicious accounts, the user can characterise them by adding information about the worldview and emotions expressed in comments, messages or tweets.

This way a group of COVID19 denialists could be isolated from the overall community in which experts and lay people are discussing the claim and its associated scientific findings. The connection between the scientific article and the presence of clickbait in associated newspaper articles could also be assessed to study the impact the claim already had in the media. All these pieces together would contribute to obtain a nuanced picture of the events while fostering users' fact-checking abilities and investigative capacity.

6 Discussion and Conclusion

After the COVID19 pandemic it is evident the need for official authorities to prevent, debunk and stop infodemics from the start. In this article we propose to adopt a human-in-charge (HIC) approach in the design of the Misinformation Widget (MsW). MsW is an expression of human-centred security. MsW toolbox and methodology propose to semi-automate the investigation of disinformation campaigns built around sensitive scientific controversies that can be included under the category of *cloaked science*. By cloaked science we mean the weaponisation of false or fabricated scientific information within a wider disinformation campaign to achieve a political or economic gain.

Briefly MsW includes: (a) a methodology meant to promote users' critical thinking and capacity to verify the accuracy of claims and the credibility of sources; (b) a toolbox that consists of a REST API integrating a number of new and available AI solutions suitable for fact-checking and cyber-attribution. By constantly moving from small to big data in their investigative efforts, users can triangulate findings, revise their assumptions and reach robust conclusions. Another advantage of MsW as a REST API for advanced users is its adaptability and the possibility of developing and integrating more investigative tools to the MsW toolbox. By promoting users' critical thinking, MsW is also a promising tool for improving the quality of data labelling and helping users becoming more aware of their own ideological and psychological biases. The HIC approach adopted is based on the assumption that AI should never replace human intelligence, but rather complement it, and that only humans can be politically and legally responsible of performing attribution tasks needed to distinguish mis-from dis-information.

Even though since 2014 there has been an exponential growth in the number of active fact-checkers, there are still no specific applications helping users to tackle the problem of scientific disinformation or cloaked science. By focusing on the interdependence between the veracity of claims and the credibility of sources, MsW includes a robust, recursive approach toward the epistemic challenge of separating truth from falsehood. Considering the relevant operational, judicial and public policy implications disentangling mis- from dis-information, we invite all concerned stakeholders to adopt MsW methodology and toolbox to foster the collaboration between fact-checkers, who focus on debunking misinformation by verifying content accuracy, and cybersecurity researchers and law enforcement agencies, who concentrate their efforts on identifying malicious actors - either criminal groups or State-sponsored agencies. As the investigation of disinformation demands to collect evidence to identify malicious agents and infer their motivations, it is important to ensure humans take full responsibility and control of the entire process and AI tools support, never replace, human judgement.

Furthermore, MsW is aligned with new paradigms emerging in the domain of national security to foster the collaboration between private and public actors in fighting disinformation. For example MsW can be used within the DISARM framework, which is a working tool derived from MITRE ATT&CK framework methodology that includes *Adversarial Misinformation and Influence Tactics and Techniques* (AMITT) [17]. DISARM is increasingly adopted within NATO allies to label information and build datasets describing disinformation campaigns. MsW is compatible with DISARM and can be deployed to support the investigative work of fact-checkers, civil society as well as law enforcement agencies. Finally, MsW toolbox can be customised and can benefit a variety of stakeholders. It can be used by law enforcement agencies in the investigation of disinformation campaigns as well as to promote investigative journalism.

Acknowledgements. This work was partially funded by European H2020 project TRESCA (Grant Agreement No 872855), national project XAI-DisInfodemics (grant PLEC2021-007681 funded by MCIN/AEI/10.13039/501100011033 and by European Union NextGeneration EU/PRTR), and regional project "CYNAMON - Cybersecurity, Network Analysis and Monitoring for the Next Generation Internet" (funded by "Programas de Actividades de I+D entre grupos de investigación de la Comunidad de Madrid en tecnologías 2018" P2018/TCS-4566; BOCM. No. 304; 21/12/2018).

References

1. Antenore, M., Camacho Rodriguez, J.M., Panizzi, E.: A comparative study of bot detection techniques with an application in Twitter Covid-19 discourse. Soc. Sci. Comput. Rev. 08944393211073733 (2022)
2. Cresci, S.: A decade of social bot detection. Commun. ACM **63**(10), 72–83 (2020). https://doi.org/10.1145/3409116
3. Donovan, J., Nilsen, J.: Cloaked science: the Yan reports. Media Manipulation Casebook (2021). https://mediamanipulation.org/case-studies/cloaked-science-yan-reports
4. Garimella, K., Morales, G.D.F., Gionis, A., Mathioudakis, M.: Quantifying controversy in social media. CoRR abs/1507.05224 (2015). http://arxiv.org/abs/1507.05224
5. Hounsel, A., Holland, J., Kaiser, B., Borgolte, K., Feamster, N., Mayer, J.: Identifying disinformation websites using infrastructure features. In: 10th {USENIX} Workshop on Free and Open Communications on the Internet ({FOCI} 2020) (2020)
6. Islam, M.S., et al.: Covid-19-related infodemic and its impact on public health: a global social media analysis. Am. J. Trop. Med. Hyg. **103**(4), 1621–1629 (2020). https://doi.org/10.4269/ajtmh.20-0812
7. Jonason, P.K., Webster, G.D.: The dirty dozen: a concise measure of the dark triad. Psychol. Assess. **22**(2), 420 (2010)
8. Mosqueira-Rey, E., et al.: Human-in-the-loop machine learning: a state of the art. Artif. Intell. Rev. **56**(4), 3005–3054 (2023)
9. NATO: Nato's approach to countering disinformation: a focus on Covid-19 (2020). https://www.nato.int/cps/en/natohq/177273.htm
10. Nilsen, J., Donovan, J., Faris, R.: Cloaked science: the Yan reports. Inf. Commun. Soc. **25**(5), 598–608 (2022)
11. Oliva, C., Palacio-Marín, I., Lago-Fernández, L., Arroyo, D.: Rumor and clickbait detection by combining information divergence measures and deep learning techniques. In: Proceedings of the 17th International Conference on Availability, Reliability and Security, pp. 1–6 (2022)
12. Oliva, C., Palmero Muñoz, S., Lago-Fernández, L., Arroyo, D.: Improving LSTMS' under-performance in authorship attribution for short texts. In: Proceedings of the 2022 European Interdisciplinary Cybersecurity Conference, EICC 2022, pp. 99–101. Association for Computing Machinery, New York (2022). https://doi.org/10.1145/3528580.3532994
13. Oliva, C., Palmero Muñoz, S., Lago-Fernández, L., Arroyo, D.: Improving LSTMS' under-performance in authorship attribution for short texts. In: Proceedings of the 2022 European Interdisciplinary Cybersecurity Conference, pp. 99–101 (2022)
14. Palmero Muñoz, S., Oliva, C., Lago-Fernández, L., Arroyo, D.: Advancing the use of information compression distances in authorship attribution. In: Spezzano, F., Amaral, A., Ceolin, D., Fazio, L., Serra, E. (eds.) MISDOOM 2022. LNCS, pp. 114–122. Springer, Cham (2022). https://doi.org/10.1007/978-3-031-18253-2_8
15. de Paz, A., et al.: Following negationists on Twitter and telegram: application of NCD to the analysis of multiplatform misinformation dynamics. In: Bravo, J., Ochoa, S., Favela, J. (eds.) UCAmI 2022. LNNS, vol. 594, pp. 1110–1116. Springer, Cham (2022). https://doi.org/10.1007/978-3-031-21333-5_110
16. Rasmussen, A.L.: On the origins of SARS-CoV-2. Nat. Med. **27**(1), 9 (2021). https://doi.org/10.1038/s41591-020-01205-5

17. Terp, S., Breuer, P.: Disarm: a framework for analysis of disinformation campaigns. In: 2022 IEEE Conference on Cognitive and Computational Aspects of Situation Management (CogSIMA), Salerno, Italy, pp. 1–8 (2022)

18. de la Torre-Abaitua, G., Lago-Fernández, L.F., Arroyo, D.: A compression-based method for detecting anomalies in textual data. Entropy **23**(5), 618 (2021). https://doi.org/10.3390/e23050618

19. Tsikerdekis, M., Zeadally, S.: Detecting online content deception. IT Prof. **22**(2), 35–44 (2020)

20. Varol, O., Ferrara, E., Davis, C., Menczer, F., Flammini, A.: Online human-bot interactions: detection, estimation, and characterization. In: Proceedings of the International AAAI Conference on Web and Social Media, vol. 11 (2017)

21. Wadden, D., et al.: Fact or fiction: verifying scientific claims. In: Proceedings of the 2020 Conference on Empirical Methods in Natural Language Processing (EMNLP), pp. 7534–7550. Association for Computational Linguistics (2020). https://doi.org/10.18653/v1/2020.emnlp-main.609

22. Wang, X., Li, J., Srivatsavaya, E., Rajtmajer, S.: Evidence of inter-state coordination amongst state-backed information operations. Sci. Rep. **13**(1), 7716 (2023)

23. Ziems, C., He, B., Soni, S., Kumar, S.: Racism is a virus: anti-Asian hate and counterhate in social media during the Covid-19 crisis. arXiv preprint arXiv:2005.12423 (2020)

Author Index

A
Abdulsalam, Yunusa Simpa 327
Akgün, Mete 265
Almutairi, Amirah 77
Arroyo, David 385

B
Benkaouz, Yahya 327
Bouamama, Jaouhara 327

D
Degli-Esposti, Sara 385
Deng, Yanxiang 195

F
Fadhel, Nawfal 77
Fu, Shaojing 195

G
Gadyatskaya, Olga 3
Gjøsteen, Kristian 137
Gómez-Espés, Alberto 385
Greuet, Aurélien 283

H
Hamidy, Gilang Mentari 305
Hao, Feng 345, 363
He, Shiqing 217
Hedabou, Mustapha 327
Hernandez-Matamoros, Andres 177
Herodotou, Samuel 345

J
Joosen, Wouter 305

K
Kang, BooJoong 77
Kanno, Satoki 46
Kikuchi, Hiroaki 177

K
König, Hartmut 23
Kourtellis, Nicolas 93
Kuzuno, Hiroki 61

L
Laidlaw, Elliot 363
Larangeira, Mario 114
Li, Rui 3
Lian, Zhuotao 235
Lin, Qiuzhen 217
Liu, Lin 195
Luo, Songwei 195
Luo, Yuchuan 195

M
Matsunaka, Takashi 155
Mehr Nezhad, Mahshid 363
Mimura, Mamoru 46
Monreale, Anna 249
Montoya, Simon 283

N
Nakamura, Toru 155
Nan, Kaixi 235
Naretto, Francesca 249

P
Palmero-Muñoz, Santiago 385
Paphitis, Aristodemos 93
Paul, Andreas 23
Perera, Maharage Nisansala Sevwandi 155
Pérez-Miguel, Luis 385
Pfeifer, Nico 265
Philippaerts, Pieter 305

R
Raikwar, Mayank 137
Rizzo, Simone 249

S. Li et al. (Eds.): NSS 2023, LNCS 13983, pp. 397–398, 2023.
https://doi.org/10.1007/978-3-031-39828-5

S
Sakurai, Kouichi   155
Schuster, Franka   23
Sirivianos, Michael   93
Su, Chunhua   235
Su, Xiangyu   114

T
Tanaka, Keisuke   114

U
Ünal, Ali Burak   265

V
Vermeersch, Clémence   283

W
Wang, Jia   217
Wang, Shixiong   195
Wu, Shuang   137

Y
Yamauchi, Toshihiro   61
Yokoyama, Hiroyuki   155

Z
Zhang, Chen   235

Printed in the United States
by Baker & Taylor Publisher Services